The Unexpected Minority

Other Books of the
Carnegie Council on Children

All Our Children: The American Family Under Pressure
by Kenneth Keniston and the Carnegie Council on Children
Harcourt Brace Jovanovich, 1977
First Harvest/HBJ Edition, 1978

Small Futures: Children, Inequality, and the
Limits of Liberal Reform
by Richard H. de Lone
for the Carnegie Council on Children
Harcourt Brace Jovanovich, 1979

BACKGROUND STUDIES:

Child Care in the Family: A Review of Research
and Some Propositions for Policy
by Alison Clarke-Stewart
Academic Press, 1977

Minority Education and Caste:
The American System in Cross-Cultural Perspective
by John U. Ogbu
Academic Press, 1978

John Gliedman and William Roth
for the Carnegie Council on Children

The Unexpected Minority

Handicapped Children in America

Harcourt Brace Jovanovich
New York and London

Excerpts from "Effects on Parents" by Kathryn A. Gorham, Charlotte Des
Jardins, Ruth Page, Eugene Pettis, and Barbara Scheiber, in *Issues in the
Classification of Children,* vol. 2, ed. Nicholas Hobbs, used with permission
of Jossey-Bass Inc.
    "Analysis of a Boy with a Congenital Deformity" by André Lussier,
"The 'Exceptions': An Elaboration of Freud's Character Study" by Edith
Jacobson, M.D., and "Narcissistic Ego Impairment in Patients with Early
Physical Malformations" by William G. Niederland, M.D., from *The Psycho-
analytic Study of the Child,* reprinted by permission of International
Universities Press.
    "Excerpts from the Analysis of a Child with a Congenital Defect" by
Robert A. Furman, reprinted by permission of the author and *International
Journal of Psycho-Analysis.*
    Excerpts from *The Making of Blind Men: A Study of Adult Socialization*
by Robert A. Scott, © 1969 by The Russell Sage Foundation, New York.
Used with permission.

Set in Linotype Baskerville

Printed in the United States of America

Library of Congress Cataloging in Publication Data

Gliedman, John.
The unexpected minority.

Includes bibliographical references and index.   1. Handicapped children—
United States.   I. Roth, William, 1942–   joint author.
II. Carnegie Council on Children.   III. Title.
HV888.5.G58   362.4'0973   79-1823
ISBN 0-15-192845-2

First edition
B C D E

Contents

Contents

Contents

Acknowledgments

We owe a special debt of gratitude to the members of the Carnegie Council on Children for their advice and encouragement throughout the five years that it has taken to complete this book. Above all we thank Robert J. Haggerty, William Kessen, and Faustina Solis for their wise insights, their penetrating criticisms, and their unstinting patience with the countless drafts of this manuscript. In addition, we have benefited greatly from the comments and suggestions of Kenneth Keniston, Laura Nader, and Harold W. Watts. While this book does not speak in the Carnegie Council's name, it owes a great deal to the efforts of individual Council members to make it better.

Many other friends have given generously of their time and energy. Our colleagues on the Council's research staff provided crucial intellectual assistance and moral support, especially Peter O. Almond, Richard H. de Lone, Georgia Goeters, John U. Ogbu, and Katherine P. Messenger. In New Haven we also profited from numerous discussions with Lucy A. Cardwell, Stephen Decanio, Rafael Greenberg, Leo Molinaro, Vahid Nowshirvani, Richard Sugarman, and James W. Thompson. The following people were good enough to provide us with detailed critical readings of the manuscript: Margot S. Adler, Gene Bell, Christopher T. Cory, David Jhirad, Samuel J. Meisels, Anna Reid, Bruce Thomas, Cheryl R. Towers, Deborah Klein Walker, and the late Paul Ronder. Their scrutiny has improved the book in many ways, though we alone take responsibility for its views. Our many conversations with handicapped children, parents of handicapped children, and disabled adults have shaped our thinking in more ways than we can possibly begin to enumerate, and probably in more ways than we are aware of. We particularly thank the persons who have permitted us to quote them in these pages. We have tried to show our gratitude by respecting their confidence.

Arlene Gurland, Margaret Jackewicz, Sheila Meyers, Arlene Piazza, and Sylvia Rifkin typed the early drafts of the manuscript in New Haven and transcribed countless hours of tapes. They set a standard of excellence and personal generosity that was matched by Judy Distephano, Missle Wodajo Hankerson, Karin Kaminker, and Michele McLean, who typed later drafts of the manuscript in New York. Ethel Hinberg in New Haven and Darlene Cope-land in New York provided administrative support that also went far beyond the call of duty. Cheryl R. Towers, managing director of the New York Dissemination Office, has been a constant source of help and encouragement.

During the early stages of the project Susan Hunzinger helped with the editing. Ronnie Shushan and Jill Kneerim bore the brunt of the work, with an invaluable assist from Christopher T. Cory. Toward the end the manuscript was improved by Thomas A. Stewart's keen logic and fine sense of style. Marjorie Williams and Carol Meyer helped oversee the final transition into the printed word.

We owe special thanks to three of our editors. Christopher T. Cory provided crucial moral support during many a dark night of the soul, as well as deploying his blue pencil with unerring accuracy. Ronnie Shushan endured the book's many transmo-grifications with astonishing good humor and was unflagging in her efforts to tighten and clarify our arguments. To Jill Kneerim we are indebted for personal kindnesses that go far beyond her superlative job of editing. She offered wise counsel and constant encouragement, suffered the passing of more broken deadlines than we care to recall, and was steadfast in her commitment to the project's integrity. It is impossible to imagine this book's coming into being without her organizing presence.

John Gliedman thanks the Center for the Social Sciences at Columbia University for extending visiting scholar privileges to him in 1977–78 and 1978–79. He also thanks the Yale Medical School Library for its cooperation and assistance. Al and Ann Kent of Edgartown, Massachusetts, supplied something just as essential: months of solitude at a place in the woods where large portions of this book were written.

Foreword

Of all American children, those who are handicapped are the least identifiable as a distinctive social group. They share no common physical, psychological, or cultural characteristics: the blind child, the child with cerebral palsy, and the child with minimal brain damage are generally less like each other than each is like his or her able-bodied age mates. What distinguishes handicapped children is above all a *social* fact: they differ from the able-bodied norm, and for this reason they are assigned a stigmatized and deviant social role.

As this book documents, that social role has far-reaching and often disastrous consequences for children who must constantly interact with an able-bodied world from which they deviate. What makes the handicapped "special" are the attitudes and reactions of others who are not handicapped; and the greatest harm to the handicapped child or adult stems from this socially engendered impairment of daily life, self-concept, and future—not from functional impairments themselves.

In making this central point, Gliedman and Roth take issue with all of the dominant paradigms for understanding and "treating" handicap. Of special importance is the medical model of disability, upon which most current thinking and policy are based. The medical model starts from the fact that many (though by no means all) handicapped children are physically different from other children. It then defines this difference as a medical problem to be treated in the same general way as, for example, a strep infection. From this definition a host of consequences follows. Medically certified as "ill," the child becomes a full-time (and often lifelong) patient. Both the child and the parents are expected to accept passively the medical establishment's superior knowledge and therapeutic instructions. The child is defined as having "something wrong," and the goal is to "get well," which of course the child can never do. Indeed, the medical model sometimes suggests that all other activities, including planning for the future, are to be suspended until the child is "cured."

Gliedman and Roth show how this paradigm underlies not only federal, state, and local policies that affect handicapped children, but the most enlightened of private attitudes as well. Even today, control of programs for handicapped children usually resides in the hands of medically oriented personnel; the prevailing emphasis on "rehabilitation" points to an underlying conception of handicap as akin to a disease from whose ravages assiduous therapy can help the patient recover.

The difficulties with the medical model, however, are overwhelming. To begin with, it is simply inapplicable to handicapped children. The essence of illnesses is that they can be cured, but what distinguishes handicapped children and adults is that they will continue to be as they are—of a different form from other people. Most doctors and therapists, far from possessing superior knowledge about handicap, know much less about how to live life in this "special form" than do the handicapped child and his or her family. Nor can the child be expected to make dedicated and heroic efforts to "get well," since he or she is not "sick" to begin with. And far from suspending normal activities to concentrate on "cure," the child needs most of all to get on with the business of learning how to lead a full life.

The other major problem with the medical model is that it blinds us to the overwhelmingly social nature of the handicapped role and to the social origins of many of the problems of handicapped children. Defining the situation as essentially medical relegates it to the realm of physiological defects and assigns central responsibility to a specialized group of professionals. What is omitted is everything that is most vital to the lives of the handicapped: the socially learned preconceptions and reactions of the able-bodied; the absence of societal place and provision for people like them; the socially communicated sense of stigma and doom; the socially generated expectation that handicapped children have no real future as adults. And, conveniently for the able-bodied, the medical paradigm absolves them of all responsibility.

This same definition of handicap also stands in the way of research on the psychological and psychosocial development of handicapped children. The authors speculate that many of the "universal" laws of child development do not apply, for example, to the cognitive or emotional growth of blind or deaf children, whose development may have a logic all its own. Similarly, the study of the resourcefulness and courage of handicapped children and their parents in dealing with social discrimination, prejudice, and pessimism would have much to teach about the way other groups adapt to prejudice and overcome adversity.

In the course of this work, Gliedman and Roth discuss virtually every aspect of disability, enlivening their book with anecdotes, with critical research analyses, and with interviews with handicapped children, their parents, and handicapped adults. They discuss in detail the potentials and dangers of new federal and state legislation intended to bring handicapped children into the mainstream of school and society. They explore the many research questions that disability poses for developmental psychology and special education. They look ahead to the employment problems that await today's handicapped children a decade or two hence. They examine the physician's responsibility in chronic care. And they provide an unusually detailed critique of the thickets of bureaucratic impersonality and incomprehension that lessen the effectiveness of the existing network of social services for the handicapped child and his parents.

But above all, this book provides a new and sharper lens on the situation of handicapped people in American society—as well as children. The reason current efforts to "help" the handicapped are so often ineffective or counterproductive is precisely because they rest on a flawed paradigm. What distinguishes this work is that it offers a different perspective, one that is both common-sensical and obvious, yet revolutionary in its implications that the able-bodied unwittingly create most of the problems of the handicapped. Further, this new perspective not only yields understanding but points the way toward new policies. *The Unexpected Minority* is a major contribution to the liberation of all handicapped people from misunderstanding, discrimination, and misguided social policy.

This book, the last of the books to be published by the Carnegie Council on Children, also illustrates the objectives of the Council. Early in its work the Council came to believe that a small private commission had a special opportunity to do more than make recommendations; in addition, and perhaps more important, the Council tried to ask whether the lens through which Americans analyze and prescribe for children is adequate. In general, our answer has been that we have consistently seen our children and families through a flawed lens, one that magnifies the problems of individuals and their personal responsibility for self-help but obscures the broader societal forces and responsibilities that are often more important in determining what children become. Redefining handicap as a "social" problem, Gliedman and Roth fulfill and extend the Council's objectives.

Throughout their work the authors have had advice from other staff and Council members. The book is published as one of the Council's publications, although credit and responsibility must rest with its authors.

KENNETH KENISTON

Massachusetts Institute of Technology, 1979

Speaking for myself, I too believe that humanity will win in the long run; I am only afraid that at the same time the world will have turned into one huge hospital where everyone is everybody else's humane nurse.

Goethe, Travels in Italy, May 27, 1787

The Unexpected Minority

Introduction

A child's lot is inextricably bound up with the world he lives in.
This perception dominates many recent discussions of children's
issues. Some writers, stressing the role that social context plays in
every child's life, have called attention to the economic and social
pressures that limit the choices parents can make for their children.[1] Others have observed that the child is exquisitely alive to
society's treatment of the adults around him: what he sees and
understands may profoundly shape his sense of self, his expectations of the future, and even the importance he places upon
doing well in school.[2] Strangely enough, discussions of the nation's 5 to 10 million handicapped children have rarely reflected
these perspectives. Even today the child with a handicap is approached in the traditional manner; he is examined in isolation
from the social world around him. Our book seeks to redress this
oversight.

A new idea—simple, yet wide-ranging in its ramifications—
informs our vision of disability. It is that handicapped children
and adults are an oppressed minority group. Their oppression
takes many forms: outright prejudice against handicapped people
of all ages, job discrimination against disabled adults, and well-

meaning but destructive misconceptions that exaggerate the true limitations of many handicaps. Frequently oppression is compounded by professionals who define the child's academic and psychological needs exclusively in terms of deviations from the norms of an able-bodied childhood and heavy-handed experts who alienate and demoralize the child's parents in the name of a spurious ideal of professionalism. Increasingly, handicapped adults are themselves adopting a civil rights analysis of their problems. They are demanding better social services, but they are demanding more: an end to prejudice and discrimination against people with different bodies.[3]

Unlike blacks and Hispanic Americans, the disabled do not form a distinct cultural community (although their oppression bears striking resemblances to that practiced against ethnic minorities). Nor are handicaps produced or transmitted in a way that parallels the perpetuation of racial characteristics from one generation to the next. (Most handicapped children have able-bodied parents, and most disabled parents have able-bodied children.) Yet, as the social psychologist Kurt Lewin long ago noted, the members of an oppressed group often have little in common except the fact that society singles them out for systematic oppression.[4] Examples abound: European Jews during the 1920s and 1930s and, closer to home, women, gay people, and the elderly in present-day America. Similarly, handicapped children and adults are an oppressed minority, not because of a shared cultural heritage, but because society exposes most of them to a common set of socially produced hazards. Discrimination—much of it systemic rather than personal—constitutes what we shall call the sociological situation of the handicapped. This "interdependence of fate," to recall Lewin's useful term, imposes from without a social identity upon the otherwise heterogeneous collection of children and adults who happen to have handicaps.

Even so, not all handicapped children fit the minority-group model. Perhaps 10 percent of all handicapped children possess a disability so limiting mentally or emotionally that they would not be able to lead normal lives even if prejudice against them melted away.[5] Some moderately retarded children fall into this category, as do nearly all children with severe or profound mental retardation. So do most victims of childhood psychosis and other severe emotional disturbances. At the other extreme, children with mild or borderline handicaps may escape serious stigma altogether. But others are less fortunate: their socialization experiences have more in common with the seriously disabled than with the able-bodied. Most fall somewhere in between, sometimes being treated as handicapped, sometimes being treated as able-bodied. To the extent that a mild handicap—or an unjustified handicap label—places a child at special social risk in his family, school, or community, our minority-group analysis illuminates his needs.

Estimates of the numbers of handicapped children are highly unsatisfactory.[6] Many children are incorrectly classified as handicapped; others possess undetected disabilities. There is wide variation in the criteria used to assess the severity of a handicap. Many estimates rely heavily on data collected by the public schools, yet their widespread mislabeling of many perfectly normal minority children has long been common knowledge.[7] More recent research suggests that the schools may be just as inept (and nearly as racially biased) in their diagnoses of many physical and sensory disabilities.[8] The normal child who poses a management problem gets the label, and, quite frequently, the child with a real disability is overlooked.[9]

It is possible that the 1979 survey conducted by the National Center for Health Statistics and the new questions about disability to be included in the 1980 census will lead to greatly improved estimates of the incidence of different disabilities among children and youths. Until the results of these surveys become available in the mid-1980s, the figures assembled by James S. Kakalik and his associates are as good as any.[10] Kakalik's estimate may well overstate the true prevalence of many handicaps. But it probably does not overstate the number of children who, at one time or another while they are growing up, will be perceived as handicapped by peers, parents, professionals, or others who count. Our best guess is that between one-quarter and three-quarters of the children singled out by Kakalik are exposed to *prolonged* stigma and discrimination because of a true handicap or an incorrect diagnosis that labels them handicapped.[11] Of the rest, all but the most seriously retarded and emotionally disturbed live on the border between the world of the handicapped and the world of the able-bodied.

Physical disabilities, sensory handicaps, and chronic health impairments may be twice as common among poor children as among other children. We believe this is the case, but the health survey data are ambiguous, and most of the data are consistent with the view that the majority of these handicaps are evenly distributed throughout the population.[12] In any event, the larger size of low-income families implies that a disproportionate number of poor families have at least one child with a handicap.

Handicapped Children and Youths to Age 21 in 1970*

Type of Handicap		Number of Children and Youths
Visual impairment		193,000
Partially sighted	148,000	
Legally blind	45,000	
Hearing impairment		490,000
Deaf	50,000	
Hard of hearing	440,000	
Speech or spoken language impairment		2,200,000
Crippling or other health impairment		1,676,000
Mental retardation †		2,800,000
Mildly retarded (IQ 55–69)	2,100,000	
Moderately retarded (IQ 40–54)	420,000	
Severely retarded (IQ 25–39)	224,000	
Profoundly retarded (IQ under 25)	56,000	
Emotional disturbance (autism, childhood psychosis, and less severe emotional problems)		1,500,000
Learning disability		740,000
Multihandicapped		50,000
	TOTAL	9,550,000 ‡

* The total number of handicapped children and youths in Kakalik's estimate comes to 11.4 percent of the entire population to age twenty-one in 1970 (83.8 million). Because of the great uncertainty in this and all other estimates, we prefer to present Kakalik et al.'s absolute figures rather than to adjust them upward in order to reflect population growth since 1970.

† These figures require a word of explanation. At least 80 percent of the children classified as retarded are labeled "mildly retarded," and most of them bear no resemblance whatsoever to popular stereotypes about the retarded. The great majority of mildly retarded children (those with no symptoms of organic brain damage or any history of institutionalization) are virtually indistinguishable from normal children except in some academic settings. (The popular stereotype of the retarded child is perhaps most closely approximated by the child with Down's syndrome, a condition that affects one in every 600 to 900 children. Mongoloid children—as the victims of Down's syndrome are sometimes called—compose between 2 and 4 percent of all children in the retarded category, or between 10 and

20 percent of all children with IQ's below 50.) Note also that the ranges given in the table are those established by the American Association on Mental Retardation. The schools employ a somewhat different system. They classify children with IQ's in the 60–79 range as Educably Mentally Retarded (EMR) and children with IQ's in the 40–59 range as Trainably Mentally Retarded (TMR). If, as is customary when making estimates of the prevalence of mild or "borderline" retardation, one assumes a normal distribution of IQ scores and a standard deviation of 15 points, the schools' inclusion of children with IQ's in the 70 to 79 range would add about 5.8 million more individuals up to age twenty-one to the mentally retarded category (about 6.91 percent of the total 1970 population in this age range).

‡ This figure includes some 100,000 institutionalized children and youths. About 8,000 were in chronic disease hospitals; the rest were divided fairly evenly between psychiatric institutions and custodial institutions for the retarded.[13]

There is better evidence about adult disability.* About one-third of all mothers receiving Aid to Dependent Children were classified as disabled by the Old-Age, Survivors, Disability and Health Insurance program (OASDHI).[21] And most of the million or so disabled workers eligible for benefits from OASDHI were formerly employed in manual or blue-collar occupations.[22] Many surveys have questioned adults about their health status.[23] Data collected by these studies suggest that most major disabilities are one and a half to three times more common among people of modest means than among the affluent.[24] These differences are most pronounced in middle age, when disabilities that limit a person's capacity to hold down a job or to keep house may be nearly four times as common among the poor as among middle-income adults. Disabilities that prevent the carrying out of either of these activities are perhaps ten times more common among poor people.[25] The survey data do not establish whether low-income blacks (and the members of other ethnic minorities) are at greater risk of becoming disabled than poor whites.[26] But there is some evidence that when a black worker becomes disabled, he suffers a

* Statistical convention makes it impossible to compare the total numbers of handicapped children with the total numbers of handicapped adults. Most surveys of adult disability do not include learning disabilities or speech disabilities; nor do they include more than a tiny fraction of the many mentally ill or mentally retarded people who live outside institutions.[14] Of those disabled people surveyed, the great majority reported that they became disabled during adulthood.[15] It appears that about 90 percent of the nation's half-million blind and 2 million deaf are over the age of twenty-one.[16] A little more than half of all blind people are probably in their sixties or older.[17] All told, something like 20 million working-age adults reported a sensory disability, a physical handicap, or a chronic health impairment when queried in the 1960s and 1970s, or about 15 percent of this age group.[18] Perhaps a quarter of all adults age sixty-five or older have similar disabilities, 5 million out of a total population of about 20 million.[19] These estimates are the best available, but they represent only the crudest of approximations.[20]

sharper earning loss in his subsequent employment than a white worker of similar general characteristics.[27]

While working with handicapped children, we have found that the social problems of the mentally normal child with a handicap often provide insight into the problems of any child who, rightly or wrongly, is perceived by someone else as being handicapped. The trajectory of our analysis reflects this observation. Throughout, the problems of the blind, crippled, or severely health-impaired child will be our touchstone. Indeed, because of our emphasis upon the socially invented aspects of disability, we will not always distinguish sharply between the problems of children with genuine disabilities and the problems of normal children who go through life mislabeled by the school, by a social agency, or by their parents. To anticipate our central theme: many of the most incapacitating aspects of severe disabilities such as blindness or paraplegia are just as much social inventions as the discrimination sometimes directed at the mislabeled child. This strategy does not mean that we ignore the serious problems raised by the inadequacies (and racial bias) of present diagnostic and classificatory procedures. But, unlike most critics, we will be chiefly concerned with the implications of these shortcomings for the education and the future employment of children with genuine handicaps. It goes without saying, of course, that we recognize the great importance of recent legal and scholarly efforts to curtail or eliminate the mislabeling of children.[28]

In this book we shall not attempt anything like a comprehensive reexamination of all the needs of the mentally normal or near-normal child with a handicap; such a task would require an expertise that we lack and a study many times longer than this one. Rather, our intention is to lay before the reader the main lines of our minority-group analysis and then to apply this analysis to those aspects of childhood disability which, in our judgment, are most in need of reinterpretation. In Part One we sketch out our approach, first asking why American society has traditionally failed to view the handicapped as an oppressed social group. In Part Two we criticize and then offer constructive alternatives to the ways that psychologists usually study how handicapped children grow up. Part Three focuses upon the professional and some of the most important services he provides to handicapped children and their parents. In Part Four we discuss the appalling ignorance and confusion that surrounds the employment problems of today's generation of disabled adults—problems that, unless they are soon remedied, will blight the lives of today's handicapped children some decade or two hence.

Two crucial social services issues are discussed in the appendices. In Appendix 4, Katherine P. Messenger and John Gliedman survey the medical needs of handicapped children, the role that preventive medicine can play in combating disability, and the need for a national health insurance scheme that can defray the often ruinous medical expenses that attend many handicaps. In Appendix 5, we call for the creation of a national insurance plan to help defray the often considerable *nonmedical* expenses that are incurred in raising a handicapped child. The first three appendices supplement the minority-group analysis presented in the text.

Our use of footnotes requires a word of explanation. Because we have attempted to address a broad audience of specialists and nonspecialists, we have constantly balanced the requirements of readability against the need for a certain technical rigor, especially when we have tried to go beyond merely criticizing traditional approaches to handicap to presenting constructive alternatives. As much as possible, we have used the notes to expand the arguments presented in the text and to explore issues of interest to the specialist but of little concern to the nonspecialist.

Since so much of our discussion will touch upon the ways that society misconstrues the child's abilities, it would be useful to have a pair of contrasting words that clearly distinguish between the biologically and socially produced limitations of a disability. No such pair exists. Responding to this need, many writers have proposed new and highly restrictive definitions for *disability* and *handicap*. Unfortunately, there is no consensus about which of these definitions should prevail. Some writers define *disability* as the biological component and *handicap* as the social component; others employ the reverse usage.[29] Dictionaries add to the confusion by defining *handicap* and *disability* as synonyms. The *American Heritage Dictionary* is typical: a *handicap* is "a deficiency, especially an anatomical, physiological, or mental deficiency, that prevents or restricts normal achievement," and a *disability* is "a handicap." [30] In our own work we have found it useful, but only as a kind of mental scaffolding, to denote the purely biological aspect of disability by the words *allomorph* and *allomorphism*, coinages formed from the Greek roots for "other" (*allo*) and "shape, form, or structure" (*morphos*).[31] It is possible that there is a place for these rather awkward terms in highly technical discussions where one sometimes wants to avoid the overly negative connotations of words such as *deficit, deficiency,* or *disabled.* But in these pages we will trust the reader to infer from the context when we are speaking of the child's allomorphism, society's contribution to the allomorph's problems, or both the biological and social components of a handicap.

This book is the record of an attempt at intellectual emancipation. When we began, we believed that the traditional definition of the handicapped child's needs was perfectly satisfactory—that all that was really required was more of the same kinds of services for handicapped children. Only gradually did we come to see our initial error. By failing to think through the implications of the "civil rights lens" for the *child,* we had unwittingly committed ourselves to making the same kinds of mistakes about disability that were made about other groups of disadvantaged children a generation ago. Every discipline has its blind spot. And the more we thought about our own, the more typical it seemed to be. Society's role in handicapping disabled people is always mentioned in the textbooks. It is the subject of a large research literature and a kind of cliché among rehabilitation workers. Yet for all that, discrimination against the disabled is one of the great unexamined commonplaces of our field and, indeed, of American life. Its exploration is what this book is all about.

Part One

The Situation of Handicap

Chapter 1

Handicap as a Social Construction

Suppose that somewhere in the world an advanced industrial society genuinely respected the needs and the humanity of handicapped people. What would a visitor from this country make of the position of the disabled individual in American life—especially the 10 or 20 million mentally normal people with serious physical, sensory, or health-related handicaps?

To begin with, the traveler would take for granted that a market of millions of children and tens of millions of adults would not be ignored. He would assume that many industries catered to the special needs of the handicapped. Some of these needs would be purely medical because many handicaps require special drugs and appliances to ensure the normal operation of body functions. But many would not be medical. The visitor would expect to find industries producing everyday household and domestic appliances designed for the use of people with poor motor coordination. He would look for cheap automobiles that could be safely and easily driven by a paraplegic or a quadriplegic. He would anticipate a profusion of specialized and sometimes quite simple gadgets designed to enhance the control of a handicapped person over his physical world—special hand tools, office supplies, can openers, eating utensils, and the like.

Backing up this family of industries he would expect to find a research and development base, a network of laboratories and institutes at least as numerous as the research and development base of the Apollo space program—the only instance so far of our society's bringing to bear its vast technological resources to design special prosthetic devices (i.e., the elaborate support systems necessary to allow a man to travel in space and to walk upon the surface of the moon).

Coming across discussions of America's energy crisis, he would look for long-term energy strategies that took into account the special needs and concerns of handicapped people. He would assume that advocates of high-technology solutions emphasized the potential benefits of a high-technology future for disabled people. He would take for granted that defenders of "soft paths" to energy stability just as vigorously claimed that their commitment to a simpler, decentralized life-style was in the interest of the nation's handicapped minority.

As he examined our newspapers, magazines, journals, and books, as he watched our movies, television shows, and went to our theaters, he would look for many reports about handicap, many fictional characters who were handicapped, many cartoon figures on children's TV programs and many characters in children's stories who were handicapped. He would expect constantly to come across advertisements aimed at handicapped people. He would expect to find many handicapped people appearing in advertisements not specifically aimed at them.

The traveler would explore our factories, believing that handicapped people were employed in proportion to their vast numbers. He would examine the industries that build and design factory machinery in the expectation that a significant amount of research and development was devoted to increasing the productivity of mentally and physically handicapped workers.

He would travel across the country by car, staying overnight in our motels and hotels. He would take our planes and trains and buses. He would fly overseas, he would book passage on our ocean liners. He would walk the streets of our towns and cities. And everywhere he went he would expect to *see* multitudes of handicapped people going about their business, taking a holiday, passing an hour with able-bodied or handicapped friends, or simply being alone.

He would take for granted that in many families one or both parents were disabled. He would assume that an elaborate network of services existed to help them in raising their children and that a parallel and partially overlapping service network existed to serve the needs of able-bodied parents who had handicapped children.

He would explore our man-made environment, anticipating that provision was made for the handicapped in our cities and towns. He would look for ramps on curbs, ramps leading into every building. He would expect the tiniest minutiae of our dwellings to reflect the vast numbers of disabled people.

Observing our elections, he would take for granted that the major parties wooed the disability vote just as assiduously as they pursued the labor vote or the black vote. He would assume that disabled individuals had their share of elected and appointive offices. He would expect to find that the role played by the disabled as a special interest group at the local and national levels was fully commensurate with their great numbers.

The visitor would examine our trade unions, believing that many labor leaders were disabled. He would canvass high corporate management, expecting to find many handicapped businessmen. He would go into our schools, looking for handicapped teachers and principals. He would assume that there were many disabled doctors, lawyers, and scientists.

The traveler would expect all these things because roughly one-tenth of all children are handicapped, one-fifth of all adults are handicapped, and at least *half* of all able-bodied adults have a disabled spouse, child, parent, or close friend.

Instead, this is what he would find:

Vast numbers of nursing homes and hospitals where disabled men, women, and children are left to rot in solitude.

Work practices and hiring procedures that systematically discriminate against disabled workers, millions of disabled adults who are able to work but are unable to find jobs even during periods of peak employment, a vast underrepresentation of the disabled in the professions and other well-paying jobs, and a network of sheltered workshops where 200,000 adults earn an average wage of less than a dollar an hour.

He would find a kind of "precapitalist" market structure in which information about new devices for disabled individuals is poorly transmitted; in which innovation is slow and funds for capitalization of new ventures are difficult to obtain; and in which, as with prescription drugs, the main mediators of information about new products are professionals. Not only are the handicapped generally denied a work identity; they are also denied an independent identity as *consumers*.

The visitor would also discover a nearly complete neglect of the needs of the handicapped in our man-made environments, from the most humble artifacts of domestic life like plumbing and doors, to our transportation systems and the organizations of our factories, towns, and cities. And he would find a set of impressive laws prohibiting architectural and transportation barriers that are still not being enforced.[1]

In our media the visitor would find the disabled individual portrayed as a child. In fact, most of the disabled he would see in the media *are* children, even though handicapped adults greatly outnumber handicapped children and even though *able-bodied* adults appear far more frequently in the media than *able-bodied* children. In addition, the visitor would note, in media attempts to explore the problems the disabled face in American society, a striking tendency to portray the severely retarded individual—who in a sense is a perpetual child—as typical of all handicapped people. But perhaps most of all, the visitor would be astounded by what, given the huge number of handicapped individuals and able-bodied individuals with a direct interest in handicap, is a near blackout on news, stories, and documentaries about disabled people.

In many respects he would find the handicapped in the United States as politically weak as blacks were before the legal breakthroughs of the 1950s and 1960s; and, indeed, in cities such as Los Angeles he would discover to his amazement that many disabled adults must go to great lengths to exercise their right to vote because many polling places are still inaccessible to the wheelchair bound and other voters with mobility limitations.

What is it in our society's vision of disability that has concealed the injustice of all these facts from the huge numbers of able-bodied adults with a direct stake in the well-being of a disabled relative or close friend? What has permitted the able-bodied adult with a disabled spouse, a crippled child, or a blind classmate not merely to acquiesce in this political and social oppression but simply not to perceive this oppression as oppression? What does the able-bodied individual *see* when he sees a handicapped person? Why is society so *mystified* by handicap?

Social life—as well as science—is dominated by what the historian of science Thomas Kuhn has called paradigms, theories of how the world works that selectively emphasize certain aspects of experience and overlook others.[2] These interpretive structures in large part determine the way social issues are perceived, formulated, and attacked.

For many generations mainstream society's attempts to deal humanely with the disabled and the professional's vision of the nature of disability have been shaped by a host of mutually reinforcing paradigms. Starting from very different intellectual premises, these frameworks have converged to produce a set of flawed assessments of the disabled person's needs and the place of the disabled in American society. Indeed, despite their condemnations of prejudice toward the disabled, these models share far more with longstanding myths and stereotypes about handicap than has generally been recognized.

Like all social paradigms, the lenses that have shaped the traditional visions of disability are exceptionally resistant to change. Faced with what seems at first to be a flat incompatibility between these ideas and the emerging civil rights model of disability, it is easy for anyone whose thought has been shaped by the old paradigms to revise the civil rights analysis unconsciously until it becomes so compatible with traditional views about handicap that it remains a civil rights analysis in name only

The naturalness—as well as the unconscious character—of this mechanism of accommodation or constructive misunderstanding must be emphasized. As the psychologist Gordon Allport has noted: "While most of us have learned to be critical and open-minded in *certain* regions of experience, we obey the law of least effort in others. A doctor will not be swept away by bold generalizations concerning arthritis, snake bite, or the efficacy of aspirin. But he may be content with overgeneralizations concerning politics, social insurance, or Mexicans. Life is just too short to have differentiated concepts about everything. A *few* pathways are enough for us to walk in." [3]

These general characteristics of social paradigms—their adaptive "cunning"—must be directly confronted by an attempt, such as ours, to approach the handicapped child by means of a minority-group lens. Indeed, unless we first subject the old paradigms to critical scrutiny, there is every possibility that they will exert a powerful unconscious influence upon the way in which we ourselves reinterpret the handicapped child's needs and problems.

The Lay Culture's Disease Diagnosis of Handicap[4]

It is from the philosophers of science that we learn that even the most apparently objective perceptions of the world are conditioned by our theories of how the physical world works. What is involved is not too different from what perceptual psychologists call "mental set." Nature, like language, is intrinsically ambiguous. Like those queer drawings used by psychologists in which, depending upon our expectations, we see one or two equally possible figures, the simplest act of seeing is a "theory-laden" activity.

Indeed, there was a time when even a sunrise appeared to be a different kind of objective fact to different people. This was when astronomers still actively disagreed about whether the sun revolves around the earth or the earth revolves around the sun. The sixteenth-century astronomer Tycho Brahe saw one thing when the sun rose in Prague; his pupil Kepler saw something quite different. Brahe, a believer in the Ptolemaic or earth-centered theory, "saw" that the moving sun had once again cleared the horizon of the stationary earth. But he did not deliberately *will* this perception: to recall the psychologist Hermann von Helmnoltz's useful term, theory and raw sense data were fused together into an "unconscious inference." [5] Brahe *saw* the sun move around the earth. But Kepler, viewing the same event, *saw* something very different. For him it was the earth that moved, rotating on its axis and circling the stationary sun.

What is true for observations of nature holds with redoubled force in social life. To a large degree, the first task of any interaction between people is interpretation. Each person seeks to reduce the inherent ambiguity of the other's social persona to a manageable level. This attempt takes the form of conscious and unconscious theorizing that is analogous to the way that scientists build and test their theories about nature.[6] Drawing upon certain tried and true interpretive strategies, through a process of trial and error we construct a model of the other person's character—and a model of his model of our character. Like the scientists, we treat certain items of information as crucial. Some of these are evident upon first meeting the person—age, race, sex, manner, dress, speech patterns. Others must be learned either from the person or from others with knowledge about the person—religion, profession, key aspects of personal history, and so on. These pieces of information direct our interpretive efforts and foreclose certain possibilities from the start. We communicate our self-image to the other, our state of mind, our character, our social status, and our feelings about the other. We communicate to the other whether we think he has a future and whether we might have a future together, in our private or professional life; whether we might be compatible acquaintances, business associates, friends, or lovers.

In a first encounter the knowledge or perception that a person is handicapped is among the most important of clues that we can obtain about his character. Indeed, in many instances the sudden discovery that the person is or is not handicapped suffices to transform our perception of his social persona completely. Consider your own reaction to a figure limping down the street. At a distance you may feel pity, revulsion, or an interest in the unusual. You may, if you have had a normal upbringing, deliberately not see anything. As the person draws closer, you notice that the leg is in a cast, indicating a temporary injury. Many feelings you experienced at the outset vanish, replaced by a sense of relief, mild curiosity, even empathy. As the person comes closer yet, you see on the cast autographs and a stick drawing of a figure on skis somersaulting through the air. Now virtually every feeling changes. You know the cause of the injury (a skiing accident), and you know that it is temporary. The person had to be enough of an athlete to ski in the first place. Further, the signatures show the person had friends in the injury, conspirators after the fact, displaying to one and all that the person is not disabled but temporarily injured—and also that the victim has been able to make a joke of it, that the injury is fast becoming a story to be related and savored.

We autograph casts. When a friend is temporarily confined to a wheelchair, we joke about it, and he lets us borrow the wheelchair to try it out, to "go for a spin," to play with it. The reason for joking is that one needs a way to signal to the bystander—and to oneself—that appearances are deceiving. "I look as if I am crippled for life," says the person temporarily in a wheelchair, "but in fact, I will soon be up and about in the world. Therefore I joke about my condition, and ask that you join with me in making fun of it."

The situation changes if you see a metal leg brace instead of a cast. Unlike temporary injuries, a handicap is considered by others to be integral—"essential"—to the handicapped person's social being. He is treated differently because of his handicap, and he is expected to behave differently. "I soon learned," writes a man crippled in an automobile accident, "that it was considered bad form for me to behave like a normal person in certain situations." Not surprisingly, such a person soon starts to think of himself in a different light, namely, as "disabled."

To be visibly handicapped, one might say, is to possess a body that does not emit social cues in the way normal bodies do. It is to speak a social language that most able-bodied individuals do not understand. Talking with a blind person can initially be as disconcerting as watching television and having the video portion of the program flicker on and off or suddenly dissolve into snow; only with further acquaintance does one learn to disregard the blind person's misleading facial expressions. Continuous drooling does not signify that a man with cerebral palsy is a baby. That he grins and nods wildly in agreement does not mean that he is naive. The dramatic wave of the hand may not indicate that he wants to interrupt but only that he is reaching for his cigarettes. Disabilities that interfere with articulation may make the speaker seem offensive, unbalanced, or incompetent, as many a stutterer and deaf person has learned. Oddities of syntax or vocabulary that reflect the handicapped person's special socialization experiences can misrepresent his character to the world.

But it is not just the obvious difference that imposes a systematic distortion upon social communication with disabled people. As with all language, there are few aspects of the cues that determine interpersonal perception which are not themselves intrinsically ambiguous. Does the mysterious *Gioconda* smile mean mirth or mockery? Is the high-pitched tone of voice a sign of strain or arrogance? Can we take the other's public persona at face value or must we discount it as the artifice of a skilled salesman or manipulator? In constructing our theory of the other person we frequently rely upon indirect information about the person to resolve these ambiguities.[7] Here, too, the disruptive role played by the disability is often crucial. Even when the handicap is invisible, if we know that the person has epilepsy, is mildly retarded, or has a hidden physical disfigurement, that knowledge often overwhelms our other perceptions of the person and causes us to interpret his behavior very differently from what we would read into it if we believed him to be able-bodied. To recall Erving Goffman's useful definition of stigma, the fact that the person possesses an invisible handicap labels him with "a stigma, an undesired differentness from what we had anticipated" that casts his behavior and other social attributes into an entirely new and usually unfavorable light.[8] The facial expression, the tone of voice, the flawless front presented to the world take on entirely different meanings depending upon whether or not we *know* the person is an epileptic, is mildly retarded, or has a shameful, if invisible, deformity.

Handicaps short-circuit the conventions that regulate the interactions between individuals with normal minds and bodies. Whether the disability is immediately apparent or is merely known to exist, the handicapped person is placed at a social disadvantage. The able-bodied person is likely to interpret the other's "presentation of self" according to rules and conventions that discriminate against him in the same way that they discriminate against an individual who behaves according to the canons of an alien culture. This potential for misunderstanding is often magnified by the reverberating character of human interactions—and self-awareness; for not only do we reflect upon the results of our own thinking—i.e., our theory of what the other thinks—but we also take into account our theory of what the other person thinks we are thinking.[9] The result of this wheels-within-wheels character of human behavior is to give many encounters between able-bodied and handicapped individuals something of the Byzantine structure of a lovers' quarrel. Initial misunderstandings are magnified rather than overcome. Rather than correcting traditional stereotypes and misunderstandings, the relationship merely confirms each side in the correctness of its original views.

None of these problems is, of course, a once-only affair. Far more is involved than what occurs at the given moment of an encounter between two individuals, one able-bodied and the other handicapped. Handicapped individuals meet the able-bodied every day. Inevitably their self-image—and their images of able-bodied others—has been conditioned by this history. A lifetime of these often demoralizing interactions—or simply a childhood full of them—cannot but affect many individuals' self-image and ability to communicate. It is a history of *learned* inferiority.

Handicap and Racial Prejudice

The stigma of handicap bears many general resemblances to the stigma of race. Just as disability crucially influences the able-bodied person's interpretations of the other, so, too, race plays a decisive role in determining the inferences the racially prejudiced individual draws from the cues of interaction. To the racist, the same tone of voice, gesture, or manner of dress signals very different "facts" depending upon the speaker's race. An agreeable, assertive tone of voice in a white man is interpreted as a sign of "uppitiness" and unreliability in a black. A sudden wave of the arm to emphasize a point may pass unremarked from a white but may be interpreted as a physical threat from a black. And a style of dress that confirms the white person's respectable and conservative persona may strike the racist as a comic or irritating parody of the white world when adopted by a black.

Frequently the discovery that a person has epilepsy, an amputated leg, or some other concealable handicap dramatically changes our sense of who he is. There is a perceptual "snap," a sudden reinterpretation of the cues of interaction. Similar shifts in gestalts were common in race relations a generation ago, when the color line was still a powerful reality and the phenomenon of "passing for white" fascinated the popular imagination: "At a session of summer school an irate lady of middle age approached the instructor, saying, 'I think there is a girl of Negro blood in this class.' To the instructor's noncommittal reply, the lady persisted. 'But you wouldn't want a nigger in the class, would you?' Next day she returned and firmly insisted, 'I know she's a nigger because I dropped a paper on the floor and said to her, "Pick that up." She did so, and that proves she's just a darky servant trying to get above her station.' " [10]

Like racists, able-bodied people often confuse the results of social oppression with the effects of biology. The able-bodied person sees that handicapped people rarely hold good jobs, become culture heroes, or are visible members of the community and concludes that this is "proof" that they cannot hold their own in society. In fact, society systematically discriminates against many perfectly capable blind men and women, cripples, adults with reading disabilities, epileptics, and so on. In other instances —and again the parallel with white racism is exact—beliefs about the incompatibility of handicap with adult roles may be no more than a vague notion that "anyone that bad off" cannot possibly

lead an adult life, and no more respectable than the vie
a handicapped person is mentally or spiritually inferior t
he is physically different or that "people like that" have n
ness being out on the streets with "us regular folks." Like race
prejudice, a belief in the social incapacity of the handicapped
disguises ignorance or bigotry behind what we "see" to be an
obvious biological fact. For, like Tycho Brahe watching the sun
"move" around the earth, we do not see our belief. We *see* a
handicapped person.

There are, of course, differences between the discrimination
blacks face and the discrimination the handicapped face. In some
ways, the handicapped are better off: they meet no organized
brutality, no lynch-mob "justice," no Ku Klux Klan rallies. But
in other ways the handicapped are, surprisingly, much worse off.
There is the matter of pride, for example; blacks can, do, and
should be proud of their skin color and not want to change it;
but no one argues that mental retardation is good, that blindness
is beautiful, that doctors should stop research into the causes and
cures of cerebral palsy.

Perhaps the most important differences concern the diagnosis
of social ability that each entails; again, the handicapped come
off worse in the comparison with blacks. The racist did not deny
the black a place in normal life. Rather, he asserted that the
"innate" biological limitations of the black "race" made it necessary to restrict the black to the lowest rungs of the social ladder
—servant, field hand, unskilled manual laborer.[11] Only when he
encountered a black who refused to observe the color line did
the racist place the black in the sociological no-man's-land known
as deviance.[12]

The stigma of handicap, on the other hand, hampers its bearer's
ability to assume virtually *any* positive social persona. This
stigma is reflected in the common definition of *handicap,* which
the dictionary describes as a "deficiency, especially an anatomic,
physiological, or mental deficiency, that prevents or restricts normal achievement." Perceived only as a blind man, a cripple,
or a dwarf, the handicapped person is assumed to be incapable
of assuming any normal social functions, even the most humble
and demeaning: "I knew a man who had lost the use of both
eyes. He was called a 'blind man.' He could also be called an
expert typist, a conscientious worker, a good student, a careful
listener, a man who wanted a job. But he couldn't get a job in
the department store order room where employees sat and typed

orders which came over the telephone. The personnel man was impatient to get the interview over. 'But you're a blind man,' he kept saying, and one could almost feel his silent assumption that somehow the incapacity in one aspect made the man incapable in every other." [13]

The full consequences of this stress upon social incapacity are apparent only when one recognizes that the possession of an exclusively negative social identity (i.e., always being considered incapable of normal function) is psychologically and socially synonymous with being denied any human identity whatever. As Erving Goffman notes, "By definition, of course, we believe the person with a stigma is not quite human." [14]

Thus, the perception of a person as handicapped produces perhaps the most radical act of social declassification possible. Traditional racial stereotypes segregated the black *within* the lower reaches of normal society; only rebels and revolutionaries were defined as deviants. [15] But stereotypes about disability are different. They deny the handicapped any place at all in normal society. No wonder few of us find it strange that tens of millions of mentally normal disabled people are segregated from the mainstream of daily life. We simply don't expect to find them among us.

At one time or another society has perceived many groups of people besides the disabled as deviants—everyone from criminals to feminists to members of religious minorities. But regardless of the attributes that lead to exclusion from the normal community, if a person is perceived as a deviant it seems natural to diagnose the cause of his deviance as a kind of sickness or disease. [16] For example, those who believe homosexuality is a form of deviance frequently disagree about its causes. The psychoanalyst blames early childhood experiences. The neurophysiologist speculates about abnormal brain structures induced by hormonal imbalances during pregnancy. And the fundamentalist blames the homosexual for freely choosing the path of sin. Yet it is equally natural to call homosexuality a disease in all three of these paradigms.

The ease with which we diagnose deviance as a diseaselike state promotes confusion in our perceptions of handicapped people. A kind of vicious circle is often at work. Our misconceptions about the incapacitating consequences of a disability cause us to see the person as a deviant, as one who cannot fit into any of the roles assumed by normals in everyday life. Then the culturally determined associations of deviance with disease states encourage us to single out those aspects of the individual that are disease-like. For many handicapped people the result is that their very real biological limitation—their blindness or their paraplegia—provides instant legitimacy to the social stereotype that it first elicited. A car accident may cause paraplegia, but there is no meaningful sense in which a car accident causes the intense job discrimination that many qualified paraplegics experience. By assigning a medical cause to the paraplegic's deviance—his putative inability to assume any normal roles in society—lay society denies its responsibility for excluding the individual from normal life.

Racists have never applied a disease diagnosis so consistently to blacks. Only when the individual protested his oppression did they redefine him as deviant and transform the stigma of race into the symptoms of a diseaselike moral condition. The Uncle Tom accepted his "biological destiny" and was granted an "honorable, although humble," place in society. Nat Turner was perceived as a diseased madman precisely because he challenged his oppression. Today it is doubtful that many whites perceive black activists as diseased; thanks to generations of struggle, blacks have won a measure of legitimacy for their efforts at political organizing. Perhaps only in situations of real physical danger does something like the older disease diagnosis surface, as when we share a deserted subway platform at five in the morning with a young tough who looks as if he just stepped off one of the stage sets for *The Warriors.* But most able-bodied people remain the prisoners of traditional misconceptions about disability. Here it seems obvious that the diseaselike characteristics of handicaps *cause* the disabled person's deviance—especially when the stigmas of disability are genuine medical conditions like paraplegia. It requires a great effort of the imagination to recognize that the judgment of deviance comes first. The diseaselike condition, the handicap, dominates our perception of the person's social nature only because we have already decided that he is a deviant.

Perceptions of Handicaps Reflect Decisions about Deviance

In her biography of Moshe Dayan, the general's daughter writes that after he lost his right eye in battle, her father was mystified by the fascination his injury seemed to hold for many women. Dayan's handicap is one of the few that change dramatically in phenomenological appearance depending upon whether the person is a child, a woman, or a man. The nature of this change clearly shows how the able-bodied person's decision whether or not to treat a disability as a stigma of social deviance influences his perceptions of the handicapped person.

Conjure in your mind a military man with an eye patch. Is there not something romantic and heroic about the injury? Doesn't it suggest a dark and complex past, a will of uncommon strength, perhaps a capability for just enough brutality to add an agreeable trace of sinister and virile unpredictability to the man? Depending on one's politics, it can suggest a resourceful ally or a dangerous enemy. Mustn't a man be very tough and very competent to escape so lightly from a brush with death? No doubt these reactions explain why the only time Madison Avenue used a disability to enhance the glamour (and salability) of a commodity was in the Hathaway shirt ads of the 1960s.

Now replace the image of the Hathaway man who wears an eye patch with the image of a seven-year-old girl who wears one. For most people, something strange happens. The romance and mystery disappear; what we see is a handicapped child. There is something sad and even pitiful about her; we fear for her future and worry about her present. We think: This poor kid is going to have a hard time growing up and making it in this world. Whereas the presence of an eye patch made the Israeli leader seem even more of a hero, the presence of an eye patch on a child is a sign of damage, a cause for pity, an indication that this is a child whose ability to fit into some adult role in the future is in jeopardy.

Similar shifts in valence occur with a host of minor disfigurements or cosmetic blemishes, as an acquaintance of ours learned to his astonishment when, after a hiking accident that left him hobbling about for several weeks, he was told by a number of friends that he looked so distinguished using a cane that he should consider always using one. Needless to say, this is not something that anyone says to a young child who is forced to use a cane.

Many striking illustrations of the impact of social function upon one's perception of a handicap are provided in films. For example, in Jean Renoir's film *Grande Illusion,* Erich von Stroheim plays the part of a man with a brace under his chin, a lame leg, a body scarred by burns, and a back injury which requires that he wear a steel corset. While this enumeration suggests a severely disabled man, we do not perceive the commandant as handicapped when we watch the film because our tacit social grammar responds to his character, his job, and the period during which the film is set in such a way as to make his handicaps recede into the background.*

To begin with, the movie is set during wartime. During war our tacit definitions of disability are relaxed. We adopt a saner approach. What counts is not so much how a man looks (within limits) but whether he can still function; and the German officer is perfectly capable of discharging the duties of his assignment behind the lines.[17]

In addition, the social identity of the character played by von Stroheim helps to block our tendency to view the man as handicapped. An old Prussian aristocrat with a spartan sense of morality and honor, his fidelity to the symbols of his social position —fastidious appearance, perfect manners, a deliberate cultivation of an aesthetic sense—makes it impossible for us to cease viewing the man as a social adult. Finally—and perhaps most important— the aristocrat's military duties as commandant of a prisoner-of-war camp directly conflict with the attribution of social powerlessness which stands at the core of able-bodied society's definition of handicap. As commandant he controls the lives of hundreds of able-bodied prisoners.

Similar transformations in our conventional perceptions of particular disabilities are wrought when the bearer is a movie villain—one of those real-world deviants who are granted a conditional legitimacy in our fantasies, provided, of course, they are defeated in the end. Here, too, even severely incapacitating handicaps can signal that, far from being a pitiful social incompetent, the villain is unusually resourceful and cunning. Hence the false arm of Dr. No in the James Bond thriller *The Island of Dr. No,* or the gleaming, sinister hook on the arm of Captain Hook in *Peter Pan;* similarly, the cluster of disabilities that afflicts Dr. Strangelove in Stanley Kubrick's film of that name—the arm

* This shift in the social significance sometimes accorded disabilities during wartime was dramatically reflected in the employment experiences of disabled manual workers during World War II. All kinds of job qualifications that had effectively barred physically and sensorily disabled adults from work were suspended for the duration of the wartime labor shortage. With the return of normal labor-market conditions at the war's end, countless thousands of highly productive disabled workers were laid off.

that is not fully under his control, the partial paralysis that results in his being pushed about in a wheelchair and wearing
braces on his legs—do not always cause us to view the president's
adviser as handicapped.

Each of these examples of "positive" handicaps represents a
kind of gift of social convention, a physical trait that, in certain
settings and for certain social roles, enhances, or at least does not
actively undermine, the individual's claim to be taken seriously
as a social being. The magnitude of this gift commands our attention. The racist's perception of a black individual as a member
of the "Negro race" is unchanged regardless of whether the black
is perceived as a deviant (e.g., a Nat Turner) or as a loyal and
capable house servant. In contrast, there is no such thing as a
"good" handicap. That is, in those rare instances in which the
able-bodied world's social grammar decrees that a certain disabled person in a certain setting is not socially incapacitated, the
person is simply not perceived as suffering from a condition at
all: he is permitted to pass over into the world of social normals.

Needless to say, matters are very different for the great majority
of handicapped people. In nearly all instances the cripple, the
blind man, even the adult who admits to a reading disability, must
contend with the belief that, until proven otherwise, the handicap renders him less capable than an able-bodied person of similar
age, sex, and social background. Overcoming this presumption of
inferiority is not impossible, but it may require a very special kind
of sociological tour de force. Defined by society as a conspicuous
failure, one way out is open to all: the possessor of a negative
handicap can always prove that he is the exception to the general
rule *if* he can achieve conspicuous success in some area of life.

Perhaps no single example demonstrates more dramatically the
arbitrary character of the able-bodied world's perception of handicaps as biological conditions than the impact of success upon the
way in which almost any disability is perceived and remembered.
We do not think of Franklin D. Roosevelt as a great crippled
president; we think of him as a great president who, among many
other things, happened to be crippled. Nor do we customarily
think of John F. Kennedy as a handicapped president cut down
before he could redeem his promise. Yet he suffered from Addi-
son's disease, a chronic illness that qualifies its bearer to carry the
handicapped label. And while both Alexander the Great and
Julius Caesar were epileptics, it takes Jose Luis Borges (himself
blind but not considered handicapped) to remind us that in

Caesar's case, a handicap changed the course of history. While swimming in the Rhine, Caesar had an epileptic fit and nearly drowned. Only the presence of a soldier on shore saved his life. As a result of the incident, Caesar decided not to mount a major invasion of what is now Germany.

Nor do we remember that Lord Byron had a club foot and Alexander Pope had curvature of the spine. Elizabeth Barrett Browning was a paraplegic. Milton was blind when he wrote *Paradise Lost,* Beethoven was deaf when he wrote the Ninth Symphony, Nietzsche was a syphilitic, and Dostoevsky was an epileptic. Edison was deaf, and Freud spent the last sixteen years of his life wearing a prosthesis on his jaw. To speak of these men and women as handicapped seems a contradiction in terms. It seems so, we believe, because success defines a chronologically adult individual as carrying out certain adult functions so well that his inability to carry out other adult social functions is judged irrelevant.[18] We remember FDR's cigarette holder better than his wheelchair.

Again, note the contrast with society's traditional racist perceptions. We never forget the blackness of Paul Robeson, Jackie Robinson, and James Baldwin. Because they cannot escape their racial identification, their conspicuous success works to discredit traditional demeaning role stereotypes concerning blacks. But when a person successfully violates our preconceptions about disability, something very different takes place. The person's unusual accomplishments do not challenge our beliefs about disabled people as a social group. They seem to set the person apart, to exempt him from membership in the group. At most we view him as the exception that proves the rule, the one in a million who has made his mark despite the crippling inferiority of being handicapped. More often still, as our examples of famous disabled people suggest, we simply assume that he is able-bodied.

If a similar state of affairs prevailed in race relations, every black would lose his original ethnic identification the moment he enjoyed a measure of economic success. Upwardly mobile blacks would be classified as whites, and society would reserve the term *black American* for those individuals who remained in poverty.* While this analogy may seem somewhat extreme, it not only captures the logic of lay society's traditional vision of disability, but

---

* Something like this may be the case in Brazil, where social status appears to alter perceptions of race membership significantly and where, as the Brazilian saying goes, "money whitens." [19]

it represents the operational definition of disability that has been employed in nearly all government surveys of the general demographic characteristics of disabled adults. Virtually all surveys of the employment of disabled adults have traditionally excluded from their count any blind man, cripple, or other person who does not describe himself as economically disabled by his handicap—i.e., the successful.

All of these examples illustrate how our apparently objective perceptions of handicaps as socially incapacitating biological conditions are the perceptual products of a prior—and unconscious —social construction. Only when our tacit social grammar decrees that the disability is a stigma of deviance do we *see* a handicapping condition. But the moment that our social grammar decrees otherwise, either because of conspicuous success or because of some combination of social role and setting, we cease to perceive a handicapping condition. Far from being a response to an inflexible fact about biology, our perception of a handicap nearly always reflects an arbitrary, unconscious decision to treat normal social function and the possession of any handicap as mutually exclusive attributes.

Chapter 2

The Handicapped Role

In middle-class American society it is usually considered bad taste to make fun of the handicapped. Although often honored in the breach, this ideal of tolerance toward the disabled exerts a profound influence on how handicapped children and adults are treated. On the interpersonal level, the ideal provides the able-bodied with a purchase on dealing with the irrational fears that may be provoked whenever an individual is perceived as a social deviant, as well as the special fears aroused by the culture's emphasis on disability as a disease- or injury-related deviance.[1] On the community level, the ideal serves to define the nature of society's general obligations to the disabled and to suggest the most appropriate ways these obligations can be met. In performing these private and public functions the model plays the same role for disability as contemporary ideals of racial tolerance play in race relations. Tragically, this similarity in general social function is not matched by a similarity in the depth and clarity of the analysis of the nature of handicap that is provided by the model.

Tolerance toward Race and Tolerance toward Disability

Racial tolerance begins with an assertion of the equality of all racial and ethnic groups. This assertion takes the form of a direct challenge to the racist's perceptions and the racist's theories of race difference: blacks are not "self-evidently" inferior. In contrast, the lay culture's notion of tolerance toward handicapped people takes for granted the reality of the "self-evident" inferiority of the handicapped person. Instead of challenging this vulgar prejudice, it makes its analytic point of departure the negative feelings that our naïve perceptions of handicapped people often provoke in us. Yes, we say, handicapped people are indeed as helpless and incompetent as we believe them to be. But our response is unfair. Precisely because handicap is a diseaselike condition, we should treat the handicapped person as a sick person, a person who poses no threat to us but who requires the kind of mature tolerance that we automatically extend to a friend or neighbor who falls ill.

Thus, whereas contemporary ideas of racial tolerance challenge the legitimacy of traditional stereotypes about race, society's tolerance toward the disabled focuses upon disarming the able-bodied world's negative response to its stereotyped perception of disability as a form of deviance. That is, the ideal does not deny that a disabled person is socially deviant. Nor does it challenge the "rule" that a deviant person is incapable of fulfilling any positive social role unless he proves otherwise. Instead, it tries to exempt the handicapped person from the moral opprobrium that usually attaches to deviance.

Perhaps the best way to illustrate the difference between society's model of racial tolerance and its model of what, with some awkwardness, one might call "disability tolerance" is to examine what happens in two kinds of social encounters—those where an initial perception of a person as handicapped subsequently proves to be mistaken, and those where the disabled individual's behavior forces the able-bodied person to perceive him as a member of a socially and economically oppressed minority.

To begin with, consider the following hypothetical situation. On a trip abroad, we are invited to a party being held at the home of two professors who teach physics at the university. Before we meet our hosts, the doorbell rings and a new guest appears. It is their son. He is short, about four feet tall, with an unusually large head, light skin, and tight, peppercorn hair. His arms seem too long for the rest of his body, and his legs are unusually short. He has a broad, flat nose, full lips, and curiously Mediterranean eyes. Though his manner signals that he is adult, he moves with the agility of a child.

While we are taking all this in, we overhear a foreign woman in a bright print dress murmur, "What a pity. And he seems so intelligent, too."

"Not at all," replies her companion, a tall, handsome black man. "Here in Zaire, there are many people like him; as it happens, his parents are of pure Pygmy descent."

The shift in tolerance is instructive. As long as we believe the short man at the party to be disabled, we perceive him as the victim of a handicapping condition. There is something disturbingly incomplete about the man, and the sense of this taints our perceptions of his personality and his abilities. We don't know him; we haven't even met him yet; but we already suspect that he is crucially flawed mentally and morally. Quite possibly we experience a vague uneasiness and discomfort in his presence. There is a diseaselike taint attached to the man, and disease quite frequently arouses very complex feelings of fear, revulsion, guilt, and anxiety in the healthy.

Confronted with our first impressions, our conscience accepts them at face value and is at pains to reassure us that it is perfectly natural for us to feel the way we do, for the man's diseaselike deformities probably have warped his mind and character. However, continues our conscience, what is not appropriate is to blame or to punish the man for his diseaselike problem. Instead, we must attempt to hold our uneasiness and discomfort at arm's length and to relate to the man in the same fair and charitable way in which we seek to relate to the victim of any seriously incapacitating medical condition.

Should we now discover—as is illustrated in the example—that the man is not handicapped but the member of a racial minority, a new vision of the person snaps into place, and with it, a new vision of what it means to behave in a tolerant and open-minded manner. We may well still feel discomfort and uneasiness in the man's presence, but if we are honest with ourselves, we will readily admit that these feelings represent traces of a racist mentality and that we should extirpate them, root and branch. Because we now perceive an able-bodied man who belongs to a minority group, we know that we *should* treat him as a mental and moral equal in every respect, that any condescension on our part is paternalistic, and that there is no conceivable moral justification for feeling at all uneasy about his physical differences.

An equally great shift in our perceptions and in the model of tolerance that seems appropriate occurs when a disabled person talks about handicapped people engaging in political action. How can we keep alive our vision of him as the helpless victim of a handicapping condition when he is putting together a political organization and agitating for change? [2]

We interviewed such a man. From a purely medical point of view, he was seriously handicapped. Paralyzed from the waist down, lacking voluntary control of his bowel and bladder functions, he was confined to a wheelchair from morning to night and could get in and out of bed only with the greatest difficulty. He told us:

A few years ago I was selling medical equipment, and one day it suddenly hit me that there were a lot of people like me out in the real world, and that if we got ourselves organized and raised a little hell we could begin to get the able-bodied world to recognize that we had special needs and to take those needs into account when designing buildings, transportation systems, job requirements, and the like. Too often disabled adults and the parents of disabled children are afraid of raising hell. Action inevitably involves disturbing the status quo; for power to realign, it must first be disturbed. An important job for political organizations is the political education which teaches people that they do in fact have efficacy, power, and dignity.

The other day I went to a department store and found the whole place inaccessible. I said I would like to talk to whoever was in charge of physical facilities. They said okay and referred me to the manager. If I had said, "I want you to put ramps in this store," the manager's response might have been, "That's a good idea. Why don't you put it in the suggestion box?" But when I said I represent an organization that wants ramps in the store, then I had more pull. What matters when you confront an opponent is not really how strong your organization is, at least at this initial confrontation, but rather how strong he thinks it is.

The manager of the department store said he would talk to his board of directors, probably thinking that I would go away. Knowing that promises of some future action are frequently a ploy to get rid of some current nuisance, I pressed the issue and said I would be willing to meet with the board of directors or help the manager in designing the ramp.

It's important to align yourself with as many people as possible. I pointed out to the manager that there are advantages to ramps for people other than those in wheelchairs. I told him that I saw a lot of women in the store with babies in strollers who were having trouble getting up the stairs. I pointed out to him that a lot of old people have trouble maneuvering the same sorts of architectural barriers that are barriers to me. Even if a guy is not too crazy about disabled people, it'll be hard for him to knock mothers and old people.

So, you approach a businessman, a social worker, hospitals, places with rehabilitation, schools, parents; you talk to people. You find out where they are at. You tell them what you want to do. You organize and do it. And if you are able to make people realize that they can move, then they will move. And then you have accomplished a few things and the word seems to go out. And you meet more disabled people, and they start showing more interest. Sure, some are not politically oriented, but they realize that what you are doing is good for them and they will support you. I'm not saying that organizing is easy. But I am saying that it is necessary because, when all is said and done, we *are* an oppressed minority group.

These examples make something very plain.[3] By accepting the disease diagnosis of handicap, our ordinary ideal of tolerance and fairness to the disabled reinforces society's most damaging, demeaning, and unfair confusions about the nature of disability. A certain kind of paralysis may well be a permanent condition. But the social obstacles to adulthood encountered by the crippled child and adult are arbitrary, unfair, and of considerably greater importance than the biological limits to normal function that are imposed by the paralysis. A reading disability is a major and highly vexing diseaselike condition in a literate society. But the job discrimination and the social discrimination practiced against adults who cannot read is far more disabling than the frustrations in assimilating information through other channels. Blindness imposes obvious limits, but it is society that excludes the blind from the social and economic mainstream by refusing to make reasonable (and inexpensive) provision for the blind in its architecture, transportation systems, work requirements, and work practices and procedures.

The Handicapped Role

Talcott Parsons has observed that while most forms of social deviance condemn the individual to an unconditional exile beyond the perimeter of the normal social world, there is one extremely common form that does not. This is the deviance that stems from physical injury or accident. Provided the sick or injured person fulfills special obligations that apply when one is sick, society does not deny or demand constant new proof of the person's claim to a positive social identity.[4] Instead, society agrees to excuse him temporarily from his usual role obligations so that he can get well and return as soon as possible to his normal duties. Society extends to the sick or injured individual a "medical tolerance."

In Parsons's classic formulation, the sick role has four main characteristics, of which the last is by far the most important:

1. The patient is exempted from normal role obligations.
2. He is not held responsible for his state.
3. The state of being sick is considered conditionally legitimate *if*—
4. The patient cooperates with the source of help and actively *works* to achieve his own recovery.

A fifth characteristic, not explicitly mentioned by Parsons but strongly implied by his formulation, is the presumption that the sick role will be temporary.

A similar indulgence is accorded the handicapped person. He, too, is treated with a specifically medical tolerance. Like the victim of acute illness or temporary injury, he is excused from his "normal" role obligations and expected to fulfill the obligations of the sick role.

On the surface, the "handicapped role"[5] seems just as humane and fair as the sick role. Handicap is not viewed as a punishment for sin, nor is it invested with mysterious supernatural associations. A matter-of-fact, scientific approach is taken. Because the handicapped are portrayed as the victims of impersonal accidents, disease processes, and genetic imperfections, stigma and prejudice are obviously out of place. The handicapped cannot help being handicapped any more than the victim of acute disease can help being sick. What is needed is understanding and assistance.

Of course, there will always be people who take advantage of their handicap, just as there are people who use sickness to manipulate others and to shirk their duties and obligations. But, in general, handicapped people want to overcome their handicap, and the handicapped role clearly indicates what the obligations of the able-bodied world toward these people should be. As individuals and as a society, we must provide whatever assistance we can to help the handicapped conquer their disabilities. Thus, the handicapped role establishes a tacit social contract between the able-bodied and the handicapped. Being an ideal, the handicapped role also interprets the nature of handicap to both the handicapped and the able-bodied. It provides members of the society with a way to chart unprejudiced attempts to cope with the complexities of handicap—a conceptual map that also provides the able-bodied with a moral standard against which to measure their feelings and reactions to handicapped people. Yet because the culture's diagnosis of handicap as a diseaselike problem is seriously flawed, the application of the medical model of disease to handicap brings unexpected complications. The medical model of the handicapped role mystifies—or obscures—the important sociological dimension of handicap. It lends objective confirmation and moral legitimacy to the culture's diagnosis of handicap as a diseaselike problem. It explains—and prescribes—the most important social characteristics of handicapped people. And because it is so genuinely humane in intention—and draws upon the immense prestige of modern medicine—the handicapped role fatally obscures from view the disastrous psychological and sociological consequences that follow from expecting a handicapped person to fulfill permanently the role obligations expected of a good patient.

From the sociological point of view, the most remarkable characteristic of medical deviance—as ostensibly defined by the sick role—is its reversible character. Nearly every other kind of deviance—such as alcoholism, drug addiction, mental illness, or crime—confers a moral stigma on the individual that is generally not canceled by being pronounced "cured" or rehabilitated.[6] As Kai Erikson has noted, the individual "is ushered into the deviant position by a decisive and often dramatic ceremony, yet is retired from it with hardly a word of public notice. And as a result, the deviant often returns home with no proper license to resume a normal life in the community. Nothing has happened to cancel out the stigmas imposed upon him . . . earlier."[7] By viewing the disabled through the lens of medical tolerance, then, lay society chooses the most humane option that is compatible with its initial and prior classification of the handicapped as a deviant. However, this strategy, though well intentioned, is doomed at the outset by the peculiar irony inherent in assigning a role designed for curable illness or injury to what is perceived as an incurable condition—i.e., a handicap. Since no role expectation, however well intentioned or benign, can change the underlying biological reality of handicap, the fact that handicaps are incurable or chronic immediately reestablishes precisely the sociological link between disability and the many kinds of irreversible moral deviance that the handicapped role is intended to deny unequivocally. To engage in metaphor, the handicapped role establishes, on the plane of thought as well as on the plane of emotions, an open frontier between the categories of moral deviance and handicap—a network of analogical bridges and formal similarities that offers a constant temptation for the unprejudiced person to respond to a handicapped person as if the individual were somehow indelibly tainted morally or spiritually.

In short, because of the way the role asserts and seeks to mobilize the claims of the conscience, it generates new ways for disability to arouse fear and uneasiness in the able-bodied.

Guilt by Association

Although no one will openly condemn a handicapped child or adult as a moral failure, the implication of taint and moral inferiority is there all the same, and the handicapped role, in its formal resemblance to other permanent roles that are derived from temporary roles, subtly encourages and reinforces these negative feelings.

Disease is expected to be temporary. The natural assumption is that when one falls ill, either one will get well or one will die. (Only later, when the early crisis of the illness is past, does anyone begin to consider the possibility of a chronic disorder, and it always seems to take them by surprise.)

The sick role, although temporary, belongs to a certain class of temporary roles. The sick person is granted leave from his normal duties precisely so that he can return to them as quickly as possible. Provided that the patient cooperates with the source of the help and actively works to achieve his recovery, he is not held responsible for his failure to perform his normal duties, and his status as a patient is viewed as perfectly honorable and legitimate. Thus, in certain respects the sick role resembles the role of the apprentice in a trade, the student role, the role of the promising young politician, writer, or man of science, the role of the child. After a decent interval—long in the case of childhood, shorter in the case of the apprentice or recruit—a person is expected to move on and enter a permanent adult role. Apprentices become craftsmen, students assume adult careers, promising young people realize the promise of their youth, children grow up, recruits become soldiers. In each of these cases, the temporary role is viewed as a means to an end. In each, too, allowances are made for the individual's conduct as long as he is in his stage of apprenticeship.

Another, closely related family of temporary roles involves the integration of newcomers into cohesive social groups. Regardless of their characteristics, newcomers are forced into these roles as a kind of initiation into the group life. Words like *tenderfoot, greenhorn, novice,* and *nouveau riche* refer to such roles.

Finally, there is a most interesting class of roles in which behavior that is strongly condemned as immoral, immature, wasteful, and foolish if practiced all the time is countenanced as long as it is temporary. Spending otherwise condemned as profligate is considered by many people to be permissible and praiseworthy as long as it is done during the Christmas shopping period. All manner of riotous conduct is condoned during Mardi Gras. Behavior that would otherwise earn students or adults the label of agitators or revolutionaries is tolerated by the authorities as long as it takes place during or after a sporting event and does not last too long. While students are supposed to graduate, it is certainly permissible if they take a year off to "find themselves." And a level of immediate gratification and purposelessness, not to mention playfulness, that is otherwise frowned upon is permitted during vacations and the custom known as the honeymoon. To this category of deviant behavior that is sanctioned provided it is temporary we—following Parsons—would add sickness.

Each of these temporary roles involves an important deficiency in control or mastery. In the many apprenticeship roles, the deficiency is clearly in skill and experience. In the many novitiate or "rookie" roles, the individual is deficient in his ability to command respect, cooperation, and support from the members of the group who define him as a newcomer. In the many "holiday" or "breather" roles, a relaxation of control over one's emotions and impulses is temporarily sanctioned (regression, acting out, immediate gratification, passivity are all briefly permissible).

Conversely, when an individual persists overlong in any of

these roles, when, in fact, he transforms a temporary role into a permanent one, it is precisely that formerly sanctioned lack of control that now inspires disapproval.

The promising young man who does not realize his promise is accounted a moral failure. The "perpetual student" becomes first an object of concern and then, as the years drag on, a cause of irritation and an object of contempt. Newcomers who remain unintegrated into the group too long are thought of as failures and are reclassified as morally suspect outsiders. Children who fail to grow up are either handicapped (retarded) or sick (mentally ill). And people who try to live their lives as one long holiday, festival, or Christmas are considered playboys, debauchees, and profligates. In each case the transformation of a temporary role into a permanent role subjects its bearer to disapproval, contempt, and the stamp of failure.

However, nearly all temporary roles possess ways of deferring this ultimate moral reckoning. The student can justify taking unusually long to get his degree on the grounds that he has been physically or mentally ill. Bright young men struck down by disease before they can prove themselves will be given a second chance if they recover. The erstwhile playboy can explain his years of self-indulgence as the result of emotional problems that medication and psychotherapy have finally brought under control. One can avoid for a while being considered a dropout, a failure in one's career, or a dilettante by appealing to extenuating circumstances such as illness.

In invoking this excuse, the individual seeks the temporary shelter of the sick role. He ascribes his continued deficiency in control or mastery to a temporary breakdown of his physical or mental faculties. He seeks an additional grant of time—a supplementary leave of absence—so that he can regain his normal powers and bring his house into order as soon as possible. (Sometimes what is sought is not more time, but a reinterpretation of one's past, a retrospective leave of absence: in short, a second chance.)

Tragically, only the handicapped person is denied this valuable social option. Because his role represents the permanent version of the sick role, he cannot seek a reprieve from society's harsh moral judgments by invoking the *temporary* protection of the sick role. That is, the social category of "handicapped" defines a class of people who explain their inability to get well (and therefore to assert normal social mastery) by appealing to extenuating circumstances—an accident, a congenital defect, a chronic illness, all things beyond their control. As a consequence the handicapped cannot *escape* from being classified as permanently sick (and therefore handicapped) by appealing to circumstances beyond their control, for it is precisely that appeal which has landed them among the handicapped in the first place. Indeed, the only way that the handicapped role provides for redeeming one's social failure (a redemption available in all temporary roles that have become permanent) is the achievement of great success or power, as in the careers of FDR, Elizabeth Barrett Browning, or Feodor Dostoevsky.

The Transformations of Content and the Denial of a Social Identity

Perhaps the cruelest irony of lay society's attempt to deal fairly and honorably with handicap is this: what is a fair exchange in the sick role is transformed, by the attribute "chronic," into a restatement in scientific and apparently objective terms of the most oppressive traditional stereotypes about the social ability of handicapped people:

• The sick role's grant of a temporary exemption from normal role obligations changes into a permanent exclusion from normal opportunities—a refusal on the part of able-bodied society to believe that the handicapped person is capable of leading a normal social life.

• The sick role's decision not to hold the patient responsible for his state becomes a generalized inability to take seriously the handicapped person's attempts to assert his social abilities: instead of recognizing that when the handicapped person refuses to behave like a good patient it is because he is not just a patient, we treat legitimate acts of self-assertion as lapses of conduct for which the patient must not be held morally responsible and which require psychiatric assistance. That is, they are considered *symptoms of maladjustment.*

• The sick role's insistence that the patient actively cooperate with the source of help to achieve his own recovery turns into a permanent denial of a person's rights and dignity as a human being: we see nothing wrong with placing him under the perpetual tutelage of those experts who provide him with help, and we believe that the "patient" should constantly subordinate his own interests and desires—which include leading a normal social life—to the therapeutic goals and programs decreed by the professional who is providing the help.

This last transformation of the sick role is especially devastating because it reinforces the culture's primary definition of the handicapped person as socially incompetent in every respect. The handicapped person is not merely defined as powerless because he is "sick." He is defined as doubly powerless because he cannot even master the role obligations of an ill able-bodied individual of the same age. The able-bodied individual succeeds at getting well. Precisely because the handicapped person's biological deficit is not yet susceptible to cure, he "fails" to assert a similar mastery over his "ailment."

Thus, to relate to a person through the lens of the handicapped role is to imply that the person has been reduced to a state of absolute social incapacity. But note that a person incapable of discharging any social function is no longer a social creature; he is an isolate. Or, to recall the original Greek meaning of the word, he is an "idiot." For people identified by the handicapped role have been stripped of their social being. They have been reduced to mere biology.

Chapter 3

Handicap and the Social Pathology Model

Because lay society has perceived disability in terms of disease, it has granted the professional who specializes in handicap the same kind of blanket authority for dealing with all aspects of disability that it has accorded the physician who specializes in acute illness. Like the doctor in acute medicine, the professional has been expected to do far more than provide specialized services to the disabled and their families. The professional has been expected to formulate policy, to translate the growing store of specialized medical and social science knowledge about disability into a form understandable to able-bodied and disabled laymen, and, in general, to interpret the meaning of disability to society at large. The professional has also been expected to chart funding priorities for basic and applied disability research and to take responsibility for undertaking this research.

This delegation of responsibility confers enormous importance upon how the professional views disability. If the professional looks at disability the way laymen do, the handicapped person will have no one in the able-bodied community to whom he can turn for personal or political assistance. Both as individuals and as an oppressed social group the disabled will be trapped between the mutually reinforcing mystifications of layman and expert. If, on the other hand, the professional's vision honors the immense complexity of disability, the handicapped will have a potent political and personal ally. Precisely because society expects so much from the professional, he is in an especially favored position. The professional's immense prestige also provides him with the opportunity to help change the way that lay society views handicap and to help raise the political consciousness of the disabled and their families.

Tragically, professionals have played a very different role in handicap. Until quite recently, most professionals have exaggerated the biologically imposed limitations of handicaps just as much as the lay culture has done. A mere decade ago, a leading critic of the rehabilitation system for the blind wrote that the "attitudes and beliefs about blindness among [many] workers for the blind [are] not noticeably different from attitudes and beliefs of the general public." [1]

Even those professionals who reject lay society's misconceptions about disability have rarely attempted to assume responsibility for fostering social change and political organization. All too often a withering pessimism about the prospects for social change has prevailed. In the 1950s and 1960s, when other oppressed social groups were making impressive strides in attacking traditional patterns of discrimination, experts on handicap were saying that similar progress for the disabled would require *centuries*. The pessimistic thinking of professionals who rejected the disease diagnosis and the handicapped role was summed up this way as recently as the early 1970s: "Our culture has a well-developed value system relating to variations in physique. To change the negative attitudes of the culture towards those who are judged to be disabled may require hundreds of years of systematic labor. In the meantime we are confronted with the practical problem of helping the handicapped to live with some measure of usefulness and happiness." [2]

Despite the important changes now occurring in the field of handicap, many professionals continue to subscribe to these traditional beliefs. Just as crucially, even the most ardent advocates of specific civil rights reforms often inadvertently perpetuate the spirit of traditional stereotypes and pessimism in their day-to-day work as service providers, researchers, and policy makers. They do so because of the special problem-solving paradigm that the professional employs when defining and seeking to meet his professional responsibilities. It is a paradigm that continues to dominate the conduct of civil rights advocates as well as more traditionally minded professionals.

What is the paradigm? Simply, the notion of professionalism, the professional's vision of what it means to conceptualize and to approach a problem in a specifically professional way—a vision that is inculcated in human services professionals during their training and is then reinforced and "confirmed" by the structure of the professional's relationships to his peers and to his clients. Thanks to this paradigm, the professional seems to possess an objective, scientific method for discerning the clinical issues, the research issues, the service delivery issues, and the public policy issues that are raised by any group of people whose problems are so overwhelming as to require public assistance and private philanthropy. In addition to the disabled child and the disabled adult, these groups include alcoholics, drug addicts, mental patients, and underprivileged racial minorities. Following traditional practice, we shall refer to the paradigm as the social pathology model.[3]

At first glance, the professional's formulation seems to represent a distinct improvement over conventional views of disability. Both the disease diagnosis and the handicapped role, it will be recalled, blame *biology* for the social inferiority of the disabled. The cripple is said to be incapable of assuming normal social roles because the loss of the use of his lower limbs exerts a depressive influence upon all his social abilities; the blind man is incapable of all but the most menial work, such as is offered in sheltered workshops for the blind, because the loss of sight is believed to "cause" an equally grave loss of mental ability and positive personality characteristics. In contrast, the social pathology model takes no fixed position on the cause of the handicaps. The model argues that the disabled person's problems may be caused by environmental factors (such as how the person was raised, or the prejudice and discrimination he has experienced on account of his disability), the innate biological limitations of the handicap (as is the case for the profoundly retarded individual), or a complex mixture of biological and social factors. Thus, whereas lay society dogmatically says biology causes incapacity, the social pathology model encourages the professional to approach the question of cause in an unbiased scientific manner or, to recall a common synonym, a *professional* manner.[4]

However, the professional's problem-solving paradigm fails to follow up on this promising beginning by making a clean break with lay society's vision of disability as a kind of social deviance. Though the details of the professional's deviance analysis may differ considerably from the biologically oriented analysis, the net result of the continued emphasis upon disability as deviance is once again to place the spotlight of attention on what the disabled person is not—*not* achieving at grade level in school, *not* having achieved a satisfactory emotional adjustment to the biological and social realities of his handicap, *not* possessing the compensatory skills required for gainful employment.

Perhaps the best way to suggest the hazards of applying the social pathology model to handicap is to mention briefly some of the criticisms that have been directed at the model in human services areas outside handicap.* All of these criticisms converge upon this common theme: by relying exclusively upon a deviance analysis, the model frequently frustrates the professional's good intentions. Indeed, instead of providing a humane alternative to lay society's prejudices about people in need, the social pathology model often encourages the professional to behave in ways that are perfectly consistent with society's harsh and unfair stereotypes. Thus, in recent years psychiatrists and legal experts have pointed to the abuses of civil liberties that have been sanctioned by employing the social pathology model in the rehabilitation of prisoners and the treatment of institutionalized mental patients.[5] Sociologists and political philosophers have warned of the hazards of relying too heavily upon a model that reduces all moral and political issues to apparently "objective" questions of deviance and health.[6] Social historians and social scientists have attacked the use of the model to curtail sharply the family's traditional responsibilities for child rearing and justify the increasingly dominant role of experts as arbiters of child-rearing practices and goals.[7] Indeed, within medicine itself, there is a growing awareness that the medical model has fostered serious confusions about the moral and psychological dimensions of medical care.[8]

Until the late 1960s professionals looked at the needs of black children and black adults almost exclusively through the social

---

* To the best of our knowledge, the relevance of the social pathology model to disability has never been seriously questioned, let alone comprehensively reexamined. One of the side effects of our survey of the handicapped child's needs through a minority-group lens is that we will also be able to present what we believe to be the first thoroughgoing critique of the application of the social pathology model to handicap.

pathology lens. More recently, this reliance upon the traditional paradigm has come under heavy attack. These criticisms provide an invaluable perspective on the limitations of applying the social pathology model to the handicapped individual.

To begin with, critics have noted that the social pathology model defines the problems of the underprivileged black child in terms of his deviations from the established norms of behavior for middle-class children—children who grow up in a vastly different social world.[9] This deviance analysis of the child has concealed the fact that every child, black or white, able-bodied or handicapped, constantly responds to the social context in which he grows up and to the vision of his future options in adulthood (and therefore his future adult identity) that is transmitted to him by the world around him. The black child who seems maladjusted when judged by the norms of mainstream society may be very well adjusted indeed to the social life that the mainstream imposes upon his minority group.[10]

In its most extreme forms, the professional's middle-class bias has led many professionals in the past to approach the black child as a small deviant, an isolated individual whose educational and psychological needs could be met by strategies devised for middle-class children who failed to attain the norms of their social class. When the professional has tried to relate the black child's problems to the child's family life, the social pathology lens has frequently led him to assess family child-rearing practices by middle-class standards, to explain the child's problems as being caused by the observed deviations from middle-class family norms, and to then devise "cures" that attempt to persuade minority families to adopt middle-class child-rearing practices. All too often this emphasis has meant that the professional has forgotten that family life can be understood only in terms of the family's social context—and that what may represent a pathological adaptation in one stratum of society may represent a highly positive adaptation in some other stratum of society.[11]

A second criticism of the application of the social pathology model to the problems of black children has focused on the interpersonal consequences of the professional's exclusive focus on helping the child correct his deviance. This focus leads some professionals to treat the black child as a small patient—to expect the child to subordinate all his other concerns to the task of cooperating with the care giver; and when the child instead persists in behaving like a child, the professional is encouraged to cite this failure to fulfill the expectations of the sick role as evidence of the child's maladjustment.

Similar criticisms have been directed at the professional's relationships with the child's parents, for here too the professional often expects the client to submit to the rules of the sick role—either because the professional views the parent as part of the problem (perhaps because of "incorrect" child-rearing practices, for example) or because the professional expects the parent to subordinate all other concerns to making sure that the child meets the remedial goals set for him by the professional.

Many critics have noted a closely related failure, which also stems from the professional's use of a deviance lens—an inability to recognize that the minority-group parent must mediate among a host of competing demands that range from the insistence of other professionals that everything be subordinated to *their* particular management plans, to the parent's need to take account of his own insight into the child's needs and strengths, to the often overwhelming task of locating and obtaining a proper mix of services, to paying for these services as well as for the hidden expenses that attend many handicaps. The professional fails to perceive these daunting managerial demands because his model of service delivery encourages him to emphasize the importance of the parent's following *his* instructions. For similar reasons the professional either refuses to satisfy the parent's appeal for emotional support and counsel (because counseling is not his specialty) or meets this need in a way that fails to do justice to the magnitude of the parent's managerial responsibilities for the well-being of the child.[12]

Yet another criticism of the application of the social pathology model to blacks has focused upon the theory of social change that is frequently associated with the model. The theory asserts that the best way to improve the social position of an underprivileged minority relative to other groups is to provide the minority individual with a set of services that seeks to minimize his deviation from the mainstream—especially first-rate education and vocational training.[13] This approach is useful, but it seriously oversimplifies the problem of achieving social change in the face of prejudice and discrimination. In a racist society such as our own, direct political assaults on the mechanisms of structural discrimination are at least as important as education and vocational training.

Thanks to these—and similar—cirticisms, the professional's vision of the minority child's needs and problems has begun to undergo dramatic change. The need for an equal emphasis upon attacking systemic discrimination against racial minorities and the provision of services to individuals is generally recognized. An increasing number of professionals who work with minority groups are aware of the ease with which they can inadvertently force their clients to obey the dictates of the sick role. There is a freshening trend against the public schools' traditional ethnocentrism, as well as the ethnocentrism of the psychologists, social workers, and other psychotherapeutically trained professionals who have worked with and studied minority children and their families in the past. An awareness that all behavior is an adaptation to the social context in which the individual lives—and therefore can be understood only by means of that context—is growing. And there is a new respect for the many ways that the adult's daily experience of discrimination indirectly shapes the pathways of childhood.

Professionals in handicap have traditionally approached the handicapped in the same way that professionals have traditionally approached minorities. By failing to heed the recent criticisms of the application of the social pathology model to racial minorities, those who work with handicapped people run the risk of continuing to reproduce all their traditional mistakes—and those of professionals in minority areas—during a period in which public awareness of the problems of the disabled reaches an unprecedented level of intensity. For the professional committed to a civil rights analysis of disability there is a special irony in this continued acceptance of the social pathology model. Even as he denounces lay society's misconceptions about disability in the name of a civil rights analysis, he is likely to propose clinical, research, service-delivery, and policy strategies that are perfectly compatible with the traditional view of handicap. This irony finds its counterpart in lay society. Translated into popular form, the social pathology model represents a humanized version of lay society's ideal of medical tolerance toward the disabled, a version that avoids society's crude exaggeration of biology. As more and more professionals emphasize the abilities of the handicapped in the name of a civil rights analysis, there is a real danger that many able-bodied people will confuse the social pathology model with a civil rights analysis of handicap. Here, too, what we earlier called the "law of least effort" is likely to play a major role in perpetuating a new set of misunderstandings about handicap. The professional's traditional lens is likely to gain widespread popularity in lay society precisely because it requires far fewer modifications of the conventional wisdom about disability than the minority-group analysis.

In this section we have explored the three most important ways in which lay society and human services professionals have viewed the handicapped individual and his problems. Although each paradigm has its own unique shortcomings, a common flaw dominates. Each of these models treats disability as a kind of deviance, a departure from the biological or behavioral norms of the able-bodied world. This emphasis upon the negative characteristics of handicapped individuals accounts for the most serious shortcomings of society's attempts to deal positively and humanely with the handicapped child and adult. For while the biological limitations of a handicap can certainly be approached as a deviation from the norms of biological health or completeness, the deviance lens imposes a tragic simplification of the social dimension of disability.

To do justice to the complexity of disability—and to dismantle the structures that have excluded the disabled from the mainstream—we must all learn from the example set by blacks and other oppressed groups in the past generation. Disability must be approached from two complementary—and equally crucial—perspectives. A *political perspective* is essential because only a civil rights movement, supported by a massive federal commitment to integration, can end the exclusion of handicapped people from the social mainstream. Just as important, however, the immediate needs of each person with a handicap must be approached from an *ethnographic perspective* that also draws upon the minority-group lessons of the past decades: we must discard the intellectual straitjacket of the social deviance analysis and devote as much effort to understanding the handicapped person in terms of his own norms and social situation as to seeking to reduce or cure his specifically biological limitations. In the pages that follow, we shall seek to implement this two-pronged strategy. We shall regard the handicapped child as a member of an oppressed minority rather than as a small patient or a small deviant. Rejecting the artificial distinction that traditional discussions of handicap draw between the problems of childhood and the problems that await the individual in adulthood, we will follow the practice of recent students of minority problems and explore the child's need for a viable adult future as well as his needs during childhood. In the largest sense, our task is one of both integration and discovery. Some of the most important questions about handicap rarely, if ever, have been asked. By the same token, of course, we do not wish to forget or to ignore what is of value in the traditional strategies. By selectively rethinking the spectrum of the handicapped child's needs and problems, we hope to contribute to the emergence of a minority-group model of handicap that conserves as much as it innovates—a model that honors what is best in the past even as it seeks to replace the traditional vision of the handicapped child with a vision that is more in accord with the child's needs and abilities.

Part Two

The Undiscovered Childhood

Chapter **4**

The Case for a
Developmental Psychology
of Handicap

"It is not surprising," said the sociologist Kai Erikson, "that the members of the community seem reluctant to accept the . . . deviant on an entirely equal footing. In a very real sense they do not know who he is." [1] This is certainly the case for the handicapped child. There is a crucial sense in which not only the society at large and the professionals entrusted with his care, but even his parents, do not know who he is.

A leading authority on handicap has put the matter this way:

Suppose you are approached by a mother who has a deaf child. "I understand that deaf children tend to become maladjusted," she says. "What can I do to prevent this?"

"Well," you say, "how old is your child? Is it a boy or a girl? How much hearing does he have? . . . How old were you when the child was born? . . . Is anyone else in your family deaf or hard of hearing? Does the child show signs of maladjustment now?"

The questions, of course, can be endless. A curious thing about them is that there are only common sense reasons, or often no reasons, for believing the answers have any direct relationship to the child's behavior. After the answers are received you may say, "Treat him as if he were normal, but *don't* expect as much of him as if he were

55

normal. Don't spoil him, but on the other hand, *do* make allowances for his disability. A special nursery school for deaf children would be a good thing, but then he has to live in a world with normally hearing people, so a regular nursery school for deaf children would be a good thing too. It all depends upon what kind of child he is." In other words, we don't know. We don't know in general, and we don't know what it depends on. The responsibility is passed back to the parent with directions that are contradictory and impossible to fulfill.

Similarly, suppose a parent brings a six-year-old cerebral palsied child and raises the specific question: "Can my child get along in school?" Often we don't know. After asking innumerable questions all that can be said is, "Let's try him out and see." If he gets along, then he gets along, and that's fine. Of course, the waste, frustration, anxiety, and psychological damage to the child if he doesn't get along are unfortunate but inevitable. Clearly this is an unsatisfactory state of affairs.[2]

Nor is the professional's ignorance and uncertainty confined to the child's psychological and social needs. We also know little about how to educate the handicapped; as one expert recently noted: "Theory and practice in special education today are rarely based upon scientific evidence because so little good research has been done on ways to help disabled children learn." [3]

The professional's ignorance is compounded by the ignorance of parents. The overwhelming majority of parents with handicapped children are themselves able-bodied. The complications introduced by this crucial difference between parents and their handicapped children is suggested by imagining what raising a black child would be if, like handicap, skin color were distributed more or less at random from one generation to the next— both at birth and as the result of childhood disease and injury. Suppose that every couple, regardless of their skin color, had a one-in-eleven chance of having a black baby and a ten-in-eleven chance of having a white baby. Suppose, in addition, that every white child had a one-in-one-hundred chance of becoming black —as a result of a disease or injury—sometime during childhood or youth. Lacking the autonomous cultural tradition possessed by black parents, white parents in our hypothetical world would be able to take nothing for granted when raising a black child. They would have to invent and improvise, all the while having to cope first with their shock, guilt, and anger at having a black child at all, and second with the prejudices and misconceptions about the abilities of blacks that are part of their cultural heritage, just as the disease diagnosis and the handicapped role are part of the cultural heritage of most able-bodied parents with handicapped children.

Because few parents have had the experience of being handicapped themselves, there is no cultural tradition that tells a parent how to raise a handicapped child. Nor is experience in raising an able-bodied child often a sufficient guide. Indeed, experience with a normal child may make the parents' task even harder by constantly fostering comparisons between the handicapped child's behavior and the behavior of able-bodied siblings when they were the same age. In such a situation, reliable scientific information about the special developmental needs of handicapped children is not simply a useful source of supplementary information for the parent. It comes close to being a necessity.

Here, then, is what we consider the most important reason for establishing a tradition of uncompromising excellence in studies of the psychology and social psychology of handicap. It is not because we prefer science to parental wisdom, cultural tradition, or the insights of the experienced clinician or teacher. Rather, it is because our society seems to lack anything like a tradition for raising reasonably happy, reasonably self-fulfilling handicapped children that we are prepared to ascribe an importance to basic research out of all proportion to its importance for other groups of stigmatized children. Science must work overtime to provide information that can be integrated into that mixture of love, anger, inspiration, and obstinacy that we call parenting.

Toward a Developmental Psychology of Handicap

Traditionally, a very narrow vision of childhood dominated disability research. Leaving the study of normal development to their colleagues who worked with the able-bodied, psychologists focused upon pathology. In the main, they explored two interrelated questions: how does a child adjust to being disabled, and how does the disability restrict or impede the child's ability to function normally? [4] Such was the prestige of the social pathology paradigm that researchers often explicitly treated the child as a small deviant. Able-bodied norms of behavior prevailed, and rarely, if ever, did investigators question the relevance of these norms to children with handicaps.

Even today most disability research conforms to this pattern. Nowhere else in psychology does one find so many studies which, by seeking to identify a difference, any difference, between a handicapped group and a normal group, parody the individual difference psychologies of the late nineteenth and early twentieth centuries.[5] And nowhere else, too, can one find theories that were discarded years ago in other areas of psychology still guiding research.[6] This barrenness is compounded by the unusually poor technical quality of most disability research, the methodological weaknesses so often noted in research reviews.[7]

Fortunately, there have recently been some signs of change. A small but growing number of studies have begun to apply developmental models to the handicapped child.[8] The perspective on disability implied by these approaches is strikingly different from the one that prevailed in the past. Developmentalists assert that the child plays an active role in his development, that he grows as a result of his interactions with the physical and social environment. Emphasizing the positive, they propose that all but the most severely retarded or emotionally disturbed possess the potential to develop normally. They speak of the need to foster this development rather than the need simply to correct deficiencies. And they stress the importance of providing every child with the kind of emotional and intellectual stimulation that is appropriate to his stage of development.

So far, however, developmentalists have made a crucial oversight. They take it for granted that theories constructed for able-bodied children can correctly interpret the developmental significance of the handicapped child's behavior. The importance of this research shortcoming cannot be emphasized too much. Because of stigma and misunderstanding, handicapped children often live in a social world that is radically different from the one inhabited by their able-bodied peers, and their physical or mental disabilities often impose sharp constraints on the ways that they can obtain and analyze experience. These social and biological differences raise a fundamental theoretical question for the field of child development: *do some handicapped children develop according to a healthy logic of their own?* By ignoring this question developmentalists do more than imperil the value of their research; they run the risk of sometimes perpetuating the traditional deviance analysis of disability in a more subtle and more socially acceptable form.* It is simply not enough to apply mainstream developmental theories to disability. Psychologists must first assess the applicability of these theories to each of the many groups of children with handicaps.

This conclusion is supported by several independent lines of inquiry, much of it with ethnic minorities. Studies suggest that inner-city children often display their greatest mental and social sophistication in areas of life that conventional developmental tests overlook—such as coping with the dangers of street life, rising in the hierarchy of a gang, taking responsibility for younger siblings, and fashioning a positive sense of self in a racist society.[10] A number of recent studies have concluded that conventional theories of personality and social development are biased against women in a similar way.[11] Still more support comes from one of the very few longitudinal studies of handicapped children. This work focused upon Canadian children born deformed because their mothers had taken the drug Thalidomide during pregnancy.[12] Researchers discovered that, contrary to expectation, the severity of the child's physical handicap was of only secondary importance in affecting his overall emotional and intellectual development. As Thérèse Gouin-Décarie and Monique O'Neil observe:

. . . This problem is not primarily a medical problem. It is first and foremost a social problem. Let us but mention a single indication of this fact. The initial reactions of mothers of Thalidomide children, their perception of their child's handicap (which, moreover, continued to evolve over time) and their emotional relationship with their child was always a function of the social norms of the surrounding social milieu. In every case the seriousness of the malformation only played a secondary role.[13]

Findings like these led Gouin-Décarie and O'Neil to conclude that personality theories developed for able-bodied children simply don't seem to fit the facts of the Thalidomide children's lives.

Finally let us note . . . that the categories so often used in the work dealing with handicapped children (acceptance, rejection, over-pro-

---

* The small French literature on the intellectual development of handicapped children also suffers from this shortcoming. Piagetian tests have been used for decades, but they have served as diagnostic tools rather than as a point of departure for careful studies of the relevance of Piagetian theory to handicapped children. By and large, this literature simply records the fact that some groups of handicapped children seem to deviate from the developmental norms established by Piaget in his work with able-bodied children.[9]

tection, guilt feelings, etc.) appear to us to be neither adequate nor functional. The phenomena in question are so tightly intertwined with sociological context that the methods of analysis of social psychology (especially those used to treat the problems of minorities) appear to be far better able to do justice to the reality [of the child's handicap] than the methods of analysis of clinical psychology. . . .[14]

But if conventional theories are "neither adequate nor functional," it seems that the place to begin is where they leave off—by closely examining how mainstream personality theories fail to do justice to the ways in which the handicapped child's growth is "tightly intertwined with the sociological context" of the handicap. Similar questions, we believe, must be directed at present-day theories of social development and of intellectual development.

We systematically explore these issues for the first time in our discussion of gaps in psychology's understanding of how handicapped children grow up. Throughout we will probe the ability of present-day developmental theories to do justice to the social context of disability. We will assess their relevance for children who are subjected to the special socialization experiences of a handicapped childhood. Needless to say, precisely because our enterprise is exploratory it can offer no secure conclusions about the chief characteristics of the handicapped child's development. What it can do is to offer a number of plausible working hypotheses about the most fruitful points of departure for future research in this area. It is our hope that by going beyond a narrow critique of the existing handicap literature we can take the first steps toward initiating serious and responsible debate about how best to integrate the study of the handicapped child into the mainstream of clinical and experimental child psychology.

Our emphasis upon the social context of a handicapped childhood is by no means exclusive, and from time to time we will examine some of the ways that the child's own response to the biological aspects of his disability may affect development. But our strategy will result in one significant omission in our survey of research issues: because of limitations of space and time, we will not consider the impact of the specifically biological limitations of the child's disability upon his growth. Our decision is made easier by the existence of excellent summaries of recent work done in this area. Thus, we will not examine the questions raised by the distinguished series of studies of the intellectual and personality development of blind children which have emanated from the groups centered around Selma Fraiberg at the

University of Michigan Medical Center and Dorothy Burlingham at the Hampstead Child-Therapy Clinic in London. The results of this work have been published in a series of books and papers that could well stand as a model for the rest of the field.[15] Nor will we discuss the important research conducted in the past decade into the cognitive and linguistic development of deaf children by Edward S. Klima, Ursula Bellugi, Hans Furth, Eric Lenneberg, and others. Here, too, excellent surveys are readily available, and the research has focused on the impact of the biological handicap upon development, rather than on the impact of social stigma.[16]

We must also signal a very different kind of omission, one forced upon us by the impossibility of anticipating the results of future research. Someday, when the field of handicap has joined the mainstream of experimental psychology, an important literature will concern itself with the interaction between development and the dynamics of the handicapped child's family. A kind of family sociology or anthropology will be constructed.[17] Personality differences will be explored. Differences in social background will be taken into account. Special emphasis will be placed upon comparing families with able-bodied parents to families in which at least one of the parents shares the child's disability and to comparing these families with those in which a handicapped parent does not have the same kind of handicap as the child. In the meantime, we can only say that normative data are absent, that any good clinician has a point of view on the matter, and that anyone with some familiarity with the general literature on families and a good imagination can construct almost any kind of theory that he wishes about the interaction of a particular handicap with family life. What is needed, in our view, is the elaboration of a kind of taxonomy in which typical family "solutions" to the problems posed by raising a seriously handicapped child are traced out. Ultimately, we would like to see this descriptive framework supplemented with more detailed models of family structure as well. However, long before this is possible, simpler naturalistic studies that might be of great interest could be carried out. No one, for example, has sought to locate those factors of family life that correlate strongly with a handicapped child's achieving independence and self-respect later in life. Something similar is the case for nearly every other aspect of the child's social experience, and for nearly every group of handicapped children. Wherever one looks, basic descriptive work is lacking.

The Relevance of Handicap to the Interests of Mainstream Developmental Psychology

Remarking on the generally poor quality of disability research, many critics have emphasized the need to attract first-rate investigators from other areas of psychology. As Saad Z. Nagi has observed, part of the problem is institutional. Just as services for the handicapped are hopelessly fragmented and underfinanced, so, too, research "suffers from limitations of support, fragmentation of R & D activities, and the absence of a major institute or center to serve the function of a clearing house." [18] Because of these shortcomings, we strongly endorse Nagi's call for the establishment of a National Institute of Handicap. If funded on a scale commensurate with the incidence of handicap in the population, such a center could serve as a powerful force for upgrading the quality of research. It could begin to persuade some of the best scientists and most promising students in psychology to devote some of their time to handicap, thereby helping to establish the institutional foundations for integrating handicap into the mainstream of experimental psychology.

But something else is also required. Psychologists in other areas of child development need to reassess the relevance of disability research to their own theoretical interests. They need to be persuaded that disability provides an opportunity to perform socially useful research while investigating difficult questions about the nature of the mind. Support for these contentions will be forthcoming in the survey of research issues. However, our emphasis upon the needs and problems of the handicapped may overshadow one question of such potential importance for the rest of psychology that it deserves special mention here. This is the possibility that the study of how handicapped children grow up may provide the developmental psychologist with a crucial litmus test, a way to sort out the degree to which today's theories of personality, social behavior, and intellectual growth are culture-bound or culturally unbiased.

Alone among children, the handicapped child can be given all the material and emotional "perquisites" of childhood and still be denied a chance to grow up because of the cultural definition of his handicap that he confronts at every turn. He may enjoy all the great emotional constants of childhood—the presence of loving, affectionate, decent parents and a comfortable standard of living—but still confront inconsistencies in his social experience fully as great as any faced by even a schizophrenic child. In effect, handicap represents a vast and cruel "experiment of nature." It joins a profound distortion of the child's social relations (which is usually the end result of a pathological family life) with what is found only in a normal family life—loving parents, affection, sensitivity, and a decent level of material comforts.[19] This gruesome "experiment of nature" may well be of crucial importance for attempts to study the development of able-bodied children.

In every culture, however different its social organization, its customs, and its technology, the normal course of childhood involves certain general experiences and expectations. A normal child can assume he is like his parents and siblings. He can also assume that in the fullness of time he will become an adult. He also encounters at every turn a complex network of social and biological links between himself, his parents, and the community. True, he may belong to a despised and persecuted minority, but even the lowliest untouchable has his kith and kin, his family and the society of other untouchables. For these great constants of childhood to be disrupted requires a severe rent in family life —the death of one's parents and relatives, the dislocation of a shantytown slum, famine, or the equally disorganizing effects of mental illness or parental malevolence. Only for the handicapped child can these features be altered without invariably being accompanied (in our culture) by a pathological transformation of his family.

If this argument is correct, a conclusion of great importance follows: when seeking to assess the universality of theories of development—and the relative roles of nature and nurture in child development—one may be well advised to study handicapped children as well as able-bodied minority children and children in non-Western societies. Indeed, in certain possibly decisive respects, it is possible that the socialization experiences of some handicapped children (e.g., those with severe disabilities raised in reasonably normal homes) may be far more different from the white middle-class average than the socialization experience of even the child who grows up in the most exotic of non-Western cultures.

Invariably, theories of development are based upon experience with white middle-class children.[20] In attempting to overcome their ethnocentrism, many investigators have sought to devise culture-free measures of development or to construct indices of

development that take into account the specific differences between the culturally defined priorities presented to white middle-
class children and those presented to minority-group children.
Others have sought to study children in non-Western cultures.
So far, at least, these efforts have foundered on the same rock.
Because the overlap between cultures is partial, every attempt to
study the growth of a child in a culture other than one's own
requires the investigator to make a tentative construction of the
main outlines of the child's culture.[21] Without this construction
one has no guide to what kinds of questions involving cognitive,
moral, or emotional development are relevant. Yet with this
construction one risks constantly confusing elements of the child's
culture with projections of one's own cultural world view, and
the results of one's studies remain inconclusive.*

It is conceivable that the handicapped child may provide the
investigator with an opportunity to study groups of children who
do not pose such profound cross-cultural problems because they
belong to his own culture, yet who are subjected to an array of
socialization experiences that are even more alien to the norms
of an able-bodied American childhood than those of a child who
grows up in a non-Western culture. Should this prove to be the
case, the implications for constructing meaningful tests of theories
of child development would be staggering. For years psychologists
have rushed off to faraway places in the hope of testing the
relative importance of nature and nurture, the universality of
Piaget's stages of cognitive development, Kohlberg's stages of
moral development, and various psychodynamic theories of emotional development. Is it possible that all this time the best group
of children with whom to explore these and other crucial developmental issues has been quite literally staring us in the face?
Is it possible that the study of the handicapped child represents
the best way to deepen our understanding of how all children
grow up?

One should add, of course, that even if this turns out to be
the case, it will hardly be a cause for celebration. America's treat-

---

* Moreover, there appears to be something about our own socialization experiences
that makes it almost irresistible to ascribe the inferior performance of a minority-
group child on a middle-class test to the inferiority of the subculture or to genetic
differences in innate ability. As Marvin Harris shows in his brilliant *The Rise of
Anthropological Theory*, a vulnerability to racism and cultural chauvinism is part
of the cultural baggage of Western man.[22] Like the concept of handicap, it is not
something that requires the active operation of malevolence; it is one of the ways
of viewing experience that we automatically imbibe from tradition.

ment of its handicapped children is, quite simply, a national disgrace. But the fact remains: parents and professionals have a desperate need for reliable information about the best ways to foster a stigmatized child's optimal development. They are not getting that information now, and it is most unlikely that they will ever get it as long as disability remains a backwater. Changes in federal funding priorities will help. But more than money is needed. Disability research must become intellectually respectable among mainstream academics. It must begin to attract psychology's brightest talents. Nothing would better serve these ends than the discovery that the best way to pursue the great issues in contemporary developmental psychology is to study how handicapped children grow up.

Again and again in the history of child psychology breakthroughs have occurred whenever a way is found to view the child's world not as it appears to the adult investigator but as it appears to the child himself. While none has been more than a crude and imperfect approximation of the child's construction of the world, these attempts have always represented major advances over the naïve assumption that the child is a miniature adult. Thus, from Freud we learned that a three-year-old, a seven-year-old, and an eighteen-year-old live in very different emotional worlds and respond to the same "objective" set of circumstances quite differently. From Piaget we have learned that something similar is the case in rational problem solving. The way intellectual problems are perceived, as well as the tools available to the child to solve these problems, changes dramatically with age. And from the psycholinguist we have learned that the language of small children is more than an imperfect version of adult speech: it is a different and simpler language unto itself, complete with its own semantic and grammatical rules—a code that, like the child's thought and character, evolves over time. In each of these instances we have learned to think of the child as an individual who views the world through different lenses at different ages and who has available to him radically different sets of emotional, linguistic, and conceptual tools at each stage of life.

These hard-won insights into the gradations of growth in ablebodied children cannot be taken for granted by those who work with handicapped children and study their development. They must be painstakingly tested anew because the social and biological constants of a handicapped childhood are often very different from those of an able-bodied childhood. If the psychology of handicap is to do justice to the children it studies, it must take the initiative in assessing the relevance of able-bodied developmental norms to children with disabilities. In Piaget's phrase, we need a psychology that is not only developmental in spirit but also ethnographic in spirit, a psychology that does not shirk from exploring the possibility that some handicapped children develop according to a healthy logic of their own.

Chapter 5

Social Development

What reason do we have to believe that the special social situation of the handicapped child might radically alter the stages through which he grows up? Why do we propose that even if the content of each stage of development is the same, the order in which the handicapped child traverses these stages may be different?

Perhaps the most tantalizing clues come from the few published case histories of handicapped individuals.* Here and there a striking discovery is reported. Because of the handicapped child's different biological and sociological destiny, the analyst finds it necessary to revise drastically his expectations about the "normal" or healthy course of emotional development in childhood. Sometimes the surprised therapist notes that behaviors commonly considered regressive in an able-bodied child prove to be powerful tools for growth for the disabled.

This small clinical literature is an intellectual and emotional oasis. It again demonstrates that the best work in disability has usually been done in areas where intuition has been given the freest hand and where rigorous and systematic scientific investiga-

* A selection of these psychoanalytic case histories is presented in Appendix 1, p. 305.

tion has not begun. Yet, with so little available book learning, we cannot assume that every handicapped child will have a therapist willing or able to challenge the inadequate conventional wisdom of the field. Nor do we want every sensitive therapist to have to reinvent the wheel, to discover that his or her theoretical framework is much less adequate for the disabled than for normal people.

What the child, the clinician, and the experimentalist need is a comprehensive body of research that treats the handicapped child on his own terms. We need studies that do not uncritically impose on the handicapped developmental and behavioral expectations derived from research with able-bodied children. The developmental framework (or frameworks) to summarize this information would, in effect, systematically expand upon the clinical literature's most crucial insight: that the ultimate goals of childhood are the same for the handicapped and the able-bodied child, but that the means used to attain these goals may be radically different—so different that behavior that is clearly pathological in an able-bodied child may on occasion serve a developmentally progressive function in a handicapped child.

Toward a Theory of Social Development

Lacking many relevant studies of handicapped children, we must engage more extensively than we would wish in supposition and analogies to the experiences of the handicapped adult. Nonetheless, precisely because it is so easy to misunderstand, misrepresent, and misconstrue developmental questions, we believe it is imperative to go beyond generalities and to map out, in as much detail as possible, some of the most important issues to explore, to explain why they are important, and to describe how we would like to see them approached.

Because we believe that the social consequences of handicap have been underemphasized and misunderstood by psychologists, we will concentrate upon the interaction of the social situation of handicap with development, fully recognizing that a mature developmental psychology of handicap will not neglect the many ways in which the character of the child's biological difference (his handicap per se) may also affect development.

Although our position represents a new departure for handicap, some of the questions it raises are in line with recent attempts by Carol Gilligan and others to construct models of social and personality development that are better adapted to describing the development of girls and women than traditional male-oriented frameworks.[1] However, to avoid prematurely complicating our discussion, we will not try to anticipate the systematic differences that may well exist in the developmental paths followed by handicapped boys and girls. As with such other crucial social factors as class and ethnicity, we shall assume as a matter of course that attempts to implement our research perspective must explore the undoubtedly complex interactions of handicap with sex.

What we need now is to move from the general to the particular. We need to gain a better sense of the concrete character of the sociological distortions introduced by a child's disability into his everyday life. Having identified some of these distortions, we can then view them from the perspective of the developmental psychologist: how do these distortions affect the child's emotional, social, and intellectual development at different stages of his life? How might these distortions change the child's idea of the central emotional issues of his life at a given stage? Might these distortions render the handicapped child precocious in certain areas of social behavior and backward in others? Might these precocities and backwardnesses, in turn, have important ramifications for the child's emotional and intellectual development? We will not, of course, be able to prove that any of these social factors affects a a child in a given way, but we can make a plausible case that they may. And that, after all, is our point—to indicate good reasons for studying the handicapped child's development from the ground up, for setting to one side preconceptions derived from study of the able-bodied, and for attempting to discover for the first time the main constancies, the milestones and "tasks," of the handicapped child's development.

First of all, we need to fashion a crude map of the distorted social space that our society makes the handicapped child inhabit. To do so, we would ideally draw upon a large body of empirical studies of the way able-bodied adults and children interact with handicapped children. Unfortunately, these studies do not exist. Given this dearth of information about the sociological situation of the handicapped child and adolescent, we are forced to rely almost entirely upon what is known about the situation of the handicapped adult and what handicapped adults remember about their childhoods. Both sources of information are also far from satisfactory. If one sets to one side the vast but nearly useless literature on attitudes toward handicap, most social psychological and sociological research has focused upon the behavior of handicapped and able-bodied strangers—interactions between an able-bodied and a handicapped person who have just met for the first time.[2] The extensive literature of autobiographical accounts suffers from other shortcomings. Though suggestive, these narratives must be approached with caution because they describe how it was to grow up handicapped a generation or more ago, because memories of childhood are notoriously unreliable, and because those who write autobiographies may not be typical of the disabled population at large.

Though this fragmentary and often frustrating source material is no substitute for an adequate sociology of the handicapped *child,* we believe that it still can suggest some of the main social pressures experienced by many handicapped individuals in middle and late childhood. We base our belief upon a clinical principle which, despite its theoretical difficulties, possesses an undeniable practical value: what adults say they experience as adults and what they remember about their childhoods often put into words features of social settings and social interactions that children and adolescents respond to emotionally long before they can verbalize these experiences themselves.

Having drawn upon existing microsociological data as well as provided some new data of our own, we will then reframe the sociological issues raised by our survey from a perspective typical of developmental psychology. This perspective views the child as an active builder of theories about his social world as well as about the physical world. Reserving for chapter 7 a consideration of the many difficult theoretical issues raised by this model of the child, such as how he frames his theories, how he tests them, and the extent to which they are conscious or unconscious, we will practice a drastic simplification in order to bring out the essence of the developmental approach. We will ask two simple questions: first, what kinds of theories about able-bodied people and the able-bodied world might we reasonably expect a handicapped child to form as a result of his interactions with able-bodied people? Second, how might these theories influence his social development and his personality development?

The answers to these questions will help us rethink the relevance of mainstream theories of the able-bodied child's social development to handicap.

The Social "Grammar" of Handicap:
A Naturalistic Overview

What is it like to live under the gun of the disease diagnosis of handicap and the handicapped role—time and again to come up against the wall of able-bodied people's expectations of what is proper and possible for a disabled individual? Few areas of the handicap literature are more moving than the accounts of childhood written by handicapped men and women. The psychiatrist Jerome D. Frank has suggested that the "primary function of all psychotherapies is to combat demoralization . . . through restoring the patient's sense of mastery." [3] If one thing is clear from the autobiographies of the handicapped, it is that the first hazard many face is the demoralization that can result from having one's competence as an individual constantly challenged while one is growing up—not because one actually is incompetent but because the able-bodied *think* one is.

Consider this autobiographical statement quoted by Erving Goffman in *Stigma*: " 'I think the first realization of my situation, and the first intense grief resulting from this realization, came one day, very casually, when a group of us in our early teens had gone to the beach for the day. I was lying on the sand, and I guess the fellows said, "I like Domenica very much, but I would never go out with a blind girl." I cannot think of any prejudice which so completely rejects you.' " [4]

Reviewing literature of this kind, Barker and his associates have emphasized the ensuing "marginality" of many disabled people.[5] Again and again one reads in autobiographical chronicles by the handicapped how the presence of the handicap poisons in advance and blows up out of all importance the most trivial and inconsequential encounters. Except with good friends—and even here there is often excoriating doubt—one simply doesn't know in advance how the disability will affect the other person. "The blind, the ill, the deaf, the crippled," writes Barker, "can never be sure what the attitude of a new acquaintance will be, whether it will be rejective or accepting, until the contact has been made. This is exactly the position of the adolescent, the light-skinned

Negro, the second generation immigrant, the socially mobile person and the woman who has entered a predominantly masculine occupation." [6] Moreover, adds Goffman, this uncertainty, this fatal ambiguity (which, let us reiterate, bears a certain similarity to the double-bind situations of the schizophrenogenic family) undermines the superficially favorable encounter as well. At least from middle childhood on the handicapped person can never be quite sure. Some part of him knows that despite the pretty words and good manners, "in their hearts the others may be defining him in terms of his stigma." [7]

A second important source of clues about the nature of the social space in which handicapped children move comes from handicapped adults who have described their encounters with able-bodied strangers. Many handicapped adults—as well as many clinicians—agree that these interactions illuminate many aspects of the handicapped child's social experience. Perhaps most important, this literature helps to provide a sense of the finer detail of the handicapped person's encounter with the able-bodied world —the way that the able-bodied individual choreographs his behavior in accord with his expectations about the handicapped role. It is a dance in which many disabled people find themselves constantly being treated in ways more appropriate to a perpetual patient than to an independent adult. The following comments by handicapped people in Davis's important paper are typical:

I get suspicious when somebody says, "Let's go for a uh, ah [imitates confused and halting speech] push with me down the hall," or something like that. This to me is suspicious because it means that they're aware, really aware, that there's a wheelchair here, and that this is probably upppermost with them. . . . A lot of people in trying to show you that they don't care that you're in a chair will do crazy things. Oh, there's one person I know who constantly kicks my chair, as if to say, "I don't care that you're in a wheelchair. I don't even know that it's there." But that is just an indication that he *really* knows it's there.[8]

One night when I was going to visit a friend two of the people from my office put me into a taxi. I could tell that at first the taxi driver didn't know I was blind because for a while there he was quite a conversationalist. Then he asked me what these sticks were for [a collapsible cane]. I told him it was a cane, and then he got so different. . . . He didn't talk about the same things that he did at first. Before this happened he joked and said, "Oh, you're a very quiet person. I don't like quiet people, they think too much." And he probably wouldn't have said that to me had he known I was blind because he'd be afraid of hurting my feelings. He didn't say anything like that afterwards.[9]

Now, where this affects them, where this brace and a crutch would affect them, is if they are going someplace or if they are doing something, they feel that, first, you would call attention and second—you wouldn't believe this but it's true; I'll use the cruelest words I can—no cripple would possibly be in their social stratum.[10]

I was visiting my girl friend's house and I was sitting in the lobby waiting for her when this woman comes out of her apartment and starts asking me questions. She just walked right up. I didn't know her from Adam, I never saw her before in my life. "Gee, what do you have? How long have you been that way? Oh gee, that's terrible." And so I answered her questions but I got very annoyed and wanted to say, "Lady, mind your own business." [11]

The first reaction a normal individual or good-legger has is, "Oh gee, there's a fellow in a wheelchair," or "there's a fellow with a brace." And they don't say, "Oh gee, there is so-and-so, he's handsome," or "he's intelligent," or "he's a boor," or what have you. And then as the relationship develops they don't see the handicap. It doesn't exist any more. And that's the point that you as a handicapped individual become sensitive to. You know after talking with someone for awhile when they don't see the handicap any more. That's when you've broken through.[12]

The large social gathering [says a young paraplegic man] presents a special problem. It's a matter of repetition. When you're in a very large group of people whom you don't know, you don't have an opportunity of talking to three, four or five at a time. Maybe you'll talk to one or two usually. After you've gone through a whole basic breakdown in making a relationship with one—after all, it's only a cocktail party—to do it again, and again, and again, it's wearing and it's no good. You don't get the opportunity to really develop something.[13]

The case histories cited by Davis provide us with another level of detail. But to begin to gain a sense of some of the generic differences between able-bodied and handicapped strangers, we need to focus upon a single interaction and to trace out its elaborate social "choreography" in some detail. Recalling our earlier discussion in chapter 1 of the ultimately perceptual consequences of the handicap role, remembering that seeing is a "theory-laden activity," we must ask, If what we see when we meet a handicapped person is the result of our largely hidden social theories of handicap, what happens when an able-bodied person meets a handicapped person who doesn't fit into the handicapped role?

Tom Murphy (able-bodied) meets Larry Jones (disabled) [14]

"Tom Murphy" is a bright, young apprentice sociologist working in the area of handicap. "Larry Jones" is an executive in Chicago and quite successful in his business. The men have many roles in common: being male, in their thirties, well educated, and in reasonably high-status occupations (though Jones's is higher than Murphy's). They also share an openness to each other and a desire to learn. These sociological facts precondition the theories by which they interpret each other as well as the following crucial social difference: Murphy is able-bodied; Jones is handicapped.

Murphy did not initially know that Jones was handicapped, having been referred to him by a former teacher who had described Jones as a businessman interested in the problems of the handicapped. What did Murphy *see* in the other? What did he feel in the encounter? And in what sense is what he saw Jones communicate the result of a "theory-laden" activity? Here is Murphy's account of the meeting as told to us:

> Being a person concerned about the way I present myself to others, I had half rehearsed the beginnings of a telephone conversation: "Hello, how are you? My name is Tom Murphy." I also had developed an image in my mind of the young executive, very smooth and articulate, of higher status than my own, well dressed, gifted, and other constructions which I made knowing only the teacher who had recommended him, his position in the business world, and the secretary who connected us.
>
> The conversation began abstractly about the problems of the disabled. To this abstract background I imported the category of stranger both as a description of myself and of the man whom I will call Larry. I abstractly discussed the possible similarities which might exist between different forms of strangerness. But with this abstract conversation voice cues started to assert themselves. At first he had a slight stutter, I thought. Then it didn't seem like a stutter and I was reminded of an Irish writer, Christy Brown,

whom I had met. He had cerebral palsy and trouble with his speech. The image was probably important. I respected Brown and was set up to respect Larry. The strategy I used to find out whether the person at the other end of the telephone was severely physically incapacitated was to ask: "Should I meet you at your office, or would you like to come to mine?" In my mind was the deeper question of "Which is easier?" If he answered this question by saying something like "It's hard for me to negotiate the city, I'd prefer it if you'd come here," an option open to him, my dilemma would be resolved. When he said, "Why don't I come over and we'll go someplace for dinner," my construction of him was dissonant with that fact, which better suits my construction of people who are not handicapped.

Instead of the usual things involved in an encounter of this sort—"How will he size me up? How will things go intellectually? How will he be dressed?"—I was concerned about my own reactions to a physical disability as yet unclear. Age, manner of speech, family background receded before the question of physique.

I opened the door, paused a second, and shook hands. He was dressed very casually. That surprised me. I think that beneath my construction of Larry's physical handicap I had a great investment in the construction of him in a three-piece suit. I started to discuss sociology with him, I think, because I wanted to stay on an abstract level: that of sociologist and informant. I was reluctant to treat the person as a full human being, in some way wanting to divert our encounter to the abstract level of disembodied intellect. I was relieved to have seen Larry, probably because all of the questions in the construction had become more important in a certain sense than the handicap itself. Those questions were resolved on sight. Many other questions remained unresolved, however. I accepted him graciously without surprise: this was the pretense. There were two chairs in the room, one much more comfortable than the other. I didn't want to ask which chair Larry would like because that would be an acknowledgment of the fact of his handicap. My secretary was in the room and I watched her reaction. If you're not sure how to react, watch what somebody else is doing. But I could get no cues from her.

Everything that we did in our encounter in the office,

which lasted about a quarter of an hour before leaving for a restaurant, became, to use a sociological word, "problematic." I wanted to offer him a drink, which would have been natural. I was uncertain of that. Perhaps I feared that he would spill it. More probably I feared that this action would become problematic to him. On leaving the office, when I picked up Larry's coat to help him on with it, an old Irish custom, that too became problematic for me. I wondered if he would interpret this act as my going out of my way to do something I would not ordinarily do because of his handicap. I started to question the appropriateness of an Irish custom in an American setting, which is to say that my perception of my own actions became problematic as well. Each little detail which we take for granted in our encounter with strangers cannot be taken for granted in the case of two people who are strangers in another sense, in Simmel's sense. Each detail—standing up, sitting down, putting on coats, opening doors, closing doors—becomes invested with a question mark. Can he do it? Will he be insulted if I do it? Will he be insulted that I do not offer to do it?

Usually when one is trying to construct another person, and further, when one is trying to construct his construction of you, you pick up cues and modify your behavior so that his construction of you will be what you desire it to be. This was made more difficult by the "noise" existing in our communication. I began to have feelings that Larry was manipulating me, that he was so detached from reality that he could play with it, unconcerned about how others would construct him. These feelings undoubtedly came from me.

For some reason Larry would not admit the sociologist-informant relationship. This made things more difficult for me. I attributed maliciousness to him for that. Perhaps I wanted to block out the physical reality by intellectual exchange and was angry that I was not allowed to do so.

Walking to the restaurant, I was quite conscious of my pacing. Was I walking too fast for Larry? Could my pace be interpreted as walking too slow because of his handicap? I wanted to say, "How fast should we walk?" But I didn't. I slowed down on a pretext. On noticing that he deliberately had to slow down I concluded that the pace we had adopted was a natural one. Or was it? Was Larry walking at my pace so that I would not have to feel awkward about accommodating myself to his pace? I wondered if he was thinking that I was thinking these questions. I wondered if this sort of situation was not so commonplace for him that he'd developed an ability to detect the existence of these questions in the mind of an able-bodied person.

Larry chose the restaurant. As we went in he was greeted by the host, who knew him. This immediately put him into a social context. We take it for granted that strangers we meet go out, meet people, eat, are sociable, party, interact with others, unless there are positive cues that the other person is extremely shy. My seeing Larry in the context of a social creature immediately brought all of the attributes of a social creature to him. He became, in a sense, able-bodied, outward-going. Everything changed with the perception that he had not allowed his handicap to prevent him from being a social being. He further embedded himself in a shared world as we went into a preliminary discussion of American politics, about which he was extremely knowledgeable. But why should that be surprising? But it was. I think that everything in the encounter with a handicapped person is problematic until it is filled out by definite cues. It is almost as if one starts in the interaction with a handicapped person as if he were not a social creature, but has to offer evidence of being social like the rest of us. It is normally taken for granted that man is a social creature. Yet nothing is taken for granted in the interaction with a disabled person. He has to prove himself innocent and is assumed guilty, rather than innocent until proven guilty. Usually people are social and human until proven otherwise. With Larry, somehow he had to prove to me that he was social and human. When all things were flowing more smoothly in my mind, awkwardness and questions continued to reassert themselves.

I had a sense throughout the conversation that Larry was a stranger and of my being a stranger in the interaction of two strangers trying to feel each other out. I used the word *normal* about myself and then put my fingers up to put quotation marks around it. Larry told me I should take the quotes off *normality* and this allowed me to realize that by using the normal I was not insulting him. I confided some personal details about myself and then became conscious of having done so and wondered whether I was not saying,

"Look—there are these strange things about me, too; don't feel so bad."

The crucial transition from the stranger and stranger situation to an interaction of acquaintance or friendship involves being able to predict the behavior of the other. This is, needless to say, facilitated by communication, and when Larry indicated that talking about certain things was something that he would accept, that is to say when he took the quotes off the word *normal*, that was his cue to proceed beyond the handicap. Once I got beyond the physical handicap, all of the other details which had been hiding behind it manifested themselves: business executive, sophisticated about food, wine, and restaurants, knowledgeable about current affairs—all of these played the role that they should have played from the very beginning. Each piece of new information became less surprising. Somehow, I'm not sure how, the other details which are certain in social humanity —the newspapers one reads, the records one listens to, the woman to whom one is married—become less surprising. Yet this passage from stranger to acquaintance is dangerous and at times I felt that I wanted to retreat to the stranger role, and the safety of the sociologist and informant role, which would have denied the physical presence of his body at the level which it would have taken before I got to know Larry as a social human being.

As the conversation progressed, the intellectual Larry stretched itself. His questions were incisive. What with the distinctions he drew and the points I was forced to elaborate, I found myself caught up in a very rewarding and challenging interaction. The physical self was kept in the background, but not artificially as indicated before.

Larry's handicapped self did constantly improve, but something had changed. He looked at his watch and reached for a telephone book. I wanted to get it for him. I stopped myself. I felt uncomfortable at stopping myself. Then I concluded that if he wanted me to assist him he would have asked, and this conclusion seemed less arbitrary than the earlier conclusions regarding putting on his coat.

Larry had a social engagement. He was transformed from a handicap looking up a phone number to a social creature involved in a network of social relationships which I became very conscious that I knew very little of. The social self reasserted itself. And the handicapped self intruded again as I helped him with his coat, and the social self intruded as we said good-bye, agreeing to meet again, as he left for an engagement that is in the context of his life.

It is a complex relationship. I guess, should we ever have the occasion to become friends, many unresolved aspects of it will become unproblematic. I'm sure that if you had a chance to talk to Larry, his version of it would be as complex as mine. Things did change during the course of it. I'm left with the problem now of realizing that I made him prove himself. And then I realized that he may not have seen it that way, which would have made it not that way at all.

Having so far focused upon the able-bodied individuals' approaches to handicap in this section, we now want to look at some of the ways in which disabled individuals try to cope with the social reality imposed upon them by the able-bodied.

The situation of handicap represents something like a pure case of the kind of stigma that other "deviant" groups are subjected to when they venture outside their prescribed roles. For the compass of the permitted roles for handicapped people is so small that unless they are almost completely isolated, they will constantly be crashing through the limits of the roles society sets them and into the sociological limbo that lies beyond. The coping maneuvers and strategies of the handicapped represent the other side of the many sociological barriers between able-bodied and disabled—barriers that often affect the disabled individuals' ability to communicate with themselves quite as much as their ability to communicate with others. To confront this "other side," however briefly, is to be forcibly reminded of the immense human toll the handicapped role exacts in terms of frustration, demoralization, humiliation, anger, despair, and identity. It is also to be reminded —as if it were needed—that the sociological situation of the handicapped is a national disgrace.

To begin with, consider the disabled executive's version of the Murphy-Jones encounter as he told it to us.

Larry Jones (disabled) meets Tom Murphy (able-bodied) [15]

Look, you have to understand something. I am a pretty busy man. So I probably wouldn't have returned Murphy's call had not my secretary mentioned the name of Harris, an old teacher of mine to whom I owe a lot. I don't forget my debts. My secretary connected me with Murphy and the first thing I noted was his voice. At first I thought it was British. I have never thought in a sense that it was possible to be Irish. You know, leprechauns, blarney, and St. Patrick's Day. The first line sounded like a con job. I remember it well: "Hello, how are you? My name is Tom Murphy." It sounded like a con job because Murphy went quickly from "how are you" to the next sentence. He didn't leave me any room. I wondered why, and then as he said "Murphy" the Murphy clicked with the accent, and then in a certain sense I knew who I was talking to.

They say that first impressions in business are important. I believe that one thing that separates the good executive from the average executive is the ability to decipher these first impressions. It can save you a lot of time. I have become quite good at it and now I always rely on my instinct. They are not exactly instincts, mind you; they are things we have learned. Although the way he rapidly strung together the first sentence with the last bothered me and told me that he wanted something from me, I detected from his voice a friendliness, and, since I have never met an Irishman, I agreed to meet him that night.

Murphy started talking with me about our both being strangers. That put me off. I guess it disturbed me because he had the audacity to consider that our strangerness was a basis for talking. Then, I realized that maybe such an opinion of strangerness might be common among immigrants from countries who are basically occupied, you know, subservient. I guess his being Irish really intrigued me—when I was an adolescent I had read some books by an Irish writer called Christy Brown. Brown had C.P. [cerebral palsy]. He talked about that experience in Ireland. I guess I wondered if Murphy's reactions to me might round out the description of Irish reactions and him.

With that in mind I decided to meet him on his grounds. This was so he would feel as comfortable as possible. Also what he wanted to talk to me about was being disabled. I figured that that would be a hard subject for him and if the conversation was to be anything but a complete disaster it would be best to conduct it where he had every opportunity for comfort. In addition I wanted to get out of my office, probably out of my world. My world tends to define itself more restrictively than I would like and I welcomed the chance to enter the world of another. I changed clothes in the office. I work in a conventional system because I found that that is the only place that I can work. I found it very hard to get the kind of work which will pay me enough for my expensive life-style, which includes things like prosthesis polish, heavy drugs, and cab fares (which can come to quite a lot in Chicago). But off the job I like to live a life among friends; and my friends are hip. By hip, I don't mean the Pepsi generation, I mean artists, writers, people who in general will at least, I feel, take me for what I am instead of for a stereotype. Or maybe better, what I think I am, and what they think I am is the same thing. So I slid into my blue jeans, flannel shirt, and put on a heavy sheepskin jacket. I realize that this may sound like changing roles, but I just happen to have found it necessary.

When I entered Murphy's apartment I had the option of talking first and acting first, not leaving any room for Murphy to ask questions which might be hard for him. Instead I left him room. I was curious as to the sort of questions that he would ask. What other people do at the beginning of an interaction with them tells me a lot about the person. It is more than first impressions, somehow; being handicapped, first impressions about me are much more accurate predictors than later impressions. This isn't to say that the situation doesn't change dramatically as I get to know somebody better. Invariably it does, but the way in which it changes has something to do with what you can already see at the beginning. I don't think I can explain it any better than that. Sometimes I just think that my world and the world of an able-bodied person must be so different that it doesn't make any sense to even talk about things like this. I was particularly interested in Murphy's body. He was holding himself loosely, which I usually take to be a good sign. He lit a cigarette and, being a European, he offered me one. I don't usually smoke so I wasn't sure that it didn't mean a lot to him to have this gift accepted, and also I wanted to establish contact with him on something past the verbal level. When I took the cigarette from his hand, my hand shook and I think he felt that. The shaking didn't seem to bother him; that was good, too. Anyway, the cigarettes were English.

I don't drive because I can't, and Murphy doesn't drive because he never learned how. So when I suggested that we go to a restaurant, I naturally suggested one within short walking distance. I had other reasons for wanting to stay in the neighborhood anyway.

I hadn't been to the restaurant, a small Italian place, for about four years. The same manager who had been there said hello to me. One of the first things that I learned is that I am a hard person to forget. I guess I stick out in their minds. I looked at the menu, ordering not mainly for what I like to eat but for what I could eat without making myself too conspicuous. That cut out spaghetti. I didn't know Murphy and I only eat spaghetti with friends. What I mean by that is I only let down my guard, which has to do with all kinds of moods predicated on my handicap, in the presence of people I trust. I guess I went a little further than that, too. I wanted to impress Murphy and so took the leeway that he gave me to talk about things that I wanted to talk about. I wanted to talk about things in which I was an expert. . . .

Murphy started talking about disability as opposed to normal. His fingers hung in the air making quotation marks. I told him to take the quotation marks off of *normal*. The effect of this was that Murphy confided to me that he had been in a mental institution. I couldn't really see what the connection between that and my reassuring him was, but I have long since resigned myself to the fact that there are things about people which are simply unbelievable, and in fact I've come to enjoy that.

At first, before I got to know Murphy, I held him at a distance. I guess some of the ways that I did this was by shifting roles, impressing him with myself, and for that matter even choosing the setting of the restaurant which he hadn't heard about and I knew. We became good friends— I mean good for the two hours we spent together—and I expect we will be seeing each other again. I was unable to spend the evening with Murphy because I had a date that night, although I found myself getting so involved with the conversation, which was becoming fascinating to me, that time slipped by. When I first looked at my watch, I was already ten minutes late. I got the phone book to find Carol's number. I was in too much of a hurry to bother with the formalities inherent in the first time you ask somebody to do something for you, so I looked up the number myself. We returned and said that we would see each other soon. It is probably stupid to say this but it continues to amaze me just how interesting and complex people are. Everybody is different. But everybody is the same. Getting to know somebody is impossible unless, while you are doing it, you forget how impossible it is and then for some reason it becomes easy.

There are many striking differences between Jones's narrative and Murphy's because the social theories that undergird their perceptions of the encounter are not the same. Small but revealing examples are the ways in which Jones's taking the cigarette and being recognized in the restaurant signify very different things for the two men. A far more important example—and one worth dwelling on—is the manner in which Jones is aware (and must be aware) of the significance of his acts for Murphy in a way that Murphy is not (and need not) be aware of the significance of his actions for Jones. Whereas Murphy is a sociologist in his *professional* life, Jones—like most handicapped people—has come to be a consummate sociologist in his *private* life. The reason for this difference is clear if one examines the very different things that are at stake for the two men in the encounter.

Murphy's identity as a functioning adult—a social being—never is in doubt for either Murphy or Jones. To himself, Murphy is simply Murphy. A man perplexed by his reactions to Jones, he quickly overcomes some but not all of the obstacles to communication between him and the executive. To Jones, Murphy is an able-bodied adult stranger whose initial reactions pose a certain threat, although a predictable one. To speak of Murphy fluctuating from his intellectual side to his able-bodied side to his social human being side to his self-that-reacts-to-handicap would sound equally odd to both men. Yet Murphy practices this kind of fractionation on Jones. Initially preoccupied by the "handicap," even at the end of the encounter Murphy does not see a single unitary adult by the name of Larry Jones. He sees an individual who snaps back and forth among different identities. One moment he is "a handicap looking up a phone number—" (because, in Jones's words, "I was in too much of a hurry to bother with the formalities inherent in the first time you ask somebody to do something for you"), and the next moment Jones is "transformed" into a "social creature." At other times the "intellectual Larry" stretches himself and "Larry's handicapped self did constantly improve."

Jones's social behavior displays a similarly segmented character, but for a different reason. Throughout, the executive constantly recalibrates his presentation of himself in order to persuade Murphy to see him as an adult social being. This recalibration is paralleled by the emphasis in Jones's narrative upon social facts —jobs, friends, adult settings—that serve to "prove" Jones's adultness. Whereas Murphy practices a fractionation on Jones, the executive pursues a strategy that maximizes the impact of his integrated adult identity upon the other.

Nowhere is this contrast in aim clearer than in the emotional undertow of the two narratives. For all Murphy's sensitivity, his account radiates confidence about his own identity as an adult. And despite Jones's successful attempt to "prove himself" (the insight is Murphy's), there is an almost adolescent tension in his version, a braggadocio that seems compounded in equal parts of the resentment of an actor forced to present a command performance against his will and the desperation of a soldier before a military tribunal. Murphy is playing a more conventional game— impressing Jones with his competence as a sociologist. But Jones is playing to secure parts of his adult identity that Murphy can take for granted. It is a game in which, whatever the outcome, the main emotional pressures are borne by Jones.

The strategies evolved by the handicapped individual to help cope in social interactions are as numerous as they are complex. Here we will discuss a number of the most important—what the philosopher Jean-Paul Sartre has called "bad faith," what sociologists call "passing," and the broad family of strategies that go by the name of "gamesmanship." [16] All of these strategies are employed in childhood as well as adulthood.

A self in the presence of another expects to be taken seriously. He assumes that the other will take his performance as indicative of his true self—that he will divine from it its true attributes. On the self's own part, there are two possible extremes: he may believe in his own performance, believe that he is behaving authentically; or he may adapt his performance to the stereotypes of the other, perhaps to make the most of a situation in which the self lacks the power to compel respect from the other. This second approach, a conscious or unconscious decision to "act in bad faith," often leads to an attitude of uninvolvement mixed with bitter self-contempt in which the child or the adult may take a perverse pleasure. As an example, in a male-dominated society many women have been forced to play the part of the "dumb female" or "weak child" in order to manipulate their parents, brothers, husbands, or lovers. Many have bitterly hated themselves for their humiliating deceits yet have also taken a perverse pleasure in carrying off the charade.

What has historically been the case for most women and for other stigmatized groups such as blacks has often been the handicapped individual's sociological destiny as well. As Jones's remarks about Murphy illustrate, the handicapped person is usually a shrewd sociologist. But Jones—a successful executive—is the relatively fortunate exception. What his narrative does not show is the frequent contempt, demoralization, habitual dishonesty, and uncertainty about the true self that is often the other side to the disabled person's sophistication. This is the price in bad faith that many must pay for the social awareness needed to survive in an able-bodied world.

Lurking behind the decision to "pass" are its potential costs—costs that sometimes include the possibility of bad faith. Passing requires time and energy. It requires ingenuity and usually subjects the individual to considerable emotional strain. Most of those who pass successfully live in constant fear of being found out—e.g., the child with a reading disability, the adult who has spent time in a residential institution for the mildly retarded, the child with a chronic illness such as epilepsy which many consider to be shameful, the adult with a concealable defect or disease that exerts an influence upon his fears that is out of all proportion to able-bodied society's attitudes toward the disability.[17] Most crucially of all, passing undermines the self's sense of authenticity and genuine worth. I *seem* to be a regular guy or a normal kid. But is this able-bodied persona, this careful fabrication, the real me? And if I must always dissemble to hide my handicap, who is the real me? Am I leveling with myself, or am I acting in bad faith? Passing is a kind of social "white lie"—perfectly understandable yet unpredictable in the devastation it may wreak on an individual's ability to know where the mask leaves off and the true person begins. Insecurity, rigidity, extreme conformity, and overdramatization of the role one assumes are among the occupational hazards of the individual who successfully passes.

Finally, there are the strategies of gamesmanship. Precisely because the disabled individual finds the sociological deck stacked against him in many childhood and adult encounters, he may seek to overcome this disadvantage by a subtle manipulation of those remaining cues which convey competence that are under his control. The ways this can be attempted are legion. But whether the tools used are an authoritative tone of voice, a tendency to manipulate language in aggressive ways, or an exaggeratedly dependent and apologetic manner—which itself can be highly manipulative— the tools are in the service of a view that sees interactions as contests. Moreover, because many handicaps—such as blindness or cerebral palsy—make one dependent on or vulnerable to the other in ways unimaginable to the able-bodied, the biological component of one's handicap supplies an additional incentive for, in effect, constructing a social prosthesis to help compensate for one's physical limitations as well as for one's social limitations.

There are great dangers in seeing interactions as contests for control. What is gained in casual encounters in some school settings and in the workaday world may be lost in situations of intimacy such as the family; although since handicapped adults are frequently denied either a position in the world of work or anything like the opportunities for intimacy that the able-bodied take for granted, many adults who have grown up with handicaps are unlikely to experience this disadvantage firsthand.

Mainstream Theories of Social and Personality Development

By means of example and analysis we have adumbrated a few features of the social context in which many handicapped people grow up. Lacking anything like a developmental sociology of handicap—a body of work that traces out the main characteristics of able-bodied/handicapped interactions at different ages—we have focused upon the one area of behavior that has been studied in any depth, namely, first encounters between able-bodied and handicapped adults. Precisely because this work involves adults, its relevance to the experiences of handicapped children is problematic, although it is our clinical impression that it captures an important aspect of interactions in late childhood and adolescence.

But for us, at least, the accounts presented here possess a value that goes far beyond their literal application to childhood. They

are like lightning bolts that briefly illuminate a sociological landscape whose existence was barely suspected. What they show is
enough to put the burden of proof on those who would assume
that the paths of development followed by handicapped children
are adequately captured by developmental theories constructed
for able-bodied children. And the need for a systematic rethinking
of our theories of child development before they are applied to
handicapped children is, after all, what we have been arguing for.

In many respects the task now before us is rather like trying to
shuffle together two imaginary decks of cards. In one deck is a
small number of case histories of handicapped children and adults,
full of clues about how the different sociological situation of the
handicapped child might alter his chief developmental problems
and issues. In the other, we have the autobiographical accounts
and the small number of studies of adult interactions that we
have just reviewed. The danger of attempting to integrate this
material is clear. We know very little about the social development of able-bodied children, let alone of handicapped children.
And even in mainstream psychology it is always easy to raise
fascinating and weighty questions that cannot yet be studied
empirically. The hazard we face with handicap is not in suggesting
too little, but in suggesting too much. To this point we have
resisted the temptation to go beyond an impressionistic and highly
schematic account of what we know about the social situation of
the handicapped child and adult. Now we must present an equally
lean and impressionistic account of why we need a developmental
psychology of handicapped children—an account that balances
between too much theoretical sophistication and too little theoretical sophistication.

Most theories of development in child psychology point to a
set of stages—of, for example, social development—that most children seem to go through. Although they often describe the characteristics of each stage in some detail, none of these theories can
explain why the child passes through the particular stages described. Nor can they account for a universal property of all
stage theories—the "fact," if indeed it is a fact, that for any given
theory of development, the order in which a child traverses that
theory's stages is invariant; it is simply observed or asserted that
the order is invariant. Related to this point is a third limitation
of most stage theories. This is that they cannot supply any explanation for why a child *moves* from one stage to the next instead of
staying put in a certain stage all his life. Nor can they explain

what set of properties makes a given stage more or less advanced than any other stage, except that, empirically, stage A always precedes stage B.

These properties of mainstream models of social and personality development—their ladder character, their insistence that the "rungs" of the ladder are invariant, and their failure to provide a principled account for stage invariance and for why the child moves from one rung to the next—make it essential that we proceed with great care before we apply theories of the able-bodied child to the handicapped child. Suppose, for example, that the rungs on the handicapped child's ladder have a different order. Suppose he uses an entirely different kind of ladder. Suppose he follows a different strategy up the ladder, skipping certain rungs and coming back to them much later in life when he can finally handle them. Suppose there are different styles of growing up among the handicapped and each style, although leading to the same end result, maturity, reaches that end by means of a different ladder or a different developmental strategy. Suppose there are systematic developmental differences related to sex, ethnic group, class, and whether or not one has a disabled parent or sibling.

All of these possibilities seem to us to be plausible. Should any of them be correct, our entire approach to the handicapped child might have to be revised. By not systematically exploring these possibilities we risk harming many handicapped children even when we seek to help them.

Lawrence Kohlberg's typology of moral stages provides a useful standard against which to reassess mainstream stage theories of child development in the light of handicap. Kohlberg's schema is worth singling out both because it is typical of most approaches to moral and social development and because it probably exerts more influence in the fields of education and judicial reform than any of its rivals. When we turn to questions of personality development in chapter 6, we will examine a typical developmental theory in this area—Erik Erikson's stage theory of personality development, one of the most humane and suggestive of the many ego psychological theories to be advanced in recent years. Besides being extremely influential, Kohlberg's and Erikson's theories have the advantage of being relatively easy to summarize. They both also possess the typical strengths and weaknesses of mainstream theories of personality development and moral development.

Theories of Moral Development

In many respects the questions studied by the moral psychologist cut to the very heart of all social behavior. The moral psychologist studies the child's developing notions of what is just and unjust. He studies the child's changing ability to take the other person's point of view in conflict over *resources*. The child's changing notion of normative rules (his ability to play games and to participate in collective endeavors) forms part of the subject matter of moral psychology, as does the narrower and related question of the child's ability to cooperate with a friend at different ages. Though social behavior is studied in many different ways in mainstream psychology, the moral psychologist studies the key social theories that guide social behavior at different ages. By challenging the adequacy of mainstream theories of moral development for the handicapped child, we are, then, asking a set of questions that extend far beyond the narrow issues suggested by the everyday connotations of the phrase "moral development"; we are challenging the applicability to the handicapped child of some of the most important insights about the social development of the able-bodied child.

All theories of moral development from Baldwin to Piaget to Kohlberg distinguish among three broad stages in a child's interactions with other people: an "unprincipled" opportunistic stage in which behavior is governed by fear of punishment and other people are in some sense used as tools; an overly principled stage in which one takes rules and laws so seriously that one honors them to the letter even when doing so means (to an individual at a higher moral stage) violating their spirit; and a principled but flexible stage in which one seeks to honor one's moral principles by obeying their spirit even if this sometimes means an apparent conflict with the letter of the law.[18] Put another way: a child progresses first from following the law of the jungle, to rigidly following the rules set down by an authority figure or by the community, to learning to make exceptions to the norms of his society; from raw opportunism, to rigid justice, to justice tempered with mercy. As with all developmental theories, no one knows why children pass through these broad stages. Nor have attempts to prove that the sequence of stages represents a logical ordering been well received by logicians and philosophers.[19] About the most that can be said is that until the child is capable of adult reasoning (what Piaget calls formal operational thought), his level of cognitive development places a ceiling on his ability to verbalize his moral decisions.[20] Even so, it remains to be seen whether the ability to verbalize is any more relevant to learning about a child's morality than it is to learning about an adult's morality.[21]

Two key assumptions made by all developmental theories of morality are crucial to knowing whether the theories apply to handicapped children. The first involves the claim—tacit in Piaget, explicit in Kohlberg—that social development progresses through interactions with social equals, in which one is gradually forced to take increasingly sophisticated roles. According to this view, it is only with his equals that a child is exposed to the full consequences of his actions. And only when he cannot achieve his way through whim or force do other modes of conflict resolution (such as sharing) become salient. "Moral role-taking," writes Kohlberg, ". . . may have many affective flavors . . . e.g., empathy, guilt, disapproval, and respect. . . ."[22] But all these different modes of role taking are premised upon "a common structure of equality and reciprocity, between selves with expectations about one another."[23]

The second assumption is that the child views both the world and the rules he is forced to obey as basically just. Whether or not one reads Baldwin, Piaget, or Kohlberg, social development—and with it, moral development—is presented as a process of improving one's theory of how a just society works. In Piaget this process culminates with the adolescent taking his place in a mature adult society in which the basic norms of social behavior represent a Kantian version of the Golden Rule; strongly influenced by Durkheim, Piaget's views of the collective reflect a peculiar mixture of the archaic and the modern.[24] In Kohlberg there is no talk about modern society being regulated by neo-Kantian structures. But the basic premise about justice remains. As in all other moral theories developed with able-bodied children, the possible role of *injustice* in affecting one's notion of social behavior is ignored.

Taken together, these two assumptions generate the working hypothesis that underlies all theories of moral development: that moral principles are basically principles of role-taking. Each stage of moral development ascribes a different meaning to the phrase "everyone's perspective" and then proceeds to tell the individual to "act so as to take account of everyone's perspective on the moral conflict situation." [25] All theorists agree, for example, that the most primitive stage of moral development interprets "everyone's perspective" to mean: Keep in mind what your parent (or similar authority figure) will do to you if he catches you! And keep in mind that your parent (or similar authority figure) will reward you if you do it. Similarly, there is agreement among moral theorists —though not among their critics, the moral philosophers—that the highest moral stage interprets the phrase "everyone's perspective" to mean following the Golden Rule.[26] In a deep sense, then, "moral development is fundamentally a process of the restructuring of modes of role-taking." [27]

This view of moral development requires that we accept as our working hypothesis that the character of the handicapped child's social development is likely to differ in many significant respects from the developmental paths traced out by his able-bodied peers. For at the very least we must assume that the handicapped child will be leading a double life—partaking of the role-taking experiences typical of able-bodied children his age within the family circle and possibly with a few select friends, while simultaneously being systematically exposed to the alienating social pressures of handicap. In sum, the handicapped child will undergo one form of moral learning predicated upon the existence of equals and the assumption of a just world, and another form of social learning in which he constantly encounters the injustice of the world. Without speculating about how pure this split between his social experience and moral learning can be, or even how soon in life it can occur, it would seem inevitable that when it does appear it will have important and perhaps decisive effects on every aspect of the child's social development.[28]

Something of the range and variety of possible developmental differences between handicapped and able-bodied children is suggested by viewing the fine-grain structure of Kohlberg's stage theory from the perspective of a social analysis of handicap. To do so, we must briefly describe the main characteristics of the six rungs of Kohlberg's developmental "ladder." [29] The first two of these rungs correspond to different kinds of opportunistic behavior—at stage one the child is portrayed as attending only to whether or not he will be punished or rewarded by those in authority if he acts; the characteristics of the other selves in the conflict situation are relevant only insofar as they are powerful or weak.[30] At stage two the child is a more sophisticated opportunist. A miniature Machiavellian, he will show considerable subtlety in using the other people in the conflict situation for achieving his ends; he has become a manipulator of other selves. The two middle rungs of Kohlberg's ladder correspond to different kinds of rigid law-abiding behavior. Stage three is the "goody-goody" stage. The child adjusts his action in order to receive praise and approval from the others. He is a conformist and acts in accord with his stereotypical notions of what is the majority or normal behavior. Stage four represents a shift in the child's loyalties from individuals who might praise him to an abstract notion of the law. He respects the social order, believes in the value of authority, and considers right behavior as "doing one's duty." The two top rungs of Kohlberg's ladder involve more flexible and tacitly philosophic orientations that almost never appear before adolescence. Stage five captures the essence of liberal utilitarianism. A respect for the relativity of all personal and social values is joined with a willingness to submit to a set of procedural rules that will maximize our ability to go our own ways. Stage six retains the emphasis on the practical importance of procedural rules to maximize our individual liberty, but it reverses the moral relativism of the preceding stage. It does so by extracting from these procedural rules an absolute though abstract definition of what is good. Kohlberg often cites the Golden Rule and Kant's categorical imperative as examples of stage six morality.[31]

What is most striking about each of these stages of "moral role taking" is that the interaction strategies of handicap—bad faith, passing, gamesmanship—work to undermine any straightforward progression through the developmental ladder. Or, rather, we should say that the burden of his stigma might compel the child to pursue a set of social strategies very different from those typical of the able-bodied child. Thus, both bad faith and passing seem highly refined techniques for coping with a stage one world, a social world where one is weak compared to the able-bodied world and where one is punished for being handicapped by being assigned demeaning roles. Bad faith is a way of living with this punishment; passing is a way to escape it. In a similar fashion, the strategies of gamesmanship seem to represent a sophisticated response to a stage two moral world—a world where the handicapped individual's social survival, his ability to escape the handicapped role, depends upon living on his sociological and manipulative wits. Yet at the same time, if the child has a supportive family life, one can be sure that he will be asked to play roles corresponding to the notions of reciprocity embodied in higher levels of moral development. It is this double character of the handicapped child's role-playing experience that leads us to expect a very different path of moral development or a very different kind of morality.

Three developmental possibilities strike us as especially likely and seem worthy of serious investigation.

The Hobbesian Exception. If I have been treated as a pariah by my classmates and family, I will have little incentive to be a nice boy (Kohlberg's stage three), or to believe in law and order (stage four) or to believe that "reasonable men can compose their differences within the framework of a utilitarian setting" (stage five). Even the morality of the marketplace (stage two) may seem irrelevant precisely because I have discovered again and again in my personal dealings with others the impossibility of reciprocity. Thrust outside the normal social laws, I may conclude that these laws are bogus, that what counts is whether or not you get caught (stage one), or I may find solace in a notion of humanity sufficiently abstract to render the fact of my handicap irrelevant and to provide me with moral support in my stubborn determination to be myself (a Kantian ethic stressing rationality and autonomy such as Kohlberg's stage six). But with further experience I may conclude from the behavior of others toward me that most men are not rational, that the Kantian ethic is appropriate only for the small number of individuals who have in fact achieved the age of reason; for the rest of humanity I may decide that in my dealings with them what counts is whether or not I get caught (stage one). With still more experience (perhaps of being caught too many times for comfort), I might adopt a law-and-order stance (stage four) on the Hobbesian grounds that given most people's attitudes toward handicap, a handicapped person is safer if the law is obeyed to the letter than if it is amended or honored in the breach. For such a person the trajectory of his moral development might be one, six, one, four.

The Concealers. Contrast with this the path that a person might be predisposed to follow if it were possible to conceal his disability and pass as normal. Here the "logic" of stage one might be especially seductive. For, granted that the fact of being disabled (i.e., punished) is *prima facie* reason for believing that one has done something wrong, it also follows by the logic of stage one morality that one can redeem one's morality through the "simple" expedient of hiding the fact that one has been punished. At the same time, as one's knowledge of the social world grew, one's knowledge of what it means to pass successfully would grow more sophisticated. Fear of ever causing suspicion would lead one to value conformity above all else, which in time might lead one to evince a stage four law-and-order morality.

The Controller. Finally, suppose that I decide to make the goal of maximizing my control over the physical and social world an end in itself as well as a means to other ends like self-esteem, love, friendship, and success in school. Imbued with this perspective, I will have a very special relationship to my models of moral role taking. My insistence on control will define a theory of moral action, and I will assess the validity of my theories of the social world primarily in instrumental terms, by whether or not they help me achieve my goal of mastery. This extreme pragmatism may lead me to employ all six kinds or moral theories in different areas of my life. It may also lead me to traverse the Kohlbergian stages in a different order, one that reflects the exigencies of achieving control in my environment rather than the social demands that are characteristically made upon able-bodied children in my culture. Perhaps most crucially, shifts in the ways that the social and physical environment frustrates my thirst for control at different periods of my life may confer a cyclic character to my moral development. For example, from adolescence onward, I may shuttle back and forth between stage four and stage six morality, depending upon the kinds of obstacles to control that I encounter. When it is possible for me to master a new physical or social challenge if I throw myself wholeheartedly into the task, I may favor the law-and-order morality of stage four. (For unless *everyone* obeys the rules to the letter, the immense effort that I must put into mastering these rules is devalued.) On the other hand, when the obstacle is impossible to overcome, I may preserve my self-esteem by adopting the humanistic perspective of stage six morality. Alternatively, I may buttress my self-esteem by downplaying the importance of taking any system of social rules too seriously; I may become an apostle of moral and cultural relativism and adopt a stage five morality. Given these possible ways of using different kinds of moral theories as tools, my moral career might be better described as consisting of recurring patterns of moral motifs rather than as a straight-line developmental sequence from lower to higher stages.

The root of the matter is this: each stage of social development presupposes a certain balance of power between the child and the social world. Further, it opposes to this balance of power a

clear-cut set of expectations of what ensues if the rules governing social behavior (as the child perceives them) are obeyed. For
a handicapped child both sides of this equation are altered by
the devastating social meaning of his handicap. On the one hand,
at every age he possesses less social power outside the family than
his able-bodied peers. On the other hand, he is constantly exposed
to incompatible kinds of moral role-taking experiences. Both
within the charmed circle of the family and in the outside world
the handicapped child is constantly defined in two socially contradictory ways—as a complex, growing child who, among other
things, happens to have a handicap, and as a handicap, a freak, a
perpetual patient, an object of pity, contempt, or despair. In the
lives of some children the lines of this division in social experience roughly parallel the division between the family and the
outside world: they are usually treated as persons in the home
and almost always defined as handicaps elsewhere. For other children the sociological chasm cuts across all boundaries: both at
home and in the outside world they encounter in full measure
both kinds of experiences.

Even without taking into account such other complicating factors as how much the child blames himself for his predicament,
it is clear that any theory of moral development derived from
experience with able-bodied children risks seriously misreading
the developmental pathways followed by handicapped children.
Further speculation on this point is premature because we simply
do not know enough about how handicapped children grow up.
What is desperately needed by parents and professionals alike is
carefully designed naturalistic studies of the social development
of handicapped children, studies that recognize that the developmental approach requires far more than the uncritical application
of conventional models of development to handicapped children.

Chapter 6

Personality Development

If we need to rethink mainstream theories of moral and social development before applying them to handicapped children, the need to examine theories of personality development is even greater. Most personality theories still represent the distillation of the wisdom of a particular group of clinicians, rather than testable scientific theories.[1] The usefulness of these distillations, even to the lay reader, is incontestable. But the peculiar generality in which theory is framed and the reliance upon evocative terms that are ill defined make personality theories both seductive and easy to abuse. It is all too simple for the professional or the parent to reconcile any kind of behavior to the theory's predictions by labeling the behavior a pathological deviation from the norm.* In a society that has traditionally treated the handicapped as deviant and therefore inferior, the resilience of psychoanalytic theories poses a special danger, for every time a therapist confuses a healthy deviance with maladjustment, he places the immense prestige of his profession on the side of society's negative stereotypes about handicap.

---

* This problem is compounded by the richness of the analyst's explanatory tools. The psychoanalytic literature currently recognizes some *thirty-nine different kinds of defense mechanisms* alone.[2]

To illustrate the problems besetting any attempt to study the personality development of handicapped children and adults, we propose to show in detail how a typical model of personality development lends itself to an almost automatic adaptation to handicap. After we have offered our "case history" we will briefly suggest some of the reasons why such adaptations should be considered at best to be working hypotheses that require rigorous empirical testing of a sort that is without precedent in present-day personality theory.

The theory we shall discuss is Erik Erikson's theory of the eight stages of man. Erikson's theory is especially useful for our purposes because, while it formulates personality development in terms of a ladder of crucial life problems, its discussion of each of these problems draws heavily upon the tradition of ego psychology (of which it is a notable example) and, through this tradition, upon Freudian notions of the mechanisms of the unconscious and the crucial role of early life experiences. Because of this parallelism between Erikson's stages of life problems and the tough Freudian substrate, the dangers besetting the application of Erikson's theory to handicap are typical of an extremely wide range of other psychoanalytically inspired theories.

As noted earlier, the logical form of Erikson's theory is not unlike the moral typologies of Baldwin, Piaget, and Kohlberg. Development is conceived of as a ladder. The rungs in the ladder are fixed, and the successful resolution of the problems typical of a given rung on the ladder is viewed as a precondition for successfully resolving the problems that appear at the next highest rung. However, in contrast to theories of moral development, failure to resolve the problems of one stage does not prevent one from encountering the problems of the next. Rather, failure vastly complicates one's attempt to solve these new problems. Instead of seeing them in their true light, one reacts to them in terms of the earlier, unresolved stage; for example, instead of responding to one's boss as one's boss, one responds to him as one's father and proceeds to act out one's unresolved problems with one's father—problems that presumably should have been "worked" out much earlier. (This, in essence, is the theory of neurosis common to all psychoanalytically inspired theories.) Finally, the content of each stage, as well as the fact that everyone traverses the stages in the same order, is a clinically derived generalization, not a logical property that can be derived deductively from a precise description of the theory. Something similar is the case for most other theories of personality. Whether the theorist be Freud or Erikson or any one of the numerous other personality theorists, we are almost always confronted with empirically (or clinically) derived typologies. The empirical or quasi-empirical basis of these theories is, of course, one of the most powerful reasons for insisting that they be carefully reexamined before being uncritically applied to handicapped children.

Erikson's Eight Stages and Handicap [3]

Erikson characterizes each of his eight stages in the life cycle by the struggle that characterizes that stage. Infancy is marked by the struggle of "basic trust versus basic mistrust."

During this period what William James called "the blooming, buzzing confusion" of the infant's initial sensations and perceptions gives way to a perception of temporal patterns and regularites. The infant learns that separation from his mother does not mean abandonment, that she is still out there and will return to him when he needs her. This knowledge—which establishes correlations between inner needs such as hunger and familiar and predictable events in the outer world such as the return of the mother—provides the first rudimentary sense of ego identity and trust in oneself: "not only has the infant learned to rely upon the sameness and the continuity of the outer providers," but the infant trusts its own ability to cope with the flux of inner sensations that structure its life and its ability to accept nourishment and affection in a manner that does not elicit rejection by the care provider.

The successful negotiation of this stage is difficult for every infant. But it may be particularly difficult for the handicapped infant because of complications introduced by the handicap itself —the separation of mother and child during periods of extended medical treatment, and the special physical or sensory obstacles (such as blindness) to establishing a firm correlation between the inner population of feelings and sensations and the outer population of predictable events.

A crucial complicating factor in this and later stages is the parents' attitude toward their handicapped child. As Erikson notes, basic trust requires more than "sensitive care of the baby's individual needs." Children trust their mothers because their mothers trust themselves, possessing "a firm sense of personal trustworthiness within the . . . framework of their culture's life style." Thanks to the disease diagnosis of disability and the handicapped role, all too many parents lack a positive cultural framework to draw upon while raising their child. Lacking a sense of self-confidence in what they are doing, they find it especially difficult to provide the infant with that essential component of their patterns of parental "prohibition and permission— . . . a deep, almost somatic conviction that there is a meaning to what they are doing." In amplifying on this remark, Erikson makes an observation that is relevant to every stage of the handicapped child's development: "Ultimately, children become neurotic not from frustrations, but from the lack or loss of societal meaning in these frustrations."

Erikson calls the second stage of life the time of "autonomy versus shame and doubt." It occurs when the infant is learning to move around under his own control—learning to crawl and walk, learning how to control his bladder and bowels. As the child's muscular control increases, he begins to experiment with holding on and letting go. Both urges can express themselves positively or negatively. Holding on can become "a cruel retaining or restraining," or it can be caring and thoughtful—"to have and to hold." Letting go can express itself negatively as an unleashing of destructive forces, or it "can become a relaxed 'to let pass' and 'to let be.' "

During this stage the child is especially prone to take on more of the world than he can handle or understand. He can grasp a glass jar and bang it on the floor. But when the jar breaks and cuts his hand, the accident comes out of the blue, and the mastery produced by giving the jar a good thump may give way to feelings of shame and doubt. The parent's job is to supply the missing discretion to the child's still indiscriminate will. This requires "firm yet reassuring outer control." Without this external guidance, the child's experiences with an still unpredictable world are likely to drive him back within himself. "Instead of taking possession of things in order to test them by purposeful repetition," he will become obsessed by his own repetitiveness. He will seek a series of small victories in order to reassert his mastery of the environment. But these victories will be hollow because they are "the infantile model for a compulsion neurosis."

Again, the risks of this period seem magnified when the child is handicapped. What, for example, represents the right balance between autonomy and protection when the child is blind or deaf and therefore must explore the social and physical world in ways that are profoundly different from the ways of the able-bodied child, or when the child is more vulnerable to injury or illness because of a chronic disease or a crippling disorder? Just when does protection become overprotection? And conversely, how can the parents help to provide the handicapped child with the kinds of experiences with the physical and the social world that can foster the positive expression of the child's urges to hold and to let go?

A special problem for handicapped children during this period is presented by the child's newly acquired ability to feel shame and to be shamed. This sense develops "as the able-bodied child stands up and as his awareness permits him to note the relative measures of size and power." Because of their disabilities—e.g., crippling deformities, lack of normal energy induced by a chronic disease, a missing limb, impaired hearing—some handicapped children may acquire an exaggerated sense of their powerlessness. The intense shame that accompanies this powerlessness may lead the child to hate himself and to "wish for his own invisibility." Some children, "shamed beyond endurance" by their handicap, may be goaded into secret or open defiance. Perceiving the adults around him as saying that his deformed body, his self, and his desires are "evil and dirty," the child may come to question the infallibility of his judges and "to consider evil only the fact that they exist: his chance will come when they are gone, or when he will go from them."

The concerns of the preceding stage are amplified and transformed by the third stage, the Oedipal crisis, a time dominated by the conflict of "initiative versus guilt." The great danger of this period is a "sense of guilt over the goals contemplated and the acts initiated in one's exuberant enjoyment of new locomotor and mental power." This risk is greatest as "infantile jealousy and rivalry . . . now come to a climax in a final contest for a favored position with the mother; the usual failure leads to resignation, guilt, and anxiety. . . . This, then, is the stage of the 'castration complex,' the intensified fear of finding the . . . genitals harmed as a punishment for the fantasies attached to their excitement." For the handicapped child the hazards at these stages are exacerbated by the very fact that, in contrast to other children and his parents, the child bears a very real special mutilation of the body —a crippled limb, a speech defect, a palsy, a cosmetic disfigurement. Whereas the able-bodied child escapes from the Oedipal terrors of fantasized mutilation by introjecting or internalizing the identity of the powerful parental rival, this psychic maneuver possesses a special ambiguity for the handicapped child. The integrity of the child's sexual organ is preserved, but the handicap remains—a paradox that may lead to a displacement of feelings about sexuality from the sexual organ to the disability or to those activities that are rendered impossible or especially difficult for the child by the biological limitations of his disabilty.

Even when the core hazards of the Oedipal period are successfully navigated, the handicapped child may face many crucial secondary hazards. With increasing age, limitations on mobility, communication, object manipulation, and social interaction may assume greater significance because they cut the child off from more and more of the activities and experiences that are appropriate to his age. Of still greater importance is the possibility that parental misunderstanding combined with rejection by his peers will prevent the handicapped child from fully benefiting from one of the most positive characteristics of this stage of growth. As Erikson notes, "the child is at no time more ready to learn quickly . . . to become bigger in the sense of sharing obligation and performance. . . . He is eager and able to make things cooperatively, to combine with other children for the purpose of constructing and planning . . . to profit from teachers and to emulate ideal prototypes." For the able-bodied child, but not necessarily for the stigmatized handicapped child, the grown-up world offers the child a secure and glamorous reality "in the form of ideal adults recognizable by their uniforms and their functions," which is "fascinating enough to replace the heroes of picture book and fairy tale" and in which the able-bodied child can feel that he has a place.

Around the time that the child enters school, he enters into a fourth developmental stage whose principal conflict is that of "industry versus inferiority." During this period "violent drives are normally dormant." The child sublimates his earlier concerns and "learns to win recognition by producing things." This turning outward represents the consolidation of two earlier streams of development—the child's purely physical mastery of his body (walking, bowel and bladder control, etc.) and the acceptance that he cannot remain a baby all his life, that "there is no workable future within the womb of the family."

Both processes may, however, be delayed or rendered incomplete in the case of a handicapped child. Paternal overprotection —what Solnit and Green have called the "vulnerable child syndrome"—may foster a continued dependence on the womb of the family, and the biological limitations of the child's handicap may decisively impede that mastery of the body that the able-bodied child has achieved by now. It is at this time, as well, that the child is likely to grasp the scale and the significance of the stigma that is associated with his handicap. Like the black child, he may begin to feel that his handicap "rather than his wish and his will to learn will decide his worth as an apprentice, and thus his sense of *identity*," a hazard that raises especially complex problems when the child's handicap—e.g., a reading disability or a stutter— is both highly stigmatized and a genuine impediment to learning or the mastery of crucial interpersonal skills.

Should these special hindrances undermine the handicapped child's exploitation of his new capacities, he may succumb to the special danger of this stage of life—a sense of inadequacy and inferiority. Despairing "of his tools and skills or of his status among his tool partners, he may be discouraged from identification with them and with a section of the tool world." Feeling himself "doomed to mediocrity or inadequacy," the child may regress back into "the more isolated, less tool-conscious familiar rivalry of the oedipal time."

With the fifth state—"identity versus role confusion"—the individual enters into the turbulent storms of adolescence, a period during which he must "refight many of the battles of earlier years" because of the achievement of sexual maturity and the other dramatic physical changes that accompany maturation. Able-bodied and handicapped alike have an exaggerated sensitivity to their physical appearance, and both "are concerned with what they appear to be in the eyes of others as compared with what they feel they are" as well as with the question of what they will become in adulthood, the question of their career. Unsure of their new bodies, unclear about their future careers, all adolescents are bedeviled by the problem of personal identity.

However, the handicapped adolescent—like the able-bodied minority youth—frequently knows that he faces a far bleaker economic future than his normal peers. He may have little to look forward to in adulthood—perhaps a life on welfare, perhaps the make-work of a sheltered workshop, perhaps jobs that are both demeaning and meaningless because they tap so little of his potential. Frequently, this bleak and entirely realistic career prospect is supplemented by an equally bleak social prospect—a diminished chance of being able to afford to raise a family, or, indeed, a diminished chance of marriage in the first place.

Faced with the loss of identity or the role confusion that is brought on by the career crisis, the able-bodied adolescent draws upon a host of coping strategies. Each of these strategies is either less readily available to the handicapped or is more likely to serve a negative rather than a positive function. One of the most common ways to shore up temporarily a diffused identity is to "over-identify, to the point of apparent loss of identity, with the heroes of cliques and crowds." For the able-bodied adolescent, this merging provides a temporary framework for the self. But because almost all adolescent heroes are able-bodied, a similar kind of identification by the handicapped adolescent may actually serve to enhance his role confusion by leading him to reject his disability and to deny the cruel social (and physical) reality of his handicap.

One of the most important devices used by adolescents to protect against identity confusion is to be "remarkably clannish, and cruel in their exclusion of all those who are 'different.' " All too often the handicapped adolescent finds himself on the receiving end of this exclusion; and while the stereotypes imposed upon him by the able-bodied do define an identity of sorts, this identity reinforces the worst elements in the culture's definition of disability as a diseaselike problem. Far from providing the disabled adolescent with some temporary, if negative, structure during a period of role confusion, his exclusion from the group represents a significant step in making him feel like a despised outsider.

Finally, the stigma and isolation that the handicapped adolescent experiences frequently rule out relationships with members of the opposite sex. The consequences of this exclusion extend far beyond the obvious impact on sexual development. To a large extent, adolescent love represents yet another strategy that the self uses to clarify its identity—a strategy that involves "projecting one's diffused ego image on another and by seeing it thus reflected and gradually clarified," that process of talking and more talking that explains "why so much of young love is conversation."

Erikson's sixth stage of development is characterized by the conflict between "intimacy versus isolation," which takes place during young adulthood. Having found himself, the young adult is now capable of risking what was most precious in the preceding stage: "He is eager and willing to fuse his identity with that of others." He is ready for, intimacy, "able to face the fear of ego loss in situations which call for self-abandon: in the solidarity of close affiliations, in orgasms and sexual unions, in close friendships and in physical combat. . . ." The great risk of this stage is the "deep sense of isolation and consequent self-absorption" that may occur if the individual shuns these experiences out of a fear of ego loss.

The achievement of intimacy may be especially difficult for the handicapped person. Throughout his life he has been forced to dissemble, manipulate, and lie. His emotional survival has often depended upon the use of elaborate stratagems to hold at bay the able-bodied world's insults and humiliations. Not a day has passed when he has failed to draw sustenance from his habitual defenses against the injustices practiced upon him in even the most casual encounter. By now many of these protective strategies are second nature. Yet unless he can learn to selectively set them aside, he will be incapable of attaining the reciprocity and equality that define true intimacy. Discerning how and when it is not only safe but *necessary* to let go in a relationship may be one of the most daunting tasks faced by the handicapped person who has survived by never letting his guard down.

But even as we underline the special psychological hazards of this period it is good to recall—as Erikson does for the able-bodied —the new ways that society intensifies the individual's problems now that he is an adult. Being members of an oppressed minority, many handicapped people have circumscribed work options. Many also have severely limited sexual options. Frequently, the economic preconditions for marriage do not exist; indeed, because of restrictions on mobility, the disabled individual may have extreme difficulty in even meeting members of the opposite sex, let alone in forming relationships or finding privacy. The handicapped person may find himself rejected by potential lovers because he is thought to be "different," "sick," or "ugly."

The stigma and exclusion experienced by the disabled individual, weigh heavily upon his ability to resolve the great crisis of the seventh stage of life, that of "generativity versus stagnation." Just as social and economic discrimination make it harder to establish a long-term intimate relationship, these factors (along with a continued commitment to tried-and-true ego defenses against stigma and prejudice) may make it much harder for the handicapped adult to fulfill the central task of this period of life— the rearing of a family or the forging of some other equally meaningful link between the concerns of the self and future generations. "Generativity," writes Erikson, "is primarily the concern in establishing and guiding the next generation." Where this "enrichment" of the sphere of ego interests fails to take place, the individual often regresses "to an obsessive need for pseudo-intimacy . . . often with a pervading sense of stagnation and personal impoverishment." He enters into relationships where an obsession with self becomes a substitute for genuine intimacy. A special hazard of this stage—and one to which it is only too natural for the handicapped adult to succumb—is that "where conditions favor it, early invalidism, physical or psychological, becomes the vehicle of self-concern."

"Ego integrity versus despair" marks the great crisis of the eighth and final stage in Erikson's schema. To navigate this crisis successfully is to achieve a ripeness, an acceptance of death, and the "acceptance of one's one and only life cycle as something that had to be and that, by necessity, permitted of no substitutions." Though fully aware of the relativity of all life-styles, the individual knows that "for him all human integrity stands or falls with the one style of integrity [the one life-style] of which he partakes." Viewing his life as one of the possible expressions of his culture, he affirms his bond with the past and with the future of his culture. He accepts that he is a man of his time and thereby becomes a man of all times—"so that a wise Indian, a true gentleman, and a mature peasant share and recognize in one another the final stage of integrity." The dangers of this stage are a fear of death, a rancor at the passage of time, and a despair that "the time is now . . . too short for the attempt to start another life and to try out alternate roads to integrity." Here, too, the special obstacles of a handicapped life—those many hazards that we have surveyed in the past few pages—may make the achievement of this final stage of ego integrity and ego integration especially difficult for some disabled individuals.

Erikson Reconsidered

At first glance, our abbreviated attempt to apply Erikson's stage theory to handicap seems promising. It is clear, for example, that Erikson's theory is fully capable of accommodating many of the special issues that a handicapped child may encounter in his development—the problem of parental attitudes, peer prejudice, the concrete and symbolic significance of the biological limitations that are associated with the handicap, and so on. However, in a deeper sense the attempt seems unsatisfactory.

Perhaps the most crucial shortcoming of the approach is epistemological. In order to remain faithful to Erikson's typology, we have been forced to describe the disabled person's development negatively, in terms of the special hazards that some handicapped individuals may face when seeking to negotiate the Eriksonian stages. This emphasis upon potential hazard has committed us—albeit in a subtle and humanistic form—to approach disability by means of a deviance analysis, looking at the problems of the handicapped by identifying specific areas of *potential* deviance for each stage. As a consequence, we have been forced to prejudge precisely those developmental questions about handicap which, above all others, require painstaking empirical investigation before even the most tentative answers can be given. For example, instead of impelling us to ask if failure to master a given stage-dependent crisis (such as autonomy versus shame and doubt) possesses the same meaning for the handicapped child's development as for the able-bodied child's development, our deviance analysis commits us to asserting this similarity as a basic axiom. Just as crucially, we are not encouraged to ask if the eight stages identified by Eriksonian theory adequately describe the optimal development for at least some groups of handicapped individuals; here, too, a correspondence between the development of the able-bodied and the handicapped is postulated in advance. Moreover, we have been forced to assume that at every stage of life—and for every group of handicapped individuals—each defense mechanism and, indeed, each unit of behavior possesses the same developmental meaning for the able-bodied and the disabled. Last, but not least, we have had to assume that the order of Erikson's eight stages corresponds to the optimal ordering of these developmental stages for handicapped individuals. Thus, despite—or perhaps because of—the ease with which the Eriksonian framework can be adapted to handicap, it is by no means clear that it adequately captures the chief developmental stages that are followed by different groups of handicapped children.

Still another problem with uncritically applying Eriksonian theory to handicap is the theory's insistence that all psychologically successful individuals pass through the eight stages of development in the same general way. One of the beauties of Erikson's theory, when applied to the able-bodied, is that each higher stage incorporates within itself the most salient features of lower stages. It is not, for example, that questions of trust and mistrust are definitively solved in infancy, but that infancy is the time when they first appear.[4] In later stages of life questions of trust and mistrust are elements of the dominant problems of the period. One cannot, for example, achieve intimacy in early adulthood (Erikson's fifth stage) without mastering the problem of trust and mistrust in the new and far more complex form it attains in adult relationships. In the language of philosophy: resolution of the problems of an earlier stage represents a necessary but not a sufficient condition for the mastery of the new form these problems take in the next stage of life. For the able-bodied, then, Erikson's stages have something of the character of a set of Chinese boxes. Each stage contains within it the set of smaller boxes that preceded it. The issues represented by each of these smaller boxes take on a new and more sophisticated meaning in the context presented by later stages of life.

The Eriksonian model seems far too simple for many disabled people because the clear-cut nesting relationship of one stage to the next is constantly being undercut by the interaction of their physical limitations with their social situation. As a result, many of the early conquests of the able-bodied child—the control over his body functions (autonomy versus shame and doubt, Erikson's second stage)—are never definitively resolved even in their most primitive form. For a paraplegic who must constantly monitor his kidney functioning and worry about urinary tract infections—not to mention managing the matter of bowel movements—there is a provisional quality to his mastery of primary biological functions that is absent in the able-bodied. At the same time, to the extent that the paraplegic is dependent upon an attendant (or a family member) to help him, there is an "infantile" quality to the way he must assert his mastery over his body. Like the young child who must call on his mother for help, the physically handicapped person must sometimes relate to his own body by means of another (able-bodied) person. Sometimes the individual is an attendant, as with a paraplegic. Sometimes he is a stranger, as when a blind person asks for help in crossing a street. Often it is a doctor. In each case the sociological situation of handicap tends to exaggerate the analogy between the handicapped person's dependence upon the other and the young child's dependence upon his parents. Here—as well as at other stages of development—increases in physical and social mastery that are once-and-for-all conquests in the life of the able-bodied must constantly be reaffirmed by an act of will directed at a person whose help is needed, or at a body that may have less stamina and that will often be hampered in big and small ways by needless environmental barriers, and at the forces in oneself that counsel an all too easy and sometimes seductive passivity.

It is a common observation of clinicians that handicapped children and adolescents often display great precocity in their interpersonal behavior. Just as the Eriksonian model seems incapable of doing justice to the complex ways that a disabled person's different body may interact with development, so the theory seems poorly adapted to coping with the many ways that a social precocity may dramatically influence the course of his healthy development. For example, many handicapped adolescents are certainly preoccupied with questions of identity; but, at least in our experience, these questions are frequently bound up with issues of intimacy versus isolation (stage six), generativity versus stagnation (stage seven), and most especially with ego integrity versus despair (stage eight) in ways that simply burst the bounds of an Eriksonian characterization of the able-bodied individual's adolescence.

Yet even assuming the improbable—that the theory's description of an ego integrity crisis in old age does justice to an ego integrity crisis in a handicapped adolescent—a crucial problem remains. The preferred solution to the stage eight crisis takes on an entirely different character when the crisis occurs at the threshold of adult life rather than at the end of the life cycle. The resolution that seems appropriate for old age—a certain tranquillity and sense of wise fullness joined to an acceptance of the inevitable—might well be a highly regressive and "infantile" solution for an adolescent for whom the only possible way that he will be able to achieve a meaningful adult life is through living by his psychological and social wits. Despite its apparent immaturity when judged by able-bodied standards, an almost obsessive egoism might be a much more healthy strategy with which to face the daunting prospect of attempting to lead an active adult life with a severe physical disability. Similar difficulties, we believe, effect the theory's preferred resolutions for the crises of stages six and seven when these crises are played out in an adolescent setting.

What the limitations of handicap deny the blind or the crippled —a once-and-for-all mastery of the body's world and the world of objects—is also frequently denied the person in the social realm. Integration in the group, a sense of interpersonal ease, a secure, positive social identity—protecting these hard-won achievements of childhood and adulthood is difficult enough for the able-bodied. But it is even more difficult for a person who lives in a social world where, thanks to the handicapped role and prejudice, no positive social acquisition is entirely safe. At any moment he may be forced to prove himself to others in terms that reproduce an old developmental crisis. At other times the demoralization of being misperceived and mistreated may revive old wounds and encourage states of mind that call into question earlier gains. The paradoxes of freedom have been explored at length by philosopher-psychologists such as Jean-Paul Sartre. What the existentialists urge upon the able-bodied individual—the conscious recognition that he is "condemned to freedom," that what counts is what he does in the present moment, not what he has done in the past—seems built into the sociological destiny of many of the disabled.

Nothing sets the handicapped more completely apart from most of society than their special relationship with pain and death.[5] Traditionally, the problem of mortality—its significance, how one copes with the passing of a loved one, how one prepares for one's own demise—has been the dominant concern of Western culture and Western religion. Throughout the nineteenth century death remained a constant preoccupation of novelists and playwrights: not death in the impersonal, bureaucratic form it has achieved in this century, but death in the form of the private tragedy—the death of a beloved child, the death of a parent, the death of a mother in childbirth. With the rise of modern medicine we have become a culture that represses death rather than openly exploring and working through its significance for our private lives.

Members of a society that no longer has any place for death and dying, the handicapped share the same fate as the elderly: both suffer by being unable to draw upon the kinds of cultural "solutions" to mortality that once were everyone's birthright. In the place of these myths and ceremonies they are given medicine and a culture that pretends immortality by idealizing youth and violence. Excluded from the "youth culture," the handicapped and the aged have also benefited the least, in a cultural sense, from medicine's banishment of death to the periphery of life. Indeed, they *are* that periphery. Even when a handicapped person is not in danger of dying, his disability marks him as one who is, in a sense, prematurely aged.[6] Perhaps of even greater importance is the pain that is often associated with the disability or with the medical or rehabilitative procedures that are required to combat it. Speech therapy and physical therapy are often an agony for the palsied and the crippled. The pain and suffering that attend renal dialysis and kidney transplants is beyond the pale of a normal childhood. The impact that these factors can have upon the unfolding of a life is suggested by a moving letter that appeared in *The New York Times*:

> At 23, I have spent one-third of my life in and out of radiology clinics. I have often thought that the experience of sitting in a radiology clinic for long periods of time is an excellent although brutal lesson in learning the terrible truth that life is ruled by chance. Only fools and cowards can possibly believe that life can be ruled by a striving for anything.
>
> I do not believe that anyone has ever chosen to acquire a cancer or to become mentally ill. Anyone who has ever experienced either knows that no one could ever choose such unspeakable pain.[7]

Here, too, the handicapped individual may find himself or herself "unstuck in time," cut off from others by the very different developmental tasks that are posed by a premature confrontation with death, disability, and the absurdity of existence.

At the opposite pole from pain and death are the questions raised by the ability to love and to achieve intimacy. Here, too, the Eriksonian framework may sometimes require modification. Moderately and severely disabled children often have fewer opportunities for gaining sexual experience than able-bodied children. Many factors can be responsible—stigma, mobility limitations, long periods of time spent in institutional settings, and stereotypes about disability that either deny the child's sexuality or, as in the case of the retarded, sometimes view it as a dangerous force that must be suppressed. Frequently the child's social exclusion means the deferral into early adulthood of many aspects of normal adolescent psychosexual development. While this delay is not necessarily harmful, it must be reckoned with in any appraisal of the developmental issues faced by a handicapped individual: behavior that might be regressive in an able-bodied person may have a different meaning for a person who has grown up handicapped. The interpersonal survival strategies mentioned earlier introduce additional complexities. These and other ego defenses against victimization may sometimes impede growth (which was suggested in our discussion of Erikson's sixth stage of development, "intimacy versus isolation"), but they may also function in the service of health.[8] As in areas outside sexuality, the psychological goals served by the person's strategies for contending with stigma and discrimination may not be fully understood if he is judged by norms constructed for the able-bodied.

There are many other systematic differences between the experiences of able-bodied children and handicapped children. For example, parents and professionals often place great emphasis upon fostering the child's adjustment to the limitations of his disability and his acceptance of the discrimination that attends his physical or mental difference. The desirability of a realistic accommodation cannot be questioned—provided, of course, that one can agree upon what is "realistic." * But even the adults' best-conceived attempts to persuade and encourage can sometimes provoke unintended developmental consequences that intensify the differences between the pathways pursued by able-bodied and handicapped children. Some children with disabilities may rebel violently against "adjustment" precisely because of the emphasis placed upon it by their elders, who are usually able-bodied. Other children may retreat into a premature and equally destructive "wise maturity"—a coming to terms with life before they have gotten to know life; that is, a flight from experience in the guise of maturity. For some individuals, at least, the need to arrive at a balance between too much accommodation and too little may define the characteristic crisis of a particular stage (or stages) of childhood or adolescence.†

A more familiar set of hazards is also of great developmental significance—the handicapped child's often excessive exposure to institutional settings and relationships with professionals in which he is tacitly or overtly defined as a patient. Of course, virtually all children encounter some doctors, some dentists, some

---

* Nowhere has this complex question been explored with greater sensitivity and humanity than in *Awakenings,* Oliver Sacks's study of adults who have been severely disabled by Parkinson's disease.[9]

† Do similar crises of accommodation play an equally important role in the adult development of some individuals with handicaps? It seems likely, because each new advance in maturity brings not only a greater degree of ego integration for the person but a new set of insights into the price that one has paid on account of one's disability. At least at some periods of adulthood, these new insights might be the sort to reopen the question of how to strike a balance between too much and too little acceptance.

teachers, and some counselors who fit them into the mold of the sick role or treat them in a high-handed manner that is perfectly consistent with any one of a number of such low-status identities in our society as female, black, or handicapped person. What sets the handicapped child apart is the likelihood that he will be chronically exposed to these negative experiences because of the responses that he may provoke in his teachers and because of his frequent contacts with groups of professionals (e.g., doctors, physical therapists) whom other children see far less often while they are growing up. And whatever the professionals' reasons, the impact upon the child of much of their treatment is to reinforce the culture's image of him as a perpetual patient, a person who is defined in terms of his disability and whose actions are of value and meaning only insofar as they are directed toward overcoming the limitations of his disability and escaping from his deviant status.

The special importance of taking into account these kinds of socialization experiences for the chronically ill child has been emphasized by Barbara Korsch: "If you try to think what this child actually does all day, what his life is like, you realize how much time he is spending in various therapies. His whole interaction with the health care delivery system is something that is a visible, measurable aspect of a sick child's life. Is there something about the way the child interacts with health professionals that we, as a group of health professionals trying to assess those children, could try to make our arena of observation and that would tell us about this child's life and independent functioning?" [10]

Our survey of Eriksonian theory suggests that the burden of proof must rest squarely with those who maintain that theories of able-bodied personality development can be applied without modification to the handicapped. Yet, even so, we have not begun to enumerate all the differences in social experience that may make the developmental trajectories of some children with handicaps very different indeed from those postulated by conventional theories. Nor have we addressed the important theoretical issues that are raised by the possibility that the handicapped child sometimes develops according to a healthy logic of his own. We have not attempted to distinguish between types of handicaps or to take into account the undoubtedly complex interactions of disability with social class, ethnic group, sex, and other factors. We have remained silent about the impact of family life upon the optimal developmental pathways for a specific child with a specific disability in a specific time and place. We have not addressed the question of whether handicapped people are too diverse as a group to be encompassed by any one typology of personality development, whether psychologists will need to construct many different scenarios for growth, if some of these versions of the life cycle will be associated with particular handicaps, or if all of them will cut across disability categories. We have ignored or enormously oversimplified these and other crucial issues because there are so few naturalistic studies of the personality development of handicapped people and because neither personality theory nor social psychological theory, in their present state of refinement, lend themselves to rigorous theoretical analysis. But above all we have simplified in order to underline the central importance of approaching the handicapped child on the child's terms, rather than on terms spelled out in advance by personality theories developed for able-bodied children and adults. We must take nothing for granted about the applicability of any existing personality theory to handicap. To settle for anything less at this stage of research is to risk perpetuating society's most misleading stereotypes of inferiority in the guise of scientific objectivity.

Chapter 7

Intellectual Development

Studies of the intellectual development of children are dominated by Jean Piaget. Piaget's theory operates on a far more complex level of analysis than theories of moral behavior or personality. Instead of providing a simple qualitative description of each stage of growth, Piaget attempts to provide a formal structural description, complete with quasi-algebraic equations and elaborate experimental designs, of the range of logical abilities that underlie the child's problem-solving behavior.

Even in a book written specifically for experts in cognitive psychology, a critical review of Piaget's position on the relation between cognitive development and social development would be a daunting task. Yet despite the obstacles, we believe it urgent to perform such an analysis before developmental traditions become well established in handicap. For many reasons—not the least being Piaget's notoriously vague and contradictory prose style —Piaget's views on social development are widely misunderstood even by professionals. As most psychologists interpret Piagetian theory, there is no way that the special social experiences of handicapped children could possibly alter the nature of their intellectual development. That is, the orthodox view of the relation between social and cognitive development implies that Piagetian theory can analyze the handicapped child's cognition just as well as it can analyze the able-bodied child's cognition.

Every theory directs its adherents to raise certain questions in their research and to take for granted the answers to other questions. If psychologists take for granted the suitability of Piagetian theory as a tool for studying the handicapped child, a deviance analysis may prevail by default: able-bodied norms will be *assumed* to be appropriate for handicapped children, and any negative deviations from these norms will be automatically treated as reflecting a problem in the child's development rather than a problem with the theory. This is why we shall reexamine the orthodox interpretation of Piagetian theory: in our view, the first item on the Piagetian's research agenda for handicap should be a systematic attempt to test the theory's relevance to handicap.

Earlier, we stressed that no mainstream model of moral or personality development can account for either the content of the developmental stages they posit or the apparent empirical fact that able-bodied individuals always pass through these stages in the same order.

Kohlberg's theory of moral development describes a series of stages as fixed and invariant as the rungs of a ladder, but it cannot explain why a given stage occupies a given place, in the developmental hierarchy. Erikson's personality theory describes stages that basically nest one within the next. This nesting, which is characteristic of most psychoanalytically inspired personality theories, represents a significant increase in logical complexity over the simpler ladder typologies of which Kohlberg's theory is an example. But as the proliferation of rival theories to Erikson's suggests, there remains an arbitrary character to the choice of labels one assigns to them. For Erikson, the first great issue of life is the problem of trust and distrust. But for Freud, the first issue is not trust but sexuality; for Adler, it is power. None of the three can justify its choice of where to begin; none can explain why.

Piagetian theory is also characterized by stages, and it is a still more powerful typology. It goes beyond the ordering of classes of behavior to the description of the logical structure of behavior. This shift from an exclusive focus on content to an approach that focuses on form as well as content represents a considerable advance in conceptual sophistication and explanatory power. One of the most striking examples of this advance lies in the theory's ability to account, on purely logical grounds, for the ordering of some (though not all) of its stages.

Piaget divides cognitive development into four great periods. The first stage—which extends from infancy to about age two—is called the period of sensory-motor thought. The second is called preoperational thought and spans the ages from two to seven. Middle childhood (ages seven to thirteen) is characterized as the period of concrete operational thought. The final and most advanced stage of thought begins during adolescence and reaches full maturity in early adulthood. This stage is called the period of formal operational thought. The logical relationships between Piaget's first two stages remain unclear because the detailed characteristics of sensory-motor thought are only now beginning to be explored, and the nature of the mental structures that underlie preoperational thought are still cloaked in mystery. Of all Piaget's stages, the preoperational period is the least understood.[1] Matters are very different for the third and fourth stages of Piaget's developmental hierarchy. Here the theory provides sufficiently precise algebraic descriptions of the logical abilities characteristic of each stage to explain why concrete thought not only is more primitive than formal thought but may be its necessary precursor.

The germ of Piaget's explanation goes like this. It is possible to view the problem-solving behavior of well-educated adults as consisting of a fixed number of basic logical strategies that can be used singly or in combination. These strategies are superior to those of middle childhood in two crucial respects: they are able to deal with more variables at the same time and they are much less context-bound. Piaget argues that adult thought represents the fullest possible generalization of the logical abilities that must be presupposed in order to account for patterns of problem-solving behavior displayed by children during the period of concrete operations.

To describe the formal properties of adult thought, Piaget uses the propositional logic developed by Bertrand Russell, Alfred North Whitehead, and other logicians in the twentieth century. For concrete operational thought (middle childhood), Piaget draws upon another strand of twentieth-century logic, the theory of groups, although here he introduces some modifications of his own. In both cases Piaget was the first to apply to psychology some of the new logical techniques that were perfected after 1900; these techniques made it possible to describe the logic of nonmathematical problem solving with the same kind of rigor as constructions of mathematical proofs. Although logicians are sharply, even bitterly, divided on the merits of Piaget's borrowings and innovations, his attempt to describe the algebraic structure of child thought and adult thought represents a milestone in the history of psychology.[2]

A rough sense of the power, the scope, and the ambition of Piagetian theory can be gained by looking a little more closely at the logical structure of concrete operational thought, the mental stage characteristic of middle childhood.[3] According to Piaget, concrete operational thought involves eight basic cognitive strategies which are called "*groupements*." * Each of these groupements embodies a basic idea of how to think about classes, how to state the way in which different classes of objects stand in relationship to one another. (For our purposes a "class" is anything that can be named—e.g., a particular individual, a concept, a species, etc.) Each of the groupements one through four captures a different way of grasping how two classes can be similar in some respect (e.g., Jack and Jill are human beings). Groupements five through eight represent a complementary way of conceiving of class relationships—comparing two classes in terms of how they differ from each other (e.g., Jack is older than Jill). The mastery of the logical skills which the groupements contain represents a great advance in the child's ability to think. But there is a limit to how far the child can go with these structures—like a mysterious injunction in a fairy tale, a child can use only one logical strategy at a time. This limitation stems from the autonomous character of the logical strategies embodied in the groupements. Each represents a separate "logical track." Pursuing a train of thought down one track, the child has no logical spur that allows him to switch onto another logical track. The metaphor is remarkably exact. Given a task whose successful solution requires the application of several of the strategies typical of the groupements, the child finds himself derailed. When

---

* *Groupement* is often translated as "grouping" in English. However, in French *groupement* figures in many constructions in which the English analog would be "group"—i.e., *groupement politique* ("political group"), *groupement tactique* ("tactical group"). Moreover, *groupement*'s primary meanings lack the vagueness of "grouping"—e.g., the act of forming a group, a meeting of the members of a group, the bringing together of a collection of objects that form a group. All of these senses of the French word are consistent with Piaget's vision of cognitive development as arising from an active manipulation of objects, a *savoir faire*, to recall the phrase recently used by Piaget in his *Réussir et Comprendre*. Because "grouping" conveys none of this sense of active interaction with the world but seems both pallid and opaque, we shall use *groupement* throughout our discussion.

117

he tries to make the switch, in his attempt to view the problem from the fresh perspective of a different logical strategy, he forgets where he is. He becomes confused and falters. Or he ends up garbling things and producing a distorted answer. Only with the achievement of formal operational structures in adolescence or adulthood does thought finally become capable of proceeding down several tracks at once, or switching smoothly from one to another.

These two properties of groupements—the extremely basic character of the logical ideas they embody and the mutual incompatibility of these ideas for the young child—are best illustrated by a simple example. A child can recognize that the Tin Man, the Scarecrow, and the Cowardly Lion all share certain important characteristics—they are Dorothy's friends, they are all afraid of the Wicked Witch of the West, and they all want something from the Wizard.* And a child is also capable of recognizing that the Scarecrow is more intelligent than the others, the Tin Man more sentimental, and the Lion more brave.† For an adult, nothing is simpler than keeping both the resemblances and the differences between Dorothy's friends in mind and perceiving them as one powerful group that can defend and support Dorothy. But Piaget claims that the concrete operational child cannot systematically connect these facts. The child can grasp the similarities between Dorothy's friends, and he can grasp the differences. But he cannot unite them into a stable perception of the three characters as a group. Indeed, a Piagetian might speculate that some of the terror and endless fascination that we all feel as children when we listen to fairy tales come from the way that the crucial features of the plot constantly dissolve and reform into new and contradictory patterns in much the same way that, as adults, we are tricked by the impossible staircases and archways in M. C. Escher's paintings. Just as the adult eye cannot integrate Escher's contradictory perspectives into a single whole, so too the child's mind may not be able to weave the different logical threads of the fairy tale into a single all-embracing pattern.‡

* Groupement one embodies the idea that two different things can be similar because they possess overlapping properties.

† Groupement five embodies a way of stating the relationship between objects in terms of their dissimilarity.

‡ In recent years there have been many structural studies of myths and fairy tales. These studies might repay examination from the point of view outlined here.

Piaget's Theory: The Orthodox Interpretation

Throughout this book we have emphasized that handicapped children often grow up in a social world that is radically different from the world of able-bodied children. What are the implications of this difference in socialization experience for attempts to apply Piagetian theory to the handicapped child? Piaget's general position on the relationship between social experience and cognitive development provides a useful point of departure. As we will see, his general position (he has never extensively discussed the development of mentally normal children with handicaps) is not what it first seems.

In one of his sociological essays he addresses the question head-on: "Does the structure of collective interactions . . . determine the structure of intellectual operations?" he asks.[4] Does the child "become capable of rational operations because his social development renders him capable of cooperation?" [5] Or is it the other way around? Does the child's cognitive development provide him with the necessary intellectual tools for making sense of the social behavior of children his age and "therefore make it possible for him to cooperate?" [6] Which comes first, the chicken or the egg, the logic or the social experience?

In fact, concludes Piaget, the structure of the individual's social behavior is always the same as the structure of his cognitive behavior for any stage of his cognitive development. Social behavior and cognitive behavior are different expressions of "one and the same integrated logical system in which the social aspect and the logical aspect are inseparable both in the form and the content." [7]

At first glance this answer seems clear and unequivocal. However, a close reading of the main texts in which Piaget talks about social behavior—such as *The Psychology of Intelligence*, the chapter on adolescent thought in *The Growth of Logical Operations in Childhood and Adolescence*, *The Moral Judgment of the Child*, the relevant passages in *Structuralism*, and the essays in his *Études Sociologiques*—reveals that when Piaget says "social behavior" he always means one very restricted class of social behavior: the ability to cooperate with other people in a manner deemed to be characteristic of one's age.

When discussing social behavior, Piaget is interested in showing the connections of cognition with the ability to cooperate—whether this be the ability to understand what the other is saying in a rational argument, the ability to share or to participate in a common task, or the ability to participate in a game with other children. Consistently, what seems to fall outside the boundaries of his discussions are all those other social strategies that even young children use when they display great insight into the other's character, intentions, and feelings; the strategies children use when they act out of a desire for self-preservation; when they act selfishly and greedily; when they act in desperation; when they seek to manipulate, cheat, and pass as something they are not; when the issue in their minds is not cooperation but social or emotional survival.

Speaking of twentieth-century British philosophy in the tradition of Austin and the later Wittgenstein, Iris Murdoch has observed that it is perfectly adequate when one is interested in exploring what one does or intends or means when performing the everyday tasks of life—going to the post office to mail a letter, accepting an invitation to dinner, borrowing a book from the public library—but that it utterly fails to shed any light on what we do when faced with any great emotional or moral crisis.[8] It is not overstating matters to apply the same criticism to Piaget's discussions of social behavior. Piaget's emphasis upon the orderly aspects of middle-class and upper-class life seems curiously out of touch with the turbulent history of our time, and especially poorly adapted to the experience of such oppressed groups as the handicapped.

This narrow limitation in what Piaget means by social behavior casts an entirely different light on his claim that social and cognitive behavior develop in tandem. Even if we provisionally grant that Piaget's ladder of developmental stages may capture the logical structure of the child's growing ability to cooperate, the theory would appear to be neutral on the question of the relationship between the development of the child's noncooperative behaviors (and modes of social cognition) and cognitive development. In this regard, a remark by the logician Charles Parsons in his trenchant critique of Piagetian theory is apt.* Speaking of the logical strategies that compose the eight elementary groupements of the concrete operational stage, Parsons notes that while these strategies may "yield the richest algebraic

---

* To avoid burdening our text, more technical discussions of many of the issues raised by our discussion will be found in the notes.[9] A few notes are directed to the nonspecialist seeking an amplification of a point made in the text or the definition of an unfamiliar Piagetian term; e.g., notes 24, 38, 39, and 40.

structures" and may "play the most important role in the cognitive acquisitions of this stage," they do not by any means exhaust the logical strategies that "occur constantly in ordinary life and science" and that are susceptible to the same kinds of "logical operations" as the operations that characterize the algebraic structures of concrete thought (e.g., the operations known to the logician as composition, conversion, and negation).[10] In short, Piaget's descriptions of the sophistication of a child's thought and behavior may be exactly accurate as far as they go. But they may not go far enough. It is entirely possible that in areas not studied by Piaget, a child will display a greater logical sophistication, in both the structure of the child's unconscious behavior and the structure of the child's representational thought.[11] For example, the child's representational thought in "non-Piagetian" areas of social life may well display a mastery of certain logical skills (i.e., reversible operations) long before the child enters the concrete operational stage in those areas of his life that Piaget and Piagetians have studied.[12]

Piaget's failure to mention, let alone study, most of the social survival strategies of children is perfectly consistent with the goals of his theory and research. For Piaget, child psychology is a means to an end, not the end in itself. His real interest is epistemology—the nature and origin of knowledge. He has studied children in the hope that their more primitive thought processes will shed light on the great unsolved problems of philosophy and logic—just as the molecular biologist studies the primitive genetic code of the virus and the microbe in order to gain insight into the operation of the genetic material in the infinitely more complex human being.[13] From Piaget's perspective, therefore, it is most important to study the thought processes that seem directly relevant to such basic epistemological questions as the nature of number, space, motion, time, and causality. The ways the child copes with all the disorderly aspects of social life—power, oppression, unfairness, stigma, guilt, etc.—represent at best interesting but epistemologically irrelevant questions; at worst they are complicating factors—contaminants and irritants that must be carefully excluded from the experimental situation before the study of cognition can begin. A similar epistemological fascination permeates the technical descriptions of the theory. Indeed, it is impossible to read Piaget's detailed discussions of the groupement model without wondering if a psychologist less interested in epistemology and more interested in, for example, cultural anthropology would have singled out for special attention the same collection of logical abilities.[14]

But even if one focuses exclusively on what might be called the "classic" Piagetian structures of cognition (the eight groupements of concrete operational thought and the prepositional logic of the period of formal operations), there are compelling reasons for challenging Piaget's assertion that social and cognitive competences develop in tandem. Thanks to the cross-cultural studies of cognitive development carried out by Michael Cole and his collaborators, it now appears that *"cultural differences in cognition reside more in the situations to which particular cognitive processes are applied than in the existence of a process in one cultural group and its absence in another"* (italics in original).[15] Thus, if one wishes to chart the cognitive development of a non-Western child or a child raised in a minority subculture in the United States, traditional Piagetian tests of cognition may focus on the wrong set of problem-solving situations.

Cole's research suggests a similar conclusion for handicapped children. That is, when problems of interaction with other people assume a central role in the handicapped child's life, it seems perfectly reasonable to entertain the possibility that the child may sometimes display more sophisticated logical abilities in the social realm than in his attempts to solve the kinds of problems posed to him by classic Piagetian tests of development—even if by "logical abilities" we mean only those algebraic structures singled out for attention by Piagetian theory.[16]

Should any of the objections that we have raised to Piaget's position on social development prove correct, the implications for attempts to foster the handicapped child's social and cognitive development may be very great indeed. At present, Piagetian theory is unable to account for how the child achieves a new level of cognitive development or how, once this level is achieved in one area of problem solving, the child gradually generalizes his new logical competence to other problem-solving situations.[17] But if handicapped children frequently display their greatest logical sophistication (either by Piagetian criteria or by other logical criteria) in certain areas of social problem solving, a new possibility presents itself. Cognitive advances (as registered by conventional tests) may sometimes occur when the child learns how to apply an advanced social competence to Piagetian tasks on which he reasons less complexly.[18] The understanding of development gained by testing this hypothesis may have important practical applications. Educators may be able to design teaching strategies and curriculum materials that help the child build bridges between those (social) areas where his logical abilities have attained their greatest scope and the problem-solving situations posed by schoolwork and other classroom activities. Much may also be learned about how best to facilitate and assess the child's social maturation, and measures of mental aptitude and cognitive development may be greatly improved.

Where Does the Handicapped Child First Demonstrate Mastery of the Logical Structures Described by Piagetian Theory?

In our discussions of Kohlberg's and Erikson's simpler stage theories of development, we were obliged to draw analogies between what is known about the handicapped adult and what may be reasonably expected to be true for the handicapped child. Throughout, our aim was not to prove that our proposals were correct but to demonstrate that they possessed enough surface credibility to warrant taking them very seriously before one undertakes any programs of research into the handicapped child's development. As we turn to our specific proposals about intellectual development, we find ourselves in a similar position; there is a great dearth of relevant research and we cannot draw upon a body of secure knowledge to make our points. Here, too, we must develop plausible working hypotheses and rely heavily upon illustrative examples.

Two psychoanalytic case histories of handicapped children form the core around which we develop the argument of this section. (The two case histories appear in full in Appendix 1.) Each illustrates the kind of conscious problem solving that one would expect to find if our conjecture is correct—that is, if for handicapped children some of the classic Piagetian algebraic structures make their first appearance in representational thought in areas of social behavior overlooked by Piagetian research. In exploring this possibility, we must, of course, emphasize that no retrospective analysis of a child's behavior (and one often performed at two removes at that) can possibly be more than illustrative. But if we do not claim that our two examples *prove* anything, we can hope they help to bring home to the reader the vital importance of seriously exploring the effect of the social meaning of the child's handicap upon every area of his intellectual development.

The first case history involves a boy born with a congenital deformity of his arms. At the time that analysis began, at age thirteen, Peter's arms measured scarcely eight inches in length, his shoulders were deformed, and his hands had three fingers each and no thumb. Speaking of Peter's astonishing ability to overcome the physical limitations of his handicap, his analyst observes that the most unexpected development was "the extent to which Peter was able to make constructive use of fantasy in the formation of ego abilities. . . ." [19] It is to the implications of Peter's use of fantasy for egocentric thought in childhood and adolescence that we wish to turn.

Given Peter's handicap, it was not surprising that he should have an intense and rich fantasy life; and since he was an adolescent, one would expect these fantasies to follow the usual course. "Adolescent intellectuality seems merely to minister to day-dreams. Even the ambitious fantasies of the pre-pubertal period are not intended to be translated into reality." [20] Speaking of these kinds of fantasies, Piaget and Inhelder observe:

The indefinite extension of powers of thought made possible by the new instruments of propositional logic at first is conducive to a failure to distinguish between the ego's new and unpredicted capacities and the social or cosmic universe to which they are applied. In other words, the adolescent goes through a phase in which he attributes an unlimited power to his own thoughts so that the dream of a glorious future or of transforming the world through ideas . . . seems not only fantasy but also an effective action which in itself modifies the empirical world. This is obviously a form of cognitive egocentrism. Although it differs sharply from the child's egocentrism (which is either sensory-motor or simply representational without introspective "reflection"), it results, nevertheless, from the same mechanism and appears as a function of the new conditions created by the structuring of formal thought.[21]

And indeed, some of Peter's fantasies did fit this pattern—they were fantasies and nothing more. But others did not. These followed a pattern typical of neither childhood nor adolescent egocentric thought. His analyst wrote:

. . . Other fantasies and hopes, which my colleagues and I admittedly felt to be equally unattainable, remained for some time as central points of interest until these too were dropped one by one from the analysis but for quite a different reason. They moved out of the realm of fantasy into actual accomplishment. During the analysis Peter learned to play the trumpet well enough to plan a career as a per-former. He learned to swim and dive well enough to earn a life-saving certificate. In this he measured up to the standards required of all applicants; no special allowances were made for his deformity. And he learned to ride a bicycle in the face of the opposition of his appre-hensive parents. These accomplishments showed that Peter had a more generous and, at the same time, more realistic assessment of his capa-bilities than did his parents, his analyst, or the other professional consultants.[22]

Speaking of the significance of Peter's fantasy life, André Lus-sier, his analyst, observes:

So far as physically disabled people are concerned, surface observa-tion shows that, according to their reactions, they can be divided into two categories, the active and the passive ones, the doers and the dreamers. Apparently, in the analytic literature, more attention has been paid so far to the passive than to the active type. . . . Peter . . . dared to put his "dreams" to the test. For him there was nothing mutually exclusive between the appearance of compensatory fantasies on the one hand and compensatory actual improvements in ego per-formance on the other. Peter's real achievements were so well inte-grated, so positively egosyntonic, that it seems we must look beyond pathological mechanisms for a comprehensive explanation. . . . Peter's activity . . . was creative. There seems no doubt that Peter is an ex-cellent example of an "active disabled" person. The people who belong to this category do not usually seek psychiatric help, and their reac-tions are usually dismissed as "normal." Whether or not Peter's drive towards activity [i.e., his "adaptive" use of fantasy life] is characteristic of all the indivduals who belong to this group, or whether we have to regard him as exceptional, will have to be decided in the future when more detailed analytic studies of such persons are made avail-able.[23]

The point about Peter's compensatory fantasies is worth re-peating because it signals the importance of attempting to track cognitive development (as measured on Piagetian tests) as one studies the psychodynamic development of "active disabled" per-sons. That is, does the appearance of Peter's special use of fantasy as a tool for real achievement correlate with any special cognitive milestone? Does it, for example, represent the first place where formal operational thought manifests itself—i.e., a grandiose theory typical of the first bloom of formal operations, a "fictional finalism," to use Adler's useful phrase, which is discarded when it ceases to be fictional? If so, this is an instance where the locus of what Piaget calls a horizontal *décalage* (the transfer of a new logical skill from one domain of problems to another) is firmly rooted in the affective life and in social life.[24] Should this be the case, one can ask if other intellectual skills typically appear first in social and emotional life in the disabled child, and, if they do, how parents, teachers, and doctors help the child apply these precocious abilities to school behavior and other important areas of the child's life.

The second case history concerns Cindy, who was congenitally blind in one eye. She was in therapy from about age three and a half to the end of her sixth year. Speaking of Cindy, Robert Furman, her analyst, points to an apparent paradox. "On the one hand this little girl's deformity became involved in every stage of her development, making her psychological growth truly different and more complex. On the other hand her analysis helped her most by enabling her to delineate and restrict her difference from others to just the sightlessness of her left eye, restoring her self-esteem by limiting her damage to its proper reality proportions." [25]

Cindy's analysis allows us to ask the same question we asked about Peter, but this time about an earlier stage of cognitive development. Does Cindy's ability by the end of analysis (when she is almost seven years old) to "delineate and restrict her difference from others to just the sightlessness of her left eye" represent the first area of her behavior where she manifests the transition from preoperational thought to concrete operations? [26]

The matter is brought out clearly by the analyst's moving description of what Cindy calls "the problem about this eye-water." Early in the analysis it became clear that Cindy could not handle sadness. "Every time a sadness would have been appropriate she either became excited in her head-rocking or left the office to urinate." [27] Later, even after she had cried several times in the analyst's presence, she "complained constantly that she could not be sad because she could not cry." [28] At another time "she told me she was sad but could not cry because 'she didn't understand about this eye-water.' " [29]

Then, near the end of therapy, something extraordinary happened. A fact that had hitherto seemed anomalous and had been powerless to change her belief that she could not be sad suddenly took on new meaning and significance. In the course of a session with her therapist, Cindy once more burst into tears. Then: ". . . After a moment, [she] ran from the office. She returned promptly, most pleased through her tears. She had gone to the bathroom to look in the mirror and had seen that both her eyes had cried. She wasn't different about the tear-water; her eye was different just in that it could not see. She readily agreed that what was so important was that her feelings were not different; it was just the sightlessness of her one eye." [30]

Reading through Furman's description, it is tempting to interpret it this way: before the appearance of concrete operations little children cannot handle class inclusion relations in any consistent manner. That is to say, as the child understands it, one is either like others or different from them; one can't be different in one way and like in other ways. (In Piaget's notation, the pre-operational child cannot handle the class inclusion relations symbolized by $A + A' = B$.) Still less can he or she handle the idea that one can be different in a small way and like in all the important ways. Faced with the fact that her eye was different, Cindy could not defend herself from concluding that "therefore" she was different in *every* respect from all other children. This deduction seems implied in the following exchange, which occurred before her "crucial experiment."

Another danger with her anger came up much later in her analysis. She had brought an Oedipal anger in the transference in the wish that could she get her hands on my wife she would stuff her in the trash can and then burn her up. When I interpreted this as a feeling she must have had with her mother, she was horrified. I said I knew all little girls had these feelings about their mothers. She replied that I did not understand: with her it was different; when she wished her mother dead, she really wished her dead. I again said that I thought it was this way for all little girls. Cindy was adamant; for her it was different. I asked if it was because she had so many things she was angry at mother about, like about being a girl or about her eye. She firmly said no: it was because her eye was different, she was different, and so her anger was different. [31]

With the achievement of the first stage of concrete operations (the part-whole relations of groupement one) the notion of simultaneously being like and different becomes for the first time conceptually possible. Earlier Cindy seemed to have reasoned: my eye is different, therefore I am different, and I can't be sad, and I can't cry, and my anger is different. Now, when she breaks down in therapy, she hesitates a moment and then runs to a mirror. She has seen tears flow from her blind eye before. But now she "sees" the significance of what those tears mean. Her eye is different, but not her tears. The observation has the force of a crucial experiment. An interpretation of her handicap typical of the preoperational period collapses and, thanks to her therapist, is replaced by a new interpretation that, drawing upon the new logical resources of concrete thought, is far less demoralizing and also more in accord with reality.

An important question is raised for us by this possible interpretation of Cindy's behavior. What was the therapist helping Cindy to accomplish? Usually one thinks of psychoanalysis as a process in which the therapist helps his patient generalize formal operational thinking to areas of his emotional life where he has customarily reasoned on a more primitive level; that is, therapy is a way of facilitating horizontal *décalages* or the transfer of cognitive skills from less emotional domains of behavior to more highly charged domains. But with children an additional element of complexity is added, the ceiling placed on understanding by the child's level of cognitive development. The relevance of this constraint is an open question. It is not inconceivable that the main transactions in child therapy involve noncognitive areas of knowing. But should there be cases where the child's cognitive stage is relevant (and as our interpretation of Cindy suggests, it seems plausible that at certain periods of a handicapped child's life it may be quite relevant) then one can begin to ask if one of the functions of therapy is to provide a set of social learning experiences that directly nourish cognitive growth rather than indirectly nourishing it by, say, removing certain emotional obstacles to growth. Cindy's initial conclusions about her disability—that her feelings were different because her eyes was different—strike us as perfectly rational given the formal limitations of preoperational rationality. Far from appearing to satisfy some devious unconscious need, they seem to represent an accurate (and terrifying) set of facts about reality as it is structured by preoperational thought. What is for us most striking about her is the sense one gets that she is actively grappling with an objective problem. Her behavior with the mirror has about it the quality of a sudden inspiration, a solution to an intractable dilemma that has long haunted her. Given this reading of her behavior, why shouldn't Cindy first display concrete operational thought here, in the one area of life where she needs it most—i.e., with respect to thinking about the implications of her being "different" because of her blindness? And this being so, why shouldn't some of the structural characteristics of the therapeutic interaction provide the means to facilitate this surge of growth? [32]

The Problem of "Diadic Thought"

In the next few pages we will briefly examine some of the main structural properties of the interpersonal strategies that we described in chapter 5. These strategies—bad faith, passing, and gamesmanship—all involve thinking about self and other in interpersonal encounters. We will call this kind of cognition diadic thought. Diadic thought poses severe problems for Piagetian theory. It is too complex for the concrete operational period and not complex enough to qualify as fully developed formal thinking. It represents a synthesis of logical abilities that does not fit neatly into any of Piaget's boxes—precisely the kind of algebraic structure that the logician Charles Parsons faulted Piaget for ignoring. Most seriously of all, Piagetian theory, as presently constituted, simply cannot account for problem-solving behavior as complex as passing or gamesmanship until the achievement of formal operations during adolescence. By nearly ignoring complex human interactions, Piaget and his followers have overlooked a crucial possibility: that, in general, the child's problem-solving abilities in the social world may far outstrip his problem-solving abilities in the physical world.[33] This oversight may have especially disastrous consequences for our understanding of the cognitive development of handicapped children.

Speaking of the diad, Laing, Phillipson, and Lee have observed that "Some philosophers, some psychologists, and more sociologists have recognized the significance of the fact that social life is not made up of myriad I's and me's only, but that you, she, or us may indeed be as primary and compelling (or more so) as the experience of 'me.' The critical realization here is that I am not the only perceiver and agent in my world. The world is peopled by others, and these others are not simply objects in the world: they are centers of reorientation to the objective universe. Nor are these others simply other I's. The others are you, him, them, etc." [34]

This view of the other is exceedingly complex. Like the deep structure of language, it involves level upon level of nested dependencies—chains of inference about how the other views me, wheels within wheels. "I may not actually be able to see myself as others see me, but I am constantly supposing them to be seeing me in particular ways, and I am constantly acting in light of the actual supposed attitudes, opinion, needs, and so on which the other has in respect to me." [35]

Thus, suppose that an adolescent is caught by a teacher smoking in the bathroom in school. He knows that he is supposed to look sorry and apologize. Moreover, he knows—if this is his first offense—that if he does these things he will probably avoid serious punishment. In effect, the adolescent adopts a strategy of "passing" as repentant. Despite the trivial character of this behavior, its logical structure is rather complex. R. D. Laing and his associates have studied this structure, and Laing has popularized their analysis in such books as *Knots*.[36] There are at least three levels to the adolescent's thinking, three wheels within wheels.

• What I feel about what I've done; i.e., I'm not in the least repentant about smoking in the bathroom.

• What I think the teacher thinks I feel; i.e., she thinks that I am repentant.

• What I think about what the teacher thinks I feel; i.e., she thinks that I am repentant, but I'm not repentant and therefore I've fooled her.

There are other complexities—the teen-ager's evaluation of the best strategy for avoiding punishment, for example—but already it is clear that this kind of thinking is tremendously intricate. To clarify its structure Laing and his colleagues have developed a useful descriptive notation and a theory of interpersonal behavior in children, adolescents, and adults.[37] The theory makes sense and seems to work equally well for describing the power games that four-year-olds play with their mothers and the conspiratorial thinking of mature statesmen. And that's the rub—for Piagetian theory simply cannot account for the logical complexity of the young child's most sophisticated interpersonal behaviors. Like his linguistic competence, they presuppose an array of logical abilities that do not come together in cognitive behavior until a child enters the period of formal operations at around thirteen years.

Diadic thinking presupposes the ability to shuttle back and

forth between the self's point of view and the other's point of view, what Piagetian theory calls "decentration." According to Piaget, this mental flexibility requires the mastery of the logical operations that mark the onset of the period of concrete thought in middle childhood. As a consequence, the theory is unable to account for how a preoperational child could behave in a way that is consistent with the Laing, Phillipson, and Lee model.[38]

Diadic thinking requires the individual constantly to integrate judgments involving classes and subclasses (the qualitative aspects of self's and other's performance) with judgments concerning relations between different classes (comparisons of self's and other's relative credibility; judgments of the relative value, probability, or appropriateness of different strategies toward the other, etc.). This task presupposes an ability to integrate one's thinking about class similarities and class differences into a single coherent chain of reasoning, something that Piagetian theory claims to be impossible for the concrete operational child.* That is, diadic thinking requires the simultaneous use of types of algebraic structures that are never joined together in a systematic way by the concrete operational child—structures that display the reversibility of groupements one through four (inversion) and structures that display the reversibility specific to groupements five through eight (reciprocity).[39] Diadic thought also requires an ability to think about propositions and to think hypothetically, two abilities that Piagetian theory defers until the period of formal operations.[40]

Finally, in order to account for improvement over time in one's diadic behavior, the Laing, Phillipson, and Lee model implies that the child's inferences about the other at least sometimes have the form of a theory of the other that is submitted to empirical test—a method of analyzing experience that, according to Piagetian theory, is also the unique preserve of formal operational thought.

The contrast between the properties of diadic thinking we have just outlined and the logical properties of preoperational thought (or even concrete operational thought) could scarcely be greater.

---

* We see no prior reason to expect the algebraic structures employed in diadic thought to be identical to either the structures defined by the eight groupements or the structure of formal operational thought. Again, the logician Charles Parsons's remarks on the somewhat arbitrary character of Piaget's groupements seems apt (see pp. 120–21). However, this issue is too complex to go into here, and we will be deliberately vague about the precise form of the algebraic structures that are presupposed by diadic thought.

Yet precisely this wheels-within-wheels reasoning is required to account for the handicapped child's ability to "pass" (recall our example of the adolescent caught smoking) as well as for the child's ability to manipulate the other and to use the role thrust upon him by the able-bodied for his own ends. Were we attempting to assess the ability of Piagetian theory to account for the social ability of able-bodied children in this chapter, we would also observe that a similar complexity of social behavior is imputed to the young child by psychoanalytic theory and is beginning to be suggested by the mounting evidence that infants engage in extremely complex social interactions with their mothers. Since our focus is handicap and the needs of the handicapped, we merely note that the diadic abilities of very young handicapped children seem to embody in an exaggerated and extreme form the social abilities that many able-bodied children evince during the preoperational stage.

Let us now turn to a possible example of a young child using her diadic ability to think consciously about the meaning of her handicap. When Cindy, the girl of the second case history, was about three and a half years old, the following sequence of events occurred between her and her therapist:

Our first insights came at the time of the initial separation from me over a Christmas vacation. *She became worried about the two windows in my office. What would happen if she got angry enough at me to break one of those windows? She answered her own question by saying that then she would not be able to see at all.* We were not able fully to clarify this for a number of weeks until she was preparing herself to go to the eye doctor for a routine twice-yearly examination. *She began denying the permanency of the blindness of her left eye* and insisted it was not because she was afraid of being sad or angry. *"If I know that my eye will never see ever, then I'll be so angry at everyone with two eyes that can see I will want to blind one eye in everyone and then people will do it back to me and then I won't be able to see at all"* [italics added].[41]

To us, the italicized passages suggest a chain of reasoning that integrates logical characteristics which, according to Piagetian theory, are not integrated into a coherent algebraic system until adolescence. Cindy begins by denying the permanency of the blindness of her left eye, a denial that presupposes the ability to employ the kind of negation (inversion) typical of groupements one through four. She then justifies this denial by providing an explanation that appears to require a highly sophisticated mastery of the kind of reversibility typical of groupements five through eight.

Cindy's apparent ability to employ logical strategies reminiscent of some of the groupements that focus upon class differences is especially striking. Again and again in nursery school, three- and four-year-olds come into conflict over the possession of toys. In the course of these conflicts they display the typical inability of egocentric thought to view the conflict from the other's point of view. Yet at the same time, children of this age are peculiarly susceptible to adult presentations of the other child's point of view. This susceptibility, in Piagetian terms, is itself a consequence of the limitations of egocentric thought. It stems from the young child's inability to coordinate his self-interest with the other child's self-interest. By presenting him with the other child's point of view, one in effect distracts him from a contemplation of his own. For a space he is aware *only* of the other child's point of view. And while he is, he is led by its inner logic to act in the other child's interest. " 'When Dan had had his turn, he insisted on holding the end of the rope while Tommy was using it. Tommy asked him to let go, but at first Dan would not. Mrs. I. asked him, "If you were doing it, would you want Tommy to hold the rope?" He replied "No," and let it go. Harold responded to the same sort of appeal, when he was angrily threatening to "throw dust" at Mrs. I. because she had interfered with what he was doing. Mrs. I. said to him, "Would you want me to throw dust at you?" He said, "No." "Then please don't throw it at me." Harold smiled and gave up his hostility at once.' " [42]

Now consider what Cindy is able to accomplish in her retaliation fantasy. First, she poses to herself the other's point of view and coordinates it with her own, a classic example of decentration. Second, she doesn't desist (in her fantasy efforts to blind everyone) because the other's self-interest temporarily becomes her own. Instead, her decision is the result of drawing the logical consequences of the other's reaction to her action. She desists because the other's retaliation will restore the original asymmetry and, worse, will lead to a qualitative worsening of that asymmetry: "Then I won't be able to see at all." It is this double accomplishment that seems to render the structure of her fantasy beyond the capacities of preoperational thought.

In certain respects Cindy's reasoning seems to weave together logical characteristics of groupements one through four and groupements five through eight in ways that exceed the capacities of even the concrete operational child. A case in point is her conclusion that having two blind eyes when others have one blind eye is much worse than having one blind eye when others have no blind eyes. Viewed from the perspective of the purely comparative (or quantitive) structures of groupements five through eight there is no difference between the two states; in each instance one has one fewer good eye than other people. Appreciation of the immense qualitative difference between having one blind eye and having two blind eyes seems to require logical abilities resembling those found in groupements one through four.[43]

The linkage of Cindy's assertion that she *must* deny the permanence of her blindness with a coherent justification of the necessity of this denial is also noteworthy. To assert the necessity of not changing her mind requires a recognition that she can change her mind if the facts warrant change. A sensitivity to this logical possibility seems to require the reversibility typical of groupements one through four—an ability to shift back and forth between her actual belief and a hypothetical contrary belief.* Yet in justifying why she does not change her mind, Cindy provides an explanation that, as we have seen, seems to require the mastery of the reversibility typical of groupements five through eight. This sequential use of both kinds of logical reversibility in a single coherent line of reasoning also seems to exceed the logical capacities that Piaget ascribes to the concrete operational child.[44]

If we ignore the logical form of Cindy's statements, they fall readily into the category of what Piaget calls a mental experiment, a typical device of preoperational thought: "that is, an isomorphic, step-by-step mental replica of concrete actions and events. Rather than schematize, re-order, and generally refashion events as does the other child, the young child simply runs off reality sequences in his head just as he might do in overt action." [45] But if we instead examine the logical form of Cindy's fears, matters are very different. For then the question becomes, What in real life is she copying by rote in her "mental experiment"?

One possible answer is that her fantasy is not a simple copy of anything in real life; instead it represents the understandable fear

* Recall that Piaget claims that an ability to think hypothetically rather than concretely is not possible until the period of formal operations.

of a little girl with one blind eye.[46] But in that case we have not disposed of the problem of logical structure which her expression of this fear represents. Rather, we have displaced the problem to the realm of Cindy's imagination.

However, even were Cindy's fantasy simply to reflect an event that she has somehow perceived, its derivative character would not explain away her logical precocity. As Piaget, Inhelder, and Sinclair have demonstrated in their studies of memory, our ability to reproduce a memory image is a function of our cognitive competence.[47] That Cindy may have reproduced the logical links of another person's behavior—and applied it to her own fears—presupposes precisely what is at issue, a series of logical abilities far beyond the capabilities of preoperational thought. Her fantasy cannot, therefore, be a simple copy of something she has viewed through the lens of preoperational thought. It cannot represent the simple running of "reality sequences" in her imagination just as she might do in "overt action," because it possesses a formal structure which, at age three and a half, Cindy can neither reproduce in her own cognitively guided behavior nor understand (cognitively) when it takes place right in front of her.

A similar flaw vitiates any attempt to explain away Cindy's precocity by postulating the operation of unconscious defense mechanisms that distort her original perceptions of a real event or her memories of this event. While such suggestions may well have a place in attempts to understand Cindy's apparent precocity, they do not in themselves provide an explanation. Indeed, they greatly complicate matters by postulating that even Cindy's unconscious thought processes have a precocious logical sophistication and then requiring that the child's conscious fears and fantasies faithfully mirror this complexity.

Listening to Cindy talk about her retaliation fears, one is reminded far more of Piaget's characterization of intellectual interaction between individuals capable of formal operational thinking than of his picture of the egocentric child: "Intellectual interaction between individuals is thus comparable to a vast game of chess, which is carried on unremittingly and in such a way that each action carried out with respect to a particular item involves a series of equivalent or complementary actions on the part of the opponent: laws of grouping are nothing more or less than the various rules ensuring the reciprocity of the players and the consistency of the play."[48] One is, in fact, reminded of precisely that diadic competence that many therapists and much of current personality theory assume exists in even young children.

But, of course, we are not Cindy's therapists. What we know of her is only what her analyst's case history tells us. Without knowing far more about this little girl who struggled so valiantly with the mystery of her blind eye, we can say nothing definite. Before we could even begin to impute to her thinking about handicap the logical abilities of diadic thought we would want to approach the work of analysis keeping in mind the logical abilities implied by the way she grapples with her problems during her interactions with the therapist.[49] All the standard topics of psychotherapy—defense, symbolization, displacements, etc.—would have to be scrutinized from an experimental perspective that emphasized their underlying logical form.[50]

A single overarching conclusion emerges from the discussion of developmental issues presented in these pages. Whether the area be moral behavior, personality, or cognition, the automatic application of mainstream theories to handicap commits the researcher in advance to a deviance analysis of disability; yet, because of the special complexity of the handicapped child's social experience, a deviance analysis is completely unwarranted given our present state of knowledge. Indeed, should such an approach ultimately prevail in handicap by default, all of developmental psychology will be the poorer because of it.

But much more is at stake in how psychologists decide to study the handicapped child's development than the fate of a field of research. Psychology has assumed the status of an autonomous cultural force in middle-class American society, and what it says in future decades about the developmental characteristics of handicapped children is going to be taken very seriously indeed. It is here that a rigid conception of development is likely to exert the greatest harm. For the professional—who views his job as working to correct the child's harmful deviations from the norm—psychology's emphasis on the child as a small deviant will provide constant confirmation of what the social pathology model has already taught the professional to expect to see. As for the layman, it is hard to imagine any other explicitly developmental program that is better adapted to preserving the essence of the handicapped role and the disease diagnosis than one that judges the handicapped by able-bodied standards and defines as pathological all negative deviations from these norms. Thus, a wooden and mechanical application of mainstream developmental theories to handicap may not only lead to a sea of findings that are intellectually irrelevant and sterile; it may provide powerful, widely accepted, and apparently objective support for society's traditional mystifications of disability.

Convinced of the pressing need for research of a type for which there is almost no precedent in the field of handicap, we have singled out what seem to us to be some of the most important developmental questions for psychological research to ask about handicapped children.

1. Above all else we must simply look at handicapped children in different settings and watch them grow up. We must approach the handicapped child from the perspective of the naturalist or the cultural anthropologist. Setting aside our expectations about what is normal and abnormal, healthy and regressive in able-bodied children, we must study handicapped children on their own terms in their own settings. Perhaps the most important of these settings are the family, the school, and psychotherapy. In each case we must look for behavioral strategies that prove especially conducive for growth. As naturalists or cultural anthropologists, we must be careful to take into account social class, ethnic group, gender, the nature of the handicap, and its sociological significance in the child's milieu. The potential value of this kind of research was suggested in our discussion of the naturalistic work on the development of blind children in chapter 4 and in the two case histories of handicapped children presented in this chapter.

Our remaining points represent elaborations and refinements of this first one.

2. There are cogent reasons for believing that the handicapped child's psychological development indeed differs in significant ways from the psychological development of able-bodied children.

The great social constants of childhood are as different for a handicapped child as for the child in the schizophrenogenic families studied by Bateson or Laing. But the great emotional constants of childhood—which are absent in the pathological family —are not necessarily absent in the family life of the handicapped child. Handicapped children often find themselves loved at home and hated by society.

3. The behavioral strategies fostered by these experiences, this contradiction between home life and social life, provide ample reason for believing that the handicapped child's social and moral

development may differ significantly from the able-bodied child's. In fact, there are many good reasons for believing that all existing theories of moral and social development may have to be significantly revised before they will adequately describe the development of handicapped children.

4. There are compelling reasons for believing that theories of personality development and perhaps cognitive development may need to be substantially modified for the handicapped.

In contrast to every other disadvantaged child, the handicapped child is not raised by parents who share his sociological destiny. Whereas the parents of the black child, the Mexican American child, the Native American child can draw upon a rich cultural tradition to help guide them in raising their children, the parent of the handicapped child lacks any such tradition. Indeed, the main advice that our culture offers to the parent is negative— a destructive definition of the child as a perpetual patient whose "childness," whose ability to grow up, is gravely imperiled by his handicap. And while the parents of other disadvantaged children can draw upon their own childhood experiences—and their experience raising other children—the relevance of these traditional sources of insight for the parenting of a handicapped child is more problematical. Of course, the advice of wise and sensitive professionals can help parents a great deal. But professionals also suffer from the absence of a mature developmental psychology of handicap. Just as the social situation of the handicapped represents something like the extreme case of the stigma directed at other disadvantaged groups, the dilemma faced by parents with a handicapped child represents the extreme case of the problems encountered by all parents because of the decline of the family and the increasing irrelevance of traditional solutions to the problems of child rearing. Precisely because parenting—and, for that matter, clinical practice—is such an intuitive art, it is essential that intuition be supplied with the kind of information about the developmental characteristics of handicapped children that is rarely forthcoming from the parents' own culture, their firsthand experiences, or the findings of mainstream child psychology.

Part Three

Services and Service Providers

Chapter 8

Parents
and Professionals

If a single word could adequately sum up the status of the handicapped child in American society—and no word really can—it would have to be *vulnerability*. Tensed between biology and society, every handicapped child is made vulnerable not only by the genuine limitations of his handicap but also by the destructive, demeaning, and entirely unnecessary stereotypes and role expectations that are the destiny of those who grow up handicapped.

Nowhere is this vulnerability greater than in the child's relationships with those who provide him with specialized medical, educational, and other services. In countless ways, large and small, many professionals define the child exclusively in terms of his handicap and teach him to identify his true self with the image contained in the handicapped role. Yet the child and his parents desperately need many kinds of help that only experts can provide.

Every disadvantaged group encounters a similar contradiction in the social services they receive: invaluable assistance conjoined with oppression. This contradiction is especially destructive for the handicapped child because of the unique importance of services in his life. Even today, when many basic needs often go unmet because of lack of funds, professionals bear a day-to-day responsibility for the well-being of the child and his family that is without parallel for any other social group.[1]

The need for services—and their often oppressive character—dominates the concerns of many thoughtful parents and professionals. (Handicapped adults are just as concerned with these issues; if anything, the adult finds the contradictions of the service establishment even more difficult to bear than do the parent and the handicapped child.) Unfortunately, criticisms of services to handicapped children have underrated the ways that professionals confuse the relation between society and biology in their work. As a result, reformers have rarely perceived just how far their reforms must break with tradition if even the boldest moves —such as the legal and legislative gains in special education during the 1970s—are not ultimately to prove hollow. Despite the advances of the past few decades, every handicap service still needs to recast its *conception* of the proper relationship between professionals and clients in terms that honor the dignity and humanity of the handicapped child and his family. Just as crucially, every nonmedical service, from education to social work, must systematically scrutinize its claim to possess expert scientific knowledge about handicap. All must purge themselves of a deviance analysis of disability and deal with the handicapped on their own terms.

A comprehensive overview of all services for the handicapped would be unmanageably long. We shall instead focus on what most discussions of services for handicapped children leave out —the many ways that traditional models of disability either promote pseudoexpertise or prevent the professional from establishing cooperative, nonoppressive relationships with the handicapped child and his parents. Again, for economy's sake, we will discuss the premier service areas of handicap: medicine and special education. It goes without saying that services we discuss briefly or not at all—such fields as social work, vocational rehabilitation, and research and development programs in technology for the disabled—are beset by similar problems.

While all these handicap services are deeply flawed because of their reliance upon traditional models of disability, it must never be forgotten that each of them still accomplishes far more good than harm. This point bears special emphasis in the case of medical services. Here a host of conceptually straightforward improvements—such as more funds for preventive medicine and programs targeted at those children who are most likely to become handicapped—could accomplish prodigies in reducing the incidence and the severity of childhood disability.* It would be tedious to reiterate this point at every stage of our discussion. Yet as that analysis unfolds, it is essential that the reader keep in mind that our aim is not to be balanced or comprehensive; rather, it is to suggest a fresh way of thinking about service issues that can act as a supplement or a corrective to the traditional way that policy makers and civil rights advocates alike have approached the service needs of handicapped children and their parents.

The problem of client-professional relationships touches upon some of the most troubling issues of our age. In a society that routinely creates or expands its publicly funded social service organizations in response to perceived social needs, the question of the proper relationship between the client and the professional is increasingly synonymous with the question of the proper relationship between the citizen and the state. Our own position in these matters is conservative and is best stated beforehand. We are alarmed by the long-standing practice of service organizations viewing their clients through a medical or quasi-medical lens that transforms political or moral issues into apparently objective questions of "social pathology" or "preventive medicine." This misuse of medical reasoning makes it especially easy for policy makers to think of handicap—or, indeed, any major social problem like crime or poverty—as a social disease.† On an individual level, the implications of the social pathology model make it equally natural for the professional to assume that because he is

---

* For a discussion of these issues that complements the psychologically and sociologically oriented analysis of medicine presented in this section, see Appendix 4, "Medicine and Handicap: A Promise in Search of a National Commitment," by Katherine P. Messenger and John Gliedman.

† This mind set is well illustrated by the tendency of the federal bureaucracy to extend the traditional cultural definitions of groups of handicapped people to groups that have not traditionally been considered handicapped by the general culture. For example, the new HEW regulations for implementing Section 504 of the 1975 Vocational Rehabilitation Act define alcoholics, drug addicts, and juvenile delinquents as handicap groups. The framers of the regulations originally wanted to go further and also define homosexuals as a handicap group, but this decision was dropped in the final form of the regulations. See the interesting discussion of these questions in the statement of the proposed regulations that appears in the *Federal Register* for July 16, 1976.[2] Also see our discussion of the social pathology model in chapter 3.

an expert in a technical specialty, he has the right (and, indeed, the obligation) to override or to undermine the client's judgments about himself or a parent's judgments about a child. In both realms moral choices that were traditionally assumed to be the exclusive prerogative of the individual have increasingly come to be seen by many professionals and laymen as falling within the boundaries of what Talcott Parsons has called the "legitimate authority" of the professional and his service institutions.[3]

A similar transformation has affected the notion of expertise. To be acknowledged to be an expert, one must obtain formal credentials and formal licenses. With few exceptions, neither laymen nor professionals respect the self-taught expert without proper credentials. The awe of credentials is widespread but also very recent in American culture, dating only from the rise of professional societies in the late nineteenth century.[4]

This enthusiasm needs two qualifications. To begin with, it is essential to distinguish between a professional's formal expertise and his ability or willingness to employ it on behalf of his client. Often, service institutions—such as the hospital or the school—severely constrain the professional's ability to use his or her expertise to full advantage. No other child demands more flexibility and ingenuity from the professional than does the handicapped child. Yet, as David Kirp and his colleagues note, "organizations such as school systems devise routinized ways to handle recurring issues," even when there *is* no routine way to meet the child's special needs.[5] Like other institutions, the organizations that deliver services to handicapped children and their parents encourage their members to "limit uncertainty, increase predictability, and centralize functions and controls."[6] These pressures subtly tilt the professional's perceptions of the child's strengths, limitations, and needs in ways that ultimately serve the institution's self-interest.[7] The parent of a handicapped child labors under no such institutional constraints. Nor, despite the obvious complexity of all parental motives, is any other adult likely to have the child's best interests more constantly at heart.

Just as important, parents often know more about their children than the experts whom they consult. While many professionals acknowledge this fact, their training and ideology encourage them to ignore it in practice. All too often the only parents allowed relatively free give-and-take with professionals are parents who possess some independent professional standing as experts in a specialty that bears upon childhood—medicine,

144

clinical psychology, social work, law, etc. A more striking abuse of our culture's concept of the expert cannot be imagined: to be taken seriously, the parents' claim to expertise about their own child must be backed by a socially recognized formal credential that "proves" that they are experts about children in general.

Not that parents are, on the whole, any more rational about their children than the professional is. Quite the contrary; parents are at least as vulnerable to irrationality and to confusions of their self-interest with the child's interest as is the professional. Parents themselves may be influenced by the handicap role and the presumption that the handicapped are childlike. All of us are affected by the culture's presuppositions about disability, often in ways we do not even perceive. In focusing upon the professional's shortcomings, we do not wish to idealize or romanticize the parent's strengths. But we do wish to reassert certain traditional cultural priorities that are often forgotten by professionals: namely, that the parent's rights over the child take precedence over the professional's personal moral views. To put it bluntly, the professional exists to further the parent's vision of the handicapped child's future. Should the professional disagree, he has every right to try to *persuade* the parent to adopt a different view. He also has every right to give advice when the parent is confused and seeks guidance and emotional support. But except in the most extreme instances of parental incompetence and brutality, such as child abuse, the professional has no right to use his immense moral and practical power to intimidate or to manipulate the parent.

In every handicap specialty it is essential that parent and professional actively work together on the child's behalf. Cooperation may be essential for medical reasons: medication that is not given the child by the parent is medication that may as well not be prescribed. Collaboration is also necessary because neither the parent nor the professional possesses a monopoly on the truth, and each can serve as a check on the shortcomings and limitations of the other. But before a partnership can genuinely exist, there must be give-and-take, mutual respect, and something like moral and cultural equality. Both the parent and the professional must attempt to understand the other's point of view, special moral concerns, and culturally determined priorities for the child. Both must relate to each other as adults who possess complementary expertise and responsibility for the child. In the rest of this chapter we shall examine some of the most important obstacles to achieving this commonsensical—and very traditional—ideal of parent-professional cooperation.

The Sick Role and the Parent

The occupational hazards in the relationships between experts and parents have been well summarized by the medical sociologist Eliot Freidson in his description of the average physician's conception of the patient: "The customary professional characterization of the client [in medicine] . . . insists upon his ignorance and irrationality. Such characterization is the prime justification for the professional's inclination to make the client at best a passive participant in the work—to, in essence, remove from the client his everyday status as an adult citizen, to minimize his essential capacity to reason and his right to dignity. Expertise in general claims its privilege by claiming the client's incapacity." [8]

This general tendency of experts inside and outside the field of handicap (a tendency shared by bureaucrats) is reinforced when the object of the professional's services is a child. Perhaps a child has cerebral palsy and needs physical therapy, or his hearing is impaired and he needs speech therapy, or he has a reading disability and needs special educational services—in each instance the average professional defines his relationship to the child in much the same way as would a physician treating a patient for an acute infection such as pneumonia. He views the child in accord with the dictates of the social pathology model. The child has a special problem. The problem falls under the umbrella of the professional's special expertise—his "rational authority." [9] The professional then seeks to approximate a service relationship in which the child obeys the strictures of the sick role.

At this point, however, the fact that the client is a child greatly complicates the picture. No matter how much the expert might wish to focus exclusively upon that part of the child that falls within his expertise—the child's muscular coordination, speech articulation, or chronic disease—he cannot avoid taking into account the child's parents. This need follows from the fact that as a rule children are not willing to follow the dictates of the sick role or, for that matter, any role formulated by an adult. The parents become the doctor's enforcers, seeing to it that the child obeys the doctor's orders. This doctor-parent collaboration is relatively inconsequential when it is short-term, but it becomes particularly crucial in the case of handicap because most interventions are long-term.

Obviously the physician, for example, cannot ensure that a child will follow the delicate regime prescribed for diabetes; that job—which from a structural point of view means enforcing the canons of the sick role upon the child—is up to the parents. Nor can even the most devoted special education teacher help students with homework in the evenings or provide a supportive home environment. That, too, is up to the parents.

The obligations of the sick role, it will be recalled, are:

1. The patient is exempted from normal role obligations.

2. He is not held responsible for his state.

3. The state of being sick is considered conditionally legitimate *if—*

4. The patient cooperates with the source of help and actively *works* to achieve his own recovery [i.e., follows the doctor's orders].

5. Implied but not stated explicitly by Parsons is the presumption that the sick role will be temporary.[10]

Unfortunately, most parents who take a handicapped child in for treatment are soon nudged into accepting most of these obligations for themselves. They get treated as if they were patients: proposition one gets reformulated, in effect, to read "subordination of one's own idea of parental prerogatives and duties to the professional's conception of parental priorities and duties now that the child is under the professional's care."

It is striking to observe how often the structure of the professional's relationship to the parent automatically transforms the parent, in the expert's eyes, into a kind of patient. A good example is provided by the role parents are usually forced to play when they are lucky enough to find a comprehensive diagnostic center in a large hospital where a great variety of specialists can examine their handicapped child and where an overall plan of attack on the disability can be mapped out.[11] To begin with, during the several days in which the experts test the child, the parents are usually excluded. Finally, when the diagnosis and plan of attack are complete, the parents are summoned to a conference in which one professional—generally the social worker—"interprets" the results of the diagnosis to the parents. But he also tells the parents that they will never be able to see the diagnosis. Only other professionals (with the parents' written permission) will be able to see it.

Speaking of this process, Beatrice Wright observes that it has three negative effects: "(1) The parent gets the feeling that much is being said and done behind his back. (2) Decisions and conclusions are made, albeit in the form of recommendations, without his active participation. This always carries the danger that the parent will be unable or unwilling to carry them out. (3) It places the parent in the position of a child who has to be told what to do without having a real say in the telling or doing." [12]

Thus, from the very outset, the social worker's task in this encounter reduces to coping with the parent's negative reaction to being treated like a *patient* rather than like a *parent*.

Any layman who has ever had to cope with hospital red tape or sought benefits from a government program understands this. The "client," he finds, is thrust into a position of passivity and powerlessness in which it is made clear to him in no uncertain terms that he must accord the bureaucrat all the respect and compliance due a physician. Like doctors, bureaucrats who provide services for the handicapped treat parents as if they were patients. If the parents will not cooperate with the role being imposed, the bureaucrats often threaten to withdraw their services from the child.

In recent years, sensitive professionals have expressed concern about the way services for handicapped children seem organized to exclude the parent from the decision-making process. This concern has been voiced in numerous calls for an increased awareness of the parent's rights as a parent and in a host of proposals for administrative reforms designed to include the parent in the decision-making process. However, even the most parent-centered administrative reform can be undermined by the many subtle pressures that often keep parents from speaking up and pressing their objections when asked to participate in a review process with professionals. Still more important are the obstacles raised by the professional's conceptions of his rights and prerogatives as a professional. These role expectations and norms of proper parental behavior are often at serious variance with the parent's prerogatives concerning the child. As a consequence, many conflicts between parents and professionals hinge upon their basic disagreements about deeply felt personal values. These differences are highly unlikely to be resolved in favor of the parent in any simple review process in which the parent stands alone against an array of diploma-bearing experts.

The problem begins with the vast asymmetry in need between

the parent and the professional—the fact that in most of these encounters the parent needs the professional far more than the professional needs any one parent. The parent's concerns are concentrated on one handicapped child; the professional has many children as clients and in almost no instance does his emotional commitment to a specific child come near the parent's. Handicap services are poorly organized, expensive, hard to find. For the parent, merely finding the threshold of the professional's offices requires inordinate time, money, and hard work. Professionals don't seek out parents; professionals are sought out, sought after, and treated with great care lest the parent find himself turned away from the threshold and forced to start the exhausting process anew. The very structure of the time pressures on the professional conspires to put the parent at a marked disadvantage. The half-hour spent discussing the child's problems with a physician is fraught with significance for a parent. It is anticipated. It is remembered. It is dwelt upon. The hopes and fears of the parent organize themselves around it. No matter how conscientious the professional, he must see the half-hour in a different, less intense light, if only to protect himself from the impossible strain of going through every minute of every day at the high emotional pitch the parent brings to his brief interview with the professional. These asymmetries are further magnified if what is at stake is not a consultation with one professional but a comprehensive review of the child's problems by a group of professionals. The structure of this event in the parent's eyes is even more likely to intimidate, to silence, and to push the parent toward compliance completely independent of the individual professional's intentions.

Yet these are not the only impersonal pressures that can subvert genuine dialog. Perhaps the most common weakness of specialists is to overreach and mark out for themselves an area of expertise far exceeding their real special knowledge. Many a busy professional misperceives a conflict in personal values between himself and a parent as a challenge to his expertise and, therefore, to his professional identity. Does a mother expect the special education school to be accountable to her for the quality of the education it provides her child? The school's first impulse is to assert the primacy of its own bond with the child over the parent's by claiming that the question of the child's educational needs is far too complex to be dealt with seriously by a layman. Does the parent contemplate suing a vocational rehabilitation counselor for malpractice (perhaps because the experts tried to persuade a newly blinded youth that the vocation appropriate for a blind man is to make brooms in a sheltered workshop)? The very idea of a malpractice suit brought by a client or in behalf of a client strikes the specialist as absurd.[13] As the professional sees it, the client's or parent's role is not to evaluate the quality of the service provided, it is to make the most of the opportunities provided by the service—to study hard or to encourage the child to study hard, to implement the advice of the rehabilitation counselor, or to help the child pass through the rehabilitation process. In short, the professional rarely recognizes in his expectation that the parent ought to behave in a cooperative, patientlike way a personal value judgment rather than a necessity born of the professional's specialized knowledge. This error frequently leads the professional to equate a challenge to the sociological structure of the parent-professional relationship with a challenge to his claim to possess expert knowledge. The moment this confusion occurs, the professional may find himself employing a host of explicitly coercive strategies in what he believes to be a perfectly legitimate cause—defending his professional integrity against an "irrational" parent.

A final twist is added to the professional's error—and the parent's predicament—by the ease with which models of psychological explanation lend themselves to viewing any perceived challenge to legitimate professional authority as a symptom of emotional "maladjustment." [14] In one stroke the professional erects a new tier of obstacles to learning from his firsthand experience with parents that he should not expect them to behave in a patientlike manner. As for the parent, the circle is closed and he finds himself in a double bind: either submit to professional dominance (and be operationally defined as a patient) or stand up for one's rights and risk being labeled emotionally maladjusted (and therefore patientlike).

Still other coercive pressures find their source in those great constants of American life which are often ignored in discussions of handicap—race and class. Even sensitive professionals who acknowledge the serious barriers to communication imposed by cultural differences sometimes seem to lose their heads when they talk about how they have overcome these barriers by spending enough time with the parents to work through initial misunderstandings and suspicions. For surely something more than time is necessary to bridge the gap between an upper-middle-class white professional and a family from the *barrio* or the ghetto. Insight into the stereotypes, role expectations, and manners of the subculture to which the parents belong is also essential. Without this insight—and some way of learning from initial mistakes— even the best-intentioned and most time-consuming intervention can misfire. The professional may behave in ways that actually intimidate and threaten the parents even when he thinks he is being most open and flexible. The phenomenon of the ugly American is not restricted to middle-class Americans overseas.[15]

The most subtle coercive forces often stem from what distinguishes the client-professional relationship at its best from a mere economic transaction in the marketplace—the feeling of a shared goal and a sense of community that can impart to the relationship an ethical and emotional quality and transform the bond into a kind of friendship.[16] Anyone who has ever experienced such a relationship with a professional will acknowledge that very often the preservation of the special bond becomes an end in itself. Even if one disagrees with the professional, one hesitates to go too far for fear of transforming the "friendship" into a mere commercial transaction or an out-and-out political struggle. Precisely because the professional is sensitive and kind, he may encourage a process of self-censorship in the parent that conceals the professional's sociological mistakes and leads the parent to act against his own self-interest in the relationship.

Indeed, the tragedy of all the coercive pressures we have briefly surveyed is that the professional does not even notice them unless he takes great pains to probe beneath the surface of his relationships with parents. Between the intimidation he inadvertently practices on the parent, his tendency to equate differences in personal values with challenges to his expertise, his overuse of psychology to explain away parents' dissatisfaction with his prescriptions, and a host of other perceptual, cognitive, and structural factors, the professional is denied essential feedback, and a sociological misunderstanding of major proportions is perpetuated. The parent is the most immediate victim of this misunderstanding, but ultimately the child will suffer as well.

An indication of how the professional's pressures and misunderstandings can undermine an apparently flexible and open review process is provided by the typical problems parents experience with public schools. School is the one institution that has traditionally claimed to possess informal procedures designed to give the parent a say in all important decisions concerning the child. The following story, an encounter of one parent with a system designed to deliver special education, occurred *before* the implementation of the new reforms mandated by Public Law 94–142. It suggests how easily the professional's structural dominance can cast parents in the role of patient even when, on paper, the system appears to be making every effort to honor the parents' rights.

Although Danny had been slow in learning to speak and was somewhat withdrawn in kindergarten, his troubles actually began in first grade. His teacher had been trained in the phonovisual method and "knew" that that was how all children learned to read. By midyear Danny not only had not learned to read but was frustrated and miserable. He hated to go to school. Mrs. Burns [Danny's mother] scheduled several conferences with the teacher and found that the teacher saw him as a daydreamer who needed extra work assignments. She had been keeping him in at lunch and after school for drilling. To his parents she delivered the verdict that they expected too much of him, that he was reacting to pressure to perform at too high a level.

It did not take much longer for Mrs. Burns to land in the principal's office. The principal admitted that a professional diagnosis of Danny's difficulties could be helpful, but she discouraged the family from using the school psychologist, explaining that she was so overburdened by requests that there might be a wait of five or six months. The parents turned to their family doctor, who recommended a neurologist and a psychologist. The neurologist reported that Danny's condition could be described as *minimal brain dysfunction* and commented on some of his symptoms in detail. The psychologist assured his parents that Danny *could* learn. They recommended placement in a class for children with learning disabilities.

"It was a relief to know that it wasn't our fault," Mrs. Burns recalls, "but actually we had no idea what Danny needed. Then we were told by the school system that placement in an 'LD class' was extremely difficult, and not many children were accepted. When placement *was* arranged, we were told how lucky we were to receive these services for Danny."

The label *learning disability* was Danny's admission to the class the following fall; he had to take a bus to and from the class. His new teacher explained that he could not be expected to show much progress for a while, since he was far behind and had suffered a severe blow to his self-esteem. Although there was indeed very little progress, the parents were content to wait, because Danny at first seemed happier and more relaxed in a small class without the pressure to compete.

But problems began to surface. Danny began to complain about doing "dumb work." He wanted to write and spell; he was sick of connecting dots on a piece of paper. He became increasingly unhappy about the other children in the class. One started fights, climbed shelves, threw books. One cried incessantly. Another pretended he was a bell and "rang" a lot.

Danny's mother was told at a conference with the teacher that he had to learn to get along with others, that while it might not *appear* to be so, he was really doing well academically. When Mrs. Burns suggested that the class include some study of history and nature, she was told that it would take too much time away from learning "skills." And besides, the other children were not interested.

Mrs. Burns appealed to the school principal, who told her that she and her husband had not accepted Danny's handicap. As the year went on, the message was repeated: Danny was lucky to be in this special class.

Danny was again sullen and irritable about going to school, but his family felt that they had no alternative. When the next year began, he was once again on the bus to his special class assignment. But that fall, when Open School Day came around, Mrs. Burns was the first parent in class. And she stayed all day.

When she got home, she pulled out her typewriter and began to write. She described the classroom she had just observed: the difficulty the teacher had restraining children who were hyperactive; the boredom of other youngsters, who spent hours "tidying" their desks or doing work from piles of dreary worksheets left day after day in their shelves; the isolation of children who were not even allowed to mix with children from other classes in the playground. She wrote that her son was not learning and that he had no interest in going to school. She expressed her growing doubt that the teacher was actually qualified to teach children like Danny. And she demanded an immediate conference of all the school personnel who were involved. She sent copies of her letter to the principal, the school psychologist, the supervisor of pupil personnel services—and the superintendent of schools.

One week later a special meeting was held to talk about Danny Burns. Present was everyone who had received a copy of the letter (except the school superintendent). Everyone was angry. Teacher and principal faced the parents as accusers. It was clear to them that Danny was a "learning-disability child" and had been placed in an appropriate class. What more could these parents want? The pupil personnel worker, consulting Danny's record, stated that he would *not* recommend a change in placement—because Danny had not progressed academically. The school psychologist declared that Danny was too easily frustrated and too sensitive to be permitted a change in placement. The director of placement supported the views of his coworkers, documented by Danny's records, in maintaining that he "could not allow" Danny to leave the LD program.

The parents held their ground, insisting that the teacher was not aware of Danny's abilities, that he was not progressing, that the school situation was causing deterioration, not growth. Then an education specialist, who had been attending the session, spoke up. She had first-hand experience with all the available LD classes and stated that none of them offered what Danny needed: a combination of supportive, special help with specific skills and an opportunity to be with his peers in a regular class setting for other activities which would stimulate and interest him. She recommended, as a start, a new summer program which would use a wide variety of techniques to help youngsters lagging seriously behind their grade level.

The specialist prevailed, and that summer Danny "bloomed." It was a turning point.[17]

Despite the provision in the system for consultation, Danny's mother was still treated like a patient by the school staff. Whenever she contested the school's programs for her child, her views were dismissed as irrelevant and perceived as irrational and obstructionist. In effect she was constantly criticized by professionals for failing to conform to the usual definition of the sick role—for failing to be passive, cooperative, and completely in accord with the decisions of the experts. Indeed, reading the narrative, one is reminded of Millman's description of the patient on a hospital ward who was "caught" reading about his disease in a medical journal.[18] Here too, the experts in the school system seem to view each attempt by Danny's mother to contest their diagnosis of her son's needs and their programs for her son, as an unwarranted intrusion of the "patient" into matters best left to professionals.

What is especially striking about the experiences of Danny's mother is that none of the professionals involved needed to think of her explicitly as a patient in order to define her as a patient operationally. All that was necessary was for the various school specialists to ignore her complaints.

The Limits of "Caring"

Faced with an example such as the case of Mrs. Burns, the reaction of the professional genuinely interested in parent-centered services is frequently misplaced. Instead of concluding that ways must be found to reduce the professional's power and therefore to reduce the harmful consequences of his role definitions and his human shortcomings, the concerned professional often puts all the blame on the individuals with some professional responsibility for a child like Danny. No litany is more familiar in discussions of parent-profesional relationships in handicap than the appeal to be sensitive, to take the time to go beyond the stereotype, to care for the parent as a unique human being. Now obviously, empathy, warmth, concern, and dedication to the welware of the parent are essential ingredients in any good social service system. But to respond to the failure of what in principle appears to be an adequate consultation process by appealing to the need to "care" is to oversimplify the problem dangerously by once again resorting to the traditional social pathology model. More is needed to make service delivery genuinely parent-centered than formal provision for parental participation in the review process and an attitude of genuine concern on the part of the professional. The parent must have ways of protecting himself from the pressures that so often favor the professional and that make it so difficult for the professional to detect the harm he may do.

One of the most flexible and mutually rewarding of parent-professional relationships is that between an expectant mother and her physicians. Nothing could be more open and parent-centered than the many warm, caring relationships established by the obstetrician with his client. If genuinely caring were all that was required to make an ideally flexible and parent-centered relationship work out in practice, one would expect it here. Yet when a mother gives birth to a handicapped child, serious problems often develop between the mother and her physicians. Since the formal character of the relationship remains unchanged and since it is unlikely that the physician has suddenly turned harsh and uncaring, a third factor must be responsible for the sudden transformation of the relationship. By examining what can go wrong in such circumstances, we will set the stage for exploring another essential ingredient in any parent-centered social service.

The mother of a child with Down's syndrome, in a long interview with us, gave a disturbing account of her experiences with physicians and other professionals when the child was born and in the first few years thereafter.* Carla's experiences were extreme

---

* Down's syndrome, otherwise known as mongolism, is a genetic disorder marked by severe to moderate retardation (with most IQ's of those afflicted falling in the 20 to 40 range), by a greatly increased likelihood in childhood of heart disease, and by certain other physical infirmities.

even by the standards of a major handicap, but the reasons are diagnostic of the sources of many parent-professional conflicts in handicap: a conflict in basic personal values which a number of concerned and sensitive professionals misperceive as maternal "maladjustment," an instance of a mother's decisions about her child being dictated by shock, guilt, anxiety, and anger concerning the handicap. As we shall see, it is a conflict and a misperception that the traditional client-professional relationship is largely powerless to resolve.

Carla's Story [19]

When I gave birth to Julie I had a Caesarean section. This was at seven-thirty on Tuesday night. Wednesday morning at eight a strange doctor came into the room. He had made his rounds of the nursery. He came to me and said, "Well, I saw the baby and I don't know how much she weighs."

I said, "I know. She's five pounds, twelve ounces. The doctor told me that last night."

And then he said, "But, well . . ."

"What?" I exclaimed. "Is there something wrong?"

He answered, "Well, we're not sure. We think she has a chromosomal defect."

"What's that? What's a chromosomal defect?"

"Do you want me to go into specifics?"

"You're damn right," I answered. "You're talking about my baby, aren't you?"

"Yes," he said.

"Then you'd better be specific if you're telling me something's wrong with her. She has a chromosomal defect. What does this mean?"

"Well," he began, "I can't go into details now. We have to take a test and see what happens. You know, see what the test result is."

And, of course, I was getting more panicky with every word he said, and I broke down and cried.

"Now, now," he said, patting me on the shoulder, "now, now, that's life."

"Get the hell out," I told him, "and never come back into my room again!"

My obstetrician came in about, oh, about half an hour later, very broken up, tears in his eyes. I thought to myself: Something terrible must be wrong with my baby.

Finally, he said, "We think she's a mongoloid."

"Will you please call my husband and tell him?" I answered. Then I said, "I'm very angry with you because you should have gotten in touch with my husband first instead of sending in this strange man to tell me."

(And, you know, I had some experience with mongoloid children. I was in a convent for fifteen years. One of our schools was a school for exceptional children. I never taught in it. But I had been there to see the children. And I didn't think they were such monsters that everybody had to go around with tears in their eyes about them.)

Had you seen your baby yet?

No. They wouldn't let me see the baby. Of course she was premature—two weeks, just about two weeks. But nobody would come near me and talk to me. The nurses and the aides who had been so friendly the night before were all avoiding me. And, of course, that made me feel very bad. I couldn't imagine . . . Then I began to think, What have I done? I must have done something very terrible that nobody wants to talk to me, that nobody wants to look at me.

How did you feel the first time you saw your baby?

Well, I thought she was a pretty little baby. And everybody was making such a terrible fuss. And I had kind of mixed feelings. I just didn't know how to understand this whole thing. You know, it was overwhelming at the time. Except that I had no feeling that I would reject this child. There was nothing like that in my mind at all for one minute. And in fact I was so angry with everybody for their reactions to me and the baby. I was so furious . . . that they had treated me so badly. I mean, I was very sad, but it didn't devastate me. What devastated me was the way the doctor told me. All of this kind of ostracization. You know, not coming near me. I thought, Well, gosh, there must be something wrong with me.

Why do you think they wouldn't come near you?

Oh, I think because they didn't know how to handle the situation. I don't think they knew what to say to me. They knew, I think, that most people reject these babies. And they didn't know how I was going to react. So they didn't know what to say or how to act. I mean—first I was furious about their insensitivity. But I've come to realize that most people don't know how to handle human feelings or . . . human experiences. If something is not perfect, not what society thinks is perfect, an aberration, then most people don't know how to deal with it. They don't have any inner resources. There's something lacking in them as people. They can't face a reality. So they make abnormal what is normal in our lives. You know, American society considers anything less than perfect an abnormality. And that can be stretched pretty far. Even the kid who's ugly—who has no potential for beauty—is considered an abnormality in our society. And that kid really suffers because of it. A whole gamut of people who are less than perfect suffer because society has this thing that anyone less than perfect is abnormal. It's everywhere. We're bombarded with it on the TV, in the movies, and in advertisements. I'm very sad that people have been so weak with me.

Why do you think so many people are afraid of people who are different?

They're afraid because of this whole mentality of perfection and achievement. If you can do something, you're fine. If you can't, you're forgotten. It's true for kids. It's true for adults. When a man retires—when he's too old to produce—society forgets that he's a human being. When you are out of the market, you are out of everything. So, it's our whole mentality of achievement and doing instead of being oneself—not being a psychologist or a teacher, just being.

Did you ever lose faith that you were right during your stay at the hospital?

No. The only doubts I had came when people were avoiding me. I thought maybe I had committed some terrible crime. You know, I just wondered what I had done that was so bad. And when they talk about guilt feelings about having this child; I don't have any guilt feelings about the baby, about giving birth to a mongoloid child. I mean, it's a genetic thing that happened. It's an abnormality. And . . . some people—oh, maybe they feel they've been punished by God. But I have never felt that way. If God punishes and curses people, I don't believe in God. That's not the God I believe in. And I haven't lost faith in God because I have never felt that God is up there meting out punishments and rewards. I think God makes us free so that we can just choose. He doesn't intervene. So, to be guilty, I feel you have to be a free agent. And in the choice of the baby we just were not free agents. We were free to choose whether we would keep her home or not. That's different. Now, if I had put her away, then I would feel guilt. I'm sure I would.

Let's imagine for a moment that you had put her away. What would you be feeling now?

I don't think I could live with myself. It's hard for me to even imagine that. I would feel terrible. She has a heart condition . . . my pediatrician spoke about institutionalization when I brought the baby to him for a checkup. He said his brother had had Down's syndrome and had caused unbelievable hardship in the family because his mother had kept him at home. And he told me some of his experiences. But that didn't deter me from keeping Julie. I couldn't even consider an institution for Julie unless something happened that made me absolutely unable to take care of her myself. And I couldn't foresee anything like that.

How many children do you have?

I have two. Susan, who is five and normal; and Julie, who is two years old. But I've taught children for fifteen years. I've been with little children, and I love children. I think that's part of my whole mentality. I've never rejected a child. I've had some really tough kids to work with, and I don't think I have ever rejected a child.

A moment ago you said that Julie has a heart condition. Did you have any trouble getting it treated because she suffered from Down's syndrome?

Yes. When they discovered the condition, Dr. Brewer, the pediatrician, said to me, "Well, I think . . . you could see a cardiologist if you want to pursue it."

"What do you mean by that?" I shot back.

"Well, you know," he said, "if you want to pursue it you could see a cardiologist."

"What do you mean, do I want to pursue it? You wouldn't

say that to a mother with a normal baby. Do I want to pursue it? Why, you could even make the appointment," I replied.

And he said, "Well, I'll give you the name of a good cardiologist."

But when I tried to get the cardiologist from City Hospital he was all booked up. This was in April. He was booked up until July and wouldn't see the baby.

So I went back to my pediatrician and he said, "Why don't you just keep trying to get an appointment?" This made me furious because that answer meant "this would be a good chance to just let her die." "If I want to pursue it"—he wouldn't say that to a mother with a normal baby. He would immediately say, "You'd better see a cardiologist because this kid is in trouble."

Well, I searched for a cardiologist, and on Saturday I found one who could see Julie at the Children's Hospital at the end of the next week. Then came Sunday. It was Easter. I'll never forget it. Julie vomited all day. I was frantic. The next day I called the Children's Hospital and told them I had to see the cardiologist right away. When we got there he said, "It's a good thing you brought her in today, because she wouldn't live another day." Later, when they released her from the hospital, I found a new pediatrician who was recommended by the Center for Exceptional Children.

How did you find out about the center?

On my own. After three months of asking people where we could go, I called Aid for the Handicapped. I called Child Service, but nobody recommended the center. The Child Service said they would put me on a waiting list. Aid for the Handicapped said they would put me on a waiting list. But I wanted help now. So I called a friend at the Children's Hospital and the doctor she was working for recommended the Center for Exceptional Children. It's only about ten minutes away from us. But evidently the people at City Hospital, where the baby was born, were not aware of it. At least nobody recommended that I go there.

Besides giving you the name of another pediatrician, did the Center for Exceptional Children help you in any other ways?

No. If anything, it made things worse for me. For a while

I saw a social worker there, but the woman was domineering, authoritarian, and closed-minded. Talking with her was like running into a brick wall. I used to keep saying to her, "Look, tell me about this baby. Tell me what you're going to do to help me with her." I had some very strong arguments with her about how I felt. I resented her saying that before we had this kid, we had no feelings about mongoloid children. I said, "God damn it, don't tell me that. Don't say that to me because that's not true. You don't know me. You don't know my background. So don't come and say that I felt a certain way about these children because it's a damn lie." You know, I think it's criminal of them to do that, to categorize everybody as feeling a certain way. People are so complex. I mean, I don't even understand myself, my own feelings. I'm not saying that psychologists or social workers can't help. But let them first listen before they start telling people about how they feel or what they think.

Why did you decide to organize a parents' group?

Desperation. I was so disgusted and depressed that there was no help. I was getting kind of panicky about it. That's what upset me most of all—that there was nothing for these children. Most of them are institutionalized. And the rest aren't eligible for any program of help until they are at least three. Well, I say that three is just a little bit too late for these kids. If you want to help them develop their full potential you've got to start with infants.

What kinds of things is your group going to do?

We want to set up our own center staffed by professionals whom we hire and who provide our children with the kinds of education programs that are simply unavailable anywhere else in the community. We're looking for people who are sensitive to the needs of parents, who are not going to threaten parents, who are sensitive to the child and the needs of the child, people who are not rigid about what they have learned and read. We want people who are creative and innovative and who are going to build a program centered around the child and the family. Not a great big beautiful outline that the kids have to fit into—and if this kid doesn't fit, he's out of the program. That's what happens in some of these places in the city where they do an evaluation and if they feel that the child fits into their program, then he's accepted. To me that is absolutely asinine because it's not meeting the needs of people. It's an elitist kind of thing. What we want to do is to have an open program. We have some general ideas of how children learn and what is good. But we're not going to base entrance into the program on the child's ability to fit into a cubbyhole. We will try to be creative enough and loving enough to meet the needs of every child and every family as much as we can.

We also want to help new parents while they are still in the hospital. We plan to meet with them and give them an alternative to institutionalization. We don't want to go in evangelizing. We simply want to present an alternative. We also want to go into the home and show the mother what she can do to stimulate her child. We would have a kit to bring in and give her some ideas. And if she needs help emotionally, we'd try to help her here too. We've done some of this with a few of the new parents at the center.

Do you ever find yourself worrying about Julie's future?

Yes. I find myself worrying about it a lot. You know, that's where I really get discouraged. We just don't have the programs that would really suit the kind of future I'm thinking of for Julie. Say our program really is successful, and she can function—not only Julie, but the other children —can function at a good level. Where do they go from our program? Even in the near future, we have to be sure that there are programs in our area where Julie can go. And then I think of adulthood. If she ever reaches adulthood. You know, we don't even know if she will, because she's going to have surgery when she's five.

What's wrong with her heart?

Oh, gosh, she has two holes in the septum, and then she has a cleft valve. So we really don't know if she's going to reach adulthood. But what is there for a mongoloid adult? Suppose she does outlive us. How is she going to feel when we're dead? She'll be lost if we don't make sure that she somehow gets out into society—that there is a place for her, that she has friends, that there is a hostel maybe, with normal people that she can relate to and be happy relating to. But I also wonder. Would she really be happy in a normal setting? Say they're teen-agers, and these other teen-agers are functioning at a much more sophisticated level than Julie. Even now you can see Julie a little lost sometimes when there are normal children around playing.

There's another problem: I don't want Julie to be a burden on her mentally normal older sister. I don't want to say, "Susan, it's your duty to take care of your sister." Right now there's no problem—Susan's five and Julie's two. But in ten years, things will be very different.

Up to now you haven't spoken of Julie as a burden.

Not for me—for Susan. It would be a burden for Susan to take care of Julie when she's a young adult, when Susan has dates and whatnot. Or if she marries. I don't mean they have to separate completely. I don't want that to happen either. But I don't want to thrust an obligation on Susan which would be unfair. We don't know what Julie's going to be like when she is older, and I don't want Susan to feel guilty. I don't want her to feel that she has to. If she decides on her own, fine. Wonderful. But I'm not going to torment her with saying that she has to take care of Julie. I think that would be unfair. Right now Julie is doing very well. But what she will be doing later on, we don't know. Nobody can foresee that.

Would you raise Julie differently if you knew that she would not live to adulthood?

No. Because what I'm doing for Julie, I feel, is my way of loving her, my way of caring. And whether she lives to fifteen or fifty, I would be obliged—I mean I would be obliged to myself and to Julie—to do this. Whether she lives to fifteen or fifty is inconsequential to me. If she can live a happy fifteen years, with as full a life as she can, fine. If I can provide that, I will.

You wouldn't want to just make her happy and not worry all that much about making her independent?

No, I wouldn't, because I think that's part of the happiness . . . her finding happiness is being independent. Yes, even now she's happier when I let her go and let her do what she wants. You know, running around and getting into the cupboards. She's happy doing that and she's learning to be independent. She's making choices as she's sitting with all the pots and pans and pulling them out. Even something like that. I could say, "Oh, my God"—which people do with normal children—"oh, she's going to get hurt. She's going to do this." But I don't, because I believe that you've got to let children explore and to be happy as they explore.

Independence is pretty important to you, isn't it?

Yes. If you really love your children, you have to guide them to be independent and free of you. That's our role as parents. At each step to make them as independent as possible, whether we like the way they think or not. Their ideas may be different. Their aspirations may be very different from what we have for them. But that doesn't matter. Our job is to love them for themselves, and to love and to be detached at the same time. It's very hard for me to say what I mean by that. There has to be a loving bond. But not the kind of thing that keeps them tied to the umbilical cord. We have to lead them to whatever life *is*—to what they want to pursue and discover. I think it's so great if I can take my child by the hand and say, "Look, I've taken you this far and my happiness will be in your discovery."

It may be tempting simply to call most of the experts whom Carla encountered callous, uncaring, obtuse, high-handed, and selfish; but this would be a gross oversimplification. Far more is involved in the picture of the health care system Carla describes than the lack of a caring attitude. Indeed, there is ample evidence in her narrative that most of the experts who misserved her did indeed care—the halting speech of her obstetrician, the circuitous language in which it was suggested to her that she should allow Julie to die by refraining from taking the child to a heart specialist, the social worker's attempts to get Carla to talk about her feelings. These are not the actions of people incapable of emotion and indifferent to Carla's welfare. Quite the contrary, they are the actions of individuals torn by feelings of compassion, guilt, and anguish at Carla's tragedy. One can, for example, imagine Carla's pediatrician heatedly replying, "I do care a lot. I grew up with a retarded brother. Don't you think I *know* what it's like to have a mongoloid child in the family? Sure she doesn't want to institutionalize. But just wait. In the long run she'll realize that it was the best move for everyone." To reduce the problem encountered by Carla to a matter of caring or not caring is to do the professional a great injustice. It is to confuse the destructive effects of the professional's actions with his often impeccable intentions.

The issues raised by Carla's extreme experiences with the health care system vividly illustrate the weakness of an approach to service delivery which assumes that adequate administrative and legal safeguards of the parent's rights in regard to the child plus dedicated professional care are alone sufficient to ensure a genuinely parent-centered service delivery. Carla's legal rights to custody of Julie were never in doubt and, indeed, Carla's decision not to institutionalize prevailed. Nor do we believe that the suffering visited upon Carla by the treatment of her nurses, doctors, and social worker could have been forestalled or moderated by a formal review process built into the hospital setting or initiated from outside by a monitoring agency run by professionals. For such a review to serve its intended function of curbing professional abuses, the professionals participating in the review must be able to overcome their powerful perceptual biases toward the parent of a severely handicapped child—biases that are every bit as powerful as the biases that are triggered in the layman by learning that a stranger is handicapped.[20] The discrediting, condescending character of these biases is well summarized in a still widely read description of parents such as Carla by the Group for Advancement of Psychiatry:

The "righteous indignation" of parents of the retarded child can be one of the most difficult problems with which the physician must deal. He should be aware that the anger of the parents is not personal, but rather that they are using him as a convenient target for the projection of their hostility. It is important that the physician try to help the parents recognize why they are reacting as they are, and equally important that he not counter with his own hostility. The parents should slowly be led to an awareness that their own resentment is derived in part from their guilt feelings and also from their inability to accept the fact that this really happened to them.[21]

Everyone connected with Carla knew—or soon learned—that Carla was a devout Catholic, had spent many years of her youth as a nun, and had fifteen years' experience working with retarded children in a church-run nursery. Viewed through the therapeutic lens, this biographical background appears irrelevant, or it may be treated as further proof that Carla is prone to be irrational in matters concerning a handicapped child. As long as facts such as these are routinely ignored by most professionals— or obscured by the adjustment-psychology model that so often provides professionals with an "objective explanation" of the resistance they encounter in their contacts with parents—a review process dominated by professionals is only likely to provide the professional with a new occasion for seeking to impose his therapeutic morality on the parent.[22]

How can the professional sift out instances when the parent's resistance to advice is indeed irrational from instances in which the parent's resistance reflects the professional's inadvertent abuses of his immense informal powers in any relationship with a parent? Given the pervasiveness of the social pathology model among professionals, how can one imagine that the average professional is capable of even recognizing the existence of moral claims made by parents like Carla when the conflict in values does not concern other professionals and other parents, but instead occurs in the professional's own personal practice? [23]

It is now more than a generation since the political scientist Harold Lasswell coined the term *virocracy*, meaning rule by an elite recruited on the basis of vigor, vitality, and prowess.[24] By analogy to Lasswell's term, one might describe the errors of Carla's professionals as stemming from their inappropriately medical—or iatrocratic—model of the client-professional relationship.* Incapable of honoring the moral passion of a former nun, Carla's professionals were able to perceive only her *passion*; they could not distinguish Carla's moral claims from the grief, guilt, and anxiety that Carla undoubtedly felt because she had brought a handicapped child into the world. Having disposed of all moral categories not explicitly recognized by the medical model, the professionals were then able to define their obligation to Carla exclusively in terms of their interpretation of the psychiatric meaning of her pain. The social worker tried to help Carla work through all the old, unresolved psychological conflicts provoked by the "reality crisis"; the others believed that they were trying to protect Carla from the consequences of decisions arrived at while she was incapable of "normal" adult function. It would be wrong, however, to say that any of Carla's professionals conceived of themselves as being obliged to make moral choices on behalf of the "maladjusted client"; for the concept of moral choice is predicated on the existence of competing moral alternatives, and

* *Iatrocratic* is formed from the Greek words for "doctor" (*iatros*) and "to govern" (*crateo*). We will not strain the reader's patience by continuing to use this ugly neologism in the text. We employ it here to bring out the singular fact that the language lacks any other word to denote *either* the wanton abuse of medical models of explanation outside medicine *or* medical behavior that is destructive in a psychological or a sociological sense precisely because it is inspired by an inappropriate use of a medical model of explanation.

the essence of the medical model is to dissolve all moral alternatives into a single therapeutic mandate: relieve suffering, whether physical suffering occasioned by disease or "maladjustment." By their own lights, Carla's professionals acted rationally and compassionately. They followed the only moral course that their view of the client permitted: they sought to relieve her suffering and treat what they defined as her maladjustment.

Is there any hope of restructuring professional education in such a way that every professional would begin his career imbued with the skills needed to make a serious attempt to draw the line between questions of specialized knowledge (where the expert ought to prevail) and questions of personal values (where the parent ought to prevail)? If there were, it might be possible to construct a genuinely parent-centered service delivery system without venturing beyond the boundaries of the conventional model of client-professional relationships. This strategy would rescue the traditional paradigm by defining a new service need: the need to mitigate the professional's glaring abuses of his authority and power. But experience suggests that professional education is far more resistant to major changes than society at large —at least when these changes involve a redefinition of the professional's role that stringently reduces his power and authority. Moreover, even were such Draconian reforms in professional education possible, it seems likely that the many structural, cognitive, and perceptual factors that help maintain professional dominance in the parent-professional relationship would inevitably resocialize the professional back into the same patterns that characterize his behavior today. Indeed, we suspect that long after the handicapped individual has assumed a respected place in the mainstream of American life, critics will still be documenting the excesses of professional behavior in the helping services.

Improving Parent-Professional Cooperation: The Political Prerequisites

If one believes that parents require constant guidance and tutelage in order to act in the best interests of their children, the hazards of professional intervention we have explored in this chapter will appear to be necessary evils. Our own position is quite different. We believe that the parent-professional relationship in handicap should be in accord with the traditions of civil society. Instead of professional dominance, there should be parental coordination, and not just by the affluent and well-educated parent who comes from the same cultural milieu as the professional. Parents should oversee and orchestrate the services that professionals provide their children. Parents of all races and social classes should be able to pick and choose among different experts, obtain outside opinions when dissatisfied with the services or advice provided by a professional, and constantly evaluate the professional's performance in terms of the overall needs of the growing child.

Every society seeks ways to distinguish between legitimate and illegitimate power. It does so by imbuing certain social roles—such as judge, policeman, and parent—with the moral right to exercise authority over other members of society in well-defined settings and circumstances. During the last century—and at an ever-increasing rate—the traditional moral justification for authority has been supplemented and frequently supplanted by a justification based upon expertise. Often, the expert's claim to authority is amoral. The engineer does not decide to build the bridge, he merely possesses certain specialized knowledge that makes it possible to build the bridge.

In the human services, however, the tendency toward specialization implicit in the concept of the technical expert has gone still further. As even a cursory glance at such areas as child development will show, many professionals find it natural to believe that they are experts about the kinds of values that parents should possess and inculcate in their children. Much of the conflict and confusion that occurs between parents and professionals in handicap stems from the almost self-evident character of the professional's intuitive feeling that he is a moral expert as well as a technical expert.

Not the least of the benefits of urging the parent to assume an executive role *vis-à-vis* the professional is that this strategy takes the parent's traditional claim to moral authority and adds to it an appeal to the very different claim to legitimacy of managerial authority. Unlike the parent's moral claim, which often seems pallid and suspect when ranged against the professional's appeal to his expertise, the administrator's moral authority can hold its own. The administrator specializes, as it were, in being a generalist—in cultivating an ability to grasp the big picture that so often eludes the narrow specialist. By meeting the expert on the expert's own ground, the authority of the manager seems as natural, as self-evident, and as uncontaminated by arbitrary and subjective factors as the specialist's own claim to authority.

Unfortunately, what is culturally obvious often remains unexplored. Outside the field of handicap, the idea of parent-as-manager has obtained considerable currency in recent discussions of how to improve social services. Perhaps because the model seems so intuitively obvious, much less attention has been devoted to the need to empower parents in ways that permit them to exercise the discretionary and coordinating powers of the administrator in their encounters with professionals.

Insight into what the average parent needs in order to function as a manager is provided by mentioning some of the structural advantages that administrators possess when they consult experts. Our purpose in alluding to some of these advantages is not to tell the reader anything he does not already know but to suggest that what the reader knows about the realities of power and expertise in large organizations is of the highest importance in any discussion of how to enable more parents to function as executives in their relationships with professionals.

To begin with, when a professional advises an executive, the professional is dealing with an organization rather than with an isolated individual. As a consequence, even the outside consultant is likely to feel that his career is on the line every time he provides a service to the manager. The professor who consults for the government will be at his best because he wants to be asked to consult again, or perhaps because he also wants to be appointed to a prestigious government review panel. Since most individual parents are not rich, famous, or powerful, their satisfaction with the professional's services is much less crucial to the professional's career prospect. The different "schedule of reinforcements" that the professional encounters in advising organizations is, of course, directly reflected in how seriously the professional treats the social side of his relationship with the administrator. It is only common sense to take pains in establishing a relationship that the administrator perceives to be satisfactory. Indeed, because the cards are so heavily stacked in favor of the administrator, the professional will often have to choose between speaking honestly and thereby harming his career prospects, or being "realistic" and tilting his advice to make it more palatable to his employer's ears. Finally, professionals often share the culture's respect for the special kind of authority vested in the administrator. This respect is often a significant factor in conditioning the expert's behavior toward an especially powerful administrator in government or private industry—i.e., the head of a large and powerful bureaucracy or a highly placed executive in a firm. As we have seen, professionals often lack an equivalent respect for the moral authority vested in the parent.

Here, then, is what it means to say that the parent should assume a managerial role. He must have power—the kind of power that comes with occupying a position of administrative authority in a large organization. Without it, even the best-intentioned attempts to reform the way professionals deliver their services risks frustration. Good intentions and a genuine desire to help are simply not enough if the deck remains stacked against the client. The parent, not the professional, should be the one to set the terms of the relationship.

For most people—all but the most wealthy, clever, and influential—this power must spring from the same source as that of the administrator—the group. Perhaps more than anything else, it is essential that parents of handicapped children organize themselves into self-help groups. These can provide the parent with access to alternate information about services in the community, consultations with outside professionals, and moral support. Just as important, membership in active local groups is likely to exert a subtle influence upon the weight professionals give to establishing a mutually satisfactory relationship with the parent. Viewed as isolated individuals, few parents are likely to seem important enough to the average professional to have much influence on his future career. As the member of a group of powerful local parents' organizations, the parent's ability to influence the professional's career prospects is greatly enhanced. Something of the deference that characterizes the professional's relationship to the lay administrator may enter into the service relationship. This deference need not be Machiavellian. Most people adjust their behavior unconsciously *to reflect the prevailing structural asymmetries in a relationship.* What seems "inappropriate," "unreasonable," and a threat to professional privilege when the deck is stacked in the professional's favor may seem only natural and appropriate when the professional senses that his career depends as much upon parental satisfaction as it depends upon his relationships with his colleagues.

Some of the most important benefits to ensue from a great increase in political organizing by parents are likely to involve the expectations that many parents currently bring to their encounters with professionals. Professionals are not, of course, alone in preferring to view the parent as patientlike. Despite the examples of parents like Mrs. Burns and Carla, many parents share the professional's traditional model of client-professional relationships and believe that professional authority takes precedence over their own authority. Where such an attitude prevails among parents, even the boldest attempt to improve the professional's accountability is menaced by failure because of the possibility that parents will not take advantage of their new rights. Moreover, when parents and professionals share the traditional model of intervention, a common response to difficulties encountered in implementing new reforms (such as those now under way in special education) is foreseeable. Instead of trying to make the reforms work by seeking ways to transform the traditional client-professional relationship into a relationship of rough equality between parent and professional, the cry will go up among parents that the short-term difficulties encountered by the reforms "proves" that the old was better and that most of the responsibility for service decisions concerning the child should be left in the hands of the professional, who "knows best." Parents' organizations can do much to forestall the failure of reforms in the first place, as well as providing other explanations for whatever difficulties do occur.

A good grass-roots parents' group can accomplish many other things. It can provide the kind of continuity from year to year that fosters the emergence of a folk wisdom about how to meet specific crises in the family's life. It could be the place where parents swap ideas and experiences in the manner that parents have, from time immemorial, gotten together to share ideas about child rearing. By bringing together parents with similar experiences, it could go a long way toward reducing the sense of isolation and abandonment so often induced in parents by the strain of raising a child with a handicap. It could serve as a corrective to unrealistic hopes about medical miracles and educational breakthroughs. It could give parents the lowdown on the local social service agencies for handicapped children and provide the latest word on how to make the most of them. It could give parents a chance to meet successful disabled adults and to gain from them a more balanced understanding of the relative role of society and biology in their own child's handicap. In short, local self-help groups could be the place where parents with handicapped children came together to form a community of like-minded people—not a "therapeutic community" managed for them by professionals, but a community that they themselves control.

Of course, parents' groups are not panaceas. They are just as vulnerable to the forces of decay, corruption, and ossification as other institutions.[25] What starts as a genuine "participatory democracy" may turn into a private empire administered by a few politically astute parents for their own gain. And a sense of community can become a sense of oppression by a small-minded majority. Political inexperience is another problem. Parents of handicapped children are no more experienced in local political organizing than other parents. They are just as liable to make mistakes as any other group of politically inexperienced people. They may unnecessarily polarize issues between themselves and professionals in the community. And they may become easily discouraged when quick victories are not obtained, or when the group settles down to the often wearing day-to-day routine of practical politics. None of these hazards is unique to parents' groups, however. Indeed, they are common to all organized groups.

Discussions of parent-professional relationships hinge upon a fundamental question of values. Who is to be considered as fully adult in the encounter: the parent and the professional or only the expert? All too often the social pathologist doesn't want to entrust parents with the power to make decisions on behalf of their handicapped children. He believes that he should routinely determine what is in the child's best interest. We hold to a different morality. We believe that professionals should treat parents as adults.

Chapter 9

Special Education at a Turning Point

Every revolution changes our moral and intellectual vision of the world. Over the past decade parents, advocates, and educators have achieved a set of legal and legislative victories that many believe to define a new and revolutionary idea of the public school's obligations to the handicapped child and his family. As recently as the 1960s "special education," the name given to the special instructional services provided handicapped children, was a stepchild. While the nation was seeking to improve the quality of the minority child's schooling, the handicapped child's educational needs remained forgotten, even though these needs were easily as great as those of the most cruelly disadvantaged able-bodied children. At that time perhaps one handicapped child in eight—over one million handicapped children—received no education whatsoever, while more than half of all handicapped children did not receive the special instructional services that they needed.[1]

In the intervening years, special education has changed rapidly. During the early 1970s, court decisions triggered a major reorientation in the goals and priorities of the state-run public school system. Reflecting these shifts, the education amendments of 1974 (Public Law 93-380) marked the first time that Congress formally recognized the handicapped child's right to an education and his right to procedural due process. Not long afterward Congress passed and the president signed into law the Education for All Handicapped Children Act of 1975 (Public Law 94-142). "It is the purpose of this Act," states the law's preamble, "to assure that all handicapped children have available to them a free appropriate public education which emphasizes special education and related services designed to meet their unique needs, to assure that the rights of handicapped children and their parents or guardians are protected, to assist State and localities to provide for the education of all handicapped children, and to assess and assure the effectiveness of efforts to educate handicapped children." [2]

When the law's provisions came fully into effect in September 1978, the child and his family possessed a set of rights that many would have found unthinkable a decade before. P.L. 94-142 guarantees every handicapped child, regardless of the nature and the severity of his disability, a free public education. It directs the schools to tailor this education to the child's individual needs, and it stipulates that whenever possible the child should be educated alongside his able-bodied peers. Just as importantly, the law tries to take the parent into account. It establishes an elaborate administrative procedure designed to ensure that parents have a say in every educational decision the school makes about their child—everything from the evaluation of the diagnostic tests the school psychologist gives the child to the construction of the child's individualized educational plan. When one compares P.L. 94-142 to previous educational policy toward handicapped children, it is little wonder that many educators refer to it as a "quiet revolution" in special education. In the words of one respected educational reformer, the new law "reflects the dream of special educators and others concerned about the education of children with handicaps." [3]

We have serious reservations about P.L. 94-142. They go far beyond the frequently expressed belief that the costs of fully implementing it will be far greater than anticipated, and that staggering practical and political problems stand in the way of constructing workable versions of the newly mandated administrative and organizational changes.[4] What principally concerns us is that P.L. 94-142 does not take a clear stand against the medical paradigm that has traditionally formed the schools' vision of the handicapped child's needs and its vision of parent-school relationships.

The law's ambiguity is at once a cause and a symptom of perhaps the greatest weakness of the reform movement in special education. Despite all the talk of revolutionary changes, there are fundamental differences among reformers about the nature of this revolution, and these differences are almost never discussed. Instead, a situation reminiscent of minority education in the 1960s prevails. Shared rhetoric conceals the lack of anything like a shared vision of the parent-school relation and the handicapped child's needs.

The great majority of reformers still subscribe to the traditional paradigms. They treat handicap as a disease and they see nothing wrong in the medical ideal of client-professional relationships. They have one overriding concern: to correct the school's historic failure to effectively and equitably put these beliefs into practice. As they read it, P.L. 94-142 represents a dramatic breakthrough in society's commitment to meet the handicapped child's needs as these needs are defined by the social pathology paradigm. Other reformers interpret P.L. 94-142 in a diametrically different way. They believe that the new law challenges the traditional deviance analysis of the child's needs and the medical conception of parent-school relationships. Somewhere in between are those who accept the deviance model but reject the traditional parent-school model. Their reading of the revolutionary character of P.L. 94-142 reflects this mixed attitude toward the social pathology paradigm.

While these differences continue—and they will persist if they are not openly discussed—reformers will have little say in the direction that reform takes. Getting the schools competently to implement the social pathology model is a task of daunting proportions; but here, at least, professional and reformer speak the same language (after all, every service institution inside and outside handicap conceives of its primary mission as seeking to implement more efficiently the ideals of the social pathology model in its own area). Transforming the schools' vision of the handicapped child's needs and the parents' rights is inherently much more difficult because it challenges the schools' claims to expertise about handicapped children and adults, and because the professional's training and experience encourage him to dismiss criticisms of his paradigm as irrational, incomprehensible, and unprofessional. To achieve a change of this magnitude in special education will require constant pressure from a reform movement that knows exactly what it wants and will stop at nothing to achieve it. Without this focused pressure, the schools will succeed in interpreting even the boldest legal and legislative innovations in accord with their

175

traditional ideas. Should this be the fate of the new reforms in special education, a precious opportunity will have been lost. What might have been a revolution will, at best, result in a series of managerial innovations that permit the schools to do a bad thing better.

The ambiguities, inconsistencies, and silences of the special education reform movement are not new. They have existed from the very beginning of the "quiet revolution." A brief review of this history will set the stage for our examination of the many ways that P.L. 94-142 fails to make a decisive break with the traditional philosophy of special education.[5]

The Right to a Free Public Education

Of all the handicapped child's educational problems, school exclusion is the easiest to confront. Regardless of one's views about the schools' deviance analysis of handicap (or, for that matter, the generally poor quality of public education), there is no justification whatsoever for denying huge numbers of children a free public education on account of their handicaps. Even an inferior education is better than none at all. And in a society that expects every normal child to attend school, few things seem more likely to shatter a child's sense of self-esteem than to deny him schooling just because he is different.

The Constitution does not establish the right of every child to an education, but it does assert the individual's right to equal protection under the law. This right has frequently figured in legal decisions involving education. Two lawsuits in the early 1970s marked the turning point in the fight to extend the principle of equal educational opportunity to the handicapped child. In 1971 the Pennsylvania Association of Retarded Children (PARC) went to court on behalf of the many retarded children in Pennsylvania who were receiving no public education whatsoever. The federal district court ruled in favor of the parents' group and required that the state provide every retarded child with access to a free public education. It was not long before the precedent established in the *PARC* case was greatly expanded. In *Mills* v. *Board of Education of the District of Columbia* (1972) the courts decreed that every school-age child in the District, regardless of the nature or severity of his handicap, was entitled to receive a free public education. In both the *PARC* and *Mills* cases, the court ruled that school exclusion placed the handicapped child at such educational, emotional, and intellectual risk that it violated the equal protection clause of the Fourteenth Amendment.

Yet even here, where the issue seems so clear, the broader implications of the ruling meant different things to different reformers. Some saw a major victory for those who had long sought to improve the implementation of the medical model in handicap by increasing the number of children receiving special education services. For others the new educational mandate represented far more: it was a beachhead for ideas about education that were commonplace in minority education but had little or no precedent in special education—such ideas as discarding the traditional deviance analysis of the minority-group child's educational problems or restructuring the relationship between the parent and the professional.

The Parent and the School

During the 1960s the courts had focused increasing attention on the ways that the social pathology paradigm led to serious abuses of the civil rights of prisoners, institutionalized mental patients, juvenile offenders, and other deviant groups frequently subjected to enforced therapy.[6] The *PARC* and *Mills* cases established crucial precedents for applying this body of legal opinion to the problems of special education.

Traditionally the school administrator made all the important decisions about the handicapped child's education: whether or not the child could be given schooling at the public school; if so, what diagnostic label should be assigned to him; and what programs he should be placed in to meet his special educational needs. These decisions were frequently reached unilaterally, without any expert assessment of the child's educational needs and without any involvement of the parents. Many handicapped children who *were* accepted by school administrators were misclassified (with regard to their handicap), and even if they were properly classified, they were assigned to educational programs or tracks that bore little relationship to their needs. A learning-disabled child might be classified as retarded by the school and placed in a class for slow learners from which he might never escape. A retarded child might be correctly classified as retarded but placed in a class of emotionally disturbed children. Indeed, in some instances the only consistent criterion for acceptance, classification, and placement of children in particular classes was administrative convenience.[7]

Both courts that ruled in the landmark cases found this state of affairs intolerable. In the *PARC* case, the district court ruled that the Pennsylvania school system had violated the retarded child's right to the protection of procedural due process as defined in the Fifth and Fourteenth amendments. Shortly thereafter the district court in *Mills* v. *Board of Education of the District of Columbia* extended the right to procedural due process to all handicapped children in the country.

To anyone familiar with the history of civil rights litigation in the 1960s, these decisions marked an explicit attack on the special education school's medical model of parent-school relations. However, most professionals working with handicapped children were not familiar with this legal history. (Nor were most parents.) From a perspective bounded by experience in special education, the educational philosophy that informed the *PARC* and *Mills* decisions was more ambiguous. The new guarantee of due process could be interpreted in either of two ways: as a necessary device to safeguard the parent against occasional abuses of the traditional parent-school relationship or a major step toward the redefinition of that relationship in terms of a contract between two equals.[8]

The Right to an "Appropriate Education"

The most sophisticated attack on the social pathology model was not launched from within the field of disability at all. It came from the civil rights movement. In a series of crucial lawsuits, civil rights advocates charged a host of public school systems with selectively overlabeling minority-group children as educably mentally retarded (EMR) and emotionally disturbed. Once placed into these categories, the children were assigned to special classes. Since children labeled EMR or emotionally disturbed seemed to do just as well academically when kept in the regular classroom, the net result of the overlabeling of minority children was to subject them to the potential stigma associated with a handicapped classification and to perpetuate traditional patterns of racial segregation in a new guise.

The *prima facie* evidence that racial discrimination sometimes marched under the flag of special education in many school systems was especially compelling: the incidence of handicaps that stem from a physical or genetic cause is roughly the same among all ethnic groups, yet minority children were greatly overrepresented in such categories of handicaps as mild retardation or mild emotional disturbance, where no clear physical or genetic cause could be imputed. For example, in 1971 blacks composed 9 percent of the students in the California school system, 12 percent of all severely or profoundly retarded students, and 13 percent of all physically handicapped students—but 27 percent of all children labeled "mildly retarded." In New York State in the 1960s a black child was twice as likely to be classified mildly retarded if he attended a racially mixed school than if he attended a school that was mainly or entirely black.[9] In other words, when black children were not already receiving a segregated education by virtue of segregated residential patterns, the school frequently perpetuated segregation within the programmatic framework of integration by overlabeling black children "mildly retarded." A particularly flagrant misuse of handicap classification was discovered in the Missouri school system.[10] There virtually no black children were placed in classes for the learning-disabled, whereas black children made up about one-third of the students in classes for the educably mentally retarded. Learning disability, it seemed, obeyed the color line in Missouri.[11]

In order to satisfy the courts that the racial imbalances in special education classes did not reflect systematic differences in the mental ability or emotional stability of white children and minority-group children, civil rights advocates subjected the classification procedures used by the public schools to minute scrutiny. Again and again a similar pattern emerged: the public schools assessed minority-group children by norms established for white middle-class children. The courts ruled that these assessment procedures were highly discriminatory and that the overrepresentation of minority-group children in the classes for the EMR and the emotionally disturbed represented a hitherto unseen form of racial discrimination.

If the schools' present classification procedures were flawed, what procedures should replace them? As the courts pondered this point, a crucial opportunity was lost, a chance to attack the discriminatory character of the norms used to assess children who were genuinely handicapped. Instead of systematically questioning the diagnostic procedures used by the special education school, civil rights advocates introduced into disability litigation the same double standard that characterizes society's very different ideals of racial tolerance and tolerance toward the disabled.* Toward minority-group children in such "suspect" classifications as emotionally disturbed and educably mentally retarded, the courts mandated the application of pluralistic procedures—diagnostic tests and clinical practices that explicitly took into account the child's cultural background and assessed his mental abilities and emotional maturity by the standards of his social group rather than by the standards of white middle-class society. But the court's sensitivity to the need to tailor assessment procedures to the child's social world went no further than race and ethnicity. Instead of extending the concept of pluralistic criteria a step further, in order to respect the special socialization experiences of the handicapped, the courts accepted the traditional—and highly discriminatory—simplifications of special education. They assumed as a matter of course that it was perfectly appropriate for the schools to assess a handicapped child's mental ability and emotional maturity by judging the child according to the norms established for able-bodied children.

The courts did enunciate two crucial education principles.† First, the schools were directed to individualize their programs for handicapped children, to tailor each child's educational program to his specific needs, to teach the child rather than the handicap category. Second, the courts accepted the arguments of special educators on behalf of what is increasingly being called the mainstreaming "belief." This is the belief that, all other things being equal, it is better psychologically, socially, and just possibly academically to educate the handicapped child with able-bodied children rather than to educate the handicapped child exclusively with other handicapped children.[13] ‡

* This distinction was discussed in chapter 2.

† In both cases, the courts justified their intervention in new areas on pragmatic grounds. To ignore the character of the education provided the child, the courts argued, would risk rendering meaningless any decisions concerning the classificatory procedures used by the schools or decisions concerning the handicapped child's right to a public education. As Kirp put it, "The Supreme Court has often noted [that] a court of equity has vast powers in framing its decree 'to go beyond the matters immediately underlying its equitable jurisdiction and decide whatever other issues and give whatever other relief may be necessary under the circumstances.' "[12]

‡ Of course all other things are not always equal.[14] One crippled child may be emotionally better off in a segregated setting, whereas another crippled child would

Unfortunately, these principles reproduced all the shortcomings of the analysts of school classification procedures. The courts overlooked the discrimination against the handicapped that is built into special education's diagnostic tests, instructional techniques, and curriculum materials—what one might call the "normalist" bias that pervades nearly every aspect of the field. Similarly the court failed to reckon with the many ways that the social pathology paradigm can undermine the intent of the mandate to mainstream handicapped children whenever possible with their able-bodied peers. Once again the schools' deviance analysis of disability remained unchallenged.

In the years following the path-breaking decisions of the early 1970s, special education changed enormously. By 1977 all but one state had adopted legislation calling for the mandatory education of at least the majority of its handicapped children.[16] By 1974 twelve states were required by statute to provide the parent or guardian with due process procedures, and another thirteen states were similarly required by regulations issued by the appropriate state educational agencies.[17] Headway was also made in implementing the appropriate educational mandate. States such as Illinois and Massachusetts established laws or regulations instructing the schools to draw up an educational plan for each handicapped child that included the specific educational objectives to be attained.[18] By late 1975, twenty-two states had either statutes or agency regulations requiring that handicapped children be placed in regular classes at least part of the time.[19]

Despite this impressive progress, the legacy of the courts' ambiguous position toward the schools' paradigms clouds the prospects for future reform. Special education is in the throes of an administrative revolution without a clear intellectual center. The

---

flourish in a regular classroom. Other children may have a specific instructional need —e.g., speech training, learning to read Braille—that is often best carried out in a special segregated class. Mildly retarded children or children with a learning disability may sometimes benefit by having special remedial teaching sessions in segregated settings (or with individual tutors) scheduled unobtrusively within the overall framework of a mainstream education. For handicapped children requiring long stays in hospitals, concurrent periods of segregated education may be unavoidable. And there are certain groups of handicapped children, such as autistic, psychotic, severely retarded, and profoundly retarded children, who can greatly benefit from special programs but who must be taught in segregated settings.[15] The courts recognized the existence of this continuum of necessary instructional settings from the first and spoke of the need to educate the handicapped in the "least restrictive" (i.e., least segregated) setting that was consistent with meeting their special emotional and academic needs.

institutional apparatus of the field is being transformed from top to bottom, but many of the ideas that have traditionally formed the schools' educational practice continue to prevail because they have not yet been subjected to a clear-cut challenge. Nowhere is the lack of a center clearer than in the legislation that will set the tenor of reform in special education for the next generation—the Education for All Handicapped Children Act of 1975. The fundamental character of P.L. 94-142 makes it the natural and inevitable point of departure for any systematic exploration of the ambiguities and inconsistencies of approach that currently plague special education.[20] Deferring to the next chapter a discussion of P.L. 94-142's impact upon the child—mainstreaming and the individualized education plan—we shall first explore the shortcomings of the law's attempt to reform but not to restructure fundamentally the parents' relationship with the school.[21]

Parents' Participation in Educational Decisions: An Unresolved Issue

P.L. 94-142 calls for the parents' active participation in virtually every stage of the schools' formal decision-making process—from the initial diagnosis of the child's handicap, to the evaluation of his educational needs, to constructing and implementing the individualized education program (IEP), to choosing the least restrictive environment in which to educate the child. The contents of the IEP that the school must construct for every handicapped child provides a good idea of the scope of the parents' projected participation. As set forth in the implementation regulations issued by the Department of Health, Education and Welfare, the IEP must consist of the following components:

1. a statement of the child's present levels of educational performance;

2. a statement of annual goals in the child's education, including short-term instructional objectives;

3. a statement of the special educational and related services to be provided to the child, and the extent to which the child will be able to participate in regular educational programs;

4. the projected dates for initiation of services and the anticipated duration of the services; and

5. appropriate objective criteria and evaluation procedures and

schedules for determining, on at least an annual basis, whether the short-term instructional objectives are being achieved.[22]

Unfortunately, the law is unclear about what it means by "active participation." As we noted in chapter 8, the phrase possesses a radically different meaning when it is applied to a patient or to an individual expected to behave in a patientlike way. Instead of meaning that the parent should play an active role in every educational decision made about the child, the phrase means just the reverse of what it seems to mean—that the parents are expected to cooperate with the recommendations of the school's expert, to do their utmost to fulfill the obligations of the sick role.

The public schools, of course, have a long history of treating parents in precisely this manner. As Kirp has observed:

Even where state law [in 1973] requires parental consent before a child is assigned to a special education class, that requirement is often either ignored or satisfied by coercing parental acquiescence. Parents are informed that a particular placement is the only option available and occasionally threatened with criminal sanctions if they reject it. Misunderstanding or intimidation become even more common when parents speak little or no English, and school officials speak only English. Schools are unwilling to discuss sorting decisions with parents for many of the same reasons that they object to formal review: such discussions take time, they require that educational decisions be rendered in a language comprehensible to laymen, and they necessarily invite challenges over matters that the school treats as its prerogative.[23]

Given this history, it seems inevitable that many schools will interpret the law's mandate in conformity with their traditional medical model of how parents should behave. Instead of willingly treating the parent as an adult, they are likely to continue to expect the "mature," "cooperative" parent to behave in a *patientlike* manner in the decision-making process.

If the intent of P.L. 94-142 is to be acheived, the average parent must be able to relate to the public school in the way that a manager relates to a consultant rather than in the way a patient relates to a doctor. To establish this new relationship despite the schools' reliance upon the medical model of client-professional relations will require the kind of clout and savvy that can be provided only by powerful, well-organized parents' groups. By not explicitly encouraging the creation of such countervailing centers of power, the new school law promises far more than it can deliver.

Nowhere is the gap between legislative promise and social reality more readily visible than when one contemplates the kinds of nonpolitical strategies that common sense would suggest are best calculated to help the parent actively participate in the schools' decision making. Merely to work one's way through a compendium of these strategies—such as the following list prepared by Kathryn Gorham and her associates—is to underline the powerlessness of the average parent when the parent must confront the school and its bureaucracy without any institutional supports of his own.

Suggestions for parents:

1. You are the primary helper, monitor, coordinator, observer, record keeper, and decision maker for your child. Insist that you be treated as such. It is your *right* to understand your child's diagnosis and the reasons for treatment recommendations and for educational placement. No changes in his treatment or educational placement should take place without previous consultation with you.

2. Your success in getting as well informed as you will need to be to monitor your child's progress depends on your ability to work with the people who work with your child. You may encounter resistance to the idea of including you in the various diagnostic and decision-making processes. The way you handle that resistance is important. Your best tool is not the angry approach. Some of your job will include the gentler art of persuasion. Stay confident and cool about your own abilities and intuitions. You know your child better than anyone else could. You are, obviously, a vital member of the team of experts.

3. Try to find, from among the many people whom you see, a person who can help you coordinate the various diagnostic visits and results. Pick the person with whom you have the best relationship, someone who understands your role as the principal monitor of your child's progress throughout life and who will help you become a good one.

4. Learn to keep records. As soon as you know that you have a child with a problem, start a notebook. Make entries of names, addresses, phone numbers, dates of visits, the persons present during the visits, and as much of what was said as you can remember. Record the questions you asked and the answers you received. Record any recommendations made. Make records of phone calls too; include the dates, the purpose, the result. It is best to make important requests by letter. Keep a copy of your notebook. Such documentation for every step of your efforts to get your child the service he needs can be the evidence which finally persuades a program director to *give* him what he needs. Without concise records of whom you spoke to, when

you spoke to him, what he promised, how long you waited between the request and the response, you will be handicapped. No one can ever be held accountable for conversations or meetings with persons whose names and titles you do not remember, on dates you cannot recall, about topics which you cannot clearly discuss.

5. Make sure that you understand the terminology used by the professional. Ask him to translate his terms into lay language. Ask him to give examples of what he means. Do not leave his office until you are sure you understand what he has said so well that you can carry the information to your child's teacher, for instance, and explain it to her in a clear, understandable language. (Write down the professional terms too. Knowing them might come in handy some time.)

6. Ask for copies of your child's records. You probably will not get them, but you *could* ask that a tape recording be made of any "interpretive" conference. It is very hard to remember what was said in such conferences.

7. Read. Learn as much as you can about your child's problem. But do not swallow whole what you read. Books are like people. They might be offering only one side of the story.

8. Talk freely and openly with as many professionals as you can. Talk with other parents. Join a parent organization. By talking with people who "have been through it already," you can gain a perspective on your particular problems. Besides, you will receive moral support and will not feel quite so alone. Get information from parent organizations about services available, about their quality. But bear in mind that a particular program might not help your child even though it has proved helpful for another child. Visit programs if you have the time and energy to do so. There is no substitute for firsthand views.

9. Stay in close touch with your child's teacher. Make sure you know what she is doing in the classroom so that, with her help, you can follow through at home. Share what you have read with her. Ask her for advice and suggestions. Get across the idea that the two of you are a team, working for the same goals. Make your child a part of that team whenever possible. He might have some great ideas.

10. Listen to your child. It is *his* point of view that he is giving you, and on that he is an expert.

11. Work hard at living the idea that differentness is just fine—not bad. Your child will learn most from your example. Help him to think of problems as things that can be solved if people work at them together.[24]

The cultural traits, tastes, and abilities presupposed by this sound advice are perhaps most frequently approximated by the tiny fraction of parents who are well-to-do and well educated. Such parents are more likely to be comfortable obtaining information from books. They are more likely than less affluent parents to have experience keeping records and to have a life-style compatible with record keeping. They are more likely to possess enough self-confidence to mingle freely with professionals, to insist that the professional always make himself clear. Being more likely to be of the same race and class as the professional, they are also more likely to be able to ask their questions and raise their objections in ways that do not threaten or irritate the professional. And they are more likely to have the time, the tact, and self-confidence to establish a close working relationship with the teacher—to get across the idea that parent and teacher "are a team."

Yet even the parent who possesses these traits in abundance is likely to encounter severe resistance from many schools. The experience of Mrs. Burns, the mother of a child with a learning disability whose frustrations with the system we quoted in the last chapter, is not atypical. As we saw, the school did not greet Mrs. Burns's aggressive action on behalf of her child with open arms. Although formal recognition was given to her rights to consult with teachers and staff, Mrs. Burns was opposed at every step of the way in her efforts to correct the school's educational errors. She was told that only experts could pronounce on what kinds of programs were appropriate for her child. She was treated as irrational, troublesome, and uncooperative. And although Mrs. Burns finally prevailed, she did not do so entirely unaided—it was only the intervention of one of the school's own, a special expert in learning disabilities, that decided the case in her favor. In short, the school was perfectly willing to let Mrs. Burns talk. But it was incapable of listening to her as an equal—and modifying its educational practices in accordance with her will.

Had Mrs. Burns been black, worn shabby clothes, or mouthed her concerns in the accents of a minority or a white working-class dialect, one doubts if, unaided by the threat of calling upon a political group, she would have received even the runaround she did get from the school. Given the prejudices against all lower-class parents that commonly dominate city school systems, one suspects that the school's reaction would have been much harsher —a threat to put Mrs. Burns's child into an even less appropriate class, or, if Mrs. Burns were a welfare mother, perhaps a word or two with her case worker, in the hope of exerting indirect pressure in order to quiet the troublesome mother.[25]

It would be far too simple to ascribe such examples of school resistance to ill will. As we argued in our general discussion of professional conduct, a lack of good intentions and sincere concern is rarely the cause of the professional's inability to share decision-making power with the parent. Rather, the problem is, in the broadest sense, perceptual. As a general rule, the professional has extraordinary difficulty in seeing when and where he oversteps the bounds of his legitimate authority. We have every confidence that the schools will seek to live up to the spirit of the new educational law. Our fear is that the schools will often ride roughshod over the parent's rights even while sincerely believing that they are honoring these rights to the full.

The gravity of the schools' perceptual problem is well illustrated by the ease with which even the most high-handed and arbitrary professional can genuinely believe that he is implementing guidelines designed to ensure that he shares decision-making power with the parent. Gorham has also set out a typical set of parent-centered guidelines that look like this:

Suggestions for professionals:

1. Have the parent(s) involved every step of the way. The dialogue established may be the most important thing you accomplish. If the parent's presence is an obstacle to testing because the child will not cooperate in his presence, the setup should include a complete review of the testing procedure with the parent. (Remote video viewing or one-way windows are great if you are richly endowed.)

2. Make a realistic management plan part and parcel of the assessment outcome. Give the parents suggestions for how to live with the problem on a day-to-day basis, with the needs of the child, the capacities of the family, and the resources of the community all considered. Let the parents know that you will suggest modifications if any aspect of the management plan does not work.

3. Inform yourself about community resources. Give the parents advice on how to go about getting what they need. Steer them to the local parent organization.

4. Wherever possible, make the parent a team member in the actual diagnostic, treatment, or educational procedures. It will give you a chance to observe how the parent and the child interact.

5. Write your reports in clear, understandable, jargon-free language. Professional terminology is a useful shortcut for your own note-taking; and you can always use it to communicate with others of your discipline. But in situations involving the parent, it operates as an obstacle to understanding. Keep in mind that it is the parent

who must live with the child, help him along, shop for services to meet his needs, support his ego, give him guidance. You cannot be there to do it for him. So the parent *must* be as well informed as you can make him. Information that he does not understand is not useful to him. The goal is to "produce" a parent who understands his child well enough to help him handle his problems as he grows up.

6. Give copies of the reports to parents. They will need them to digest and understand the information in them; to share the information with other people close to the child; and to avoid the weeks or months of record-gathering which every application to a new program in the future will otherwise entail.

7. Be sure the parent understands that there is no such thing as a one-shot, final, and unchanging diagnosis. Make sure he understands that whatever label you give his child (if a label must be given) is merely a device for communicating and one which may have all kinds of repercussions, many of them undesirable. Make sure he understands that it says very little about the child at present and even less about the child of the future. Caution him about using that label to "explain" his child's condition to other people.

8. Help the parent to think of life with this child in the same terms as life with his other children. It is an ongoing, problem-solving process. Assure him that he is capable of that problem solving and that you will be there to help him with it.

9. Be sure that he understands his child's abilities and assets as well as his disabilities and deficiencies. What the child *can* do is far more important than what he cannot do, and the parent's goal thereafter is to look for new abilities and to welcome them with joy when they appear. Urge him to be honest and plain speaking with his child. Tell him that the most important job he has is to respect his child, as well as love him, and to help him "feel good about himself." Tell him that blame, either self-blame or blame of the child, has no part in the scene. *It is no one's fault.*

10. Warn the parent about service insufficiencies. Equip him with advice on how to make his way through the system of "helping" services. Warn him that they are not always helpful. Tell him that his child has a *right* to services. Tell him to insist on being a part of any decision making done about his child.

11. Explain to him that some people with whom he talks (teachers, doctors, professionals of any kind, other parents) may dwell on negatives. Help train the parent not only to think in positives but to teach the other people important in his child's life to think in positives.[26]

The single most important obstacle to implementing these guidelines is often the average professional's special "perceptual disability"—his often tragic inability to view his behavior through the eyes of the parent. Though often willing to acknowledge in principle that the parent has a right to participate actively in educational decisions concerning the child, the expert lacks sociological insight into the perceptual, cognitive, and structural characteristics of his relationship with the parents of a handicapped child, and therefore all too often he misinterprets parental reactions to his abuses of his power. Instead of reexamining his own behavior, the expert interprets parental anger, resistance, challenge, and counterthrust as evidence of the parents' emotional maladjustment, bad faith, or arrogance.

Again, Mrs. Burns's experience is instructive. Except for the suggestion to "steer the parent to a local parent organization," it is perfectly possible that all the school personnel encountered by Mrs. Burns might have heartily subscribed to each of Gorham's recommendations. After all, wasn't the heart of the conflict between the school and the parent over whether or not the school had constructed a "realistic management plan"? And wasn't the fact that Mrs. Burns was able to consult with her child's teachers, and even to force a meeting of the school personnel to discuss her case, proof that the school was ready and willing to see that the parent was "involved every step of the way"?

Unable to see what the parent sees in the encounter, the professional is denied essential feedback. Unable to learn from his mistakes with parents, he risks viewing the consequences of each new abuse of his power as merely confirming his pessimistic appraisal of the abilities of most parents.

Given the professional's tendency to rationalize his mistakes, it seems to us that the only way to break the vicious circle is to provide the parent with the kinds of political support that will make it possible for more parents to carry off what Mrs. Burns managed unaided. If the school is to become more responsive to parents, it must be made very clear to the school that it is often more trouble to resist the parents' complaints than to give in and try to meet them.

When the parent comes from a minority-group background, the professional's feedback and communication problems are greatly increased. In what meaningful sense, one wonders, can the average teacher or special education expert connect with a West Virginia coal miner and his wife, or treat a Hispanic welfare mother as a "team member" in their professional deliberations? A leading professional in the field of rehabilitation has written: "Sometimes we might as well be speaking Chinese as trying to reach disabled young Negroes in slum housing in our big cities, people who have been on relief for three generations. Too often we do not know how to talk to these people or how to make any real contact with them, and it takes a very dedicated and unusual type of professional individual who can emerge from a middle class psychological upbringing to be really effective in this kind of milieu." [27]

In the immediate future, parents' groups and other advocacy groups hold out the best hope for translating the new legal mandates for parental participation into reality. The groups can supply parents with advice, emotional support, legal assistance, and, in some instances at least, professionals willing to offer expert consultations. These groups can also provide the parent with the kind of political clout that forces the expert to stand up and take notice of what the parent has to say and to learn from his mistakes. In the long run, however, economic strategies seem worthy of serious consideration.[28] We see no inherent reason why private contractors could not compete with the school in providing educational services to the child, or why parents should not be given vouchers with which they can elect to purchase instruction from the public school or from a private contractor. Certainly the general quality of the education provided by most public schools is so low that a society that believes in the free enterprise ethic might at least give serious consideration to the "radical" possibility of using free enterprise to improve the quality of education and the accountability of the school to the parents.

When the Consultation Process Breaks Down

P.L. 94-142 comes somewhat closer to confronting the need to change the traditional model of parent-school relationships in its approach to breakdowns in the parents' participation in the schools' decision-making process. When parents feel that their views are being ignored, they have somewhere else to go; they have a formal right to appeal any school decision about their child to a higher authority.[29] Unfortunately, as presently formulated, the provisions concerning procedural due process suffer from the same kinds of limitations that beset the law's attempt to ensure that parents participate actively in the schools' process of decision making. Once again, the law presupposes the possession of cultural styles, personal abilities, and financial resources that few parents possess. Despite the great potential of the reform, the average parent is likely to find that it changes little—unless he can draw upon the resources of a parents' group or some other advocacy group when appealing the school's decision.

The correction of two oversights in the law would greatly improve the parents' ability to take full advantage of the new appeals procedure. At present, the law makes no provision for defraying the costs of outside expert consultations, expert advice, legal counsel, and translation services incurred by parents while exercising their right to an administrative review or while exercising their right, as a last resort, to challenge the decision rendered by the review process in the courts.[30] Just as important, the law fails to confront the problems raised by possibly extensive delays in the due process procedure or in any ultimate court review.

The general outlines of the due process procedure stipulated by P.L. 94-142 are impressive. The school must provide the parents with prior written notice of *every* decision concerning the identification of their child's handicap, the diagnosis of their child's educational needs, the construction of an individualized education program (IEP) for their child, and placement of their child in special and regular programs. By "every" the law means every. Notification must be given if the school is making a decision for the first time (e.g., constructing an IEP for a first-grader), changing an earlier educational decision (e.g., reclassifying a child originally labeled "mildly retarded" as learning-disabled), or responding to a proposal by the parents concerning identification, diagnosis, the IEP, or placement. Unless it is "clearly not feasible," all written communications to the parents must be in their native language.

Should the parents disagree with the school's decision, they are entitled to an "impartial due process hearing." This hearing must be conducted by an educational agency of the state. The law leaves it up to the states to decide whether this hearing takes place at the local, intermediate, or state level. The law stipulates that the official in charge of the hearing cannot be involved in the education or care of the child.

As part of the due process procedure, parents have the right to obtain an independent educational evaluation of their child. Parents also have the right to examine "all relevant" records concerning the child, that is, records concerning the identification of the child's handicap by the school or by medical diagnosis paid for by the school; records concerning the school's evaluation of the child's mental, physical, and emotional abilities; records concerning the school's construction of the individualized education program for the child; and records concerning the actual placement of the child in the school programs stipulated in the IEP.

In all hearings and appeals, the parents as well as the representatives of the school have the following rights: "1) The right to be accompanied and advised by counsel and by individuals with special knowledge or training with respect to the problems of handicapped children; 2) the right to present evidence and confront, cross-examine, and compel the attendance of witnesses; 3) the right to a written or electronic verbatim record of such hearing; and 4) the right to written findings of fact and decisions." [31]

When all possibilities for resolving a dispute within the administrative review structure of the school system are exhausted, a final option remains: the parents (or the school) can go to court.

The educational status of the child during the dispute is defined as follows. If the parents and the school can agree to an interim plan, that plan is to be followed. If agreement is impossible, a child entering school for the first time is to be placed in the standard public school program for able-bodied children, provided the parents agree; if the child is already in an IEP at the time of the dispute, he remains in that program until the dispute is settled.

Before the hearing, the parents are likely to incur substantial expenses if they exercise their right to obtain an independent evaluation of their child from an expert outside the school system. They are also likely to have to spend money for expert advice if they exercise their right to examine all relevant educational records concerning the child. Such records will typically consist of test scores, psychological write-ups, teacher evaluations, and medical diagnoses. If the parents do not feel competent to interpret these records entirely on their own, they will want expert assistance. In looking for help they are certainly not going to want to seek advice from the school's own experts, perhaps the very experts who are responsible for the school decision that the parents are seeking to contest.

A similar oversight characterizes P.L. 94-142's provisions for the hearing. There, the parents possess the right to present witnesses, to submit evidence, to confront, cross-examine, and compel the attendance of witnesses. They also have the right to be accompanied and advised by counsel, the right to a written or electronic verbatim record of the hearing, and a written record of the hearing's findings. Here, too, an unfair financial burden is placed upon the parent of modest means who wants to hire a lawyer for the hearing and pay for the time of experts who testify on the child's behalf. An additional problem exists for parents who are not fluent in English. Although P.L. 94-142 requires that the school make all reasonable efforts to inform the parents about prospective educational decisions in their native language, it makes no provision for providing the parents with free translator services during the hearing, or for translating school records.

If the parents are not satisfied with the results of their administrative appeal, a final recourse remains. They can go to court and initiate a civil suit against the school. The law is silent about the financial burdens that litigation in the courts places on the less affluent parent.

A second shortcoming of P.L. 94-142 is that it does not recognize the need for dispatch in all review procedures concerning the child—after all, children grow older and a year misspent in a school is a serious matter. If even a small fraction of the parents of the 4 million children in the relevant mild-handicap categories challenge the school's classification and instructional decisions, the review process is likely to be swamped. Delay might not misserve children previously labeled "normal" who are later classified as handicapped. As noted earlier, the child cannot be transferred into a new program until any dispute is resolved. Since the great majority of "mildly retarded" and "emotionally disturbed" children and youths do not receive these labels until puberty, the number of parents potentially capable of benefiting from this provision of the law is very great.

By the same token, however, the parent who fails to exercise his right to challenge an original classification decision is at a great disadvantage should he subsequently change his mind and decide to challenge the school's decision. Serious questions are raised by the possibility that some school systems will formally or informally establish administrative procedures that provide for speedy review of challenges to initial classifications and program placement and much slower review of attempts to have the child reclassified or placed in different programs. In the past, only about one child in ten has escaped from a special program for the emotionally disturbed, mildly retarded, or perceptually handicapped and returned to the regular classroom.[32] Should a similar pattern characterize school-initiated proposals to transfer such children back into regular programs (and/or to reclassify them as nonhandicapped), it seems quite likely that parents' proposals for changes in the program and reclassification of the child will greatly outweigh school proposals. In such an eventuality, speedy review of challenges to initial classification and placement and a slow review of attempts to reclassify would be in the institutional interests of the school.

Parents' attempts to monitor the *quality* of the education provided their children seem especially vulnerable to the problem of administrative and judicial delay. As we will see in the next chapter, neither the traditional special school nor the traditional regular school containing some handicapped children has been any more successful at meeting the special instructional needs of mentally normal children with physical handicaps than it has been able to meet the educational needs of any other disadvantaged minority. Here, as well as in questions concerning the discriminatory bias of curriculum materials and intelligence tests, the alert parent is likely to take full advantage of the opportunity provided by the review process for prodding the mediocre public school into giving the child a good education.

The procedural approach to parental rights adopted by P.L. 94-142 attempts to convert matters of substance concerning the child's education into formal issues that are settled by educators not directly involved in the care or education of the child. Overcoming these difficulties should be a major concern of legislators and the courts in the coming years. Ensuring swift administrative review and financial relief for the less than affluent parent would represent a major improvement over the present law. It is quite possible that in many school systems meaningful review will become a reality only when the parent possesses something stronger than the right to an administrative review and, as a last resort, litigation. One possibility worth considering is that the parent should be able to veto any educational decision made concerning the child. A precedent for such a veto is contained in the existing HEW regulations governing educational decisions made about a child referred by the school or any other public agency to a private institution.[33] These regulations stipulate that the private institution cannot initiate any change in the child's individual education program without the consent of *both* the public agency and the parents.

Whatever the changes made in the present legislation, however, it seems clear that more than good laws will be required to restructure the school's traditional, medically inspired conception of its rights and obligations toward the child and the child's parents. The active involvement of parents' groups, advocacy groups, and other parent-centered or parent-run groups is essential. Without extensive group supports, the provisions for parents' participation and procedural due process of P.L. 94-142 risk the fate of most legal rights in our society: that only the wealthy can afford to have them enforced.

Chapter 10

The Handicapped Child in School

From the beginning the revolution in special education has emphasized the need to provide each handicapped child with an "appropriate" set of educational services. Again and again the courts, state legislatures, and educational agencies, and now P.L. 94-142, have stipulated that the school must not employ diagnostic procedures that discriminate against the child, and that a specific plan of educational services must be designed to help the child realize his full intellectual potential. The importance of educating handicapped children as much as possible with able-bodied children has also been recognized by the educational reforms. P.L. 94-142 stipulates that each child is to be educated in the "least restrictive" environment consistent with meeting his educational needs; whenever feasible, the child is to be "mainstreamed," or educated along with his able-bodied peers.*

* The current approach to mainstreaming in educational policy is exemplified by the following statement adopted by the Delegate Assembly of the Council for Exceptional Children in April 1976: "Mainstreaming is a belief which involves an educational placement procedure and process for exceptional children, based on the conviction that each such child should be educated in the least restrictive environment in which his educational and related needs can be satisfactorily provided. This concept recognized that exceptional children have a wide range of special

But what is meant by the terms *appropriate* and *nondiscriminatory*, and what model of tolerance is to inform the schools' attempt to mainstream the child whenever possible? Here, too, P.L. 94-142 tries to resolve basic questions of educational philosophy by means of an exclusively procedural approach. It establishes an impressive set of new administrative mechanisms—the individualized educational program (IEP), the regulations concerning diagnostic procedures, the guidelines for mainstreaming. But each one of these innovations is ultimately no better than the vision of the handicapped child that informs its implementation. If the vision conforms to the schools' long-standing deviance analysis of handicap, the great hopes raised by P.L. 94-142 may be cruelly disappointed regardless of how well or how poorly the schools translate the law's provisions into practice.

Beyond Compensation: The Need for Pluralistic Teaching Strategies

To anyone familiar with the massive educational programs directed at the inner-city child in the 1960s, the strategy that informs the schools' implementation of the IEP for handicapped children may seem all too familiar. During the 1960s minority-group education was also dominated by the social pathology paradigm. The minority-group child was assessed by educational norms constructed for white middle-class children. Where the child fell short of meeting these norms, he was, at least in principle, to receive special help. This help took the form of compensatory programs designed to make good the child's cultural limitations and educational backwardness. The results of these programs were disappointing. Even when the schools proved themselves capable of implementing a technically adequate compen-

---

educational needs, varying greatly in intensity and duration; that there is a recognized continuum of educational settings, which may, at a given time, be appropriate for an individual child's needs; that to the maximum extent appropriate, exceptional children should be educated with non-exceptional children; and that special classes, separate schooling, or other removal of an exceptional child from education with non-exceptional children should occur only when the intensity of the child's special education and related needs is such that they cannot be satisfied in an environment including non-exceptional children, even with the provision of supplementary aids and services."

sation strategy, the benefits for the child were far smaller than had been hoped.

If the compensation strategy does not work with minority-group children, why should it be an effective pedagogical technique with handicapped children? In posing this question we do not dispute the value or the importance of helping the child compensate for the specific functional limitations of his handicap—teaching blind children Braille, providing speech therapy to the palsied child, developing special programs for the child with a reading disability. What concerns us is the vision of the child's learning abilities that informs not only these attempts but virtually all of the educational services that schools provide handicapped children.

Our skepticism about the pedagogical value of the philosophy of compensation is rooted in our analysis of the developmental psychology of handicap in Part Two. Because of the special stigmatizing experiences associated with growing up handicapped, many disabled children and youths move through two radically different social worlds—one in which they are treated as growing human beings by their immediate families and the other in which they are often treated as stigmatized inferiors by peers and by many adults. This second world of experience is *at least* as alien to normal middle-class life as is the world of the inner-city child. Like that of the ghetto child's life, the cumulative impact of the two worlds of handicap can be both impoverishing and highly stimulating. It narrows because most moderately and severely handicapped children are cut off from many of the peer experiences common to able-bodied children their age. This lack of experience with other children is often joined with less firsthand contact with many areas of everyday life—and a greater dependence upon television for vicarious experiences. Yet at the same time, the contrast between his family's love and support and the social stigma the handicapped child encounters inside and outside school (as well as the great stresses often produced by the presence of a handicapped child in the family) is likely to nourish an almost uncanny sociological precocity, an ability to "psych out" others, to manipulate social encounters, and to see through adult pretense —a "street smarts" like the ghetto child's. This tension between a social world in which the child finds himself accepted as a human being and a social world in which the child finds himself treated as a freak, a victim, or an inferior is often rendered even more complex by the presence of a disability that imposes significant limitations on the child—blindness, a problem with fine motor coordination, deafness, or a speech impediment. How these very different physical and social factors interact with cognitive, emotional, and social development is, as we have argued, one of the great unknowns of modern psychology. While we are at least beginning to understand some of the most important ways inner-city children differ from middle-class children in cognitive style, with handicap all we know is that we don't know.

Our ignorance renders the schools' unreflective acceptance of compensatory strategies suspect and possibly perverse. In one stroke a host of crucial pedagogical possibilities and options are ruled out. Whether the schools seek to teach a child a compensatory skill such as Braille or to teach an academic subject such as social studies, the compensatory model biases them in favor of emphasizing the child's weaknesses and limitations rather than helping him to draw upon the strengths and coping abilities that he may have developed in response to the special socialization experiences that attend a handicapped childhood in any social strata.

A Potential Alternative: "Contact Strategies"

As one seeks ways out of the dead end of the compensation approach, the experience of programs directed at minority-group children again seems relevant. In the course of attempting to reach the disadvantaged child, a variety of innovative educational strategies was developed in the 1960s. Called "contact strategies" by Mario Fantini and Gerald Weinstein, they all share an ethnographic perception of the learning needs of the minority-group child.[1] Instead of viewing the child as necessarily less gifted than his middle-class peer, they view him as a foreigner living in a culture where the educational rules are rigged against him. The point of the contact strategies is to help the child learn these rules as efficiently as possible and in a way that emphasizes the dignity and value of his own subculture. The four most important of these strategies for teaching are:

1. mapping out the way inner-city children learn and then adapting one's own teaching techniques to take advantage of the child's cognitive style—for instance, seizing on the game orientation of many inner-city children to teach about the operation of the courts by having the children act out courtroom situations;

2. making the content of the curriculum reflect the child's own interests—building reading skills by using racing magazines, stories about such people as Muhammad Ali, etc., rather than by using standard readers geared to the putative interests of white middle-class children;

3. the use of children teaching children or youths teaching youths—i.e., learning through teaching; and

4. the use of educational assistants or paraprofessionals who come from the same social milieu as the child.[2]

Of course, to call for a concentrated attempt to map out the special learning styles of different groups of handicapped children is one thing. To anticipate what these styles will look like—and how much they will differ from or resemble the style of the able-bodied—is quite another question. In our critique of Piaget, we argued that one task of a pedagogy for the handicapped should be to help a sociologically adept but academically backward child to apply his advanced logical abilities to the range of problems encountered in the classroom. This idea seems to us to be a promising point of departure for research into the handicapped child's learning style—i.e., how do children with different kinds of handicaps and from different class backgrounds learn about adults and peers? Are there some handicapped children who can be most easily reached by appealing to their sociological sophistication, perhaps by constructing games in which they are encouraged to use their great ability to cope with the disorderly aspects of social life? Are there others—perhaps adolescents—who would benefit from such teaching devices as role playing, or courses on the psychology and sociology of able-bodied individuals' responses to handicap, etc.?

Equally intriguing questions are raised by the possibility of adapting the curriculum to the interests of the handicapped child. Again what seems required is an ethnographic perspective, a willingness to watch and carefully test one's observations against one's experience with particular groups of handicapped in given social settings.

Parallel questions are raised by the remaining contact strategies in our list. For example, it seems to us likely that the best way to teach a young deaf child grammatical written English is to have an older deaf child more fluent in written English teach the younger child, using signing as the medium of commentary and nonwritten instruction. Provided that the ultimate effect does not lead to the inadvertent stigmatizing of the disabled individual, it seems to us that having older handicapped children teach younger handicapped children might sometimes be beneficial and, as has been the case with inner-city students, trigger dramatic progress in the older child's studies. The usefulness of handicapped teachers' aides and paraprofessionals also seems to us well worth investigating. Besides serving as positive role models for the child, disabled adults may sometimes be in the best position of all to help the child build bridges between his sociological experience and the demands of the classroom. They may sometimes make the best possible teachers and administrators as well.

Despite the attractiveness of contact strategies, it is essential that an attack on the compensatory approach not replace one oversimplification with another. Handicapped children are individuals. Because of the almost endless ways that different factors can interact in shaping the experience of a handicapped person, it is possible that as a group, handicapped children show an even greater range of individual variation in their learning strategies than able-bodied children of similar background. A pluralistic approach to the disabled should not be wedded to any specific set of diagnostic or educational procedures. By the same token, however, our strategy is more than just another appeal to treat each child as much as possible as an individual. Perhaps it is best described as ethnographic in spirit.

Learning from Psychotherapy

A host of important pedagogical issues are raised by the many parallels between the problems faced by teachers and by psychotherapists.* Psychotherapy and education share a similar gap between the model and the achievement. In both fields new theories or techniques often burst upon the scene by registering impressive successes in small-scale demonstration projects or their equivalents. Yet after the initial success, the effectiveness of the innovation soon wanes and the technique proves to be no more successful than traditional procedures. A similar phenomenon sometimes

---

* Needless to say, we do not have in mind the problems encountered by psychotherapists who apply the social pathology model to psychotherapy. We mean therapists who adopt an ethnographic or pluralistic approach in their therapeutic interventions. For a detailed discussion of a client-centered model of psychotherapy, see chapter 11.

occurs in medicine, where a new operative procedure can yield impressive success in pilot studies but fail to live up to its initial promise in larger and longer-term trials. Here, too, it is plausible to suspect that the enthusiasm and faith of the proponents of innovation are responsible for its initial success. This enthusiasm, communicated to the client, accounts for the apparent initial superiority of the new technique. Later, when the procedure is a routine affair, the client responds to it less favorably. This pattern is often called the "placebo effect" in the medical literature, where it is generally dismissed as at best a medical curiosity and at worst a serious obstacle to assessing the objective value of new medical techniques.* We prefer to view the placebo effect as an example of a widespread social-psychological process in which "healers," "therapists," and "teachers" are sometimes capable of mobilizing their clients' belief systems on behalf of recovery.[3]

A second parallel between education and psychotherapy concerns the overall effectiveness of strategies that seek to apply different theoretical orientations. It is hard to find a single pedagogical approach in the history of public and private education that, when applied on a mass scale, yielded results appreciably superior to any other pedagogical strategy. Psychotherapy is no different in this respect. Despite the great theoretical differences between schools (Freudian, Jungian, Adlerian, Rogerian, etc.), the recovery rates reported by these schools are about the same.

Finally, both education and psychotherapy recognize the importance of charisma. Both speak of the rare individual who is capable of achieving extraordinary results, the master teacher or the great healer. (In psychotherapy such figures often establish their own theoretical schools. In education it is often lamented that the successful teacher is rewarded for his success by being promoted to a nonteaching job.)

At this point, however, the parallel breaks down. So far, only psychotherapy has been willing to study itself from an ethno-

---

* *Placebo* comes from the Latin, "I please." Originally the word referred to any physiologically inert substance (such as a sugar pill) when, thanks to the force of suggestion, that substance produced powerful physiological or psychological effects in a patient—effects that frequently mimicked those produced by well-known drugs such as morphine or alcohol. More recently *placebo* has come to mean any kind of suggestion effect in medicine. The new usage roughly corresponds to what industrial psychologists and economists mean when they speak of the "Hawthorne effect" in industry—i.e., the temporary improvement in industrial output that frequently follows any innovation in a factory quite regardless of the objective economic value of the change.

202

graphic perspective—and somewhat fitfully at that.[4] In the past two decades research has identified a host of findings relevant to education. Some of the most suggestive research concerns the relative importance of personality factors.[5] When successful psychotherapeutic encounters are scrutinized, success often seems related to the client's and the therapist's having compatible personalities (and perhaps compatible tastes in theorizing). Other patterns emerge when the actual therapeutic behavior of experienced and inexperienced therapists is compared. Experienced therapists belonging to different schools have more in common with each other than they have in common with inexperienced therapists who share their theoretical orientation.

Building upon the findings in studies of psychotherapy, we would like to see the following research questions asked in special education (and, for that matter, in minority education as well):

• Ignoring the personality characteristics of the teacher but attending to those of the child as well as to sociocultural variables, can one construct tests that discriminate among children on the basis of the pedagogic strategy that they are most likely to benefit from? For example, can one identify those children who would benefit from a strict authoritarian strategy, those who would benefit from a contact strategy?

• How important is the educational strategy once the teacher's personality is taken into account? Is there any value in trying to devise ways to match children with teachers on the basis of compatible cognitive styles and personalities? And if so, would this matching process reduce or eliminate the need to concern oneself *at all* with different pedagogical theories?

• What is a good teacher? Anyone somewhat familiar with education can point to master teachers who perform educational miracles with children the school has given up on. Do these teachers share personality characteristics? Can one speak of an archetypal personality profile (or behavior profile) equally potent in all sociocultural settings and with all groups of disabled children? Must finer-grain distinctions be made, ones that identify master teachers for a given milieu and perhaps for a given subset of all handicap groups with it?

Like the other research proposals we make in this chapter, there are many practical barriers. One cannot rush into the classroom with a preconceived hypothesis, issue a questionnaire, and write up the results. Every step of the way will require painstaking ethnographic field work in which the greatest emphasis of all is placed upon watching teachers and students interact and then testing every tentative hypothesis against further naturalistic observations. To perform this kind of work requires highly experienced clinical observers who are capable of devoting five or ten years of their professional lives to a project whose success is by no means assured at the outset. Again, the example set by Selma Fraiberg and her colleagues in their study of the development of blind infants and young children is exemplary.

Diagnostic Procedures That Discriminate Instead of Diagnose

Educators have come to accept the need for diagnostic tests that do not penalize able-bodied minority-group children for their cultural differences. Because of the schools' fierce resistance to the idea of pluralistic assessment criteria for any social group, P.L. 94-142's insistence upon diagnostic criteria that do not discriminate racially or culturally represents a great advance over traditional practices in special education. However, this advance is not the only one needed. Tests need to be devised that take into account the special socialization experiences of handicapped children from many different cultural backgrounds. Special education has not even begun to confront this crucial issue. Both in theory and in practice the schools fail to take seriously the possibility that many of the disabled belong to a cultural minority whose norms for optimal development may differ in significant ways from *both* the norms of able-bodied minority-group children *and* the norms of white middle-class children.

The root problem is again the deviance analysis of disability that pervades the schools' approach to handicapped children. Virtually all diagnostic procedures in special education measure the child's mental ability or social development according to norms that are appropriate for able-bodied members of his social group or able-bodied children in general. The handful that attempt to establish special norms for children with specific handicaps do so in a way that renders the norms meaningless for educational purposes because of the educators' reliance upon a deviance methodology in test construction.

The flaws of the schools' conventional intelligence tests are typical of what is wrong with its deviance approach to the handicapped child's abilities.* Consider first the intelligence tests' presumption that the handicapped child has partaken of the experiences common to able-bodied children of his ethnic group and social class. Clearly, to the extent that the handicapped child is excluded from this normal range of experience—many children are—the test measures their cultural deprivation, not their intellectual ability. Thus, questions such as "How far is it from New York to Chicago?" or "What does COD mean?"—which are found on the Wechsler Intelligence Scale for Children (WISC)—presuppose that the child travels or is familiar with different kinds of mail.† Again and again in our talks with special education teachers we have been struck by how little one can assume about the moderately or severely handicapped child's mastery of such everyday knowledge, especially if the child has lower-class parents. A child who doesn't know how to use a public phone or how to ride a bus will be penalized by the intelligence tests' premium on general knowledge about the world.

A somewhat different problem is presented by the special emphasis such tests place on vocabulary. Precisely because many handicapped children have socially impoverished or socially deviant lives, one would expect their vocabulary to depart from the vocabulary of their peers. At the very least, this difference will lower the tests' reliability. Often, we suspect, it will represent a subtle way of penalizing the child for being different.

A second major way intelligence tests discriminate against handicapped children is the premium these tests place on speed, short-term memory, sensory ability, and motor coordination. The child with cerebral palsy is especially vulnerable to this kind of discrimination. Testers employ bits and pieces of tests designed for able-bodied children and take great liberties in both test administration and test interpretation. As a result of what one authority has described as a "smorgasbord approach," intelligence estimates for such children are frequently pulled out of a hat and then turned into an authoritative-looking number.[7] Just as crucially, the mechanical difficulties of conventional test administration divert the tester's attention from the basic fallacy of attempt-

---

* By intelligence tests we mean tests administered individually as well as group tests. According to school convention, IQ tests are individually administered, whereas aptitude tests are group tests.[6]

† Many of the schools' most widely used tests—such as the Wechsler—are also biased in favor of white middle-class children.

ing to assess the palsied child by the norms of any group of able-bodied children.

Yet another kind of discrimination stems from the logical structure of intelligence tests. Although it has been said many times, the point bears repeating here: for all their usefulness in helping the conventional school single out good educational risks among the able-bodied of all social classes, intelligence tests are not diagnostic devices and shed no light whatsoever upon the *causes* of poor or mediocre performance in a conventional setting. This limitation is not a result of the tests' present state of development but stems from the underlying logic of their design. An IQ or aptitude test has been designed through a process of trial and error to produce scores that correlate fairly well with subsequent academic performance. Why these scores correlate well is anyone's guess—as is immediately apparent when one asks a tester why, for example, vocabulary items bulks so large on intelligence tests. The answer given is circular rather than explanatory: vocabulary scores have been found to correlate fairly highly with academic performance.[8]

Useful perspective on what an intelligence test score means is provided by the following example. Suppose we know two things about a child who has limb deformities like Peter's, the boy with short arms and incomplete hands: first, that he does poorly in his schoolwork, and second, that his IQ falls within the mildly retarded range, say at 65.* Our instinctive reaction given these two pieces of information is to use the low IQ to "explain" the poor school performance. We say, "Peter does poorly in school because he is mildly retarded," and the explanation seems to shed light on his academic problems.

Suppose, however, that we replaced the phrase "mildly retarded" with the only piece of information about Peter that is actually provided to us by his IQ score of 65—i.e., "does poorly on a test whose scores correlate fairly well with academic performance." Now our sentence reads, "Peter does poorly in school because he does poorly on a test whose scores correlate fairly well with academic performance." Though the sentence is awkward, it does bring out into the open the fact that one cannot explain school performance by pointing to a score that merely correlates with school performance. Indeed, for all the light that Peter's IQ sheds

* The full case history appears in Appendix 1.

on his poor work, one might as well have spared oneself the expense of the test and simply said, "Peter does poorly in school because he does poorly in school."

A similar conceptual flaw vitiates the special intelligence tests that educators have developed for blind children. These tests rank the blind child relative to the test performance of a representative group of other blind children. Judged narrowly by the traditional goals of intelligence tests for the able-bodied, the tests are fairly satisfactory: retest reliability is high, and there is a fairly good correlation between test scores and academic performance.[9] To the extent that IQ tests for the blind can predict academic performance, these tests serve a useful, if minimal, screening function. Like their counterparts for the able-bodied, these tests identify a small subset of blind children who can be expected to do fairly well in the conventional special classroom and who, one can assume, are being reasonably served by existing educational procedures. However—and this is the singular weakness of the logic of the conventional intelligence test—the IQ test for the blind can say very little about the mental potential of the vast majority of blind children who neither score exceptionally well on the test nor do exceptionally well in school.*

All of the intelligence tests that we have discussed embody a deviance analysis of the handicapped child's abilities. Instead of seeking to identify the special characteristics of the child's cognitive strategies, they assess the child according to norms that make no allowance for these differences. Tests designed for able-bodied children assess the handicapped by norms that may have no relevance whatsoever to the child's intellectual development. The special tests designed for blind and deaf children perpetuate the normalist fallacy in a more subtle guise, by remaining faithful to the logic of the conventional intelligence test.

At the risk of repetition, let us emphasize this point: an IQ test for able-bodied children or even one designed specifically for handicapped children can identify good academic risks (given conventional teaching procedures), but it cannot diagnose the causes of poor or mediocre school performance. As with other minority-group children, we know that stigma, emotional problems, the

---

* Educators have also constructed intelligence tests for deaf children along similar lines. But these tests are unsuccessful even by the standards of conventional psychometrics. Try as they will, testers have not been able to design a test for deaf children that correlates very well with academic performance.[10]

strains of family life, and the special premium that the social situation of handicap puts upon using one's intelligence in areas of life not tapped in schoolwork all play a dominant role in limiting many handicapped children's academic achievement. For these children the impact of any conventionally designed intelligence test is likely to be negative. The schools have demonstrated time and time again their predisposition to misread the significance of intelligence test results and to transform them into self-fulfilling prophecies. It is essential that handicapped children who are good academic risks in a conventional setting be identified. But it is also essential for the schools to recognize that any test score that suggests even moderately below-average intellectual potential probably is revealing more about the harmful impact of the child's social experiences than it is about his "innate" ability to learn.

If all this isn't bad enough, the schools' basic diagnostic oversight is compounded by the testers' failure to design any tests that even try to honor all the social variables that may cause the path of a handicapped child's optimal cognitive development to diverge from able-bodied norms. The special tests for the blind and the deaf make no allowance for ethnicity and social class. Tests specifically designed for minority-group children are aimed at the able-bodied (some of whom are mislabeled handicapped by conventional intelligence tests); as a consequence, the black or Hispanic child with a major physical handicap is judged by the same ethnic group norms as his able-bodied peer. And the mainstay of the schools' psychometric effort—intelligence tests with a white, able-bodied, middle-class bias—ignores all three factors.*

Experienced workers in the field of handicap readily acknowledge the serious weakness of intelligence tests, and, indeed, all psychometric procedures as diagnostic tools.[11] But even experts in special education frequently overlook both the theoretical reasons for these shortcomings and the need to reckon with at least social class and ethnicity when designing diagnostic instruments. Just as important, school personnel entrusted with making diagnostic decisions about the child rarely display the caution and pragmatism that characterize the way that the best diagnosticians treat all formal assessment procedures.

---

* Gender is also likely to be of critical importance in helping to determine the kinds of cognitive strategies that a child with a given handicap will develop in his or her social milieu.

Strategies to Minimize Mislabeling

If P.L. 94-142 does not speak to the diagnostic needs of the handicapped child, does the law at least propose an adequate set of diagnostic procedures for eliminating the schools' traditional over-labeling of minority-group children as mentally retarded and emotionally disturbed? Because decisions about emotional disturbance are much less dependent upon testing procedures than upon clinical judgment, the law's guidelines will probably have little effect in and of themselves upon the schools' traditional abuses of this handicap classification. (However, the provisions for procedural due process discussed in the preceding chapter could dramatically reduce this and all kinds of mislabeling if parents take full advantage of them.) The impact of the new rules on decisions concerning mental retardation is more complex. If faithfully implemented by the schools, the new procedures will undoubtedly reduce the extent to which minority-group children are erroneously classified as mentally retarded. But for all their value, the new reforms are flawed in ways that make it virtually certain that many minority-group children will continue to be over-labeled as retarded. Just as importantly in the long run, the new reforms perpetuate some of the schools' most harmful misconceptions about the nature of psychometric assessments—misconceptions that harm handicapped children as well as those able-bodied children who are mislabeled as mentally retarded.

We have no quarrel with the law's insistence that whenever possible all diagnostic tests must be administered in the child's native language or mode of communication, a procedure that seems to us to represent elementary common sense. Our concern focuses upon the vagueness in the law's attempt to protect the child against the school's traditional overreliance upon intelligence tests. The law stipulates that no single assessment procedure "shall be the sole criterion for determining an appropriate educational placement." [12] As generally understood in the special education literature, the "multiple-criteria" strategy mandated by P.L. 94-142 most often means ad hoc modification of traditional assessment procedures that reduces the numbers of children who are labeled "retarded" but that retains the white, able-bodied, middle-class bias of the school's traditional reliance upon the single criterion of an intelligence test score. Instead of assessing the child's learning potential by means of one discriminatory test (the conventional intelligence test), the multiple-criteria approach assesses the child's ability by means of a battery of tests, *each one* of which is biased —in tests of verbal ability, reading comprehension, or social maturity, as well as conventional intelligence tests.

Just as important, the law's multiple-criteria strategy encourages the school to adopt potentially self-defeating pedagogical strategies. Faced with an array of scores on tests that presume to assess different aspects of the handicapped child's mental abilities, the school finds it natural to attack the child's academic weaknesses in isolation from his strengths. Instead of attempting to build bridges between areas in which the child functions well academically or socially and areas where the child functions poorly, the school provides the same remedial instruction to *all* children who do poorly in a given academic area. This approach is bad for the school, which can hardly attempt to build bridges between areas of competence and weakness when the members of a remedial reading class have little else in common academically and socially save their poor reading. And it probably contributes to the stigma and low status that remedial classes have acquired in many schools. It is a common observation that children who do especially poorly in some or all of their school subjects often try to limit as much as possible the impact of this poor performance on their self-image and their social image. One is poor in math and good in everything else. One is a rotten student but a great athlete. By defining the remedial project as an attack upon the child's academic weakness in isolation from the rest of his character, the school can seriously undermine the child's attempt to maintain his sense of self-worth and dignity. Instead of turning the remedial class into an experiment in which teacher and child attempt to extend the area of the child's academic and social conquests, the class defines the child in terms of his perceived "failures" and his status as a stigmatized deviant.

Perhaps nowhere are the shortcomings of the multiple-criteria approach more clearly visible than in the way that it performs a diagnosis of mental retardation. As Jane M. Mercer notes, the school interprets the labels "educable retarded" and "trainable retarded" to refer to "persons who are presumed to be constitutionally subnormal and to have a very low potential for learning." [13] Given the extensive evidence of cultural bias in all conventional psychometric assessment procedures, it seems self-evident that one cannot perform the diagnosis of constitutional subnormality and very low learning potential for a lower-class white child or a minority-group child or handicapped child of any race or class unless the child scores in the retarded range on *all* the tests administered to him. A score in the normal range on any one of the tests would suggest that either the other tests were not fairly assessing the child's potential because of their cultural and class bias, or that emotional or other experimental factors prevented the child from functioning up to his full potential on the other tests. Except when there is convincing neurological evidence of brain damage or a genuine learning disability, the following generalization seems to reflect the present state of psychological and educational knowledge: any child who has mastered the cognitive strategies necessary for adequate performance in one area of social or academic life probably possesses the innate ability to master the necessary cognitive strategies for adequate performance in other areas of social and academic life.

Unfortunately, the multiple-criteria strategy, as usually applied in special education, embraces a very different approach to the diagnosis of retardation. To escape the label of "retarded," a child must score above the retarded range on a completely arbitrary number of the tests that are administered to him. For example, Garrison and Hammill's influential study of children placed in classes for the retarded in the five-county greater Philadelphia school system employs five separate tests and counts as retarded any child who failed more than one of the tests.[14]

Mercer has recently developed a far more promising version of the multiple-criteria approach.[15] Her "pluralistic evaluation procedure" consists of two different parts—the administration of a conventional IQ test and the administration of a questionnaire to the child's parents that is designed to assess the child's general level of social behavior in nonacademic situations. In interpreting a child's test scores, Mercer compares her score with those obtained by other children from similar sociocultural backgrounds. Only a child whose IQ and social adaptation scores are very poor in comparison to the norms of his sociocultural group is labeled "retarded." Thus, no absolute meaning is assigned to any test score. Knowing, for example, that a child's IQ score is 75 does not allow one to say that his IQ is very close to the traditional psychometric definition of mild retardation (IQ's in the 50 to 69 range). One must also know the mean IQ scores obtained by the child's sociocultural peers. An IQ of 75 falls within the normal range for Mexican-American children from lower-class Spanish-speaking homes; it falls well within the retarded range for white upper-middle-class children.

Especially noteworthy is Mercer's emphasis upon identifying areas of nonacademic functioning in which the child performs near his subculture's norms. Only children who matched the criterion for retarded for their subculture on both the intelligence test and the social adaptation test are labeled "retarded." Thus, Mercer's "double failure" criterion means that the hypothesis that a child is retarded will be rejected whenever the tester finds a single convincing example that the child functions normally in some area of social life.

Mercer's attempt to construct a pluralistic intelligence test for minority children is far from satisfactory. Many of her decisions about proper test instruments and sociocultural norms seem arbitrary.[16] And when she argues that "a pluralistic clinical perspective would require abandoning the supracultural stance of the customary clinical perspective when evaluating persons who *are not biologically damaged*" (italics added), she inadvertently perpetuates some of the most unfortunate of our culture's stereotypes about the handicapped.[17]

Still, Mercer's work points the way toward the kinds of diagnostic procedures that would encourage and in some degree permit the pursuit of pluralistic educational strategies by the schools —strategies that would honor the sociocultural diversity of our society as well as the special socialization experiences of the handicapped. We are especially impressed by the way that Mercer's pluralistic approach emphasizes the need to perform fine-grain discriminations among children who do very poorly on conventional intelligence tests.

Mercer's own work clearly distinguishes in principle among four groups of children who are often labeled "educably retarded" or "trainably retarded" and treated similarly. These are (1) the "quasi-retardate," who fails Mercer's pluralistic IQ norm but passes Mercer's pluralistic social adaptation norm; (2) the "behaviorally maladjusted," who passes the pluralistic IQ norm but fails the social adaptation norm for his sociocultural group; (3) the "low normal," who passes both the pluralistic IQ and social adaptation forms; and (4) the "nondisabled retardate," who fails both the pluralistic IQ norm and the pluralistic social adaptation norm.[18]

Distinctions such as these clearly point the way to much more sophisticated educational programs for children who do poorly in school. Speaking of those children who fail the pluralistic IQ norms but pass the pluralistic social adaptation norms, Mercer suggests a strategy that we would like to see followed with all handicapped children, as well as with all minority-group and lower-class children: "Having demonstrated by his adaptive behavior that he can cope intelligently with nonacademic situations, programs could be developed . . . based on the assumption that he has problem-solving ability not evaluated in the intelligence test situation. Programs could be addressed to his specific verbal and cognitive difficulties on the assumption that he has the potential for learning, given appropriate educational experiences." [19]

Beyond the Deviance Analysis: Pluralistic Diagnostic Strategies

A first step toward the construction of better diagnostic procedures would be to apply Mercer's pluralistic approach to handicap. Handicapped children should, whenever possible, be assessed by pluralistic norms that explicitly compare them to children with similar handicaps and similar sociocultural backgrounds. Although there are many practical difficulties in constructing tests that meet this objective, we believe that even imperfect tests modeled fairly literally on Mercer's own tests for minority children could greatly reduce the mislabeling of disabled children as retarded.

However, perhaps the most important benefit of a commitment to pluralistic assessment strategies is the kinds of problems that this commitment would force the field to confront directly. Many special education specialists are mesmerized by the mechanical difficulties of communicating with a deaf, blind, or speech-disabled child. They are perplexed by the obstacles that stand in the way of giving these children the same IQ test that able-bodied children receive. Despite the cautions of some of the leading figures in the field, little attention is paid to what could be learned from conventional tests even if they could be easily administered to these groups of children. A commitment to pluralistic assessment criteria would force the educator to reexamine some of his most cherished stereotypes about the disabled child. Rather than judging the child's social and emotional development by standards constructed for the able-bodied, the educator would be forced to ask what is normal for a child of a given age, with a given disability, in a given sociocultural group. Instead of assuming that all children who score in the lowest 3 percent on intelligence tests are retarded, the tester would have to determine through experimentation where to establish cutoff points for his tests—a task that will once again require the cultivation of an ethnographic sensibility. Most important of all, a commitment to a pluralistic perspective will lead the educator to ask questions about the child's development in a way that will reveal once and for all the intellectual poverty of the traditional psychometric approach.

When dealing with children suspected of being retarded, we want our tests to distinguish between children who have very low innate intellectual potential and children who function poorly in school and even on conventional measures of social adaptation developed with able-bodied individuals but who nonetheless display normal or above-normal cognitive sophistication in some areas of their social life (for instance, in their ability to manipulate adults to their advantage).

When dealing with other groups of handicapped schoolchildren, we are just as interested in the overall landscape of their cognitive functioning; discrepancies between the level of sophistication of academic and nonacademic performance are potentially just as important for the child who performs satisfactorily in school because such discrepancies can reveal a pattern of social backwardness that also requires special recognition. For all children with different bodies, one diagnostic concern should dominate: identify the child's areas of cognitive strength so that one can then seek to build bridges that will allow the child to apply his most sophisticated reasoning strategies to problems in other areas of his life where he displays less developmental sophistication.

In pursuing these vital questions, psychometricians inevitably will have to reckon with the developmental theories of Piaget. Unfortunately, two major obstacles stand in the way of employing a Piagetian approach to surveying the overall cognitive abilities of handicapped children.

The first stems from the continued vigor of a set of misconceptions about conventional IQ tests that were discarded in mainstream experimental psychology decades ago. These misconceptions, which center upon the belief that an IQ score measures a child's cognitive development, are evinced most dramatically in the practice of translating a disabled child's IQ into an "equivalent" mental age. Even today one finds leading figures in the assessment of the disabled perpetuating this naïve misunderstanding of mental development.

The evidence that IQ's in or near the mildly retarded range correlate poorly with mental age or intellectual development comes from many quarters. Our discussion of the overlabeling of minority children points to one line of evidence. Most minority-group children who score poorly on IQ tests function normally outside the classroom. Since functioning adequately outside the classroom often requires as much intelligence—but applied to different ends--as functioning well in the classroom, the poor correlation between social behavior and IQ probably reflects a poor correlation between the logical complexity of a child's social behavior and his IQ.[20] Similar conclusions are suggested by data from much more culturally homogeneous societies such as Great Britain and Sweden.[21] Evidence that a normal IQ correlates poorly with mental development is provided by Zigler and his associates in comparative studies of low-IQ (mildly retarded range) and normal-IQ children who live in custodial institutions.[22] Contrary to the assumptions of many earlier investigators (including Piaget and Inhelder), Zigler found that both groups of children functioned at the same developmentally immature level: judged by developmental measures, the normal-IQ children were cognitively retarded.

Finally, there is a growing body of data that suggest that the correlation between Piagetian stage of cognition and IQ is equally poor at the other end of the IQ scale.[23] Thus, it appears that a ten-year-old with an IQ of 150 does not solve problems in the same way as a fifteen-year-old with the same IQ. He is, as it were, "kid smart" (i.e., concrete operations smart), not "adolescent smart" (i.e., formal operations smart). Though smarter than most other ten-year-olds, he appears to use the same family of cognitive strategies and suffers from the same kinds of cognitive blind spots as ten-year-olds of average intelligence. Similarly, a ten-year-old with an IQ of 50 does not employ the mental problem-solving strategies of an average five-year-old, although the parents of retarded children are often given a "mental age" equivalent of their child's IQ.

The second obstacle to employing an ethnographic approach in the assessment of the handicapped child's mental ability and educational needs stems from the usual way in which Piagetian theory is applied in mainstream educational psychology. We have already criticized this practice tacitly in chapter 7, where we argued that existing Piagetian tests tap too narrow an area of intellectual behavior and that before we can adequately assess a child's actual levels of intellectual performance, we will have to apply a Piagetian approach to the study of his interpersonal and emotional behavior.

Further perspective on the limitations of existing Piagetian tests is gained if one recalls that Piaget started his career by examining the wrong answers and the explanations for answers given by children to questions on the French IQ test, the Binet-Simon IQ test. Beginning with an interest in the same domain of behavior as the tester, Piaget has in general concentrated upon understanding the developmental path taken by the child in this domain, rather than going beyond it. Because this point is often not appreciated, it is good to underline it. As we saw in chapter 7, Piagetian tests are designed to elucidate the logical characteristics of the kinds of problem-solving behaviors deemed to be involved in academic performance.[24] As in all scientific enterprises, the progressive elaboration of Piaget's testing instruments has resulted from a mixture of luck, trial and error, intuition, and happy inspiration. At each step along the way, the direction to be taken has been indicated by the needs of the theoretical enterprise as defined by the structure of the theory. Aptitude testers look at the same family of behaviors as Piagetians, and they draw upon similar creative forces, but here these forces are used to a different end. The evolution of aptitude tests has been guided by the need for performance on the test to correlate strongly with academic performance and, as a check on the progress of the test in its early stages of development, the need to correlate highly with established aptitude tests. Because of these different aims and constraints, it is hardly surprising that performance on Piagetian tests should correlate so poorly with performance on aptitude tests, even though both Piagetian and aptitude testers begin by looking at the same kinds of problem-solving behavior. Like two hereditary lines descended from a common ancestral stock, Piagetian tests and aptitude tests have evolved away from each other in response to the different selective pressures generated by Piaget's desire to study logical structure and the desire of aptitude testers to predict academic performance with ever greater precision.

Earlier, we saw that the school classification lawsuits of the 1970s focused on the schools' discriminatory overlabeling of minority-group children as mildly retarded or emotionally disturbed. P.L. 94-142 fails to integrate this important legal tradition with an awareness of the special ways that traditional diagnostic procedures can discriminate against handicapped people of all races and social classes. Instead, the new law concerns itself almost exclusively with measures for reducing the mislabeling of able-bodied minority-group children. These measures, although imperfect, are important, and they will represent a landmark achievement if and when the schools fully implement them. However, a law that seeks to transform the content of special education in America must attempt more than simply sparing the able-bodied minority-group child the added stigma of handicap. The central diagnostic mission of the field is to diagnose correctly the needs and abilities of children of all backgrounds who have real biological handicaps—blind children, crippled children, children suffering from chronic disease such as diabetes, children with genuine reading or math disabilities. Here the new school legislation falls down badly. Admittedly, the schools' continued misunderstanding of the nature of intelligence tests and the narrowness of traditional Piagetian procedures represent serious obstacles to the construction of pluralistic assessment procedures for handicapped children. But until these obstacles are removed, the claims in Public Law 94-142 that "diagnostic procedures and methods have advanced to the point that . . . state and local educational services can . . . provide effective education to meet the needs of handicapped children" will have a hollow ring.

Mainstreaming

A common flaw vitiates P.L. 94-142's conception of nondiscriminatory diagnostic procedures and the individualized education program: both reforms are good, but they don't go far enough because they leave untouched the domination of the social pathology paradigm in education for the handicapped. Something similar is the cause for the third pillar of the "appropriate education" mandate—the commitment to educate handicapped children as much as possible with able-bodied children rather than to segregate them from the general school population as has generally been the practice in the past. Here, too, the force of a good reform is likely to be blunted by the educator's traditional vision of the handicapped child's needs and abilities.

At the very least, mainstreaming promises to provide the parent with an invaluable set of options—being able to place his child in the best public school in the community, being able to shift the child back and forth between mainstreamed and segregated settings in accord with the child's overall needs, being able to use the threat of changing the child's placement to force the school to improve its services to the child, being able to extricate the child from any educational setting, mainstreamed or segregated, that is clearly disastrous to the child's mind or emotions. But this new ability to pick and choose between the best (or, more realistically, the least bad) options offered by segregated and mainstreamed options in the community is not enough. The animating vision of the new mandate is more generous. It is to bring the handicapped child into the mainstream of childhood. It is to end his exclusion from social experience appropriate to children his age. It is to provide him with an education that no longer reinforces—however inadvertently—society's traditional misconceptions and stereotypes about the abilities of handicapped individuals. It is the same vision that informs school desegregation for minority children: to improve education by breaking down the barriers of prejudice and misunderstanding that have excluded the handicapped from the mainstream of American life for so long.

For all these reasons, the last thing we should want is for the school to introduce into the mainstreamed classroom all the discriminatory practices that so often have made segregated special education a vast "factory for failure."

Perhaps the greatest single obstacle to achieving the positive goals of mainstreaming stems from the continued dominance of the social pathology model in special education. Most teachers recognize that stigma and prejudice are often far more constricting to a child than the strictly biological limitations of his handicaps. Yet when they intervene in the child's life, they often act upon this knowledge negatively, treating the sociological status quo of handicap as a given, a "fact of life" that is as immutable as the biological limitations of severe mental retardation. Depending upon the teacher's perceptions of the child's intelligence, the social pathology paradigm suggests the following basic strategies. For the gifted child, do whatever is possible to help the child fully compensate for the social and biological limitations of his handicap because he has a fighting chance to succeed as an adult on society's terms. For the average or below-average child, do what one can to help the child exploit the inferior social options that greet him in childhood and await him in adulthood. For all children, place special emphasis upon inculcating a healthy acceptance of their social and biological fate.

Taken one by one, all these strategies are unimpeachable. The gifted child needs to be given every possible chance to excel academically because intellectual success provides one of the few ways for him to make it into the social mainstream. Less talented children need programs that are matched to their abilities. And nearly every child with a major disability needs help in coming to terms with the injustice of his social and biological fate. Yet traditionally, these individually good strategies have combined with other expressions of the social pathology paradigm—the emphasis upon compensatory pedagogical strategies, the use of diagnostic procedures that assess all the handicapped by the norms of able-bodied society—to create an extremely destructive mind set in special education. It is a mind set that leads to an almost perfect disassociation between the teacher's analysis of the social basis of most handicaps and the teacher's actual practice in the classroom.

Many special education teachers criticize the culture's undervaluation of the abilities of handicapped people. Explicitly or tacitly they reject lay society's disease diagnosis of disability and the handicapped role. Yet because of their constant emphasis upon helping the child to compensate or to adjust, these same teachers frequently treat their students as small patients. A disabled adult active in programs to improve special education related the following experience to us:

Recently our group did some work with a program designed to teach handicapped kids basic living skills. You know, the things a non-disabled kid takes for granted—like how to use a pay telephone, or how to buy a dress in a store. Even self-care skills in some instances. Well, the strange thing is this. We frequently find in our classroom demonstrations that the able-bodied teacher—and her able-bodied helper—don't give the kids a chance to ask questions or enter into the discussion. Instead, the teacher and her helper do all the talking for them—much as a patient's personal physician will do all the talking when an outside consultant comes into the hospital to examine the patient. When we point this out after the class to the teacher and suggest that next time she try to get the children actively involved in the discussion, the usual reply is "Say, that's a good idea. Why didn't I think of that myself?" It's tragic. Even people who have worked with handicapped children all their lives sometimes fall into the trap of seeing them as passive onlookers on life, rather than as kids who can ask questions for themselves and who are perfectly capable of taking responsibility for many areas of their life right now.

Just as crucially, "realism" about the diminished future that awaits many of the handicapped has traditionally led many teachers to *overcompensate*, to hold unrealistically low academic standards. Knowing what awaits the child as an adult, the school has sought to "spare" the child "needless" frustration and disappointment by actively foreclosing the child's intellectual and psychosocial options during childhood. Believing that a second-class adulthood awaits the child, many teachers have believed that it is more humane to provide the child with a second-class childhood as well. The rationale for this strategy is, as we have seen, very different from the rationale provided by lay society when it imposes the handicapped role upon the child. Society believes that the child's biological limitations doom him to be a perpetual patient who must be excused from the normal role expectations of childhood. The special education teacher emphatically rejects this exaggeration of biology. But by treating society as if it were as immutable as biology, she has frequently subjected her pupils to an academic double standard that ends up treating them as if they were indeed perpetual patients.

Nowhere is this convergence between lay society's model of tolerance toward the disabled and the teacher's professional vision of the child more destructive (or more striking) than in the virtual exclusion of science from special education curricula. Although common sense would suggest that a scientific career is particularly suited to the physical limitations of many mentally normal handicapped children, common sense has not prevailed in special education. Frequently, science has been considered "too difficult" for sensorily and physically handicapped children.[25] In other instances, the need to modify standard laboratory equipment to allow blind and physically disabled children to perform experiments has provided the schools with an excuse for not offering an adequate science curriculum. In still other instances, educators have claimed that physically and sensorily handicapped children are "not interested" in science—a claim that must be considered in the light of the finding by two recent surveys that "most handicapped students in public and private schools simply have not been exposed to science teaching."[26]

Whatever has inspired special educators to put science out of the reach of seriously handicapped children, the choice has had tragic results. The American Association for the Advancement of Science (AAAS) is one of the few groups recently to have taken an active interest in science education for the handicapped. According to the AAAS Project on the Handicapped, "There are virtually no professional scientists who have been handicapped since birth or early childhood." [27] The project staff believes that the elementary schools are primarily responsible: "Without an introduction to science vocabulary and to development of concepts and problem-solving in elementary schools, the student is unable to continue to higher levels." [28]

Fortunately, many schools, parents' groups, and disabled adult groups are attempting to correct this long-standing denial of the child's future. Although basic reforms in the schools' approach have not taken place, there has been a proliferation of programs that supplement the conventional curriculum by providing the handicapped child with information about possible careers and by permitting the child to meet active disabled adults with whom he or she can identify. The Center for Independent Living, a disabled self-help group based in Berkeley, California, has been a pioneer in developing such programs. In the words of C.I.L.'s Larry Biskamp:

The point of our career program is to bring disabled people into the school who are successful independent adults. One thing most handicapped children desperately need is good role models. It's vital that every child realize that he or she has a future. Unless you believe that you have a future, how can you think of yourself as a person? The career program is a first step in trying to bring home to these kids that they have a decent future waiting for them after they leave high school. We say to them: "Here are some of the ways to cope with being disabled. They're not the dead ends you've learned to expect from life." We say: "Look at us. We're not dead ends. We lead independent lives. We're grown up like your parents." And right away, something is kindled—an awareness of the vast possibilities for change, a way of looking at yourself differently, a way of seeing yourself as something more than a helpless cripple, as something more than a person forever isolated from society, a person who can be an active participant. It's also very important to know that when your parents die you won't have to be placed into a nursing home. That's the other side to a disabled kid's thinking about his future, and one which the career program can also begin to address.

Despite these beginnings, many teachers and administrators in special education continue to curb the handicapped child's intellectual achievement in the name of a misguided "realism" about the adult future that lies ahead. Here, for example, is the advice that the leading textbook gives for prospective teachers and educators in special education: "Not all intellectually normal physically handicapped children should be advised to go on to college. Certainly great care should be taken in advising such young people to enter professional schools. One of the great tragedies in modern society is that of the overtrained, unemployable, physically handicapped adult." [29] The prescription given for avoiding this tragedy is not, as one would suppose, a vigorous effort to stop job discrimination against physically disabled individuals with professional degrees, the one group for whom even a severely disabled body means relatively little, but instead to dissuade the gifted youth from becoming a lawyer, a computer programmer, or a scientist. The textbook continues:

Many young people with serious physical handicaps should appropriately have only the enrichment experiences of a liberal arts education. The goal of such an experience, however, should be thoroughly understood by both the child and his parents as well as by the college or university officials, that is, that it should be for enrichment. The unemployable physically handicapped person who has a good mind will have enforced leisure time. The goal of the liberal arts education is to help him fill such periods of inactivity with intellectual activities, with reading, with the healthy pursuit of music, drama, and the fine arts, with such creative activities with which he is capable of coping both at the high school and the college or university level. This is the goal for the seriously disabled cerebral palsy youth or for others with comparable untreatable and irremovable physical disabilities.[30]

Translated into the educational practice of the average teacher or administrator, statements such as these can only perpetuate the exclusion of handicapped people from the economic mainstream by encouraging teachers to lower academic standards for them (after all, what difference will it make?) and to dissuade gifted but severely incapacitated children from obtaining precisely those skills best calculated to get them jobs or to win lawsuits against prospective employers who show a discriminatory bias in hiring.

Imagine the statements above being made about blacks! Such comments were made, years ago, in the debate about the merits of "industrial" education versus regular education that raged among black leaders in the South from post-Reconstruction days to World War II. Some, like Booker T. Washington, endorsed an educational philosophy similar to the philosophy that still dominates many areas of education for the handicapped—a belief that the black child should be provided special "industrial" or "vocational" training that would prepare him for the restricted occupational opportunities he would possess as an adult. Others, like William Du Bois, believed that black children should receive the same kind of education that white children received, lest the content (as well as the quality) of black education help to perpetuate the inferior status of blacks. For their part, southern whites enthusiastically supported the concept of industrial training because they wanted to preserve the caste system.

The argument runs: Negroes are, and must be, servants, farm laborers, and industrial workers; they should, however, be trained to do their work better; then, in their "place," they would be better citizens too. What is needed, consequently, is a Negro education which bothers less with bookish learning and more with life in a humble status, daily duties, and the building up of character. The play of these arguments can be observed today [1938–1940], when, for instance, one accompanies the State Agent for Negro Education in a rural county trying to persuade the local white leaders to spend money to improve Negro education.[31]

Social workers, psychologists, social psychologists, and psychiatrists also unwittingly serve to trim the cloth of the handicapped individual's childhood to reflect the excluded status of handicapped adults in the present-day United States. Again and again the goal of psychotherapeutic intervention is to teach the child to be the handicapped equivalent of Stepin Fetchit, to help him "adjust" to the social status quo of handicap, to adopt a life-style in childhood that will prepare him for the stigma, exclusion, and dependence that awaits so many handicapped individuals in adulthood.

A comparison of this adjustment philosophy to the philosophy that prevails among professionals concerned with the problems of black children is particularly instructive. Rarely in the field of race relations (or in discussions with professionals who work with black children) does one find anyone arguing for the need to use psychological techniques to help the black child (and the black adult) adjust to the "facts" of his reduced social situation more "realistically," and, ultimately, by means of a reorientation of values, to realize that being black is really not all that important. Indeed, it would be nothing less than obscene for a leading expert on the black problem to urge that the psychotherapist seek to help the black child move from feeling that "I am nothing but an incomplete injured person who has always to mourn his loss" to a stage of wise maturity in which he recognizes that "I am as I am, and though I don't have all the possible assets that can be *imagined*, my life is full." [32]

Quite the contrary, an early (and probably overly psychoanalytic) study of the repercussions on character and personality of the traditional situation of the black, Abram Kardiner and Lionel Ovesey's *The Mark of Oppression*, concludes this way:

The psychological expressions of the Negro personality that we have described are the *integrated* end products of the process of oppression. Can these be changed by the *education* of the Negro? The answer is no. They can never be eradicated without removing the forces that create and perpetuate them. Obviously, Negro self-esteem cannot be retrieved, nor Negro self-hatred destroyed, as long as the status is quo. What is needed by the Negro is not education, but *reintegration*. It is the white man who requires the education. *There is only one way that the products of oppression can be dissolved, and that is to stop the oppression* [italics in original].[33]

Contrast this with the following observation by a leading authority in the field of handicap:

Disability appears to be as much a problem of the nondisabled majority as it is of the disabled minority. Maladjustment in normal individuals with respect to physical disability is widespread. However, we cannot change our society overnight, and social attitudes often present problems that can be dealt with only indirectly.

It appears that a dead end has been reached. If disability is relatively fixed and society is relatively inflexible, that leaves only the person.[34]

Statements like this are so common in books on the handicapped (and in discussions with professionals in special education and other fields) that they pass unremarked. And because they possess an obvious measure of truth (one can hardly seek to turn every handicapped child into a potential civil rights activist), it is easy to overlook the degree to which the adjustment philosophy embodied in these assessments of the social status quo of handicap help to prepare a new generation of handicapped individuals for the same demeaning, demoralizing, dependent lives endured by today's handicapped adults. Suppose, for example, that one encountered the following reasoning—which captures the logic of the adjustment paradigm—in a discussion of the problems of blacks:

1. The most devastating problems a black child faces stem from the racist character of American society, a society that treats blacks as an inferior social group.

2. Therefore, the best way to help the black child cope with problems of growing up in a racist society is to do everything possible to help the child adjust to the often bleak social facts of life.

But reasoning like this is not the only obstacle that stands in the way of achieving the full social potential of mainstreaming. A host of well-established school practices and priorities are likely to perpetuate many of the worst features of segregated special education within the programmatic framework of the new reforms quite regardless of the teacher's own attempts to treat the child as a social equal.

Tracking—or the grouping together of children of similar academic accomplishments—seems especially likely to undermine mainstreaming's egalitarian intent.* Because so many handicapped children do poorly in school compared with their able-bodied peers, it is quite possible to imagine instances in which most mainstreamed children end up being segregated in ability groups of poor students. Besides reproducing the pattern of segregated education within the programmatic framework of mainstreaming, there are special hazards associated with tracking any child. Researchers who have studied the social psychology of tracking agree that labeling a child "bright" or "slow" sets up self-fulfilling prophecies in teacher, student, and classmates.[37] Furthermore, these prophecies reinforce and transmit existing negative stereotypes about the classes of children who most often wind up in the low-status tracks. Especially ugly possibilities are raised when handicapped children are mainstreamed in schools that contain able-bodied children from many class and racial backgrounds. It is hard enough on a lower-class black child to be placed in the

---

* Educators are beginning to be aware of the dangers of tracking handicapped children in either mainstreamed or segregated settings, and some of the most interesting work in special education involves experiments with "open classroom" formats. These innovations are excellently summarized in a recent volume edited by Samuel J. Meisels, *Special Education and Development: Perspectives on Young Children with Special Needs*.[35] Unfortunately, much of this work suffers from the same conceptual shortcomings that we explore elsewhere in this chapter—a general reliance on conventional interpretations of Piaget and a use of diagnostic tests that measure the child against able-bodied norms.[36]

"slow" groups in a school with a white middle-class majority. The prospect of the slow group's being expanded to include most of the newly mainstreamed crippled and chronically ill children seems designed to reinforce existing class and racial stereotypes as well as existing stereotypes about the disabled.

The dangers in tracking seem all the more tragic because there is not a scrap of evidence to suggest that it is a valuable educational strategy. As the National Education Association has noted, there is "a notable lack of empirical evidence to support the use of ability-grouping as an instructional arrangement in the public schools." [38] Indeed, perhaps the most carefully executed study of the educational impact of tracking concluded that ability grouping tended slightly to favor (i.e., improve the educational performance of) the above-average pupils, whereas random grouping tended slightly to favor the below-average.[39]

If the schools are to treat the handicapped as social equals, they must do more to make a clean break with special education's traditional tolerance of tracking, low standards, and restricted curricula. They must provide curriculum materials that connect with the handicapped child's experience and do it in a way that attacks society's conventional stereotypes about disabled people, the fears aroused by the disease diagnosis of handicap, and the misguided notion of tolerance that is embodied in the handicapped role. Here, too, the schools' deviance analysis of disability makes them incapable of perceiving the need for curriculum materials to combat society's well-meaning misconceptions about disability *as well as* negative prejudices and fears. Committed to emphasizing the deficiencies of the handicapped, schools find it only natural that children's books about the handicapped concentrate upon increasing the able-bodied child's understanding and tolerance for the inferiorities of his handicapped peers.

Two stories for children in grades one through three in the Albert Whitman "Concept Books" series are typical. *He's My Brother,* billed by the accompanying promotional literature as about the problems of a child with a learning disability, confuses matters greatly.[40] "Jamie suffers from 'the invisible handicap,' " writes the author at the end of the book. "Children like him cannot be pigeonholed. They are not retarded." Yet, after reading about this child, who represents a composite picture of all the possible kinds of problems that a child with a learning disability may have, the identification with mild mental retardation seems complete. In other words, a book apparently intended to break down the stereotype instead reinforces it. *Howie Helps Himself*, a story about a child with cerebral palsy, appears to be aimed at satisfying the young able-bodied child's curiosity about this handicap.[41] It casts the handicapped child entirely in the handicapped role: he is not a person, he is a handicap. We see Howie struggling back and forth between his home, where his only playmate is his older sister, and a segregated special education school where the main activity seems to be Howie's attempts to move about in his wheelchair. The book ends after Howie has finally mastered the use of his wheelchair.

Reading these texts, one wonders: Where is the fantasy, the sense of future, and the freedom of an inventive children's book? Why can't handicapped children have handicapped heroes who solve crimes, pilot spaceships, and even face down some of the nasty prejudice they encounter in school? Why can't someone publish children's books that go beyond the mechanics, the physical dimensions of the handicap? Why can't we have books that do more than appeal for "understanding" and sympathy? Most of all one wonders about the impact of books like *Howie Helps Himself* and *He's My Brother* on the self-image of the handicapped children who read them, as well as on the able-bodied readers' stereotypes about the abilities of handicapped children.

Some of the most important obstacles to successful mainstreaming stem from the schools' exaggerated deference to the medical implications of a child's handicap. There is a pecking order in the helping services, and special education stands much lower in this hierarchy than rehabilitation medicine, speech therapy, pediatrics, or any of the other specialties that can provide discreet, potent, compensatory therapies. Because they perceive their educational mission as helping the child to compensate for his deficiencies, school administrators and teachers have found it only natural to subordinate their claims on the child's time to the claims of the medical specialties. The result for the child with a major handicap such as cerebral palsy has frequently been an education in name only. In the words of one expert, "We're still taking kids out of class to give them therapy; so that kids are still going to school . . . for five hours and maybe receiving two hours of education."[42] " 'I would be in arithmetic class,' " recalls an adult with cerebral palsy who is now a counseling psychologist, " 'and someone would come and say, "It's time for therapy," and they would pull you out of class. I never learned the times tables, for example. I never learned English grammar, as every time

English grammar was being taught I was being taken to therapy, so there are chunks missing from my elementary and secondary education.' " [48] Practices such as these not only interfere with the child's education by destroying continuity and making it hard to keep up with the schoolwork. They generate a constant stream of situations in which the teacher must excuse the child's poor academic performance precisely because the child was receiving a specific medical therapy. Did the child fail to do his homework? Perhaps it was because he was unusually fatigued by physical therapy. Or perhaps it was because he was taken out of the reading class before the meaning of certain new vocabulary items was clearly explained. Similarly, the objective constraints on the time available for academic subjects—and the continuity of teaching that is possible—force the teacher to tailor his academic goals and his expectations to the realities of the day. At best, these compromises force the sensitive teacher to lower his academic standards. At worst, through the attitude change process known as cognitive dissonance, the teacher's adjustment to administrative realities may induce completely erroneous beliefs about the low academic potential of many handicapped children. Either way, however, the final impact upon the child is very similar: a second-rate education that subjects him to a network of teacher priorities, expectations, and tolerances for academic mediocrity and failure that reproduce most, if not all, of the formal characteristics of the handicapped role.

The degree to which the schools' overemphasis on medical priorities can effectively segregate the disabled child within an officially mainstreamed school is clearly brought out by another experience related to us by C.I.L. member Larry Biskamp. It is a story that again illustrates the potential role that parents' groups and disabled adult groups may play in helping the school to overcome the blind spots induced by the social pathology model.

A bunch of us from C.I.L. recently visited a mainstreamed high school. We had been invited to lead a discussion about sexuality and disability in a class on sexual self-image containing only disabled students.

Well, the school seemed very nice and all that, but one thing struck us as funny as we were being shown around before the class. Despite the fact that none of the stairwells were ramped, we didn't see any disabled students using the school's elevators. When we commented on this, we were told that the elevators were off-limits to all students. Only the staff could use the elevators. Why was this? Well, the elevators were too dangerous, always breaking down or something. Strangely enough, though, none of the staff had ever suffered any serious inconvenience, let alone injury, from the unreliable elevators.

Of course, the result of this overprotectiveness was that the physically disabled students were not only fully protected from the school's "dangerous" elevator system, but they were, for all practical purposes, imprisoned on one floor. Now remember, this was a school in which the staff, from the principal down, believed in the value of mainstreaming because it encouraged healthy interactions between able-bodied and disabled kids. Can you imagine what a monkey wrench such a dramatic and all-pervasive lack of mobility throws into a disabled adolescent's ability to interact as an equal with his able-bodied peers? Can you imagine the extra reason for perceiving the disabled student as "queer" and "shameful" that this school regulation places in the head of your average able-bodied adolescent?

We filed this all away in our heads as we rode into the classroom in our electric wheelchairs. We temporarily set it aside and threw ourselves into leading a discussion on sexuality and disability. A number of people at C.I.L. have put together a really excellent "stigma tape," in which they let it hang out about how it feels to be treated like dirt because you're disabled. To start things off, we played the tape. Then we followed this up with a very frank and open discussion about our own sexuality. Well, the kids responded in kind. They came out and asked us all sorts of questions about themselves which they had been too embarrassed to ask their able-bodied teachers. And since everything is interrelated, we started talking about other aspects of self-image. We spoke about how we had initially felt we were helpless because of our disability, but how we no longer felt helpless. We spoke about how important it is to take control of one's life, and to not let oneself be pushed around by able-bodied people, even if the people doing the pushing mean well and act out of ignorance.

Everything is interrelated. A week later the students went on strike, demanding they be given keys to the elevators, so that they could be as mobile as the able-bodied kids. And they won.

Research Priorities for Mainstreaming

Although basic and applied research can never be a substitute for direct attempts by reform groups such as C.I.L. to change the schools' vision of the handicapped child, research can sometimes help an institution to perceive the importance of change and to adapt more swiftly to this perceived need. If done with care and sophistication, attitude change research can speak the schools' language, yet demonstrate conclusively that the schools' deviance analysis of disability leads them to structure mainstreamed classrooms in ways that promote prejudice or prevent positive social interactions between handicapped and able-bodied children.

Unfortunately, the existing body of research in this area is deplorably poor.[44] Rather than remain bound by the present-day limitations of handicap research, we believe that investigators should acquaint themselves with social-psychological studies of racism.[45] This literature contains by far the best existing information about the complex relationships between the structure of social interactions and attitude change.*

Perhaps the most important lesson to be learned from the race relations literature is that the *quality* of the interactions between able-bodied and handicapped children is likely to be crucial.[47] Simply mixing together seriously handicapped and able-bodied children is unlikely to change existing negative stereotypes. For positive attitude change to occur, ways must be found to integrate the handicapped child socially as well as physically. Unless social integration is accomplished, mainstreaming can actually serve to induce negative attitudes toward disability among able-bodied children and thus can badly demoralize the seriously handicapped child.

Research in race relations suggests that successful mainstreaming requires the achievement of at least the following goals:

• The teacher must succeed in establishing a norm of friendly interactions between handicapped and able-bodied.

• Group projects must be provided that allow handicapped and able-bodied children to cooperate toward achieving a common goal, such as performing a school play, undertaking a piece of scientific research, or constructing an exhibit.

• Whenever possible, the teacher should do her best to ensure

---

* This literature is not without its limitations, too. Thus, though developmental studies of racial attitudes are abundant, there has been very little research into ways to induce attitude change in children. In the past thirty years there have been eight studies, six of which involved high school students.[46] Moreover, as is also true for attitudes toward handicap, very little is known about how parents affect the formation of their children's racial attitudes. Nonetheless, despite these limitations, the race relations research represents the best information we currently possess about precisely those issues that are of paramount importance in mainstreaming handicapped children or, for that matter, in attempting to minimize stigma in segregated settings. We should take its findings very seriously indeed.

that handicapped youngsters occupy positions in the informal and formal hierarchy of the class that are in no way inferior to the positions occupied by able-bodied children.

• Opportunities for informal interaction between able-bodied and handicapped children must be facilitated.

Because of the special physical and communications limitations of many groups of severely disabled children, the achievement of these goals is likely to be much more difficult than when the school seeks to reduce racial tensions between blacks and whites.

The need for the teacher to encourage friendly interactions and to discourage hostile and unfriendly interactions seems straightforward. But if the teacher perceives severely handicapped students as patientlike, she may inadvertently reinforce the handicapped role by imposing norms for friendly behavior that are appropriate for interactions between patients and healthy people. This problem is especially likely to occur during adolescence, when the frequently exaggerated solicitude and sentimentality of the able-bodied adolescent is likely to be just as threatening to the severely disabled adolescent's self-esteem as forthright expressions of social rejection, mockery, and hostility.

The challenge presented by successfully using group projects to improve social integration is equally great. Young people are exquisitely sensitive to insincerity in adults. The token participation of a severely handicapped child in a group project is not going to fool anyone. Yet if the teacher sees the severely handicapped child as patientlike, token participation is likely to seem both natural and appropriate to the teacher. What is necessary is to find ways in which the severely handicapped child can provide the group with a skill or make a contribution that the group genuinely needs.

The need to find ways for the handicapped child to participate in group projects as an equal rather than as a mascot or charity case seems still more acute when one considers the society of the classroom. From middle childhood on, this society becomes increasingly complex and independent of the teacher's control. Parallel to the official social structure of, say, an eighth-grade class, with its class president, student council representative, and so forth, is the informal network of cliques and friendships that determine popularity and prestige. A sensitive and skilled teacher can do much to help the disabled youth exploit what options for social participation exist in the class, but by the same token, clumsy and heavy-handed attempts to help him can exacerbate the difficulties he encounters with his able-bodied peers. These problems can be increased even more if the school's reliance upon ability grouping reproduces the traditional pattern of segregated education for handicapped children. When most severely disabled children end up being placed in slow-learner groups, they are likely to find themselves isolated from the most prestigious cliques in the class, as well as laboring under the special stigma that sometimes attends placement in a below-average ability group.

Opportunities for informal interaction with his able-bodied peers will not in themselves guarantee social integration of the seriously disabled child, but a lack of them can virtually guarantee social isolation. In general, ability grouping has this effect. The special service needs of many handicapped children can compound the problem, since the time they have to spend in physical therapy, speech therapy, or mobility training can cut heavily into opportunities for informal social encounters. Unless the school makes special efforts to encourage able-bodied and handicapped children to mingle during recess periods, gym classes, and lunchtime, still other opportunities for informal encounters will be lost. Children with major physical or sensory handicaps face another critical social problem. From middle childhood on—and most of all during adolescence—the character of in-school friendships and interactions is strongly influenced by one's ability to pursue school contacts after school. Unless the blind or crippled child can easily visit his school friends outside school, he is almost automatically going to be cut off from social equality in the classroom. Mobility is a prerequisite for such after-school socializing. In the cities, architectural barriers and mass transit systems frequently restrict the mobility of people with different bodies. In the suburbs and in rural areas, access to a car is a prerequisite. Although the schools cannot solve these problems, they must do their best to take them into account. They can encourage after-school activities that take place in the school building—yearbook, newspaper, plays, etc.

In and of themselves, most kinds of social-psychological research are unlikely to affect how the schools mainstream handicapped children. This being said, we must briefly single out some of the most important kinds of research questions that need to be answered for the school that is capable of breaking with tradition and carrying out a sensitive, child-centered policy of mainstreaming; for such is the size and variety of the public school system (and such is the diversity of the school reform movement in special education) that there will always be a saving remnant of schools that implement the spirit as well as the administrative letter of the mainstreaming mandate.

To begin with, information about the community's attitudes toward different kinds of handicaps and the role expectations that it holds for handicapped people could be of great benefit in *planning* a mainstreaming program.[48] It is especially important to determine where community attitudes are more tolerant of disability than might be expected. The last thing that a school wants to do is to recommend the placement of a blind child in a segregated setting on grounds of his social vulnerability when relatively little stigma attends blindness in the child's subculture.* Attempts to *evaluate* a school's experiences with mainstreaming are also closely dependent upon a thorough knowledge of community attitudes and role stereotypes concerning handicaps. Indeed, there is simply no way of determining the causes of a successful or an unsuccessful mainstreaming program unless one possesses a kind of ethnographic profile of community conceptions of disability.† For example, one sometimes hears in private conversation with special educators generalizations such as the observation that "Scandinavian-American communities seem to be relatively tolerant of physical handicaps, whereas Greek-American communities seem relatively intolerant of them." Is this true? If so, one can easily imagine situations where ignorance about ethnic or class factors could lead to entirely spurious findings about the relative merits of two different strategies for mainstreaming physically handicapped children.

Social psychology may also be able to provide the schools with invaluable information about the best and the worst ages at which to mainstream children in different communities. In our own conversations with severely disabled youths and adults, we have been struck by the extreme variability of their social experiences during adolescence, regardless of whether they were mainstreamed or edu-

---

* Such variables as the age and sex of the able-bodied children in the mainstreamed class are also crucial. Thanks to the work of Stephen Richardson, we now know that in some communities, at least, there are significant shifts in the attitudes toward the handicapped held by able-bodied boys and girls as their age increases.[49] These important findings need to be followed up in detail for many different ethnic groups and social classes.

† Traditionally, studies of attitudes toward handicaps have not attempted to relate expressed attitudes to the community's general conceptions of illness and its model of appropriate illness behavior. We believe that this approach—which flows from the analysis of disability presented in Part One—may help to inject order and clarity into an area that is badly in need of both.

cated in a segregated setting. Some told us that mainstreaming was the best possible strategy for them during adolescence. Others were equally positive about preferring to go through adolescence in a segregated setting. We have encountered similar variation in attitudes toward mainstreaming and segregated schooling while a child. Discerning any underlying patterns to what makes for success in different school settings at different ages (and for different sexes) will not be easy. But the practical payoffs of such information would well repay the effort.

Changing the traditional premises and priorities of segregated special education will, it is clear, require far more than the successful implementation of P.L. 94-142, for nearly every aspect of the schools' traditional educational vision can be reproduced within the framework of the new law. Must reformers again heed the example of their counterparts in minority-group education? Is further reform in special education ultimately contingent on the success of the disability movement to end discrimination and to achieve the economic and social integration of the handicapped person in American society?

As long as attention is restricted to the low expectations that educators hold for handicapped children, we believe that the answer is yes. School reform is indeed closely dependent upon the social gains of the handicap civil rights movement, as well, of course, as upon the efforts of reform groups such as C.I.L. to get the schools to bring their educational practice into conformity with these gains. For example, if there is almost no chance that even the best-qualified adult with moderate or severe cerebral palsy can earn an independent living in American society, this fact will profoundly affect the way parents raise their palsied children, the ways teachers educate palsied children, the advice counselors give palsied chlidren, and the goals pursued by those who provide psychotherapy to palsied children. If, as a result of litigation, lobbying, and other advocacy efforts, the exclusion of palsied adults begins to end, this improvement in the present-day situation of the adult will influence the way that school personnel relate to children with cerebral palsy.

Fortunately, perhaps for the first time in the history of the handicapped in America, a climate of growing optimism and rising expectations among parents, professionals, and handicapped adults prevails. This climate has been created by the impressive victories of the burgeoning handicap lobby and the still embryonic handicap civil rights movement. And while traditional modes of thought continue to dominate the practice of special education, it must be said on the schools' behalf that never before in their history have they been more disposed to reconsider their aims and programs for children with handicaps. As long as this revolution of rising expectations continues, the schools—and, indeed, every professional group with an interest in handicapped children—will become increasingly open to a new and more generous vision of what is "realistic" for the handicapped child. If the political and legal momentum of the 1970s is sustained—and one must emphasize the *if*—then the schools will become more and more able to implement the spirit of the "Quiet Revolution." Educators will take the child's intellectual and social potential even more seriously. And more reform groups will prod them to do so. Bright children with major handicaps will less frequently be given second-class educations in the name of realism and compassion. "Difficult" subjects like science will not be considered inappropriate for children with handicaps. More attention will be paid to the vision of disability contained in curriculum materials. Gradually, the schools' present-day reliance upon the philosophy of adjustment will come to seem as strange to future educators as the application of adjustment philosophy to black children seems today. As American society learns that the handicapped deserve the same kind of tolerance as that accorded racial minority groups, the schools will change.

However, as we have tried to suggest in this chapter, the reform of special education requires far more than changing teacher expectations about the handicapped child's abilities. The school, like all institutions composed of professionals, possesses its own autonomous traditions. These traditions will greatly complicate the schools' response to further social change in favor of handicapped people. Nothing in the schools' traditional analysis of disability is incompatible with the aims of a disability civil rights movement. But nearly every aspect of the educational practices sanctioned by the social pathology paradigm blunts or undermines the schools' ability to educate the handicapped in accord with the movement's pluralistic goals. As the experience of the black civil rights movement demonstrates to surfeit, the schools possess a nearly unlimited capacity to reconcile major changes in the status of a disadvantaged group with a continued reliance on the social pathology model. If anything, the adaptability of the paradigm in special education should be greater, for, as we have seen, the social pathology model provides the schools with a fair and humane critique of lay society's analysis of the nature of disability while advocating educational strategies that are often indistinguishable from the ones that the disease diagnosis and the handicapped role would suggest. For all these reasons, then, it is of the utmost importance that reformers recognize the need for the schools to discard their traditional educational paradigm and to adopt in its stead a pluralistic model of the handicapped child's needs and abilities.

In this chapter we have sought to clarify the differences between the educational strategies suggested by the social pathology paradigm and the pluralistic paradigm. To do so we have singled out a host of basic issues:

• the need to build bridges between the academic concerns of the classroom and the concerns of the handicapped child (the need to develop "contact strategies" for handicap);

• the ways that tests designed to assess the intelligence of handicapped children inadvertently discriminate against them, and, therefore, the need to design new, nondiscriminatory tests;

• the ways that even the diagnostic procedures mandated by P.L. 94-142 continue to discriminate against able-bodied children from minority-group backgrounds;

• the hazards of mechanically applying Piagetian theory to the instructional needs of handicapped children, and, therefore, the need to apply the approach toward the handicapped child's development outlined in Part Two of this book to the pedagogical challenges of handicap;

• the ways that the schools' emphasis upon helping the child adjust to the "realities" of disability can frustrate the egalitarian goals of mainstreaming, and the way that a host of other school practices and procedures can also undermine the intent of mainstreaming;

• the need to develop first-rate science curricula for physically and sensorily handicapped children, and the need for the design of curriculum materials that combat (or at least do not perpetuate) the prevailing negative stereotypes about handicap in the general culture;

• the need for mainstreaming programs to draw on the rich fund of practical experience and scientific knowledge concerning attitude change that has been gathered by students of race relations.

Over the past decade special education has witnessed a set of changes that can only be called revolutionary. Yet a crucial ambiguity clouds the new reforms. Do they mark the beginning of the field's emancipation from an educational paradigm—the social pathology model—that is increasingly recognized as obsolete? Is the field to spring to the forefront of educational innovation in America? Or will the schools read the reforms as mandating a long-overdue attempt to adequately implement their traditional diagnosis of the handicapped child's needs? If so, it is likely that educational history will repeat itself, and the mistakes made in minority-group education in the 1950s and 1960s will be made by special education in the 1980s. We believe that today's generation of handicapped children deserves better.

Chapter 11

The Psychological Effects of Medical Care

Generations of physicians have lamented the low priority placed upon the psychological dimension of medical care. Outside observers have also criticized medical care for focusing exclusively upon the "organ system" rather than also taking into account the impact of disease and cure upon the whole person.[1] Criticism of the typical physician's relative neglect of psychological factors has been especially sharp from those specialties whose concerns overlap with medicine and psychology—psychiatry and psychosomatic medicine. Although written nearly a generation ago, the following description of the "dual personality" of the average physician remains telling.

Within the medical community, the practitioner can afford to assume a "scientific" attitude which is essentially only a dogmatic antipsychological attitude. Because he does not know exactly how this psychic element works, because it is so contradictory to everything he has learned during his medical training, and because the recognition of the psychic factor seemingly disrupts the consistency of the physiochemical theory of life, such a practitioner tries to disregard the psychic factor as much as possible. As a physician, however, he cannot entirely disregard it. Confronted with his patients, his therapeutic conscience forces him to pay primary attention to this detested factor, the importance of which he instinctively senses. He must deal with it, but in doing so he excuses himself with the phrase that medical healing is not only a science but an art as well. He is unaware that what he refers to as medical art is nothing but the deeper, intuitive—i.e., unverbalized—knowledge which he has obtained during the long years of his clinical experience. The significance of psychiatry, particularly of the psychoanalytic method, for the development of medicine lies in that fact that it supplies an efficient technique for the study of the psychological factors in disease.[2]

The relatively low importance accorded to psychology is tragic. No one would tolerate a program of medical instruction that forced the student to spend ten or twenty years acquiring his basic medical skills by trial-and-error experience with his patients, yet this is precisely how he is expected to obtain psychological expertise.

Perhaps no area of medicine, with the possible exception of terminal care, suffers more from the failure to stress psychological sophistication than chronic medicine. In the pages that follow we shall examine some of the most important reasons why this is so. The issues we explore will complement the concerns of our earlier discussion of parents and professionals. Here the focus will be on the other half of the traditional client-professional relationship in handicap—the physician's own conception of his professional responsibilities to the child and his parents.[3] In making the case for a more holistic medical vision we shall advance a model of psychotherapeutic intervention in chronic care that eschews the simplifications of psychiatric models inspired by the social pathology paradigm.

When the physician sees an able-bodied child with an ear infection, the cure is straightforward and swift and makes relatively modest demands on the parents. The physician examines the child, writes a prescription for a multispectrum antibiotic, gives the parents such specific instructions as "Be sure that she keeps taking the medicine even if she seems fine in a day or so," tells them to call if any unforeseen difficulties arise, and arranges for a checkup in a week. The entire episode is self-contained and structured around the premise that, barring the unforeseen, the antibiotic will do its job.

Medical intervention in chronic illness and handicap is often very different. Frequent stays in the hospital for extensive tests, corrective surgery, or other kinds of treatment may be required—

experiences whose psychological impact upon the child and his parents is often extremely negative. There may be a need for outpatient services such as hemodialysis, which can be terrifying events for the child and enormously stressful for the family. Even when frequent hospital visits are unnecessary, the task of carrying out the physician's instructions for managing the child's chronic illness requires major commitments of the parents' time and energy.

From the physician's perspective, implementation of his strategy may seem to require no more from the parents than prudence, a rational concern for the well-being of their child, and an ability to stick to routines. Yet unless the child is to be permanently sequestered in a hospital ward, management of a chronic disorder never takes place in a vacuum; it must be carried out within the context of ongoing family life, where management of the child's biological condition is only one of many pressing demands that the child makes upon the parents (and often not the most urgent). Regardless of their level of education, cultural background, ability to verbalize problems, or intelligence, the parents' actual ability to implement the physician's plan will reflect their conscious or unconscious response to such difficult day-to-day questions as the following: When does the child's need for social experience or self-confidence take precedence over what seems medically prudent? How does one manage the child's medical problem without turning into an overprotective parent or turning the child against the whole idea of medical care? How does one cope with the possibility that one's child has a reduced life expectancy and may even die at any time? How does one prepare a child for an independent adult life?

Earlier we saw that detailed studies of the psychological and social "ecology" of the family with a handicapped child are urgently needed. Even the terribly crude existing studies of such families suggest something of the especially demanding family context within which parental attempts to manage the child's biological disorder take place. In general, children with major handicaps display problems of emotional adjustment perhaps twice as often as able-bodied children of similar background.[4] Just as striking, the frequency of emotional problems among the handicapped child's able-bodied siblings is also extremely high.[5] And while statistics on parental discord and divorce have not been systematically collected, it seems reasonable to suppose that marital problems for parents with a handicapped child are at least as common as among parents with no handicapped children, and thus perhaps one handicapped child in three must live through a divorce.

To address the problem of helping the parents, the physician must first of all be a skilled interviewer and observer. Styles of communication vary enormously within subcultures. Some parents are loquacious and aggressive; others have great difficulty talking about their problems. When the physician and the parent come from different subcultures, communication difficulties are intensified. Additional problems are posed if the parents speak an unfamiliar (or low-status) dialect of English (e.g., black English), or if their native language is Spanish, Haitian French, or some other tongue.

Once the physician has surmounted these barriers, he must in addition possess enough psychological expertise to settle on the best strategy for helping the parents implement the program.[6] For some parents, psychotherapy may be necessary. For others, clear and detailed explanations of the reasons behind each step of the management plan may be central. Other parents may simply need an opportunity to blow off steam in a supportive setting. The style of the physician's intervention is also a matter of responding to the parent's individual characteristics. An authoritarian manner may work well with some, whereas a more egalitarian approach may be required with others. Some parents may require a great deal of structure; others may prefer very little. Group settings may be best for some, individual encounters for others. Finally, some parents may need no special help at all, but even then the physician must take special pains to make sure that parents who appear to be coping successfully are indeed coping. This need to go beyond the mere appearance of success is especially great because many "doctors . . . are prone to interpret passive comformity and 'good behavior' [by the parents] as evidence that things are going well. . . ." [7]

We shall call the many skills a doctor needs to find out what the parents are saying, where they are having problems in implementing the management plan, and how best to help them a general psychotherapeutic ability—meaning by this phrase the complex of interpersonal strategies singled out by the psychiatrist Jerome D. Frank in his model of the therapist's role in psychotherapy.[8] Eschewing doctrinal assertions, Frank's analysis draws heavily upon what has been learned about the common traits shared by all successful psychotherapists regardless of their particular theoretical orientation. These traits define a client-centered model of intervention that stands in sharp contrast to the model of intervention often employed by those physicians who do make at least a minimal attempt to meet the psychological challenge of chronic care.

In acute medicine, the physician tries to apply a fairly inflexible criterion of health and disorder to his patients. Without this, diagnosis of disease would be impossible. Indeed, the physician's rough rule-of-thumb definitions of health and morbidity seem so natural that when he does encounter patients whose bodies partly conform to a different set of norms, he frequently greets their claims to be medically different with disbelief. Such is often the case when an individual with cerebral palsy or paraplegia receives treatment for an injury or disease unrelated to his disability. The palsied individual's warning that his muscle spasms make it impossible to take a routine blood sample or to obtain a clear X ray are often ignored.* A paraplegic injured in a car accident may have difficulty persuading accident-room personnel that a bone in the paralyzed area is probably broken.†

The research summarized by Frank suggests that in successful psychotherapy the traditional medical definitions of sickness and health are stood on their heads in all but the most severe cases of disorder (i.e., the psychoses). Whereas the physician tends to fit the patient's symptoms into relatively unchanging pigeonholes—measles, pneumonia, influenza—the psychotherapist attempts to dispense with preexisting interpretations and seeks to approach

---

* One woman with cerebral palsy related her experiences with medical personnel before undergoing minor surgery as follows: " 'There's no way in this world that you're going to X-ray me. You can take pictures, but you'll have blurs. . . . At first they [the X-ray personnel] tie you down and, of course, the ties break [because of involuntary thrashing]. There you are, you're upset because your straps have broken, and then four marine-types come and hold you down. It sounds funny, but it's really quite humiliating. Here I am, a 33-year-old professional woman saying, "You cannot X-ray me. . . . If you give me anesthesia, I'm sure you will get a few good pictures, but awake there is no way." There is no way to take blood from me. They tell me, "Put your arm out so we can take some blood." "Okay, here's the arm." The next thing you know, the blood is gushing all over the place.' " 9

† Speaking of her treatment in a hospital accident room after a car accident, a woman with paraplegia told us: "They were treating me as a nondisabled person. They were asking me to wiggle my toes, trying to elicit reflexes, saying, 'What makes you think your leg is broken if it only hurts a little?' Because I'm a paraplegic, dummy, and if it hurts it must be bone pain. X-ray it. 'Oh, well, we'll humor her, we'll X-ray it.' I felt as though I was totally responsible for myself, and I dared not get hysterical." 10

the symptoms of mental distress as a foreign language whose grammar and semantics must be learned from the patient. And while the physician's model of good health possesses roughly the same content from one patient to the next, the experienced psychotherapist appears to let the client define the goals of psychotherapy and, therefore, the ideal of mental health toward which therapist and patient direct their efforts.

Of course, not all psychotherapists employ this client-centered model in their actual clinical practice. Some adopt a strategy that translates the social pathology paradigm into psychotherapy.[11] Especially in mental institutions and in encounters with individuals labeled as deviant by the law, psychotherapists tend to impose their own notions of health and sickness, good adjustment and maladjustment, upon the patient. In calling for the physician to employ psychotherapeutic skills in chronic care, we do not mean to imply that the physician should use these skills in the coercive manner that characterizes some psychotherapy.[12] Nor, for that matter, do we mean that the physician should remain ignorant of the obstacles to achieving an ethnographic perspective posed by that cluster of poorly defined phenomena that are somewhat misleadingly called "labeling effects"—distortions in the therapist's perceptions of the client's behavior that are induced by the therapist's own value biases and by the often partial (or slanted) information that the therapist possesses about the client.[13] Where such effects dominate, a vicious circle can be created. The therapist sees what he has been led to expect to see by his stereotypes and by the information he possesses about the client, and instead of learning from experience he generates a self-fulfilling prophecy about the client's behavior.

Further light on the physician's need for psychotherapeutic expertise is provided by an apparently unrelated problem—that of evaluating the effectiveness of the management plan even when the parents successfully implement it.[14] This difficulty stems directly from the special character of medical intervention in chronic medicine. Because medicine can only manage most handicaps, not cure them, the improvement brought about by the physician's biological intervention is especially vulnerable to being masked or outweighed by the child's psychological reaction to the intervention and also by the effect his siblings' and parents' reactions have on him. Often perceiving a clear relationship between the effectiveness of his intervention and the deportment of the acutely ill child, the physician finds that the connection between treatment and behavior is far more problematic in chronic medicine (e.g., encouraging laboratory data on blood chemistry may or may not be accompanied by improvements in the child's school performance or overall state of mind). Since most physicians intend their medical interventions to increase the patient's general "well-being," "functional level," "health," or "functioning," the lack of a clear-cut causal relationship between these vague but commonly accepted goals of intervention and the management program is perplexing and often frustrating. In the words of one pediatrician: "Most of us are ill prepared to deal with children who do not get well, with children in whom small progress in improved function is all we can hope for, and with parents of such children who, in having to live daily with the burden, can be forgiven for being less openly grateful to us, for we have done so little for them." [15]

Faced with a child who seems worse off as a person even though neurological function or laboratory indications have improved, a physician may find the perspective afforded by a psychotherapeutic viewpoint to be of great use. By emphasizing that major disabilities are not just biological disorders but are complexly psychosomatic, the nature of the physician's biological intervention is clarified. When an antibiotic cures a child's ear infection, the biological intervention works more or less automatically: the fever goes down, the earache goes away, the child's energy returns, and in a few days he is back to normal. In contrast, the successful biological management of a chronic disease such as diabetes does not produce a straightforward outcome. Instead, management provides the child with important biological options that the child may or may not exploit, depending upon his psychological reactions to the intervention and such other important factors as his family life and school experiences.

By clarifying the difference between providing the child with a biological option and helping the child take advantage of his option, a psychotherapeutic lens can greatly clarify the issues that are involved in assessing the impact of intervention in chronic disease. Just as helping the parents implement the management program requires a specifically psychotherapeutic perspective, so, too, helping the child take advantage of the benefits of intervention again requires a psychotherapeutic perspective. In a sense, the physician in chronic medicine must not only take an unusually active role in implementing his medical strategies, he must also take an active role in making the child receptive to their success.

244

A handicapped child's experience of disease, doctors, hospitals, and medicine is obviously likely to have a strong effect upon his perceptions of himself and others. The most suggestive studies of this subject have been carried out by Barbara Korsch and her associates. Working with children who have undergone hemodialysis or received a kidney transplant, Korsch has found a consistent pattern of poor personal adjustment as measured by standard psychological tests.[16] The most striking impact of the illness on these children was their extremely low self-esteem.[17] Unfortunately, Korsch and her coworkers are just beginning to collect data on the psychosocial status of children with kidney disease *before* they undergo treatment. As a result, it is not yet possible to isolate the specific psychological effects of the treatment on the child. "We are having a difficult time in weighing (1) what we are actually doing to the patient (including the trauma of treatment) against (2) the remaining physical disability, and expressing these factors in terms of what we would consider to be a good outcome. Interaction between the two [factors] is colossal, and this continues to be a problem." [18] But even when medical intervention is less traumatic, it is clear that the child's psychological response to the care giver and to the intervention is a complex and subtle matter that can play as large a role in determining the child's general level of physical and social well-being as purely biological improvement can. An increasing number of pediatricians acknowledge this point, yet little systematic research on this subject has been conducted. The present state of affairs in chronic medicine has been succinctly stated by I. Barry Pless: "Although a case can be made from the viewpoint of the specialist for assessing the success of his treatment or intervention *only* in terms of reduced morbidity, this approach does not reflect the orientation of modern, comprehensive pediatrics. The issue, rather, is that of treating the child, not simply the disease. We must convert this rhetoric into something approaching reality." [19]

To raise the need for sophisticated assessment of the psychosocial impact of disease and medical care on the child is to return in a new form to one of the central themes of this book. At best the physician, the educator, and the psychotherapist can only assess the handicapped child's psychological and social development by means of tests and theories of child development that have been constructed by studying able-bodied children. This limitation of existing models and tools casts a long shadow over the physician's attempts to interpret his clinical experience with handicapped children. Before the doctor can even begin to sort out the impact of his intervention on the child, he may have to function as a cultural anthropologist and determine the meaning of medical intervention for the child's family or even for the social milieu in which the child is raised. In this regard it is useful to consider the findings of Gouin-Décarie's study of children born with missing or deformed limbs because their mothers had taken Thalidomide during pregnancy. (See chapter 4, pp. 59–60, for a brief summary.) The parent's behavior toward the child seemed to depend very little on the severity of the child's disability. The best predictor of the mother's behavior was her social milieu. A study of polio patients by Fred Davis suggests that physicians are not immune to the effects of social milieu either. Davis found that the higher the socioeconomic class of the patient's family, the less severe the physician rated the physical limitation and the more optimistic the physician was about an eventual restoration of physical function.[20] Engel has recently noted the importance of taking into account both the doctor's and the patient's personality when attempting to assess the overall impact of care. This approach recalls the way that many researchers have attempted to evaluate the outcome of psychotherapy.[21] But even Engel's strategy, which represents a quantum leap in methodological sophistication, is likely to fall short unless it is supplemented by careful attention to the sociological variables discussed in our survey of developmental psychology.

In approaching the problem of assessment, we believe that again the physician will be best served by employing the ethnographic ideal sketched out in Jerome D. Frank's model of psychotherapy. Whether the physician is confronted with the question of using a test that has been standardized on an able-bodied population, or is studying a group of children from varied socioeconomic backgrounds, or is trying to honor the role of personality variables in the doctor-patient relationship, it is essential that he take nothing for granted about the interpretive structures he uses to make sense of the "data." Precisely because we do not yet possess a developmental psychology of handicap or adequate psychometric tests for handicapped children, the highest premium must be put on clinical intuition and sensitivity.*

---

* Our general position is sketched out in chapters 4 through 7. We discuss the limitations of intelligence tests in chapter 10; similar conceptual flaws beset tests that assess personality development or social behavior.

How far some physicians are from possessing the sensitivity required in chronic care is brought out well in a number of recent studies of physicians' behavior outside the field of handicap. These studies document a pattern of medical rigidity that is hard to reconcile with the profession's humanistic goals and ideals.[24] Although similar studies have yet to be performed in chronic medicine, we have been impressed by the similar picture disabled adults paint of their medical experiences in childhood and adulthood. Perhaps because physicians can dismiss the reports of disabled individuals as symptoms of emotional maladjustments, little attention has been paid to their complaints.[25] Yet far more than rationalization, projection, and unconscious anger is involved. The picture of the human quality of medical care that emerges in conversations with disabled adults is remarkably close to the picture that emerges in private conversations with concerned physicians. The main difference is that disabled persons are more willing to speak for the record than physicians, who must contend with powerful pressures to refrain from criticizing the profession in public.[26]

A sample of what we heard again and again about medical care in childhood and adulthood from adults who grew up with a chronic illness, a sensory handicap, or a physical handicap is provided by this segment of an interview with six people.*

> *Let's talk a bit about your reactions to doctors, hospitals, and the medical system. Who wants to start?*

> SUSAN: An alarm goes off in my head saying "avoidance."
> WILLA: I have nothing to do with doctors. I haven't been

The need for subtlety in the doctor's techniques of assessment is especially important because of the growing interest among physicians in applying cost-benefit measures to the apportionment of medical resources in chronic care. Berg has recently raised this issue on the policy level.[22] Pless has posed a similar problem on the level of clinical practice. Speaking of the attempt made by the University of Rochester health care teams to assess the impact of medical care in a variety of areas (physical functioning, psychological functioning, and school functioning), Pless notes that "the great conundrum remains: [in] which of these [areas] is [improvement] most important if, by a given change in care, an equal degree of improvement cannot be achieved in each of these areas?"[23]

* To preserve their anonymity, we have altered the names of the participants. Tom and Susan have spina bifida. Willa contracted polio at age three and was crippled by the disease. Jack was crippled by polio at age fifteen and received a disabling injury in an automobile accident when he was twenty. Beatrice is a paraplegic; her disability stemmed from an injury incurred during birth. Alice was born with cerebral palsy.

to a doctor for years; I don't want to go; I can't stand hospitals. I haven't explored it that much. When I look back, I never had anyone explain what polio meant, why it happened to me. I thought I'd done something bad, that God was punishing me. And I couldn't figure out what I'd done that was so bad when I was only three.

Just three years ago I had to go to a hospital for something. I cried most of the way there. It's totally irrational behavior and I keep working on it, telling myself I'm going to be okay whenever I'm sick.

Is it totally irrational or is it also based on a rational conception of the medical system?

WILLA: I guess most of it's based on never having been treated as a real person when I was young and in the hospital. I never had things explained to me. I always had to wait for two or three hours for the doctor to see me for fifteen minutes. I never knew what he meant by things he said, and I never knew why I should come back or where I should go next.

SUSAN: What the hell's irrational about that? You know, I've been telling myself for years, on and off, "Now Susan, you're being irrational." And recently it's come to me that to some extent this reaction may come from people telling me, "Susan, you're being a baby," "Susan, you have no right to feel this way," so that it's Big Mama who's telling me I'm irrational. And given the situation, maybe it's not so irrational.

TOM: Well, I think there's something irrational about it—it's rational and irrational at the same time. I think that when you have a handicap, you have a long history of being dependent in various ways, and if you're dependent you develop anxieties about the people whom you're dependent on. At least I've found that in my development I've grown to be very distrustful and I think I can relate that to being dependent: hating to trust but having to trust.

SUSAN: I spent years being most frightened of people who said things like "We're only trying to do you good." I'd trust the people who were there for business reasons, but when they said, "We only want to help you," the alarm would go off in my head.

JACK: I think that those of us with a lot of hospital experience have gained a certain amount of expertise about the medical care system that breeds a certain amount of distrust.

TOM: That's true. The more you know about what goes on in hospitals, the more you realize that these people are fallible, all too fallible, and you feel that you cannot rely on them. When you're in the hospital, you have to make damn sure that you get what you're supposed to get, because if you don't, they'll mess you up.

SUSAN: Did you ever find they were getting hostile with you because you wanted to know before you swallowed it what medicine they were throwing at you that day? I got a reputation as a bad patient. I always followed orders, but I always wanted to know what was going on and they got mad at me for it.

BEATRICE: What happened to me after my fusion was a prime example. I was in the operating room eleven hours or something; they realigned my whole body. It was this fantastic surgery and I trusted the surgeon. I went in and had the operation and came out of it fine. But a few weeks later I came down with this virus and became deathly ill. For three weeks I went through hell because they wouldn't give me simple fever-reducing pills like Tylenol until my fever reached a certain level, because they wanted to make sure I had the fever even though I was dying. And I'm not sure whether it was the virus that nearly killed me. It may have been my allergic reaction to the antibiotic they gave me for about a week; the reaction affected my hearing and left me with some permanent nerve damage.

But when you talk about your having to tell them about your condition, when I was in the hospital I was on an orthopedic floor because of the fusion, but I had other problems. I had a plastic surgeon and I had a decubitus ulcer that had to be treated. The nurses didn't know how to treat me. The doctors gave me instructions and I had to train each nurse that gave the treatment two or three times a day and they didn't like it. They didn't like receiving their training from me, but I insisted that they listen.

Do you think these problems are special to handicapped people?

SUSAN: I think it's just something that goes with anyone who is chronically ill as well as disabled.

BEATRICE: I think there is one important difference. I think a nondisabled person who goes into a hospital has never really had very much experience with the medical environment. He goes in there in awe, saying, "Boy, these doctors and nurses, they really know what they're doing and there's something up there."

SUSAN: So you're saying the difference is that the handicap gives you an experiential background that someone with a newfound illness may lack?

BEATRICE: Well, when he's somebody who has had experience in the past, so he knows that the medical personnel aren't infallible.

JACK: My guess is that this added experience would cut both ways. I have a feeling that we have more expertise than a nondisabled person. But I think in a hospital situation we're more often than not dismissed by the medical personnel because we have a chronic rather than a curable problem.

BEATRICE: Yeah: "Here comes another crip." You're right. Medical personnel have the same kinds of stereotypes as the general public.

JACK: There's another problem. I suspect most of us don't fight as much as a nondisabled person might precisely because of the dependence that most of the time we still have. In other words, I've found that it takes much more to get us to fight for what our rights are.

SUSAN: I've also felt that there's a tendency on the part of medical people to devalue practical experience. We don't know about electrolytes; we know we're supposed to drink a bunch of fluids. We don't know all about wonderfully sophisticated stuff, and if we can't frame our views in the appropriate medical jargon then our ideas are devalued. I often felt that way. I know all about how to avoid getting a decubitus ulcer on my heel but they wouldn't pay any attention to me because I was eleven years old and kids aren't supposed to know that kind of stuff.

ALICE: My experience with doctors was that I didn't trust them because of my family situation. My parents had always said that doctors were quacks. When my parents put me into the hands of doctors, I got scared and I was very upset with them, but I had to go along because they were my parents. I would be a lot better off today if I had gone with the program of physical therapy that was prescribed for me. I've started physical therapy again just to get back at those doctors who, by their insensitivity, turned me off about physical therapy when I was young. I want to get back at those doctors who were so mean and so insensitive to my needs, those doctors who refused to explain things to me, and who made me feel like—"Gee, fellows, here's another patient; it's on the table, let's do this and this to her, and then send her on her way."

SUSAN: Yeah, at the hospital I felt I was being treated like a piece of furniture. They'd talk to my parents about the leg, and "Do you like the finish?" and "What do you think of the upholstery?"

How many of your doctors when you were kids talked to you instead of your parents?

ALICE: My father didn't know what to say either, because it was never fully explained to him just exactly what was going on. It wasn't until I became about fourteen or fifteen years old that I could actually say to my father, "I don't want this operation." And they would finally explain things, sit me down, to convince me to go their way.

BEATRICE: You know, it's really not unusual—the fact that medical people don't talk. I think another example is the fact that from the time I was about five years old when I was a patient at the Children's Hospital in Boston, and no one at the Children's Hospital ever told my parents that there was a school for handicapped children located in Boston. I was being taught by home teachers from the public schools on a two- or three-hour-a-week basis.

SUSAN: Well, hospitals didn't know about those kinds of things. All hospitals are into is medicine.

TOM: I think in some ways that it's precisely because they are our benefactors that there is such resentment against physicians and other medical personnel. I think it's somehow natural to want to bite the hand that feeds you, and to resent people who combine an ability to provide really vital medical services with a tendency to put themselves on a pedestal, to be stand-offish and unwilling to relate as people to the patients they help. Because handicapped people are always in the position of being helped by others, handicapped people are probably especially sensitive to

the slights and rebuffs that so often go along with help
that's supposed to be disinterested. Those slights intensify
the handicapped person's sense of being a burden on others,
as well as his sense of being impotent and being unable to
control his own life.

SUSAN: Can I just say something else about hospitals that
I think may be truer of persons who are handicapped or
have a chronic disease? At least for me, early on there was
a tendency to objectify myself and my body because I was
"the case." I was the one with the ostomy, the this, the that,
and I was accustomed to the idea early on that I had absolutely no reason to have any desire for modesty, or a sense
of privacy, and my body was sort of in the public domain
for doctors to look at and practice on. Frankly, I think
that was an important factor in my growing up, too.

*What would you say to doctors who come in contact with
handicapped kids?*

TOM: Well, I don't know. I think the whole issue here is
complex because it comes down to finding ways to improve the way doctors and patients relate to each other.
Personally, I've been very lucky for the past few years. I
have all I need in terms of medical care for my problems.
Yet I also have a doctor who makes it about as easy as possible for me to talk to her. She's not too busy to explain
things to me. She thinks of me as a whole person, not just
as a medical case. She relates to my needs as a whole person, not just my body's medical needs. She seems interested
in what I have to say. She seems flexible and willing to
modify her medical recommendations to take my needs as
a person into account. She's willing to listen to me when I
say, "Yeah, this new medical procedure sounds good, but
it's going to interfere terribly in the way I'm leading my
life."

She learns from you, too.

TOM: Yes. You know, if I say I can't do this because it's
going to interfere terribly with what I want to do in terms
of my personal activities, we reach some kind of compromise that may not be ideal medically but that lets me
function the way I want to. I have the feeling that my doctor sees the practice of medicine as something that's meant

to support and enhance life—my life, in my case—and not as an end in itself.

The Physician's Responsibility in Chronic Medicine

From the need to honor the immense complexity of the psychological dimension of chronic care, it is but a small step to what is perhaps the central ethical dilemma in chronic medicine: what is the doctor's professional responsibility in situations where he cannot cure a disease but can only manage or ameliorate a chronic disorder? Is it to view the psychological dimension of care as no more than a vital adjunct to his specifically biological mission? Or where medicine cannot cure, should doctors adopt a different definition of their primary function?

For us, medical history provides the best answer to these questions. Before the triumphs of clinical medicine in the nineteenth century, the physician viewed himself as a healer who used every resource at his disposal to help his patients cope with their infirmities. While these resources included biological remedies, the most important of the physician's tools were, in the largest sense, psychotherapeutic.[27] Indeed, most of what was considered medical technique was really one form or another of psychotherapy. Whether by harnessing the "placebo effect" on the side of health, or by providing solace, moral support, and counseling, the physician's main curative impact was achieved through helping the patient mobilize his own physical and spiritual defenses against disease.[28]

How can physicians be encouraged to adapt existing models of medical care to the special demands of handicap? One way is through their medical education. Although we are pessimistic about the ability of schooling to improve materially the average physician's psychotherapeutic sensitivity we are fairly sanguine about education's potential to inform the future physician about the special kinds of nonmedical service problems posed by chronic care. What is involved is not a radical break with medical tradition but a straightforward adaptation of widely respected models of medical care, an attempt to persuade the physician that someone must cope with the psychological dimension of care.

Along these lines, we support the creation of centers where physicians and other medical personnel could receive specialized training for working with handicapped children and their parents. Useful models are provided by the relatively few medical schools that take chronic disease and disability seriously and offer wider experiences in nonmedical settings during their training programs (the University of Rochester is one). Moreover, several schools of public health (such as Berkeley, North Carolina, and Michigan) offer programs of specialization in handicap in their maternal and child health departments.

The centers we propose could mesh nicely with other proposals for moving much of medical school and pediatric training out of the hospitals and into communities. A deemphasis on acute disease in general should help highlight the everyday problems of handicapped children—and the degree to which their needs are similar and dissimilar to those of other children.

Beyond this, we believe that there is a place in the training experiences of all pediatricians, family practitioners, obstetricians, and internists for firsthand contact with disabled individuals who dramatically violate our cultural expectations concerning handicap. This contact should be designed to provide the future physician with a sense of the enormous potential present even in individuals with severe physical disabilities and the progress being made by the disabled to achieve full integration into the mainstream of American life. Some such awareness seems necessary because these groups of physicians are frequently involved in providing advice on nonmedical decisions concerning a disabled child, such as whether or not to institutionalize a mongoloid child or to encourage a blind or palsied child to try to become more independent. Indeed, the family physician's nonmedical advice in these matters is often given as much weight by the worried parents as the physician's recommendations in areas about which he has some expertise. Even in specifically medical areas, the doctor's advice can be colored by an excessive pessimism about the child's potential, or by ignorance of the emotional and developmental costs entailed in the treatment he prescribes. These shortcomings can, we believe, be traced in part to a common source, the isolation and one-sided nature of present-day medical education. More exposure to handicapped children and adults who do not end up in the back wards of state institutions and to consideration of the problems from the viewpoints of parents, other professionals, and patients would alter these inappropriate responses. Precisely because of the enormous prestige of the physician, we must do everything possible to ensure that when a parent asks his advice, that advice reflects the most up-to-date information concerning the "social prognosis" of the handicap, rather than information that is *one or two generations* out of date.

Besides an increased emphasis on handicap in medical education, we need to provide postgraduate refresher courses for physicians who want to deepen their familiarity with disability. Ultimately, many of these courses might most effectively be provided by information centers similar to those proposed by Kakalik and his associates in the mid-1970s, although orientation programs presented by service groups staffed and run by disabled adults (such as the Center for Independent Living, the group discussed in chapter 10) provide a still more appealing way for joining an intensive educational experience with an opportunity for the physician to confront some of his own most deeply ingrained misperceptions about the severely disabled.[29] In any event, two broad kinds of educational formats seem necessary: in-depth surveys of particular nonmedical problems that the physician encounters in his attempts to help handicapped patients, and comprehensive overviews of the array of specialized services for the handicapped that exist in the community. To these should be added programs more appropriately carried out by physicians —attempts to acquaint the nonspecialists with the latest advances in diagnosis, treatment, and prevention of specific disabilities.

Reforms of this sort in medical training and postgraduate education will be expensive. Support for them might be most appropriately provided by the federal government, but questions of financing must await a large-scale, prestigious group study and report on the ways to improve disability education. In 1910 Abraham Flexner, then on the research staff of the Carnegie Foundation for the Advancement of Teaching, produced a report (*Medical Education in the United States and Canada*) that stimulated long overdue reforms in the standards, organization, and curriculum of American medical schools. We believe that a similar kind of report, funded by the government or by a prestigious national foundation, could play a crucial role in focusing key educational and funding priorities.

Changes such as these would go a long way toward increasing the number of new physicians capable of taking the psychological dimension of chronic medicine seriously. But medical education is itself enormously resistant to major change, and toward nothing does it display a more fixed and settled resistance than proposals to emphasize the humanistic dimension of care. All the "scientific instincts" instilled in medical educators by their own training and experience argue against such a radical redefinition of the physician's role. Although there are exceptions, most who teach in the medical schools prefer to view the psychological dimension of medical care as a residual category whose importance constantly diminishes with each new medical advance. For these reasons it is possible that rather drastic measures may be required to change medicine's traditional indifference to those aspects of medicine that go beyond biology.

As in special education, an opening wedge for reform may be provided by litigation carried out by parents' groups or individual parents who accuse a physician of malpractice because he failed to work actively with them to implement his management plans. Such suits would explicitly confront the courts with the need for two separate legal criteria for good medical care—one that is appropriate to chronic medicine and one that is appropriate in short-term interventions. Should the courts accept this challenge, one could expect them to give legal standing to the importance of "good-faith efforts" by the physician to assist the parents actively in implementing his management program for the child.

As in special education, the courts would probably stress the need for procedures and processes rather than hold the physician accountable for his failure when he could show that he made a reasonable attempt to fulfill his extramedical obligations. But whatever the particular formulas worked out by the courts, the creation of legal precedents might help move medical education and medical practice toward a greater respect for the psychological dimension of care. For example, accreditation committees might be persuaded (or induced by further litigation) to require medical schools to devote more attention to physician-parent communication in residency programs for pediatricians and specialists in childhood disability. The federal stick and carrot might also be brought into use. Federal support of medical schools might be made partly or wholly contingent upon the schools' providing evidence that they were making a reasonable attempt to train physicians in chronic care who would be capable of meeting the legal criteria of good care in chronic medicine.

We are fully aware that encouraging malpractice suits is highly controversial, and that any workable legal formulas for determining physicians' liability in suits charging a lack of effort to communicate with the parents or to treat "the whole child" will be as imperfect as the formulas that now govern the adjudication of conventional malpractice suits. We are also fully aware that any attempt to use legal precedents to change medical education will be even more controversial. But the medical profession's dislike of controversy must be balanced against the enormous resistance to change of medical education and the equally great resistance of practicing physicians to changing the traditional definition of their professional obligations, even when these definitions are as manifestly insufficient as they are in chronic medicine. Moreover, in extreme cases—such as hemodialysis, where a patient must spend three or four hours several times a week attached to a machine, generally in a clinical setting—the physician who makes no provision for the psychological dimension of chronic care is just as guilty of providing incompetent medical care as the surgeon who performs an unnecessary operation or the clinician who prescribes the wrong drug.[30]

Part Four

Employment and the Achievement of Adulthood

Chapter 12

The Theft
of the Future

Were society's disease diagnosis of disability correct, the handicapped person's problems would not materially change with the achievement of his majority. Perpetual patients age, but they do not develop sociologically; they remain "unstuck in time," citizens of a therapeutic state where there are only good patients and bad patients, not grown-ups and children. Condemned by biology to endless physical and mental dependency, every handicapped person's life would indeed be bounded by service needs from cradle to grave: good medical care, special counseling, schooling when young, sheltered workshops (or some other form of occupational therapy) when older, and a vast reticulum of custodial institutions, hostels, and halfway houses to provide for the day when his parents die or become unable or unwilling to keep him at home.

For perhaps one child in ten who is classified as handicapped, there is more than a measure of truth in this vision of the future. Barring major scientific breakthroughs, the intrinsic biological limitations of profound mental retardation or childhood psychosis condemn most of their victims to lives outside social time, to a kind of sociological stasis in which their enduring inability

ormal roles forces the able-bodied world to treat them
ere indeed perpetual children. Others in this 10 per-
have a more ambiguous fate. Such is the case for the
ntal retardation often associated with Down's syndrome.[1]
gree of mental infirmity restricts the individual to a
futu. that lies somewhere between the independence of a normal adulthood and the boundless dependency of the profoundly
retarded. Many of these children will someday be capable of assuming certain adult roles, but only on condition that they receive
supervision and guidance from able-bodied counselors.[2]

However, as we have emphasized throughout this book, the inherent abilities of the great majority of handicapped children
do not conform to this pattern. Most handicapped children are
mentally normal or nearly so. Providing that their often immense
service needs are met in childhood, not only will they mature
physically, they will also mature mentally. Far from being exiled
by their defective biology to a life outside normal social time,
there is every reason for them to enter the social mainstream as
adults—to hold jobs, make careers for themselves, and raise families.

Yet quite regardless of how well these children have prepared
themselves for the achievement of adulthood, severe, sometimes
crushing, job discrimination awaits them when they grow up.
This discrimination is most intense for individuals with major
physical or sensory handicaps. But widespread job discrimination
also clouds the future prospects of children with epilepsy, stuttering, chronic disease, mild mental retardation, and so on.

Economic discrimination is by no means the only new problem
that the handicapped encounter as adults. Indeed, we have argued
in earlier chapters that the stigma surrounding a person's handicap may decisively affect the nature of his developmental crises
in adulthood as well as in childhood. And, as we note in Appendix 2, "The Sexuality of the Severely Disabled," society's misconceptions about the sexual needs of people with major physical
handicaps often cruelly delays their sexual development. We
take it as axiomatic that the last thing any of us should want
for a handicapped child is an adult life in which his only available "career" choices are those of the deviant—unemployment
sustained by a steady stream of welfare checks or the often meaningless and demeaning make-work of the sheltered workshop.
Obviously these options, although rebarbative in the extreme,
may well be the only ones open to some or even to many indi-

viduals who grow up handicapped. But we need to be able to distinguish clearly between instances where exclusion from the able-bodied economy is the only realistic option and where exclusion is merely convenient.

Perhaps just as important, society's economic exclusion of the disabled casts a long shadow over the way that many handicapped children are raised. We have already spoken of how teachers and administrators in special education tailor the handicapped child's education to the diminished economic future that lies ahead. The impact of job discrimination on the way able-bodied parents raise their handicapped children is not clear.* But the sociologist Melvin Kohn's monumental ten-year study of the relationships between work experience and parenting patterns strongly suggests that the ending of job discrimination may have a profoundly beneficial effect; for if Kohn's conclusions should prove to hold for the parenting of handicapped children, no single factor is of greater importance in determining how parents raise their handicapped children than their firsthand experience of the economic meaning of disability in their own occupations.[3]

Any discussion of job discrimination against the disabled faces an obstacle that does not exist for discussions of the economic needs of other oppressed social groups. At present, economic statistics reproduce lay society's presumption that the disabled are intrinsically inferior to the able-bodied. As a consequence, although data are collected about disabled workers, there is no way to determine what proportion of the disabled worker's higher unemployment rate, lower work force participation rate, lower average wages and income, and below-average representation in better-paying occupations stems from biological limitations and what proportion stems from job discrimination.[4]

Worse, it is by no means clear whether most of the people reported as disabled are actually disabled. Existing estimates may be too high (or too low) by perhaps 50 percent.[5] † Moreover, virtually no information is collected about three-quarters of all

* Note, however, that one of the most important ways that job discrimination against the minority-group worker affects the way minority-group children are raised is not widely paralleled in handicap. Job discrimination against the disabled does not have a direct economic impact on most families with handicapped children because most parents of handicapped children are able-bodied.

† The scale of this uncertainty is one of the two main reasons why existing statistics tell us nothing of substance about job discrimination (i.e., huge numbers of able-bodied people may well be included in the statistical count, and their employment experience may seriously distort the overall picture). The other reason is that sur-

individuals classified as handicapped when they are children—the learning-disabled, the emotionally disturbed, and the mildly retarded.[6] And although information about onset of disability is collected, the data are so flawed as to be utterly worthless.[7] The consequences of this last point bear special emphasis: lacking reliable information about onset, it is impossible, even were existing surveys otherwise satisfactory, to single out for special attention the employment problems faced by those individuals with whom this book is especially concerned, individuals who grow up handicapped.*

Faced with this dearth of data, we have decided upon a strategy that may well seem unnecessarily academic and scholastic to readers with personal experience of the crushing job discrimination that awaits the handicapped individual in the job market. We shall simply take for granted the existence of this discrimination and focus, in this section, on the kinds of questions that researchers must begin to ask so that we will possess satisfactory quantitative information in the future. Before embarking upon this path, some explanation for the importance that we place upon basic and applied research about job discrimination is clearly in order.

The Case for Research

Every oppressed group in America faces a primordial political task. It must persuade itself and the rest of society of the moral legitimacy of its claims for social and economic equality. In pursuing this objective the group faces a crucial political obstacle: society's presumption that the biological characteristics that define the group explain the group's inferior economic and social status.

---

veys have traditionally included only those individuals who both described themselves as handicapped on a questionnaire *and* said that their handicap hindered their ability to find work; if the experience of minority-group antidiscrimination litigation is any guide, many do not realize that they are the victims of job discrimination.

* The point is far from trivial. Everything we know about the job entry problems of minority-group youths suggests that the discrimination faced by individuals entering the job market with a disability may be even worse than the discrimination faced by workers who become disabled on the job.

In the past, this biological rationalization of oppression has been straightforward. At the turn of the century educated opinion believed that native-born Americans were innately superior to the new immigrants from southern and eastern Europe, and this belief provided a politically convincing justification for the social and economic exploitation of these new immigrant groups.[8] A generation or two ago similar beliefs about the innate inferiority of blacks supplied an equally potent political justification for racial discrimination. And even today beliefs about the biological inferiority of women command wide political support (as is evinced by sentiment against the Equal Rights Amendment) and provide powerful rationalizations for the traditional exploitation of women by men in our society. The assertion that a social group is innately inferior, when judged by the norms of mainstream society, still remains the most effective way to discredit the group's claims for social equality in the eyes of the general public. However, with the rise of the social pathology model as an instrument for social policy, new ways of justifying the social status quo have taken their place alongside the traditional expressions of racial, ethnic, and sex bias. Nowadays opponents of social change frequently cloak their racism or sexism in the humane language of therapeutic morality. They do not come right out and say that the oppressed group is inferior; instead, they seek to prove, often by drawing upon pseudoscientific evidence, that the group in question contains a sufficiently large percentage of people with disabilities to warrant a social policy that, as a first approximation, treats the entire social group not as an oppressed group but as a collection of disabled individuals.

This redefinition has far-reaching political implications. An oppressed group's claims for a fair share of jobs and income has an absolute character. There is no possible moral justification for resisting them.[9] But the moment that a group is defined as a collection of handicapped people, one's social priorities insensibly change. One need only read the writings of scientists such as Arthur Jensen and Hans Eysenck, who believe that, on average, blacks are mentally inferior to whites, to see how this happens.[10] Questions of stigma and structural discrimination, though not denied, recede into the background; and first priority is placed upon *treating* the putative inferiority. Just as when we meet a disabled stranger, the handicap at first blots out the person's other social attributes, so, too, the claim that a social group possesses a biological inferiority galvanizes the attention, and it is easy to fall into the trap of assuming that because the difference exists, it must be important. Hispanics and feminists constantly find their demands for social justice menaced by those who seek to redefine them as handicapped—the victims of mental or emotional disabilities. But no special act of political and economic redefinition is necessary for individuals with biological differences that society automatically labels as disabilities, for the culture provides a host of ready-made reasons for common sense to take for granted that the biological inferiorities cause their economic problems. Indeed, so pervasive is this cultural bias against the disabled that even economists in the forefront of attempts to improve existing definitions of disability often succumb to this oversimplification. Here, for example, is how Monroe Berkowitz, one of the leading innovators in the economics of disability, summarized the economic problems faced by the disabled participants at the 1977 White House Conference on the Handicapped Individual: "The current status of the people who are the focus of this Conference stems from any of several causes, each of which is essentially medical." [11] For many disabled adults (those whose handicaps place no significant limitation on their ability to work but who do suffer intense job discrimination because of them) Professor Berkowitz's remarks have something of the same disingenuous quality as arguing that the economic problems of black Americans are *caused* by the unfortunate medical fact that they have inherited from their parents a set of genes that code for Negroid characteristics.

Here, then, is our central reason for placing such importance upon the collection of systematic information about job discrimination: "handicapped" is not simply the residual category into which society places individuals whom it believes incapable of assuming adult roles; it is also a political classification—a label that can be used to deny the rights of any legitimate political group on medical grounds. By collecting and widely publicizing information about job discrimination, "handicapped" will begin to lose its traditional economic and political meanings. It goes without saying that more than information about discrimination will be needed to change society's actual treatment of disabled people. Indeed, we have stressed throughout this book that a grass-roots disability civil rights movement is essential —a movement that uses every weapon in the political arsenal to compel the integration of disabled people into the mainstream.

But even if such a movement does not materialize, the patient accumulation and publicizing year in and year out of the facts about job discrimination could play an important role in correcting the shortcomings of the traditional medical model of tolerance toward the disabled. Indeed, short of constant demonstrations in the streets and acts of civil disobedience, we believe that nothing could more effectively undermine society's misconceptions about disability than for the disabled and their allies to hammer away constantly at the theme of job discrimination; for, by definition, one can only discriminate against people who *deserve* to be treated as social equals.

There are many other political reasons for collecting systematic and unimpeachable evidence of job discrimination against the handicapped. A decade after racial minorities and women achieved the enactment of tough antidiscrimination laws concerning employment, the Rehabilitation Act of 1973 granted similar legal protections to disabled workers. Section 501 of the law requires the establishment of affirmative action hiring programs on behalf of the disabled in all federal agencies. Section 502 builds on earlier legislative efforts to ensure that public and private buildings are made accessible to handicapped people. Section 503 mandates affirmative action programs of all federal contractors doing more than $2,500 worth of business a year with the government. And Section 504 explicitly bans job discrimination against the disabled in any public or private agency that receives federal funds.

Like the education legislation enacted during this period, the Rehabilitation Act of 1973 marked a great advance over the past. But the new reforms were not the result of grass-roots pressure from the disabled and their able-bodied allies. A sympathetic Congress, the efforts of diligent lobbyists, and the receptiveness of the federal bureaucracy, at least in principle, to the idea of treating the disabled as another disadvantaged minority group all contributed to the relatively unpublicized passage of this landmark legislation. Implementation of the new laws has lagged badly. Three full years elapsed before any federal agency even adopted regulations for implementing the new amendments; as of this writing many federal agencies have still not issued implementation regulations.

To compel the enforcement of the employment legislation of the 1970s the disabled will have to achieve a degree of political organization that they do not yet possess.* However, granting this, there is still a very large place for data about job discrimination. Such information can play an important role in focusing the disability civil rights movement's attention on the most crucial employment problems, mobilizing public support for attacks against job discrimination, providing policy makers with specific program options, providing a sound framework with which to judge policy proposals, monitoring the success (or lack of success) of specific antidiscrimination strategies, and carrying out successful litigation to compel company and industry compliance with the antidiscrimination laws.

A good example of the importance of systematic information about job discrimination is provided by the experience that minority and women's groups have gained in their attempts to attack job discrimination in the courts.[13] Broadly speaking, strategies to implement fair employment laws concerning nonwhites and women over the past few decades have focused either on dealing with individual complaints of discrimination on a case-by-case basis or on initiating broadly based legal suits designed to attack a "pattern or practice" of discrimination in a given plant, company, or industry, under the provisions contained in Title VII of the Civil Rights Act of 1964. Experience has shown that attempts to attack systemic patterns of discrimination are much more effective than the case-by-case approach.

Consider first the cost of enforcing a fair employment law on a case-by-case basis. Unless the enforcement agency has a large budget, the agency is likely to be inundated with far more complaints than it can handle. This danger is well exemplified by the federal government's experience in trying to establish machinery to enforce the Civil Rights Act of 1964. Created under the 1972 Amendments to Title VII of the Civil Rights Act of 1964, the Equal Employment Opportunity Commission (EEOC) was given the task of investigating all complaints by individuals con-

---

* The problem of architectural barriers provides another example, if one is needed, of the importance of political organization and public support.[12] The Architectural Barriers Act of 1968 (P.L. 90-480) stipulated that all new federally funded public buildings and all federally funded renovations of existing public buildings should take into account the special needs of the physically disabled. However, because the disabled and their allies failed to marshal the necessary political pressure needed to ensure enforcement, P.L. 90-480 has never been effectively enforced. Even though Section 502 of the Rehabilitation Act of 1973 sets up machinery for enforcing the earlier law on architectural barriers, the federal government still continues to drag its feet. If anything, political pressure will be even more crucial to enforcing the employment provisions of the Rehabilitation Act of 1973.

cerning job discrimination because of race or sex. By 1977 the commission had a backlog of over 100,000 unadjudicated complaints. Because of delay in the courts, it is now common for Title VII cases to be held up for five to ten years—during which, of course, the employment practices that have been challenged can continue.

Most important of all, a case-by-case strategy does not reach the most deeply embedded kinds of discrimination. Individual complaints are generally inspired by a glaring departure from established practice. If the practice itself is broadly discriminatory, individuals are less likely to perceive a personal grievance and bring a personal case.

The moral for efforts to achieve meaningful integration of the disabled worker into the economic mainstream when today's handicapped children are adults seems clear. The moment one goes beyond the very important step of removing obvious physical barriers to employing the disabled—installing washrooms that paraplegics can use, providing ramps, encoding elevator buttons in Braille—one needs to be able to initiate class-action suits that demonstrate—through "objective statistics"—the existence of a *pattern* of discrimination against disabled individuals in a given plant, company, or industry.* As described in *All Our Children*, a report of the Carnegie Council on Children:

* It goes without saying that we wholeheartedly support attempts to eliminate all barriers to mobility. Removing these barriers is a vital necessity for a host of social reasons that have nothing to do with the potentially great economic value of mobility—it will increase the ability of many disabled people to lead an active social life, to vote (in 1979 many polling places were still not accessible to wheelchair-bound voters), to move about freely in their own homes, and, in general, to be at least physically if not economically capable of leading an independent adult life. Moreover, the moment that significant inroads against job discrimination are achieved, the elimination of barriers to mobility will obviously assume great economic importance.

But there is absolutely no reason to believe that, in and of itself, the elimination of physical barriers will substantially increase the numbers of disabled adults who can find work or the job options open to disabled workers who already are employed. Studies of architectural and transportation barriers to mobility frequently do make this claim, but the studies base their claim on what disabled people with mobility limitations *believe* to be the case, not on a realistic assessment of the kinds of job discrimination that currently home-bound adults would face once they actively entered the job market, or the kinds of job discrimination that currently employed people might encounter should they start applying for jobs that they formerly believed were unobtainable because of mobility barriers. Job discrimination against able-bodied minority workers and women has never been impeded by the fact that neither group faces the barriers to mobility that large numbers of disabled adults face.

Since systemic discrimination takes the form not of outright or open exclusion of women or minorities but rather of apparently neutral practices like the credentials "required" for a job, those who suffer from discrimination more often than not *do not even realize* that they are victims; only work force statistics or other objective data will reveal it. Responsibility for challenging allegedly discriminatory, established employment policies on a plant-wide, company-wide or industry-wide basis should be separated from the very different function of resolving individual claims of unfair treatment. The deeply rooted patterns of job discrimination in this country will not be changed by attacking them case-by-case.[14]

Sooner or later, attempts to enforce the new employment laws on the books will have to follow this route. The disabled and their allies are going to have to take employers and whole industries to court, and in convincing the courts of their case, the advocates of integration will have to present compelling statistical evidence to prove the existence of systemic patterns of discrimination against disabled workers.

To be sure, because the economic exclusion of the disabled adult is so complete, there *is* an important place for the kinds of symbolic breakthroughs in employment that helped raise black hopes and expectations in the early 1960s. In achieving these relatively modest but easily publicized advances, the disabled and their allies need not worry about the deplorable state of economic information about job discrimination. And when the newly hired individual is highly visible and the first of his kind, the symbolism of the individual's employment can have a powerful effect. However, as the civil rights movement learned in the 1960s, American business is better at making symbolic gestures on behalf of integration than substantive changes in employment practices. Moreover, what appears as a moving symbolic gesture the first time—say, the hiring of a deaf person in a highly visible and attractive job—quickly becomes just another example of tokenism if systematic discriminatory patterns remain unchanged. In the next few years, it is reasonable to expect that the disabled will register many symbolic advances in the field of employment. However, by the time today's handicapped children reach maturity, the ability of the economy to absorb disabled workers without substantial reforms will probably have been exhausted. Disabled workers will be somewhat more visible, somewhat more mobile, and somewhat better off economically. There may even be a tiny elite of disabled individuals who owe their high status and high-paying jobs to the willingness of American society to make token accommodations to the economic demands of all disadvantaged minorities. But barring structural changes, the vast majority of disabled adults—including today's handicapped children—will face just as bleak an employment future as they face today.

There is another future issue of some importance. It is likely, although by no means certain, that the economy that today's handicapped children enter in the 1980s and 1990s will be profoundly different from the growth economy of the great post–World War II boom. Thanks to the energy crisis and the environmental crisis, growth alone may no longer be a way to placate the demands of the disadvantaged, and social reformers of all political colorations may be forced by harsh economic realities to link their demands for social justice to programs that involve significant redistributions of wealth and income from the affluent to the needy.[15] Such programs represent, in effect, a basic renegotiation of the social contract between society and its members.[16] The less the disability civil rights movement and its allies know about the quantitative characteristics of job discrimination against the handicapped, the harder it will be for them to hold their own against competing social groups in a no-growth economy. Similar considerations hold if conservative trends increase economic inequality, perhaps in the name of stimulating the development of new energy technologies, increasing the competitiveness of American industry in world markets, cutting taxes, or implementing Draconian energy conservation measures. Here, too, the less economically sophisticated the disability coalition proves to be, the more likely that it will be gulled, outmaneuvered, or simply cheated out of its fair share of jobs, income, and economic opportunity. Moreover, continued ignorance about systematic patterns of job discrimination is very likely to conceal some of the most important bonds of economic and political self-interest between the disabled, women, and minority groups. In our experience—and in the experience of many others—job discrimination against the disabled falls most heavily on minority-group workers and women.

Finally, because this book focuses on handicapped children, we must say a word about why so many parents of handicapped children and so many professionals who work with handicapped children place a low priority on collecting quantitative information about job discrimination. The reason is not that parents and professionals are indifferent to the employment problems that await the child. Rather, it is because they continue to believe that education is the sovereign social strategy for reducing and ultimately eliminating economic injustice against the disabled. Given this reliance on education, detailed statistical information about job discrimination seems to be a frill: why bother to collect data about a problem when nothing that one could possibly learn would alter the fact that the best way to help handicapped children in the adult world is to provide them with the best possible education? Unfortunately, this faith in education as a tool for social change flies in the face of everything that reformers outside handicap have learned about what must be done to end job discrimination against able-bodied minority-group workers. Thanks to the research of a generation of economists, it is now clear that improvements in a minority group's education have little effect upon the group's share of jobs and income when members of the group face prejudice and systemic discrimination in the job market.[17] In the absence of political and legal attacks on discrimination, major shifts in a minority group's proportionate share of income and jobs have occurred only during the acute labor shortages that prevailed during major wars, when normal exclusionary practices were temporarily suspended. With the return to a peacetime economy the gains made during wartime were eroded.[18]

Historically, the main role of improved education seems to be negative. Like the Red Queen Alice meets in *Through the Looking Glass*, who must run faster and faster simply to stay in the same place, education seems to need constant improving to allow an underprivileged minority to hold its own. For example, during the years of peacetime boom in the late 1940s, the 1950s, and the early 1960s the absolute size of the economic pie grew prodigiously and even underprivileged groups who received less than their fair share of jobs and income benefited in absolute terms. During this period, minority education as measured by such indices as average number of years of schooling improved considerably. Yet this improvement in education was unable to increase the minorities' share of jobs and income (black/white job income differentials in most occupations remained remarkably constant during this period), although improved education probably helped keep minority workers from losing ground to more privileged economic groups.[19] As the Red Queen remarked to Alice, "*Here*, you see, it takes all the running you can do to keep in the same place. If you want to get somewhere else, you must run at least twice as fast as that!"

Improved education will not eliminate the unfair advantage enjoyed by white workers over minority workers. The advantages include whites' higher pay for the same work, whites' wider choice of occupations, whites' better likelihood of promotion, whites' better chance of finding work in the first place, and whites' reduced chance of becoming unemployed. Similar unfair disparities exist between the employment opportunities and experiences of men and women. Exclusively educational strategies are singularly incapable of reducing these kinds of job discrimination, because education changes the behavior of the work applicant, not the behavior of the prejudiced employer or supervisor. This is true whether one focuses upon improving the academic quality of the education provided minority students or upon providing minority workers with special vocational training. Decades of attempts to attack job discrimination against minority-group workers by means of education-centered strategies testify to the powerlessness of education alone to reduce discrimination. What is needed is a concerted attack upon the network of overt, tacit, and sometimes inadvertent discriminatory practices that perpetuate unfair economic inequality.[20]

Chapter 13

The Presumption
of Economic Inferiority

To study discrimination the economist must first define the basic statistical category of his field—the category of "disabled workers" —in a way that does not assume that all workers with handicaps are less productive or in some other way economically inferior to their able-bodied counterparts.* Since many professionals in the

---

* Some readers may wonder why we say nothing in this chapter about vocational rehabilitation (VR) programs for handicapped youths; for surely the experience gained by these programs is relevant to a discussion of job discrimination. The reason is that we have not been able to find unambiguous statistics about the populations served by VR or about the long-term effectiveness of VR.[1] Information about the effectiveness of the much larger VR program for disabled adults is also unreliable; although it is clear that job placement is a major problem (during the 1970s about half a million disabled workers a year received retraining at the nearly 3,000 VR workshops in the nation, and only one rehabilitated worker in ten subsequently found work).[2] Better placement *has* been achieved by small-scale pilot projects that involve private industry at every stage of the rehabilitation process.[3] But this strategy attacks systemic discrimination in too piecemeal a fashion ever to make a major impact upon traditional exclusionary practices, at least until it is part of a comprehensive federal strategy to end job discrimination.[4]

Others may wonder why we say nothing about the need to change employer attitudes toward disabled workers, since it is often said that attitudes are the biggest barrier the disabled worker encounters.[5] We do so because attitude change campaigns have consistently failed to change hiring practices.[6]

human services emphasize that even major handicaps such as blindness or paraplegia are irrelevant for some jobs and quite limiting for others, one would expect to find a similar sophistication about the nature of disability in economists who study disabled workers. Traditionally this has not been so. Even today the statistical category "disabled worker" is a medical category.[7] That is, it is defined by analogy to the categories "unemployed" or "sick," rather than by analogy to the categories "female worker" or "black worker." [8]

The distinction is subtle yet all-important. *Disability*, as economists have traditionally used the term, refers exclusively to those physical or health conditions that limit an individual's ability to work. No consideration is given to the fact that disability is also a social characteristic, like being black or being female, that exposes an individual to unfair job discrimination.

With disability thus defined, the economist proceeds to assume that it can be measured in the same way one measures unemployment. Therefore, he simply asks a representative sample of individuals if they possess any chronic injury or illness that affects their ability to work; he simultaneously collects information about their employment, income, race, and other standard econometric variables; and then he tabulates the results for each major physical and mental disability by severity of the reported "work disability."

Thus, the economist's first error is to collect the wrong data. A similar error characterizes analysis of the data that he has collected. Here he assumes that the medical condition known as a disability (the biological limitations that attend a given handicap) *caused* the work disability. The more severe the medical condition (total blindness versus visual impairment), the more severe the economic condition or the so-called "work disability." * For example, he assumes that those individuals with cerebral palsy who report that they have a severe work disability are actually more severely limited physically than those palsied individuals who report a moderate work disability.

Looked at sociologically, the economist's definition of disability is patently absurd. It commits him to the proposition that a physi-

---

* Strictly speaking, the economist concerns himself only with "work disabilities" and the "work-disabled" adult. In practice the economic literature uses *disability* and *disabled* interchangeably with these more technical terms. As will become apparent, the economist's use of *disability* and *disabled*—words that possess in everyday speech a very different meaning from the technical definition of "work-disabled" and "work disability"—leads to endless confusion in the field.

cian's definition of physical or mental impairment accurately reflects the job abilities of handicapped people who seek employment in jobs requiring either minimal physical labor or minimal mental labor. It completely overlooks the role that stigma, inaccurate expectations about ability (such as those perpetuated by the economist), and employers' uncertainty about ability may play in influencing employment experience.[9] And it ignores the impact on employment performance of such important sociological and psychological factors as being socialized into a passive, dependent role by parents or other adults whose vision of what is possible for the handicapped is tragically narrow. There is no place in the economist's definition of a disabled worker for the fact that one crippled adult spends his life in a nursing home while another serves more than three terms as president; no place for honoring the fact that while some people are mentally or physically limited in ways that are indeed relevant to their employment, many others are different in ways that subject them to stigma, structural discrimination, and prejudice fully on a par with blacks; and no place for taking into account the findings presented by Robert A. Scott that the blind man who is classified as "severely work-disabled" often entered this economic category not because of his blindness but because of a set of beliefs about the abilities of blind men that were drummed into him when he was "rehabilitated" by a private social agency for the blind.[10]

At the same time, the economic definition of disability also appeals to the commonsense notions of disease and injury possessed by the economist and his audience. The more severe the disease or injury, by definition, the more it impairs one's ability to function as an adult; and conversely, the more severe the work disability, the more severe the medical condition of the worker can be presumed to be. Far from seeming like a sociological absurdity, this appears to be elementary logic. But, to begin with, it does not take account of one extraordinary fact: that the successful handicapped worker—an individual like the disabled executive interviewed in chapter 5—is automatically excluded from any statistical count of disabled workers. To qualify for membership in the economic category "disabled workers," one must be considered in some way inferior to an able-bodied worker. When one's economic or social success makes this judgment impossible, one is simply not included in the reckoning of "disabled workers."

Again, we must emphasize that the absurdity of this statistical decision is by no means self-evident if one conceives of disability as primarily a medical problem.* Given a medical definition of the "disabled worker" as "economically sick," the exclusion of the successful but handicapped worker makes perfect sense: if he is successful, he is, by definition, "cured" of his economic "illness" and is of no more interest to the economist and his policy-making audience. It is as if the economist, treating the category "black worker" as a condition that one escaped with affluence, excluded all middle-class and upper-class blacks from surveys of black employment.

In this book we have often insisted on the importance of the able-bodied individual's tacit social theories about handicap in accounting for what he *sees* when he first meets a severely disabled stranger. Can an economic definition of disability that flatly asserts that the possession of a disability is incompatible with economic success be any less important in determining what an economist *sees* when he turns his attention to the employment problems of the disabled? Is it any wonder that the economist who occasionally devotes his attention to handicap sees nothing odd in routinely assuming that the "disabled" worker is obviously less productive on average than his able-bodied counterpart in most work settings? Is it any wonder that many economists believe the best and most practical way to solve the disabled worker's employment problems is to put him into the economic equivalent of the custodial institution and the chronic care ward—the sheltered work-

---

* Indeed, this medical emphasis is quite understandable. The technical literature on disability economics speaks to the practical needs of policy makers and administrators in charge of state and federal programs that provide some kind of service or transfer payment to adults who qualify as disabled.[11] These programs include workmen's compensation for job-related disabilities, income maintenance for those unable to work (Supplementary Social Security Insurance), vocational rehabilitation, sheltered workshops, Medicaid, Medicare, and a number of other income-transfer and service programs that are either specifically targeted at the disabled population or, because of the frequent association of disability in adulthood with poverty and old age, serve a whole population with an unusually large proportion of disabled individuals.

These institutional consumers carry clout. Every year, government and private agencies spend enormous sums on disability. One estimate placed the 1975 figure at $111 billion, with about half of this money coming from the federal government.[12] Between 1967 and 1975, disability expenditures grew at twice the rate of the gross national product. Published projections suggest that by 1980 more than $160 billion a year will be spent annually by private and public sources.[13] Clearly, the sheer scale of the social services dimension of disability makes it mandatory that economists devote a great deal of their time to these questions.

However, it is increasingly clear that the economist's traditional medical model of disability is seriously flawed even as a tool for guiding social services policy.[14]

shop? The economist sees individuals who by definition are in some way inferior. He *sees* work disabilities.

New Departures in the Economics of Disability

Beginning in the 1960s, some epidemiologists and economists in the field of handicap began to express serious reservations about medically based economic definitions of disability. Although this definition still reigns supreme, attempts have now been made to work around it—to make distinctions that avoid some of the pitfalls of the medical model. In the mid-1960s Lawrence D. Haber pioneered in introducing measures of "functional limitation" into surveys of disability, and the study he organized, the 1966 Social Security Survey of the Disabled, provided unequivocal evidence that the traditional equation of medical severity with economic disability was seriously flawed. In general, he found that the severity of the individual's functional limitations was very poorly related to the severity of his work disability.[15] In the intervening years it has become almost commonplace for economists to introduce discussions of disability with the caution that disability is really very complex, that the economic impact of a given medical condition varies widely with the individual, that one blind man may end up being a famous popular singer while another from a similar background may end up operating a vending concession in a federal building. But once this warning is issued, economists generally ignore it.[16]

A beginning toward ending this conceptual confusion was made in 1976, when the economists Monroe Berkowitz, William G. Johnson, and Edward H. Murphy from Rutgers advanced a model of disability that, although it leaves the traditional economic definition intact, attempts to modify the medical vision of disability that it embodies.[17] The Rutgers team proposed that "work disability" be viewed as the end product of a social process, rather than as a state. The process is the encounter of a person possessing certain physical limitations with the physical requirements for the kinds of jobs that, given the person's demographic profile (age, sex, race, years of education, etc.), he might be expected to seek. The authors propose that one single out those functional limitations that are relevant to the job and call them "job impairments." Individuals with impairments are then defined as work-disabled.

Though sociologically obvious, this modification is immensely significant. For the first time it becomes possible in principle for the economist to distinguish between people whose functional limitations are irrelevant to their ability to perform work and people whose functional limitations in some way compromise their work ability. Once this distinction is acknowledged, it becomes possible (again in principle) for the economist to consider posing the central question of all studies of discrimination in areas outside handicap: given a person whose handicap is not relevant to his job, are his employment experiences the same as those of an able-bodied individual possessing similar demographic characteristics? A finding that this handicapped person does worse in the job market—for instance, that his group suffers higher unemployment rates, lower work force participation, lower average income, fewer hours worked per year, exclusion from or underrepresentation in certain occupations open to his able-bodied "twin"— would be presumptive evidence of the existence of job discrimination. More generally, the economist can now ask (in principle) when and where the employment experiences of a specified group of disabled workers seem worse than appears warranted by the degree of job impairment associated with the handicap. Finally, it is good to note that the Berkowitz, Johnson, and Murphy formulation also makes it possible for the economist to recognize the importance of including in his enumeration of disabled workers all those handicapped people who have been excluded from existing statistical surveys because they did not describe themselves as "work-disabled." [18]

Berkowitz, Murphy, and Johnson are the first to acknowledge that it is hard to distinguish in practice between the limitation and the impairment that attends many kinds of disabilities.* Identifying the actual physical requirements for a job is notoriously complex, and existing definitions are unsatisfactory.[19] As the literature on minority-group employment suggests, specifying the kinds of education and experience required for many jobs is equally difficult.[20] Obtaining reasonably accurate assessments of a person's physical limitations—strengths, stamina, ability to compensate efficiently for a missing limb, etc.—is also no simple matter.

Perhaps the easiest and cheapest solution to this problem is the

---

* The difficulties are perhaps smallest for sensory handicaps such as blindness and deafness and physical disabilities that do not usually impair stamina such as congenital orthopedic malformations.

one employed in existing surveys of disabled workers—to ask the individual to assess his or her own physical limitations. Because of the appeal of this approach—and its wide acceptance—it is necessary to examine its shortcomings in some detail.

To begin with, it is nearly certain that self-estimates of the nature and severity of physical impairments will often prove to be systematically related to important personality characteristics such as "introvert" and "extrovert," as well as to such important social characteristics as sex, race, age, social class, and even the individual's perceptions of the general economic climate.[21] The reliability of self-assessments of one's "work disability" are equally suspect.[22] In short, the raw data that the economist must collect to make meaningful statements about discrimination against disabled workers require much more sociological and psychological sophistication than the kind of data that the economist is accustomed to collect when he asks respondents questions about race, education, sex, employment, unemployment, or nonemployment: the answers to these questions are much less contaminated with social-psychological "noise." If the economist had good reason to believe that all the variables that influence self-estimates of physical limitations canceled each other out, the questionnaire method might still be tenable.[23] But there is absolutely no reason to assume that this convenient state of affairs actually obtains.

Another factor likely to affect significantly self-estimates of physical impairments is the age of onset of the disability. Given what is known about the special psychosocial hazards of growing up handicapped, it seems likely that within certain social milieus there will be significant differences in self-estimates of disability between, for example, the congenitally blind individual and the individual who loses his sight in early middle age. Unfortunately, there is a convincing suggestion in existing data files on disabled adults that self-reports of onset are riddled with major inaccuracies. For example, our analysis of the data collected on onset by the 1966 Social Security Survey of the Disabled suggests that self-reports of onset of disability before age eighteen may either greatly overestimate or greatly underestimate the number of individuals who actually grew up disabled.[24] (Moreover, while the Social Security Surveys contain direct information about childhood onset for a small group of adults, the disabilities possessed by these adults are highly unrepresentative of the overall pattern of disabilities encountered in handicapped children and youth.) [25]

Some of the most troubling problems raised by the possible

biases built into self-reports concern attempts to assess changes in job discrimination against disabled adults from one year to the next.* This information is equally essential for the policy maker and the activist. The point is obvious yet bears emphasis. The last thing we want are statistics suggesting that job discrimination is decreasing when it is actually unchanged or increasing. Conversely, when job discrimination is diminishing, we want our statistics to reflect that fact. Nor do we want our employment data to indicate sizable increases or decreases in job discrimination when, in fact, discrimination has remained constant. Unfortunately, the sensitivity of self-reports to the interviewees' subjective judgments of themselves and their future make it quite likely that at least in some social milieus estimates of job discrimination based upon self-reports of physical limitation are liable to perpetuate precisely those kinds of distortions.[26]

This problem is best illustrated by a deliberately oversimplified, imaginary example. Imagine that disabled adults could be conceived of as a single, perfectly homogeneous group. Now imagine a ten-year survey of job discrimination that reveals a significant increase in discrimination. Such a finding, of course, could be accurate. But if one knew nothing about the impact of social-psychological factors upon self-reports of functional limitations, the survey result could be 100 percent wrong. The interpretation would go something like this. Let us say that between 1980 and 1990 public awareness of the needs of the disabled grows, the disabled themselves become a potent and respected political force, and the stigma and mistaken role stereotypes of disability lessen. Because of these important changes, the disabled individual's belief in his abilities and potential improves, and he gives more realistic (or unrealistically optimistic) estimates of his functional limitations. In short, an improvement in the meaning of being disabled in America might lead to an entirely spurious statistical increase in job discrimination.

Conversely, consider a finding that job discrimination *decreased* between 1980 and 1990. Here, too, it is possible that a shift in the

* As documented in earlier notes, it goes without saying that similar problems are raised by relying upon self-reports for obtaining estimates of such basic economic parameters as employment, work force participation, and unemployment. Indeed, the striking differences between the results of the 1966 and 1972 Social Security Surveys of the Disabled suggest that estimates of the total number of disabled adults based on self-reports contain huge errors that stem from the systematic distortions introduced by exogenous social and social-psychological factors. (These issues are discussed at some length in notes 21 and 22.)

sociological and psychological meaning of disability might have been responsible for the observed finding. Even though real improvement in the situation of the disabled might occur during the decade, the improvement might not be great enough to satisfy the aroused expectations of the disabled. The individual might look around him, see many more successful handicapped people than in the past, and blame himself for not being a success. Out of discouragement he might overstate his limitations relative to 1980.

Or suppose the promise of the 1970s is not fulfilled and disability relapses into its traditional backwater status. Such a relapse might also lead many people to overstate their limitations. Then, with cruel irony, the able-bodied culture might well end up confusing a consequence of the collapse of the disability civil rights movement with evidence that important progress had indeed been made in eliminating job discrimination between 1980 and 1990.

Conceivably, it will turn out that the distortions in self-reports are so clear-cut, so stable, and so closely related to easily measured demographic variables that we will be able to take these distortions into account when analyzing data obtained by the self-report method. If these and other sources of systematic distortion could be roughly controlled, it is possible that self-reports would be usable. In the meantime, however, great caution is in order. Because we are completely in the dark about the relative importance of systematic biases in data based on self-reports, we must assume these data are worthless for ascertaining the most elementary facts about disabled adults—their numbers, their rate of work force participation, their unemployment rate, and, of course, the scope and character of the job discrimination that is practiced against them.*

The Special Discrimination Practiced against Disabled Workers

Whenever the economist can control for productivity and other economically relevant differences between disabled and able-bodied workers, it will be possible to accumulate the same kind

---

* As we noted in chapter 11, physicians may well be strongly influenced by sociological variables when making assessments of the severity of a person's disability.[27] If so, detailed physical examinations and work tests of every adult surveyed might still yield biased data (as well as being a very expensive way to assess the characteristics of a national survey of thousands of people). We believe this question merits serious study.

of data about discrimination against disabled workers that are routinely collected about minority-group workers and women. However, in and of itself, this research will not be able to identify two kinds of discrimination that are uniquely experienced by disabled workers: work practices and work environments that do not take into account the special physical limitations of such handicaps as paraplegia yet, with economically feasible modifications, could take into account the needs of at least some groups of disabled workers. Broadly speaking, research into these kinds of discrimination would deal with two groups of disabled adults: those able to find work but whose ability to compete with able-bodied workers is impaired by the physical structure of the work environment and existing work practices, and those who are excluded from the work force altogether because of these factors.

Clearly, establishing suitable definitions of work practice and work environment discrimination raises a host of issues with no parallel in studies of job discrimination against the minority-group worker or studies of minority-group-type discrimination against disabled workers. First, the investigator must estimate where to draw the line between an economically feasible modification and one that cannot be justified on economic grounds; just where he draws this line will depend on his political philosophy and on how much weight he gives to the goal of integrating the disabled into the able-bodied economy. Second, the investigator must undertake aggressive empirical research to determine just what kinds of modifications are possible, and when and where these modifications meet the preestablished criterion of economic feasibility. The rehabilitation literature is full of examples of how sometimes trifling modifications of the environment or established work practices can greatly increase the employability of some categories of disabled workers.[28] But ad hoc examples will not suffice. Systematic research is necessary if we are to gain any idea of the needless burden placed upon the disabled by a work establishment that has evolved from one generation to the next in response to the abilities and limitations of the able-bodied work force.*

* As Gerald W. Scully has noted, economic productivity is always defined relative to an existing network of relationships that links the individual to other workers and to the physical organization of the workplace.[29] Thus, from a formal point of view, the economist defines productivity in the same way that the social psychologist defines the handicap that is associated with a given disability: ". . . it cannot be said that a person has a disability without specifying the situation in which he is expected to behave. Disability is not an objective *thing in a person,* but a social

Of all disabled adults, those who are currently excluded from the work force may have most to gain from this research. At present, all discussions of the employment needs of the severely disabled assume that sheltered workshops are the only realistic alternative to welfare.* Yet, surely, any social policy for the severely disabled should begin by asking a very different question: given the present-day economic climate, existing technology, and foreseeable economic needs, what is the best balance between two possible policy goals—a policy of integrating as many disabled adults into the able-bodied economy as is technologically possible regardless of the expense involved, or a policy that restricts itself to combating minority-group-type discrimination against the handicapped and to fostering relatively inexpensive and obvious modifications of work setting and work practices? It is easy—and intellectually trivial—to assert that no qualified paraplegic should be denied a job because of door frames too narrow for a wheelchair and the lack of adequate washroom facilities.† But should the nation invest billions of dollars, say, to redesign automobile assembly lines in Detroit so that paraplegics can work side by side with able-bodied workers? ‡ Most readers would probably agree with us that the investment would not be worth the ensuing social benefits. But what of investments in conversion that fall somewhere between the easy extreme of widening a door and the prohibitively expensive extreme of redesigning an industry from the ground up? For example, given X dollars, how does one design a plant that marks the "best" compromise between maxi-

---

value judgment. A society makes a disability by creating a culture in which certain tools are required for behavior. Variations in physique by themselves have little psychological meaning out of the frame of reference in which they are evaluated." [30]

* Research has lagged even here: such straightforward policy issues as the trade-off between sheltered employment and a straight minimum-wage transfer payment to the unemployed and chronically unemployable are only now just beginning to be explored. Though existing studies on this point are useful, their value is compromised by their failure to treat the trade-off problem as a social welfare issue in which the importance of providing as many disabled individuals with meaningful lives is taken into account.[31]

† Intellectually trivial but, as our discussion of minority-group-type discrimination suggests, by no means politically trivial: even when the paraplegic is able to wheel himself into the office he still has to persuade the employer to hire him.

‡ Our example is purely hypothetical. We have no idea what substantial conversion of Detroit's automobile assembly lines would cost, or even if such conversion is technologically feasible today. We also have no inkling of the economic benefits that would flow from such a strategy even should it be technically possible.

mizing able-bodied workers' productivity and maximizing the employment of various target groups?

Somewhere between these extremes lies a family of solutions that, given existing technology and existing limitations on resources, represents the fairest compromise—a compromise consisting of considerable modifications of the able-bodied work place, a sheltered workshop system for individuals too severely disabled to fit into the able-bodied world, and a system of transfer payments for individuals too severely disabled to perform any meaningful work.* In such a world large numbers of disabled individuals now excluded from the able-bodied world of work would be able to compete effectively. Others would be able to perform meaningful work in a sheltered setting (in contrast to the demeaning make-work so common in today's workshops), and still others unable to work at all would at least receive an adequate income from the government. An additional feature of policies lying in this region of "reasonable compromise" might be the provision of wage subsidies to employers hiring disabled individuals who, although capable of working with the able-bodied, are less productive than comparably qualified able-bodied workers. These subsidies would help to achieve the goal of integrating as many disabled individuals as possible into the general work force.†

The Missing Disabilities

Earlier we noted that existing employment statistics omit something like three-quarters of all individuals classified as handicapped during childhood—the mildly mentally retarded, the learning-disabled, and the emotionally disturbed.[33] At present it is impossible to estimate the economic impact of all but the most severe of the disabilities falling into these categories; still less can any meaningful judgment be made about the relative eco-

* For a brief overview of the present status of policy-oriented discussions of sheltered workshops and other employment-related social services programs, see the references presented in notes 2 and 11.

† Studies are also needed of the relative merits of quota systems and wage subsidies to employers hiring "underproductive" disabled workers and paying them the same wage as their more productive able-bodied peers, on the one hand, and, on the other, placing these underproductive workers in sheltered workshops.[32] This research would, of course, seek to take into account the costs of conversion versus the construction and administration of sheltered workshops.

nomic importance of discrimination and the limitations that attend the handicap. Even to begin to answer these questions we need to make cross-sectional studies of the adult population. Since self-reports are likely to be unreliable, other strategies will have to be employed. The correlation of mental disturbance in childhood with mental disturbance in adulthood is so poor that it may be impossible to identify a representative sample of adults who were labeled "emotionally disturbed" in childhood without access to school or medical records. For the remaining "missing disabilities" the simplest procedure may be to administer to the population sample a battery of tests designed to detect academic disabilities. These test results, when joined to information about the individual's family background and present-day demographic characteristics, should make it possible to determine which disabilities (and which degrees of severity) are directly relevant to adult employment experience, and why. In addition, careful experimental design may make it possible to identify a subset of individuals whose academic disability was relevant only because it made it impossible to gain the educational credentials important in obtaining the kinds of jobs individuals with similar family backgrounds normally obtain. In short, one may be able to identify instances in which the best way to help the child with, for example, what the schools call a math disability would be to prevent colleges or graduate schools from discriminating against an otherwise qualified individual who was unable to meet the institution's basic math requirements (e.g., on college boards or graduate records) when clearly intending to specialize in areas such as law, English literature, or history, in which mathematical ability is irrelevant or marginally relevant.*

* Our concern here is not so much with the youth who does exceptionally well in verbal aptitude and very poorly in math, or vice versa. It is the student with an average or moderately above-average score in one area and a very poor score in the other area who seems most likely to suffer serious discrimination.

Chapter 14

Increasing Employment Even When Discrimination Persists

The research we have called for in the preceding chapter will be especially important if a powerful disability civil rights movement comes into existence. However, despite the large numbers of disabled adults and the even larger number of able-bodied adults with a direct stake in disability, it is possible that the disability civil rights movement will never become a coherent, powerful, well-organized force in American political life. While these considerations are no excuse for defeatism, they do underline the need for finding ways to improve the employment picture that do not require such major and therefore politically demanding alterations in the economy.

In the pages that follow we outline some of the key issues that this complementary research should address. In doing so, we will go over some of the ground already covered in the preceding chapter, but from a perspective that will shed additional light on the problem of employment. The premise throughout will be that the economy greatly underutilizes the abilities and talents of the nation's pool of disabled workers. We assume further that there is no reason to believe that this underutilization stems exclusively from prejudice, systemic discrimination, architectural discrimination, or work organization discrimination. Rather, it is arguable that a significant portion of this underutilization is perfectly rational given the special margin of uncertainty in the information currently available to employers about the economic value of disabled job applicants and disabled job holders—the extra margin of "noise" in their formal and informal credentials and records. To simplify matters, we focus exclusively upon delineating this margin of uncertainty and exploring its impact upon a perfectly unprejudiced employer—that is, an employer whose only interest is in maximizing his firm's ability to compete with other companies.[1] As further simplification, we focus only on the most employable members of the underutilized population of disabled workers, those individuals whom the unprejudiced employer would probably hire if he possessed a reliable way of singling them out from less qualified disabled job applicants.

Despite these simplifications, we believe that our main points apply to virtually all managerial decisions that are made about disabled job applicants and disabled workers. There is a great need for basic and applied research which, by seeking to improve the economy's efficient use of disabled adults, demonstrates that it is in the firm's economic self-interest to change its personnel policies to benefit the disabled job applicant and the disabled workers.*

Before proceeding, it is advisable to forestall a possible misunderstanding of our position. There is a crucial distinction between the immorality or unfairness of structural forces and the motives and morality of the people who perpetuate these forces or act in ways that reinforce the effects of these forces. Certainly employers exist who are prejudiced against disabled workers, and these prejudiced employers are indeed morally wrong. But it is perfectly possible—although as yet impossible to document—that many employers would be willing to hire disabled workers if they knew that the disabled worker was fully competitive with the

---

* Although we do not develop this point in the text, it will become clear as our argument progresses that research on the impact of changes in the organization of work and the physical structure of the work environment may also provide management with new knowledge that will make it in the firm's economic self-interest to improve its employment policies concerning the disabled.

We should add that we do not mean to suggest that employers will always put to use the new knowledge that is gained by the research we shall describe. But it will be infinitely easier to persuade private firms—or to persuade the federal government to force private firms—to adopt new hiring and promotion policies for disabled workers when it can be conclusively shown that these new policies are in the firm's self-interest.

able-bodied workers seeking the same job. By singling out some rational reasons why an unprejudiced employer might well doubt this, we explore a potentially important source of the continuing structural discrimination against disabled workers.

Some major disabilities are perfectly irrelevant to an individual's job ability; other disabilities cruelly reduce it; and often it is hard to tell which is which. Naturally, people who work with disabled children must raise heaven and earth to help the child fully exploit his full human potential, however reduced his abilities may be in certain areas. But the economy is not run according to a similar principle. Employers seek to make the highest profits or ensure their firm's growth; managers seek their own advancement within the firm. Few if any employers place their employee's ability to grow and develop before other concerns, and given the rules of the marketplace it is probable that any employer who did run his company like a school or a charity would soon go out of business. Moreover, while every parent would undoubtedly like the economy to treat his or her child as a unique individual with a unique pattern of needs and strengths, it is unlikely that most parents would accept the sweeping social changes required to ensure that the economy treated every disabled person in a similar way.

Writers in other areas of employment frequently point out that individual employers profit from paying the minority-group worker and women lower wages for the same quality work as that performed by a white male. To the extent that similar practices characterize the employment of disabled workers, only the most unstinting political pressures are likely to change the employer's behavior. However, discrimination takes many forms, and some of these forms hurt the employer almost as much as the employee. When a firm turns away an especially well-qualified worker because of race, sex, or disability, or fails to reward a worker with promotions commensurate with his or her ability, both the worker and the firm suffer, the worker because he or she doesn't get the job, the firm because it hires or promotes a less talented worker. If the employer is prejudiced, the firm's loss can be defined as the price that the employer is willing to pay for his prejudice, and where prejudice is involved, political pressure will be required to change the firm's behavior, pressure that makes prejudice in hiring and promotion too costly even for the most highly prejudiced employer.

But there is still another kind of discrimination in which the failure to hire or to promote the qualified minority-group or female worker stems from inefficiency and inability on the part of management to recognize a highly qualified black or Puerto Rican or woman when they see one. Of all the kinds of discrimination practiced against a minority-group worker, this last kind is in principle the easiest to end—but it is by definition the hardest to see.

Precisely because other forms of job discrimination are so deeply entrenched, it is essential that the disabled and their political allies determine the relative importance of managerial inefficiency in accounting for the difficulties encountered by disabled workers in finding work and in being promoted according to merit. By focusing on the legitimate uncertainties that enter into an unprejudiced employer's decisions about hiring a disabled person, we focus on precisely these kinds of problems. The research we discuss should point the way to establishing the relative importance of managerial inefficiency for different industries, disabilities, and occupations. Our research proposals will also suggest ways to improve the employer's decision making concerning the disabled worker. In addition, we will suggest ways of reimbursing the employer for the added risk that he incurs when he decides to hire a disabled worker despite the greater uncertainty that almost always attends his decision.

Finally, let us emphasize that economic research should not be devoted to helping employers skim off and employ only the cream of the disabled population; it should be devoted to expanding employment for the entire spectrum of disabled individuals. But we see no reason why attempts to resolve the far more tractable problems of the most employable individuals should be deferred until we possess a comprehensive understanding of the employment needs of all groups of disabled people. Indeed, as we have seen, contemporary economics lacks the necessary conceptual tools to assess the full spectrum of the employment needs and problems of disabled individuals. One of the most urgently needed of these tools is an analytic base line against which more ambitious attempts at social reform and experimentation can be measured— attempts such as the ones briefly outlined in the preceding chapter. Information about the scope, nature, and scale of improvements that can be achieved through minimal changes in the employment status quo represent an invaluable component of this framework.

What Information the Employer Needs

What occurs when a disabled youth graduates from high school or college and seeks his or her first job? This is the point at which most discussions of handicapped children and youths break off. Consider the hypothetical (and simplified) example of an employer who holds no prejudice against handicapped individuals and who seeks to base his hiring decisions exclusively on what is in the firm's economic self-interest. Suppose that an able-bodied youth and a disabled youth, both with degrees from a prestigious university, apply for the same job. Let there be no reason to believe that the disabled youth's handicap is at all relevant to his ability to perform the work adequately, and let both youths possess equally impressive paper credentials. Let us suppose that the employer must base his hiring decision upon the information provided him by an academic transcript, letters of recommendation from former teachers, personal impressions of the applicant formed during a job interview, and scores on any vocational aptitude tests administered by the employer. Given this array of information, are there any reasons why an unprejudiced employer would consistently favor the able-bodied applicant over the disabled one?

Unfortunately, there are many reasons. To begin with, the fact that a youth is disabled injects a special measure of ambiguity into his academic records and letters of recommendation. Without making extensive inquiries, the employer has no way of knowing if the applicant's grades have been unfairly inflated or unfairly depressed because his teachers were biased for or against him. Nor does the employer have any way of knowing if the applicant's grades were depressed by emotional problems which he has now outgrown. Perhaps his grades were depressed by the special "handicaps" stemming from the presence of significant architectural and transportation barriers to mobility on the campus—difficulties in using the library or attending laboratory sessions of science courses, undue fatigue from having to maneuver around a large campus many times a day because campus bus and jitney services are not capable of serving the wheelchair-bound, etc.

Letters of recommendation are no clearer. Is the youth being greatly overpraised because of his handicap? Is emotional instability being concealed? Are his intellectual abilities overrated?

Or do the recommendations understate the youth's strengths and abilities because those who wrote them are consciously or unconsciously prejudiced against handicapped people? Again, only if the employer makes an elaborate investigation can he begin to reduce the ambiguity associated with the letters of recommendation to a par with the recommendations the able-bodied youth has presented.

Additional ambiguities arise in the interview with the disabled youth. These ambiguities, which we explored at length in chapters 1, 2, 4, and 5, reinforce the employer's difficulty in getting accurate information about his prospective employee.*

At worst, the employer is likely to misinterpret the physically or sensorily disabled person's different body movements. At best, the employer will frankly admit that, unless he takes more time to get to know the applicant than is possible in a standard interview situation, he really is not in a position to assess adequately the personal characteristics of many handicapped applicants.[2]

More generally, a disabled person's presentation of himself is often a response to social and psychological stigma and may bear little relationship to his economic abilities or disabilities. Nor does an understanding of the problems encountered by disabled people lessen the uncertainties that surround the interview situation; all that this knowledge can contribute is a warning: *caveat emptor*; the disabled applicant is just as likely to undersell as to oversell himself.

Even the applicant's scores on vocational aptitude tests are ambiguous. If the employer understands the premises that underlie these tests, he will realize that their rather limited predictive value has been confirmed only for able-bodied workers and that there is absolutely no reason whatsoever for believing that they will be of any value in predicting the actual job performance of many groups of disabled workers.[3]

For many physically or sensorily disabled individuals, the information ambiguities are further compounded by an employer's uncertainty about what effect their handicaps will have on their flexibility and their productivity. All too often both the employer and the economist who studies handicap assume that anyone with a major disability is automatically less productive and less flexible than an able-bodied worker with comparable experience, educa-

---

* These ambiguities occur whether the handicap is immediately obvious, as cerebral palsy is, or it is not so superficially obvious but appears on the applicant's medical or academic record (e.g., diabetes or mild mental retardation).

tion, and background. However, an impressive number of small-scale studies of employment suggest that the real pattern of productivity differences resembles differences in physical ability or athletic prowess between men and women.[4] All other things being equal, a paraplegic may be less productive in a given job than his able-bodied counterpart.* But many paraplegics will be just as productive as the average able-bodied worker, and some will be more productive. Given this overlap in economic attractiveness, an unprejudiced employer should be perfectly willing to hire the minority of paraplegics who are as productive as or more productive than the average able-bodied worker.† However, before we can expect the employer to hire qualified paraplegics, some way must be found of accurately distinguishing the highly qualified paraplegic from the less qualified. Lacking a battery of tests or a special credential that certifies that the disabled applicant is indeed highly qualified, economic self-interest requires the unprejudiced employer to base his hiring decisions on the *average* properties of the two groups. And since, on average, the employer is more likely to draw a good worker from the pool of able-bodied applicants than from the pool of handicapped applicants, the employer will have every reason to restrict his hiring to the able-bodied.

What we have described are some of the formal and informal credential problems that await many handicapped children when they grow up and enter the job market for the first time. These entry problems—as well as the similar problems that arise in an employer's decisions about promotion and firing—represent an *information barrier* that in some instances, at least, is every bit as serious as outright prejudice against disabled adults. As long as this information barrier remains, the unprejudiced employer will often take a much greater risk if he hires a disabled job applicant than if he plays it safe and hires an able-bodied appli-

* Note that we ignore the question of why these productivity differentials exist—i.e., whether they reflect the inherent biological limitations of paraplegics or also reflect the influence of social factors such as being socialized into a dependent, passive role. We believe that a substantial portion of the productivity differential stems from social factors.

† For the sake of simplicity we ignore here such real-world complications as the number of new workers the employer seeks and the relative numbers of able-bodied and paraplegic job seekers. For example, if the demand for new workers is low, all employers may be able to satisfy their work force needs by restricting their hiring to the most economically attractive subset of workers. Given our assumptions, very few paraplegics will be in this subset.

milar qualifications. Thus, rational economic consid-
ne—and not prejudice or fear—will dictate preferring
lied applicant to the disabled applicant.

n a generation ago, Roger Barker and his colleagues
l the chief uncertainties that many employers had
been found to express on one occasion or another about the
added risks of hiring handicapped workers. It is a stunning commentary on how low a priority is placed upon increasing the job
opportunities of the disabled that little has been done in the
intervening years to study most of these uncertainties.

1. The lower production rate of the disabled leads to increased cost
of production and lowered wages, when wages are based on total
output.
2. The disabled increase accident rates, leading to:
 a. Increased insurance rates
 b. Increased liability for compensable injuries particularly where
 a second injury greatly increases degree of loss.
3. There is greater danger to the disabled and others in emergen-
cies: fires, earthquakes, explosions, etc.
4. There is greater absenteeism among the disabled because of effects
of illness, weather, etc.
5. The disabled increase costs of sick benefit plans, leading to dissatisfaction of other employees.
6. The disabled can perform only a limited number of jobs, leading
to inflexibility in personnel.
7. The disabled cannot be accepted into the regular hierarchy of advancement because higher jobs usually require greater versatility.
8. The disabled cannot meet the demands of the apprenticeship period; e.g., a lame boy can do jewelry repairing or press feeding but
cannot enter these trades as a messenger, which is often required.
9. The handicapped require special considerations—altered machines,
special exits and ramps, help in arriving and leaving—leading to increased costs and interference with routines.
10. Special placement programs with added job analyses and check-
ups lead to increased costs.
11. Fellow workers do not like the disabled, and special considerations are resented.
12. Customers object to a place that looks like a charity organization.
13. The employer's sympathy inevitably will be aroused and he will
demand less of the disabled employee, give him special considerations, and be unable to fire him when he should.
14. Disabled persons have disagreeable personality characteristics:
they are depressed, nervous, temperamental, and demand special
privileges.

15. Because of seniority rights in labor contracts, industry cannot afford to saddle itself with employees whom it cannot fire and who cannot adjust easily to changed production requirements.

16. State safety laws make it difficult to employ the disabled.

17. Trade unions oppose the employment of disabled persons because they are subject to wage exploitation and are more easily subverted by employers.*

18. The employer has a responsibility to his own disabled workers; this is all he can handle.[6]

These observations are nearly as appropriate today as they were when Barker made them in the early 1950s.

In rising to the challenge of the employer's information needs, the federal government should explore a number of different possibilities simultaneously. Pilot programs should be launched in which employers are reimbursed for the additional risk they take when hiring certain groups of disabled workers; when designing these programs it is essential that a wide range of reimbursement schedules be explored so that rough estimates of the responsiveness of employers' hiring practices to increasing reimbursement levels can be explored. Furthermore, it is essential that reimbursement programs be designed in such a way that they do not inadvertently encourage an employer to fire newly hired disabled workers at the end of the subsidy period so that he can then lure a new group of subsidized workers to replace the ones just fired. Although American industry is extremely resistant to the idea of job quotas for any disadvantaged group, we believe that a careful examination of the quota systems in such countries as Great Britain, Sweden, and West Germany may provide useful ideas about how to stimulate industry into making a greater effort to locate and hire qualified disabled workers.[7]

Because the goal of these subsidies is to provide the employer with the monetary means to equalize the differential uncertainty —and therefore the differential risk—associated with employment decisions about able-bodied and handicapped workers with similar credentials, it is possible that the most effective programs will prove rather different in character from either the subsidized

---

* Space prevents us from exploring the role played by labor unions in restricting the employment of disabled adults and in perpetuating other forms of discrimination. Yet as is forcefully noted by the Urban Institute's *Report of the Comprehensive Service Needs Study,* research is needed in this area because "(1) union policies may operate as barriers [to the employment of disabled adults]; (2) unions are in a powerful position to force employers to change the policies which tend to restrict job opportunities for the disabled."[5]

short-term work experience provided by such experimental programs as those being conducted as part of the National Supported Work Demonstration or the long-term wage subsidies that some European countries have used in quota systems that reserve a certain number of jobs in the competitive market for underproductive disabled workers.[8] We are particularly interested in comparing—and perhaps combining—schemes that provide employers with a monetary incentive to hire qualified disabled applicants with schemes that focus on protecting employers against the economic consequences of the added risk that, at present, is often built into the employer's decisions about hiring or promoting a disabled adult. These later schemes would attempt to make good the difference in losses of productivity that were above and beyond what one would ordinarily expect from the inevitable mistakes made in hiring decisions involving able-bodied workers. Here the aim would not be to provide employers with incentives for retaining inefficient disabled workers, but in providing meaningful incentives for taking more chances in their hiring decisions about the disabled.

Ultimately, basic research into the scope and character of job discrimination against disabled workers may provide an opportunity to construct new tests for distinguishing between good and bad job risks among handicapped workers. The development of such tests might also be profitably pursued in conjunction with the development of new kinds of psychometric tests called for in our discussion of special education. Despite the fact that existing personnel tests have relatively low predictive value for able-bodied workers (for even the best tests the average correlation between test performance and work performance is about .35), the prestige enjoyed by such tests in private industry would make worthwhile the construction of nondiscriminatory tests designed especially for handicapped people.[9] Moreover, the special ambiguity of most information that the employer obtains about handicapped people places a special premium on any device that substantially reduces that ambiguity. A second possibility is to arm the disabled job applicant with a set of special credentials that industry would respect. In principle, the provision of such credentials is one of the chief tasks of vocational rehabilitation (VR) programs. In practice, these programs are very poor at placing their graduates—a comment on the quality of the programs, their credibility with employers, the intensity of widespread job discrimination against the handicapped, or some combination of these factors.[10] In any event, the construction of special credentials requires extensive experimentation, for a special credential can serve its intended purpose only if it does indeed accurately predict a disabled worker's subsequent employment performance.

To avoid confusion in our discussion we have singled out only one of a host of areas in which managerial inefficiency (or ambiguous information) *may* play a significant role in affecting the employment experience of disabled adults. Other areas include the hiring and rehiring of newly disabled adults and decisions concerning promotions. It is also possible that in jobs where productivity or flexibility is difficult to judge objectively, employers frequently and unintentionally underestimate the economic value of some disabled employees and inadvertently underpay them.

In calling for basic and applied research into all these areas we must emphasize that this research will be just as costly, time-consuming, and frustrating as the research described earlier. Generalizations from one industry, from one kind of handicap, or from the race, sex, or social class of handicapped people are likely to be difficult. The same basic set of questions will have to be asked about a bewildering range of individuals, occupations, and disabilities which in its diversity is a microcosm of American society.

Yet, like research into job discrimination, research into the efficiency of managerial decision making about disabled workers will provide the raw material out of which tomorrow's economic platform and programs for the disabled adult must be constructed if these social initiatives are to have any hope of success.

Conclusion: The Special Urgency of Basic and Applied Research

In this section we have taken for granted that mobilizing a moral and political commitment to integrating the disabled adult into the economic mainstream is a key priority for everyone concerned about handicapped individuals. We have also assumed that the parents of handicapped children—and professionals who work with handicapped children—are deeply concerned about the employment obstacles that await today's generation of disabled children in adulthood. Taking these assumptions as our point of departure, we have attempted to survey the kinds of questions that must be extensively studied if integration is ever to be an economic reality.

Again let us reiterate: research alone will not eliminate job discrimination against disabled adults or lead to modifications of the work environment and the organization of work that increase the number of disabled adults who can compete with able-bodied adults in the labor market. Nor will research alone necessarily ensure that unprejudiced employers will take advantage of new knowledge. A serious political and moral commitment to integration is absolutely essential if the possibilities created by research are to be translated into action. But by the same token, even the most powerful political commitment to integration will in and of itself be unable to increase significantly the employment of many groups of disabled adults because integration strategies based upon the traditional medical model of disability or upon a mechanical application of the civil rights model to handicap will simply not work.

To sift out when a given handicap is economically relevant and when it is not, to chart and understand the nature and extent of job discrimination, to probe how productivity and job flexibility may be altered by changes in the organization of work and in the physical structure of the work environment, to construct techniques to help or to encourage unprejudiced employers to hire more disabled workers, to win class-action lawsuits claiming systemic patterns of discrimination in a company or an industry—these tasks all presuppose a basic and applied research effort of major proportions. Tragically, the shortcomings of the field of disability economics are unequaled in any other specialty save perhaps the developmental psychology of the handicapped. Given these deficiencies, there is only one way that the necessary research effort can be begun in time for today's generation of handicapped children to benefit from it: that is for the parents of handicapped children, professionals outside economics, disabled adults, and others with an interest in handicap to take the initiative. They must demand that research into the employment problems of the disabled be placed on the same intellectual footing as research into the employment needs of women and able-bodied minority workers.

For the next few years—and conceivably for the next decade—there will be a great need for symbolic breakthroughs in employment. These breakthroughs can help educate the general public to the fact that disabled people are far more capable of leading productive lives than is commonly supposed. By focusing attention on such easily understood obstacles to employment as architectural barriers in buildings and public transportation, the disabled and their allies can raise the political consciousness of the public about disability. At the same time, disability superstars, the Paul Robesons, Jackie Robinsons, and Ralph Bunches of disability, can help dramatize the unfair exclusion of the disabled from the economic mainstream by challenging specific acts of job discrimination practiced against them.

However, while these and other strategies can help to publicize the employment problems of the disabled, there is no reason to believe that in and of themselves they will make a meaningful dent in the needs of the overwhelming majority of disabled adults. Most handicapped adults are not superstars. And the vast majority of adults who will benefit from the elimination of barriers to mobility will almost certainly be denied work because of the many other kinds of discrimination that disabled workers face. Instead of being excluded because he cannot get his wheelchair through the office door, the paraplegic will be denied work because existing hiring procedures strongly discriminate against hiring paraplegics in many jobs for which paraplegia is completely irrelevant.

To go beyond tokenism will require a direct attack on the structures of exclusion that currently restrict the employment options of millions of disabled adults. With the exception of attempts to improve the efficiency of managerial decisions concerning disabled workers, virtually all attacks on the existing structures of job discrimination will require major political and social reforms. Because these reforms will be designed to eliminate the unfair advantage conferred upon the able-bodied worker in today's market, they will require taking jobs away from less qualified able-bodied workers and giving them to more qualified handicapped workers —a process fraught with great potential for political controversy. Moreover, when attempts are made to increase the employment of the disabled by modifying work organization and work environment, very serious issues of expense will also be raised.

The symbolic value of token advances in integration and attacks on physical barriers to mobility will probably begin to wear thin at just about the time today's handicapped children and youths enter the job market in large numbers. If political momentum is not to be lost, the disabled and their political allies will have to address the much more difficult problem of achieving systematic integration. Always assuming that disabled people organize themselves into a potent political force in the first place, the knowledge gained by the research called for in these pages will be of critical practical importance in shaping realistic program goals and political priorities. However, only if a major redirection of basic and applied employment research is made in the very near future is it at all reasonable to expect that the results will be available in time to help the disabled and their allies a decade or so from now.

Without new knowledge, the battle for substantive (as opposed to symbolic) integration will be fought on terms that are extremely unfavorable to the disabled. At best, one can anticipate the proliferation of well-intentioned programs and policy goals patterned upon the experience of able-bodied minority workers and women. These programs will be doomed to almost certain failure. The employment problems of many groups of disabled workers are too complex to fit naturally within the framework of existing minority models; new strategies, which are possible only if the research called for in this chapter is carried out, are necessary to translate a civil rights commitment to integration into terms that do justice to the special problems posed by handicaps. At worst, the present domination of the medical model in discussions of the employment of the disabled may continue. As often occurs today, even activists in disability may confuse demands for more and better welfare services with programs designed to increase as much as possible economic integration. The call may go out for still more welfare programs for the millions of disabled adults who want to work; or civil rights leaders may conclude—as many economists do today on the basis of their ignorance of handicap—that the only practical program is to invest billions in a huge sheltered workshop program, a system of economic hospitals, where fully grown adults can be given make-work in the mistaken belief that "there is nothing else that one can do for these people."

The Unexpected Minority

It was Rousseau who first glimpsed the void that underlies our commonsense perceptions of nature, who intuited something of the full extent to which what is ascribed to biology and what is ascribed to society is itself the product of a social construction. Much of what seems most biologically determined about the handicapped child is also a cultural invention, a judgment about the significance of the disability which presents itself in the guise of a self-evident biological truth. The life of every handicapped child is shaped by this paradox. To grow up handicapped in America is to grow up in a society that, because of its misreading of the significance of disability, is never entirely human in the way it treats the person within.

Blacks, women, gay people, and the elderly encounter many of the same kinds of oppression as the handicapped—prejudice, stigma, job discrimination, the moral arrogance of professionals. And scholars once studied the black child in the same self-defeating way that they still study the handicapped child. But powerful metaphors of disease and health dominate our perceptions of disability, and these metaphors obscure the full extent of society's oppression of handicapped children and adults.

The problems of most disadvantaged groups elicit conflicting responses among laymen and professionals. No single ideal of fairness prevails; no interpretation dominates the national debate to the exclusion of all others. Are poor blacks genetically inferior to whites, the victims of such diseaselike conditions as cultural deprivation, or an oppressed minority for whom political organization and struggle must be central? Is alcoholism a disease or a vice? Should we help mentally ill people or ostracize them? Are women's rights advocates members of a valid political movement or malcontents who should be ignored? Are lesbians mentally ill, depraved, or the victims of political oppression? Opinion on all these questions is divided. Though often influential, the social pathologist's deviance analysis, his therapeutic morality, is only one approach among many.

Disability is different. Here there is nearly perfect agreement between cultural beliefs about what is fair and tolerant and the expert's preferred analysis. No professional needs to convince us that disability is a kind of deviance. Just as we see that handicaps are diseaselike conditions, it seems only natural that the handicapped role defines the legitimate needs of handicapped people. This triumph of a therapeutic morality is without parallel in any other area of civil society. It is exceeded only in those "totalizing institutions" where the professional's abuses of the social pathology model have been most pronounced—prisons, nursing homes, chronic disease hospitals, mental hospitals, residential schools for the handicapped, residential schools for Indian children run by the Bureau of Indian Affairs, and custodial institutions for the retarded.

Thus, what many social critics have perceived as a future threat for society at large has long been a bitter reality for many handicapped children and adults: the disabled already live within a therapeutic state. In this society of the "sick" there is no place for any of the hallmarks of a present or future adult identity; no place for politics, no place for work and sexuality, no place for choice between competing moralities. All political, legal, and ethical issues are transformed into questions of disease and health, deviance and normal adjustment, proper and improper management of the disability. Language itself changes. "Respecting the child's individual needs" means focusing upon the child's deviance to the exclusion of everything else. "Special education" means providing the child with schooling that usually is neither special nor education in the ordinary sense of these words. "Maturity" means learning to accept one's social oppression as well as the true limits of the body. "Portraying with sensitivity and understanding the problems of handicapped people" becomes an Orwellian euphemism for perpetuating the handicapped role's vision of disability in the media. Is it any wonder that the minority-group characteristics of the disabled so often come as a surprise, that the handicapped child and the handicapped adult are an unexpected minority? To recall Sheldon Wolin's fine phrase, the "sublimation of politics" has proceeded furthest with handicapped people. Of all America's oppressed groups, only the handicapped have been so fully disenfranchised in the name of health.

Psychological Aspects of Handicap

From *The Psychoanalytic Study of the Child* 15 (1960): 430–53:

Analysis of a Boy with a Congenital Deformity

by André Lussier

(London, England—Montreal, Canada)*

This paper is based on the analysis of Peter, a thirteen-year-old boy born with malformed shoulders and abnormally short arms terminating in hands having only three fingers and no thumbs. When Peter entered analysis, the over-all measurement from his shoulders to fingertips was scarcely eight inches. As far as is known, the psychodynamic implications at the unconscious level of so severe a congenital deformity have not previously been described in psychoanalytic literature. The positive results presented here are to be attributed to the inspiration and close collaboration of the staff of the Hampstead Child-Therapy Clinic under the direction of Anna Freud.

* This case was treated by the author in the Hampstead Child-Therapy Clinic under the individual supervision of Dr. Ilse Hellman which is gratefully acknowledged.

The Hampstead Child-Therapy Clinic is maintained by grants given by the following Foundations: The Field Foundation, Inc., New York; The Ford Foundation, New York; The Foundations' Fund for Research in Psychiatry, New Haven, Connecticut; The Anna Freud Foundation, New York; The Grant Foundation, Inc., New York; The Estate of Flora Haas, New York; The Old Dominion Foundation, U.S.A.; The Psychoanalytic Research and Development Fund, Inc., New York.

A special objective of the analysis was to compare the castration anxiety associated with such a gross bodily handicap with that of a neurotic youngster having no physical abnormality.

A finding of unusual interest in this analysis was the specific constructive function assumed by the fantasy life in the development of a number of permanent skills and ego abilities.

Background Information

Much of the information about Peter's family background came from the reports of social workers and Hampstead Clinic personnel who had interviewed Peter's mother at various times prior to and during his analysis.*

The whole subject of Peter's birth and early childhood was fraught with anxiety for his mother. She said she had never got over the shock of seeing him for the first time . . . it was terrible! Never before had she spoken of this to anyone.

She was certain that Peter's deformity had been caused by her mother-in-law with whom she had not got along at all well. The mother-in-law, she said, used to "row" her during the pregnancy. This quarreling she knew to be bad, and one day to avoid a scene on the street she tried to pass the mother-in-law "without taking any notice of her." The ruse failed and the incensed mother-in-law seized her by the shoulders to bring her to a halt. While she was not injured, she was greatly upset by the encounter and her feelings were hurt. She was three months pregnant at the time and was sure that Peter's deformity was a direct consequence.

Peter's birth was an easy one, his mother reported. She was not told of the child's deformity at the time of the delivery and discovered it only when the baby was first brought to her. The sight was a terrible blow. "His arms were so tiny," she recalled.

The Parents

Peter's mother said she had had a happy childhood and had been devoted to her own mother. She described herself, however, as having always been high-strung and according to a medical report had suffered from neurasthenia when she was thirteen years old.

Her husband was the first boy ever to take notice of her. Their marriage followed a five-year courtship. In 1940, when Peter was a

---

* Mrs. Bianca Gordon, psychotherapist with the Hampstead Clinic, saw Peter's mother at regular intervals.

year and a half old, the father was called up for army service, and the mother took Peter back to her native town to live with her parents. Except for leaves, the father was away until 1946.

A second child, a daughter, was born in 1941 when Peter was three.

When Peter was five, his maternal grandmother took ill and Peter's mother had then to keep house for four men—her own father and her mother's three brothers.

The maternal grandmother died three years later. Peter's mother said she thought at the time she would never get over her mother's death. In fact, she said, it had kept coming back into her mind ever since, accompanied by what she described as horrible thoughts.

Peter's mother was a Roman Catholic but did not attend church. Her husband, she reported, did not believe in religion. Actually, the mother had little to say about the father. He was an engineer's mate, and while not regarded as an impressive figure for his son was nonetheless looked upon as the authority in the family. Following his return from the war, he got along well with Peter, then seven, and often played with him.

After the war, the family lived in a poor district and the parents were far from satisfied with their housing. The mother said she would like to have had a house with a garden where Peter could have played without being seen by the passers-by. Moreover, the fact that Peter had to sleep in the same room as his sister disturbed his mother, especially in view of Peter's handicap.

Peter as Baby and Boy

Peter's mother breast-fed him until he was two months old, when she had to wean him because of cracked and festered nipples caused, she felt, by her own worrying. She had found it difficult to handle Peter because he could not put his arms around her. In the bath she would support him with one hand under his neck and was constantly fearful he might slip out of her grasp and drown.

During the first six months Peter cried almost nightly. To comfort him his mother would carry him about and give him "gripe water" but would not feed him because she "kept to a schedule." Apart from this, he was a healthy baby and no trouble. His mother started training him to use a pot when he was two months old and said she had persevered in this training to have him clean and dry by about seven months.

During his first year Peter was twice separated from his mother for periods of about six weeks each while he was in the hospital for surgical interventions to separate the webbed fingers of his right hand and to provide greater mobility in shoulders and arms, one of which, the left, had no elbow.

From early infancy, Peter was clever with his feet and could pick up things with his toes. While learning to walk, he would fall down frequently because he seemed top-heavy.

The mother told the social workers that she had taken Peter to doctor after doctor, always in the hope that he could be "cured" although she had been repeatedly told that his condition was beyond remedy. When the doctors explained that Peter's left arm had no elbow she at first accepted the fact but soon began to believe she could see one and even that Peter was beginning to bend his arm a little.

When he was three, the sister was born. Physically normal, Mary was the second and last child. During this pregnancy the mother had imagined she was going to have another boy whom she was already calling "Stephen." She told Peter about "Stephen" and when Peter was naughty she would threaten him by saying that "Stephen" would not come to life because of his bad behavior. She claimed she had never been afraid that this second child would be deformed.

The mother reported that Peter and Mary got along well together, that Peter was fond of his sister, and that Mary, in turn, would "stick up" for Peter. Sometimes, however, Peter would torment Mary and his mother had to "smack him." During the analysis, very little emerged about the sister. Clearly, Peter compensated for his insecurity by regarding the little girl with her normal arms as no more than a baby, and consequently no threat to him.

When Peter's mother took him out as a baby and young child, she would cover him up to hide his arms. She said she felt very ashamed of him. She was especially embarrassed when people stared, and this uneasiness continued right up to the beginning of the boy's analysis. On his part, Peter would react to stares by turning to his mother for reassurance, but she would "just feel ashamed" and could not comfort her son. She realized she was failing Peter, causing him suffering and making him more insecure. Even so, she did not believe in spoiling him, although, she said, it was hard at times not to do so.

By the time Peter was about ten years old, he had acquired the hard-earned skill of feeding himself, even being able to use a knife and fork, although still needing help to cut meat. He was described as a very clean eater. He could partially dress himself. He could put on his socks and shoes but could not do up his laces and needed help with some garments. He also needed help in the toilet right up to the beginning of his analysis. Shortly thereafter, however, the slight growth of arms and shoulders associated with puberty made it possible for him to take care of himself in the toilet.

Peter started going to school at the age of three. He was enrolled at a regular neighborhood school and did well there. At seven, he was transferred to a special school for the physically handicapped. Here he gradually lost interest in schoolwork, becoming more and more preoccupied with his daydreams. His studies suffered to the degree that he was regarded as a backward pupil. His backwardness was, in fact, one of the motivating factors in the later decision to give him analytic treatment.

When he was about eight and a half, Peter began arriving home from school with his pants soiled. This continued for about four months. His mother blamed the school, explaining that Peter was too shy to ask for help when going to the toilet. The soiling never occurred at home.

Only two months after this problem had been overcome, Peter began wetting the bed. This happened right after another hospitalization for surgical intervention preparatory to the fitting of artificial arms.* He continued wetting the bed nightly for about five months until medication prescribed by his physician gradually cleared up the symptom. Enuresis, however, recurred a year later. His mother blamed herself for these troubles as she was still upset by the comparatively recent death of her own mother.

At the age of nine, when Peter was still able to read only a few words, mostly two-letter or three-letter words at that, he was given a Revised Stanford-Binet intelligence test which rated him as a low normal (IQ 85–90). Subsequent observations suggest the rating did not do justice to his intelligence.

The Problem

Manifest behavioral difficulties already referred to were instrumental in bringing Peter into analysis at the age of thirteen. The nocturnal enuresis appearing at the age of nine following the surgical intervention, and recurring at ten, was one of these. The backwardness at school was another. But, as soon became clear during the analysis, the fundamental problem was an emotional disturbance expressed in a continuous and inventive evasion of factual truth and in the creating of a fantasy life of remarkable complexity and color. There were, too, some depressive tendencies.

For a boy with Peter's handicap and experiences, such difficulties were to be expected. But unexpected was the way in which Peter failed to exhibit either masochistic satisfaction, passivity, or self-pity —three characteristics only too readily associated in our mind with the psychology of many disabled people.†

Peter did not like to be handled, nor did he want to be regarded as

---

* Before his physical growth stopped, surgical work had to be done to the inner articulations of the shoulder as a preparation for the future fitting of better artificial arms.

† Conclusion drawn by Anna Freud following her diagnostic interview with Peter.

an object of pity. He did not seem to derive or want to derive gain
or gratification from his disability. Dominant in his behavior was the
active striving toward the achievement of his goals.

The Analysis

The analysis proper, consisting of intensive work in daily sessions
five days a week, lasted for about twenty months. Contact was maintained for a further sixteen months, but during the last year Peter's
visits were irregular, varying from about once a week to once a month
toward the end.

Compensatory Mechanisms

The early stages of the analysis produced many illustrations of the
psychological mechanisms Peter was using to cope with his deformity.
Three were dominant. He sought to push his handicap out of existence by intensive denial of its reality; he built a fantasy world from
which he excluded his physical handicap; and he developed certain
reaction formations as defenses against insecurity and inferiority. His
aim, both consciously and unconsciously, was always to prove to the
world that whatever anybody else could do with normal arms he
could do as well or better with short arms and without artificial aids.

Early in the treatment, the sessions were filled with talk of his splen-
did exploits and great hopes. He would see himself excelling in all
kinds of competitions and activities in none of which he would make
even the slightest allowance for his handicap. In his fantasy he was
a remarkable tree climber, for example, and also something of a
champion at cutting down trees, both obvious impossibilities. He
boasted how skillfully he could ride a bicycle. He liked to imagine
himself, too, as the youngest trumpet player in the world. "I want to
be the best, alone on top, no one better than me." His greatest wish
at this time was to own a trumpet.

The need to show off was continuously apparent in his behavior
and his fantasies. He wanted his analyst to know that he was physically the strongest of his gang. He did, in fact, carry a large dagger at
his side which he would brandish as a symbol of his prowess. Heroic
in its denial of the deficiency of his arms was his boast that he could
"slap the other boys in the face so hard!"

Again and again he would tell how he planned to organize special
shows in London at which he would be the featured attraction, diving
headlong from the Tower Bridge to the astonishment of the skeptical
crowd.

Peter especially liked to acquire things that other boys did not have, so that he could provoke their envy. "Look, you haven't got what I've got." "See my big dagger, mine is bigger." He expressed this kind of feeling more vehemently and more frequently than would the average boy.

His deep-seated insecurity due to his deformity constantly impelled Peter to essay exceptional feats of daring or skill. The day he started taking swimming lessons he commented: "I am looking forward to swimming with my girl friend; I want to show her that I can swim; perhaps she does not think I can do it well. . . . If I have enough pride, I will get my swimming certificate." Then he recalled an earlier incident at the pool when, feeling unsure of being accepted by the poolside gang of young swimmers, he had climbed to the upper springboard to display how fearless he was. When the other boys saw him up there, he said, they became frightened for him, and when he realized they were frightened, he jumped into the water. The boys were impressed. They applauded him and accepted him. This story shows how desperately hard Peter was working to prove he was in no way inferior to his peers in achievement.

During the first months of the analysis, it could be said that the intensity of Peter's fantasy life was so great as to verge at times on pseudologia phantastica and to carry him close to borderline capacity in reality testing. One day, full of excitement, he reported: "I have just won a bike by answering questions." The fact was he had entered a daily newspaper contest by answering questions and sending in the contest entry. At the time, this action was all the foundation he needed on which to build the belief that he had already won the bicycle. Moreover, he had moved on from this belief in ownership to the planning in minute detail of a 400-mile trip.

At this stage his fantasies were so intense that their realization in actuality seemed to him to be at most no more than a matter of time. This conviction led him into a number of dangerous situations such as that resulting from his bravado on the high-diving board.

Castration Anxiety

Peter's castration anxiety soon assumed a paramount place in the analysis. Paradoxically, his anxiety was in no way different in type from that of any physically normal neurotic boy except in that he had a permanent unconscious need to compensate for the lack of normal arms.

Peter's castration anxiety was related to masturbation fantasies and activities, to oedipal strivings, and to the resulting guilt and fear of punishment. In his case, the arm defect was unconsciously feeding the castration complex. The defective arms were, in a sense, equated with "defective" genitals and thus were unconsciously taken as evidence of actual castration.

Peter had all the classic masturbation fantasies but with unusually strong exhibitionistic components. In these, his symbolic exhibitionistic masturbating was always followed by symbolic castration.

The exhibitionism was shown in the fantasies in which he performed as a trumpet player and was cheered by huge, delirious crowds. Similarly in other fantasies, he performed notable exploits on a bicycle for which his photograph would appear in the daily papers.

The sense of guilt arising out of his strong sexual feelings for his mother and the consequent fear of punishment were shown through such actual dreams as this: He was riding his bicycle at great speed . . . he became more and more excited, then started going down a steep hill . . . his mother was there watching his performance . . . she laughed and was quite "thrilled" . . . a crowd of bystanders was equally thrilled . . . at the peak of his excitement he found he could not control the speed at which he was racing downhill. "I am going so fast it isn't possible to put the brakes on. I can't stop. I have an accident and break my leg."

It is interesting that Peter had a variety of fantasies revealing oedipal strivings in which he had to go to the hospital for a broken leg, not an arm.

In some fantasies so much emotional significance was attached to cycling that Peter's legs symbolically became his genitals. Cycling was sexualized and consequently injury to legs represented punishment by castration. The same process was also apparent in those trumpet fantasies in which the trumpet was broken.

This sexualization was so intense that Peter said he had to avoid thinking about his bicycle or trumpet at night. "It makes me feel too hot and too excited, and then it is hard to fall asleep."

Still another instance of phallic displacement was Peter's frightening dream of lying in bed, face down, and finding a big snake under his tummy. Peter used to masturbate at night lying on his stomach.

During the period in the analysis in which Peter was longing for a bicycle or a trumpet, there were a few episodes of homosexual anxiety. He had indeed to miss some sessions to avoid becoming "too excited" while talking to his analyst.

The Significance of Enuresis

From the material provided by the analysis it became evident that the enuresis associated with Peter's intense oedipal fantasies had two meanings for him, as it does for most enuretics. It meant prohibited sexual activity accompanied by castration as punishment. And simultaneously, it had the reassuring meaning of an undamaged, well-functioning penis. For Peter, castration anxiety was intensified because unconsciously he equated his arm defect with castration. This unconscious equating of a real with a symbolic handicap intensified both his denial of his deformity and his great need to overcompensate for it. The arm defect, in itself a visible handicap, also greatly increased his need for displaced phallic exhibitionism.

Most of Peter's dreams show that this phallic exhibitionism was a basic factor in his bed wetting. For example, he had many dreams involving airplanes. In front of an amazed crowd including either his mother or the Queen, he would pilot a plane at a terrific speed. Then he would crash in water and break his leg. The dream sequence was obviously one of masturbation-erection, enuresis, castration-punishment. After Peter had been in analysis for about a year, the enuresis disappeared.

The Construction Role of Fantasy

The extent to which Peter was able to make constructive use of fantasy in the formation of ego abilities was the most unexpected development of the analysis.

As mentioned earlier, the boy entertained, for a time, a number of unrealizable fantasies such as climbing and cutting down trees. These soon dropped out of the analysis completely. But other fantasies and hopes, which my colleagues and I admittedly felt to be equally unattainable, remained for some time as central points of interest until these too were dropped one by one from the analysis but for quite a different reason. They moved out of the realm of fantasy into actual accomplishment. During the analysis, Peter learned to play the trumpet well enough to plan a career as a performer. He learned to swim and dive well enough to earn a lifesaving certificate. In this he measured up to the standards required of all applicants; no special allowances were made for his deformity. And he learned to ride a bicycle in the face of the opposition of his apprehensive parents. These accomplishments showed that Peter had a more generous and, at the same time, more realistic assessment of his capabilities than did his parents, his analyst, or the other professional consultants. Moreover, he seemed to have at his disposal an almost inexhaustible fund of energy.

That Peter should talk about his hopes and fantasies just so long as they remained in the realm of unreality was an unusual and fascinating aspect of the analysis. He presented a succession of foci of intense interest—the trumpet, the swimming, the bicycle, and others. Each of these was talked about with great excitement, elaborated in imaginative detail, then dropped abruptly the moment Peter took action to make it a reality. For example, the entire subject of trumpet and music dropped out of the analysis when Peter was finally given a cornet. The analyst would therefore have been unaware of the details of the boy's real achievements but for the reports of the therapist who interviewed the mother.

It could be said, then, that the analysis dealt at any one time only with the residue of Peter's fantasy world, and the work of the analysis could be described as the continuing transformation of fantasies into ego abilities executed in reality. Peter was using fantasy to conquer reality. And through this process he was seeking a secure ego identity.

It was significant also that Peter's most highly charged fantasies all revealed strivings toward a masculine identity. This was particularly apparent in the way the trumpet and the analyst served alternately as means of achieving masculinity. When Peter felt he was gaining enough satisfaction from his trumpet, he felt he could dispense with the analyst by missing sessions.

Multiple Mechanisms

At this point it might be well to note that any one of Peter's activities must be recognized as having been brought about as the result of the interplay of more than one mechanism. Phallic displacement, overcompensation, and reaction formation were involved in the trumpet playing before large audiences, in the display of badges won in swimming, diving, and lifesaving, and in the wearing of a dagger at his side. One striking instance betraying the extent to which Peter's short arms threatened his masculine pride was the determined attempt at fourteen years of age to win membership in a fishing club whose minimum age requirement was sixteen. He set his heart on this goal because he was convinced that, should he succeed on grounds of actual performance as a fisherman, the world would cease to entertain doubts about his potentialities. He would then belong to the category of men. Moreover, membership would entitle him to wear "a big badge" on his coat which he could show to all his friends. Here again, drawing upon his tremendous reserves of energy, Peter did win the coveted membership on merit despite his age.

From Fantasy to Reality

Some considerable time after Peter's fantasies relating to the trumpet had moved out of the field of the analysis, he brought the subject back in again in an unforeseen way. One day he brought his cornet (trumpet) to the analytic session. Secure now in his real achievements and repeated successes as a musician, he somehow felt able to bring this once highly cathected subject again to the attention of his analyst.

"You want me to play?" he asked, his eyes radiant. Hesitation and shyness were brushed aside by the determination to demonstrate his skill. He communicated the feeling that nothing in the world could have prevented him from playing.

On this occasion, Peter was wearing his new artificial left arm. He said this would be his first time to play for anybody while wearing the artificial arm, and that playing would be much more than normally difficult. The wonder was he could play at all. As the artificial left hand could not grasp the cornet properly, he perforce had to use his undersized, thumbless right hand with its three slender fingers to help hold the instrument while simultaneously fingering the valves. For extra support, he put one foot up on a chair so he could rest the cornet against his knee. In this awkward and little-practiced position, he played relatively well.

After playing several selections, one of which he had composed himself, he commented that "the next time" he would play twelve tunes in a much better way without his artificial arm. After a moment's reflection, however, he said it would probably be better for him to try to learn wearing his artificial arm because the arm would give him a better appearance on the stage. The comment indicated how far removed Peter was from seeking a masochistic advantage from his handicap, or, to express it in other terms, to exhibit with his defect.

Comparisons of Peter's fantasy life with that of more physically normal adolescents revealed one fundamental difference in the relationship between sexual (masturbatory) fantasies and symbolic activity. When a physically normal youth abandons a sexual fantasy, he almost invariably jettisons all related symbolic activity and interest. Peter, in contrast, was able to transfer the interest associated with symbolic activity to constructive activity. For him, fantasy was the precursor of, not the substitute for, real striving. His early intense preoccupation with his trumpet fantasy, for example, later became the driving power that carried him over the arduous road to competence as a musician.

Observations made by Anna Freud concerning the fantasy life of the physically normal boy indicate how unusual was Peter in this respect. Anna Freud (1936) writes:

We must not suppose that an adolescent ponders on the various situations in love or on the choice of a profession in order to think out the right line of behavior, as an adult might do or as a boy in the latency-period studies a piece of machinery in order to be able to take it to pieces and put it together again. Adolescent intellectuality seems merely to minister to day-dreams. Even the ambitious phantasies of the pre-pubertal period are not intended to be

translated into reality. When a young lad phantasies that he is a great con-
queror, he does not on that account feel any obligation to give proof of his
courage . . . in real life. . . . He [the boy] evidently derives gratification
from the mere process of thinking. . . . His behaviour is determined by other
factors and is not necessarily influenced by the results of these intellectual
gymnastics [pp. 175–76].

How different is the story of Peter, the boy who left little or nothing of his fantasy world behind him with the passing of puberty.

Explanations of Peter's psychological processes must be tentative
pending corroborative findings in similar cases. A hypothesis could
be: Nothing of Peter's fantasy world could be abandoned or left
behind because every part of it had to be put at the service of an
unconscious need, the need to find substitutes for the growing of
longer arms. This mechanism of transformation would be part of a
never-ending denial of inferiority. And the deformity would be a perpetual stimulus for compensatory strivings.

Characteristics of the Disabled

The belief that "as long as one is convinced one can do something,
one can do it" has helped many people to worthy achievements. But
it can also be conveniently used to feed daydreaming while inhibiting
activity which would put the conviction to the test.

So far as physically disabled people are concerned, surface observation shows that, according to their reactions, they can be divided
into two categories, the active and the passive ones, the doers and the
dreamers. Apparently, in the analytic literature, more attention has
been paid so far to the passive than to the active type. Veterans' hospitals are still caring for many patients described as "passive-depend-
ent personalities." Typically these patients use their noncongenital
handicaps, consciously or unconsciously, as justification for passivity
and dependence. They stop striving for attainable achievements and
make inaction morally acceptable by considerations of self-pity. The
handicap becomes the pivot for a multitude of unfruitful fantasies
and excuses for resignation.

These passive individuals preserve the conviction that they could
accomplish great things by avoiding test by action. Analogous is the
frequently encountered case of the student with poor grades who does
not dare work hard for fear he might shatter the gratifying belief
that he would be at the head of his class if only he would apply himself. Here again, reality is a threat and is sacrificed. Passivity and
fantasy leave no room for achievement.

Not so with Peter. He dared to put his "dreams" to the test. For him there was nothing mutually exclusive between the appearance of compensatory fantasies on the one hand and compensatory actual improvements in ego performance on the other. Peter's real achievements were so well integrated, so positively ego-syntonic, that it seems we must look beyond pathological mechanisms for a comprehensive explanation.

Turning passivity into activity is there, but it is only part of the picture. It will be shown later that the fear of passivity played a part in spurring the boy to greater endeavors. But a purely defensive reaction cannot be the sole impetus for so many positive undertakings. If it could, it would produce reaction formations of classic, crystallized structure whereas Peter's behavior approximates much more closely that resulting from sublimation. It might be better to say that Peter's functioning could serve as an illustration of the adaptive function of fantasy life, according to Heinz Hartmann's elaborations of Anna Freud's views on the denial of reality by fantasy. Hartmann (1939) wrote:

. . . what are the positive adaptive elements of fantasy? . . . It is possible, and even probable, that the relationship to reality is learned by ways of *detours*. There are avenues of reality-adaptations which, at first, certainly lead away from the real situation.

The function of play is a good example. . . . Another example is the auxiliary function of fantasy in the learning process: though fantasy always implies an initial turning away from a real situation, it can also be a preparation for reality and may lead to a better mastery of it. Fantasy may fulfill a synthetic function by provisionally connecting our needs and goals with possible ways of realizing them . . . there are fantasies which, while they remove man from external reality, open up for him his internal reality [pp. 17–19].

Peter's condition, furthermore, should not be compared too narrowly to that encountered in certain character disorders and in manic-depressives who exhibit much compulsive, compensatory activity. Peter was all this—and something more. He looked forward while the others looked backward. His progress was more than a reactive defense. He actually achieved increasing emotional security as he went along. His actions and integration regularly operated to reduce the tension between "wanting" and "being able" to do something.

Compulsive work, counterphobic reaction, reactive compensatory mechanisms, all have something static about them. Peter's activity, in contrast, was creative. There seems no doubt that Peter is an excellent example of an "active disabled" person. The people who belong to this category do not usually seek psychiatric help, and their reactions are usually dismissed as "normal." Whether or not Peter's drive toward activity is characteristic of all the individuals who belong to this group, or whether we have to regard him as exceptional, will have to be decided in the future when more detailed analytic studies of such persons are made available.

Artificial Arms and Ego Identity

Peter had first been provided with artificial arms several years before his analysis. But for the most part he could not be induced to use them with any regularity. By using his own arms he was putting his inborn physical equipment to the test. After all, Peter had always known his body as it was. For him, his body ego was intact. While others may have been shocked by the sight of his arms, Peter himself was not. His body image had been unchanged all through his life. If there were any element of shock for him, it could only be brought about by the disturbing experience of comparing himself to others, an experience bound to jeopardize his security and self-confidence.

If, then, he so consistently refused to use the artificial arms, the reason must have been to valorize those very body parts that threatened most to feed an inferiority complex. His intense motivation toward action and achievement was a measure of this need to prove his own natural body adequate to every challenge. Yet his competition with other children was of a normal kind. The intensity with which he resorted to the mechanism of compensation in displacement was proportional to the intensity of the threat of inferiority and failure in the experiences of competition. The threat to his inner security first posed by his mother's shame served as a trigger for more compensatory performances.

We hope we correctly use Erikson's concepts and terminology (1956) in stating that the artificial arms were completely excluded from the field of Peter's identity. They were not given even the smallest part to play in his drive toward levels of performance adequate to his ideal ego identity. The sense of *self*, of *his* personality, of *his* potentialities, he felt should be based solely on the physical equipment nature gave him.

Peter's first direct reference to his arms after several months of analysis had nothing to do with his desperate wish to see them grow. On the contrary, it was a protest against having anything further done to his arms as they were. The occasion was the relating of a dream of castration anxiety in which he was walking on railway tracks when a train (the analyst) roared up to him too quickly to be avoided, hit him, and mangled his arms.

Peter himself linked this dream to the previous operations he had undergone preparatory to the fitting of artificial arms. Peter had greatly feared that the hospital doctors might decide to cut off the short arms in order to replace them with artificial ones. The surgeons had, in fact, suggested that this might be necessary in order to fit the newest, most improved type of artificial arms. Peter opposed the possibility with intensity.

Obviously such an ablation was conceived of by the boy as a brutal attack from the adult world, a cruel attempt to deprive him of any chance to reach a meaningful sense of identity. It could destroy any possibility of reaching a reconciliation with his body ego. It could be so traumatic an experience as even to pave the way for depression or devastating passivity.

It should be noted here that there was no evidence that self-pity motivated Peter's exploits. He would go out into the streets with his trumpet at Christmas and other times to play tunes and collect money from the passers-by. In this kind of activity where, if anywhere, self-pity could be expected to reveal itself in passive exploitation, Peter's whole objective was to impress people by his performance, not by his handicap.

Sexualization

The transformation of fantasies into the ego constitution was not achieved without hazard. For the main fantasy, that of becoming a musician, the process at the instinctual level was for a while a precarious one. During one phase, the musical activity was a highly sexualized, aggressive activity which threatened to interfere with Peter's musical training and performances. He enjoyed, for example, playing with the trumpet pointed as "high up in the air" as his arms would permit. When this playing with trumpet raised was accompanied by real erections in the presence of girls during a concert, Peter had to stop playing because of the sexual excitement. The resulting anxiety tended toward inhibition rather than sublimation. Fortunately, the problem was left behind after the phallic content in the activity was interpreted, thus desexualizing it without destroying it. Toward the end of the analysis Dorothy Burlingham summed up this aspect of Peter's progress: "His ego and id seem to be well lodged in his music, which might enable him really to do something with his gift." *

Reality and Depression

Two questions which presented themselves again and again during the analysis were: Why did Peter keep his real achievements out of the analytic sessions for so long? Why did he seem to cease being thrilled by anything as soon as it stopped being a fantasy?

* Dorothy Burlingham, co-director, Hampstead Clinic, during a case conference.

One hypothesis is that a coveted object (trumpet) or function (musician) was unconsciously equated to the growing of longer arms. While such objects or functions remained in fantasy, they held great emotional significance for Peter, but the moment they entered the real world, they lost their symbolic meaning. This process of converting fantasy to fact was one of painful disillusionment in that it meant abandoning a "dream" through which Peter could keep alive his deeply cherished hope for normal arms. His unconscious reaction was to devalue the real object or function. It could be expected that the process would have a depressive effect, and this did, in fact, occur. At times when he had nothing exciting to talk about in the realm of fantasy and thus felt he had to talk about himself (reality), he would become depressed.

Earlier, when the trumpet was still an object of fantasy, Peter had fully expected to receive one as a birthday present. When it failed to arrive, his disappointment was so great that he became depressed, lost interest in eating, could not sleep, and missed sessions. However, as the analysis proceeded, he developed the ability to accept disappointments of reality without experiencing such deep feelings of depression.

Important also in Peter's personality was an unconscious feeling of incompleteness expressing itself endlessly in attempts to compensate for his deformity. This feeling developed in spite of the strong body ego which made him resist the use of artificial arms. Toward the end of the analysis, it was apparent that Peter would never be able to feel he had achieved full masculine status. Unlike most physically normal men who reach a relatively satisfactory state of equilibrium in their male role, Peter gave indication that he would always need some mechanism to deal with the psychic effects of his deformity. Achievement and success would be needed again and again to bolster his masculine ego.

This mechanism was seen in operation on a number of occasions. For instance, after six successful months as a trumpeter in a band, Peter began talking about forming his own band where he would be the leader, "the boss." But, he emphasized, he had no intention of showing off. This was in contrast to the exhibitionism he had displayed earlier. In talking about "his" band, he said he would not want to make it too obvious that he was the conductor. He would just like to give a discreet signal to start the band playing. Surely the other members of the band would not like him to show off too much and he would not want to make them envy him.

Further, revealing his need to devalue arms of normal length, Peter commented that he particularly disapproved of the usual behavior of most trumpet players on the stage. He described them as "being foolish with their trumpets . . . showing off by throwing them up in the air . . . and playing in the sky." Peter, of course, could not flourish his trumpet in this fashion. In a matter-of-fact way, he summed up: "A trumpet is meant to play music, not to make a big show."

In the foregoing, Peter's psychic handling of his physical defect might be compared with the way in which young girls typically deal with a castration complex. They depreciate their own bodies but take pride in their pursuits. It is as if they were to say: "My body is of no consequence, but what I do is marvelous." Similarly, Peter's phallic exhibitionism found expression through achievement.

Oedipus Complex, Regression, and Adolescence

One day Peter came to his session fully determined, for the second time, to play the trumpet for his analyst. On the one hand, this was a sign of increasing security and reconciliation with reality. On the other, it revealed strong oedipal rivalry and forewarned of the danger of regression to a passive-masochistic state.

Unconsciously, this performance meant that he could do in front of his analyst something the latter was incapable of doing. It proved to be too daring a show of his phallic superiority as it was followed by nightmares in which his trumpet was broken into pieces and in which he was run over by horses and gorillas. In the nightmares he was reduced to a castrated, female condition. He had many ensuing fantasies, verging into real beliefs, in which his analyst was jealous of him, was unhappy that he had become a musician, and was displeased that he had got a bigger trumpet. (Peter had recently changed his small cornet for a trumpet.)

Earlier in the analysis, the rivalry in the transference and the anxiety accompanying it did not go too deeply and were expressed quite simply. He would say: "I would like to be the boss here, too, and make you talk to me and not only me talking to you. . . ." One day, a necessary visit to his dentist provoked a nightmare that was related to the transference relationship: Two very big men seized him and took him by force to the dentist; they were ugly and wanted to take out all his teeth. After relating this dream, he went on without a pause into his own fantasy: "A boy is in the dentist chair; the dentist takes a hammer, hits the boy, and takes out all his teeth. Then the boy wakes up [recovers consciousness], takes the hammer, knocks down the dentist, and takes out all his teeth." This tooth-for-a-tooth fantasy was related with great gusto.

But the feelings which emerged at this later phase presented greater difficulties. Peter was no longer cooperative and said he wished to see the analysis come to an end. He would reiterate that he did not feel like coming anymore. He would insist that he was cured, not having wet the bed for so long. His father told him it would be a waste of time to go on. It was obvious that Peter no longer found the analysis exciting. He felt he had nothing more to expect of it. It was now even disappointing. Above all, Peter did not feel like talking about his trumpet. He wanted to keep it to himself, away from the analysis, away from the analyst he was sure was opposed to his becoming independent and grown up with his big trumpet. He was convinced that the analyst was envious and consequently ill disposed toward him. His resistance at this stage almost reached phobic proportions. He was very anxious in his silences, in his avoidance of any mention of his prized trumpet. Through dreams and fantasies, it became obvious that he was afraid of being deprived of this most exciting possession. He had to keep all his strong feelings about it from the analyst. Symbolically, he was hiding away his pleasurable, exciting erection, and his unconscious fears of castration were expressed in nightmares in which his trumpet was broken while he was on his way to a session.

A little later the masturbation displacement, the guilt, and the castration anxiety became even more dominant in his dreams. In place of the gorillas of previous nightmares there appeared an even more obvious representative of the superego, the policeman. Peter reported the following nightmare: He was playing jazz with his trumpet as a member of a nightclub dance band when several policemen rushed in; he became so upset and frightened that he dropped his trumpet to the floor where it smashed into pieces. He woke up sweating profusely. Following the sessions dealing with this dream, there was a gradual lessening of the sexualization of Peter's musical activity.

Some earlier indications of the intensity of Peter's oedipal strivings were noted during the first phases of the analysis. Peter used to say that he very much liked to act in school plays, "specially the grown-up parts where I can let myself go with rage, telling off the others. . . ." He particularly enjoyed making a noise, especially whistling or sounding off with his trumpet. The significance of this can be more readily appreciated when it is known that whistling was forbidden at home during the day in order not to disturb the sleep of the father who worked night shifts. The making of noise was perhaps his favorite way of expressing his opposition to his father. Another cathected area related to his oedipal rivalry was the great temptation to remain awake as late as possible at night; this meant consciously daring to do what his father did.

In the latter part of the analysis, the mother and mother figures came more and more to the foreground. Some ambivalence had first been observed. On the unconscious, negative side, his mother was a bad, orally depriving mother. He dreamed that he had not enough to eat, that she had given him "much less sandwiches" than she had given his father. His father thus "had better chances to grow."

This negative aspect, however, was much less important in the analysis than his febrile desire to impress the mother and win her admiration and love. His yearning for her love and approval came out in a recurring daydream in which the Queen honored him for his fishing abilities by inviting him to dinner and presenting him with £1,000 for fishing equipment. Another revealing daydream found him planning to work and make money to buy a better house for his mother.

An almost incredible feat throws further light on Peter's oedipal strivings. He set himself the task of building a real bicycle without his parents' knowledge. A friend who was in on the scheme let Peter use a shed at the back of his house. Here Peter gradually assembled the parts as he was able to save his money, bit by bit, to buy them.

As the project progressed, Peter's excitement ran high. The analytic sessions were filled with vivid fantasies of how at last he would be able to perform on his bicycle for his mother. One could feel the boy's determination to let nothing stand in the way of the fulfillment of this dream, not even the disapproval he knew he could expect from his parents who had always opposed the idea of bicycle riding for Peter.

As with the trumpet, Peter surprised everyone by achieving his goal. He became a skillful cyclist.

The Mother's Changing Attitude

About halfway through the analysis, there was a significant change in the mother's attitude. She began to tell her therapist how much happier she was feeling about her son. With each of Peter's successive achievements—fishing, playing the trumpet, swimming, lifesaving, diving, and bicycling—she would express surprise and a growing pride and pleasure. More and more he was becoming an indispensable part of her life. She was finding that she liked having him around the house. One time when he was away at camp for a few days, she said how much she was looking forward to having him back and hearing him practice on his trumpet again. His deformity no longer caused her embarrassment and shame.

This change in his mother's attitude was a source of great satisfaction to Peter. As all his hard-won feats had been undertaken basically to win her love and admiration, her pleasure and pride made him very happy and promoted his growing sense of security. Evidence of the oedipal coloring of his strivings and the assurance that he was becoming "the little man" of a proud mother was the simultaneous wish of mother and son for another baby in the family. Previously both parents had maintained that they did not want another child. Now, only the father was still against the idea.

Hazards of Passivity

During the latter phase of the analysis Peter's fight against regression to a masochistic, passive-feminine relationship in the transference became a major issue. Evidence of this struggle had appeared earlier in the form of an unconscious wish to be beaten by the analyst. There was also an earlier dream of a car accident in which he received an injury that left him with an opening into the middle of his body, a condition he equated to the female sexual constitution.

While his determination to achieve independence led him to "cut" several sessions and to argue for a reduction from five to two or three sessions a week, the latent wish to become more dependent betrayed him into several slips of the tongue in which his plea for fewer sessions came out as one for more sessions, actually "seven" sessions a week.

The analytic interpretation of Peter's conflict around dependence-independence produced some therapeutic results. These were manifest in his increased self-confidence, and in an easier, freer relationship with his analyst. As should be expected in the analysis of an adolescent, this development resulted in an increasing detachment from the analyst and a decreasing interest in continuing the analysis.

At this point I realized that Peter was no longer talking to me as a patient. He had, as never before, a matter-of-fact way of expressing his intentions; he now had the direct, open manner of an adolescent boy determined to see to his own affairs. With a sense of purpose and self-assurance, he explained how he now felt about the analysis. Reasoning logically, he wanted me to understand that after school he would like to follow his friends rather than attend a session. He wanted to do what the other members of his "gang" or club did at that particular time of day; he wanted to participate in their games; he wanted to go out with girls. The more fully his passive wishes were analyzed, the more urgent became his adolescent self-assertion and revolt. Accordingly we let Peter go on his way toward the independence he was seeking—and that meant the end of the analysis.

Technical Problems

As Peter made no mention of his arms in the early analytic sessions, the question as to whether or not the analyst should himself introduce the subject was raised at a case conference. Anna Freud recommended against this, suggesting that the analysis should be conducted like any other, with no topic being avoided or introduced. Interference, she felt, could result in bypassing the full analysis of his personality. She pointed out that the material then being presented concerned Peter's fear of castration. Dealing first with this anxiety would have certain advantages. As castration was not a reality, interpretation of his fears in this area would be more reassuring than interpretation of those having a basis in reality—the malformed arms. She also saw in this procedure a safeguard against Peter's depressive tendencies.

Throughout the entire course of the analysis, the requirements of Peter's ego functioning were respected. And nothing seems to have been lost by following this procedure. His real-life activities and achievements came late but safely into the analysis. After the interpretation of much of the castration material, Peter himself introduced the subject of his arms. This occurred in a depressive context, revealing that he had been harboring the illusion that the analysis would make his arms grow. He had dreamed that he was working in a coal mine with adults; a "big accident happened" and completely cut off their air supply; he fainted and woke up in a hospital, saved from death because he had been given artificial air; and he completely recovered. In the dream, the hospitalization was followed by normal life (normal arms). But in real life, his hospital experiences for the fitting of artificial arms were not followed by "real arms." Nor did the analysis bring about the growth of longer arms. There was no magic. At long last he was able to speak of the hopelessness of his wish.

Weathering this critical period of disillusionment, Peter went on to new achievements. Gradually, the enrichment of his real abilities and his growing self-esteem made it seem likely that he would continue to make reasonably satisfactory progress toward adulthood without further help from his analyst.

BIBLIOGRAPHY

Erikson, E. H. (1956), The Problem of Ego Identity, J. Am. Psa. Assn., IV.

Freud, Anna (1936), The Ego and the Mechanisms of Defence. New York: International Universities Press, 1946.

Hartmann, H. (1939), Ego Psychology and the Problem of Adaptation. New York: International Universities Press, 1958.

From the *International Journal of Psychoanalysis* 49 (1968): 276–79:

Excerpts from the Analysis of a Child with a Congenital Defect*

by Robert A. Furman†

(Cleveland, Ohio)

As my contribution to this symposium, I would like to bring excerpts from the analysis of a young girl who was born with a congenitally deformed and blind left eye.‡

In presenting this material I want to stress an apparent paradox. On the one hand this little girl's deformity became involved in every stage of her development, making her psychological growth truly different and more complex. On the other hand her analysis helped her most by enabling her to delineate and restrict her difference from others to just the sightlessness of her left eye, restoring her self-esteem by limiting her damage to its proper reality proportions. It is possible that from understanding this apparent paradox two very simple, practical suggestions may emerge about the management of the young child with a congenital anomaly or with a severe bodily illness.

Jacobson's paper, "The Exceptions, An Elaboration of Freud's Character Study" (1959), is quite applicable here. Although physically afflicted, my little patient suffered most from being treated as different, as the exception who could do no wrong, somewhat in the manner of the truly beautiful women whom Jacobson describes.

Case Report

Cindy's parents came to me ostensibly to seek advice about discussing the sightless eye with their daughter who was then nearly 3½ years old. Preliminary interviews with the parents revealed that the congenital abnormality had aroused everyone's most neurotic reactions. The eye, for example, had never been mentioned to the little girl,

* Read at the 25th International Psycho-Analytic Congress, Copenhagen, July 1967.

† Assistant Professor Child Psychiatry, Western Reserve University School of Medicine, Cleveland, Ohio; Director, Cleveland Center for Research in Child Development, Cleveland, Ohio.

‡ This analysis was supervised by Anny Katan, M.D., and was presented for discussion six times to the Cleveland Child Analysis group. I am indebted to Dr. Katan and many others for their many helpful insights and observations.

despite the parents having observed her before a mirror passing her hand alternately over each of her eyes. Instead, Cindy had been treated like a little princess whose every wish was to be granted. Requests for a cigarette-holder like her mother's, real lipstick, a stove that really cooked had all been met.

In her enormous guilt the mother often abdicated her maternal role. She allowed Cindy to make decisions that should only have been hers, such as about choice of curtains, rugs, slipcovers for their newly acquired home. She did not intervene in situations where she knew she should have, such as in allowing Cindy to spend long weekends at the paternal grandparents where very confusing and exciting games were played. To give but one example, the aunt and grandmother played a game in which they were kidnappers, stealing Cindy and her 14-months younger brother, and only sibling, from her parents.

Cindy herself had an unusual symptom in her grotesque way of walking. She leaned backwards with both feet everted, toes pointing to the side. With every step her head rocked down towards alternating shoulders, her face fully presenting forwards at all times. The head-rocking often continued when she was not walking. Needless to remark, this bizarre gait made running impossible and stairs could only be ascended one at a time. An obvious result was that although she made herself quite conspicuous her sightless eye was hard to observe. Her left eye was just a bit smaller than its sighted mate, had an irregularly opaque pupil, but moved concomitantly with the right eye. Later in her analysis, when her expression was not distorted by anxiety and the head-rocking had ceased, the eye was not unnoticeable but did not detract from her attractive appearance.

After two months of meeting weekly with the parents, we became convinced that they could not adequately discuss the eye with Cindy, although they felt, correctly, that they would be able to support any discussions I would have with her. We also agreed that Cindy's symptom indicated treatment. She started analysis four times weekly when she was 3 years 8 months and continued until her father stopped the analysis just after her seventh birthday.

The Analysis

The first feeling about her eye Cindy brought was anal in origin. She messed and dawdled a great deal in my office, as if wanting me to become involved in the prodding interplay she had with her mother and to clean up after her each day. As we were exploring this, she got busy one day with the hand-mirror that was in the office. She complained that it was dirty, and proceeded to mess it over with clay. In cleaning the mirror subsequently, she told me of a rare brief separation she anticipated from her mother. "She always leaves me and I know why." I asked if she felt it was because she got mother so angry with her messing and fighting. She replied no, that it was because she was a mess, having only one eye that could see.

Very soon, oral aspects of her feeling about her eye made their appearance. She was complaining that neither mother nor I ever did anything for her, listing a series of impossible wishes. These finally settled on our inability to "fix" her eye. She complained then of the children in nursery school. They ate all the cookies, leaving none for her when she came back to school from her analytic session. She corrected herself that they usually left one for her. Maybe it was because they knew that if she could get at those cookies she would eat them all up so there would be none left for anyone else. We could connect then her feeling that perhaps it had been her greedy wishes that had been responsible for her just having the one eye that could see. When she returned to school that day she had a great verbal outburst of oral aggressive wishes. She became a ferocious lion that wanted to eat all the food in the school, the children, the teachers and finally the whole school building.

Her greatest difficulty with her feelings about her eye came in relation to her brother. It was hard for us to know if she was angriest at him for having a penis or for having two eyes that could see. And it was often hard to know when the verbalized anger about one covered a more intense anger about the other. Birthdays and Christmas were extremely difficult in this context as she was never able to be pleased with what she received. A milestone was reached in the work with the mother when, after a year in analysis, at Cindy's fifth birthday, her great disappointment could be simply dealt with by the mother's explaining that she knew Cindy always hoped that one birthday would bring her a new eye that could see.

Accusations that her mother, and I in the transference, were responsible for her deformity previewed her feeling that it was first her anger and then her masturbation that had caused her damage. When we were seeking a connection between her head-shaking and her masturbation, she told me of a scary dream that made her "shake" with fright. "A large bee came in the window and there was a little one on its back." She wanted to tell me more about this dream and her head began shaking. She was to be in a school play in pajamas and this worried her. She wanted to draw to tell me something. "I'll draw Mr. Shakeheader; it's my Daddy. He got in my head through the window." She then drew a picture of two window-eyes, one barred as if it were a jail with a man inside.

It took many days to clarify this, the highlights of which I would like briefly to describe. Cindy said he got in to shake her like he had been shaking mother on Channel 2 (an imaginary channel) on the television. She reported another bad dream in which the big bee, now with a big stinger, was bombed by someone or put in a big box so he could not hurt anyone. This enabled me to say that perhaps sometime she had seen something on Channel 2 that made her think Daddy was hurting Mommy and she took him inside her head to keep Mommy safe. "And he won't get out until my eye is open, until my eye can see."

The next day she wanted to tell me more about Channel 2. It was "no-on-yes." "No" equalled father, "on" meant a baby, and "yes" stood for mother. It seemed clear now that "no-on-yes," the Channel 2 show of Mr. Shakeheader, had to do with father shaking mother when making a baby. It was the slow reworking of this exposure to the primal scene, which I believe dated to about her second birthday, that paved the way for the gradual mastery of her strange gait, her "wobbly walk" as she called it.

I describe these rather isolated bits of Cindy's analysis to try to show how her eye was inextricably involved, as would be expected, with every aspect of her development, including her traumatic primal scene exposure.

And now to the difficulties Cindy had with her feelings. Our first insights came at the time of the initial separation from me over a Christmas vacation. She became worried about the two windows in my office. What would happen if she got angry enough at me to break one of those windows? She answered her own question by saying that then she would not be able to see at all. We were not able fully to clarify this for a number of weeks until she was preparing herself to go to the eye doctor for a routine twice-yearly examination. She began denying the permanency of the blindness in her left eye and insisted it was not because she was afraid of being sad or angry. "If I know that my eye will never see ever, then I'll be so angry at everyone with two eyes that can see I will want to blind one eye in everyone and then people will do it back to me and then I won't be able to see at all."

Another danger with her anger came up much later in her analysis. She had brought an oedipal anger in the transference in the wish that could she get her hands on my wife she would stuff her in the trash can and then burn her up. When I interpreted this as a feeling she must have had with her mother, she was horrified. I said I knew all little girls had these feelings about their mothers. She replied that I did not understand: with her it was different; when she wished her mother dead, she really wished her dead. I again said I thought it was this way for all little girls. Cindy was adamant; for her it was different. I asked if it was because she had so many things she was angry at mother about, like about being a girl or about her eye. She firmly said no: it was because her eye was different, she was different, and so her anger was different.

The same trend was apparent about her sadness. Early in her analysis every time a sadness would have been appropriate she either became excited in her head-rocking or left the office to urinate. I did not understand her great fear of sadness until she was sad in her guilt over being angry at me about a separation. She told me she was sad but could not cry because she "didn't understand about this eye-water." She was soon able to cry in the session for the first time when her frank wish to make a baby with me could not be gratified. She cried a second time about a year later when I did not accept the gift of a penny she brought me. This sadness we were able to understand as a transference response; it felt like her father rejecting her because she had only one eye that could see or because she was not a boy.

But despite these instances of very feelingful sadness and crying she complained constantly that she could not be sad because she could not cry. On this basis she rationalized the persistence of her masturbation fantasies or "good night tricks" as she called them as a necessary defense against her sadness. But there was more to it than this. Quite late in her analysis she brought the wish to re-enter her mother's womb. This came in the context of an excited fantasy in which she would make of herself a body penis. This fantasy became a persistent one which she was finally able to explain. If she could get back in her mother's womb she could be reborn and maybe this time she would have two eyes that could see. When I asked why that wish was so persistent, she burst into tears and, after a moment, ran from the office. She returned promptly, most pleased through her tears. She had gone to the bathroom to look in the mirror and had seen that both her eyes had cried. She wasn't different about the tear-water; her eye was different just in that it could not see. She readily agreed that what was so important was that her feelings were not different; it was just the sightlessness of her one eye.

Discussion

At the outset I mentioned that understanding the apparent paradox about differences might make possible two simple, practical suggestions about the management of the young child with a congenital anomaly or severe physical illness. The abbreviated description of the parents' management of Cindy may suffice in its bizarreness to underline the difficulty they had in dealing with what their child's deformity meant to them. In this regard, experience tells us that they were not unusual in the turmoil they encountered within themselves. I hope the description, also abbreviated, of the difficulties Cindy's deformity presented to her at each level of her development will suffice to support the point that in dealing with a child with such a deformity the parents should have available to them an understanding of normal child development that is beyond what can be expected of average parents.

With these two considerations in mind, it seems reasonable to suggest that parents faced with severe bodily illness or congenital defects in young children should be referred for assistance in dealing with their child's emotional development and should be referred as early as possible. As child analysts we should consider making ourselves available for such counseling efforts.

The second suggestion deals with one aspect of such work with the parents. Initially the goal would be to assist the parents with their feelings, their guilt, depression, and anxiety so they can be free to discuss the physical defect with their child at appropriate times. If this can be accomplished, the parents can recurrently aid their child in disentangling his feelings about the defect from the developmental conflicts which appear at each succeeding level (Nagera, 1965), trying thus to preserve the intactness of the child's self-esteem. A most significant aspect of this work throughout, and this is where the second suggestion applies, concerns the child's feelings as such. Here the parents' task is to help the child understand that although he may differ from others in body, he does not differ from them in the nature of his feelings; that he experiences worry, anger, sadness, excitement in the same way as all other children.

REFERENCES

Jacobson, E. (1959). "The exceptions: an elaboration of Freud's character study." *Psycholanal. Study Child*, 14.

Nagera, H. (1966). *Early Childhood Disturbances, the Infantile Neurosis and the Adulthood Disturbances*. (New York: Int. Univ. Press.)

From *The Psychoanalytic Study of the Child* 14 (1959): 134–54:

The "Exceptions": An Elaboration of Freud's Character Study*

by Edith Jacobson, M.D.
(New York)

Psychoanalysts know no greater pleasure than to reread Freud over and over again. Each time he grants us new insights, new discoveries, new food for thought, and new enjoyment. Recently a certain coincidence caused me to read once more, and with greatest delight, Freud's brief discussion of "The 'Exceptions'" in his study on "Some Character-Types Met with in Psycho-Analytic Work" (1915). The reason for my interest in the "exceptions" was a visit from a former patient who had been afflicted with a poliomyelitis in early childhood. Moreover, it so happened that I had just received a letter from another former patient, also a severely handicapped woman, whose life had likewise been ruled by this condition, but in quite a different, indeed an opposite manner. Both patients had been successfully treated more than ten years ago; and both since then had developed astoundingly well, in fact, beyond my expectations.

The more I thought about "The 'Exceptions'" and about my own case material, the more I felt that in this study, written forty-three years ago, Freud had sketched out a story which waited for completion.

This is the gist of the ideas expressed in Freud's study: In some patients with either a congenital injury or a physical affliction acquired in early childhood, he found a conspicuous resistance to accept the reality principle. They rebelled against the frustrations which analysis imposed upon them, claimed they had suffered enough, and behaved as if they were exceptions to whom such rules did not apply.

Their attitudes reminded Freud of the hero in Shakespeare's *King Richard III*, who, cheated by nature that has made him deformed, feels exempt from the laws by which others abide, and for this reason decides to become a villain. Why can we feel sympathy with this ruthless person? Because we too suffered narcissistic injuries in the past, says Freud, and sometimes envy those whom fate has blessed with more or greater gifts. Freud concludes his study of this character

---

* Presented in abbreviated version at a meeting of the New York Psychoanalytic Society, May 26, 1959.

type by comparing it with the psychology of woman, whose claim for privileges also rests on a narcissistic injury: her castration.

Freud's final remarks may serve as a point of departure. It seems that at some phase of our life, especially during adolescence, not only women but probably all of us may wish or even feel to be exceptions, and expect to be granted special privileges. But comparing my handicapped patients with other female patients whom I had treated, I was impressed less by the analogies than by the marked differences in their psychology. Even if notions of having been castrated are unconsciously maintained, they evidently cannot and do not have the same impact as realistic physical afflictions. However, Freud seemed to regard woman's lack of a penis as a quite realistic physical handicap. Possibly for this reason, his views concerning the psychology of women appear frequently somewhat biased. He believed that as a result of their castration, women's object relations are in general more narcissistic than men's; furthermore, that, being castrated already, woman does not have the same incentive as man to overcome her oedipal fixations and hence is unable to build up an effectual superego.

It is not important at the moment whether Freud's characterizations of woman's nature have general validity or are correct only for certain female types, as I am inclined to believe. I mentioned them only because his views on women, and especially on the female superego, have certain implications with regard to the "exceptions" which Freud did not quite spell out yet in his discussion of this character type. We realize that the paper antedates his last structural conceptions and his study of the superego; thus we are not surprised that Freud did not explore this aspect in the psychology of the "exceptions." It is significant, though, that in both of the other character types described in this paper—in "Those Wrecked by Success" and "Criminality from a Sense of Guilt"—Freud placed the focus on their guilt conflicts. To be sure, the characterological problems discussed in these three studies are closely related. However, what Freud observed in the "exceptions" and demonstrated in Shakespeare's hero is merely their refusal to accept the reality principle.

Actually, the tragedy of *Richard III* appears to be more complicated. Richard certainly is not unwilling to submit to the reality principle because he craves and hunts for pleasure. Quite to the contrary, he scoffs at life's ordinary pleasures, at sex, love, romance. In fact, he is rather a wicked plotter and schemer, who, in this activity, even shows a remarkable reality-testing ability. But his ruthless decision to become a villain points precisely to the area of his defect: his conviction that he is exempt from moral laws.

Freud does not discuss the nature of the crimes for which King Richard must finally pay his penalty. However, his remarks on women give us a fair hint, and Richard certainly announces his goals quite brazenly:

> And, if I fail not in my deep intent
> Clarence hath not another day to live:
> Which done, God take King Edward to his mercy,
> And leave the world for me to bustle in!
> For then I'll marry Warwick's youngest daughter.
> What though I kill'd her husband and her father,
> The readiest way to make the wench amends
> Is to become her husband and her father:
> The which will I; not all so much for love
> As for another secret close intent,
> By marrying her, which I must reach into.
> But yet I run before my horse to market:
> Clarence still breathes; Edward still lives and reigns:
> When they are gone, then must I count my gains.
> —Act I, Scene I

No doubt, the moral laws from which Richard feels exempt are the incest taboo and the law against patricide.* But his monologue reveals also the archaic, narcissistic-destructive nature of his oedipal strivings. Richard, hated and despised by his own mother, does not and cannot love women. They are only means on his way to success. The real driving force is his revengeful wish for power, his devouring ambition. His actual goal is the kingdom, the royal position; i.e., the ruthless acquisition of the paternal penis.

To be sure, Richard has a severe superego defect. According to Freud, in women the superego is defective too; he believes that, feeling cheated, envious or even revengeful like Richard, they can be more easily persuaded to immoral actions than men. But certainly they do not consciously abrogate and feel exempt from the moral laws, as does Richard. His superego pathology finds frank expression in the provocativeness of the prologue which is a conscious challenge, not so much to the whole world as to his own conscience which will finally overpower and destroy him.

The moving monologue in this last act—tragic counterpart of the prologue—seals his fate:

> O coward conscience, how doest thou afflict me!
> . . . .
> What! do I fear myself? there's none else by:
> Richard loves Richard; that is, I am I.
> Is there a murderer here? No. Yes, I am:
> Then fly: what! from myself? Great reason why;
> Lest I revenge. What! myself upon myself?

* Dr. Robert Seidenberg of Syracuse brought to my attention that Oedipus himself, being born with a swell-foot, may be regarded as an "exception."

Alack! I love myself. Wherefore? for any good
That I myself have done unto myself?
Oh! no: alas! I rather hate myself
For hateful deeds committed by myself.
I am a villain. Yet I lie; I am not.
Fool, of thyself speak well: fool, do not flatter.
My conscience hath a thousand several tongues,
And every tongue brings in a several tale,
And every tale condemns me for a villain.
Perjury, perjury, in the high'st degree:
Murder, stern murder, in the dir'st degree;
All several sins, all us'd in each degree,
Throng to the bar, crying all, "Guilty! guilty!"
I shall despair. There is no creature loves me;
And if I die, no soul will pity me:
Nay, wherefore should they, since that I myself
Find in myself no pity to myself?
—Act V, Scene III

Richard's complete ruthlessness and lack of manifest guilt conflicts
—almost to the very end—are probably, from the aesthetic viewpoint,
the reasons for the weaknesses of this play which abounds in brutal
crimes. And yet, this absence of conscious guilt feelings is most significant for Richard's psychology and his tragedy. He is a rebel
against his own conscience—which, as his wife Anne betrays, haunts
him every night with terrible nightmares. Consciously, he stubbornly
denies, spites, mocks at the power of conscience and at the meaning
of human love and pity. This position he reaffirms with each new
crime that brings him closer to success and ruin. Actually Richard's
hateful actions are a severely sadomasochistic provocation of fate, and
his final defeat and punishment are inevitable for inner reasons. He
is, in the words of Frederick D. Losey (1926), "the architect of his
own ruin." The last lines of his monologue epitomize his tragedy,
the crime that the world committed against him and its reflection in
his own self-destructive behavior: "I shall despair. There is no creature
loves me; / And if I die, no soul will pity me. . . ."

This dangerous masochistic need for punishment seemed to be present in all the varieties of "exceptions" which I had an opportunity
to observe. It may be warded off and cloaked by unconscious rebellion
and scorn of the laws which others must obey, as in the type described
by Freud; or, the reverse, it may be an effective defense against the
underlying rebellion and find conscious expression in the belief to be
chosen to suffer. This was the case in the second patient who will be
briefly described here as a counterpart to the first one.

In Freud's study we find a vague hint at this masochistic component
in the psychology of the "exceptions," when he refers to the great patience with which his female patient had borne her affliction before

she discovered that it was caused by a congenital injury. Possibly this admirable patience had a masochistic quality and was bound to break down anyhow under the influence of her analysis which brought her repressed rage to the fore.

No doubt we find equally contradictory attitudes in different types of neurotic women who have not resolved their castration conflict. There are the rebellious types to which Freud referred again in "Analysis Terminable and Interminable" (1937). They stubbornly refuse to give up their demand for a penis; they claim compensation or want revenge. But we also know those masochistic, overpatient, self-sacrificing female types who believe in man's inherent supremacy and privileges and willingly submit to it. Among the "exceptions" I treated or met in life, I found analogous opposing types.

My first patient was representative of the type described by Freud. Her analysis furnished convincing proof for her belief in being exempt from the oedipal laws. Moreover, her life history evidenced the unfortunate influence of her sadomasochistic provocativeness and unconscious need for punishment all too clearly.

Although suffering from a residual paresis of her right leg, this patient, an Englishwoman in her twenties, was physically attractive, charming, and seductive. Besides, she was a person of unusually high intelligence. She had been divorced after some unhappy years of marriage with a man who had cheated her and treated her very badly. She came for treatment in a very depressed state after she had broken off a new relationship with a man to whom she felt closely attached. Already during the first interviews, her relations to her family struck me as rather unusual and contradictory. She told me that her whole family—both parents and her only sister—had been killed in air raids in London. She had left with her American husband for the United States before this happened, and blamed herself, quite unjustly, for not having brought them over, too. However, despite her evident guilt feelings, their death had not reconciled her with her family. She became rather hostile as soon as she began to talk about them. She described them probably correctly, but in a somewhat merciless, derogatory manner: her father as a petit bourgeois, a compulsive, hypocritical bureaucrat; her mother as an inefficient, indolent, helpless woman; her little sister as lazy, greedy, and hopelessly dumb.

As the patient's childhood history unfolded, I certainly felt that she had ample reasons for her contradictory feelings toward her family. Like all those who claim to be treated as exceptions, the patient had indeed had a very exceptional childhood. In addition to her physical deformity, she had been weak and ill from infancy on. For many years she had been bedridden and in need of continuous treatments and physical care. At school, the children were advised to treat her with special consideration. Thus her early life had been unusually burdened; but I must also emphasize the really exceptional vitality of this patient. Born out of spite and rebellion, and supported by her intellectual gifts, it inspired her to overcome all physical and emotional hardships, to go to college, to marry, and later on to achieve a successful career. And yet, her vigorous efforts were counteracted by unconscious masochism and guilt conflicts which undermined her successes and personal happiness.

Of course, the patient's masochism originated partly in her chronic state of illness, in sexualized painful treatment experiences, and in her dependence on continuous physical care and nursing. But her profound unconscious need for punishment and her angry, spiteful rebellion against the power of her own superego were nourished by her parents' contradictory emotional attitudes: their seductive behavior coupled with unfair, reproachful hostility. Both parents were unable to hide their resentment at the suffering and sacrifices her illness imposed upon them. In particular, her mother would habitually blame her for her sickness, as if it were the result of bad behavior, and would treat her as though, if only she wanted to, she could easily walk like other children. No wonder that the little girl responded to her mother's behavior with guilt feelings and simultaneous rebellious hostility which, as in Richard's case, covered her self-contempt and her desperate cry for maternal love and acceptance. The most interesting and influential feature in her life story was probably her relationship with her father. Throughout her childhood and early adolescence their relations had been overclose, also in a physical sense; thus, the patient was certainly convinced that he had loved her more than her mother.

But there was a rival whom she could hardly defeat. A year before she was born, the parents had suddenly lost their greatly adored little boy. The patient knew that her father continued to grieve forever about the loss of his only son; that he had hoped she would be a boy and had been deeply disappointed when he got a weakly little girl, who soon contracted a polio leaving her with a physical handicap. She resolved her jealousy conflict by eager participation in her father's grief. He would tell her stories of "little Charlie" every night; talks from which the mother was strictly excluded, since the boy's name was not to be mentioned in her presence.

Thus the dead brother became "their boy." He was the father's glamorous penis that she alone, secretly, shared with him; a legitimate but unsatisfactory compensation for her physical damage, her castration. When she was three another child was born, again a girl. The patient had a very peculiar, strangely lucid memory of this event which had disappointed both father and child very deeply. She clearly remembered that father had promised her "a little boy all of her own," i.e., a realization of their common daydream: little Charlie reborn. But father came home, telling her that mother had had a little girl, and brought her nothing but a bird as a gift. She recalled her indignation that he had broken his promise and her refusal to accept the little sister, mother's pet, whom she hated ever since. The patient recounted this memory with still almost the same feeling of righteous wrath at her father's inconsistent behavior. Even now she felt that he had cheated her by giving a baby girl to mother instead of providing a boy who would belong to her alone. She never forgave her father this disappointment.

In her adolescence her father's seductive overattachment to his daughter became so manifest again that it drove her into an early marriage with a promising young physicist, a man who had deserted several girls before. Though convinced that she was in love with her partner, the patient was quite aware of the narcissistic gratifications gained from this marriage. First of all, it proved how wrong her parents and physicians had been in predicting that she would never be able to marry. Moreover, she took great pride in having found a man with such outstanding talents. And, besides, she enjoyed not only having outdone her husband's former sweethearts, but also being the first among her girl friends to marry.

Her marriage turned out a complete failure. Knowing her husband's past history, she might have anticipated that this unstable man would prove unable to be faithful. Within a year or two he betrayed her with another woman. His scientific development was quite disappointing. Yet she did not give up. She sacrificed her career to his, worked for him, supported him and persevered, carried by her conviction that she would still be able to overcome all obstacles and turn her marriage into a success. But failure was inevitable. After her divorce, she devoted herself to her career. Her success in this area did not help her; for she repeated her acting out and, in her love life, met with failure again.

The man she loved was considerably older and unhappily married. But even though he professed his great love for the patient, he had difficulties in deciding to give up his wife for her. The patient felt unable to tolerate his alternately seductive and passive, overrestrained behavior. She resented getting again into a masochistic situation remindful of her first marriage and, even more, of her relationship with her father. Thus, after a painful period of waiting in vain for a favorable change, she broke off the relationship. Thereupon, her partner decided at least tentatively to re-establish his marital life. The patient reacted to this painful experience not only with deep disappointment and depression. Feeling cheated again out of a position which her friend's love had made legitimate in her eyes, she responded as she had in her childhood when father had not given her the promised little boy. She found it as hard to forgive her friend his inconsistent behavior as she had been unable to forgive her father his, and felt bitter resentment at his wife.

During her analysis the patient's belief in being an exception to whom ordinary analytic rules did not apply presented, of course, a considerable problem. However, her intense wish to be cured won out. Thus, favorable circumstances and analytic treatment combined in helping the patient to resolve her conflicts and to gain the love she craved. She remarried and, since she had an inherent capacity for love which had been smothered only by her unusual fate, she succeeded in building up a happy relationship to her husband and young children.

I believe this case enlarges our insight into the psychology of this type of "exceptions," their unconscious motivations, the narcissistic-aggressive nature of their oedipal strivings, their rebellious, ambitious aims and claims, their resistance to accept the oedipal laws, the spiteful denial of their own conscience, the victory of their unconscious self-destructive trends and, underneath it all, their desperate cry for a love they never received.

Let us now take a glance at a quite opposite type of exception. This patient, whom I treated many years ago, also had a definite feeling of being an exception. However, it did not make her exempt from moral laws but expressed itself in precisely the opposite attitude: in the conviction of a special moral calling. She had an unconscious Christ identification and, completely renouncing worldly pleasures and ambitions, felt chosen to suffer for the crimes of mankind. It must be stressed that this girl, though severely depressed when she came for treatment after the loss of her aunt, was not psychotic and certainly not schizophrenic. If the first patient's childhood history was bad enough, this girl's life history was even worse. As a baby she had been stricken by a severe poliomyelitis which left her lower extremities almost paralyzed and all her muscles paretic. Since she came of a wealthy family, she was placed under the care of a famous physician for surgical and orthopedic treatments. These required repeated hospitalizations of many months' duration. She learned to walk with the help of a corset and braces, and to use her hands; but she remained undersized and grew hunchbacked. Her only beauty were her wonderful eyes which attested to the intensity of her feelings and her high intelligence.

After her analysis she became very active. She built up a model home for handicapped children and became prominent in organizations for the handicapped in her country. But although during her treatment she learned to permit herself active work and success in her field, she could never entirely give up her "saintliness" based on the religious conviction of her special calling. Whereas the first patient refused to submit to the oedipal laws and was overtly rather uninhibited sexually, this one had renounced men and sex in general. Not that her severe handicap had realistically excluded her from all chances as a woman. From her and from observation of some other handicapped persons I learned much about the strangely ruthless immorality of the many "exceptions" among them and about their surprising ability to attract and acquire sometimes even handsome, physically normal partners. But I also discovered that the opposite unworldly, spiritual type, of which this patient was representative, is not so rare: persons handicapped, crippled or afflicted with severe illness since early childhood, who bear it with greatest patience or even with inner happiness founded on a secret feeling that they have a special calling and that their suffering has a profound spiritual meaning. If the others live on spite, rebellion, and worldly ambition, they live on self-sacrificing altruism, humble renunciation, and acceptance of suffering.

Why had this last patient of mine developed so differently from the other one? Quite in contrast to the latter, she had had a very warm, self-sacrificing mother who gave her the most loving care during the first childhood years, probably at the expense of her two sisters. The loss of her mother when she was about seven was a terrible blow and laid the ground for her religious-masochistic development and her identification with Christ; i.e., with this saintly maternal figure who, in her fantasy, had died for her. After the mother's death a kind aunt moved into the home, whose loss later precipitated a depressive reaction, as I mentioned above. The patient's relationship with her father—a wealthy, prominent industrialist—also remained consciously good throughout her life. He, too, did his utmost to alleviate her suffering and encouraged her to obtain a professional training that might make her life more meaningful. Even though the father occasionally expressed his regret at not having a son, neither he nor her mother or aunt ever blamed her or complained about the emotional and practical burdens her sickness imposed upon them. They all showered kindness and praise on her for the wonderful patience with which she bore her illness and her painful treatments. The same atmosphere prevailed in the hospitals, where she would always become the doctors' favorite patient and friend. The special kindness with which the adults surrounded her certainly helped her to accept her suffering and even to gain secret pleasure from it. But in contrast to the severe parental ambivalence that kindled the first patient's fighting spirit, the parental overkindness here left no room for any open hostility which already in her early childhood underwent a lasting masochistic transformation. The only way in which her rebellion against her father found indirect expression was her Christian socialist leanings, to which she adhered despite her father's objections and her sisters' scorn.

These two beautiful sisters had never emulated the kindly attitude of the adult environment toward the sick girl. In general, they had shown unpleasant character traits rather early; and after their mother's death, they developed into true delinquents. Irresponsible, impulse-ridden, promiscuous spendthrifts, several times divorced, they led a self-destructive life. One became a hopeless drug addict and died of it.

From occasional violent and unbelievably cruel outbursts toward their crippled sister, I could infer that her affliction had played a significant part in their unfortunate development. Evidently it had constantly stirred up sadistic impulses causing severe guilt feelings which they warded off by even franker hostility. They treated her, indeed, as if her deformity were clear evidence of her utter worthlessness. The parents' overconcern and preference for the sick child seemed to have enraged and embittered them. Probably they felt that their father, at least, was genuinely more attracted by them than by the homely, crippled girl. That the latter nevertheless could compete successfully with her healthy, attractive, but wild sisters was unacceptable. Thus, her ability to capture people's hearts by her angelic goodness and her superior intelligence drove them to the opposite: to utter ruthlessness. In fact, the sisters as well as the patient behaved during their whole lives as if their delinquency were her fault for which she had to pay. They exploited her financially and in every other way, and the patient accepted their parasitic and insolent behavior as though it were morally quite justified. She never blamed them; she paid their debts, brought up their children, rescued them from unending calamities in continuous emergency situations. In other words, it was her special calling to suffer and sacrifice herself for them, and to pay for their sins of which she unconsciously accused herself.*

Actually the patient gained tremendous narcissistic gratifications—spiritual as well as practical—from this masochistic position. Her saintliness made her the only admirable member and hence the powerful head of her family, as later of her organizations and her institution. This secret, unacceptable victory was the reason for her inner defeat. For years it prevented her even from building up a career, for which she was qualified not only by her intellectual gifts but by her eminent sense of reality and capacity for initiative. She possessed not only educational, but also organizatory and executive talents that

---

* In the discussion of this paper, Dr. David L. Rubinfine expressed his suspicion that the patient secretly participated in her sisters' "worldly" pleasures. He was right. In certain emotional reactions of the patient and in her dream material this had become quite evident.

developed from her identification with her prominent father, and which made her outstanding in her field as soon as her treatment had liberated her ambitions for constructive practical goals.

Some years ago, when I met her again and inspected her model institution, she told me that her leading educational principle with the handicapped children was to teach them "not to regard themselves as exceptions." During the treatment I had never applied this term to the patient.

The tragic fate of her beautiful, ruthless sisters leads me to the third type of "exceptions" which I want to discuss here briefly. At a certain period of my analytic work, I happened to have a few women simultaneously in treatment who were more than attractive or pretty; they were beautiful. It struck me that their beauty seemed, if anything, to have had a devastating effect on the lives of those close to them, or on their own lives, or both. Their fates made me wonder why I had hardly ever met beautiful women whose lives had been happy or at least harmonious and peaceful. The answer might be that not only those cursed with physical affliction, but also those blessed with extraordinary gifts, with genius or with outstanding beauty, seem to be a special variety of "exceptions."

I have not analyzed persons of genius. But the biographies of great men suggest that their psychology has much in common with that of women marked by extraordinary beauty.

Probably because of Freud's reference to Richard III, I looked for a heroine in literature who might be representative of this type of "exceptions." I found her in Erskine's delightful novel *The Private Life of Helen of Troy* (1939), whose psychology mirrored in its essential features that of my beautiful patients.

In an intimate talk with her far less attractive daughter Hermione, who blames her for the evil she has brought upon the world, Helen confesses the history of her inner development: ". . . and I do see," says Hermione, "why you are different from other people. You are so beautiful that ordinary rules seem not to apply." "They didn't apply," is Helen's answer, "but they ought to have done so, and I wanted them to. That is the whole trouble. I never wanted to be different from my fellows. . . . They always said I was beautiful, but the only effect I would notice was that they treated me as if I weren't a human being. . . . I resented being excused from the ordinary rules of life. If I did wrong, when I was a child, I wasn't punished. . . . I understood what it meant when men say beauty is a curse."

In other words, already in childhood she knew that, because of her beauty, she was regarded as an exception. In contrast to the physically afflicted, it was not that she herself claimed to be exempt from moral laws, but that the others treated her as such against her wishes. They would never believe in her badness, never punish her for anything. She was immune; was loved and adored despite and for whatever wrong she did.

The Trojans never blamed her for the war and their defeat. And on the wretched trip back from Troy (with which the novel sets in) her husband's men, who went to war for her crime, do not reproach her at all. They treat her with utmost reverence. They not only blame Menelaus for his irreligious behavior, but tell him he should have listened to the advice of his divine wife.

The idealization bestowed upon Helen by the world gives no true happiness to her. If Richard III, feeling cheated of life's common pleasures and rewards, spites the voice of conscience, she feels excluded from normal human suffering and admits to her tremendous longing for punishment. When Troy fell and Menelaus entered her room with his sword in his hands, she thought at last it would come. "I even made it easy for him," she tells her respectable friend, Charitas: "I drew my robe away from my heart—so." But the sword dropped from her husband's hands. From the friend's reaction to Helen's expressive gesture one can guess that Helen here speaks with tongue in cheek. Of course she knew in advance that the sight of her beautiful breast would disarm Menelaus and bring him under her spell again. And yet, Helen, whose greatest human asset is her sincerity, tells the truth. Her exhibitionistic gesture is certainly a double challenge. It is both a seductive appeal and a provocation of punishment. Helen intends again to test the power of her charms over men, yet she waits for the strong man who will resist and at last punish and destroy her. But he never comes. She is irresistible.

Like Helen of Troy, one of my patients—a girl of uncommon beauty and intelligence, with a far less attractive sister—had thrown her spell on her father already when she was a little girl. He spoiled her, gave her whatever she wanted, and never punished her. When she was an adolescent, she told him frankly that she wanted a baby. The father (a physician) went right ahead, found a baby for adoption, and, with scant regard for his wife's wishes, radiantly brought it to his daughter.

The patient's fate was characteristic. Again, like Helen of Troy, she married, early and conventionally, a very handsome, nice, average young man of whom she was very fond and whom her father favored. Of course, like her father, he adored and spoiled her. But despite their harmonious marital relationship, she soon fell passionately in love with a brilliant, outstanding man who was likewise quite happily married. His wife was a teacher and older friend of the patient and loved her dearly. To make the situation worse, the couple had several children. In this conflict she came to me for advice and therapeutic help; she was neither willing nor able, though, to start a psychoanalytic treatment which might have led to renunciation. On my advice she tried, albeit without conviction, to stay away from her lover for some months. He, too, promised to cooperate. But after a few weeks, they were together again.

The patient's husband, who had learned about her affair, was profoundly affected. But he behaved as though she could not be measured by ordinary standards and hence was morally quite within her right. He never blamed her, continued to adore her, and patiently waited for her return; but to no avail. Her attitude to him was much the same as that of Helen to Menelaus. She felt sincerely sorry for this sweet, kind young man and did not defend her actions. But, like Helen, she could not help it; her passion was far stronger than her conscience, than her fondness and pity for him or her loyalty to her friend and teacher. She was willing to go ahead, but also to bear the consequences of her actions.

After some time the lover's wife found evidence of her husband's love affair. She was devastated, but immediately granted him a divorce. This was the signal for which the lovers had been waiting. They left their partners and were married. The patient's first husband was grief-stricken, but after some years he remarried. The betrayed wife, however, never recovered from the blow. She withdrew in bitter disappointment, led a lonesome life, and even left the raising of her children to the usurper.

To be sure, the patient had won her battle without much fight or almost with the injured partners' assistance. But hers was a Pyrrhic victory. There she was: with a husband as difficult as he was brilliant; with some disturbed stepchildren, who were soon followed by several children of her own; and, in addition, with a widowed mother, a neurotic sister, and the adopted problem child—all of them looking up to her and leaning on her for support and guidance. Life became an unending burden almost too heavy for her to carry.

When I saw her again, more than a decade later, I found her still enthralled by her husband's unusual personality. But she did not know how much longer she would be able to tolerate his unceasing emotional and sexual demands. He behaved as though he constantly had to conquer this divine being anew and assure himself of its possession. Again, I was reminded of Helen's husband. To his daughter, Menelaus confesses his belief that none of Helen's lovers had felt to be her equal and that none, not even he, had ever loved her as one loves an ordinary woman: "You can't embrace a strain of music or light on the sea."

My patient never admitted to her disillusionment, as did Erskine's heroine. Nor did she have Helen's detached, imperturbable serenity. She was torn by conflicts, tired out and frequently depressed. Undoubtedly her exceptional charms had been a curse rather than a blessing. And she was paying a heavy penalty for actions which all the world, except herself, had easily forgiven. But, like Helen of Troy, she never regretted her past decisions.

Strangely enough, the analogies between this beautiful, charming woman and my first handicapped patient are striking. Each is convinced that her father loves her better than he loves her mother. Each consciously claims a child from him. Neither of them, as she grows up, hesitates to seduce a married man and to take him away from his wife and children. And each, in her own way, pays very dearly for being deaf to the voice of her conscience.

But even though both felt entitled and were able to compete successfully first with their mothers and later with other women, the differences between them are also striking. The beautiful girl asks her father sweetly and charmingly for a baby—and gets it. Then and later, her partners adore her, forgive her, and prefer her to any other woman. Thus, externally, she always wins out, gets and keeps what she wants; naturally, without effort. Not so with the other girl. Her victories in life are the result of bitter struggles; spitefully, they announce: "You see, in spite and because of my handicaps I can fight and shall conquer the world!" But ultimately, all her conquests end in defeat and loss. She does achieve a triumph over her mother: she usurps the father's love; but the mother gets the baby from him. She is able to win men away from other women, but is apt to be cheated by them and to lose them again.

That beauty is seductive and that beautiful, charming little girls may prove irresistible already to their fathers can be easily understood. What caused the first patient's father to overstep the incest taboo is more difficult to explain. Yet I doubt whether it was coincidental that these two little girls, physically so unlike—the one sickly and handicapped, the other radiantly healthy and beautiful—both had such an irresistible appeal for their fathers. I believe what these physically opposite types have in common is their unusual narcissism, even though it develops for opposite reasons and has such different vicissitudes. We are familiar with the narcissism of beautiful women, which is a counterpart of the self-consciousness characterizing the physically afflicted or deformed. If belles love their own perfection, cripples hate their defects. But frequently their cry for beauty leads to a denial of their defects, which not rarely finds expression in an absurd vanity. Such vanity may surpass that of the beautiful woman and may result in a tendency to dress conspicuously in offensive colors and the like. This was not true of my handicapped patients; both dressed skillfully and rather inconspicuously. But the first one moved and walked with such poise and grace that, combined with her natural seductive charm, her intelligence and vivaciousness, it made men forget her physical handicap. Moreover, her dauntless determination not to give up in the face of obstacles also exerted a certain appeal.

In any event, whether the narcissistic appeal developed in the one girl as a result of her beauty or in the other from a passionate struggle for survival and self-assertion, in each of them it appeared to play a particular part in the effect upon the father and later upon other men. This does not yet explain why the handicapped patient's father behaved so seductively toward his little girl. I lack information on his individual pathology. But her analysis suggested that his motivations were partly connected with her physical defects.

The attitudes of those two fathers reflect, indeed, the opposite attitudes of the world toward the physically defective and the physically perfect. The human mind is inclined unconsciously to equate and confuse physical with moral perfection and imperfection. Physically stigmatized persons are commonly despised, feared, and treated as if their castration proved that they are morally bad. As could be seen in the second case history, such hostile-derogatory attitudes find support from projections of the sadism and the resulting guilt feelings which defective persons arouse in healthy people. The analytic material of the first patient offered sufficient evidence that the father's temptation arose not only from his sexual attachment to her, but even more from his simultaneous unconscious moral derogation of this castrated child and his own identification with her. And both father and daughter apparently felt that, being so severely damaged, she was punished already and hence immune, inasmuch as nothing worse could happen to her anyhow. It was in response to the injustice not of her physical affliction alone, but of the moral stigma her parents attached to it, that she felt entitled, in her turn, to rebel against the oedipal laws and try to achieve physical restitution through direct fulfillment of her oedipal desires.

Reversely, the human mind tends to idealize and revere physical perfection and beauty as if they were angelic, divine. This finds a reflection in the heavenly beauty of the madonna, as she is pictured by the great Italian painters. Our attitudes toward genius are similar: we find it hard to believe that persons of genius have human weaknesses and moral imperfections.* And because they have genius, we are inclined to grant them special privileges. It is significant that in con-trast to the first patient's, the father of my beautiful patient was never physically seductive with her. On the contrary, he idealized and adored his little daughter, and hence would not have dared to touch her. But he was ready to yield to any of her wishes and to give her a real baby as a present. Thus, in a different way and for opposite reasons, she too was immune; for she could not do wrong and deserve punishment. Immunity, we remember, also was the essence of Helen's

---

* This point was demonstrated by the Sterbas (1954) in the case of Beethoven.

complaints: no matter what she did, people would look up to her
and revere her like a goddess. If the physically damaged feel unjustly
blamed and punished, and thereby are moved to rebel, the beautiful
feel unjustly praised and rewarded, and therefore tempted to challenge the world and to sin.

All the "exceptions"—be they physically harmed or perfect claiming exceptional rights, or cast in their role by the outside world—
pay dearly for not submitting to ordinary rules. We saw how victory,
for the first patient, was bound to be followed by realistic defeat; how
the second patient could gain victory only through defeat (Reik,
1941), and how the last patient—to modify Reik's phrase—experienced
later defeat through victory. Characteristically, all three suffered from
recurring states of depression. In this respect my beautiful patient
was certainly quite different from Helen of Troy, who remains serene
and undisturbed by whatever horrible events happen to her, around
her, and because of her. But Helen's emotional invulnerability, her
lack of profound feelings, is precisely the penalty she and women
like her have to pay. Richard III leads a terrible, but at least a very
intense life which ends in a highly dramatic, tragic death. Helen of
Troy admits that despite her eventful life she has actually not lived
at all, since life is rich, meaningful, human only if it includes also
the experiences of suffering. Of this right to be a human being she
has been deprived by man's stubborn and blind idealization of her
beauty.

There is another writer, the German poet Erich Kastner, who gives
just as drastic and humorous expression to the handicaps which this
inhuman attitude of men inflicts on beautiful women, as Erskine in
his novel. I may close with a translation of his poem (1929):

A Damsel Complains Bitterly

I'm very beautiful, I'm known for it.
And I make people think of Botticelli.
I am not pretty. I am not a wit.
No, I am beautiful. My name is Elli.

No matter whom I meet, his eyes—expressing
a pious awe, as though he came to shrift—
contritely seem to beg me for a blessing. . . .
All men believe that I possess this gift.

Rare beauty, such as mine, is not a pleasure.
Such beauty, rare as mine, is a torment!
Men made me their ideal, by intent;
when chosen thus, one must conform to measure.

They meant to consecrate me without fail.
And no one questioned if I were a saint!

I am a girl and anything but faint,
and don't quite know why I should take the veil.

Yes, I am beautiful! Come close and see!
But don't talk gently, as if I were brittle. . . .
My figure is the noblest part of me,
it is no crime to love me just a little.

Write verse, set me to music, paint me, do!
I would not win by taking it amiss.
But don't just gape as if I were taboo!
No maiden is too lovely for a kiss!

Why should I lonesome, a mere image be?
I feel as though in church, a stony face!
My naked beauty no man yet did see.
Where is the one who dares lay hands on me?!
Your reverence for me is a disgrace.

BIBLIOGRAPHY

Erskine, J. (1939), The Private Life of Helen of Troy. New York: Triangle Books.

Freud, S. (1914), On Narcissism: an Introduction. Collected Papers, IV. London: Hogarth Press, 1925.

——— (1915), Some Character-Types Met with in Psycho-Analytic Work. Collected Papers, IV. London: Hogarth Press, 1925.

——— (1937), Analysis Terminable and Interminable. Collected Papers, V. London: Hogarth Press, 1950.

Kastner, E. (1939), Larm im Spiegel. Leipzig: Curt Weller, pp. 34–35.

Losey, F. D. (1926), Introduction to "The Tragedy of King Richard III." In The Complete Dramatic and Poetic Works of William Shakespeare. Philadelphia & Chicago: International Press, The John C. Winston Co., p. 683.

Reik, T. (1941), Masochism in Modern Man. New York: Farrar, Straus & Cudahy.

Sterba, E. & Sterba, R. F. (1954), Beethoven and His Nephew. A Psychoanalytic Study of Their Relationship. New York: Pantheon Books.

From *The Psychoanalytic Study of the Child* 20 (1965): 518–34:

Narcissistic Ego Impairment in Patients with Early Physical Malformations

by *William G. Niederland, M.D.*

(New York)

Since Freud's work "On Narcissism" (1914) many analytic papers have been devoted to the study of narcissistic disorders. Few, however, have dealt specifically with narcissistic disturbances observable in one category of patients in whom such manifestations are encountered with a certain regularity and often, in fact, are found to be the predominant features of their psychopathology. This is all the more surprising in view of Freud's statement that prominently lists among the means of approach "by which we may obtain a better knowledge of narcissism . . . the study of organic disease" (p. 82).

From the group of patients loosely described as "narcissists," that is, individuals in whose pathology narcissistic phenomena play a major role, I have selected a special category for discussion, namely, patients in whom a particular type of body defect—irrespective of the clinical diagnosis and classification—can be recognized as a nodal psychological factor in their ego development as well as a pathogenic element in the formation and maintenance of narcissistic disturbances. In view of the prevalence of compensatory narcissistic self-inflation, fantasies of grandeur, etc., among such persons, their analytic study can be expected to yield information about the role such defects play in the genesis and perseverance of certain narcissistic disturbances.

In focusing attention on such cases, I took as my point of departure Freud's papers "On Narcissism" (1914) and "Some Character-Types Met with in Psycho-Analytic Work" (1916), Jacobson's (1959) elaboration of the latter, A. Reich's (1960) contributions to the understanding of the regulatory processes involved in the maintenance of self-esteem, related studies by Bychowski (1943), Greenacre (1952, 1958), Murphy (1958, 1959), and others. I also wish to draw attention to the growing concern over birth defects—a concern which in recent years has dominated several international congresses on pediatrics, orthopedics, teratogenic effects of drugs, etc. While the tragedy of phocomelia that affected the fate of thousands of seriously deformed children has been the most alarming teratogenic malformation thus far produced, it is noteworthy that frequently the teratogenic anomalies observed have been less severe, many of them involving only fingers or toes.

Studying persons suffering from congenital malformations or physical defects acquired early in life, Freud (1916) commented on their refusal to accept the reality principle. "For reasons which will be readily understood," Freud tells us, "I cannot communicate very much about these and other case histories." He then supplemented his clinical observation with an illustration from Richard III, "a figure in whose character the claim to be an exception is closely bound up with and motivated by the circumstance of congenital disadvantage" (p. 313). From this first comment and from his example we may legitimately infer that Freud alluded to patients with gross physical pathology whose identity might have been revealed by a more detailed description of their case material. The "exceptions" described by Jacobson (1959) consisted of two groups of women characterized by conspicuous physical attributes: one group included patients with visible physical deformities, and the other included women of extraordinary beauty and charm. Similarly, Lussier's (1960) case report from the Hampstead Clinic refers to a severely malformed adolescent with readily visible body defects, while Blos's recent study (1960) on cryptorchism deals with an anatomically less obvious anomaly and concentrates exclusively on this disorder in children.

In contrast to these contributions, the present study is based on observations of adult patients who suffered from the consequences of minor physical anomalies or imperfections which were of secondary importance with regard to manifest anatomical involvement, inconspicuous in appearance, and scarcely or not at all noticeable without a medical examination. In this sense, the anomalies considered here should be understood as secret or hidden afflictions; indeed the patients tended to remain silent about their presence and to keep them concealed from themselves as well as from the outer world. It should be noted, however, that despite the relative inconspicuousness of these defects, several of them were associated with some degree of functional and other types of impairment in childhood. This fact has to be kept in mind, especially in view of the frequently stated observation that "the psychological reverberations go far beyond the actual physical disability" (Kaplan, 1959). This observation is undoubtedly correct; but what strikes the clinician as disproportionate psychopathology in terms of later development may reveal itself as proportionate to the actual impairment in early life, to its phase-specific significance, and to its far-reaching elaboration in fantasy.

Included in the group studied are two patients with minor congenital chest deformities, two with congenital umbilical hernias, one with a small bony exostosis below the clavicular region, one with inconspicuous residual cranial and thoracic deformities due to infantile rickets, one with barely visible imperfections of the left arm caused by a birth injury, and one with a congenital torticollis. Of these, only the last two patients had outwardly recognizable anomalies. One of them, the patient with the torticollis, had undergone plastic surgery in adolescence and his deformity had been so well repaired that no trace of it was noticeable when he entered analysis in his early thirties. My study thus comprises eight cases, only four of which were or are in analysis; the other four were treated in prolonged, analytically oriented psychotherapy. Five of the patients are men and three are women. In presenting my observations I shall focus on the findings pertinent to the prevalence of narcissistic phenomena in these patients and shall omit the discussion of other relevant material.

Though small in number, the present series and the data derived therefrom are not, I believe, without clinical and theoretical significance. Viewing the problem for a moment nonanalytically, it is perhaps worth mentioning that about 10 to 12 out of 100 newborn infants have congenital anomalies. Since the most frequent types of such defects are those involving the bones, joints, and other parts of the body surface—as in the cases under consideration—and since some kind of congenital defectiveness is thought to be present in about 30 per cent of the general population (if certain minor anomalies of the skeleton, teeth, skin, etc., are included) the incidence and importance of clinical manifestations directly or indirectly connected with early physical malformations cannot be negligible. The relative paucity of psychoanalytic reports * on patients with such handicaps does not necessarily militate against the mounting evidence of their clinical importance in and outside analytic practice. If the current views concerning the incidence of teratogenic effects of drugs as well as the relation between increased radioactivity and a higher rate of congenital malformations are correct, it may be expected that the pertinence of these observations may soon become more obvious.

To return to the predominance of narcissistic phenomena in these cases, it is well to reiterate that Freud (1916) recommended "among the means of approach . . . by which we may obtain a knowledge of narcissism" the study of organic diseases and related conditions. The presence of an increased body narcissism and its significant implications for the psychopathology of the patients under scrutiny could, in fact, be demonstrated in all of them. The familiar, one may perhaps say, the classic features of a narcissistic or at least narcissistically tinged disorder—compensatory narcissistic self-inflation, fantasies of grandiosity and uniqueness, aggressive strivings for narcissistic supplies from the outside world, impairment of object relations and reality testing, excessive vulnerability—were apparent in the charac-

---

* In the discussion of this paper Dr. van der Waals stated that he had never encountered similar cases (Fall Meeting of the American Psychoanalytic Association, 1960).

ter structure of all eight patients, though in varying and analytically not equally accessible degrees. Moreover, at the time the patients came for treatment—that is, as adults—the psychological reverberations resulting from their essentially benign physical anomalies and the complex, usually less benign elaboration of the latter in fantasy strikingly outweighed the organic pathology.

In what follows I wish to discuss some of the principal features which characterized the narcissistic pathology of the patients.

The Narcissistic Injury

Although each case is, of course, individual and presents its own specific pathology, it can be said that the presence of an unresolved narcissistic injury derived from basic physical experiences of an unmastered and perhaps unmasterable kind resulted in certain characteristics common to all the cases studied. The nature and permanence of the defectiveness lent to the latter a quality of nodal significance, somewhat in the manner of an organizing and concretizing experience in Greenacre's sense (1952, 1958) for the entire ego and superego development. In contrast to a variety of psychic traumata in childhood which often find a more or less spontaneous solutɩon (through mastery) in the course of further development, an early body defect tends to remain an area of unresolved conflict through its concreteness, permanency, cathectic significance, and its relationship to conflictual anxiety (primitive body disintegration anxiety, castration fear). In my patients the physical defectiveness either had existed from birth or had occurred during the first year of life; therefore, the development of the body ego had been affected virtually from the beginning. The result was a faulty, sometimes bizarre and distorted body image with strangely disfigured body contours, incompleteness of body reality, and, via projection, of external reality. In this respect the site of the injury is pertinent. The man with the thoracic deformities (pectus excavatum), a six-footer, saw himself as a dwarfish hunchback, "bent in the middle," and spoke of his deformity as being a feminizing defect in the sense of providing him with a gratuitous, nonmasculine extra cavity. One woman had a birth injury which paralyzed her left arm; during her first year of life the other arm became involved, though in a minor and not fully clarified way. This immobilization of the damaged arm had directly interfered with the formation and normal functioning of the "hand-mouth-ego" integration (Hoffer, 1960). Moreover, in later life, she showed poor reality testing as well as compensatory narcissistic self-inflation: she saw herself as a world-famous artist (a man!) of immortal greatness.

At the same time, she repeatedly complained that she could not "grasp" what was going on in the world; that, to her, people were like shadowy figures "out of reach" or like "so many fish floating by"; that at times she had no "contact" with people or events. The patient's damaged arm had been in traction throughout most of her first year of life during which time she had been forced to lie flat on her back. Thus, a part of her own body as well as many external objects had actually been "out of reach" for her, and during that period the significant figures of her immediate environment had appeared to be "floating by" in shadowy fashion, as it were. Further aspects of this experience will be discussed below.

What I have called the nodal significance of an unresolved narcissistic injury due to some type of physical defect expresses itself clinically in various ways. Some of the features have already been mentioned: compensatory self-aggrandizement, heightened aggressiveness often accompanied by outbursts of aggression and hate in word and action, the castrative aspects of the defectivenss and its bisexual and sadomasochistic elaboration. I wish to call special attention to two more characteristics: the prevalence of revenge fantasies as well as florid birth-rebirth fantasies. They usually are part of the rich and secret fantasy life which in these patients is replete with narcissistic-exhibitionistic-aggressive themes, sadomasochistic fantasies (involving especially bodily mutilation, dismemberment, etc.), erotized megalo-manic daydreams, conscious or semiconscious aspirations to greatness, immortality and eternal life. The "little man" patient whom I described some years ago (1956) saw himself as a massive conglomerate of the prominent statesmen and war leaders during the last World War. Another patient, the woman with the bony exostosis near the sternoclavicular area, dreamed that she was participating in the assembly of the eternal gods on Mount Olympus, a Greek god herself (a god, not a goddess!), looking down on the poor mortals from lofty heights.

The immortality aspects of such fantasies are of great interest, clinically and from another viewpoint as well. In several of these patients the fantasies of everlasting youth and eternal life were extraordinarily strong and, when associated with magic ideas of personal invulnerability and invincibility (in some cases, even immortality), as part of their narcissistic pathology, they appeared to assume the quality of semidelusional or even delusional beliefs—in these otherwise nonpsychotic patients. While this "eternal" feature, with its imperviousness to the passing of time and to other aspects of the reality situation, can present many therapeutic problems, especially with its implications of "interminable" analysis, the narcissistically held and often highly elaborated view of everlasting life can be readily recognized as a residue of the timeless grandiosity of infancy reinforced by later restitutive processes in which cathexes withdrawn from the object world were invested in the operations of the ego organization. It is worth noting, in this connection, that the narcissistic attributes of physical immortality and lasting value to the point of aere perennius appeared to be especially strong in the artistically gifted patients who ascribed such "eternal" qualities, if not to themselves, surely to their creative works. The fact that there were three painters, one writer, and one creative scientist among my eight patients with physical anomalies may be nothing more than a coincidence, of course. On the other hand, the presence of intense restitutive strivings which a hidden body defect experienced as a narcissistic injury of a virtually unchangeable type seems to produce; the interaction between such narcissistically imperative repair efforts, the usually strong bisexual elaboration of the bodily defectiveness, and the rich fantasy life in these people; the aggressive wish to express artistically what is concealed from the world (i.e., the physical defectiveness and the suffering it engenders)—all these strivings and psychological labors should not be ignored as potential sources of creativity in such individuals.

The unconscious reconstructive and restitutive aspects of the creative "labor" which goes into the artistic productions of some of these patients became apparent to me not only in their individual subject choice (e.g., the painting of many "naissance" and "renaissance" pictures in one case) but was also suggested by two observations. One refers to the timeless or "eternal" factor mentioned above, the other to the disproportionate disfigurement (in fantasy) of the damaged body contours. These two elements seem to find expression in the creative work as well as in the analytic productions of the patients. More specifically, the patients try to regress, in their restitutive efforts, to the time prior to the formation of the defect * or at least prior to their subjective discovery of their defect. This attempt may lead to marked pregenital preoccupation and pseudopsychotic symptomatology; but it may also induce in the artistically gifted individual that regression in the service of the ego which Kris (1952) emphasized as a requirement for creativity—here brought about through regression in the service of ego restitution. Since a narcissistic gain results from such restitution, though of course the physical defectiveness remains unchanged, the unconscious reconstructive efforts tend to go on indefinitely and may in gifted persons lead to continued creativity of an almost frantic or feverish type. I believe I have observed this creative activity (which in the deepest sense is really a restitutive, re-creative one) in some of my patients and propose to deal with these complex processes in a separate study.

* A point made especially by Dr. Bettina Warburg during the discussion of this paper.

The second factor which refers to the damaged or unusual body contours also has ego-restitutive aspects. As will be described under the appropriate heading, there exists an uneven distribution of body cathexis as a result of the defectiveness. The peculiar stimuli provided by the congenital or early acquired injury may not only contribute to the psychology of the "exceptions," as Freud (1916) has shown; they may also play a role—as yet uncharted and unrecognized —in the creativity of some of these individuals. MacKinnon (1962), studying creative factors among architects, "found the unusualness of mental associations one of the best predictors of creativity." It remains to be seen whether the unusualness of associations reflects, albeit indirectly and in certain individuals, the unusualness or unevenness of cathectic stimuli emanating from the site of an unresolved and undisclosed narcissistic injury of very early origin. At any rate, the question of a possible connection between creativity and hidden physical anomalies invites further investigation. Similar views have been expressed by other authors, e.g., Freud (1916), quoting Adler's approach to the problem of the so-called "organic inferiorities," and Rickman (1940) in his paper on "Ugliness."

Secrecy and Magic Connotations of a Nonvisible Body Defect

Most of my patients showed what Blos (1960) has called "a mysterious exclusion" of the physical malformation from the rest of the clinical symptomatology. As in Blos's patient Joe, whose cryptorchism was "inadvertently" disclosed after three years of treatment, one of my women patients revealed a rhinoplasty only in her fourth year of psychotherapy.* Patients in analysis also kept their physical imperfections concealed for a long time, though derivatives and symbolic representations sometimes emerged quite early in the treatment. The first dream of a patient with a congenital funnel chest was about a car that had an indented front fender.

However that may be, the secrecy about the defect and the fact that, though a handicap, it is usually not a major physical one not only sets this type of defectiveness apart from the more visible type of malformation; these factors also add to their narcissistic and magic implications. The narcissistic significance of the secret is well known. The invisibility achieved through the use of a magic device (Tarnhelm), in the Nibelungen, makes invincible figures of Siegfried, the young hero, and of Alberic, the dwarf. Mahler's (1942) clinical material dealing with such fantasies included two patients with con-

* This patient is not included in the series of eight.

genital deformities. According to Gross (1951), the secret ultimately refers to bodily organs and processes. Since the secrecy of a hidden body defect links it to other bodily secrets, especially to the rectum and to anal functioning with their familiar connotations of power, sadism, and magic, the concealment of the defect represents a narcissistic gain. Its narcissistic value is further enhanced by outwitting and outmaneuvering the environment. In the fantasy life of several patients a variant of the typical "Rumpelstiltskin" idea with its magic and grandiose connotations could be found ("Oh, how good that no one knows . . . !"), with the Rumpelstiltskin fantasy not just as "a pleasant pastime, but an intrinsic part of the personality" (A. Reich, 1960). Rumpelstiltskin could transform straw into gold; these patients, via the secret and its magic implications, strove to convert the defectiveness into a mark of distinction and a seat of power, thus magically undoing the narcissistic injury.* Sometimes magic oral incorporation fantasies are acted out in an attempt to restore intactness to the congenital body damage. One of my patients with a defective muscular area in the anterior abdominal wall licked and at times ate pages from sport magazines showing photographic reproductions of muscular men (a magical attempt at narcissistic replenishment). Or he would bathe for hours in a tub, retire, and awaken in the morning expecting the defect to be gone (rebirth fantasy). Such magic expectations greatly influenced the transference. The woman with the hidden bony exostosis, after having relinquished her secret, often turned to me imploring: "Make it go away!" words she remembered having addressed to her mother as a child when she discovered her malformation.

With regard to the anal and oral features, it may be recalled that Richard III, besides being "a lump of foul deformity," was also equipped by Shakespeare with teeth from the moment of his birth so that "he could gnaw a crust of bread when two hours old," a clear allusion to a hidden congenital defect in addition to his gross deformities.

Body Image, Cathectic Changes, and Defenses

Body-image distortion is an inevitable outcome of early physical defectiveness. My observations appear to confirm Hoffer's statement

---

* What can be found analytically in the fantasy life of such persons, can also be seen in actu in certain visibly deformed persons, e.g., in those hunchbacked cripples who, walking up and down before gambling houses in Italy, accost passers-by with the following words: "I am a hunchback, touch me, I shall bring you good luck." The magic property of the visible malformation, to be conveyed to the one who touches it, is obvious.

(1950, 1952) that by the second year of life the infant has established an oral-tactile concept of his own body. It forms the basis of what later becomes the intact, relatively stable, and properly cathected body image of the healthy individual; among other determinants, it is characterized by a cohesive, fairly stabilized, predominantly libidinal cathexis of the body as a unitary whole. This mental representation of the body is always influenced by the interaction of physiological (dimensional-kinesthetic-postural) factors and psychological (sensorial-emotional-exquisitely personal) experiences. Though not simply identical with the actual body, it tends under normal conditions to approximate the actual body configuration. Perception of one's self, perception of others, reality testing, and other mental activities evolve against this background of an essentially bodily self image and its cathexis. For this reason the incompleteness or disruption of the body image is bound to have an impact on a number of important ego functions. The extent to which emotional experiences can interfere with the formation of an accurate body image is exemplified by Jacobson (1954) who points to the persistence "in women of the unconscious fantasy that their genital is a castrated organ, frequently with simultaneous denial and development of illusory penis fantasies" (p. 87).

Using this familiar body-image distortion as a kind of tertium comparationis, it should be noted that in cases of congenital (or early acquired) deformity there is usually a more marked, more distorted, and insidiously pervasive discrepancy between the realistic appearance and the concrete attributes of the body in the flesh and the fantasied appearance and attributes of the body in the mind. In other words, the faulty body image caused by very early physical defectiveness cannot be viewed in the same way as the persistence of the female castration complex with its specific body-image implications, however severe the latter may be. If, for example, one of my female patients consistently feels and sees her body from the neck down as a rubbery, gelatinous mass of "some cheap, hastily put-together fabric," this fantasy—while not necessarily delusional—expresses more than the usual refutation of her female genitals. The patient is the artist whose left arm, inconspicuously deformed as a result of a birth injury, is hypocathected; for her, it hardly exists and she never mentions it. The right arm (with which she paints) and her eyes are hypercathected. More precisely, it is of course the mental representations of these body parts which are directly affected. Yet the uneven balance of the body cathexis involves more and extends further; to her, the whole body image from the neck down is that of a rubbery, gelatinous mass. This type of body feeling appears to be closely related to Mittelmann's description (1960) of the body scheme in which the skeletomuscular system holds the position of an early, quasi-independent ego structure. My patient's image, moreover, included also the body surface, i.e., the representation of the cutaneous system. In this context it should be recalled that she had been in traction and immobilized for most of her first year of life.

Closer study reveals that patients with congenital or early acquired malformations are prone to suffer from a permanent disturbance of the self-image, which in severe cases may assume semi-delusional or almost delusional proportions, have archaically tinged psychological reverberations, and present distorted or even fragmented body-image features. In some of my cases the pathological body image observed resembled that of Keiser's patients: "The body image never coalesced into a unitary whole, but persisted as a number of discrete parts which functioned independently of each other." In two of my patients the withdrawal of cathexis from the object world and its concentration on the body led to a sort of "closed unit" or "closed circle" existence in feeling, thinking, and to some extent also in action, a condition called by the patients themselves their "cocoon state," "amoeba state" or "worm existence." I am inclined to view such formations as variants of the return-to-the-womb fantasy which automatically excludes any physical handicap and restores the earliest state of narcissistic perfection. The "closed unit" type of narcissistic retreat, which in these patients appeared to be connected with the regressive pull toward attaining the fantasied state prior to the defect in the restitutive effort previously discussed, thus served to undo the feeling of physical imperfection and incompleteness. Such strivings were especially intense in patients who had unusually strong castration fear and in whose pathology the threat of loss of body parts and physical intactness constituted a major element in their ego impairment. While noting these relations between disturbed ego development and early physical defectiveness, I wish to emphasize that I do not regard the latter as the sole pathogenic influence in their clinical picture. I believe, rather, that the defect, in addition to its significance as a concretizing and organizing experience of pathogenic import from early childhood, adds a "kernel of truth" quality and multidimensional aspects to the pathological fantasies which are likely to arise during the developmental phases.

The formation of a distorted, permanently incomplete and insecure body image appears particularly intense in male patients in whom inguinal or genital anomalies such as testicular malformations, penile deformities, congenital or early acquired varicocele, open inguinal rings, etc., exist. Overly strong bisexual identifications, florid fantasies of being a hermaphrodite, and compensatory narcissistic features— ideas of being unique, of possessing special powers, magic qualities, or the like—as well as intense exhibitionistic strivings are frequently encountered in such persons. In addition, strong anal preoccupations appear to prevail in them. Equally noteworthy are psychopathic impulses and behavior. On the whole, my observations tend to support those of A. Bell (1965) and Blos (1960).

Besides the notable increase in fantasy life, most of these patients used the defense mechanisms of denial, undoing, isolation, regression, reaction formation, displacement, and projection. Although the emotional responses to the handicaps, as was stated above, differed in every individual according to the many variables and vicissitudes involved, the defenses of denial and undoing (putting the defect "out of existence") were present in all patients and could be readily observed analytically. The deeper narcissistic defenses were much less accessible and attempts to deal with them required much analytic work and utmost prudence.

Another relevant factor seems to be connected with the distribution of body cathexis in a more specific way. While the faulty body image is characterized mainly by incompleteness, marked distortions, vague feelings of altered consistency and tonus to the point of partial emptiness or disembodiment—one patient's term "rubbery" describes some of this rather appropriately—the uneven distribution of the body cathexis sometimes finds expression in still another way. In a few of my patients I have observed phenomena which suggest that, within the improper balance of the total body cathexis, a compensatory "focal" hypercathexis exists in the body-self representation at the zone of confluence between the defective bad part and the adjoining good part or, by displacement, a zone of over-cathexis which involves a corresponding body area distally (away from the defect). I have already mentioned the cathectic shift from the damaged arm to the undamaged one in the patient with the birth injury. In the woman with the bony exostosis the area surrounding the defect was hypercathected so that she felt she had a particularly attractive bust. In another patient, a very young man with a funnel chest, the altered cathexis of the total body-self was accompanied by a focal hypercathexis of the self-image in the dorsal region opposite the defective area. His back region was posturally and affectively "phallicized," the patient holding himself stiffly erect like a Prussian officer (which he was not). This focal hypercathexis not only reinforces the over-cathected phallic self image in the sense of the body-phallus equation, but also gives added impetus to the narcissistic-exhibitionistic-aggressive strivings which, through belligerent behavior, provocative action, boastfulness, arrogance, etc., make such individuals gradually obnoxious even to their devoted friends. According to Eidelberg (1948, 1959), the brash or crude actions lead to external narcissistic mortifications in an unconscious effort to undo the internal mortification. In fact, by his behavior the patient often does succeed in obtaining sufficient external punishment from the outer world, which may then serve as the external narcissistic mortification required to deny the internal one.

The phenomena suggesting the concept of "focal" hypercathexis require further investigation. Keiser (in a personal communication) commented on the fact that some afflicted persons are intensely preoccupied with their impaired body area. This preoccupation may well be the result of such focal hypercathexis of the surrounding zone rather than a masochistic fascination with the defect. Keiser suggests that the sensitivity around the body orifices or defects might be studied with these admittedly tentative findings in mind.

General Remarks on Compensatory Narcissistic Fantasies

An analytic inquiry into the narcissistic pathology of individuals with certain inborn or early acquired malformations discloses a multitude and complexity of relations which, though not excluding some aspects of Adler's "masculine protest" approach to organic inferiorities, makes his formulation appear designatory rather than illuminatory. The fantasy life, in particular, which is such an intrinsic part of these personalities and is abetted by the secrecy, the self-image distortions, the compensatory megalomanic features, the magic connotations, and the attempted or factual denial of an important sector of body reality, tends to abound in florid, at times bizarre narcissistic formations. These fantasies influence the behavior of such individuals in various ways. In gifted persons an unresolved narcissistic injury derived from physical defectiveness may act as a permanent stimulus and restitutively become a source of notable creativity and artistry. Others, bristling with hidden conceit and lifelong rancor, may be revengeful and insufferable. All shades and nuances are likely to occur, of course, and to produce unusual pathological features.

Literature perhaps more than psychology has paid attention to the character structure and behavior of malformed persons. The line of literary endeavors depicting their actions and motivations and correlating these to their disturbed physique extends from Homer's Thersites in the Iliad, Shakespeare's Richard III, to some modern writers. A contemporary novelist, A. Dewlen (1961), writing about the selection of the jury in a murder trial, has the lawyer for the defense say: "He would avoid cripples, men of small stature and people with ugly faces. These, when exalted to life-and-death power, could become cruel jurors capable of doing to the defendant as had been done unto them." While oversimplification and generalization are obvious, the statement does not appear to be entirely devoid of some astute empirical observation.

One of my patients believed he had the most remarkable brain power in the world as well as a head several times its actual size. In three patients the continued presence of an unconscious, isolated, split-off self-image of infantile origin and functioning in primitive fashion could be discerned. This self-image in the form of a "little man" or dwarf fantasy preserved the primitive self-representation of the person at the time when the recognition of the defectiveness resulted in the permanent narcissistic traumatization and in the subsequent compensatory setting up of a separate narcissistic ego structure within the total ego organization. The patients referred to this isolated, primitive segment as "little man," "the dwarf," "the imp" or the like within themselves. This split-off ego segment had remained essentially unmodified since its formation under the impact of the trauma in childhood and had not participated in the later development of the intact part of the ego. On the other hand, it had under certain conditions become the reservoir of the totality of the narcissistic-destructive-omnipotent fantasies. The analysis of the in-power and other narcissistic attributes demonstrated the early split of the ego. Most of these findings have been reported in my earlier paper (1956) and in a paper by Kramer (1955) which preceded mine.

I should like to return once more to the altered cathexis of the self-image and its focal concomitants mentioned above. With the sharpened and overly keen awareness, in a distorted way, of certain body parts, much of the cathectic distribution may center on and around the psychic representations of these parts. The cathectic distortions, through projection and further elaboration in fantasy, may then lend themselves to paranoid reactions and in severe cases to their further elaboration into bizarre and delusional or quasi-delusional formations. Less severe disturbances include sadomasochistic tendencies and behavior, difficulties in maintaining or regulating self-esteem (A. Reich, 1960), acting out, low frustration tolerance, belligerence and vengefulness, poor or volatile object relations.

The modifications of normal ego development usually set in at an early period of life. When a physical defect is found soon after birth or during the first months of infancy, there often ensues, from the time of the recognition of the defectiveness ("recognition shock") a marked disequilibrium in the relations between mother and child— a disequilibrium which hardly ever fully subsides. Some mothers go into a prolonged postpartum depression, which may later be followed by renewed depression or anxiety states. Others become oversolicitous, seductive, or otherwise defective in their nursing functions. The children are thus further traumatized through the unsatisfactory mother-child interaction, overstimulation of the body, and various physiotherapeutic or orthopedic procedures (A. Freud, 1952). Indispensable as the latter may be, the psychological vicissitudes resulting from prolonged immobilization, the necessity of wearing corrective braces, etc., and the resultant inadequate discharge of aggressive and libidinal energy, and finally, the factual or fantasied threats to bodily intactness—all accentuate the traumatic influences of physical defectiveness upon psychic development.

With their ego and superego pathology, infantile megalomania, faulty body image, bizarre and at times ominous-appearing symptomatology, persistent ego split and identity problems, some of these patients lend themselves to a diagnosis of psychotic illness. But a break with reality seems to be rare and the clinical picture, as I view it, appears to be that of a narcissistic, deep-seated, but not necessarily intractable character disorder. Prolonged analytic work with several of these patients, though not easy, has proved rewarding. Among the therapeutic tasks the correction of the faulty body image, for instance, that of being half-man, half-woman, is of considerable importance and curative value.

BIBLIOGRAPHY

Bell, A. I. (1965), The Significance of Scrotal Sac and Testicles for the Pre-puberty Male, Psa. Quart., 34:182–206.

Blos, P. (1960), Comments on the Psychological Consequences of Cryptorch-ism. This Annual, 15:395–429.

Bychowski, G. (1943), Disorders in the Body-Image in the Clinical Pictures of Psychoses. J. Nerv. Ment. Dis., 97:310–35.

Dewlen, A. (1961), Twilight of Honor. New York: McGraw-Hill.

Eidelberg, L. (1948), Studies in Psychoanalysis. New York: International Uni-versities Press, 1952.

——— (1959), Humiliation in Masochism, J. Amer. Psa. Assn., 7:274–83.

Freud, A. (1952), The Role of Bodily Illness in the Mental Life of Children. This Annual, 7:69–82.

Freud, S. (1914), On Narcissism: An Introduction, Standard Edition, 14:67–102. London: Hogarth Press, 1957.

——— (1916), Some Character-Types Met with in Psycho-Analytic Work. Standard Edition, 14:309–33. London: Hogarth Press, 1957.

Greenacre, P. (1952), Pregenital Patterning. Int. J. Psa., 33:410–15.

——— (1958), Early Physical Determinants in the Development of the Sense of Identity. J. Amer. Psa. Assn., 6:612–27.

Gross, A. (1961), The Secret, Bull. Menninger Clin., 15:37–44.

Hoffer, W. (1950), Development of the Body Ego. This Annual, 5:18–23.

——— (1952), The Mutual Influences in the Development of Ego and Id: Earliest Stages. This Annual, 7:31–41.

Jacobson, E. (1954), The Self and the Object World. This Annual, 9:75–127.

——— (1959), The "Exceptions": An Elaboration of Freud's Character Study. This Annual, 14:135–54.

Kaplan, E. (1959), The Role of Birth Injury in a Patient's Character Development and His Neurosis, Bull. Phila. Assn. Psa., 9:1–18.

Keiser, S. (1958), Disturbances in Abstract Thinking and Body-Image Formation, J. Amer. Psa. Assn., 6:628–52.

Kramer, P. (1955), On Discovering One's Identity: A Case Report. This Annual, 10:47–74.

Kris, E. (1952), Psychoanalytic Explorations in Art. New York: International Universities Press.

Lussier, A. (1960), The Analysis of a Boy with a Congenital Deformity. This Annual, 15:430–53.

MacKinnon, D. (1962), The Nature and Nurture of Creative Talent. Amer. Psychologist, 17:481–95.

Mahler, M. S. (1942), Pseudo-imbecility: Magic Cap of Invisibility. Psa. Quart., 11:149–64.

Mittelmann, B. (1960), Intrauterine and Early Infantile Motility. This Annual, 15:104–27.

Murphy, W. F. (1958), Character, Trauma, and Sensory Perception. Int. J. Psa. 39:555–68.

——— (1959), Ego Integration, Trauma, and Insight. Psa. Quart., 28:514–32.

Niederland, W. G. (1956), Clinical Observations on the "Little Man" Phenomenon. This Annual, 11:381–95.

Reich, A. (1960), Pathologic Forms of Self-Esteem Regulation. This Annual, 15:215–32.

Rickman, J. (1940), On the Nature of Ugliness and the Creative Impulse, In: Selected Contributions to Psychoanalysis. London: Hogarth Press, 1957, pp. 68–89.

The Sexuality of the Severely Disabled

So strong is the definition of the handicapped role in our society that the sexuality of the disabled is one topic on which the prudish and the "liberated" share a similar uneasiness. Not only special schools seem uncomfortable with the idea that the disabled have sexual rights like the rest of us. Cartoons in magazines such as *Playboy* and *Hustler* treat the handicapped as objects of sexual derision, and self-styled pillars of libertinage such as *Screw* magazine display all the sweaty incoherence of an adolescent on his first date when they report a conference on sexuality and handicap. Nor are most surveys of sexuality in the general adult population much better when it comes to intelligent treatment of the handicapped. The Kinsey Report omits any discussion whatsoever of the sexuality of disabled women and the Kinsey volume on male sexuality devotes one paragraph to the sexuality of disabled men.[1] The recent flurry of popular studies of male, female, and gay sexuality has also ignored the disabled.[2] Even in the gay rights movement, where one otherwise finds great openness about the varieties of human sexuality, the sexual claims of the disabled often arouse uneasiness, and a respectable proportion of disabled youths and adults are themselves homosexual.

Of all handicapped children, those with severely incapacitating physical or sensory handicaps are perhaps at greatest risk. But because of the social component of most disabilities, some children with minor or trivial limitations also find themselves being treated by parents and peers as if they suffered from a major physical limitation. For instance, stuttering, viewed exclusively as a biological phenomenon, represents one of the mildest of disabilities. Yet for certain families and in certain milieus the social significance of a mild stutter can assume tragic proportions, precipitating the child into a social universe that has more in common with the world of the physically disabled than the world of the able-bodied. Similar problems can attend mild learning disabilities, minor deformities, or even relatively mild cases of such chronic illnesses as asthma.

Whether or not his handicap is severe, when a child is raised differently because. he is perceived as severely handicapped, a host of cultural factors sanction an indifference to his real psychosexual needs. Even today, well-known experts writing in national magazines make the sexual dilemmas posed by the severely retarded child the touchstone for a discussion of the problem of sexuality in *all* handicapped children. Here is how one author made the connection:

One aspect of having a handicapped child that I found really difficult to accept cropped up unexpectedly when Bobbi [the author's mongoloid daughter] was just a baby. I took her to the doctor for a check-up. He talked about some long-range plans for her. He recommended that when she started to menstruate she be sterilized or at least put on the pill. He pointed out that mongoloids are very susceptible to rape.

Mongoloids are very affectionate. They love. They like to be loved. And they aren't too smart. It would be easy to take advantage of a mongoloid and the child might not even recognize that there was anything wrong.

There is another question about sex that has been raised about handicapped adults. Many of them are capable of expressing love sexually. Some handicapped adults can be marvelous parents. Others are incapable of raising a child. Should they be allowed to marry and become parents? Should they automatically be forced into a life of celibacy? These are not easy questions.[3]

For all its paternalism, this vision of the handicapped person's sexuality is better than most. Although it denies the possibility that the disabled can reach any kind of mental or emotional maturity, it does acknowledge that even the most severely disabled people have sexual urges like the rest of us. Many able-bodied individuals find it difficult to concede even this much to the disabled (or perhaps even to themselves). They carry the logic of the cultural definition of handicap a step further. Not only are the disabled perceived to be emotional and mental children, they are perceived as either asexual or impotent.

In private conversations with able-bodied individuals we have encountered even more offensive stereotypes that represent another and more menacing way of interpreting the culture's definition of the handicapped as childlike. While it is difficult to cast a man who moves about in a wheelchair in the role of the depraved, mentally retarded sex offender, it is not uncommon for the able-bodied to impute to the severely disabled the same anarchic, unsocialized, and perverted sexuality that is associated with the traditional stereotype of the retarded sex offender. Here, too, the able-bodied person perceives a "child" in an adult body and reacts with fear and disgust at the possible forms that sexuality may take in such an individual. (As we noted in Part One, the mentally retarded are frequently viewed in this menacing light: even today the word *moron* means a mentally retarded sexual offender in some areas of the country.)

The other main cultural response to handicap, the handicapped role, further confuses the able-bodied individual's perceptions of the disabled person's sexual identity. In effect, the handicapped role represents the culturally prescribed "solution" to the misfortune of suffering from a condition that supposedly renders one indefinitely childlike. Perceiving the handicapped as sick, it is only natural for the able-bodied to believe that they are either incapable of sex because of the "illness," or that they should not engage in sex because, as everyone knows, sexual indulgence can slow or even prevent recovery.

There are many other reasons for our blind spot toward the sexuality of the disabled. Powerful cultural taboos surround sexual behavior by or between individuals who occupy roles that provide conditional legitimatizations of states of dependency (e.g., the sick role or the role of child).[4] Intense prohibitions bar sex with one's parents, sex between any child and an adult, or sexual practices between adults that symbolize in an exaggerated form a sexual relationship between a child and an adult (e.g., sadomasochism). Sexual behavior by patients in a medical setting is also hedged with powerful taboos. All of these forbidden forms of sexuality exert a powerful fascination, as is evinced by their recurrent appearance in mainstream fiction, pornography, and in the sexual fantasies that are often expressed in psychotherapy and sometimes acted out with prostitutes and among "liberated" individuals. Since sexuality is a forbidden yet compelling aspect of many dependent roles, it is hardly surprising that some able-bodied people find it very difficult to handle the idea that disabled people have sexual needs like the rest of us.

It goes without saying that depth psychology suggests an almost endless series of specifically psychological reasons why so many able-bodied people find it difficult to acknowledge the sexual identity of the severely disabled. Some of the most important stem from the ways a handicap can key into an able-bodied person's own oedipal conflicts. A number of other possible explanations are sketched out in the typology of motives presented in Appendix 3.*

* We should add that the symbolism of dependency that surrounds some disabled individuals *can* confer on them a special sexiness in the eyes of some able-bodied

Because of the pressures in our culture to deny the sexual identity of the handicapped, it is especially important that those who work with handicapped children and adults possess a sensitive and enlightened view of sexuality. This is actually beginning to happen in the field of adult rehabilitation. Traditional taboos on sexual activity between adults in hospitals and other institutional settings still prevail, but sophisticated sexual counseling of newly disabled adults is much more common than it used to be.

Unfortunately, the attitudes of those entrusted with the education and care of handicapped children and youths are much more backward. Speaking of those responsible for special schools for the deaf in the early 1970s, Lesser and Easser note that:

. . . in our survey we have found that sex would appear to be a taboo subject despite the prominence of the role that sexual development has been given in the understanding of [child] development and in the psychoneuroses. Sexual difficulties were not even mentioned. . . . The educators of residential training in institutes for the deaf were bewildered and shocked by [our] inquiry into such matters as childhood masturbation, sexual curiosity and sexual play.[6]

A similar prudery characterizes many other kinds of residential institutions for the handicapped. The following experiences were related to us by a woman who grew up in a custodial institution for the orphaned, the abandoned, and the mentally retarded, and they are just as typical of staff attitudes in small community-based facilities as of staff attitudes in large, centralized facilities.

When you grew up in Fairview, you had to watch out even if you only kissed someone on the cheek. You had to watch out because somebody who sees you, they would snitch on you. The attendant could find out and hit you. Sometimes [a boy I liked] would give me a kiss . . . but I had to tell him to stay away. I learned that [kissing in the mid-1960s] was nasty, dirty. Fairview always gave you that idea. The attendants always gave you the idea, this is bad, don't do this; you do it and you're in trouble. It's really, really naughty. This is what they said.

Did you ever masturbate?
Well, now, this gets complicated. See, when I was small, you would see girls getting together and playing around with each other. They started at a young age. When you see someone else doing the same thing, you do the same things; and I ended up doing the same thing. You try to sneak into a place, but one time I did get caught. And when you get caught you really feel embarrassed and ashamed, because everyone knows. I felt ashamed because the

people. The small literature on the adult "adjustment" of the mildly retarded is full of examples of reasonably successful marriages in which one of the partners was labeled "retarded" during childhood and is obviously slow-witted as an adult. And many people who are crippled or missing a limb will attest that there are at least some attractive, sensitive, able-bodied people who find their disability highly erotic.[5]

attendant said, "Michele, you did something bad. You're going to get written up." What they meant by that was I would be seen by the doctor the next day. I really felt wrong.

The shortcomings of segregated education (and custodial care) are only part of the problem. Even a handicapped child educated in a mainstream setting may be excluded from the psychosexual experiences of the able-bodied peer culture. Although we wholeheartedly support mainstreaming, we believe it essential to acknowledge forthrightly the psychosexual hazards of mainstreaming during adolescence.[7] Some of these hazards are brought home in the following recollections about a mainstreamed adolescence of a man with cerebral palsy.

. . . the following is . . . an illustration [of] the kind of thing that has happened, as far as I can judge, to the kids who have transferred from special classes to regular classes quite often . . . I was 13 or 14 and my libido was starting to act up and I had a guy who I thought was a friend of mine, and he knew I had a particular crush on a particular girl. (Now, you hear kids learning about [vulgar] language in the streets . . . well, I wasn't lucky enough to be in the streets) . . . I was very [socially] backward, and he said to me why don't I suggest to this girl that we do a particular dance. (He told me the name of the dance was one of our more adorable four-letter words!) I did, and I got a rather rough come-uppance . . . Now, today, I can look back at it and see that it wasn't the trauma that I thought it was at the time. The only thing that bothers me about that is I hope that, someday, somewhere, nobody looks up a record and says, "a handicapped kid is unable to do this kind of work, because look at what this kid did in that class." [The speaker did very poorly in this class.] Obviously [the come-uppance] had an effect on how I looked at that class and how I looked at myself.[8]

For the able-bodied youth, adolescence marks the beginning of a highly disorderly but also an inevitable and socially sanctioned transfer of new social powers to the individual. It is a time when society makes good its promise of an adult future to every able-bodied individual. For the moderately or severely disabled adolescent, matters are very different. With adolescence comes not only rejection, exclusion, or a second-class membership in the peer group, but frequently a full awareness of the gulf separating one's own future prospects from those of one's able-bodied classmates. The able-bodied youth looks forward to the end of parental domination and longs to leave home. The seriously disabled youth may share this desire for independence, but he or she also confronts for the first time the fact that someday his parents will die and that, should he prove incapable of leading an independent adult life, financial pressures may then offer him no recourse except to move into an institution.

Most able-bodied youths can take a job and a family for granted in their future. Few moderately or severely handicapped youths can reasonably expect to achieve either of these goals in contemporary society except through a mixture of luck and almost superhuman perseverence. What is a long, messy, but unequivocal rite of passage for the able-bodied youth—a setting aside of the tasks of childhood for those of adulthood—is all too often a parting of the ways for the disabled youth, a definitive statement that there is going to be no real place in the adult world for him.

Because of this exclusion and the climate of sexual repression in which they grow up, many individuals with major handicaps do not even begin to think of themselves as possessing a sexual identity until their mid or late twenties or even their thirties. A woman born with spina bifida described to us what appears to be a fairly common pattern among physically disabled men and women who were handicapped as children.

I felt that my body was just another object, and that I could talk about it just as dispassionately as any doctor. My mind was really me, and my body was something that occupied a wheelchair, and was just one step removed from being in a wheelchair. I felt that I was sexually neutered. Marriage wasn't even a consideration for me in childhood and adolescence. I was so different from the rest of the human race that these concerns didn't have anything to do with me, and so didn't bother me. I perceived myself as very unpopular on two grounds: one, because I was handicapped and two, because I probably thought to myself that I had a repulsive personality anyway, and nobody could like me on any grounds. So I gave up on being liked. All the dates I had in high school was one blind date to the senior prom, and he left at nine o'clock saying he had to go home because he didn't want to break training.

How did you change?
Intensive therapy in adulthood and finding some disabled people who were finally able and willing to talk about it—both male and female—after years of having a lot of disabled people around me, all of whom had been told what I was told: "You're not supposed to talk about yourself because that constitutes feeling sorry for yourself; and you're not allowed to feel sorry for yourself." And that meant you're not allowed to explore feelings. I wasn't allowed to work with any issues because one wasn't supposed to acknowledge that there were any issues. That was my upbringing.

I recently went necking with someone just because I always wanted to go parking and I was never able to do it as an adolescent because there was never anybody to do it with. So now, here I am—thirty years old—and it was just a lark. I said, "Let's go parking, damn it." I feel like I'm rediscovering the adolescence I missed and I'm getting a boot out of it.

Listening to these remarks, a woman with cerebral palsy, who also lives independently and has a job, replied: "I had the same problems. In lots of ways I was not permitted to be a child—to get in touch with my feelings. Now that I have control of my life, I'll do things that someone else [able-bodied] may have done when they were a child, because I've never done them." Still another woman, crippled with polio during childhood, summarized the different sequence of social development imposed upon some disabled people.

I'm not sure when I got the message, but I felt deeply during childhood and adolescence that no one would ever marry me; since being married would mean that I was an adult, and I believed that I would never be an adult. And I think the first time I *did* feel that I was an adult was when I started work, which was after college, and a year of a master's program. I was twenty-three, and work meant that I had grown up. Only then did I begin to meet people. In fact, I did it [making love] for the first time this year.

Similar problems have been related to us by many physically disabled men: "I was kind of a shy kid at fourteen, and I just assumed after I got polio that sex was all over for me. No one told me different even though I can feel and move a little bit, and have good bowel and bladder control—I have all the normal sensations, yet no one ever talked to me about sex in a sensible way."

Another physically disabled man described to us how he had to overcome in himself a deep-seated belief that his sexual urges were perverse, evil, and diseased because people like himself were not supposed to engage in sex.

I remember when I went through my first sex restructuring thing. It was in the mid-1970s or something; and I happened to join a group that heavily emphasized gayness. And there was a woman in the group who was a dyke, and she started talking about all the guilt she had to overcome before she could accept that she was a lesbian. And as she talked, I felt an incredible affinity with her, because what she was saying about being gay was exactly what I had felt about my heterosexuality because I was crippled. The emotions were the same—there was the same sense of estrangement and alienation.

Listening to these accounts, it is easy to conclude that the sexual repression practiced upon severely disabled people during childhood and adolescence must leave an almost insurmountable residue of sexual neuroses and psychological disturbances. Yet the available evidence—and it *is* highly fragmentary—suggests an altogether more complex picture. It appears that one cannot always assess a severely disabled person's ability to overcome long-standing psychosexual problems by interpreting his or her symptoms of sexual maladjustment with psychological theories that have been developed for the able-bodied. At least some individuals display a striking and completely unexpected ability to change and grow in their twenties and thirties as soon as they achieve some degree of social adulthood in some other area of life—such as holding down a job or living on their own in the community. In some instances all that seems to be needed is for the person to be given the opportunity, for the first time in his or her life, to meet other disabled people in unsupervised social settings and to pursue intimate relationships away from the prying eyes and pressures of family or custodial personnel.

Recent work carried out at the Human Sexuality Program at the University of California Medical School in San Francisco supports this suggestion. As Robert C. Geiger notes:

A recurring and somewhat surprising observation . . . has been these people's [palsied individuals with varying degrees of mental and physical disability] capacity to *rapidly learn* appropriate social skills and their willingness to apply them in relationships *once the opportunity is afforded.* Most of these people have been the recipients of enormous external pressures and limitations, as well as cultural innuendos. On the other hand, they have not necessarily internalized and accepted them to the degree that they become truly "disabled." One young man, for instance, had been involved only in casual sexual experiences, always as the passive recipient of advances. He had had no long-term "give-and-take" relationships. He recently became involved in a new romance, once again as the passive member. With the young woman's persistence, however, this relationship became permanent. The couple entered the Human Sexuality Program requesting assistance in better ways to relate to each other. Counseling involved primarily techniques in interpersonal relating and some specific education regarding the basis of sexuality and sexual practices. After only a few sessions his able-bodied partner reported not only that she now received consistent sexual satisfaction but it was apparent that he had also become more assertive within the relationship. This assertiveness went beyond initiating sexual advances, which he had previously been unwilling to do, and included directly approaching interpersonal conflicts rather than passively retreating. [Italics added] [9]

Speaking more generally of the passivity of the young man evinced in the example, Dr. Geiger observes that when palsied individuals

. . . have attempted to establish relationships unsuccessfully because of inappropriate courting techniques, they tend to retreat; this retreat then forces the available partners to become assertive themselves, rather than allowing the cerebral palsied individual to assertively choose a prospective partner. This behavior pattern is not necessarily a pathologic type of passivity but a situation that can be significantly modified by experience. Given the opportunity to learn appropriate social skills, the individual is often able to function more aggressively, to modify established relationships, or more assertively establish new ones. This behavior is in contrast to the able-bodied person who may be passive because of internal characterologic factors rather than because of a stifling lack of opportunities for education in socialization.[10]

Needless to say, our present state of knowledge about the sexuality of the severely disabled is far too fragmentary to permit us to assert with any security that all or even many physically disabled people fit the pattern that we have described. Here, as in other areas of the handicapped person's personality development, much more research is needed before any generalizations of value will be possible. However, the fact that at least some disabled adults break the "rules" of psychopathology so flagrantly should alert us to the need to emphasize a side of the sexuality of the disabled that is especially easy to overlook when discussing a group of individuals who are so often defined as childlike or patientlike by the general public.

As a culture dominated by and organized to suit the needs of the able-bodied, we are still assimilating Freud's discovery that the roots of adult sexuality lie in childhood. Able-bodied adults—especially middle-class and upper-middle-class adults—spend years of their lives in psychotherapy seeking to work through and undo the effects of early traumas, frustrations, and disappointments. But while the psychoanalytic insight must rank among the great inventions of the century, it induces a peculiar blind spot in our thinking about the sexuality of the handicapped. If sexual neurosis in the able-bodied is a disease of the past, handicap is, as we have argued in this book, preeminently a disease of the future, a disorder of social time that symbolically as well as concretely denies the child a future as a viable adult.

The point is a simple one, but it is one that the "childlike" property of disability, the handicapped role, and our psychoanalytically oriented view of sexuality obscure. No foreseeable social services strategy is capable of sparing many handicapped individuals from a long and painful confrontation with their childhood once they grow up. But a strategy of political and economic reform can at least help to ensure that the individual is able to revisit his past as a social adult, rather than as a ward of his parents, a social outcast scraping by on welfare, a menial worker in a sheltered workshop, or an inmate of a custodial institution.

Since we cannot solve the handicapped individual's psychosexual needs for him in childhood, let us bend every effort to make it possible for him to solve these needs himself as an adult, when he can draw upon all the resources of adulthood. Once this complementary perspective on sexuality is granted, nearly everything we have said in our analysis of handicap as a social problem bears on the issue of sexuality.

In this note we have explored a few of the ways that society's vision of the nature of disability may hinder and alter the severely disabled individual's sexual development. But many other questions besides the ones we have singled out here require careful, painstaking research. Perhaps the best way to suggest the complexity of these issues is to reiterate some of the observations made in our discussion of social development in chapter 5.

Close attention must be paid to socioeconomic variables. A handicap like mild retardation may exert a disastrous influence on the psychosexual development of an upper-middle-class child; yet the possession of an identical degree of mental impairment may be relatively unimportant in a working-class community or in certain ethnic groups or subcultures. As we noted in Part One, systematic research into the relative degree of stigma associated with different kinds of handicaps in different social milieus is urgently needed.

Great care must be exercised in coming to any general conclusions from the clinical literature on the sexual problems of handicapped individuals. Psychotherapists tend to write up their most "interesting" examples of pathology; the individuals seen by psychotherapists represent a preselected population heavily weighted in favor of individuals with major problems; and the emphasis upon sexuality and the body in many of the 130 different schools of psychotherapy means that most discussion of the psychological problems of handicapped individuals are likely to be dominated by interpretive structures that emphasize the possible sexual symbolism of handicap.[11]

Finally, the remarks of Peter Blos and Stuart Finch are worthy of special attention. They wrote:

It is our speculation that this neglect [of the psychosocial needs of the handicapped] is analogous to the neglect accorded, until recently, the phenomena of death and dying. . . . What must often happen, we think, is an unspoken collusion between doctor, patient, family, and peers to avoid references to sexuality or, if the question is raised, to "reassure" with generalities. It is easier to keep the focus on the admittedly difficult tasks of medical management, physical rehabilitation, and vocational training. . . .

[Our impression is] that *how* an adolescent incorporates his or her own burgeoning sexuality into the totality of his personality has little to do with his *specific* handicap. We think that adaptation has much more to do with the time of onset [of the handicap] in the specific patient's life, his previous psychological development, his capacities for coping with stress, the conscious and unconscious symbolic meanings of the handicap and how it was acquired, and his ability to come to terms with the handicap as well as the family's ability to master the trauma. . . .

We would like to see . . . [the following] question studied: *How,* psychologically speaking, is a specific handicap dealt with over time by a particular individual and his family? Perhaps the concept of coping might be useful in this regard. The question would get us away from the yardstick of normality, which is really only applicable to those who have an average expectable environment, and an average expectable endowment, and help us to focus upon developmental processes. . . .

We believe that mature sexual adjustment is possible for many handicapped adolescents, as is attested by many who have achieved it. How they achieve it, what the vicissitudes of various aspects of the personality are, and how we may be of assistance deserve intensive study.[12]

Typology of Motives

All encounters have great potential for ambiguity. For the handicapped person this potential is unusually great because of the problematic character of his handicap, his physical difference, in the eyes of the able-bodied. Why are contacts sometimes so "sticky" between able-bodied and handicapped people? We shall discuss four kinds of possible explanations.

The Symbolism of Roles: The Handicapped Person as "Symbolic Other"

The first family of theories emphasizes the important symbolic overtones of handicap from a depth psychological perspective. Very pessimistically, they assert that for many able-bodied people the content of the handicap role casts the disabled individual into another role as well, the role of symbolic Other. In this role the disabled person becomes a kind of talisman, a visible incarnation of death, sexuality, and dependency, all of which arouse our deepest fears.

One possible version of such a theory might go like this.

A substantial part of able-bodied behavior toward handicapped people is preconditioned by unconscious forces. We do not treat the handicapped as authentic human beings, but as an extension of something in us. Their disabilities call forth from us anxiety about our past, present, and future; ambivalence toward our own body; and doubts about our humanity. As those who have ever *known* a handicapped person can testify, at first the handicap blots out everything else about the person like an enormous scotoma. Only later, as we get to know him, does the blind spot induced in us by the handicap contract.

What does the handicapped person *mean* for us? What does he signify?

By his very corporeality, says this theory, the disabled person evokes our deepest fears of the nonhuman and of becoming nonhuman ourselves.

We all need to believe that we are human. Yet the way that we have grown up contradicts this belief. We all learn that to achieve and prove our humanity, we must steal it and deny it in the Other. Much as our ideology of personal relationships denies it, competition, conflict, and power are at the root of most human bonds. How many people are happy because others are unhappy? In how many friendships are the partners really equals? The handicapped person—by virtue of his disability—is the incarnation of our fear of failure, of losing out, of being mutilated and conquered by the Other.

Of course, the ultimate failure is death. And here, too, the handicap possesses a symbolic importance completely disproportionate to its physical importance. For every handicapped person has, by virtue of his disability, already died a little in the mind of the able-bodied person. His lack—his blindness, or deafness, or paralysis—reminds us of the time when we shall all be blind, and deaf, and paralyzed.

But where death is, there, too, is sexuality. (The links between sex, violence, and mutilation have been noted by many psychoanalysts.) By virtue of his mutilation, the disabled person is a disturbing parody of a sexual object. No wonder that at the beginning of this century many urged castration and clitoridectomy for the retarded, the epileptic, and the mentally ill. The practice of sterilization in some states reflects to this very day the same spirit of vengeance as does our defensive denial of the sexual needs of the handicapped. For what we fear in ourselves we deny to others.

So goes one version of a depth psychology theory. A second might place more emphasis upon our defenses against the symbolic character of handicap than upon the content of the symbolism itself. One such "ego-defense" version might go like this.

In many traditional cultures there are crippled or deformed gods, and the handicapped are often imputed to have magical powers. Epilepsy is the "divine sickness." The blind are often able to "see" into the future. Often, too, the handicapped figure is granted a special license to mock the ruling conventions—and contradictions—of the day. One thinks of the trickster in American Indian myths, or Hermes in classical mythology.

In our culture all this is changed. In place of the traditional kinds of myths we have a radically new kind. This is the myth of technology —a myth whose aim is to alter the human condition, not to reconcile us to it. While there is much that is good about this myth, it is seriously flawed when it comes to helping us handle our feelings toward the handicapped.

In the large, it licenses us to deny the feelings evoked by disability by denying that the handicapped really are a problem: we soothe our conscience and our psyche by the thought that science is doing all it can to help the handicapped, and that sooner or later the problem will be solved. In the small, it interposes the frailest of defenses between us and our deep-seated ambivalences toward the handicapped. Face to face with a handicapped person, all we have to offer to him—and to fall back upon ourselves—is a cruel and easily punctured optimism that science will win out in the end. "It's really all right," we seem to say to him. "In a hundred years science will be able to cure people with your handicap."

Of course, it is not all right, and the handicapped person does not have to do very much to make it clear to us that it is not. No wonder, then, that encounters between us and the disabled are sometimes such painful failures. No wonder, too, that perceiving our defenses against our deep-seated ambivalence toward handicap to falter, we lash back with a technical fix. In effect, we tell the disabled person, "Go back to limbo. Stop reminding me that you must live your life now, not in some science fiction future where everything really will be all right."

The handicap role is not the only role which may bring in its wake some version of the role of the symbolic Other. Nor is it the only role in which the embodied symbolic Other is negative and threatening. The members of every stigmatized or disadvantaged group find themselves involved disproportionately in interactions with outsiders in which they function as symbolic Others.[1] In prewar Europe and America the Jew consistently found himself being treated as an emissary of the dark corrupting powers of money and Oriental sensuality. In a similar way, the black, with his "ebony" skin, his "greater sexual powers," and his "sense of rhythm," has evoked in whites their fears of repressed sexuality. Indeed, he has often been expected to fulfill this aspect of the role expectation as well, being the "dark" man or woman with whom everything sexual is permitted. With women, there has typically been a fissioning of symbolic role functions—one's wife being idealized and kept in a never-never land of fake gentility while one finds one's guilty pleasures with women who are poor.

Of course, what is true for discussions of these other roles is true for handicap. It is one thing to indicate a logically possible way for handicap to possess deep symbolic overtones—there are many other possible contents we have not discussed—and quite another to know if this particular logical possibility is frequently realized in real life. Similar considerations hold for the relative importance of our two subgroups of depth psychological theories. Whether the symbolism of handicap is more or less important than the difficulty the symbolism presents to our defenses is also an empirical question. At the very least it seems reasonable to expect that, like every feature of that vast uncharted landscape which is the unconscious, the emotional topography of handicap will vary as a function of the usual socio-economic, racial, and personality variables, as well as with different disabilities: the charting of this aspect of the role expectations for different kinds of handicapped individuals represents one of the great desiderata of our field. Indeed, it may well be the case that despite the ease with which one can construct possible symbolic meanings of handicap, depth psychological considerations are in many cases irrelevant. This being said, one should immediately add that for one class of handicapped individuals (children) and one class of able-bodied individuals (the close relatives of a handicapped child), it would appear inevitable that the role expectations of handicap would possess a heavy symbolic overlay. For it is in the family that we dream aloud the longest, in the family where every role assigned a member has its symbolic harmonics and overtones. And it is in the family, too, where the tragedy of role expectations formed by a misperception of the real limitations imposed by a child's handicap may be played out to the fullest.

The Cues of Interactions

The possibilities raised by depth psychology are as great as the need to determine their relative importance in the real-life experiences of the handicapped. Rather than continuing to speculate further, let us instead turn to a related way of plausibly accounting for what some-times goes on between handicapped and able-bodied individuals. Instead of emphasizing the unconscious overtones of the "semantics" of handicap, this family of explanations focuses upon the symbolic overtones of what might be called the "social syntax" of handicap—the symbolism of the handicapped person's attempts to step out of the narrow roles which are often imposed upon him even by the well intentioned. Here, too, there is considerable similarity between the problems encountered by the handicapped and the problems encountered by members of other stigmatized groups.

In what follows, we will continually point to the potential which each of the "dramaturgic" options open to the handicapped person possesses for functioning as a "hook" onto which the able-bodied can hang the role of symbolic Other. One should, however, bear in mind throughout this discussion that each of these "syntactical moves" is itself capable of creating enough uncertainty and anxiety in the able-bodied auditor to spoil the interaction even if depth psychological considerations are not at work.*

The first of these additional sources of symbolic overtones might be called adverbial. If unconscious overtones accrue to the handicapped role, they can also be evoked by the way that a disabled individual tries to carry out a nonhandicapped role. A teacher or businessman who staggers instead of walks, who drops a cigarette on his lap only to jump when it begins to burn him, even slurred or difficult-to-understand speech—each of these performative failures can serve as hooks upon which our deepest fears of incompetence, dependence, passivity, and vulnerability are caught up. At the very least—as the Tom Murphy interview in chapter 5 suggested—they can constantly keep us unbalanced, not knowing from one moment to the next what to expect.

Parallel to the way the disabled person performs an adult role is the way in which he performs the role assigned to him by the able-bodied. If he resists this role, if he steps out of it from time to time, he may once again end up being perceived as a symbolic Other.

The difference between functioning as a symbolic Other because one plays one's part to a "T" (which is emphasized by the depth psychological theories discussed in the preceding section) and functioning as a symbolic Other for performative reasons has been thoroughly explored in literature. Compare, for example, the gardener in *Lady Chatterley's Lover* (a symbolic Other precisely because he fulfills her role expectations for a working-class man) with the menace of Heathcliff in *Wuthering Heights* (which stems in part from the way in which he keeps stepping outside the role expectations proper to a person of his "station" and in part from the idiosyncratic way in which he performs the role of "lord of the manor").

Ultimately, though, the problems raised by "misleading" performative cues extend far beyond the strictly adverbial aspect of the disabled person's dramaturgic options to the "nominal" aspect of his social behavior as well: to the question of whether or not the able-bodied auditor recognizes that the disabled person is, in fact, playing an adult part. When this recognition is absent, the handicapped individual may once again find himself being faulted on performative

---

* This possibility will be explored in the next section.

grounds. Thus, it is perfectly possible to act consistently and confidently on one's own adult terms, but for all that still to seem to fail at playing any adult role adequately because one does not fit into any of the preexisting role pigeonholes of the able-bodied. Real-life examples—which involve many groups besides the handicapped —are numerous: the American woman tourist in a foreign country in which women are still treated as inferiors, the college boy arguing with a construction worker. Perhaps the most copious and instructive literary examples are presented by George Bernard Shaw, of whom it might be said that an important aspect of his genius consisted precisely in exposing the vices of society by pitting individuals playing novel roles against the ruling conventions of the day (consider, for example, John Tanner in *Man and Superman* and the old butler in *You Never Can Tell*). In such cases the performer is like a man who speaks something that sounds like a language with a grammar and that even contains many familiar-sounding vocabulary items, but is nonetheless a language the auditor cannot fully decipher. As the Murphy/Jones interviews show, the rare disabled person with a successful career finds that the "novel role" he plays as an independent adult also constantly pits him against the ruling conventions of his day.

Georg Simmel's concept of the "stranger" is worth setting out in this regard.[2] For Simmel, a stranger is someone whose reference groups are not integrated into a society—i.e., a man who, in the eyes of the mainstream, plays an unfamiliar role. According to Simmel, a stranger possesses the attributes of detachment and objectivity—attributes that may be compounded in the case of a handicapped person by his lack of connection to what others may perceive as a commonsense everyday world.

The degrees to which the disabled person constructs himself as a stranger, and is constructed as a stranger by an able-bodied Other, are not necessarily identical. The process involved in any situational encounter can be regarded as the process of making the self's perception of the Other and the Other's perception of the self "fit." Cues are used to do this. It may be the case that a disabled person, having the expectation of strangerness constructed about him, manufactures himself as a stranger to accord with that expectation. The role of a stranger may be a costly role.

Being a stranger is not unique to the handicapped. The role is shared by the drug addict, the traveler, the homosexual, many immigrants, Bohemians, etc. There are degrees of strangerness and different sorts of strangerness. There is a difference between the stranger from another culture (the alien), and the stranger who is from the same culture but from a different social location within it (the handicapped person). For the handicapped person that difference of location may be true not only socially but phenomenologically as well.

Finally, one can deliberately or inadvertently carry one's strangeness one step further and end up functioning as a symbolic Other by giving out so many apparently contradictory clues about oneself that one does not seem to cohere as a character, even a character playing an unfamiliar role. Writes the critic Frank Kermode, "Whereas there may be in the world no such thing as character, since a man is what he does and chooses freely what he does, . . . in the novel there can be no just representation of this, for if a man were entirely free he might simply walk out of the story, and if he had no character we should not recognize him." [3] Kermode is, of course, speaking in the large, speaking of long runs of behavior. In the small, however, in what Erving Goffman calls "frames," the short scenes that make up the acts of our life, what is true for the novel is true for real life. When a man puts out too many contradictory cues about himself he, in effect, has "no character" and we do not "recognize him." Even with the best of intentions, faced with a "code" we cannot crack— a person who not merely acts out of character but appears to lack a character—our reactions to him are as likely to lack coherence as his actions seem to lack coherence to us.

The Uneasiness of Ignorance

So far we have explored two broad ways in which handicap can arouse uneasiness in the able-bodied. The first involves the symbolic meaning of handicap for us. The second involves the symbolic meaning of the way a handicapped person refuses to fit into our stereotypes about him. There is a third and more optimistic family of explanations. This family ascribes much of the awkwardness of the able-bodied to nothing more serious than ignorance. One may like and respect a handicapped person and still stammer, overreact, or fall mute time and time again because one doesn't know what to do next.

Something similar occurs when one speaks with members of many disadvantaged groups and some property of their group membership comes up. One may like a gay person, but until one has some experience with gay people, one may not know how to refer to his gayness in conversation with him. More generally, the problem usually presents itself as this: how does one behave toward a member of a less advantaged group than one's own without seeming, quite unintentionally, to be patronizing or false? With handicapped people it is often the case that this last question—which at root is a function of inexperience and ignorance about the individual—is compounded by one's ignorance of the real limits on behavior imposed by the other person's handicap. In this respect, at least, the real handicap of handicap is that any handicap makes it harder for the social conventions of a given setting to operate smoothly. Only if the able-bodied person has experience in dealing with handicapped people—which many of us lack—will these special obstacles be absent. In fine, the stickiness of some initial encounters may not be due to deep-seated prejudices and fears, but to nothing more serious than inexperience.

Scott suggests one version of this approach in his discussion of interactions between the blind and the able-bodied.

Preconceptions about blindness are not the only elements of personal encounters that determine a blind man's socialization experiences; certain features of the actual encounter play an important role as well. First of all, the norms governing ordinary personal interaction cannot, as a rule, be applied when one of the actors is unable to see. Furthermore, blind people, because they cannot see, must rely for assistance upon the seeing with whom they interact. As a result, many of the interactions that involve the sighted and blind men become relationships of social dependency. . . .

One of the things we do upon meeting someone for the first time is to impute to him a familiar social identity. We label him elderly, handsome, debonair, cultured, timid, or whatever. From the identity we have imputed to him, we anticipate what his tastes and interests will be, the kinds of attitudes he will have, and how he is likely to behave. We search for clues to help us classify the person as a type of individual, and we then apply norms of conduct associated with "his type" in order to guide us in our subsequent interaction with him. Unless we can do this quickly and accurately, we are at a loss as to how to proceed, and experience the situation as embarrassing and stressful. . . .

The inability to gather accurate information on which to form impressions is not a problem only for the blind person: it leads to uneasiness on the part of the sighted individual as well. He is uncertain that the image he tries to project will be received, or, if received, accurately interpreted. He will realize immediately that his general appearance is no longer useful for conveying information about himself. His uneasiness intensifies if he does not know which nonvisual clues the blind man is using to "size him up." Is it the tone of voice or the content of words? Does his tone of voice convey something about himself that he is unaware of or wishes to conceal? He does not know how to convey to the blind man an impression equivalent to the one conveyed through sight. When visual clues to a person's social identity are missing, a difficult and awkward situation is created for both the blind man, who does not develop a complete impression, and the sighted man, who is unsure of the impression he has made. . . .

One facet of this problem deserves special emphasis. Easy social interaction is contingent upon the possession of certain skills and information that can be used as a conversation goes along. I have in mind here the most elementary kinds of things. For example, when a person meets me in my office, I may invite him to take a seat. He may wish to have a cup of coffee and a cigarette. Perhaps we will share lunch together either in my office or in a restaurant. He may wish to use the telephone while we visit. I may want to show him written materials, or he may have to excuse himself to use the bathroom. Easy, uninterrupted communication hinges on the ability of both of us to carry out the activities necessary to the encounter with ease and independence. Let us go back over the encounter as I have described it and assume that this person is blind. When he enters my office, I find I cannot simply invite him to take a seat but must conduct him to it. As I approach him, I realize that I do not know how to direct him easily, and he does not know if I can do so either. Consequently, we share an awkward moment as I try to lead him to a chair and back him into it. He in turn tries to accept my assistance gracefully while trying not to be impaled by the arms of the chair. After he is seated, I offer him coffee. When it arrives, I realize that he may want cream and sugar. It is unclear if he can manage this himself. If he cannot, and he asks me to do it for him, I may place the coffee in front of him only to find that he knocks it over when reaching for it. When lighting a cigarette, he may put a match to it yet fail to ignite it. If he continues to puff away, do I tell him or let him discover it for himself? Suppose that he flicks ashes on himself; do I point this out to him and therefore bring his disability into the conversation or do I let it pass unnoticed. When he asks to use the bathroom, what do I do? How do I direct him to a toilet or urinal or get him to the washstand? We enter a restaurant for lunch, and I realize that he cannot read the menu. How do I help him to get seated at the table? He orders meat and the question arises as to whether or not he is able to cut it. And what about things on the table of which he is unaware, such as butter and rolls? How do I help him to get these things? From its inception to its conclusion, the interaction is filled with uncertainty, awkwardness, and ambiguity, making such meetings frustrating, embarrassing, and tense. . . .

These three problems of establishing the desired personal identity in the mind of the other actor, of uncertainty as to how to interact with a blind man, and of miscommunication all work together to produce that peculiar blend of annoyance, frustration, ambiguity, anger, tension, and irritation that describes human interaction that is spoiled. The important point is that the source of this unhappy outcome is not to be found so much in the erroneous beliefs that the seeing hold about blindness, although such beliefs clearly are not entirely innocent; rather, it lies in what might be called "the mechanics" of interpersonal conduct. In this sense, the problem lies more with the relationship itself than with the erroneous conceptions held by those who are parties to it.

All of this has two important effects on the blind man's self-concept. First, he is once again reminded that he is different from most people and that the satisfying personal relationships that are commonplace to them are, for the most part, denied to him. Second, because so many of his relationships with other people are spoiled, he is denied the kind of honest and direct feedback that is so essential for maintaining clear and realistic conceptions about the kind of person he is. Often the blind man gets no feedback at all, and when he does it is usually badly distorted. As a result, the blind man can easily acquire either an unduly negative or an unreasonably positive conception of his own abilities.

Even though many of the problems that characterize encounters between sighted and blind men arise from the mechanics of inter-personal conduct, it does not always follow that blind men explain these problems to themselves in this way. On the contrary, many of them apparently assume that a normal person's behavior is caused by his beliefs. Thus, when a sighted person behaves assertively toward a blind person so as to eliminate uncertainty, the blind man infers that the other's actions are caused by a belief that blindness makes him helpless. It is for this reason, I think, that blind people have placed so much stock in the notion of an elaborate, rigid stereotype of the blind.[4]

The Promptings of Power

There remains a fourth kind of explanation for what sometimes goes awry between handicapped and able-bodied. Cutting across the other categories of explanation—or rather, always present as an unseen guest in every interaction—it requires special mention. Typically, handicapped people—and the members of other deviant or disadvantaged groups—find themselves in asymmetric power situations with individuals from outside their group. This asymmetry is not produced by the specific content of the relationships—i.e., what the particular role expectation is, what kinds of symbolic overtones and harmonics exist, etc.— but represents something more abstract, a reduction of all the multitudinous nuances of the encounter to a balance sheet in which the pluses and minuses of control are totaled up. In many interactions between nonequals a common pattern prevails: even if one assumes the best of intentions on both sides, the most open of attitudes about roles and character, and the greatest goodwill and intelligence, something yet remains which is often sufficient to corrupt the relationship against the will of both participants. It is as if there is an unconscious at work which belongs to neither individual but to the situation.

Psychology has just begun to explore the ways in which asymmetric power relations can slowly (or not so slowly) prove to be decisive in determining both the behavior and the attitudes of the members of the diad. Two well-known sets of experiments—those carried out by Stanley Milgram in the 1960s and by Philip Zimbardo more recently —are especially apposite. Both show the surprising ease with which the structure of a situation can completely transform an individual (as long as he remains in the situation). Milgram found that people from all walks of life could be induced to administer apparently painful shocks to a volunteer, provided they were put in the role of assistant to a scientist.[5] Zimbardo found that when college students played at being "guards" and "prisoners" in a simulated prison, the "guards" very quickly began to act and feel as if they were real guards and soon treated the prisoners in brutal and degrading ways.[6]

The best clues as to the importance of structural constraints come from literature. Among critics, it is perhaps Georg Lukács who best explores the ways in which individuals try to escape the hidden constraints upon their actions only to wind up becoming what they thought they would never become.[7] Indeed, all modern theories of tragedy, from Hegel onward, reflect a similar structural approach. Among novelists, D. H. Lawrence is perhaps most instructive in this regard because power is such an important issue with him. Again and again he starts with rounded, complex, promising women, throws them into relationships with men, and then traces their slow loss of freedom and integrity as the structural constraints of the traditional man/woman relation slowly win out over the woman's desire to be free and independent. The process—this slow fashioning of character by circumstance—is not unlike what the behaviorists call the "shaping" of behavior.

A handicapped person and an able-bodied person meet for the first time. Because of the uncertainty produced by his disability, the handicapped person feels that the encounter has gotten off to a bad start and fumbles, slurs his speech, or acts more clumsily than he normally does. People *fall* into roles with each other, and what they assume is often a function of the accidents of first impressions, a contingency to which the handicapped person is more vulnerable than most of us. The so-called self-fulfilling prophecy is a set of expectations one brings into a situation and which then one imposes upon the other. But there are times when it is not individual expectations but the "balance of power" in the situation which in effect generates a self-fulfilling prophecy—a prophecy that, as is demonstrated again and again in literature, can play itself out quite independently of the desires and wishes of the participants.

A doctor, for example, has a number of built-in or structural advantages in any relationship with his patients. For one thing, they need him more than he needs them. For another, he knows much more about medicine than they do. If a doctor is rather bad at explaining himself to a layman, the patient may become sufficiently rattled to become flustered and seem incompetent. And once the relation has gotten off on the "wrong foot," this initial perturbation in favor of the doctor may finally lead to an "equilibrium" situation in which the patient feels constantly oafish and ill at ease with his physician, while the physician, for his part, may consider his patient to be passive, unintelligent, poor at expressing himself, and hypochondriacal. There need be no unconscious animus on the part of doctor and patient for this to happen. Only a moderate incompetence with words on the part of the doctor and a merely average ability to empathize with his patient are sufficient.

In the past few pages we have sketched a typology of possible reasons underlying some of our typical behavior toward the handicapped individual. In the course of our discussion we have pointed to the many cases of overlap between the sociological situation of handicap, as we have described it here, and the sociological situation of other groups who suffer discrimination and stigma. It remains to raise briefly some additional questions for research.

Perhaps no area of social science research about disability is more intellectually unsatisfying than the voluminous literature on able-bodied people's attitudes toward the handicapped. With few exceptions, workers have taken expressed attitudes at face value and relied upon statistical techniques, such as factor analysis, to discern patterns in the respondents' answers.[8] As a result of this emphasis upon surfaces, there is a dearth of studies that test psychologically or sociologically interesting hypotheses about the able-bodied person's behavior toward handicapped people.[9] Attempts to elucidate characteristic (or modal) styles of interaction with disabled people are virtually nonexistent; and remarkably little effort has been devoted to establishing correlations between different kinds of personality structure (or life-style) and the behavioral strategies adopted toward the disabled. Though crude and requiring further refinement, it is possible that the distinctions indicated by our typology may suggest more interesting ways of studying how able-bodied people treat people with different kinds of handicaps—e.g., by pointing to the kinds of sociological variables that need to be examined in conjunction with personality variables. Indeed, it is tempting to expand upon Robert A. Scott's remarks about the uncertainties encountered by the able-bodied with the blind: is it possible that in many encounters the crucial determinants of the able-bodied person's behavior are less a product of depth psychological factors than of the more specifically sociological factors that we have discussed—the way that the handicapped person does or does not fulfill the able-bodied person's role expectations; the able-bodied person's own uncertainty about how to behave in a responsible manner toward the disabled person; and the asymmetries of power that so often favor the able-bodied person in his interaction with a disabled person? Careful study of the "depth psychology" of handicapped/able-bodied interactions may also contribute to the achievement of more theoretically satisfying explanations of the relative success enjoyed by certain kinds of social strategies in reducing prejudice and bigotry toward members of a stigmatized group.[10]

Some of the most interesting issues raised by our typology concern the disabled themselves. Does the typology capture the main ways that disabled adults account for their treatment by the able-bodied? Does it point to some of the most important unconscious ways that disabled adults respond to the able-bodied Other? And what of handicapped children and adolescents?

Like all explanations of behavior, those offered by our typology can be used as unfalsifiable theories; that is, no matter what the Other does, each of our four theories can provide an internally consistent explanation of his motives.[11] How do the handicapped use these explanatory models? For example, can one roughly distinguish between different groups of handicapped children and adults according to the kinds of untestable hypotheses about the Other's motives that each group prefers? Is there any regular developmental path that some handicapped children follow, first preferring one and then another unfalsifiable hypothesis? And when do falsifiable theories of motive enter the picture?

Finally, it would be extremely useful to know the rough frequencies with which interactions in a given milieu between the able-bodied and people with different handicaps are best described by the families of causality we have described. It would be surprising if these general patterns were the same for every community or were independent of such major character traits as being authoritarian or nonauthoritarian. We are especially eager to see research that relates styles of interaction between handicapped and able-bodied people to the specific content and affective characteristics of the sick role and the handicapped role in different settings, among different social groups, and for different personality types.

Medicine and Handicap: A Promise in Search of a National Commitment

*by Katherine P. Messenger ** *
and John Gliedman

Historically, American medicine has placed far less emphasis on preventing poor health than on devising cures for existing medical conditions. Prevention and cure have been viewed not as complementary strategies but as mutually exclusive ones, with prevention getting little attention and even less financing. In the field of disability, vast sums are spent treating handicaps that for a fraction of the cost could have been prevented.

As many commentators have noted, health care in this country is fragmented, disorganized, and often unnecessarily difficult to obtain when it is needed. The organizational flaws of the existing medical "nonsystem" are greatly aggravated by the lack of coherent national policy for financing medical care. For the affluent, the care provided to the handicapped child can be second to none in the world. For the working poor and the middle class, it is sometimes excellent, sometimes abominable, and all too frequently a crushing economic burden.[1]

Equally serious inconsistencies between medical promise and medical reality characterize the personal dimension of medical care.

* Katherine P. Messenger was a staff member of the Carnegie Council on Children; she is currently director of School Health Services, Division of Family Health Services, Massachusetts Department of Public Health, and lecturer in Child Health at the Harvard School of Public Health.

Designed to meet the exigencies of acute illness, traditional models of medical care have not yet fully adapted to meeting the special problems raised by the long-term care of a handicapped child or youth. All too often the physician forgets that the weakest link in the chain of medical care delivery is the willingness or ability of the parents to implement the child's medical management program. Just as important, the psychological impact of the management program on the child is also often overlooked. Trained to meet the challenges of acute childhood illness, many pediatricians draw back from those aspects of chronic care that fall outside the boundaries of traditional clinical medicine. Indeed, the physician frequently is not even able to provide the parents of the handicapped child with adequate information about other health-related services for the handicapped in the community. This breakdown of the referral systems the physician relies on when he treats a patient seems to hold true whether the doctor is in private practice, in a group practice, or in a hospital setting.

The Promise of Preventive Medicine

The single greatest contribution that modern medicine has made and, it is to be hoped, will continue to make in the field of handicap is the prevention of disability. Some prevention has taken place through public health or social welfare reforms, such as fire codes and laws banning the dangerous firecrackers that used to blind and maim many children. Much progress is also due to knowledge gained through basic biomedical research and then applied via public health intervention (such as immunization campaigns) or public health services.

Prevention can be thought of as occurring at three levels. *Primary prevention* includes actions taken to promote health or steps undertaken prior to the development of disease or disability. Examples include immunizations, the imposition of automobile speed limits, and restrictions on the purchase of hand guns. *Secondary prevention* encompasses the detection of disease or disability in its early (asymptomatic) stages as well as interventions to arrest its progress. An example would be screening for congenital metabolic disorders in newborn babies. *Tertiary prevention* involves intervention after the development of a clinically manifest disease or disability and seeks to reverse, arrest, or delay the disability's progression. Examples are the patching of a child's weak eye to prevent blindness at a later age or the aggressive treatment of cystic fibrosis to delay permanent lung damage. Tertiary prevention is closely tied to the treatment of chronic disorders with the goal of preventing secondary handicaps or prolonging functional capacities.[2] In the next few pages we will briefly explore some of the most important preventive strategies in each of these categories.

Primary Prevention

Effective primary prevention requires that the underlying causes of a disability be identified and eliminated. Four major primary prevention strategies seem of highest priority in relation to handicaps: immunizations, reducing the number of babies born with low birth weight, universal perinatal care, and improving the socioeconomic conditions of the poor.

IMMUNIZATIONS

The relationship between multiple handicaps (usually including blindness and other neurologic damage) and rubella (German measles) in the first trimester of pregnancy has led to stepped-up programs to inoculate women of childbearing age against the disease, an activity that could completely eliminate this source of disability. Similarly, immunizations against polio can protect every child from the potentially serious consequences of a disease that accounted for a large number of childhood hospitalizations and childhood handicaps only thirty years ago.

A full-scale immunization program against polio, measles, rubella, and mumps should be a top preventive priority. Polio immunization levels have fallen to dangerously low levels in some areas; only 65 percent of young children were fully immunized in 1975. Rubella can induce multiple congenital malformations and sensory disabilities in a fetus if it occurs in early pregnancy; measles and mumps can cause disabilities in children and adults who contract the disease. All these diseases are totally preventable using existing vaccines, which have small or negligible side effects. At present, the government is pushing such immunizations, but support at state and local levels is essential if present trends that show continually falling rates of completed immunizations for young children are to be reversed.

The evidence for the cost-effectiveness of a thorough rubella vaccination program has been analyzed. It is estimated that the rubella epidemic of 1963–65 left between 20,000 and 30,000 handicapped children in its wake. The added cost in special education programs alone for these children during thirteen years of schooling is close to $1 billion. This estimate makes no attempt to project the cost of other services needed by these children, nor of the enormous human toll involved in the imposition of a severe handicap for a lifetime. In contrast, only $41.6 million was authorized under the Rubella Immunization Program.[3] A recent cost-benefit analysis of rubella policy suggests that the best program would be one aimed at immunizing all females at age twelve, instead of current efforts directed at all children by age two.[4] Whichever strategy is selected, the payoff is obvious.

Polio vaccines are now conveniently given by mouth. A well-established multiple vaccine provides protection simultaneously against mumps, measles, and rubella. At present this option is passed over in many situations because the mumps component costs more than the other components, and in many states Medicaid or other public health programs will not pay for a vaccination using it.

LOW BIRTH WEIGHT

Although the biological and environmental mechanisms involved are not yet fully understood, it is clear that low birth weight is closely related to the risk of handicaps. Infant mortality statistics clearly indicate a higher risk of death for low-birth-weight infants (those of 2,500 grams or less) than for other babies, and especially extremely low-weight babies (under 1,500 grams).[5] Prematurity and low birth weight are also strongly linked to handicaps, including mental retardation, among those infants who survive. "Among premature children, that is, children born before 37 completed weeks, one must expect to find one-third of them to be handicapped with sensory defects, various school problems including learning disabilities, convulsions, abnormal EEGs, speech problems, and major brain impairment in the category of children below 1,000 grams of weight and below 30 weeks of gestation." [6]

A 1968 study of 833,000 live births in France showed that of the 40,000 children surviving their first year and estimated to be handicapped, the dominant origin of the handicap for one-third of them was "prematurity, low birth weight, . . . and related socioeconomic factors." [7]

A unique follow-up study in England which carefully compared the sequelae at ages five, six, and seven of being born prematurely ("too soon") or on time but of low birth weight ("too small")—using psychometric, behavioral, neurological, and growth assessments—strongly suggests that while both situations place the child at a disadvantage, the overall performance of the small-for-date children is significantly worse than the premature group and that the prenatal impairment of growth may be directly responsible for the later impairment.[8] (Much of the handicap associated with being "too small" at birth, however, is mild, not severe.)

In other words, to the degree that we can reduce the number of babies being born "too small," we can effect a reduction in handicap.

There are several ways to "prevent" low-birth-weight babies. Two major ones, which current policies address in some ways, are family planning and improving maternal nutrition. Family planning is a crucial preventive strategy that needs to be made readily available to women and men of all ages, incomes, and residence. There is strong evidence that pregnancies that occur too soon or too close together account for many of the high-risk births annually. The "epidemic" of adolescent pregnancies (over 1 million pregnancies and 600,000 births to girls under nineteen in 1974) highlights the problem.[9] Low birth weight is twice as likely to occur in babies born to teen-age mothers than it is in mothers over twenty; adolescents bear one-fourth of all low-birth-weight babies.[10] The handicapping risk of this situation is shown by data from a large study of births from 1959 to 1965. While only 1 to 1.5 percent of infants with mothers eighteen years old and over when they gave birth had neurological abnormalities at one year, 2 percent and 3.5 percent of those with mothers aged sixteen to seventeen and ten to fifteen respectively had neurological problems.[11] Indirect support is found from analyses that estimate that approximately one-fourth of the decline in infant mortality rates between 1964 and 1974 can be attributed to changes in the age of mother and birth order distributions.[12]

However, family-planning services, including information and provision of birth control, are still used by too few teen-agers (and others), remain inaccessible to many because of restrictive state laws or lack of funds, and are not well integrated with other health care services.[13]

Regardless of whether or not a child's handicap can be traced to low birth weight, family-planning programs are important preventives. Unwed teen-age mothers are perhaps the least equipped of any group to cope with the daunting problems of raising a disabled child. To have the problem of giving birth to a disabled child compounded by the problem of the child being unwanted to begin with is a contingency against which every parent, no matter what age, should be protected as much as is possible.

Poor maternal nutrition during pregnancy is one causative factor in the one-third of all low-weight births that are believed to be due to a retarded growth of the fetus in the womb rather than to prematurity.[14] Supplemental nutrition programs for high-risk pregnant women have been shown to result in higher birth weights, thus decreasing the chance of handicap.[15] Inadequate nutrition is also implicated in some maternal infections that can cause prenatal damage because the infection increases the likelihood that the fetus will be poorly nourished.[16]

UNIVERSAL PERINATAL CARE

In addition to preventing infectious diseases that can cause handicap and reducing the number of high-risk low-weight births, there is another broad strategy of primary prevention—the provision of high-quality prenatal and maternity care to *all* pregnant women and their newborn infants: perinatal care. (The technical term for the period including the last two trimesters of pregnancy, delivery, and the first days of an infant's life is the *perinatal period*. The term *prenatal* refers only to the time between conception and birth.)

Some factors that increase the risk of handicap occur too early in pregnancy to be affected by prenatal care, but perhaps 65 percent of handicaps that begin in infancy or before birth are susceptible to prenatal care, improved delivery, or special neonatal care.[17] Some aspects of prenatal care are secondary or tertiary prevention and will be discussed below. But there is a primary prevention component to be noted here: good prenatal care can prevent the occurrence of the high-risk birth, the development of potentially handicapping conditions, or the creation of handicap because of poor medical practice. Although definitive studies *proving* the effect of prenatal care do not exist, all associative studies show strong trends supporting the statement that infant mortality, prematurity, and fetal damage could be reduced if all women received comprehensive, high-quality prenatal care.[18] However, the amount of preventive potential is still debated. The conceptual problems involved in evaluating these issues are well illustrated by a study of maternal risk and infant death in New York City in the early 1970s. The study found that "the overall infant mortality rate would have been reduced 16 percent, to 18.4 per 1,000 live births, if mothers in each risk category had had the same pregnancy outcome as the other mothers in their ethnic group who had adequate care." [19] These findings are encouraging not only in themselves but because as the death rate for any group drops, so does the incidence of continuing damage in surviving infants. A second, more careful analysis of these data has confirmed the independent and significant effect of prenatal care on the relative risk of low birth weight, controlling a variety of factors that tend to "select" mothers into care (being more educated and hence aware of the need for good maternity care, for example). This analysis found that inadequate prenatal care increased the risk of low birth weight by 67 percent for some white mothers and about 80 percent for black mothers.[20]

Prenatal care is not magic. It works because proper monitoring of pregnancies allows difficulties to be foreseen and preventive strategies to be implemented. The mother's nutrition and diet can be improved; delivery can be planned at a specialized hospital if a high-risk birth is expected; and doctor and mother can work together to ensure that everything is done to enhance the chances that the baby will be born in good health.

HANDICAP AMONG THE RICH AND THE POOR

On the face of it, one would expect that many factors associated with poverty—poor nutrition, poor housing, misinformation about prevention and cure of disease, higher crime rates, and higher levels of generalized stress—would lead to a higher incidence of the many kinds of disabilities incurred during childhood as distinct from congenital disabilities, and to more severe degrees of disablement for at least some congenital or birth-trauma-produced disabilities. Moreover, one would expect these same socioeconomic factors to lead to a higher incidence of certain disabilities, such as chronic hypertension among adults. Because overall the poor probably live in a more polluted environment than the affluent, one would expect a higher incidence of disabilities from these effects as well. Poverty can also limit the beneficial impact of even the best-conceived public health program. It is not only in third-world countries that the effects of providing pregnant women with high-protein supplements (designed to improve the woman's health and that of her fetus) are sometimes undermined by the fact that there is not enough food to keep the rest of the family from going hungry. The economics of health care represent yet another area where poverty exerts a potent effect on health: those families who are most likely to require good health care (because of the higher incidence of disease and disability among the poor) are the ones who are least able to afford good care.[21]

Unfortunately, there is little in the way of empirical evidence to document systematically most of these commonly acknowledged problems. Ultimately, the sophisticated statistical analyses of large data sets now possible should yield hard evidence of the impact of poverty, stress, and pollution on the incidence of disability and the severity of disability among the poor. In the meantime, we can be confident that any programs improving the quality of life for the poor—programs such as income supports, pollution controls, or community services that reduce stress—are likely to have an important indirect impact on many areas of health and disability—an impact that may prove to be surprisingly large when properly controlled statistical studies are finally carried out. The educated guess of Gliedman and Roth, based on surveys not designed to measure the incidence of handicap by social class, is that medically significant disabilities occur perhaps 1.5 to 2 times more frequently among poor children than among children from affluent homes.[22]

A special moral problem is posed for the medical profession by the role that the indifferent medical care available to the poor may play in creating many unnecessary disabilities in childhood and in unnecessarily aggravating the severity of other childhood disabilities. In talks with handicapped children the authors of this book were struck by how often nonwhite children could trace handicaps such as blindness or a crippling disorder to what appears to have been inadequate or incompetent medical care, such as an eye injury that became infected and was not cared for properly until vision in both eyes was

destroyed, or by an operation to ameliorate a congenital bone malformation that actually worsened the disability. Unfortunately, the
failure of the medical profession to discipline and disbar incompetent
practitioners is only now beginning to be studied in a systematic
way.[23] But what little is known about the profession's devices of self-
regulation strongly suggests that the system inadvertently ends up
making the poor, the near-poor, and the lower middle classes bear the
brunt of medical incompetence. In place of meaningful regulation,
the profession punishes the incompetent physician by moving him to
a lower rung of the medical hierarchy; he is excluded from high-
prestige hospitals and referral networks but allowed to go on practicing in low-prestige hospitals and second-rate referral networks.

Other factors also appear to help concentrate the less able physicians in settings that deal with disproportionate numbers of the poor,
the near-poor, and the lower middle class. One such factor is the staff-
ing policies of many less prestigious hospitals. Because of the shortage
of American-trained interns and residents, these institutions have
turned increasingly to the graduates of foreign medical schools to fill
vacancies in their staffs. Yet even when these physicians are as capable
as their American-trained counterparts, serious problems of language
and even doctoring style remain. Many mistakes are undoubtedly
made because a foreign intern misunderstands a patient's words, or
because of the great contempt in which less affluent patients are held
by many physicians from rigid class-conscious societies. Here, too, the
present system of medical accountability does not provide adequate
mechanisms to protect the patient against these failures which, in the
extreme, can actually produce handicaps and often make a disability
worse than it might have been with competent care.

Secondary Prevention

The secondary prevention of handicap involves the identification of
already existing conditions or problems before they produce serious
damage. We will discuss three services with a strong secondary preventive potential: *prenatal detection of genetic conditions* and *selective abortion; screening and early treatment for genetic diseases;* and
*specialized obstetrical and newborn care.**

PRENATAL DETECTION

A large number of handicaps have their origins early in the prenatal
period, either at conception (recessively inherited and chromosomal

---

* The effectiveness of these secondary interventions is greatly enhanced if the
primary intervention of universal prenatal care is in place, so that potential risk
factors can be systematically identified; otherwise some form of outreach screening
or special program must be instituted.

diseases such as Tay-Sachs and Down's syndrome) or in the first trimester of pregnancy.[24] The French prenatal study mentioned earlier
estimates that 36 percent of handicap in children surviving at one
year is due primarily to congenital anomalies, including genetic and
chromosomal defects.[25] Amniocentesis is a procedure in which a small
amount of the amniotic fluid that surrounds the fetus is withdrawn
from the uterine cavity by a needle inserted through the abdominal
wall; it can be safely done only after the fourteenth week of pregnancy. Analysis of the fluid can now be used to identify a wide variety
of chromosomal defects and metabolic disorders. Amniocentesis is the
most common method of detecting these problems in the fetus during
pregnancy, but other techniques, such as ultrasonic imaging, direct
fetal visualization, and maternal blood tests, are also available or in
an experimental status.[26]

These techniques can reduce the incidence of handicap only if followed by selective abortion. We cannot yet correct inborn errors such
as Down's syndrome, but prenatal screening gives parents the informed option of terminating a pregnancy if the fetus shows a severe
abnormality or of sustaining it if the test is normal. This is of critical
value for parents who carry dangerous recessive traits or who are
high-risk because of parental age. Indeed, "a major advantage of prenatal genetic diagnosis is its preservation of normal fetuses that might
otherwise be aborted because of a feared genetic risk." [27] Selective
abortion may also be an option without diagnostic procedures if maternal exposure to infectious diseases such as rubella, ingestion of
drugs or harmful substances such as Thalidomide, or occurrence of
other nongenetic events indicates a high likelihood of fetal damage.[28]

Many families object to abortion on moral or religious grounds.
Thus this preventive strategy should never be expected to reduce
handicap in all possible situations. However, legal abortion is currently in danger of being made inaccessible even to those who desire
it as a possible, if imperfect, solution because of intense political
pressure to legislate restrictions on what should be a medical and
personal decision. It is both hypocritical and misleading for policy
makers to speak of promoting the prevention of birth defects and
genetic disease [29] while simultaneously advocating the legal prohibition of abortions (or the effective prohibition of them to large numbers of high-risk women by cutting off federal and state financing for
abortions) except in the case of risk of death to the mother.

Genetic counseling, a vital component of any screening program,
is still inadequately supported financially (it is often not covered by
health insurance) or practically. One study, for example, found that
most physicians do not feel that genetic screening is an important
service.[30]

SCREENING AND EARLY TREATMENT

For some potentially handicapping genetic conditions, screening in the newborn period can identify the affected infants and treatment started promptly to prevent a handicap. Perhaps the best example is phenylketonuria (PKU), an inborn error of metabolism that will, if not treated, lead to mental retardation in many children. The bad effects of PKU can be prevented by a careful dietary regimen begun in time. Thus using a blood test to screen for PKU at birth, coupled with a therapeutic diet for infants discovered to have it, can prevent or greatly ameliorate retardation, even though the initial metabolic disorder cannot be prevented.[31] At the present time, unfortunately, the technology to screen most genetic diseases exceeds our capacity to treat them. Expanded basic research in these areas could produce great benefits.

The prenatal care discussed earlier also has a secondary role to play, one that in practice generally gets greater attention than its potential for primary prevention. Preventable handicaps can be caused by failure to diagnose or monitor dangerous conditions in the pregnant woman such as toxemia (which leads to chronic fetal distress between the twenty-eighth and fortieth weeks), diabetes, urinary infection, toxoplasmosis (parasites), and blood group incompatibility between mother and fetus. According to one major study, these account for about 17 percent of handicap at age one.[32] Many of the handicapping conditions so caused can be prevented by proper prenatal care; in other cases, properly timed Caesarean section or other special delivery procedures may reduce the period of fetal distress.

"Birth trauma," or damage to the infant's central nervous system during labor and delivery, usually because of asphyxia, can also lead to severe neurological and psychological consequences. Asphyxia of the newborn has been found to be overwhelmingly the most important cause of preventable death or handicap attributable to less than adequate care at the time of delivery and is avoidable in at least half the cases by proper management of labor.[33] Specific factors include excessive or inappropriate drugs and anesthesia for the mother (causing fetal asphyxia), high forceps delivery, difficult breech delivery, and lack of appropriate electronic fetal monitoring.

Studies of low-birth-weight infants before the late 1960s led to extremely pessimistic forecasts for both their chances to live and the very high incidence of serious disabilities (especially neurological handicaps such as cerebral palsy and epilepsy) in the survivors. More recent data, however, which examine children provided with more comprehensive and specific neonatal care, contradict this gloomy prognosis and underline the importance of appropriate neonatal care in reducing disabilities. Mortality is still very high among low-birth-weight infants, but it has fallen steadily over the past fifteen years.

396

This improvement has been generally attributed to the better provision of intensive care for high-risk newborns.[34] Prospects for the survivors' normal physical and mental development have also increased. Twenty years ago, studies reported that 50 to 70 percent of surviving very small babies were handicapped in some respect. Recent studies in both the United States and Europe have painted a dramatically different picture, with the incidence of severe mental or physical handicaps in children receiving intensive care ranging from virtually none to 10 percent.* Intensive care has been particularly effective in reducing the incidence of cerebral palsy.[35]

The changes in the sophistication and effectiveness of neonatal care for the high-risk, premature, or low-birth-weight infant demonstrate the many levels at which medicine can affect handicap. From an emphasis upon isolation, delayed feeding, and minimal handling, care has shifted to a model of "neonatal intensive care units," which use teams of specially trained personnel (obstetricians, neonatologists, pediatricians, nurses, social workers, and others); sophisticated instruments and supportive environments; and intensive, active, and early intervention in marginal or dangerous conditions (resuscitation, early feeding, control of abnormal metabolic and body chemical states, etc.).[36] Parents are encouraged in most such units to maintain as normal as possible contact and caring functions for their babies; this is in sharp contrast to earlier times when "preemies" or high-risk infants were kept isolated from their parents, both as a purported health measure (to reduce risks of infection) and as an allegedly appropriate psychological preparation for the extraordinarily high death rate among such babies.[37]

Indeed, the research summarized by Klaus and Kennell[38] and others[39] now suggests that earlier practices in the prenatal care of the high-risk fetus and infant may have been an unintentional form of iatrogenic (i.e., doctor-produced) disease (or handicap) in which "remedies, physicians or hospitals are the pathogens or 'sickening agents.' "[40]

Tertiary Prevention

We can give only a few examples of the ways in which medicine can prevent handicap through treatment itself. The examples illustrate the three basic types of effective tertiary prevention:

1. Mild or otherwise nonhandicapping illnesses are treated promptly and effectively so that handicapping aftereffects do not develop.

2. Medical progress in the treatment of the handicapping condition

---

* Some of this variation probably results from the different cutoff points for definitions of low birth weight and the different measures of disability employed in recent studies.

now gives a child a longer and less disabled life although the condition itself still is unpreventable.

3. Comprehensive and thoughtful care and improved outside resources can reduce the occurrence of "secondary handicaps"—the unnecessary psychological, intellectual, and social damage that all too often accompany a biological defect and are often the real cripplers of children and families.

Strep throats and middle-ear infections are among the most common (indeed almost universal) childhood illnesses. They cause a good deal of pain to the child and provide a lot of worry and trouble to parents coping with an irritable and sick child. Middle-ear infections may also cause temporary hearing loss because of fluid in the ear. These are not, however, serious diseases; they do not require hospitalization, usually get better without any treatment, and can be cured with antibiotics. However, not all children in this country see a doctor regularly, even when they are sick. Not all parents can afford prescription drugs or fully understand the importance of giving the child all of the pills even when the child seems to be improving. (The full sequence is important because otherwise enough bacteria can remain to start a new infection quickly.)

But innocuous acute illnesses, if not treated, may lead to much more serious, permanent disability. Rheumatic fever, a potentially debilitating and deadly disease, could be virtually wiped out by prompt and adequate treatment of streptococcal throat infections.[41] Although the sore throat may go away by itself even if antibiotics are not given, some of the streptococcal bacteria can remain behind to reinfect and inflame other parts of the body.[42]

In the case of middle-ear infections, the potential threat is of repeated untreated injections causing permanent scarring of the eardrum and permanent conductive hearing loss. Since most children suffer temporary hearing loss with the infection, this can become a problem in itself if the infections are frequent. Middle-ear infections occur most frequently in young children and even this relatively mild loss (fifteen decibels or more) can be a significant risk to normal speech and language development.[43]

Prevention: Summary

Despite the scale of our remaining ignorance about the causes of many childhood disabilities, we do know enough to be able to prevent many disabilities if we could translate our present knowledge into practical programs of preventive medicine. Brewer and Kakalik observe that perhaps as many as one-third to one-half of sensory disabilities may be preventable, "but given the poor state of the data, no one knows for sure." [44] There is a need to apply systematically the knowledge we do have; as one study has emphasized for cerebral palsy and other effects of brain damage: "Prevention of cerebral palsy depends on knowledge of the causes, but action need not be delayed until understanding is complete. Much could be achieved now by using such knowledge as we have, especially in the organisation of medical services and in the application of modern standards of obstetrics and paediatrics." [45]

We have reviewed very briefly some of the advances that have been accomplished by medicine in the prevention of handicap. Collectively, they have vastly improved the lives of countless disabled children and adults. When joined to increasingly effective means of treating the acute diseases of childhood, these advances have dramatically altered the center of gravity of pediatric care in recent years. As Robert Haggerty notes, "Chronic disease is today the major health problem of children." [46] It is, write I. B. Pless and Philip Pinkerton, a problem likely to increase still more in relative importance in the future: "With the declining volume of infectious and nutritional disorders, a progressive proportion of the physician's work will involve the care of children with chronic disorders." [47]

The potential impact of preventive measures can be seen vividly when we look at our present-day national expenditures for the cure or amelioration of handicap. In the early 1970s, when $50 million per year of government funds was targeted for prevention of handicap in children, some $5 billion was provided annually by government at all levels for various services to handicapped children. [48] Thanks to such bills as the Education for All Handicapped Children Act of 1975 (Public Law 94-142), annual service expenditures will soon be well over $10 billion in 1970 dollars. Even small decreases in incidence rates could lead to huge annual savings in the service area. A 10 percent drop in the numbers of handicapped children would easily save $1 billion a year in expenditures on treatment. Considerations such as these argue on behalf of a serious expansion of preventive programs.

If prevention is to be effective, however, we must also do something that this country has never been good at: we must set up evaluation procedures that allow us to monitor the relative effectiveness of different prevention strategies. These procedures are likely to be unglamorous, intellectually uninteresting, of little use for purposes of professional career advancement, extremely time-consuming, methodologically difficult, and quite expensive by the standards of academic research (though paying for themselves many times over in eventual savings in service outlays for handicapped children). Moreover, they are likely to be difficult to justify to a lay audience unfamiliar with the importance of statistical procedures. Yet for all that, one simply cannot talk meaningfully about cost-effective preventive measures without a strong commitment to establishing a first-rate system of program analysis based upon the multidisciplinary contributions of health care professionals, statisticians, sociologists, epidemiologists, policy analysts, economists, and other social scientists familiar with the special difficulties that health services and disability present to evaluation programs.

Cure and Amelioration: The Gap between Medical Knowledge and the Delivery of Medical Care

Cure and amelioration are almost as important as prevention. Here, too, medical research has led to significant and sometimes dramatic advances. Many diseases—such as congenital heart disease, diabetes, leukemia, and hemophilia—have been rendered much less debilitating by medical procedures; the victims of these and other chronic illnesses now live longer and suffer far fewer limitations of function than used to be the case.

Thus, while muscular dystrophy remains incurable and fatal, proper medical care can "double the duration of independent ambulation while raising the quality and purposefulness of life." [49] Although a child with Down's syndrome cannot be "cured," medical intervention can ameliorate some of the physical disabilities of the syndrome—such things as dental problems, congenital heart disease, and a greater susceptibility to infection.

A particularly good example is afforded by cystic fibrosis—a complex, progressive, hereditary disease that causes major disturbances of the exocrine,* respiratory, and digestive systems. Although estimates of the incidence and prevalence of this disorder vary, it appears that in Caucasian populations about one birth in 2,000 is a child born with cystic fibrosis.[50]

Before 1953, when a sweat test for detecting cystic fibrosis was developed, diagnosis of the disease was rarely made before it caused irreversible lung damage, progressing to death—usually from pneumonia or other pulmonary problems—in childhood. But now many individuals with the disorder are living into their thirties. Improvements in prognosis have come in part from biomedical research into the prevalence and mechanisms of the disease and in part from the application of more effective treatment and management techniques. Several specific factors contribute to this picture and give a sense of the multidimensional impact of medicine on handicap.

Today, brief initial hospitalization—for diagnosis, evaluation, in-

* The *American Heritage Dictionary* provides this definition of *exocrine*: "of or pertaining to the secretion of a gland having a duct."

tensive treatment when necessary, and patient or parent education —can be rapidly followed by a comprehensive home care program for cystic fibrosis. Carefully designed nutritional programs can replace pancreatic enzymes and maintain better weight and nutrition. Aggressive physical, environmental, and antibiotic therapies can prevent or greatly delay the development of progressive lung damage by preventing primary pulmonary involvement (the accumulation of secretions in the lungs) and by more effectively treating secondary lung disease (infections and pneumonias). The key is prophylactic (preventive) instead of symptom-directed pulmonary therapy. Even when irreversible damage has already occurred, the disabling and fatal progression of the disease can still be greatly slowed down. In all cases, comprehensive follow-up care by the physician and medical care team and training of the family in home therapy techniques are essential.[51]

Until cystic fibrosis can be detected prenatally (allowing parents the option of selective abortion) or the underlying metabolic defects corrected, tertiary prevention by slowing the progression and reducing the dysfunction associated with the disease is an excellent example of medical science well applied. The inclusion of cystic fibrosis under federal and state Crippled Children's Services programs also means that medical services are financially available to most families who need them.

Medical Services for the Ongoing Problems of the Handicapped Child

None of the existing models of health care (solo practice, group practice, or specialized hospital clinics) functions nearly as well with the long-term problems of handicap as with acute illness and trauma. This is not because any of these organizational models *couldn't* work as well for the disabled but because of the failure of most physicians and policy makers to recognize that chronic childhood illness and other forms of childhood disability require some major, but not unprecedented, adaptations in the conventional arrangements of providing and paying for medical services.[52]

To begin with, there is the problem of information. Every model of health care delivery ties the physician into a network of information sources. Many of these sources are informal, especially for the solo practitioner, yet their informality does not render them unimportant. When a patient poses a problem that taxes the physician's resources, he or she draws on this network for advice, referrals to appropriate discussions in the literature, and, if necessary, formal consultations with a specialist. There is some relationship between networks of information and the models of health care delivery. In general, the more comprehensive the services offered, the more likely that the necessary information can be obtained from within the health care group rather than from outside it. Thus, whereas a partnership or small group practice might draw on its knowledge of outside services to send a patient to these services, a group of specialists or a large prepaid group practice or health maintenance organization might be able to provide the necessary services "in-house," drawing upon knowledge and resources within the group. Many of the complaints routinely directed at health care services for the handicapped are simply complaints about the lack of this kind of referral information system.

A brief review of some of the needs that the handicapped child brings into the doctor's office will suggest the scale of demands placed upon these information systems. In general, these children and their families will need *at least* the following services or capabilities: skilled and accurate diagnosis; information about the condition, its probable course, and possible interventions; proper medical treatment for retarding or ameliorating the condition; contact with someone likely to spot an undetected problem; preventive services (e.g., immunization and dental care) and routine medical care for illnesses not related to the handicap; clear assessment of any impact of the handicap on educational needs; follow-up care with treatment appropriate to the child's age; support for accompanying family needs and problems; advice about managing the financial burdens of care; and consultation with teachers, social workers, and others who deal with these children and need information about their condition. This is a formidable package indeed. It requires not only a much greater knowledge of nonmedical services for the handicapped than one can reasonably impute to most physicians or even most associations of physicians, but also an ability to keep up with the changing complexion of these medical and nonmedical services and to relate them to the patient's needs not for a span of a few months or a few years, but for a matter of decades.

Faced with the medical and nonmedical problems posed by these needs, it appears that few physicians in solo practice or even large group settings are currently able to rise to the challenge posed by a handicapped child's problems. To begin with, the parents of a child with a rare condition may not have an easy time finding a doctor familiar with the condition or sufficiently aware of his or her own diagnostic limitations to send the child to the proper specialist. At the other end of the health care spectrum, specialty clinics or diagnostic centers are still in relatively short supply. Moreover, by their very nature, specialty clinics have great difficulty handling the child with multiple handicaps or in dealing with those aspects of any handicapped child's medical needs that fall outside their specialized competence. Diagnostic clinics suffer from a different shortcoming—only rarely do they offer long-term care or follow-up. And regardless of the setting in which they practice, most physicians are poorly informed about the nonmedical services the child needs.

This point is well illustrated by a study of the care of mentally retarded patients at one of the leading medical centers in America.[53] Despite its general excellence in providing medical care as such care has been traditionally defined, the center's ability to meet the needs of parents of handicapped children was disappointing. Nearly half of the general practitioners in the center said that they knew nothing about the existence of a local mental retardation clinic; a mere 14 percent could provide the interviewer with basic data concerning the location, sponsorship, and services provided by that clinic. This ignorance was all the more startling because the clinic in question had been in existence for three years, had mailed more than six communications to each of the physicians at the medical center, and had been written up in many newspaper articles. Clearly, despite the relevance of the mental retardation clinic to the retarded children being treated at the medical center for the normal disorders of childhood and for those physical disabilities associated with many kinds of moderate and severe retardation, the existence of the clinic did not register in the minds of many physicians at the medical center as information relevant to their own professional concerns and responsibilities. Similar problems infect the practice of physicians in less prestigious group settings as well.[54]

Most of the services and approaches needed for disabled children are not part of the usual pattern of care in this country. Although the phrase "team practice of medicine" is frequently heard, it is still a rare phenomenon. Professional jealousies, distrust, and territorialities separate physicians, nurses, social workers, physical therapists, and education specialists. Thus, multiservice centers and total, coordinated plans of care, with one professional assuming responsibility for putting the family in touch with all the pieces and seeing that others fulfill their commitments, are out of the question for most families.[55]

Kakalik et al. have put the basic problem of existing health programs well:

• The provision of services is fragmented in this system, composed as it is of a melange of organized public, quasi-public, voluntary, and private agencies. There is little effective organized cooperation at the Federal level; and there is no systematic means by which relative service priorities and performance are being assessed.

• A natural outcome of the existing system structure is the absence of widely-known, locally-accessible referral services. Consequently, clients are faced with such a labyrinth of subsystems and related services that securing the appropriate mix of needed assistance is extremely difficult.

• Most medical programs are not aimed primarily at handicapped children, but are distinctly oriented to provide general health services.[56]

There are many ways that physicians could better meet the special information needs that attend chronic medical care. Two approaches, in particular, involve minimal changes in the way that medical services are delivered in America. The first concentrates on creating multipurpose facilities that can provide a wide variety of specialized medical and psychotherapeutic services and information about other nonmedical services to handicapped children and their parents. This model provides the child and his parents with access to specialists in chronic disability who are familiar with the best and newest medical procedures for coping with the disorder. Because these physicians are specialists, they are better diagnosticians than are general practitioners or generalist pediatricians. Furthermore, although extensive diagnostic experience is not always a guarantee of a good medical manner, the specialist is frequently more at ease than are general practitioners with the disabled child because he or she sees such children all the time and can distinguish between serious and less serious medical symptoms more accurately and with greater confidence than can a general practitioner or a pediatrician.

To be sure, the time has not yet come when there are enough specialists in specific diseases and disorders to provide comprehensive care to all children who suffer from handicaps that have an important medical component. Such programs, however, can make reasonable compromises. For those children who live nearby, the specialists serve as primary-care physicians giving simple, routine care, coordinating services, and also learning firsthand the overall problems and strengths of their patients. For children who live farther away, they serve as sources of regular specialist care but leave routine health care in the hands of community physicians, with whom they share records (a crucial point) and to whom they are available for consultation. For some children the program may serve only as a single-visit diagnostic facility.

This first approach, it should be noted, draws upon two important themes in medical care in America—specialization and the potential of large-scale medical organizations. A second, complementary approach would be to focus upon the other end of the medical care spectrum—the solo or small group practice. This approach would seek to provide the pediatrician in solo practice, partnership, or small group practice with enough information about the array of medical and nonmedical services available in the community to allow him or her to orchestrate the right mix of specialist, psychological, and other services for the child and the parents. Without becoming super-specialists, the physicians in this kind of arrangement can develop and maintain a special interest in chronically ill children whom they prefer not to "lose" to specialists. Close relationships with a major medical school or specialist center could enable them to refer patients without losing them and also to keep up to date on diagnostic information.

The principal virtue of this second model seems to be that it allows the nonspecialist to duplicate for the immediate community many of the coordinating functions carried out by the specialist in the multipurpose facility. Here, too, the physician can get to know the child's family sufficiently well to assess the special psychological or other stresses and strains created by the handicap. Here, too, the physician can treat the whole child rather than a "syndrome." And by maintaining clear lines of communication with specialists in the community, the generalist pediatrician can minimize the limitations placed upon him by his lack of specialized training.[57] Since specialists are generally in short supply, this model appears to be a promising way of providing a satisfactory and somewhat less expensive alternative to the larger center staffed by specialists.

We are less concerned that all care approximate the same pattern than that those at both ends of the spectrum ask more seriously what they can learn from the other, and how they can work together. For example, it is inexcusable that the primary-care physician, whether a specialist, a general practitioner, or a pediatrician, not be in contact with and share records with other care givers. Such simple measures could greatly reduce the current problems in overlapping care.

Costs

The final crucial problem confronting the present system of medical services for handicapped children is financing. Most medical care of any type is provided on the basis of ability to pay. While the majority of Americans have medical insurance, those families with the least resources are the least likely to be insured and hence are the least protected against the costs of medical care. Furthermore, since the average size of a family is greater for the poor and since the prevalence of some handicaps is correlated with family income, a disproportionate number of disabled children come from poor or nearly poor families.*

Moreover, regular health insurance may not cover a handicapped child's condition or all the treatments needed to improve it. Many policies have total benefit limits that can quickly run out with the extraordinary bills associated with disabilities such as congenital heart

---

* Recall that Gliedman and Roth estimate that childhood chronic illness and physical disability may be one and a half to two times more common among poor families than among more affluent families.

disease or with early preventive measures such as intensive neonatal care. Most policies do not cover the frequent office visits (outpatient or ambulatory care) required for good follow-up and maintenance care of many conditions. Items such as eyeglasses, prosthetic devices, hearing aids, outpatient drugs, nutrition services, physical and occupational therapy of an extended nature, psychiatric or social work consultations, homemaker care, and other "nonmedical" needs are rarely covered adequately by insurance.

Even federal and state programs specifically created to provide or finance services for those unable to pay or for those with special needs are often insufficient.[58] For example, approximately twenty states do not provide prenatal care for first pregnancies under Medicaid—yet because of both poverty and the high incidence of teen-age pregnancies among Medicaid recipients, these firstborns have an especially high chance of being handicapped and would therefore stand to benefit greatly from good prenatal care.[59]

Unfortunately, the moment we try to go beyond broad program statistics and generalities, we encounter the same problem that is faced when seeking to assess physicians' information and referral networks. Whereas some attempts have been made to survey the health care expenses and methods of payment of disabled adults, no systematic surveys whatsoever have been carried out for handicapped children. A detailed census of the health care expenses of handicapped children and methods of paying for them is of the highest priority. Such a survey might be carried out by the National Institutes of Health, which has a statistical series on disability, by the National Center for Health Statistics, or by the Social Security Administration, which has carried out some of the broadest and best-controlled surveys of adult disability in recent years.[60] Whoever carries out the survey, however, one methodological point is of great importance: the data must be collected and analyzed in a way that permits one to distinguish individuals whose disabilities impose special medical expenses. For instance, we should not lump the health care problems of the nation's 2 million or so mildly retarded children in with the problems of the visually impaired or the victims of chronic disease. In most cases mildly retarded, learning-disabled, and speech-disabled children have few special health care needs stemming from their handicaps. Yet the medical needs of these *groups* do get confused in surveys and policy studies. In this way, many discussions of the financial dimensions providing good health care to the handicapped lose track of the extraordinary importance of the low-cost option of improving the physician's general knowledge of the non-medical services available to the handicapped child in the community and do so in a way that leads to a greatly inflated estimate of the numbers of individuals who need special medical services. Since information should be much cheaper to provide than medical care, this inflation is especially unfortunate.

We believe that national health insurance offers the best hope of providing a long-term solution to meeting the many health care financing needs of handicapped children and youths. To be meaningful, however, a national health insurance scheme must make a radical break with precedent and provide adequate coverage for *all* necessary medical and health-related services of children whose handicaps impose special medical needs. Beyond this, we believe that the insurance plan should also deal with the need for physicians to provide their clients with information about nonmedical services available to the handicapped in the community, for as long as the physician enjoys his present status in American society, he or she will be expected to provide the parents of patients with a great deal of nonmedical information and advice. Parents should be reimbursed when they obtain that advice from consultations with physicians, or alternate sources of advice should be made available to them through some other federally funded program. In order that providers not abuse this potential source of extra income, counseling should be paid for only if offered in organized settings (group practices, clinics, or community agencies) where its actual provision and quality can be monitored. To every extent possible, it should be done in a multidisciplinary, interagency setting, such as the Direction Centers that Brewer and Kakalik advocate.[61]

How much would it cost to provide adequately for the needs of handicapped children and youths in a national health insurance scheme? There is really no way to form even the crudest of quantitative estimates. The "cost" of different kinds of disabilities varies enormously. A crippled child who needs an electric wheelchair might have health-related expenses ranging into thousands of dollars a year simply because of the extra cost of a van capable of transporting child and chair from place to place (amortized over the life of the vehicle) and the cost of the wheelchair—more conventional medical costs aside. A three-year-old with a minor and correctable visual impairment is likely to run up a much smaller handicap health bill for special corrective glasses.

The accompanying table provides a crude estimate of the number of handicapped children and youths aided financially and the amounts of public monies involved in various state and federal health programs in 1971, the most recent year for which any comprehensive estimate is available. Depending upon such unknowns as the amount of double counting, and the degree to which medically relevant disabilities are overrepresented among poor children, it appears that somewhat over one million handicapped youths were assisted—or perhaps 20 percent of the possibly 5 million children and youths in

1970 who we believe possessed handicaps requiring special medical services.[62,63] Our best guess is that these programs now serve a similar proportion of handicapped children and youths. Without a national survey of the health care expenses of this group, any firm estimates of the costs of improving existing health care coverage are obviously impossible. We just do not know how much it would cost to defray every handicapped child's medical expenses that are related to the handicap, how much private insurance covers now, or how much money parents are currently paying out of pocket to meet these costs.

Estimated Numbers of Handicapped Youths and Total (Federal and State) Health Services Program Expenditures, 1971*

Program	Expenditures	Number of Handicapped Youths Served
Crippled Children's Service	$ 87,897,000	485,000
Other maternal and child health programs	25,000,000	81,000
Medicaid	185,803,000	1,097,000
Rubella immunization (prevention)	16,000,000	—
Other state and federal public health programs	?	?
TOTAL	$314,700,000	At least 1,000,000 (removing double counting)

* Adapted from G. D. Brewer and J. S. Kakalik, *Handicapped Children: Strategies for Improving Services* (New York: McGraw-Hill, 1979), Tables 9.1 and 9.2, p. 256. See original for derivation of estimates and qualifications on data.

We do know, however, that while childhood disability is a vitally important problem, it is dwarfed in size and expense by adult disability. For every child and youth with a medically relevant handicap, there are roughly ten disabled adults with special medical needs. This disproportion suggests that the overall cost of national health insurance is likely to be relatively insensitive to even major shifts in estimates concerning the medical costs of childhood disability.

Interim Measures

Until an adequate national health insurance plan is enacted, there are a number of interim measures that could ease the financial burden of handicap on the parent and significantly improve diagnosis and treatment for handicapped children.

Although it is by no means perfect, the Crippled Children's Service (CCS) probably comes closer than any existing program to providing comprehensive medical service to many handicapped children. CCS is really a system of state programs, funded by federal-state grants that pay for a wide range of medical and related services (provided either by private physicians or state clinics staffed by specialists). Children with cerebral palsy, cystic fibrosis, congenital heart disease, cleft lip or palate, epilepsy, muscular dystrophy, major orthopedic problems, and complex problems requiring special coordinated services (such as kidney disease) are eligible. Financial eligibility is also determined, but limits on family income are set much higher than for welfare programs such as Medicaid, and diagnostic services are available regardless of income. In many states private physicians use the CCS diagnosis and planning capability on behalf of parents who are not receiving any other financial assistance from the government. The disproportionately large number of nonwhite children served by CCS (at least 25 percent of all children and youths benefiting from the program are nonwhite) suggests that it is at least partly successful in meeting its objective of helping the neediest families.[64] Finally, certain state CCS programs have succeeded in providing excellent medical care for handicapped children in those states; the reasons for their success appear to stem from the prime role played by medical specialists in program administration, requirements that in most cases providers be specialists, the maintenance of high standards in treatment, and doctors' acceptance of a medically based program in contrast to the welfare-based and frequently welfare-administered Medicaid program.

CCS is not without its serious drawbacks, however. Coverage is highly variable, with different states giving different preference to various kinds of disabilities, a problem brought out well by the great range in per-client expenses from state to state. Per-client expenditures averaged over $300 nationally between 1970 and 1973.[65] In 1971 they ranged from a low of $26 in the District of Columbia to a high of $249 in Ohio.[66] As the Kakalik group notes, "It is extremely hard to believe that per capita or per client CCS expenditures are equitable." [67] Nor are they adequate. The federal funding for CCS for fiscal year (FY) 1978 of $97.5 million provided services to only about 560,000 children; this is much lower than even our most conservative estimates of handicapped children.

Despite these drawbacks we would like to see CCS more publicized and financially expanded to provide more services to more handicapped children and youths until such time as a national health insurance plan that provides adequate medical care to this group is adopted. Incentives for states to increase and standardize their programs should be built into the expansion of the CCS commitment—perhaps by increasing the share of total expenses assumed by the federal government when necessary reforms were carried out. One of the greatest current problems with CCS is that the requirement that state plans be filed with the relevant federal agencies and subjected to periodic review has never been enforced. Thus, reliable statistics on populations at risk, the program's impact, and even statistics on how much it is used are wholly inadequate for good planning or program monitoring.

A second source of immediate financial assistance until national health insurance can come to the rescue could come from the implementation of the existing mandate for the federal Early and Periodic Screening, Diagnosis and Treatment program (EPSDT), established under Medicaid,[68] or its expanded version proposed by the Carter administration, the Child Health Assessment Program (CHAP).[69] On paper, the 1967 EPSDT legislation entitles most children whose families are unable to afford medical care (not just those who are otherwise eligible for welfare) to comprehensive health assessments and any needed follow-up medical care. The provisions for screening and diagnosis are particularly important both because they should encourage states to initiate screening at earlier ages and because they require follow-up services. CHAP would enlarge eligibility, services offered, and the incentives provided the states to implement a comprehensive medical care program.

Despite the fact that EPSDT legislation has been on the books for a decade, the intent of the framers of the provision has not been realized.[70] In part, this has been because necessary financing (particularly for outreach and follow-up) has not been forthcoming and because the federal-state nature of the program has limited the extent of federal control. But there are many other reasons as well. One of the most important is that EPSDT's parent program, Medicaid, is technically a *welfare* program, not a health care program, despite the fact that Medicaid is by far the largest single source of public funds for child health care. In FY 1976 total Medicaid expenditures for children were estimated to be $2.5 billion, including $1.4 billion from the federal government and $1.1 billion from state and local governments. All other public funds for child health totaled only $2.2 billion.[71] Moreover, while the enabling legislation for EPSDT provided for the defraying of doctors' bills and hospital expenses, in contrast to Crippled Children's Services, this financing was not made contingent upon local programs both being in place in the community and meeting certain federally mandated standards of quality. It is in this context that we believe proposals concerning the possible integration of CCS and Medicaid should be given special consideration. In principle, at least, one could imagine joining the comprehensive and financially open-ended characteristics of Medicaid with the best of present-day CCS state programs—their emphasis on quality care, direct provision of services, and nonwelfare orientation. To do so in a meaningful way would, of course, require considerable improvements in the existing administration of Medicaid. This joining of the best of current Crippled Children's Service programs with Medicaid and EPSDT (or CHAP) would also be an interim measure, designed to provide immediate improvement in the health care of handicapped children and youths until such time as national health insurance provides adequate comprehensive coverage of their health care needs.

A Final Plea for Special Emphasis on Preventive Medicine

Let us conclude by once more underlining the importance of prevention. Again and again we have been struck by the enormous disproportion between the federal funds currently allocated for prevention and the funds being paid to provide medical and nonmedical services to handicapped children and youths. As one contemplates the increased expenditures that will be required by national health insurance or the dramatic increases in special education funds projected for the 1980s, it seems clear that the best conceivable investment of all lies in preventing handicaps or in detecting them early enough to be able to alleviate or eliminate their disabling consequences. An adequate program of income supports for the poor will, of course, provide a good deal of indirect prevention; and any attempt to reckon the cost-benefit ratio for a national program of income supports should take into account this very considerable medical side effect. But above and beyond this indirect measure, there is a need for vastly increased direct measures. Public health has languished far too long in America. And nowhere, perhaps, could the principles of preventive public medicine be applied with greater effect—and with as great a cost-benefit ratio—as in a concerted attempt to expand our efforts to prevent handicaps.

Comprehensive
Disability Insurance

Every handicap of consequence brings with it a host of hidden expenses that go far beyond the costs of education and medical care. These difficult-to-quantify expenses stem from the family's attempts to adapt itself to the physical and emotional needs of the handicapped child, the pressures felt by the child's siblings, and, by no means least of all, the emotional strain and stress that the handicap often places upon the child's parents.

It costs money to eliminate the architectural barriers that can exclude the handicapped child from family life—doors too narrow to allow easy passage to a wheelchair, bathrooms that must be modified for easy use by the crippled child, stairs that need widening to allow the addition of a small elevator to carry the child up and down, kitchens modified to allow blind and crippled children to make their own breakfasts. Without expensive modifications in the home, many disabled children cannot participate actively in some of their own family life. Immobilized by the design of a house or apartment built for the able-bodied, the child can be structurally defined as a patient even in his or her own home. But money for the change may have to come from precious family reserves that were meant for something else—another child's college education, for example.

Parallel problems are raised by transportation. The parents of a crippled child may need a van in order to be able to take their son and his bulky electric wheelchair around from place to place as easily as if he were able-bodied. Vans may be expensive, their insurance rates may be higher than for passenger cars, and they may get very poor gas mileage, but low-cost mass transportation is rarely accessible to (let alone practical for) a handicapped child or adolescent. The private market has also been unable to provide flexible and affordable transportation services. Profit and loss considerations often require unsubsidized private companies to price their services beyond the means of many families; flat rates of twenty-five dollars for a round trip of just a few miles are commonplace. Prices like this obviously rule out using these services to sustain a normal social life for the child. Because of high costs and the resulting low demand, most private firms do not even offer weekend services or services after business hours during the work week; though much less expensive, most publicly run systems also suffer from schedule restrictions.

Transportation problems are probably most severe in the suburbs. There, where mobility is essential to full participation in after-school and weekend social life, the child without transportation—not only in adolescence, but in middle childhood as well—is condemned to an almost automatic exclusion from the social life of his or her peers. Immobility hamstrings the child's efforts to make friends with other disabled children, too. Indeed, in the suburbs, one of the most enduring obstacles to mainstreaming may well be the barrier that inadequate transportation for the disabled will impose on their socializing after school. Yet the public schools have no budget for such an expense, and it nearly always falls to whatever the child's family can devise and afford.

But it is not simply architecture and transportation that force hidden costs upon the parents of handicapped children—or force the handicapped child to pay for what his parents cannot afford to purchase. All parents need to get away from their children sometimes. When a child is moderately or severely disabled, the need to get away is often far greater. Yet because of guilt, lack of money, and the absence of anything like an adequate network of social services that could temporarily take charge of the child, few parents satisfy their own needs for a respite. When they do manage to go away for a weekend, or even to go out to a movie, they may need to hire special, medically trained baby-sitters. Parallel problems arise from the extra expenses involved in going on a vacation with a child who always needs to be within easy reach of a good doctor, and if one flies, rental of a suitably equipped van at one's destination may be impossible or prohibitively expensive. Inexpensive vacations—like camping trips— may be ruled out because of the child, resulting in higher costs.

There are many other gray areas whose financial importance cannot be anticipated without empirical studies of family consumption patterns. One of these involves the spending patterns for books, toys, and gadgets that parents interested in helping their child as much as possible might adopt. Precisely because less is known about the special developmental needs of handicapped children, it seems to us possible that a study of, at least, middle-class spending patterns would reveal a consistently higher level of expenditure for a handicapped child than for an able-bodied child in similar circumstances. Less sure of what might tease the child out of himself, or stimulate his mind, many parents may adopt a shotgun approach. While this strategy may pay off through sheer persistence, it is likely to be expensive. Every child goes through life accumulating a junk pile of books, toys, gadgets, and other treats. For some handicapped children this pile may be especially awesome. When one considers the possible reactions of able-bodied siblings to such special marks of favor as toys and treats, it is tempting to speculate that detailed studies of families with handicapped children will reveal atypical (and possibly more expensive) consumption patterns for all their children, able-bodied and handicapped.

An example of some of the extra and unforeseen expenses that make up the "handicap tax" was provided us by parents who bought an electric wheelchair for their five-year-old child.* One of the beauties of an electric wheelchair is that it gives a crippled child nearly as much mobility as an able-bodied child; but a hidden cost of this mobility is the damage inflicted in the normal course of a five-year-old's driving around the house in an electric wheelchair, which the parents we spoke with estimated at $3,000 a year. Children naturally bump into things and overturn objects; they naturally throw temper tantrums, take out their anger on objects, and revel in displays of physical mastery of their environment. When orchestrated from the cockpit of an electric wheelchair, the results of these healthy growing pains can be expensive as well as good for the child's ego. Outdoors as well, the machine that makes a more normal childhood possible conjures up visions of new and unperceived expenses. A five-year-old in an electric wheelchair can crush a flower bed, run over another child, knock down an adult, or maim a dog. Consequently, the prudent parent not only must watch over the child, but should purchase additional insurance protection.

To all these expenses one must add the cost of making as much of the house as possible accessible to the electric wheelchair, as well as

* Because the family falls into the middle-income bracket, they were not eligible for any existing program to help them buy the $1,600 wheelchair—a cost that will have to be met again and again as the child grows into larger wheelchairs. This investment, representing only the first installment of the handicap tax, ideally should be covered by a national health insurance plan, as should the special medical expenses that the couple paid out for their child.

the special cost of a van capable of safely transporting the child and his machine. Yet none of these nonmedical expenses would be covered in even the best possible mixture of existing or proposed insurance and service schemes.

We believe that the federal government should establish a childhood disability insurance system specifically designed to defray a significant part of those expenses that do not fit easily into existing definitions of service needs for handicapped children. Such a scheme would complement existing and projected medical and education programs. The plan could function like Social Security, with all families contributing against the possibility of one of their children being handicapped. We will call this proposal Childhood Disability Insurance.

Because all families are more or less at equal hazard with regard to disability, it would seem reasonable to finance Childhood Disability Insurance (henceforth called CDI) through the general tax structure. A logical administrator of CDI would be the Internal Revenue Service or the Social Security Administration.

The kinds of expenses that CDI is intended to reduce for families are so diverse and involve so many separate "consumption decisions" by the parents that any attempt to provide parents with vouchers with which to buy specific goods or services or to construct a special network of new services would probably be impractical and absurd. These decisions involve everything from whether to buy a new book or toy for the child, to whether to "wheelchair-proof" the house *before* or *after* buying a van modified for a wheelchair-bound passenger, to finding baby-sitters so the parents can go to a movie, to determining how and when to take a vacation with the family.

Before implementing CDI, two different administrative models should be carefully explored. First, CDI might be modeled on existing health insurance plans in which the individual submits an invoice of expenses and receives a cash reimbursement. This approach has the virtue of providing a way, at least in principle, of tailoring disbursements to the particular needs of each family. On the other hand, such a system would impose an enormous accounting burden on the agency that administers it; for reasonable safeguards against abusing the system will have to be created, as well as appeals procedures to protect families against inequities arising from these administrative safeguards. In practice, these necessary administrative devices are likely to reproduce many of the problems that are presented by a voucher system: in place of vouchers for certain family "consumption decisions," the parents will confront a body of regulations that determine which of these decisions is eligible for reimbursement and which is not.

On grounds of administrative simplicity, a flat fee established according to the nature of the child's disability and disbursed to the family on a monthly or yearly basis has much to recommend it. The chief problem with this approach is its lack of flexibility. The fee is likely to be enough for some families and not enough for other families. Still, because of its simplicity, we incline toward the flat fee approach but believe that both the flat fee and the reimbursement schemes should be carefully explored before a decision is made concerning which mechanism to adopt.

Finally, the question of the cost of CDI must be carefully explored beforehand. Because the insurance program is designed to help defray precisely those costs which are not addressed by existing concepts of social services, no public or private agency has collected the kinds of information about family consumption patterns that is needed before anyone can construct a realistic compromise between an insurance plan that pays *all* the hidden costs of raising a handicapped child and a plan that provides the parents with such small sums of money as to be virtually meaningless. To begin to think realistically about a CDI scheme, we must obtain realistic information about the hidden costs of raising children with different disabilities in different social milieus. On the basis of the information obtained in these studies it should be possible to determine if it is economically feasible to provide every family with a basic set of minimum benefits which at the very least would make a significant difference to the most needy families in the general population.

Council Members

KENNETH KENISTON, chairman and director of the council, has undertaken extensive studies of social change, social protest, and alienated youth: *The Uncommitted* (1965), *Young Radicals* (1968), and *Youth and Dissent* (1971). Formerly a professor of psychology in the department of psychiatry at the Yale Medical School, he is now Mellon professor of human development at the Massachusetts Institute of Technology, where he is exploring the impact of modern society on patterns of human development.

CATHERINE FOSTER ALTER, a social planner, is director of the Council on Children at Risk, an agency that does research, planning, and program development in the area of child abuse, neglect, and other populations of children at risk because of environmental factors and that serves Rock Island County, Illinois, and Scott County, Iowa. She has worked with community-based agencies and with state and county governments to assure the rights of students and to set up youth advocacy agencies and home-based day care arrangements.

NANCY BUCKLER was formerly a child care worker in a residential treatment center for disturbed children. She is now master teacher at the Loyola University Day School in Chicago, a center working with severely disturbed children and their families, and is an adjunct faculty member at the National College of Education.

JOHN PUTNAM DEMOS, a professor of history at Brandeis University, is the author of *A Little Commonwealth* (1970) and other studies of family life in the American past. Formerly acting director of the Center for Psychosocial Studies in Chicago, he is trained in psychology as well as in history. His current research interests include witchcraft in early America and the human life cycle in relation to historical change.

MARIAN WRIGHT EDELMAN practiced law during the early 1960s in Jackson, Mississippi, where she founded and directed the NAACP Legal Defense Fund. In addition to handling test cases involving children, she now directs the Children's Defense Fund, a group she founded to document and challenge unfair treatment of children in schools, courts, and the welfare system.

ROBERT J. HAGGERTY, a pediatrician, is professor of health services and pediatrics at the Harvard School of Public Health and Harvard Medical School. While at the University of Rochester, he pioneered a child health program involving many disciplines and community agencies. The senior author of *Child Health and the Community* (1975), he is now president of the William T. Grant Foundation.

WILLIAM KESSEN, professor of psychology at Yale University, has conducted numerous studies of how young children develop the abilities to perceive and think and has written about the history and philosophy of how social science approaches children. He is the author of *The Child* (1965) and editor of *Childhood in China* and, with Marc Bornstein, *Psychological Development from Infancy* (1978).

LAURA NADER, professor of anthropology at the University of California at Berkeley, has studied law among the Zapotee of Mexico and the Shias in Lebanon. She has investigated extrajudicial complaint handling in the United States and is the editor of a forthcoming book on the subject. The author of *Talea and Juquila: A Comparison of Zapotec Social Organization* (1964), she has produced a film on Zapotec court procedure (1966). With her collaborators she has written *The Disputing Process: Law in Ten Societies*, and she has edited several books on conflict, social control, and health. She is a fellow at the Woodrow Wilson International Center for Scholars at the Smithsonian Institution for the academic year 1979–80.

FAUSTINA SOLIS, associate professor of community medicine at the medical school of the University of California at San Diego, is the former deputy director of the California health department's Public Health Division. A social worker, she directed from 1967 to 1971 the first major expansion of state health services for migrant workers in California.

PATRICIA MCGOWAN WALD * is a judge of the U.S. Court of Appeals, District of Columbia. Previously, as a public interest lawyer, she was litigation director of the Mental Health Law Project in Washington, D.C. She served as a consultant to the National Commission on Civil Disorders and the National Commission on the Causes and Prevention of Violence, as co-director of the Ford Foundation Drug Abuse Research Project, and as a member of the American Bar Association's commission developing new guidelines for children's rights.

* PATRICIA WALD, who participated in the discussions that helped shape the ideas in this volume, resigned from the Council upon appointment as an assistant attorney general in charge of legislative affairs for the Department of Justice in February 1977.

HAROLD W. WATTS, senior research associate at the Center for the Social Sciences at Columbia University and senior fellow at Mathematica Policy Research Center at Princeton, formerly headed the Institute for Research on Poverty at the University of Wisconsin. He supervised the evaluation of the federally sponsored test in New Jersey of a negative income tax as an alternative to the welfare system and is currently directing a Carnegie Corporation–sponsored study of the social and economic status of American families.

Council Staff

Executive Director: Kenneth Keniston

Associate Directors: Peter O. Almond, Joan Costello,
Richard H. de Lone

Senior Editor: Jill Kneerim

Director of Public Affairs: Christopher T. Cory
Deputy Director of Public Affairs: Kathryn K. Toll

Managing Director: Cheryl R. Towers

Director of Public Relations: Adelina Diamond

Washington Representative: Virginia Fleming

Research Associates: Peter O. Almond, Robin Boger, Susan Bucknell,
Alison Clarke-Stewart, Joan Costello, Richard H. de Lone,
Peter Garlock, Mark Gerzon, John Gliedman, Rochelle Kessler,
Michael A. Lerner, Katherine P. Messenger, John U. Ogbu,
Hillary Rodham, William Roth, Elga Wasserman

Research Assistants: Chris Buckley, Deborah R. Chernoff,
Ellen Chirelstein, Laura Eby, Francesca Gobbo, Georgia Goeters,
Susan Hunsinger, Vera Wells Jones, Nina Kraut, Felicity Skidmore,
Phyllis Holman Weisbard

Statistical Analysis: Georgia Goeters

Administration: Darlene Copeland, Susan Ellison, Arlene Gurland,
Missle Wodajo Hankerson, Ethel Himberg, Jane Hyand,
Margaret Jackewicz, Karin Kaminker, Marion Lincoln,
Michele McLean, Sheila Meyers, Susan Mulford, Donna Piazza,
Sylvia Rifkin, Laurie Rosenbaum

Television Planning: Donald Dixon

Notes

Introduction

1. See, for example, Kenneth Keniston and the Carnegie Council on Children, *All Our Children: The American Family under Pressure* (New York: Harcourt Brace Jovanovich, 1977).
2. See two other volumes in the Carnegie Council on Children series: John U. Ogbu, *Minority Education and Caste: The American System in Cross-Cultural Perspective* (New York: Academic Press, 1978), and Richard H. de Lone, *Small Futures: Children, Inequality, and the Limits of Liberal Reform* (New York: Harcourt Brace Jovanovich, 1979).
3. See Frank Bowe, *Handicapping America: Barriers to Disabled People* (New York: Harper & Row, 1978).
4. See Kurt Lewin, *Resolving Social Conflicts,* ed. Gertrude Weiss Lewin (New York: Harper & Brothers, 1948). Lewin's political analysis appears in the papers that make up chapters 9, 10, 11, and 12 of that volume—"Psycho-Sociological Problems of a Minority Group," "When Facing Danger," "Bringing Up the Jewish Child," and "Self-Hatred among Jews."
5. For the basis of this estimate, see note 11 below.
6. Nicholas Hobbs, *The Futures of Children* (San Francisco: Jossey-Bass, 1975).
7. See chapter 10, "The Handicapped Child in School."
8. This conclusion is advanced by a recent study conducted by SRI International for the Department of Health, Education and Welfare; see Patricia A. Craig, David H. Kaskowitz, and Mary A. Malgoire, *Studies of Handicapped Students,* vol. 2: *Teacher Identification of Handicapped Pupils (Ages 6–11) Compared with Identification Using Other Indicators* (Menlo Park, Calif.: SRI International, Educational Policy Research Center, February 1978). (But also see note 12 below and chapter 13, note 27.)
9. See note 8.
10. James S. Kakalik, Garry D. Brewer, Laurence A. Dougharty, Patricia D. Fleischauer, and Samuel M. Genensky, *Services for Handicapped Youth: A Program Overview* (Santa Monica, Calif.: Rand Corporation, 1973), Appendix A, pp. 273–82.
11. Bearing in mind that the estimates upon which we base our assertion are exceedingly imprecise, it is still useful to set forth our underlying reasoning.

    We assume that all children in the following disability groups are at considerable risk during their childhood of being subjected to stigma and discrimination: the visually impaired, the hearing-impaired, those

423

with speech or spoken language impairment, the crippled or those with other health impairments, the mildly retarded, the learning-disabled, the multihandicapped. In addition, we include all minority children and youth who are emotionally disturbed but not autistic or psychotic. Using Kakalik et al.'s estimates, this yields a total of 7,650,000 handicapped children and youth.

Our core group—those who are most likely to experience significant stigma in adulthood as well as in childhood—composes about 60 percent of Kakalik et al.'s estimate; we include in our core group at least the following disability groups contained in the Kakalik et al. enumeration:

The mildly retarded	2,000,000
Emotionally disturbed but not autistic or psychotic:	
All minority individuals in the category (roughly 20 percent)	300,000
All individuals with some other handicap (we assume on the basis of recent surveys that such children are overrepresented among the emotionally disturbed)	300,000
Legally blind	45,000
Deaf	50,000
Reading disability or minority individual with any learning disability	300,000
Speech or spoken language impairment that persists into adulthood and, like stuttering, exposes the adult to significant stigma and job discrimination	1,000,000
Crippling or other health impairment	1,676,000
TOTAL	5,671,000

The specific numbers we adduce are much less important than what these numbers imply when one tries to apply our definition of a core group of children to any existing estimates of the numbers of handicapped children and youth. Furthermore, because estimates of the numbers of handicapped children are so sensitive to shifts in the criteria for mild handicaps, the proportion of disabled children and youths in the core group may well be still larger if, as is probable, Kakalik's data somewhat inflate the totals by including many individuals who do not deviate sufficiently from the norm to merit being called handicapped.

12. Detailed breakdowns of the fall 1976 Elementary and Secondary School Civil Rights Survey began to become available in the summer of 1978.

(This survey is conducted by the Office for Civil Rights; the Bureau for the Education of the Handicapped also conducts child counts, but, incredibly, BEH does not collect information about race.) Our preliminary scrutiny of these data found that physical, sensory, and health disabilities were generally 1.2 to 1.4 times more common among minority-group children than among white children. Since race is an imperfect—and conservative—marker for social class, this range of incidence rates is consistent with our belief that medically relevant disabilities are roughly twice as common among poor children as among children from affluent families.

But how trustworthy are the child counts being carried out by OCR and BEH? Craig and her associates report in *Studies of Handicapped Children,* vol. 2, that there is very little overlap between the children whom the schools identify as sensorily or orthopedically disabled and the children so identified by medical examinations. This finding needs to be checked. But, clearly, it is premature to base any estimates of class- or race-related differences in the incidence rates of different kinds of medically relevant disabilities on data provided by the schools.

The reliability of parents' reports is also unclear. Craig et al. find little concordance between them and medical assessments of sensory and orthopedic disabilities. In addition, racial and class differences are absent in the medical assessments of sensory and orthopedic disabilities; according to parents, these disabilities are about twice as common among black children and poor children. On the other hand, Richardson and his associates found that parents and physicians agreed 75 percent of the time. See William P. Richardson and A. C. Higgins, in collaboration with Richard G. Ames, *The Handicapped Children of Alamance County, North Carolina* (Wilmington, Del.: Nemours Foundation, 1965). Here, too, medically significant handicaps were more frequently reported by black parents and poor parents.

Richardson et al.'s own prevalence rates, based upon clinical examinations, support the view that there are important social class and race differences. Although conducted in a single North Carolina county more than a decade ago, the study remains one of the best epidemiological studies conducted in the United States. We summarize its main findings about prevalence in the table on p. 426.

Another clue is provided by the U.S. National Center for Health Statistics Survey, "Medical Care, Health Status, and Family Income, United States," in *Vital Statistics from the National Health Survey,* ser. 10, no. 9 (Washington, D.C.: U.S. Government Printing Office, May 1964); data summarized in Monroe Lerner, "Social Differences in Physical Health," Table III-5, in *Poverty and Health: A Sociological Analysis,* ed. John Kosa, Aaron Antonovsky, and Irving Kenneth Zola (Cambridge, Mass.: Harvard University Press, 1969), pp. 106–7. While there was essentially no income effect visible for chronic disabilities that did not limit an individual's activity, the incidence of chronic conditions that did limit activity was strongly associated with very low family income. For the under-fifteen age group, about 1.5 times more children in families with incomes below $2,000 per year had such conditions

Social Class and Prevalence Rates of Different Handicaps*

(per 1,000 persons under age 21)

	Upper and middle class	Lower class	Ratio of lower-class frequency to upper-class and middle-class frequency
Orthopedic conditions	64	83	1.3
Epilepsy	15	37	2.5
Vision defects	132	141	1.1
Hearing defects	22	43	2.0
Cleft palate	0	2	—
Speech disorders	60	123	2.1
Respiratory disorders	170	207	1.2
Heart conditions	11	31	2.8
Orthodontic conditions	37	54	1.5
Cerebral palsy	3	5	1.6
Skin conditions	128	175	1.4

* Based on Richardson et al., *The Handicapped Children of Alamance County*, Table 4, p. 25. The authors also report data for working-class children; these children occupy a position between the two groups described here.

than did individuals in higher income brackets. (Income effects were even more marked among the fifteen-to-forty-four-year-old group, where, of course, the greater physical and health hazards of non-white-collar work would contribute to the effect.) On the other hand, since these data are based upon self-reports of disability (or reports of parents about their child), it is possible that some or all of this difference stems from systematic biases in the responses given to the questionnaire by parents with very low incomes. (To the best of our knowledge, no studies have attempted to ascertain the existence of parental biases in reports of their children's disability that are related to income or, indeed, to any other social factor. However, there are scattered references in the literature to substantial disagreements between parental and clinical estimates of the severity of a child's disability. See, in addition to Richardson et al., *The Handicapped Children of Alamance County, North Carolina*, Ivan B. Pless and Klaus J. Roughmann, "Chronic Illness and Its Consequences: Observations Based on Three Epidemiological Surveys," *Journal of Pediatrics* 79, no. 3 [September 1971]: 351–59.)

Finally, we must note that our tentative estimates conflict with the findings of one of the best national epidemiological surveys yet carried out, that conducted in England, Wales, and Scotland in 1961. See Ivan

Barry Pless and James W. B. Douglas, "Chronic Illness in Childhood. Part I. Epidemiological and Clinical Characteristics," *Pediatrics* 47, no. 2 (February 1971): 405–14. Pless and Douglas report no social class effect. However, they do not report if they looked to see whether social class affected the *severity* of the condition (being, for example, associated with a disproportionately high incidence of severe or moderate conditions). Moreover, they use a dichotomous categorization for class (i.e., families headed by manual workers versus families headed by non-manual workers). An equally crude categorization would have concealed the association of very low family income with severity of disability shown in the U.S. National Center for Vital Statistics survey noted above. Moreover, the children surveyed in the Pless and Douglas study were born in 1946 and therefore had benefited from the free or low-cost medical care provided by the National Health Service. It is tempting to speculate that this health care may have greatly reduced differences in the prevalence rates of different disabilities (and the relative severity of disability) that might formerly have been associated with social class in the United Kingdom. (For a discussion of the prevalence of handicaps that complements the one presented here, see Appendix 4.)

13. The Urban Institute, *Report of the Comprehensive Service Needs Study* (Washington, D.C.: Urban Institute, June 23, 1975), chapter 5, Table 5-1, p. 85.

14. This question is discussed at length in Part Four.

15. See chapter 13.

16. For blindness, see Urban Institute, *Report of the Comprehensive Service Needs Study*, chapter 18, p. 424. For deafness, see chapter 19, p. 499, of the same study.

17. Ibid., p. 424.

18. For a summary of the 1966 *Social Security Survey of the Disabled* study, see ibid., chapter 4, and Part Four of this book. For a summary of the 1972 study, see Sar A. Levitan and Robert Taggart, *Jobs for the Disabled* (Baltimore: Johns Hopkins University Press, 1977).

19. For an estimate of one-quarter, see Bowe, *Handicapping America*, p. 17. For an estimate of 35 percent (which the authors consider conservative), see Dolores A. Davis and Obidima I. Onyemelukwe, "Unique Problems of the Handicapped Aging," in *The White House Conference on Handicapped Individuals*, vol. 1: *Awareness Papers* (Washington, D.C.: U.S. Government Printing Office, 1977), pp. 457–66.

20. See chapter 13.

21. Henry P. Brehm, "The Disabled on Public Assistance," *From the Social Security Survey of the Disabled: 1966*, Report Number 9, June 1970.

22. Philip Frohlich, "Denied Disability Insurance Applicants: A Comparison with Beneficiaries and Nonapplicants," *From the Social Security Survey of the Disabled: 1966*, Report Number 11, September 1970, Table 6. The figure of one million greatly understates the true toll of job-related disability. See Joseph A. Page and Mary-Win O'Brien, *Bitter Wages* (New York: Grossman, 1973), a Nader Study Group Report.

23. All of these surveys suffer from certain crucial limitations inherent in the self-report method. We discuss these limitations at length in the text

and notes of chapter 13 (see, especially, note 21 of chapter 13). For a good summary of the health survey data, see Harold S. Luft, *Poverty and Health: Economic Causes and Consequences of Health Problems* (Cambridge, Mass.: Ballinger Publishing Company, 1978), pp. 37–71.

24. Ibid., pp. 55, 64–70, and 86–88.

25. Ibid., p. 68.

26. Luft believes that when education, sex, and age are controlled, there are almost no significant race differentials (ibid., pp. 86–88). We take issue with his analysis in note 22 of chapter 13.

27. Ibid., pp. 136–38.

28. For example, the Children's Defense Fund's suit against the state of Mississippi (*Mattie T.* v. *Holladay*), which was finally resolved in favor of the plaintiffs in early 1979. For general discussions, see Hobbs, *The Futures of Children*; Craig et al., *Studies of Handicapped Students*, vol. 2; and chapter 10 of this book.

29. In 1950, for example, K. W. Hamilton proposed that *disability* be defined as "a condition of impairment, physical or mental, having an objective aspect that can usually be described by a physician," whereas *handicap* be defined as "the cumulative result of the obstacles which disability interposes between the individual and his maximum functional level." See K. W. Hamilton, *Counseling the Handicapped in the Rehabilitation Process* (New York: Ronald, 1950), p. 17, and Beatrice A. Wright, *Physical Disability—A Psychological Approach* (New York: Harper & Row, 1960), p. 9.

    But a leading figure in the epidemiology of handicap, Saad Z. Nagi, writes that *disability* "is a pattern of behavior that evolves in situations of long-term or continued impairments that are associated with functional limitations"—precisely the definition of *handicap* proposed by Hamilton. See Saad Z. Nagi, "Some Conceptual Issues in Disability and Rehabilitation," in *Sociology and Rehabilitation*, ed. Marvin B. Sussman (Washington, D.C.: American Sociological Association, 1965), p. 103.

    For an especially revealing example of how *disability* and *handicap* resist any restrictions on their meanings even in technical discussions, see Monroe Berkowitz, Jeffrey Rubin, and John D. Worrall, "Economic Concerns of Handicapped Persons," in *The White House Conference on Handicapped Individuals*, vol. 1: *Awareness Papers*, pp. 223–24. These authors endorse Nagi's distinction, then proceed to illustrate it by citing at length an author who employs Hamilton's usage.

    We ourselves have encountered in private conversations with laymen parallels to Nagi's definition of *disability* as the social component of handicap. Both a New England plumber and a recent winner of a National Book Award told us that *disability* affects the total person, whereas *handicap* refers to a specific, well-bounded physical limitation. An identical distinction between *handicap* and *disability* is made by a championship horseman interviewed in the *National Enquirer:* " 'I could accept being handicapped,' said the soft-spoken Army veteran, 'but I swore that I'd never be disabled.' " See Eric Shuman, "He's a Cowboy and Champion Rider—with One Arm, One Eye, and No Legs," *National Enquirer*, February 3, 1976, p. 37. Whether the distinction was made by the horseman or is a misquote is irrelevant for our present purpose.

30. Here are some other examples:

The Random House Dictionary of the English Language (unabr. ed.) defines *handicap* as "a physical disability," and *disability* as "a permanent physical flaw, weakness or handicap, which prevents one from living a full normal life or from performing any specific job."

Webster's New International Dictionary (3d ed.) defines *handicap* as "a disadvantage that makes achievement unusually difficult, especially: a physical disability that limits the capacity to work," and *disability* as "the inability to pursue an occupation or perform services . . . because of physical or mental impairment."

31. In mineralogy the different crystalline shapes a given chemical compound can take were formerly called *allomorphs*. The word is still current in linguistics, where it denotes any of the variant pronunciations of a morpheme. For example, the different *s* sounds in *cats*, *dogs*, and *horses* are all different phonetic realizations of the morpheme *s*. Needless to say, none of these allomorphs of *s* is superior to the rest. Our proposed usage conserves this neutrality. An allomorphism is any physical structure or behavior pattern that, justly or unjustly, is singled out by society at a given point in time and called a handicap.

1 • Handicap as a Social Construction

1. For an excellent discussion of the failure to implement the laws now on the books, see Frank Bowe, *Handicapping America* (New York: Harper & Row, 1978).

2. Thomas S. Kuhn, *The Structure of Scientific Revolutions*, 2d ed., enl. (Chicago: University of Chicago Press, 1970).

3. Gordon W. Allport, *The Nature of Prejudice*, abr. ed. (Garden City, N.Y.: Doubleday Anchor, 1958), p. 169.

4. The analysis of handicap presented in these pages has been influenced by many writers. See, especially, Norwood Russell Hanson, *Patterns of Discovery* (Cambridge: Cambridge University Press, 1969), from which we take the example of the sunrise; Erving Goffman, *Stigma: Notes on the Management of Spoiled Identity* (Englewood Cliffs, N.J.: Prentice-Hall, 1963), *Interaction Ritual: Essays on Face-to-Face Behavior* (Garden City, N.Y.: Doubleday, 1967), *Strategic Interaction* (Philadelphia: University of Pennsylvania Press, 1969), and *Relations in Public: Microstudies of the Public Order* (New York: Basic Books, 1971). We also wish to record our debt to Roger G. Barker, Beatrice A. Wright, Lee Meyerson, and Mollie R. Bonick, the authors of *Adjustment to Physical Handicap and Illness: A Survey of the Social Psychology of Physique and Disability*, rev. ed. (New York: Social Science Research Council, 1953), and Lee Meyerson, "Somatopsychology of Physical Disability," in *Psychology of Exceptional Children and Youth*, 3d ed., ed. William M. Cruickshank (Englewood Cliffs, N.J.: Prentice-Hall, 1971), pp. 1–74.

5. For a lucid discussion of Helmholtz's concept of unconscious inference, see Edwin G. Boring, *A History of Experimental Psychology*, 2d ed.

(New York: Appleton-Century-Crofts, 1957), pp. 308–11. For examples of the role played by the concept in the contemporary psychology of perception, see James J. Gibson, *The Senses Considered as Perceptual Systems* (Boston: Houghton Mifflin, 1966), and Clarence H. Graham, "Visual Form Perception," in *Vision and Visual Perception*, ed. Clarence H. Graham (New York: John Wiley and Sons, 1965), pp. 548–74.

6. Among psychiatrists it is perhaps George A. Kelley who has argued most consistently for the many parallels between interpersonal perception and the actual theory-building behavior of scientists. However, nearly all schools of psychiatry and psychoanalysis at least tacitly accept the parallel, as is witnessed by such terms as *reality testing*. See George A. Kelley, *The Psychology of Personal Constructs*, vol. 2: *Clinical Diagnosis and Psychotherapy* (New York: W. W. Norton, 1955). In addition to the many invaluable works of Erving Goffman, see R. D. Laing, H. Phillipson, and A. R. Lee, *Interpersonal Perception—A Theory and a Method of Research* (London: Tavistock Publications, 1966).

7. The perceptual effects of indirect information about a person are not restricted to lay encounters. Indirect information often biases the professional's perceptions of his client. See chapter 11, note 13, for a brief discussion of research that has explored the ways that indirect information can affect a psychotherapist's perceptions of a patient or a potential patient. We touch upon related issues in our discussion of teacher expectancy effects in chapter 10, note 4.

8. Goffman, *Stigma*, p. 5.

9. For an excellent discussion of these issues, see Laing et al., *Interpersonal Perception*.

10. Allport, *The Nature of Prejudice*, pp. 162–63.

11. For an excellent discussion of the traditional racist ideologies in America, see Gunnar Myrdal, with the assistance of Richard Steiner and Arnold Rose, *An American Dilemma* (New York: Harper & Brothers, 1944), chapters 2–5, pp. 26–136.

12. In principle, race and handicap seem capable of evoking the same range of negative reactions. (Compare, for example, our partial typology of possible ways of responding to disability in Appendix 3 with Allport's comprehensive discussion of the possible sources of race prejudice in *The Nature of Prejudice*.) However, we suspect that in some social milieus and for at least some disabilities, group stereotyping is much less important than it is in racial prejudice. That is, while some professionals who have extensive contact with the handicapped may respond to their clients in terms of sometimes negative stereotypes (see, e.g., Robert A. Scott, *The Making of Blind Men* [New York: Russell Sage Foundation, 1969]), laymen frequently respond to the handicapped as isolated individuals whose defining characteristic—being diseased—does not confer upon them membership in any distinctive social group. This *may* help to explain the perplexing finding that expressed attitudes toward most groups of disabled people have remained unchanged over the past fifty years—remaining mildly negative to mildly positive during a period in which expressed attitudes toward members of such stigmatized social groups as Jews and blacks have registered dramatic

shifts away from prejudice and toward tolerance. For an overview of
early attitude studies, see Barker et al., *Adjustment to Physical Handicap and Illness*. For surveys of more recent studies, see Nettie R. Bartel
and Samuel L. Guskin, "A Handicap as a Social Phenomenon," in
Psychology of Exceptional Children and Youth, ed. Cruickshank, pp.
75–114. For an excellent synthesis and overview, see Stephen A. Richardson, "Attitudes and Behavior towards the Physically Handicapped,"
Birth Defects: Original Article Series 12, no. 4 (1976): 15–34. On the
other hand, there is fragmentary evidence that individuals who are
highly prejudiced against Jews and blacks also are highly prejudiced
against disabled people (Bartel and Guskin, "A Handicap as a Social
Phenomenon").

13. I. J. Lee, "How Do You Talk about People?" Freedom Pamphlet (New
York: Anti-Defamation League, 1950), p. 15, cited in Allport, *The Nature of Prejudice*, p. 175.
14. Goffman, *Stigma*, p. 5.
15. When a belief in social incapacity is joined with a belief that a person's
particular handicap menaces the social order, the result can be something like a witch-hunt mentality among the able-bodied. Such was the
case in the early decades of this century, when respectable scientific opinion fostered the belief that mildly retarded people were predisposed
toward crimes of violence and sexual license—i.e., the retardate could
not clearly distinguish right from wrong and often yielded to the antisocial impulses that the normal individual successfully holds in check.
See, for example, H. H. Goddard, *Human Efficiency and Levels of Intelligence* (Princeton: Princeton University Press, 1920); R. M. Yerkes,
"Psychological Examining in the United States Army," *Memoirs of the
National Academy of Sciences* 15 (1921); and C. C. Brigham, *A Study
of American Intelligence* (Princeton: Princeton University Press, 1923).

    Among able-bodied social groups, the Jew has perhaps been most frequently defined as being a social menace because of his supposed inability to assume any positive social roles in American or Western
European society. This tendency to define Jews exclusively as a deviant
social group has a long tradition in Europe, where stereotypes about
Jews have often represented a kind of amalgam of the negative stereotypes about Jews and blacks in America, the Jew being perceived as
being both too smart and shifty *and* sensual, lascivious, and violence-prone. See Allport, *The Nature of Prejudice*, chapter 12, "Stereotypes
in Our Culture," pp. 189–99, and Jean-Paul Sartre, *Anti-Semite and
Jew*, trans. George J. Becker (New York: Schocken Books, 1948).

    Analogous attitudes toward oppressed indigenous peoples have often
been held by European and American colonial populations. See Franz
Fanon, *The Wretched of the Earth*, trans. Constance Farrington (New
York: Grove Press, 1966). An emphasis upon the black as representing
a similar potential menace has also figured prominently in American
history. See Oscar Handlin, *Race and Nationality in American Life*
(Garden City, N.Y.: Doubleday Anchor, 1957), chapter 6, "The Horror,"
pp. 111–34.

    Any social group that tries to renegotiate its place in American society may provoke a similar response in the majority. That is, those who uphold the social status quo may treat resistance to oppression as a symptom of deviance, an inability to assume any legitimate social roles. Examples are civil rights activists in the 1960s, student protesters against the Vietnam war, feminists, and gay rights activists. On the role that political action plays in conferring a new legitimacy on a group formerly branded as deviant, see Saul D. Alinsky, *Rules for Radicals* (New York: Random House, 1971). On the role that moral suasion can play, see Myrdal et al., *An American Dilemma, passim.* On the role that technocratic ideology has played in obscuring the nature of political legitimization, see John L. Schaar, "Legitimacy in the Modern State," in *Power and Community: Dissenting Essays in Political Science,* ed. Philip Green and Sanford Levinson (New York: Pantheon, 1970), and Sheldon S. Wolin, *Politics and Vision: Continuity and Innovation in Western Thought* (Boston: Little, Brown, 1960), chapter 10, "The Age of Organization and the Sublimation of Politics," pp. 352–434. We explore another facet of this ideology in our subsequent discussion of the "social pathology model" in chapter 3. (Also see chapter 3, note 4, and chapter 12, pp. 264–67.)

16. The association of disease with moral imperfection and evil is one of the oldest themes of Western culture. Plato constantly draws upon it in *The Republic* and *The Laws,* and the medicinal therapies of antiquity shuttled back and forth between a physiological and a moral model of disease. See Pedro Laín Entralgo, *The Therapy of the Word in Classical Antiquity,* trans. L. J. Rather and John M. Sharp (New Haven: Yale University Press, 1970). The linkages between disease and evil are even more extensive in Christianity. Some traditional interpretations come very close to equating chronic disease or great physical deformity with sinfulness. These views coexist with a more positive one. Like Job, the morally blameless victim of disability has been favored by God with an exceptionally difficult (and therefore meaningful) test of his faith. Others must first sin and then seek redemption and salvation through repentance and suffering. (Disability in an evil person is often viewed as punishment for sins already committed.) But the Job-like cripple achieves salvation by patiently enduring the mortification of his body by his disability—i.e., by rising above his suffering and accepting it as an expression of the unfathomable depths of the divine will. (One might say that sainthood is the preferred role for the severely handicapped.)

In this way the handicap is transformed into a metaphor for man's imperfection and the way that man can transcend his imperfection. This transformation is double-edged because of the fine line between perceiving a deformed body or diseased frame as symbolizing the corruption and sinfulness of the flesh and simply perceiving the possessor of a disabled body as sinful and corrupt.

The many parallels between lay concepts of handicap and traditional Christian concepts of the long-term degenerative and transformative impact of vice and sin upon character are well worth the attention of scholars in handicap and medical anthropology. The *locus classicus* of this theory in literature is John Milton's depiction of the progressive degeneration of Satan's character in *Paradise Lost.*

The other side of these classical and Christian motifs is the tradition of the grotesque—the use of deformity to mock the vanities of the rich and powerful, to symbolize the truth that moral worth has nothing to do with an individual's appearance or worldly position, and to humanize through laughter. In antiquity this tradition is associated with Socrates and is symbolized by the Silenus—a hollow figurine bearing the image of an ugly satyr (often said to be modeled on Socrates) on the outside and containing a figure of a beautiful dancing god within. The theme of the grotesque is especially important in the Middle Ages, when it was associated with the court jester and the Christian fool. During the Renaissance the motif became an important part of Christian humanism. (In English literature the grotesque figures especially prominently in Shakespeare and Browning.) For a brilliant overview of these humanizing uses of deformity, see Michael Bakhtin, *Rabelais and His World,* trans. Helene Iswolsky (Cambridge, Mass.: MIT Press, 1968).

17. Of course, this is not to say that the aristocrat's disabilities play no role in the film. For example, they come to represent what Europe has become as a result of the senseless destruction of the war, and they also seem to suggest the passing of the old aristocratic order.

18. The converse of this also seems to be the case; even when the handicap is an absolutely essential prerequisite for the achievement of social adulthood, it becomes very difficult to continue to think of the person's medical problem as being socially disabling.

Consider, for example, the following description of an orthopedic deformity that was first described in England in the nineteenth century: "From the heel to the great toe, the foot is unusually short, not exceeding five inches . . . the great toe . . . is bent, with a peculiar abruptness, upwards and backwards, whilst the remaining toes . . . are doubled in beneath the sole of the foot. . . . The integuments covering the heel are . . . dense, hard, resisting, . . . [and] the subcutaneous structure resembles rather the . . . sole of a horse's foot, than any human tissue. . . . But the strangest feature in this deformity is . . . that the heel and toes . . . [seem] forcibly brought together, so as considerably to diminish the whole length of the foot. . . ." (Howard S. Levy, *Chinese Foot Binding* [New York: Bell Publishing Co., 1972], pp. 288–91, slightly reordered. The extract is drawn from Bransby Blake Cooper, "Anatomical Description of the Foot of a Chinese Woman," *Philosophical Transactions of the Royal Society of London* 119 [1829]: 255–60, reproduced in its entirety by Levy, pp. 287–93.)

The deformity in question is not a natural one. Despite its resemblance to club foot, it is man-made, the result of the custom of foot binding, not the result of heredity. Practiced for nearly a thousand years in China, it was still being carried out furtively in some coastal provinces as late as the 1930s.

When reading descriptions of the custom, it is difficult to feel anything but shock and repulsion that anything so cruel could ever be inflicted upon children in a highly civilized country. And yet, when one turns from the sheer brutality of the measures taken to reduce the normal foot of a twelve-year-old girl to the bound form, one finds something curious. The custom is not inflicted upon the child without explanation; quite the contrary. During the year or so in which the child is in constant pain, the explanation is given over and over again that only grown-up women get married, raise a family, bring honor to their parents, and are accorded the privileges and respect due an adult woman. But none of these things will come to a girl unless her feet are bound. Therefore, the only way to grow up is to submit to the mutilation of having her feet bound.

It is, we believe, this syllogism—or some variant of it—that spells the difference between the mutilation's being a gratuitous cruelty and therefore a handicap, and its being a necessary step in one's socialization into the adult role. In contrast to the handicapped child of today whose question—"Why me?"—is unanswerable, there was a clear-cut, if harsh and cruel, answer in traditional China: "Because, my daughter, childhood is over and you must begin to become a grown-up woman." Quite the reverse of the gratuitous mutilations of nature, the Chinese custom resembles in its underlying structure nothing less than an urban and "civilized" version of the rites of passage required of adolescents in many "primitive" cultures.

But now reflect on one's own reaction to the custom as one first views it from without as an outsider unfamiliar with the workings of Chinese society, and then as one views it from within, as a parent with a daughter whom one loves very much and for whom one wants to do the best. For us, at least, there is a shift in our perception of the disability reminiscent of the change in gestalt that occurs when examining those ambiguous figures psychologists delight in—perhaps the one that is first a picture of a beautiful young woman and then a portrait of an ugly old crone, depending on the context in which it appears.

As outsiders we react to the mutilation not only as having been cruel and shameful in itself but as forever excluding the child from a normal life as a child and an adult. It seems to cast her from our midst. It is like a thunderbolt from the blue, an accident that is all the more terrible because it was deliberately willed and therefore could have been deliberately not willed. Far from integrating her into a group, it seems to mark her off as a pariah. We wonder how the Chinese could hate their women so much that they could do something this cruel and dreadful to them—that they should demand of their mothers, daughters, and sisters that they be handicapped.

Our reaction as an insider is not less negative. The cruelty, the harshness, the brutality, are still present, but we now see the act not as gratuitous but as the result of a terrible choice that we must make as a parent. And while the form of the choice is true to the situation of traditional China, the words we use to formulate the quandary to ourselves reflect our own time. Those words are "If I spare my daughter the terrible ordeal of foot binding, she will be handicapped for life." Handicapped. Not ruined or stigmatized or ostracized; handicapped.

19. See the discussion of race relations in Brazil in *The New York Times,* June 5, 1978.

2 • The Handicapped Role

1. For a good discussion of some of these fears, see Susan Sontag, *Illness as Metaphor* (New York: Farrar, Straus & Giroux, 1978).

2. See our earlier remarks on the way political struggle and moral dialogue can render legitimate an oppressed group's attempts to change the status quo in chapter 1, note 15.

3. Because of our interest in applying a minority-group model to handicap, we make no attempt to explore systematically all the possible models of tolerance that a member of our culture can draw upon in his encounters with handicapped people. However, one of these other models deserves special mention because of its importance in mainstream culture, in the "counterculture," and, at least in our experience, in the way that many severely disabled adolescents and young adults attempt to protect themselves from the stigma of their disability. This is the potential for a tolerance of physical diversity afforded by science fiction, or, indeed, simply by a serious interest in the existence of extraterrestrial civilizations. One able-bodied person with extensive experience with the disabled put the matter this way: "Science fiction is the one element in my life most responsible for me not being a racist or a cultural bigot." Another told us, "The only authors who are coping with the complexity of modern reality are those authors who are tied in with science fiction." For more on the flexibility promoted by the science fiction sensibility, see Robert Scholes, *Structural Fabulations* (Notre Dame, Ind.: University of Notre Dame Press, 1975).

   Because an interest in science fiction or in the existence of extraterrestrial civilizations is scorned by many as a faintly adolescent enterprise that has no relevance to the serious concerns of life, it is easy to dismiss these statements. However, one need only read the works of a science fiction writer of the first rank—such as Theodore Sturgeon—to recognize not only that the humanizing role of science fiction deserves to be taken seriously by those who study attitudes toward handicap, but that since World War II science fiction has come far closer to exploring the real complexities of disability and physical difference than any other contemporary art form. See, for example, Sturgeon's *More than Human* and *The Synthetic Man* (originally entitled *The Dreaming Jewels*). For a sense of just how seriously well-known scientists take the cultural importance of establishing the existence of extraterrestrial civilizations, see the report of the recent blue-ribbon NASA panel: Phillip Morrison, John Billingham, and John Wolf, eds., *The Search for Extraterrestrial Intelligence* (Washington, D.C.: U.S. Government Printing Office, 1977).

4. See Talcott Parsons, *The Social System* (Glencoe, Ill.: Free Press, 1951), pp. 439–47, "Definitions of Health and Illness in the Light of American Values and Social Structure," in *Patients, Physicians, and Illness*, ed. E. Gartly Jaco (New York: Free Press of Glencoe, 1958), reprinted as

chapter 10 of Talcott Parsons, *Social Structure and Personality* (New York: Free Press, 1964), pp. 257–91; Talcott Parsons and Renee Fox, "Illness, Therapy, and the American Family," in *The Family*, ed. Norman W. Bill and Ezra F. Vogel (Glencoe, Ill.: Free Press, 1969), pp. 347–60; and Talcott Parsons, "Some Theoretical Considerations Bearing on the Field of Medical Sociology," chapter 12 of Parsons, *Social Structure and Personality*, pp. 325–58.

5. While differing in many respects from our own analysis, a number of other writers have spoken of the "disabled role." See, for example, Jerome K. Myers, "Consequence and Prognosis of Disability" and "A Handicap as a Social Problem," in *Sociology and Rehabilitation*, ed. Marvin B. Sussman (Washington, D.C.: American Sociological Association, 1965), pp. 35–51, 92–93; E. W. Markson, "Patient Semeiology of a Chronic Disease," *Social Science and Medicine* 5 (1971): 159–67; Claudine Herzlich, *Health and Illness: A Social Psychological Analysis*, trans. Douglas Graham (New York: Academic Press, 1971)—Herzlich speaks of an "invalid role" in contemporary France; Gene G. Kassebaum and Barbara O. Baumann, "Dimensions of the Sick Role in Chronic Illness," in *Patients, Physicians, and Illness*, 2d ed., ed. E. Gartly Jaco (New York: The Free Press, 1972), pp. 141–54; and Theodor J. Litman, "Physical Rehabilitation: A Social Psychological Approach," in *Patients, Physicians, and Illness*, 2d ed., ed. Jaco, pp. 186–203.

6. In earlier periods of religious warfare, religious conversion represented a partial exception to this generalization: often, the member of the losing side was offered a choice between death or converting to the enemy religion and retaining a place in normal society. Something of this special potency of religious conversion still attends the deviant who, instead of being cured by an appropriate agency of the state (e.g., a prison psychiatrist or a lay professional), makes a clean break with his past as a result of a religious conversion. See William James, *The Varieties of Religious Experience* (New York: New American Library, 1959).

7. Kai Erikson, "Notes on the Sociology of Deviance," in *The Other Side*, ed. Howard S. Becker (New York: Free Press, 1964), pp. 16–17.

3 • Handicap and the Social Pathology Model

1. Robert A. Scott, "Comments about Interpersonal Processes of Rehabilitation, in *Sociology and Rehabilitation*, ed. Marvin B. Sussman (Washington, D.C.: American Sociological Association, 1965), p. 138.

2. Lee Meyerson, "Somatopsychology of Physical Disability," in *Psychology of Exceptional Children and Youth*, ed. William M. Cruickshank (Englewood Cliffs, N.J.: Prentice-Hall, 1971), p. 16.

3. For a useful overview, see Christopher Lasch, *Haven in a Heartless World: The Family Besieged* (New York: Basic Books, 1977). Also see C. Wright Mills, "The Professional Ideology of Social Pathologists," in *Politics, Power, and People: The Collected Essays of C. Wright Mills*,

ed. Irving Louis Horowitz (New York: Ballantine Books, 1963), pp. 525–55.

4. The relationship between society's medical tolerance toward disability and the social pathology model is complex. Despite the changing concepts of the nature of physical disease since antiquity, the use of disease models to discredit the legitimacy of deviant moral positions is at least as old as Christianity and, indeed, appears to have been as much a pagan invention as a Christian invention. See E. R. Dodds, *Pagan and Christian in an Age of Anxiety: Some Aspects of Religious Experience from Marcus Aurelius to Constantine* (Cambridge: Cambridge University Press, 1965). If anything, the use of disease models to guide attempts to cure moral deviance is even older. For the pre-Christian evidence, see Pedro Laín Entralgo, *The Therapy of the Word in Classical Antiquity*, trans. L. J. Rather and John M. Sharp (New Haven: Yale University Press, 1970). For a useful introduction to the vast Christian literature on the "cure of souls" (the word *cure* is used in precisely the same sense as in contemporary adjustment psychology, although the goal of the cure is, of course, radically different), see Augustine, *The Confessions*, trans. John K. Ryan (Garden City, N.Y.: Doubleday, 1960); A. D. Nock, *Conversion* (Oxford: Oxford University Press, 1933); and John T. McNeil, *A History of the Cure of Souls* (New York: Harper & Brothers, 1951). At the very least, these traditions suggest that something like the social pathology model has been used by spiritual "professionals" with moral deviants for nearly two millennia—more than long enough for it to have penetrated popular culture and become an option that occurs "naturally" and spontaneously to any nonprofessional who, for example, perceives disability primarily in terms of moral threat and moral deviance, yet recognizes the need to respond fairly and humanely to the disabled person. Of course, since the handicapped role is only a cultural option that *may* be drawn upon, American professionals may have played a crucial role in persuading some (or even all) segments of the lay public that the handicapped role should be the preferred way to relate to disabled people. Also see chapter 1, notes 15 and 16, and chapter 12, pp. 264–67.

5. See Thomas S. Szasz, *Law, Liberty, and Psychiatry: An Inquiry into the Social Uses of Mental Health Practices* (New York: Macmillan, 1963), and *The Myth of Mental Illness* (New York: Harper & Row, 1964); and Nicholas N. Kittrie, *The Right to Be Different: Deviance and Enforced Therapy* (Baltimore: Johns Hopkins University Press, 1971).

6. See Sheldon S. Wolin, *Politics and Vision: Continuity and Innovation in Western Thought* (Boston: Little, Brown, 1960), chapter 10, "The Age of Organization and the Sublimation of Politics," pp. 352–424, and Philip Rieff, *The Triumph of the Therapeutic: Uses of Faith after Freud* (New York: Harper & Row, 1966).

7. See Lasch, *Haven in a Heartless World*. Though hardly sharing Lasch's theoretical position, the Carnegie Council on Children volume on the American family also rejects the traditional medical model in its call for policies that empower the family and diminish the role played by

paternalistic family services. See Kenneth Keniston and the Carnegie Council on Children, *All Our Children: The American Family under Pressure* (New York: Harcourt Brace Jovanovich, 1977).

8. See Oliver W. Sacks, *Awakenings* (Garden City, N.Y.: Doubleday, 1974), a modern classic; and Ivan Illich, *Medical Nemesis* (New York: Pantheon, 1976), flawed but nonetheless invaluable. An enormous literature has sprung up in the past two decades that criticizes the failure of the medical model to honor the experience of dying. See, for example, Elisabeth Kübler-Ross, *On Death and Dying* (New York: Macmillan, 1969). For an example of the growing number of attacks on the medical model in the medical sociology literature, see Eliot Freidson, *Profession of Medicine* (New York: Dodd, Mead, 1971).

9. Because we discuss all these issues in greater detail in later chapters, we will confine ourselves to indicating other Carnegie Council on Children reports and monographs that touch upon similar issues.

10. See John U. Ogbu, *Minority Education and Caste: The American System in Cross-Cultural Perspective*, a Carnegie Council on Children monograph (New York: Academic Press, 1978), and Richard H. de Lone for the Carnegie Council on Children, *Small Futures: Children, Inequality, and the Limits of Liberal Reform* (New York: Harcourt Brace Jovanovich, 1979).

11. See Alison Clarke-Stewart, *Child Care in the Family: A Review of Research and Some Propositions for Policy*, a Carnegie Council on Children monograph (New York: Academic Press, 1977).

12. For a similar approach to the managerial responsibilities of *all* parents regardless of wealth and income, see Keniston and the Carnegie Council on Children, *All Our Children*.

13. See Ogbu, *Minority Education and Caste*, and de Lone, *Small Futures*.

4 • The Case for a Developmental Psychology of Handicap

1. Kai Erikson, "Notes on the Sociology of Deviance," in *The Other Side*, ed. Howard S. Becker (New York: Free Press, 1964), p. 17.

2. Lee Meyerson, "Somatopsychology of Physical Disability," in *Psychology of Exceptional Children and Youth*, ed. William M. Cruickshank (Englewood Cliffs, N.J.: Prentice-Hall, 1971), pp. 16–17.

3. Frank Bowe, *Handicapping America* (New York: Harper & Row, 1978), p. 125.

4. The flaws of the adjustment approach as a vehicle for basic research must be distinguished from the useful applied research that is often carried out in the name of measuring adjustment or establishing the determinants of adequate adjustment in the child and the family. This applied research meets an immediate clinical need for rough rule-of-thumb guides to the child's ability and the family's ability to cope successfully with the stresses and strains produced by the handicap. Ultimately, a mature developmental psychology of handicap may reveal that some or many of the premises about normal adjustment that underlie this research are flawed. But until this psychological tradition

exists, the vigorous prosecution of a pragmatic, adjustment-oriented stream of applied research seems the best way to meet the clinician's need for help in grappling with the immense complexities of handicap. See Ivan B. Pless and Philip Pinkerton, *Chronic Childhood Disorder— Promoting Patterns of Adjustment* (London: Henry Klimpton, 1975), and Gilman D. Grave and I. Barry Pless, eds., *Chronic Childhood Illness: Assessment of Outcome*, vol. 3 of Fogarty International Center Series on the Teaching of Preventive Medicine (Washington, D.C.: U.S. Department of Health, Education and Welfare, 1976), DHEW Publication No. (NIH) 76-877. Also see chapter 11.

5. The scale of this fascination with individual differences is best appreciated by reading a few recent volumes of *Exceptional Child Education Abstracts*. Also see below, note 7.

6. The most dramatic example of this is the continued survival of Kurt Lewin's "topological psychology" as a leading theoretical edifice in handicap long after Lewinian field theory was abandoned in mainstream psychology. The heuristic value of Lewin's theory for teaching purposes and for clinicians is undeniable. See the brilliant applications of field theory in Meyerson, "Somatopsychology of Physical Disability," and in Roger G. Barker in collaboration with Beatrice A. Wright, Lee Meyerson, and Mollie R. Gonick, *Adjustment to Physical Handicap and Illness: A Survey of the Social Psychology of Physique and Disability* (New York: Social Science Research Council, 1953), especially pp. 94–111 and 238–54. However, as a tool for studying the development of handicapped children—or, indeed, any group of children—the theory is severely flawed.

As summarized by Calvin S. Hall and Gardiner Lindzey, the most important of these flaws are as follows: (1) The theory merely provides a compact form for representing by way of pictorial diagrams what we already know from our common sense. (2) The diagrams hopelessly confuse representations of the individual's phenomenological life space with representations of his physical life space. (3) Despite Lewin's claim that he is interested in developmental and "historical" problems, the theory seems to exclude both approaches. (4) While "it pretends to offer a mathematical model of behavior from which specific predictions can be made . . . the model has no utility whatsoever in generating testable propositions" (Calvin S. Hall and Gardiner Lindzey, *Theories of Personality* [New York: John Wiley and Sons, 1957], pp. 248–52).

7. For excellent reviews of the literature, see Barker et al., *Adjustment to Physical Handicap and Illness*; Beatrice A. Wright, *Physical Disability: A Psychological Approach* (New York: Harper & Row, 1960); and Pless and Pinkerton, *Chronic Childhood Disorder*.

Despite the frequent emphasis upon the methodological shortcomings of research in these reviews, we do not believe that this is the field's central problem. First-rate technique is important, but one must first have good ideas. And while good methodology permits the testing of good ideas, it does not generate them. Indeed, when a field lacks many fresh ideas—as is unfortunately the case for the psychology and the social psychology of handicap—an exclusive emphasis upon the need to raise methodological standards carries its own risks. The nature of these risks has been well put by Myron Tribus in a recent discussion of the difference between physical and statistical approaches to problems in the natural sciences. See Myron Tribus, "Physical View of Cloud Seeding," *Science* 168 (April 10, 1970): 201–11. "Statistical methods are strongest," writes Tribus, "when one can do a repeatable experiment—repeatable in the sense that essentially all the variables that can be controlled or observed are kept constant in repeated trials. However, when the known important variables are not susceptible to control and are not even measured and when the general effects of the variables are known [as, we must emphasize, is the case with the psychological development of the child], statistical methods are of more limited use" (p. 208). Statistical methods are even less useful when one doesn't know what one is looking for. "Basically we are seeking a signal masked by noise. Scientific knowledge [in the form of strong hypotheses] is the filter that can hold back the noise. When we throw away the advantages of this filter, we must observe for much longer times to find the signal in the noise" (p. 208).

The crux of the matter, writes Tribus, is this: "If my claim is not that I have a solution but rather that I have the beginnings of a solution, I assert that the blind application of statistics will be counterproductive. What we need is insight into the physics. Although statistical analysis can often provide clues as to which way to look for more insight, it can be expected to do so only when applied by someone who has the physical system clearly in mind" (p. 208).

The dangers of accumulating statistically significant differences instead of seeking to obtain some understanding of the process under study has been well described by the social scientist Amitai Etzioni. "Increasingly," he writes, "scientific work may be done by what is, in effect, a trial-and-error search, rather than a focused effort. And, in consequence, the findings may be an aggregate of data rather than confirmation of a theorem. . . . Such a development would be a latter-day repeat performance of the impact the introduction of prepackaged computer programs has had on some branches of the social sciences. There, the ability to use a prepackaged program to 'analyze' a data set, say, of a random national sample of adults often results in interpretations that have all the convenience but also the bite of a precooked, frozen TV dinner. This is because existing categories are used even if they do not capture well the variables under study. Thus, opinions are analyzed in terms of sex, age, income, and size of city, even if these correlate poorly with the issues at hand. Much to-do then is made over a difference of a few percentage points between subgroupings (say young versus old), while much greater differences would be found if more suitable but less commonly tapped variables (or combinations thereof) were teased out. Finding such variables, however, requires considerable intellectual, not mechanical, effort—less use of prepackaged programs and more of scientific creativity" (Amitai Etzioni, "Effects of Small Computers on Scientists," *Science* 189 [July 11, 1975]: 93).

All of this has been well summarized by the distinguished statistician F. N. David, who observed that "it is safe to say that no really big advance in any subject would have been missed through a lack of knowledge of statistical techniques. If the research worker is good enough to see the gap in the fundamentals of his subject and to fill this gap, he will be able to do so without the use of statistics." See F. N. David, *A First Course in Statistics* (New York: Hafner, 1971), p. 1.

8. A good sense of the general paucity of developmental studies in handicap is provided by James F. Magary, Marie K. Poulsen, Philip J. Levinson, and Priscilla A. Taylor, eds., *Piagetian Theory and Its Implications for the Helping Professions, Emphasis: The Handicapped Child*, Proceedings of the Sixth Annual Conference on Piaget and the Helping Professions, University of California, 1977. Besides many papers on Piaget and handicap, the volume contains a bibliography of other Piagetian studies of handicapped children. Though a welcome indication of a quickening interest in applying developmental theories to all groups of handicapped children, the work summarized in this volume is hardly typical of the vast majority of studies of the handicapped child. Piagetian theory *is* beginning to gain a foothold in discussions of special education. But usually it is invoked to justify pursuing such commonsense strategies as open classrooms and individualized instruction for the handicapped child. We support these strategies but deplore the way that references to Piaget end up reinforcing the traditional view that handicapped children develop in the same way as able-bodied children. For a good overview of the open classroom and individualized education approach to the child, see Samuel J. Meisels, ed., *Special Education and Development: Perspectives on Young Children with Special Needs* (Baltimore: University Park Press, 1979). The volume also contains a very useful bibliography of recent studies of handicapped children from a developmental perspective. Also see Carl E. Sherzick et al., eds., *Psychology and the Handicapped Child* (Washington, D.C.: U.S. Department of Health, Education and Welfare, 1974), DHEW Publication No. (OE) 73-05000.

9. See the special issue devoted to handicap in the *Bulletin de Psychologie* 27, no. 310, 5-9 (1973–1974). In 1966 the *Bulletin de Psychologie* also devoted a special issue to the development of handicapped children and youths.

In this connection, it is worth noting that Piagetians occupy a curious position in the history of the study of mentally retarded children. For many years researchers believed that the cognitive strategies of the mildly retarded differed in significant ways from those of normal children. The notion gained important support with the appearance in 1943 of a study of retarded children carried out by Bärbel Inhelder, one of Piaget's closest collaborators (Bärbel Inhelder, *The Diagnosis of Reasoning in the Mentally Retarded*, trans. Will Beth Stephens et al. from the 2d [1963] ed. [New York: Chandler, 1968]). Some two decades later (around the time the second edition appeared with a new preface by Piaget), evidence in support of a very different view of the mildly retarded child appeared. A host of studies (often carried out from a behavioristic perspective) demonstrated that the cognitive characteristics singled out by Inhelder were typical of any child—mildly retarded or mentally normal—who had spent a long period of time in a custodial institution. For a magisterial survey of this research, see Edward F. Zigler and Susan Harter, "The Socialization of the Mentally Retarded," in *Handbook of Socialization Theory and Research*, ed. David A. Goslin (Chicago: Rand McNally, 1969), pp. 1065–1102.

10. See, for example, Michael Cole, John Gay, Joseph A. Glick, and Donald W. Sharp, in association with Thomas Ciborowski, Frederick Frankel, John Kellemu, and David F. Lancy, *The Cultural Context of Learning and Thinking* (New York: Basic Books, 1971); William Labov, *Language in the Inner City: Studies in the Black English Vernacular* (Philadelphia: University of Pennsylvania Press, 1972); Frank Riessman, *The Inner-City Child* (New York: Harper & Row, 1976); Mario Fantini and Gerald Weinstein, *The Disadvantaged Child: Challenges to Education* (New York: Harper & Row, 1970); and Richard H. de Lone, *Small Futures: Children, Inequality, and the Limits of Liberal Reform* (New York: Harcourt Brace Jovanovich, 1979). Also see the following ethnographic studies of inner-city social life: Herbert J. Gans, *The Urban Villagers* (New York: Free Press, 1962); Gerald D. Suttles, *The Social Order of the Slum: Ethnicity and Territory in the Inner City* (Chicago: University of Chicago Press, 1968); and Ulf Hannerz, *Soulside: Inquiries into Ghetto Culture and Community* (New York: Columbia University Press, 1969).

11. See chapter 5, note 1.

12. For a recent overview of this work, see Thérèse Gouin-Décarie and Monique O'Neil, "Quelques aspects du developpement cognitif d'enfants souffrant de malformations dues à la thalidomide," *Bulletin de Psychologie* 27, no. 310, 5-9 (1973–1974): 286–303. For a review in English, see Thérèse Gouin-Décarie, "A Study of the Mental and Emotional Development of the Thalidomide Child," in *Determinants of Infant Behavior*, vol. 4, ed. Brian M. Foss (London: Methuen, 1969), pp. 167–89. Also see, especially, Ethel Roskies, *Abnormality and Normality: The Mothering of Thalidomide Children* (Ithaca, N.Y.: Cornell University Press, 1972).

13. Gouin-Décarie, "Quelques aspects du developpement cognitif d'enfants souffrant de malformations dues à la thalidomide," p. 298 (translation by John Gliedman).

14. Ibid., p. 298.

15. Happily, both Burlingham and Fraiberg have recently provided excellent overviews of their work and the work of their associates. See Dorothy Burlingham, *Psychoanalytic Studies of the Sighted and the Blind* (New York: International University Press, 1972), and Selma Fraiberg, *Insights from the Blind* (New York: Basic Books, 1977). Also see David H. Warren, *Blindness and Early Childhood Development* (New York: American Foundation for the Blind, 1977).

16. See especially Edward S. Klima, Ursula Bellugi, et al., *The Signs of Language* (Cambridge, Mass.: Harvard University Press, 1979), and the forthcoming volume that will focus on the acquisition of sign language by children. For excellent older studies, see Hans Furth, *Thinking without Language* (New York: Free Press, 1966), "Linguistic Deficiency and

Thinking: Research with Deaf Subjects, 1964–1969," *Psychological Bulletin* 76 (1971): 58–72; and Eric H. Lenneberg, *Biological Foundations of Language* (New York: John Wiley and Sons, 1967). Also see Hilde Schlessinger and Kathryn Meadow, *Sound and Sign: Childhood Deafness and Mental Health* (Berkeley: University of California Press, 1972); John D. Bonvillian, Veda R. Charrow, and Keith E. Nelson, "Psycholinguistic and Educational Implications of Deafness," *Human Development* 16 (1973): 321–45; and I. M. Schlesinger and Lila Namir, eds., *Sign Language of the Deaf* (New York: Academic Press, 1978).

17. At present only tantalizing bits and pieces of such a sociology exist. These hints are scattered throughout the important literature of psychoanalytic, psychiatric, and social psychological studies of handicapped children. See the autobiographical material cited in chapter 5, the case histories in Appendix 1, and the references cited in notes 4, 7, 12, 15, and 16 of this chapter. Of special interest are clinical descriptions of handicapped children being chronically subjected to the expectations of the sick role by their parents (i.e., what we have called the handicapped role). See, especially, Morris Green and Albert J. Solnit, "Reaction to the Threatened Loss of a Child: A Vulnerable Child Syndrome. Pediatric Management of the Dying Child, Part III," *Pediatrics* 34 (1964): 58–66.

18. Saad Z. Nagi, *R & D in Disability Policies and Programs* (Columbus, Ohio: Mershon Center, Ohio State University, 1973).

19. At a certain point in our research for this book we were struck by the many similarities between the situation of handicap as we had found it and the constellation of strains and double-binds that schizophrenogenic families impose upon their children. (For a good discussion of the latter, see Gregory Bateson, *Steps to an Ecology of Mind* [New York: Ballantine Books, 1972]. Also see R. D. Laing and A. Esterson, *Sanity, Madness, and the Family*, vol. 1: *Families of Schizophrenics* [New York: Basic Books, 1965].) For a while we felt that we had to entertain seriously the working hypothesis that something similar was frequently the case in families with severely handicapped children. Only gradually did we see that we were confusing what in the case of handicap is the result of established custom and culture with what in the case of the pathological family is the result of the individual personalities of the child's parents. This distinction points to what may be unique about the socialization experiences of many handicapped children.

In a formal sense there are striking parallels between the discontinuities of social experience that are built into the social situation of the handicapped child and the parentally induced stresses that characterize the schizophrenogenic family. But in the case of handicap, the deformation is a cultural invention and is perfectly compatible with a normal range of family life-styles. Matters are very different in the double-binding family. Here the pressures imposed upon the able-bodied child define the family's pathological life-style. Far from being a cultural invention, they represent a unique family invention.

Of course, this being said, we certainly are not suggesting that pathology is always absent in the life-styles of families with handicapped children. (Would that it were!) Nor do we wish to suggest that a child's handicap never plays an important role in the development of a pathological family situation. Nor do we underplay the possible importance of hereditary factors that predispose one to psychosis. Our point is simply that in every handicap category there are a great many children whose home life falls within the normal range found among able-bodied children, and that some of these children have excellent home lives. In general, the same cannot be said for individuals who succumb to psychosis in adolescence.

20.   The shortcomings of this ethnocentrism are compactly summarized in Alison Clarke-Stewart, *Child Care in the Family: A Review of Research and Some Propositions for Policy* (New York: Academic Press, 1977). Also see the studies cited in note 10, especially Cole, Gay, Glick, Sharp, et al., *The Cultural Context of Learning and Thinking.*

21.   The general form of the problem encountered in cross-cultural studies is ultimately linguistic. The nature of this linguistic problem has been put well by the philosopher Willard Van Orman Quine: ". . . the obvious first moves in picking up some initial Kalaba vocabulary are at bottom a matter of exploiting the overlap of our cultures. From this nucleus [the lexicographer] works outwards, ever more fallibly and conjecturally, by a series of clues and hunches. Thus he begins with a fund of correlations of Kalaba sentences with English sentences at the level where our cultures meet. Most of these sentences classify conspicuously segregated objects. Then he breaks these Kalaba sentences down into short component elements—combinations which as wholes have not been translated in the direct way. He tests his hypothesis as best he can by making further observations and keeping an eye out for conflicts. But, as the sentences undergoing translation get further and further from mere reports of common observations, the clarity of any possible conflict decreases; the lexicographer comes to depend increasingly on a projection of himself, with his Indo-European *Weltanschauung*, into the scandals of his Kalaba informant. He comes also to turn increasingly to that last refuge of all scientists, the appeal to internal simplicity of his growing system . . ." (Willard Van Orman Quine, "Meaning in Linguistics," in *From a Logical Point of View*, 2d ed., rev. [New York: Harper & Row Torchbooks, 1963], pp. 62–63).

Faced with the problem of meaning, the investigator can, broadly speaking, take either the Popperian road or the Wittgensteinian road. For a Popperian approach to the ethnographer's dilemma, see I. C. Jarvie, "Understanding and Explanation in Sociology and Social Anthropology," in *Explanation in the Behavioral Sciences*, ed. Robert Borger and Frank Cioffi (Cambridge: Cambridge University Press, 1970), pp. 231–48. A Wittgensteinian approach to the problem has been advanced by Peter Winch; see, especially, "Understanding a Primitive Society," *American Philosophical Quarterly* 1 (1964): 307–24, and his comments on Jarvie's paper in *Explanation in the Behavioral Sciences*, ed. Borger and Cioffi, pp. 249–59.

22. Marvin Harris, *Rise of Anthropological Theory: A History of Theories of Culture* (New York: Thomas Y. Crowell, 1968).

5 • Social Development

1. See, for example, Carol Gilligan, "In a Different Voice: Women's Conceptions of the Self and Morality," *Harvard Educational Review* 47, no. 4 (November 1977): 481–517; Mary Belensky and Carol Gilligan, "The Role of Conflict in Moral Development: Resolving the Abortion Dilemma," paper delivered at the annual meeting of the American Psychological Association (New York, September 1979); and Carol Gilligan, "Woman's Place in Man's Life Cycle," *Harvard Education Review* 49, no. 4 (November 1979).
2. We touch upon the problem of attitude change in our discussion of mainstreaming in chapter 10, "The Handicapped Child in School."
3. Jerome D. Frank, "Psychotherapy: The Restoration of Morale," *American Journal of Psychiatry* 131, no. 3 (March 1974): 271.
4. E. Henrich and L. Kriegel, eds., *Experiments in Survival* (New York: Association for the Aid of Crippled Children, 1961), p. 186, cited in Erving Goffman, *Stigma: Notes on the Management of Spoiled Identity* (Englewood Cliffs, N.J.: Prentice-Hall, 1963), p. 33.
5. See Roger G. Barker, in collaboration with Beatrice A. Wright, Lee Meyerson, and Mollie R. Gonick, *Adjustment to Physical Handicap and Illness: A Survey of the Social Psychology of Physique and Disability* (New York: Social Science Research Council, 1953).
6. Roger G. Barker, "The Social Psychology of Physical Disability," *Journal of Social Issues* 34, no. 4 (1948): 33, cited in Goffman, *Stigma*, p. 14.
7. Goffman, *Stigma*, p. 14.
8. Fred Davis, "Deviance Disavowal: The Management of Strained Interaction by the Visibly Handicapped," in *The Other Side*, ed. Howard S. Becker (New York: Free Press, 1964), p. 123.
9. Ibid., p. 124.
10. Ibid., p. 125.
11. Ibid., p. 128.
12. Ibid., p. 129.
13. Ibid., p. 132.
14. Interview conducted by the authors, New York, May 1975.
15. Interview conducted by the authors, New York, May 1975.
16. For much more comprehensive surveys of possible ego defenses, see Gordon W. Allport, *The Nature of Prejudice*, abr. ed. (Garden City, N.Y.: Doubleday, 1958), and Barker et al., *Adjustment to Physical Handicap and Illness*.
17. For a good discussion of the problems encountered by individuals in this last category, see William G. Niederland, "Narcissistic Ego Impairment in Patients with Early Physical Malformations," Appendix 1 in this book, pp. 349–63.
18. See J. M. Baldwin, *Social and Ethical Interpretations in Mental De-*

velopment (New York: Macmillan, 1906), and *Genetic Theory of Reality* (New York: Putnam's, 1915); Jean Piaget, *The Moral Judgment of the Child*, trans. Marjorie Gabain (London: Routledge and Kegan Paul, 1932); Bärbel Inhelder and Jean Piaget, *The Growth of Logical Thinking from Childhood to Adolescence*, trans. Anne Parsons and Stanley Milgram (New York: Basic Books, 1958), chapter 18, "Adolescent Thinking," pp. 334–50; Lawrence Kohlberg, "The Development of Children's Orientations toward a Moral Order. I. Sequence in the Development of Moral Thought," *Vita Humana* 6 (1963): 11–33; "Stage and Sequence: The Cognitive-Developmental Approach to Socialization," in *Handbook of Socialization Theory and Research*, ed. David A. Goslin (Chicago: Rand McNally, 1969), pp. 347–480; and "From Is to Ought: How to Commit the Naturalistic Fallacy and Get Away with It in the Study of Moral Development," in *Cognitive Development and Epistemology*, ed. Theodore Mischel (New York: Academic Press, 1971), pp. 151–235.

19. Kohlberg stands alone in making this claim for a moral theory (Piaget's own theory antedates by nearly a decade his theory of cognitive development.) Kohlberg's attempt to provide a principled account for the ordering of his two highest stages of development (stage five and stage six; see text) has been criticized especially harshly by philosophers. See R. S. Peters, "Moral Developments: A Plea for Pluralism," in *Cognitive Development and Epistemology*, ed. Mischel, pp. 237–67; and William P. Alston, "Comments on Kohlberg's 'From Is to Ought,'" ibid., pp. 269–84.

A critique of the entire ordering of stages is suggested by Henry Sidgwick's classic objection to Kantian moral theory: Henry Sidgwick, *The Methods of Ethics*, 7th ed. (London: Macmillan, 1907), Appendix, "The Kantian Conception of Free Will," pp. 511–16. In effect, Sidgwick's objection is that it is always possible to formulate any morality whatsoever—however base or primitive—in a logically sophisticated way that satisfies Kant's definition of the highest stage of morality. Since Kohlberg defines the highest stage of moral development in his theory in explicitly Kantian terms, his ordering of moral stages is vulnerable to Sidgwick's objection. That is, there is no way on purely logical grounds to justify the superiority of any one moral stage over another. For more on Sidgwick, see John Rawls, *A Theory of Justice* (Cambridge, Mass.: Harvard University Press, 1971), pp. 254–57.

Kohlberg himself often seems to confuse a justification of the ordering of his stages on purely structural grounds with a justification that is based upon the semantic content of the different stages. Thus, while Kohlberg frequently asserts that the invariance of the stages in his or in any other "cognitive-developmental" theory can be established only by a rigorous "logical analysis" of the "development of a [e.g., moral] concept or category" ("Stage and Sequence," p. 355), he seems to mean two very different things by the phrase "logical analysis": (1) deriving stage invariance by examining the formal structure of each stage, and (2) deriving stage invariance by examining the increasing semantic differentiation of the concept of morality embodied in each stage. See, for example, such remarks as "Our moral stages represent successive forms of reciprocity, each more differentiated and universalized than the preceding form" (p. 398). However, the concept of "increasing differentiation" is especially vague and can be easily invoked to justify virtually any ordering of moral stages, including, for example, the inverse of Kohlberg's ordering of his stages. For more examples of Kohlberg's confusion of semantic description and structural description, see ibid., pp. 352–61 and 375–89.

This oversight also raises difficulties for the theory's claim to provide a way to assess the individual's stage of moral development. An empirical ordering of stages—based in part on the semantic content of each stage—may primarily reflect the child's growing factual knowledge about the world, not the growing complexity (or maturation) of his powers of moral judgment. As Gobar notes, cognitive theorists often conflate structure and content in their own research: "As a result of this illicit transition, the concrete knowledge of the subject is sometimes taken as the index of his intelligence," or, we would add, of his level of moral development. See Ash Gobar, *Philosophic Foundations of Genetic Psychology and Gestalt Psychology* (The Hague: Martinus Nijhoff, 1968).

20. That is, the attainment of a given (Piagetian) stage of cognitive development appears to be a necessary but not a sufficient condition for attaining certain levels of moral reasoning. For a review of the relevant research, see Charles Blake Keasey, "Implicators of Cognitive Development for Moral Reasoning," in *Moral Development: Current Theory and Research*, ed. David J. De Palma and Jeanne M. Foley (Hillsdale, N.J.: Lawrence Erlbaum Associates, 1975), pp. 39–56, especially pp. 40–50.

But the constraints placed upon moral development by cognitive development are sufficiently loose to permit a substantial number of reorderings of Kohlberg's six stages (i.e., permuting the order of the stages in each of the three main subdivisions of the theory or, for that matter, in destroying any ordering within each of these main subdivisions).

21. An emphasis upon verbal measures of morality is a serious shortcoming of moral theories such as Kohlberg's. At least in adolescents and adults it seems distinctly odd to assume that an ability to verbalize one's moral reasons for an action should place a ceiling upon the actual moral theory that is embodied in one's moral behavior (the algorithm, or, to use Kant's term, the "maxim," that guides one's action). We suspect that just as Piaget gradually found it necessary to discard his original emphasis upon verbal report and to look at the full gamut of cognitive problem-solving *behavior*, a similar broadening of the assessment measures is called for in the study of moral development, especially when the individuals studied grow up in a culture that, unlike mainstream American middle-class culture, places little or no emphasis upon being able to verbalize tacit moral reasoning. (Again, it is worth recalling that Piaget's main work on moral development was done early in his career, when he still placed disproportionate importance upon purely verbal measures of development.)

22. Kohlberg, "Stage and Sequence," p. 398.
23. Ibid.
24. See Inhelder and Piaget, *The Growth of Logical Thinking from Child-hood to Adolescence*, and Jean Piaget, "L'explication en sociologie" and "Les opérations logiques et la vie sociale," in *Études Sociologiques* (Geneva: Droz, 1965), pp. 15–99 and 143–71.
25. Kohlberg attributes this remark to George Herbert Mead (Kohlberg, "Stage and Sequence," p. 399).
26. See note 19.
27. Kohlberg, "Stage and Sequence," p. 399.
28. The special situation of the handicapped child is brought out well by contrasting it to Kohlberg's description of the social world in which the able-bodied child grows up: "Instead of participation in various groups causing conflicting developmental trends in morality, it appears that participation in various groups converges in stimulating the development of basic moral values. . . . While various people and groups make conflicting *immediate* demands upon the child, they do not seem to present the child with basically conflicting or different stimulation for *general moral* development" (ibid., p. 402).
29. See ibid., pp. 375–89.
30. Kohlberg finds that about half of an individual's moral responses (as assessed by his tests) fall into a given stage. The rest of the individual's responses are distributed among higher and lower stages (ibid., Figure 6.4, p. 387).
31. Relatively few individuals achieve stage six morality, as measured by Kohlberg's tests (ibid., pp. 382–86). For more on this point, see L. Kohlberg and R. Kramer, "Continuities and Discontinuities in Childhood and Adult Moral Development," *Human Development* 12 (1969): 93–120.

6 • Personality Development

1. There is a growing interest in constructing falsifiable theories of personality. For examples of some of the main lines along which this work is proceeding, see Robert R. Holt, ed., *Motives and Thought: Psychoanalytic Essays in Honor of David Rapaport* (New York: International Universities Press, 1967), vol. 5, no. 2-3, monograph 18-19 in the series Psychological Issues; Maria Nowakowska, *Language of Motivation and Language of Actions* (The Hague: Mouton, 1973); Norman N. Holland, "Defense, Displacement and the Ego's Algebra," *International Journal of Psychoanalysis* 54 (1973): 247–57; and Marshall Edelson, *Language and Interpretation in Psychoanalysis* (New Haven: Yale University Press, 1975).
2. Greta Lehner Bibring, "A Study of the Psychological Processes in Pregnancy," *Psychoanalytic Study of the Child* 16 (1961): 9–72.
3. In what follows we have tried to paraphrase Erikson's own description of his eight stages as closely as possible. All our quotations are from

Erik H. Erikson, *Childhood and Society*, 2d ed. (New York: W. W. Norton and Company, 1963), pp. 247–69.

4. For Erikson's position on this important point, see *Childhood and Society*, pp. 273–74.

5. Of all social philosophers it is perhaps Ernest Becker who has most clearly spelled out the significance of the vast change in the cultural attitude toward death which has attended the triumphs of modern medicine. See Ernest Becker, *The Denial of Death* (New York: Free Press, 1973).

6. Our focus upon the child has made it impossible to explore in any detail the problems of the elderly in American life. We believe that one of the greatest of these problems is that even the able-bodied elderly person is often forced to submit to a version of the handicapped role. For an analysis that supports this view, see Irving Rosow, *Socialization to Old Age* (Berkeley: University of California Press, 1974).

7. Carol Barth, letter, *The New York Times*, June 1, 1978.

8. For an excellent overview of these defenses, see Gordon Allport, *The Nature of Prejudice*, abr. ed. (Garden City, N.Y.: Doubleday, 1958), chapter 9, "Traits due to Victimization," pp. 138–58. Other excellent discussions appear in Beatrice A. Wright, *Physical Disability—A Psychological Approach* (New York: Harper & Row, 1960); Kurt Lewin, *Resolving Human Conflicts* (New York: Harper & Row, 1948), chapter 9, "Psycho-Sociological Problems of a Minority Group," pp. 145–58, chapter 10, "When Facing Danger," pp. 159–68, chapter 11, "Bringing Up the Jewish Child," pp. 169–85, and chapter 12, "Self-Hatred among Jews," pp. 186–200.

9. Oliver Sacks, *Awakenings* (Garden City, N.Y.: Doubleday, 1974).

10. In Gilman D. Grave and I. Barry Pless, eds., *Chronic Childhood Illness: Assessment of Outcome* (Washington, D.C.: U.S. Department of Health, Education and Welfare, 1976), DHEW Publication No: (NIH) 76-877, p. 151.

7 • Intellectual Development

1. Despite the large body of research concerning preoperational thought, the theory concerning this period has registered scarcely any advances since Piaget's summing-up over twenty years ago—see Jean Piaget, *Logic and Psychology*, trans. W. Mays (New York: Basic Books, 1954), pp. 47–48. If anything, Piaget's recent attempts to explore the relationship between the sensory-motor schemes and the appearance of concrete operations in representational thought renders the preoperational period even more mysterious from a theoretical perspective; the roughly four years that intervene between the maturation of the sensory-motor schemes around age two and the first appearances of concrete operations in representational thought around age six have been intensively studied but remain a *terra incognita*. For more on the relationship between sensory-motor schemes and concrete operational thought, however, see

note 11 below. Also see the conjectures about the importance of memory capacity in cognitive development that are discussed in note 16.

2. For excellent summaries of these criticisms, see Daniel N. Osherson, *Logical Abilities in Children*, vol. 1 (Potomac, Md.: Lawrence Erlbaum Associates, 1974), and *Logical Abilities in Children*, vol. 3 (Potomac, Md.: Lawrence Erlbaum Associates, 1975).

3. For good introductions to the structure of concrete operational thought, see Piaget, *Logic and Psychology*; John H. Flavell, *The Developmental Psychology of Jean Piaget* (New York: Van Nostrand, 1963); and Osherson, *Logical Abilities in Children*, vol. 1.

4. Jean Piaget, "L'Explication en Sociologie," in *Études Sociologiques* (Geneva: Droz, 1965), p. 90. Although the essay originally appeared in 1951, Piaget specifically reaffirms his agreement with it in his 1965 preface. (This and all subsequent translations from the *Études* are by John Gliedman.)

5. Ibid., p. 87.

6. Ibid., p. 87.

7. Ibid., p. 90.

8. Iris Murdoch, *Sartre: Romantic Rationalist* (New Haven: Yale University Press, 1953).

9. With regard to our ensuing discussion, a number of general observations are in order.

To begin with, we shall not make any attempt to deal comprehensively with the technical issues raised by our approach. Our technical notes will be designed to dispel possible misunderstandings of our position and to flesh out some of our key points.

Second, while the questions we will raise deserve to be studied for all children, the exceptional complexity of the handicapped child's socialization experiences may make studies of the handicapped the best place to explore these issues.

Third, despite our decision to focus our own discussion exclusively upon the special socialization experiences of a handicapped childhood, we must reiterate that the impact of the child's handicap upon development—and, as in the case of blind or deaf children, the complex interactions between the limitations of the disability and social experience—deserve equally close scrutiny from a Piagetian perspective.

Finally, because of the special focus of our discussion, we will not be able to discuss the growing body of Piagetian studies of social cognition. This work focuses upon an area of development that borders the issues we raise: the ability of representational thought—when viewed exclusively via the algebraic structures singled out by Piaget in his theory—to solve problems in social reasoning. For a research review, see John H. Flavell, "The Development of Inferences about Others," in *Understanding Other Persons*, ed. Theodore Mischel (Totowa, N.J.: Rowman and Littlefield, 1974), pp. 66–116. Also see note 33.

10. Charles Parsons, "Inhelder and Piaget's *The Growth of Logical Thinking*. II. A Logician's Viewpoint," *British Journal of Psychology* 51, no. 1 (1960): 75.

11. At this point it may be useful to review Piaget's position on the dif-

ferences (and the relationship) between representational thought and behavior. This review will provide us with an opportunity to clarify for the specialist some of the points that we raise in the text.

Piaget's recent work establishes a clear distinction between the logical complexity of the child's behavior and the logical complexity of his conscious thinking about his behavior. When behavior is governed by unconscious mental processes—as is the case for motor behavior—it may evince a logical complexity far in advance of the logical structure of conscious representational thought. Because of Piaget's theory of knowledge (see Jean Piaget, *Biology and Knowledge*, trans. Beatrix Walsh [Chicago: University of Chicago Press, 1971]), Piaget has focused most of his attention in experiments upon the relationship between one kind of unconscious knowledge and the emergence of the algebraic structures of concrete operational thinking into representational thought. This unconscious knowledge is that which is contained in the network of sensory-motor schemes that reach their full development around age two. From a formal point of view, the algebraic structures of sensory-motor behavior "prefigure certain aspects of the structures of categories and relations" and represent "a kind of logic of coordination of actions" ("Language and Intellectual Operations," in *The Child and Reality*, trans. Arnold Rosin [New York: Grossman, 1973], p. 116). Not until the level of concrete operations (ages seven to eleven) will "the group of displacements [which define sensory-motor thought be] . . . reconstructed on the representational plane" (*The Mechanisms of Perception*, trans. G. N. Seagrim [London: Routledge and Kegan Paul, 1969], p. 352), and it is not until the child begins to achieve the stage of formal operations (around age eleven or twelve) that the logical complexity of representational thought finally surpasses the logical complexity of sensory-motor behavior (*Réussir et Comprendre* [Paris: Presses Universitaires de France, 1974], p. 6).

Thus—and Piaget again seems to have in mind the special relationship between sensory-motor structures and the development of representational thought during the concrete operational period—cognitive development is dependent upon two separate processes: first, the progressive construction of the sensory-motor "schemes" during early childhood, and second, after the elaboration of this logic of actions, the "reconstruction on an upper level [i.e., in representational thought] of what is already organized in another manner on a lower level" ("Affective and Cognitive Unconscious," in *The Child and Reality*, p. 40).

Piaget's analysis of social behavior is much less ambitious. As noted in the text, he always seems to have in mind cooperation between individuals, as reflected by their mastery of the rules of a game or their adoption of a Kantian perspective on morality; that is, behavior whose logical form may well be captured by the algebraic structures singled out by his theory (those of concrete operational thought and prepositional logic). Having defined social behavior so narrowly, Piaget then argues that social thought develops in tandem with cognition, and that both kinds of representational thinking advance as a result of the reconstruction on the conscious plane of the unconscious acquisitions of the sensory-motor period. Piaget pays a steep price for achieving this symmetry between cognitive and social development. He must ignore altogether the many kinds of interpersonal behavior exhibited by young children that appear to possess an algebraic structure with no counterpart in his theory—especially the kind of behavior in diadic relationships that has been described by such sociologists as Erving Goffman, by psychoanalysts, and by such psychiatrists as R. D. Laing, H. Phillipson, and A. R. Lee (*Interpersonal Perception—A Theory and a Method of Research* [New York: Springer, 1966]). See our text, pp. 129–36.

If, as we suspect, these non-Piagetian forms of social behavior are initially unconscious, we must take seriously the existence of what might be called a "sensory-social" period during which their logical structures are elaborated, either in a manner analogous to the stages of sensory-motor thought or in a manner analogous to the development of language. In either case, we will need to ask the same kinds of questions about the relation between "sensory-*social*" knowledge and representational thought as Piaget and his collaborators have been asking about the relationship between sensory-*motor* knowledge and representational thought. See Jean Piaget, *The Grasp of Consciousness*, trans. Susan Wedgewood (Cambridge, Mass.: Harvard University Press, 1976), and Piaget, *Résussir et Comprendre*.

The central problem posed by the relationship between any unconscious "autonomous" competence, such as sensory-motor thought (*Réussir et Comprendre*, p. 231), and representational thought has been clearly stated by Piaget: "Why do certain sensory-motor schemes become conscious (by an expression in representative and even verbal concepts) whereas others remain unconscious?" ("Affective and Cognitive Unconscious," in *The Child and Reality*, p. 39). According to Piaget, the reason is that—in ways that must be carefully explored—many sensory-motor schemes contradict some of the child's conscious ideas about the nature of the physical world, until the period of formal operations. Where these conflicts exist, they are often resolved in favor of long-established conscious ideas: the development of representational thought during the period of concrete operations is, in fact, the record of the progressive replacement of incorrect conscious ideas about the structure of the physical world by ideas that reconstruct the information encoded in the "schemes of action." But where do the child's mistaken ideas about the world come from—e.g., his tendency to anthromorphize? Is it possible that many of these ideas come from areas of his social behavior that have been overlooked by Piaget? Might the child initially model parts of his conscious representation of the physical world on his social experience, perhaps especially those aspects of his social experience whose logical structure is not captured by any of the algebraic structures singled out for special attention by Piagetian theory—e.g., the structure of his diadic relationships with parents?

The relationship of other autonomous unconscious competences to the development of representational thought is also veiled in obscurity. Piaget himself displays great ambiguity in his writings on the relationship between language and representational thought (e.g., "Language and Intellectual Operations," in *The Child and Reality*, pp. 109–24). Theodore Mischel has recently explored the difficulties with Piaget's still vaguer attempts to demonstrate that the logical structure of the Freudian unconscious also develops in tandem with the logical structure of representational thought. See Theodore Mischel, "Piaget: Cognitive Conflict and the Motivation of Thought," in *Cognitive Development and Epistemology,* ed. Theodore Mischel (New York: Academic Press, 1971), pp. 311–55.

Even more formidable problems are presented by Piaget's need to postulate something like an unconscious scientific problem-solving competence (i.e., a formal operational competence) in order to account for the development of sensory-motor schemes during infancy and early childhood. See William Kessen, "Early Cognitive Development: Hot or Cold?" in *Cognitive Development and Epistemology*, ed. Mischel, especially pp. 305–6. Despite the important findings of Piaget's most recent work (i.e., *The Grasp of Consciousness* and *Réussir et Comprendre*), it seems to us that a similar unconscious ability to test and evaluate alternate hypotheses is needed to explain how ideas based upon preexisting sensory-motor schemes gradually replace the child's incorrect ideas about the nature of the physical world during the period of concrete operations.

An especially striking example of the need to postulate an "unconscious scientist" at work is provided by the pre-sleep monologues produced by many young children around age two when they are just beginning to learn to talk. On the one hand, the content of these monologues strongly suggest that the child is confusing his representations with reality—a confusion that is typical of the preoperational stage. Yet if one instead focuses upon the logical *structure* of these monologues, a very different picture emerges. During a period of life in which the child can neither distinguish between internal states and the real physical world nor master the rules that govern cooperative play and cooperative games, the child displays an exquisite sensitivity to the complex phonological, morphological, and syntactic rules of his native language. The child not only practices particular morphological rules (such as using *s* for the plural) and particular sentence forms, but *corrects himself in his monologues when he makes a mistake.* This ability to learn and to employ correctly complex linguistic rules seems to require that while the child's conscious representational thought has not yet even reached the threshold of concrete operations, some part of the child's mind is functioning much in the manner of a scientist when it comes to language acquisition. For excellent examples of these pre-sleep monologues, see Ruth Hirsch Weir, *Language in the Crib* (The Hague: Mouton, 1962).

12. By "greater complexity" we have in mind two main possibilities: (1) that the mastery of a specific logical operation (such as negation) may appear in the child's special behavior or representational thought about social relationships before a mastery of the same logical operation appears in the child's representational thinking about the problems

posed by classic Piagetian tests; and (2) the child's social behavior and "social cognition" may display more complex algebraic structures than the algebraic structures of Piaget's eight groupements. In the text we shall describe one algebraic structure found in social relationships which seems more complex than any of the groupings because, among other reasons, it permits the use of both the operations of negation and conversion, whereas the use of both operations in one algebraic structure is not possible in Piaget's theory until the achievement of formal operations. See in our text "The Problem of 'Diadic Thought,' " pp. 129–36.

13. Unfortunately the key works that treat these issues remain untranslated. See Jean Piaget, *Classes, Relations et Nombres* (Paris: Vrin, 1942), *Introduction à l'Épistémologie Génétique*, vols. 1 and 2, 2d ed. (Paris: Presses Universitaires de France, 1973)—the work first appeared in 1951 in three volumes, and certain sections of vol. 3 are excluded from the new edition; and Jean Piaget, ed., *Logique et Connaissance Scientifique*, vol. 22 of *L'Encyclopédie de la Pléiade* (Paris: Gallimard, 1969). We know of no lengthy treatment of Piaget's epistemological interests in English. However, see vols. 1 and 3 of Osherson, *Logical Abilities in Children*.

14. See Piaget, *Classes, Relations et Nombres*.

15. Michael Cole, John Gay, Joseph A. Glick, and Donald W. Sharp, in association with Thomas Ciborowski, Frederick Frankel, John Kellemu, and David F. Lancy, *The Cultural Context of Learning and Thinking* (New York: Basic Books, 1971), p. 233.

16. The findings of Cole and his associates point to one of the great lacunae of Piagetian theory: its failure to provide a principled account for the transfer of a newly achieved logical ability from one area of problem solving to other areas of problem solving. For example, the child usually manifests conservation of substance around age seven or eight. Yet it is not until age nine or ten that the child's representational thinking about weight also displays conservation. Conservation of volume comes still later, around age eleven or twelve (see Piaget, "Language and Intellectual Operations," in *The Child and Reality*, p. 117). Since Piaget cannot explain why conservation first appears with substance rather than with weight or volume, there is no intrinsic reason why conservation should first appear in the child's thought about the physical world; it is only Piaget's epistemological (and, one might say, metaphysical) commitment to derive all higher stages of thought from the elementary logic of sensory-motor manipulations of physical objects that leads him to exclude social interactions (in the widest sense) from consideration. (For Piaget's epistemological position, see *Biology and Knowledge*.) Later, we discuss a possible instance in which a child first displays the mastery of some of the groupements of concrete thought in her attempts to understand the meaning of her handicap (see "Where Does the Handicapped Child First Demonstrate Mastery of the Logical Structures Described by Piagetian Theory," pp. 123–29).

The social realm may prove of special significance should Juan Pascual-Leone's proposals about the role of memory capacity in cognitive development prove correct. In brief, Pascual-Leone's suggestion is that the computational space available in the "central processor" which underlies representational thought places strong constraints on the kind of problem-solving strategies that the child can employ. As this memory capacity increases with age, the constraints weaken and the child is able to employ progressively more sophisticated strategies. In this way cognitive development reflects the growth of the number of "discrete 'chunks' of information or schemes that [the central processor] . . . can control or integrate in a single act." See Juan Pascual-Leone, "A Mathematical Model for the Transition Rule in Piaget's Developmental Stages," *Acta Psychologica* 32 (1970): 301–45, and R. Case, "Learning and Development: A Neo-Piagetian Interpretation," *Human Development* 15 (1972): 339–58. Though still poorly understood, the important role of emotions in facilitating as well as impeding memory is well documented (David Rapaport, *Emotions and Memory* [New York: International Universities Press, 1942]), as is the role played by "chunking" in reducing the memory burden in many processing tasks (G. A. Miller, "The Magical Number Seven, Plus or Minus Two: Some Limits on Our Capacity for Processing Information," *Psychological Review* 63 [1956]: 81–97). One need only postulate that some handicapped children are much more efficient at encoding social information than information about the physical world to begin to have the outlines of a theoretical reason for seeking the first evidence of the child's mastery of a new cognitive stage in the realm of the social—i.e., the more efficiently encoded the information, the more memory space in the central processer that can be devoted to the cognitive strategies employed to analyze the information. This postulated encoding efficiency would, of course, be a response to the special complexity and the special salience of social experience for a child who grows up with a stigmatized handicap.

17. See notes 11 and 16 above.
18. While the theoretical perspective that we advance in this chapter is compatible with either a nativist or a Piagetian position on mental development, it is indebted in many ways to earlier nativist criticisms of Piaget. Thus, Jerry A. Fodor has stated the miniature scientist problem in the strongest possible way by emphasizing that it seems impossible for the child to extract from an analysis of his experience in the world any logical abilities that he did not already possess. See Jerry A. Fodor, *The Language of Thought* (New York: Thomas Y. Crowell, 1975), pp. 87–95. For an earlier and very useful nativist critique of Piaget, see Claude Lévi-Strauss, *The Elementary Structures of Kinship*, rev. ed., trans. James Harle Bell, John Richard von Sturmer, and Rodney Needham (Boston: Beacon Press, 1969), chapter 7, "The Archaic Illusion," pp. 98–118. It is noteworthy that although Piaget has replied to some of Lévi-Strauss's criticisms, he has avoided confronting Lévi-Strauss's central objection. See Jean Piaget, *Structuralism*, trans. Chaninah Maschler (New York: Basic Books, 1970). Also see Noam Chomsky, *Language and Mind*, ext. ed. (New York: Harcourt Brace Jovanovich, 1972), and *Reflections on Language* (New York: Pantheon, 1975). We also found J. Mehler and T. G. Bever's research

on the achievement of conservation in very young children to have been a valuable stimulus: J. Mehler and T. G. Bever, "Cognitive Capacity of Very Young Children," *Science* 158, no. 3797 (1967): 141–42. The response of Piaget and his collaborators to the Mehler-Bever work has been less than persuasive—see, e.g., Bärbel Inhelder, Hermine Sinclair, and Magali Bovet, *Learning and the Development of Cognition*, trans. Susan Wedgewood (Cambridge, Mass.: Harvard University Press, 1974), p. 8—although, as usual, Piaget has prepared a way for reconciling these results with his theory—see the discussion of "cognitive repression" in "Affective and Cognitive Unconscious," *The Child and Reality*, pp. 31–48, and note 11 above.

19. See Appendix 1, p. 313.
20. Anna Freud, quoted by Lussier, ibid., pp. 315–16.
21. Bärbel Inhelder and Jean Piaget, *The Growth of Logical Thinking from Childhood to Adolescence*, trans. Anne Parsons and Stanley Milgram (New York: Basic Books, 1958), pp. 346–47.
22. Appendix 1, p. 313.
23. Ibid., pp. 316–18.
24. In French *décalage* means "a displacement in space or time." *Horizontal décalage* is Piaget's term for the gradual extension of a newly acquired logical ability from the set of problems on which the child first displays mastery to other problems of a similar logical form. Thus, a middle-class child first begins to show a mastery of what is called the concept of conservation of *number* around age six. Asked to say which of two rows of clay pellets contains more pellets, he will give the correct answer regardless of whether the two rows are the same length or if the row with fewer pellets is more widely spaced and is longer than the row containing more pellets. (A younger child will invariably choose the longer row, regardless of the number of pellets it contains.)

But on other problems of the same logical form, the six-year-old will not display conservation. Thus, he will not recognize that the volume of a liquid is independent of the shape of the container it is in. If he is first shown that a wide, shallow container and a tall, thin container hold the same amount of water (by pouring the contents of one into the other), he will still answer that the tall, thin container holds more water when both are filled to the brim and he is asked to make a comparison. The middle-class child does not consistently give the correct answer to this question until he is eleven or twelve.

The problem of how the child learns to transfer his new logical ability from the area in which it first appears to all problems of a similar logical form is the other side of the problem of cognitive growth touched upon in our discussion of the "miniature scientist" (see note 11 above). That is, an extremely sophisticated hypothesis-testing ability not only seems to be absolutely necessary to account for transitions between cognitive stages (e.g., the appearance of the new logical skills typical of concrete operational thought), but it seems just as necessary to account for the horizontal *décalages* that occur *within* a given stage of cognitive development. Also see note 18 above.

25. Appendix 1, p. 326.
26. See note 38 and pp. 117–18 for nontechnical clarifications of this point.
27. Ibid., p. 330.
28. Ibid.
29. Ibid.
30. Ibid.
31. Ibid., pp. 329–30.
32. We must stress that our interpretation is merely illustrative and that the example is perfectly compatible with other interpretations. (One that comes to mind is that the solution to the "eye water" problem also signifies the use of a logical operation in some ways similar to the difference relation embodied in groupement five—that Cindy neutralizes rather than negates her sense of being different, something that would require combining a difference relation with its logical reciprocal.) We do not mention these alternatives in the text because they are more complex and would add nothing to a discussion that merely seeks to indicate the kinds of questions we would like to see raised in a systematic way about the social behavior of handicapped children.
33. We believe that all children will display their most complex interpersonal behavior with those children and adults who play an especially important emotional role in their lives. Certainly clinical experience and common sense suggest this—as do the speculations about memory presented in note 16 above. Unfortunately, the small number of Piagetian studies of interpersonal behavior have completely ignored affectivity. They have explored interpersonal behavior in the schoolroom rather than in the family circle. They have not studied handicapped children. Nor have they even looked for systematic differences in problem-solving ability in an able-bodied child's interactions with his best friends, his enemies, or the new member of the class. For a research review, see John H. Flavell, "The Development of Inferences about Others."
34. Laing, Phillipson, and Lee, *Interpersonal Perception*, p. 4.
35. Ibid., p. 5.
36. A brief summary of Laing, Phillipson, and Lee's theory and notation also appears in the appendix to R. D. Laing, *Self and Others*, 2d rev. ed. (London: Tavistock, 1969), pp. 154–60.
37. If we let *I* stand for what I think about something, *O* stand for what the other person thinks about something, and use parentheses ( ) to set off each "wheel" of the adolescent's wheel-within-wheel reasoning, we have something like this:

    1. (I:I) represents what I feel about what I've done—i.e., I'm not in the least repentant about smoking in the bathroom.

    2. O:(I:I) represents what I think the teacher thinks I feel—i.e., she thinks that I am repentant.

    3. I:(O:(I:I)) represents what I think about O:(I:I)—what I think about what I think the teacher thinks I feel: i.e., she thinks that I am repentant, but I'm not repentant and therefore I've fooled her.

    The potential complexity of this nesting structure is suggested by Laing, Phillipson, and Lee's example of the king and the court flatterer.

The king, I, asks what his courtier, O, really thinks of him. The courtier answers, "I can't flatter you, sire," hoping the king takes this to mean that the courtier thinks that the king knows exactly what the courtier thinks of the king: i.e., O:(I:(O:I)). But the king, used to flattery, adds another level of complexity to the interaction by thinking to himself, "That fool thinks he can take me in with that old trick": i.e., I:(O:(I:(O:I))) (ibid., pp. 157–58).

38. The preoperational stage takes its name from a very general property of the logical abilities characteristic of later cognitive stages and is a good example of the way in which what seems to the nonspecialist an apparently trivial feature of Piagetian theory is really of great importance. The property in question is that each of the logical abilities characteristic of later stages is capable of being run backward or forward —i.e., can be used to undo what it has accomplished. In formal logic, any logical rule defined as being able to be run forward or backward is called an operation. By "preoperational period" Piaget means a time of life when the child uses logic but in a curiously dreamlike way and is unable to reconstruct the original class from its members.

For example, if asked to name two animals, the preoperational child might say, "cats and dogs." But now, if one asks, "In what ways are cats and dogs alike?" the child may say, "They have ears." That is, he will point to something else the two animals have in common. He will not reliably be able to reverse his original chain of reasoning and answer "animals." Though "ears" is in fact a much more engaging answer than "animals," it is clear that being able to retrace one's logical steps is of considerable importance in problem solving, for unless one can constantly test and probe, trying out different approaches to the same problem, advancing a few steps, then retreating a few steps, only to push on again, one's abilities to think about a problem are greatly constrained.

Around age seven, middle-class children begin to display a consistent ability to reverse some (but not all) of their logical strategies. The first logical idea to exhibit reversibility is the idea of the part-whole relation of classes which is embodied in groupement one. Each of the other groupements also possesses the property of reversibility: hence, concrete operations, the name that Piaget gives to this stage of cognitive development.

The significance, then, of saying that diadic thinking seems to require the mastery of some logical operations is that young children seem to display diadic thinking long before orthodox interpretations of Piagetian theory say that they are capable of employing *any* logical operations.

39. According to Piagetian theory, when a concrete operational child thinks about similarities between classes, he draws upon the logical strategies of groupements one through four; when the child thinks about differences between classes, he draws upon the logical strategies of groupements five through eight. A crucial feature of the concrete operational child's thinking about class differences and class similarities is the

(limited) reversibility of the child's thought. This reversibility takes a very different form with differences and similarities.

Piagetian theory claims that the concrete operational child's ability to shift his mental attention from one similarity shared by a collection of objects to some other common property depends upon the mastery of an abstract logical operation—the destruction of a class by uniting it with its logical inverse. That is, before the child can shift his mental attention from the fact that lions and tigers are flesh eaters to the fact that they have tails, the child must undo his initial construction of a class of flesh eaters (to which lions and tigers belong). This ability to reverse—i.e., to negate—the result of a prior logical operation (constructing the class of flesh eaters) defines the reversibility of the thought processes described by groupements one through four.

The concrete operational child displays a different kind of reversibility when he employs the algebraic structures of groupements five through eight. In contrast to his thinking about class similarities, the child does not directly annul a perceived difference between two classes. Instead, the child neutralizes this difference by joining the difference relation with its logical reciprocal. That is, the original difference relation remains intact, but it is now neutralized by a contrary difference relation. The theory claims that a mastery of this kind of reversibility is required before the child can carry out such apparently simple tasks as ordering a collection of sticks of unequal length according to increasing (or decreasing) size. (To do so without confusion requires the child to join in a single mental structure two otherwise contradictory facts— that every stick except the first and last is simultaneously longer and shorter than its neighbors, an ability that is possible only when the child can neutralize one difference relation by joining it to its logical reciprocal.)

For Piaget, this difference between the reversibility found in the two families of groupements is absolutely crucial. Again and again he emphasizes that the concrete operational child is unable to employ both kinds of reversibility in a single chain of reasoning. The position presented in *Logic and Psychology* is typical: "no groupements are present at the level of concrete operations to combine these two kinds of reversibility into a single system" (p. 29).

Here, then, is the significance of our point about the structure of diadic thought. Piagetian theory has no way of accounting for the possibility that young children may display both kinds of reversibility in their diadic thinking.

40.   A proposition is anything that can be asserted or denied. It is what follows—or what can follow—the word *that* in sentences like "He agreed that handicap is a complex problem," or "She said that she loved him." The relationships between classes that are embodied in the eight elementary groupements can be stated in propositional form (e.g., "It is true that De Gaulle was a Frenchman," "We believe that Jill is taller than Ronnie," etc.).

This characteristic of propositional thought shows that, in a certain sense, it can be said to operate on a "higher" or "more abstract" level than concrete operational thought. That is, instead of being confined to operating directly upon groups, formal thought can begin where concrete thought leaves off. It can think about the relationships between the relationships established by concrete operations. Moreover, since the logical relationships and logical entities contained in the eight groupements represent only a tiny fraction of all the things that can be expressed in a proposition, the range and scope of formal operational thought greatly exceeds the range and scope of concrete operational thought. It is both because propositional thought operates on a "higher" level and because it does so with a larger range of logical relationships and logical entities that Piaget calls it "formal operational thought."

Thus, although it may at first seem to be hair splitting, the claim that diadic thought involves thinking about propositions is anything but trivial from the point of view of what Piagetian theory claims to say about the young child's logical abilities. As the theory is conventionally interpreted, there is simply no way that it can account for an individual displaying an ability to reason about propositions in *any* area of his social life before adolescence. If, therefore, it should turn out that very young children do indeed display diadic thinking, then either there is something very wrong with the orthodox interpretation of Piagetian theory, or on any interpretation, the theory is incurably flawed.

Similarly, Piagetian theory claims that hypothetical thinking—framing possibilities and their thinking about them—is the exclusive preserve of formal operational thought. Concrete operational thinking is concrete thinking. The child's ratiocination is directly tied to his perceptions and manipulations of concrete objects. The theory provides no way to account for the possibility that young children may construct elaborate hypothetical structures in the course of their diadic thinking about adults.

41. Appendix 1, p. 329.

42. Susan Isaacs, *Intellectual Growth in Young Children*, vol. 1 of *The Behavior of Young Children* (London: George Routledge and Sons, 1930), p. 275.

43. Cindy's ability to employ one or more logical strategies typical or similar to those employed in groupements one through four does not necessarily conflict with our earlier suggestion that her ability to gain perspective on her handicap required her mastery of groupement one around age six. The generalization of a logical acquisition in one area of diadic thought to other areas may be as slow and laborious as the generalization of logical abilities from one kind of problem to another in classic Piagetian settings.

44. One of the more attractive features of a nativist position on cognitive development is the apparent ease with which it can provide explanations for the kind of logical precocity suggested by Cindy's thinking about retaliation. For example, suppose that Pascual-Leone's proposal about precessing capacity is correct (for a discussion, see note 16 of this

chapter). Then the well-known—but poorly understood—fact that highly meaningful material is sometimes more easily remembered than less meaningful material could account for Cindy's precocity. That is, Cindy might be able to encode at least certain kinds of information about her handicap (or her beliefs about her handicap) much more efficiently than she can encode the information presented to her in classic Piagetian cognitive tasks. This greater information-processing efficiency might permit Cindy to employ much more sophisticated logical strategies when thinking about her blind eye than when attempting to solve a Piagetian task. Moreover, differences in the relative efficiency of the information-processing strategies employed when thinking about different aspects of her blindness might account for Cindy's failure to display an apparent mastery of groupement one in her thinking about the "eye water" problem until around age six; see note 43.

However, this formulation may simply covertly restate the Piagetian position in the form of a series of unanswered (and still unasked) questions about the development of increasingly efficient information-processing strategies. Indeed, it is not even clear whether the increase in digit span between early childhood and adolescence represents, as Pascual-Leone suggests, an increase in "brute" processing capacity of the "central processor" or an improvement in the information-processing strategies used to encode random digits.

45. Flavell, *The Developmental Psychology of Jean Piaget*, p. 158.
46. Laing's model of diadic perspectives is specifically designed to formalize the structure of the "fantasies" that the individual holds about himself and other people (*Self and Others*, p. 154).
47. For the briefest of overviews, see "Affective and Cognitive Unconscious," in *The Child and Reality*, pp. 44–45; the main results of the research are reported in Jean Piaget and Bärbel Inhelder, *Memory and Intelligence*, trans. Arnold J. Pomerans (New York: Basic Books, 1973).
48. Jean Piaget, *The Psychology of Intelligence* (New York: Harcourt, Brace, 1950), p. 165.
49. The possibilities raised by our purely illustrative example of diadic thinking cry out for systematic investigation. What, for example, are the detailed structural characteristics of diadic thought? Are they identical to the algebraic structures of concrete or formal operations or, as we suspect, are there important differences? Is it possible to construct a developmental typology of algebraic structures that capture the shifts that take place in diadic thinking as the individual matures? In what sense does diadic thinking proceed by means of horizontal *décalages*, and under what conditions can the logical skills typical of diadic thinking be applied to other kinds of cognition?

For an interesting application of the approach of the logician and the transformational grammarian to psychoanalysis, see Marshall Edelson, *Language and Interpretation in Psychoanalysis* (New Haven: Yale University Press, 1975). For an ambitious attempt to formalize certain aspects of social and emotional behavior, see Maria Nowakowska, *Language of Motivation and Language of Actions* (The Hague: Mouton, 1973).

50. Our discussion of Piagetian theory has focused upon the ways that the study of handicapped children may help to shed light on many crucial theoretical issues—the locus of new logical acquisitions and how they are extended to fresh areas of experience, the relationship between social experience and cognitive development, the nature of the child's thinking about diadic relationships that involve conflict and differences in power. It remains to suggest some of the areas of applied research in handicap that stand to gain the most from the kind of basic research that we have advocated.

Later, in our discussion of special education, we will briefly consider the phenomenon of "six-hour retardation," the minority-group child who in the school is labeled "retarded" but who is indistinguishable from other children the moment the afternoon school bell rings. We will also note that an IQ in the mildly retarded range tells one remarkably little about a child's academic abilities. Some children who test poorly do equally poorly in their schoolwork. Others manage to get by and never are labeled "retarded." For these and other reasons, we believe that a careful attempt to determine the mildly retarded child's logical abilities as they display themselves in every area of social life may yield important practical dividends in our understanding of mild retardation. Furthermore, we believe these studies should be carried out in conjunction with attempts to determine how congenital or learned limitations of memory capacity and information-processing capacity affect a child's ability to demonstrate particular logical skills in different areas of life.

Similarly, we believe that the diagnosis and eventual understanding of learning disabilities—as well, indeed, as moderate and severe retardation—would be greatly improved if one attempted to obtain a comprehensive picture of the child's logical abilities, memory, capabilities, and information-processing capacities in all social areas of life, rather than only in the narrow areas of behavior that are tapped by conventional Piagetian tasks and certain neurological tests.

At present, most definitions of mental disabilities tell us very little about the problem they label. We believe that the kind of Piagetian approach we have described in these pages holds out great promise for ultimately providing genuinely functional definitions of the mental handicaps.

Ultimately, one of the main reasons for studying the development of the handicapped child must be to learn how to arm him with those skills and tools that will enhance as much as possible his ability to survive as an individual in a world that seems bent on denying his humanity at every step. We want him to benefit from the improved self-esteem, parental approval, and respect of his peers that good academic performance can sometimes buy. We want him to use his great sociological strengths in the service of survival, not in the service of self-pity or self-destructive neurosis.

Two groups of handicapped children seem to us to represent the best place to begin this difficult task: those children who, like Peter, the adolescent with deformed arms, are examples of the exceptionally successful handicapped individual, and those children who, despite significant sensory or physical handicaps, appear to the casual observer to develop normally. Handicap is in many respects one of the cruelest "experiments of nature." The blind child, the deaf child, the crippled child whose mobility is severely limited, the child with cerebral palsy who is incapable of speech, all face special obstacles in learning about the world. They are denied significant families of experiences that the able-bodied child can take for granted. If normal or above-average intellectual development nonetheless takes place, it behooves us as psychologists to find out how and why. Before we can learn to help the handicapped child help himself, we must study those children who have learned on their own how to help themselves. And given the enormously greater importance of social experience in the lives of such children, it would be odd indeed if part of the secret of their success did not reside in their ability to build bridges between those areas of social life where, because of stigma or the special physical or sensory limitations of their handicap, they first display their most advanced intellectual abilities.

8 • Parents and Professionals

1. For overviews of funding needs, see James S. Kakalik, Garry D. Brewer, Laurence A. Dougharty, Patricia D. Fleischauer, Samuel M. Genensky, and Linda M. Wallen, *Improving Services to Handicapped Children* (Santa Monica, Calif.: Rand Corporation, 1974), and *The White House Conference on Handicapped Individuals*, vol. 1, *Awareness Papers* (Washington, D.C.: U.S. Government Printing Office, 1977).
2. *Federal Register* 41, no. 138 (July 16, 1976): 29548–49.
3. See Talcott Parsons, *Social Structure and Personality* (New York: Free Press, 1964), chapter 10, "Definitions of Health and Illness in the Light of American Values and Social Structure," and chapter 12, "Some Theoretical Considerations Bearing on the Field of Medical Sociology."
4. For an overview, see Christopher Lasch, *Haven in a Heartless World: The Family Besieged* (New York: Basic Books, 1977).
5. David Kirp, William Buss, and Peter Kuriloff, "Legal Aspects of Special Education: Empirical Studies and Procedural Proposals," *California Law Review* 62, no. 40 (1974): 47.
6. Charles Perrow, *Organizational Analysis: A Sociological View* (Belmont, Calif.: Wadsworth Publishing Co., 1970), p. 67.
7. For overviews, see Elihu Katz and Brenda Danet, eds., *Bureaucracy and the Public: A Reader in Official-Client Relations* (New York: Basic Books, 1973); besides many useful articles, the anthology contains an excellent general bibliography. Also see Michael Crozier, *The Bureaucratic Phenomenon* (Chicago: University of Chicago Press, 1964), and James G. March, ed., *Handbook of Organizations* (Chicago: Rand McNally, 1965).

Some of the most interesting studies of professional behavior have been carried out in medical sociology. See Eliot Freidson, *Profession of*

Medicine: A Study of the Sociology of Applied Knowledge (New York: Dodd, Mead, 1971), and *Doctoring Together: A Study of Professional Self-Control* (New York: Elsevier, 1976); and Marcia Millman, *The Unkindest Cut: Life in the Backrooms of Medicine* (New York: William Morrow, 1977). Millman's "Suggestions for Reading" provide a brief overview of the burgeoning medical sociology literature.

Useful insight into the socialization influences to which professionals are subjected is provided by the concept of the "deviant career." See Howard S. Becker, *Outsiders: Studies in the Sociology of Deviance*, exp. ed. (New York: Free Press, 1973). For good discussions of the general structural and ideological pressures that often constrain or determine professional behavior, see Albert O. Hirschman, *Exit, Voice, and Loyalty* (Cambridge, Mass.: Harvard University Press, 1970); Herbert A. Simon, *Administrative Behavior*, 2d ed. (New York: Macmillan, 1957); and Herbert A. Simon, *The Sciences of the Artificial* (Cambridge, Mass.: MIT Press, 1969). Also see Sheldon Wolin, *Politics and Vision* (Boston: Little, Brown, 1960), chapter 10, "The Age of Organization and the Sublimation of Politics"; and D. L. Rosenhan, "On Being Sane in Insane Places," *Science* 179, no. 4070 (1973): 25–258.

8. Freidson, *Profession of Medicine*, p. 353.

9. Parsons, *Social Structure and Personality*. The concept comes from Max Weber. See chapter 8, "Bureaucracy," in H. H. Gerth and C. Wright Mills, eds., *From Max Weber: Essays in Sociology* (New York: Oxford University Press, 1958).

10. See our discussion of the handicapped role in chapter 2.

11. Kathryn A. Gorham, Charlotte Des Jardins, Ruth Page, Eugene Pettis, and Barbara Scheiber, "Effects on Parents," in *Issues in the Classification of Children*, vol. 2, ed. Nicholas Hobbs (San Francisco: Jossey-Bass, 1975), pp. 160–63.

12. Beatrice A. Wright, *Physical Disability: A Psychological Approach* (New York, Harper & Row, 1960), p. 292.

13. See Robert A. Scott, "Comments about Interpersonal Processes of Rehabilitation," in *Sociology and Rehabilitation*, ed. Marvin B. Sussman (Washington, D.C.: American Sociological Association, 1965), p. 135.

14. For the institutional extreme, see Rosenhan, "On Being Sane in Insane Places"; for a somewhat overdrawn portrait of professional abuses outside the total institution, see Thomas Szasz, *The Myth of Mental Illness* (New York: Harper & Row, 1961). Perhaps the most sensitive and sophisticated discussion of the line between "maladjustment" and legitimate difference is Oliver W. Sacks's extraordinary book about the victims of Parkinson's disease, *Awakenings* (Garden City, N.Y.: Doubleday, 1974). Also see "The Therapeutic Despair," in Leslie H. Farber, *The Ways of the Will*, rev. ed. (New York: Basic Books, 1966), and Lasch, *Haven in a Heartless World*.

15. See the many illuminating examples in Lisbeth Bamberger Schorr, Wendy Lazarus, Judith Humphreys Weitz, and staff, *Doctors and Dollars Are Not Enough* (Washington, D.C.: Children's Defense Fund, 1976).

16. See Talcott Parsons's description of the "affective component" in the

traditional doctor-patient relationship in *Social Structure and Personality*. Also see the classic statements of a humanistic vision of the doctor-patient relationship cited in note 27 of chapter 11.

17. Gorham et al., "Effects on Parents," pp. 170–73.

18. Millman, *The Unkindest Cut,* pp. 194–95.

19. Interview obtained by William Roth, New York, February 1974.

20. Many factors contribute to the professional's perceptual biases besides his expectations about what constitutes appropriate conduct in a client. These include setting (see note 14 for this chapter), the kind of information that is often supplied to the professional by other professionals who refer the client to him (see the discussion of the perceptual effects of misinformation on the perceptions of psychotherapists in chapter 11, note 13), the misleading interpretations of normal interpersonal cues that are fostered by the enormous asymmetry in the respective positions of parent and professional in the service relationship (see the discussion of able-bodied–handicapped interactions in chapters 1 and 5).

21. Group for the Advancement of Psychiatry, *Mental Retardation: A Family Crisis. The Therapeutic Role of the Physician,* Report no. 56, formulated by the Committee on Mental Retardation (New York, December 1963), pp. 132–33.

    The G.A.P. has recently issued a report directed at the psychiatric consultant (Group for the Advancement of Psychiatry, *Psychiatric Consultation in Mental Retardation,* Report no. 104, formulated by the Committee on Mental Retardation [New York, October 1979]). In some ways the attitudes toward parents expressed in *Psychiatric Consultation in Mental Retardation* represent a considerable advance. For example, the report deals in an evenhanded manner with the often irrational behavior of parents and professionals following the birth of a retarded child: "Denial, anger, magical thinking, bargaining or withdrawal and depression appear as defenses against working out the narcissistic injury (the parent's witsh for a perfect child, or the professional's empathy for the parents and the wish to be omnipotent and curative)." The authors also urge the psychiatric consultant not to "under-estimate the serious stresses and frequent frustration encountered by parents of retarded children—particularly with doctors and professionals—or the tremendous strengths, patience, and constructive attitudes of most parents." But the report does not develop these generalities in any detail (though see vignette no. 17), completely ignores the kinds of complex ethical and political issues raised by Carla's narrative (even though vignette no. 18 describes in a higly abbreviated form a rather similar experience), fails to even consider the possibility that some breakdowns in the doctor-parent relationship stem from a clash of competing moralities, and exclusively relies upon psychodynamic mechanisms to "explain" any and all lapses from "rational" behavior by parents and the professionals who work with them.

22. See our remarks on the social pathology model in chapter 3, and our discussion of the shortcomings of the adjustment approach in chapter 11. Also see Nicholas N. Kittrie, *The Right to Be Different: Deviance and Enforced Therapy* (Baltimore: Johns Hopkins University Press, 1971).

23. Let us again emphasize that there is compelling evidence that experienced psychotherapists are perhaps the only group of professionals who can generally be counted on to negotiate this difficult task successfully. See Jerome D. Frank, *Persuasion and Healing*, rev. ed. (Baltimore: Johns Hopkins University Press, 1973).
24. Harold Lasswell, *Power and Society: A Framework for Political Inquiry* (New Haven: Yale University Press, 1950), p. 124.
25. For more on the tendencies of all organizations to ossify, see especially Hirschman, *Exit, Voice, and Loyalty*.

9 • Special Education at a Turning Point

1. Similar estimates were given for the number of children served in the 1970s before the implementation of the Education for All Handicapped Children Act of 1975. For a range of 450,000 to over 4 million children and youths receiving no educational services whatsoever, see David L. Kirp, "Schools as Sorters: The Constitutional and Policy Implications of Student Classification," *University of Pennsylvania Law Review* 121, no. 4 (April 1973): 724. For an estimate of 1 million, see Alan Abeson, Robert L. Burgdorf, Jr., Patrick J. Casey, Joseph W. Kunz, and Wanda McNeil, "Access to Opportunity," in *Issues in the Classification of Children*, vol. 2, ed. Nicholas Hobbs (San Francisco: Jossey-Bass, 1975), p. 271. Hobbs himself estimates that the numbers range between 450,000 and nearly 2 million; see Nicholas Hobbs, *The Futures of Children* (San Francisco: Jossey-Bass, 1975), p. 280. A figure of 1 million was adopted by the framers of Public Law 94-142.

   For an estimate of the number of handicapped children and youths served by special education programs in the early 1970s, see James S. Kakalik, Garry D. Brewer, Laurence A. Dougharty, Patricia D. Fleischauer, and Samuel M. Genensky, *Services for Handicapped Youth: A Program Overview* (Santa Monica, Calif.: Rand Corporation, 1973), pp. 59–60. A similar estimate is made in Public Law 94-142. Also see Alan Abeson and Jeffrey Zettel, "The End of the Quiet Revolution: The Education for All Handicapped Children Act of 1975," *Exceptional Children*, October 1977, p. 121.
2. Public Law 94-142, 1975, Section 3(c).
3. Frederick J. Weintraub, "Editorial Comment," *Exceptional Children*, October 1977, p. 114.
4. For example, the Children's Defense Fund had to spend four years in the courts to obtain a consent decree directing the state of Mississippi to obey the provisions of Public Law 94-142. See Gene I. Maeroff, "Suit Spurring Mississippi Efforts to Teach Handicapped Children," *The New York Times*, April 5, 1979; the Children's Defense Fund press release on the decree; and the decree itself (copies are available from the Children's Defense Fund). The 1980s are likely to see many other lawsuits that attempt to get the states to comply with a law that has been on the books since 1975.
5. In preparing this brief history we have benefited greatly from the fol-

lowing invaluable surveys: Kirp, "Schools as Sorters"; David Kirp, William Buss, and Peter Kuriloff, "Legal Reform of Special Education: Empirical Studies and Procedural Proposals," *California Law Review* 62, no. 40 (1974): 40–155; William G. Buss, David L. Kirp, and Peter J. Kuriloff, "Exploring Procedural Models of Special Classification," in *Issues in the Classification of Children*, vol. 2, ed. Hobbs, pp. 386–431; David L. Kirp, Peter J. Kuriloff, and William G. Buss, "Legal Mandates and Organizational Change," in *Issues in the Classification of Children*, vol. 2, ed. Hobbs, pp. 319–82; and Abeson and Zettel, "The End of the Quiet Revolution."

6. See Nicholas N. Kittrie, *The Right to Be Different: Deviance and Enforced Therapy* (Baltimore: Johns Hopkins University Press, 1971), and Joseph Goldstein, Anna Freud, and Albert J. Solnit, *Beyond the Best Interests of the Child* (New York: Free Press, 1973).

7. Kirp, Buss, and Kuriloff, "Legal Reform of Special Education," pp. 51–52 and note 327, p. 121.

8. Public Law 94-142 explicitly states that the school's responsibilities to the parents are not to be interpreted as defining a contract between the school and the parents. For some of the arguments in favor of establishing a contractual relationship, see Abeson et al., "Access to Opportunity," pp. 270–92.

9. Kirp, "Schools as Sorters," pp. 760–61.

10. See David J. Franks, "Ethnic and Social Status Characteristics of Children in EMR and LD Classes," *Exceptional Children*, March 1971, pp. 537–38. Eleven of the twelve Missouri school districts receiving state aid for educably mentally retarded (EMR) and learning disability (LD) classes were surveyed. Whereas about one-third of all children in EMR classes were black, only about 3 percent of all children in LD classes were black. White children accounted for about two-thirds of all students in EMR classes and about 97 percent of all students in LD classes.

11. A similar pattern is suggested by other statistics. In California in the early 1970s, 58.2 percent of all students in educably mentally retarded classes were male, whereas 80.9 percent of all students in educably handicapped (or learning disability) classes were male (Kirp, Kuriloff, and Buss, "Legal Mandates and Organizational Change," note 219, p. 369). This disproportion is precisely what one would expect if white male children with ambiguous learning problems were preferentially classified as learning-disabled while minority male children displaying similar performance problems in school were preferentially classified as mentally retarded. Also see Jane R. Mercer, *Labeling the Mentally Retarded* (Berkeley: University of California Press, 1973).

12. Kirp, "Schools as Sorters," p. 748.

13. For more on the mainstreaming belief, see "Full Educational Opportunities for Handicapped Children," Awareness Paper prepared by the Council for Exceptional Children for the (1977) White House Conference on Handicapped Individuals.

14. For useful cautions on the dangers of unthinking mainstreaming, see Donald L. Macmillan, Reginald L. Jones, and C. Edward Meyers,

"Mainstreaming the Mildly Retarded: Some Questions, Cautions and Guidelines," *Mental Retardation* 14, no. 1 (February 1976): 3–10; and Richard H. Bartlett, "Politics, Litigations, and Mainstreaming: Special Education's Demise," *Mental Retardation* 15, no. 1 (February 1977): 24–26. Insight into the complexity of the issues involved (for the mildly retarded) is provided by Reginald L. Jones, "Labels and Stigma in Special Education," *Exceptional Children*, March 1972, pp. 553–74. Also see our discussion of mainstreaming in chapter 10.

15. Kirp, "Schools as Sorters," pp. 724–27, especially p. 727.
16. Abeson and Zettel, "The End of the Quiet Revolution," p. 118.
17. Ibid., p. 121.
18. Ibid., pp. 119–20.
19. Ibid., p. 120.
20. Because of the fast-changing character of this area, we shall restrict our comments to general points and principles. For the same reason we shall not attempt to assess the effectiveness of the much more thoroughgoing reforms adopted by states such as Massachusetts. Many advocacy groups are actively monitoring state programs and national policy. Excellent sources of more information include the Children's Defense Fund, 1520 New Hampshire Avenue N.W., Washington, D.C. 20036; the Council on Exceptional Children, Reston, Va. 22090; and the Committee for State-Wide Monitoring of Chapter 766, c/o Mass. Advocacy Center, 2 Park Square, Boston, Mass. 02116.
21. Our discussion is based upon the printed text of the law in 89 Stat. 775. Also see the proposed implementation regulations that appear in the *Federal Register* 42, no. 163 (August 23, 1977), especially pp. 42490–91.
22. See Paragraph 121a.346, "Content of individual educational program," *Federal Register* 42, no. 163 (August 23, 1977): 42491.
23. Kirp, "Schools as Sorters," p. 787.
24. Kathryn A. Gorham, Charlotte Des Jardins, Ruth Page, Eugene Pettis, and Barbara Scheiber, "Effects on Parents," in *Issues in the Classification of Children*, vol. 2, ed. Hobbs, pp. 185–86.
25. For good discussions of the ways that a service bureaucracy can retaliate against a client who refuses to go along, see Francis Fox Piven and Richard A. Cloward, *Regulating the Poor: The Functions of Public Welfare* (New York: Random House, 1971); Richard A. Cloward and Francis Fox Piven, "Notes towards a Radical Social Work," in *Radical Social Work*, ed. Roy Bailey and Mike Brake (New York: Pantheon, 1976); and Rivka Bar-Yosef and E. O. Schild, "Pressures and Defenses in Bureaucratic Roles," *American Journal of Sociology* 75 (1966): 665–73, reprinted in Elihu Katz and Brenda Danet, eds., *Bureaucracy and the Public: A Reader in Official-Client Relations* (New York: Basic Books, 1973). Also see our discussion of client-professional relationships in chapter 8.
26. Gorham et al., "Effects on Parents," pp. 183–84.
27. Mary E. Switzer, "Remarks," in *Sociology and Rehabilitation*, ed. Marvin B. Sussman (Washington, D.C.: American Sociological Association, 1965), p. 11. Switzer was commissioner of the U.S. Vocational Rehabili-

tation Administration at the time she contributed to the Sussman volume.

28. See Albert O. Hirschman, *Exit, Voice, and Loyalty* (Cambridge, Mass.: Harvard University Press, 1970).

29. For excellent treatments, see Buss, Kirp, and Kuriloff, "Exploring Procedural Models of Special Classification," and the overlapping discussions in Kirp, Buss, and Kuriloff, "Legal Reform of Special Education," and Kirp, Kuriloff, and Buss, "Legal Mandates and Organizational Change."

30. On the potential problems raised by such oversights, see Kirp, "Schools as Sorters," pp. 788–89, and Kirp, Kuriloff, and Buss, "Legal Mandates and Organizational Change," pp. 359–60.

31. Public Law 94-142, Section 615(d).

32. Kirp, Buss, and Kuriloff, "Legal Reform of Special Education," p. 45.

33. See the *Federal Register* 42, no. 163 (August 23, 1977), § 121a.347, "Private School Placements," p. 42491. A few state plans—such as the Massachusetts plan—already give the parent a veto over every educational decision made by the public school. Also see the useful discussion of the "individual education contract" in Abeson et al., "Access to Opportunity," pp. 270–92. While some states—Massachusetts, for example— have established such a contract, the language of Public Law 94-142 —especially as interpreted in the proposed implementation regulations (*Federal Register*, § 121a.349, "Individualized education program—accountability," p. 42491)—rules out a formal contract between the parents and the school.

10 • The Handicapped Child in School

1. Mario Fantini and Gerald Weinstein, *The Disadvantaged Child: Challenges to Education* (New York: Harper & Row, 1970).

2. Frank Riessman, *The Inner-City Child* (New York: Harper & Row, 1976), p. 89.

3. A small number of older studies have viewed the placebo effect as one of the many ways that the physician can mobilize the "forces" of suggestion on behalf of the patient. See M. Levine, *Psychotherapy in Medical Practice* (New York: Macmillan, 1942). For a comprehensive overview of this stream of medical thought, see Arthur K. Shapiro, "A Contribution to a History of the Placebo Effect," *Behavioral Science* 5 (1960): 109–35, especially pp. 126–30. For a brief overview of more recent research, see Henry Byerly, "Explaining and Exploiting Placebo Effects," *Perspectives in Biology and Medicine* 19, no. 3 (Spring 1976): 423–36. For a more detailed discussion of the placebo effect, see chapter 11, note 28.

4. There is, of course, a growing literature concerning "teacher expectancy effects." Unfortunately, the value of this literature is vitiated by severe methodological flaws. Attempts to demonstrate long-term effects on pupil performance of biased information provided the teacher at the

beginning of the school year (e.g., fake IQ scores) have yielded results in accord with common sense. See Robert Rosenthal and Lenore Jacobson, *Pygmalion in the Classroom: Teacher Expectation and Pupil's Intellectual Development* (New York: Holt, Rinehart and Winston, 1968). But these studies have been heavily criticized on methodological grounds. See, for example, the devastating reanalysis of the Rosenthal and Jacobson data in Richard E. Snow, "Unfinished Pygmalion," *Contemporary Psychology* 14, no. 4 (April 1969): 197–99. On the other hand, numerous studies have demonstrated short-term effects of teacher expectancy on pupil performance in such laboratory tests as learning nonsense syllables; a useful review of some of these studies appears in Rosenthal and Jacobson, *Pygmalion in the Classroom*. Still other studies have demonstrated that false information will affect teachers' behavior toward students immediately after the information has been provided. See, for example, the studies of Rubovits and Maehr, which examine teachers' behavior in a thirty-minute experimental period immediately after the teachers were provided misleading data about the IQ's of a group of schoolchildren—Pamela C. Rubovits and Martin L. Maehr, "Pygmalion Analyzed: Towards an Explanation of the Rosenthal-Jacobson Findings," *Journal of Personality and Social Psychology* 19, no. 2 (1971): 197–203; and Pamela C. Rubovits and Martin L. Maehr, "Pygmalion Black and White," *Journal of Personality and Social Psychology* 25, no. 2 (1973): 210–18.

These demonstrations are useful, but their value would be greatly enhanced if personality and contextual variables were also examined. A suggestion of the potential value of such explorations is provided by a study that did examine the impact of personality variables on receptivity to biasing information. After dividing teachers into two groups, those who believed that their actions had an impact on the world ("internally controlled") and those who viewed events as outside their control ("externally controlled"), R. Carter gave members of each group fake psychological reports about a group of preschoolers. Each teacher was then asked to teach sight vocabulary to the children. In a finding that invites comparison with the Langer and Abelson study of behaviorist and psychoanalytically oriented therapists discussed in note 13, chapter 11, Carter found that the externally controlled teachers were immune to the expectancy effect, whereas the internally controlled displayed a strong expectancy effect—e.g., they taught more vocabulary items to the children whom the fake psychological reports had described as more intelligent. See R. Carter, "Locus of Control and Teacher Expectancy as Related to Achievement of Young School Students," unpublished doctoral dissertation, Indiana University, 1969, summarized in Nettie R. Bartel and Samuel L. Guskin, "A Handicap as a Social Phenomenon," in *Psychology of Exceptional Children and Youth*, 3d ed., ed. William M. Cruickshank (Englewood Cliffs, N.J.: Prentice-Hall, 1971), p. 89.

In attempting to overcome the limitations of the existing teacher expectancy research, researchers could benefit greatly from a familiarity with the much more sophisticated body of work that has explored the determinants of successful interactions in psychotherapy. An excellent and comprehensive discussion of these factors is provided by Jerome D. Frank, *Persuasion and Healing* (Baltimore: Johns Hopkins University Press, 1973).

For a general review of this research, see L. Luborsky, M. Chandler, A. H. Auerback, J. Cohen, and H. M. Bachrach, "Factors Influencing the Outcome of Psychotherapy: A Review of Quantitative Research," *Psychological Bulletin* 75 (1971): 145–85. A useful review also appears in the important experimental study reported by Adolph O. Di Loreto, *Comparative Psychotherapy: An Experimental Analysis* (Chicago: Aldine-Atherton, 1971). For a useful critique of earlier studies, see Barbara Lerner and Donald W. Fiske, "Client Attributes and the Eye of the Beholder," *Journal of Consulting Psychology* 40, no. 2 (1973): 272–77 (this important study is briefly discussed in note 13, chapter 11); Barbara Lerner, *Therapy in the Ghetto: Political Impotence and Personal Disintegration* (Baltimore: Johns Hopkins University Press, 1972); Hans H. Strupp, "On the Basic Ingredients of Psychotherapy," *Journal of Consulting and Clinical Psychology* 41, no. 1 (1973): 1–8; and Sol L. Garfield, "Basic Ingredients or Common Factors in Psychotherapy?" *Journal of Consulting and Clinical Psychology* 41, no. 1 (1973): 9–12.

We cannot conclude this note without some mention of the possible role that the school principal may play in ultimately determining the expectations that students have about their abilities. For a small-scale study that supports this conjecture, see C. F. Palfrey, "Headteachers' Expectations and Their Pupils' Self-Concepts," *Education Research* 15 (February 1973): 123–27. A similar view seems to inform the educational experiments now being undertaken by the Rev. Jesse Jackson in Chicago.

The importance of the principal in setting the general tone of teaching in the school has been emphasized perhaps most forcefully by Seymour B. Sarason in *The Culture of the School and the Problem of Change* (Boston: Allyn and Bacon, 1971). Following Sarason's suggestion, it is tempting to speculate that researchers in education and special education should be paying at least as much attention to principal-teacher relationships as to teacher-student relationships.

5. The placebo literature (for a brief review, see note 28, chapter 11) and the labeling literature (for a brief review, see note 4, above and note 13, chapter 11) cry out to be integrated with studies of the role that personality factors play in successful teacher-student interactions—and, indeed, in all attempts to understand interactions between care givers and clients. As far as we know, little attention has been paid to the role that personality variables play in teachers' susceptibility to the biasing information contained in such labels as "retarded" or "emotionally disturbed," as well as the influence of personality on perceptual biases induced by other sometimes misleading "information" generated by the school about the child. Yet if one accepts the plausible hypothesis that some of these perceptual effects reflect processes similar to the psychological mechanisms at work in placebo responses (where information affects the individual's physiological reactions rather than his

interpersonal behavior and perceptions), the positive association of placebo reactions with anxiety noted by Arthur K. Shapiro raises an extremely interesting question, namely, are high-anxiety teachers more likely to act in a stereotyped (and therefore negative) way toward handicapped children who enter the classroom with a diagnostic label or a dossier of diagnostic information about their disabilities? Are high-anxiety able-bodied children and youths more likely to be affected by the knowledge that a classmate is handicapped than are low-anxiety students? And what of the handicapped child himself? Are those children and youths with high manifest anxiety more likely to be scarred by the stereotypes that surround their handicap in their milieu? Similar questions are also raised by Shapiro's observation that "hysterical patients with *la belle indifference* . . . are reported to react poorly to placebos, despite the fact that they have traditionally been considered to be among the most susceptible of patients" (Arthur K. Shapiro, "Placebo Effects in Medicine, Psychotherapy, and Psychoanalysis," in *Handbook of Psychotherapy and Behavior Change*, ed. Allen E. Bergin and Sol L. Garfield [New York, John Wiley and Sons, 1971], pp. 439–73. Also see Arthur K. Shapiro, "Factors Contributing to the Placebo Effect: Their Implications for Psychotherapy," *American Journal of Psychotherapy* 18, suppl. 1 [March 1964]: 73–88).

These questions also invite comparison to our remarks about the possible impact of personality factors on expectancy effects discussed above in note 4. Both the Langer and Abelson study of psychotherapists and the Carter study of teachers distinguished between personality types by means of cognitive criteria (i.e., behaviorist versus psychoanalytically inclined, "externally controlled" versus "internally controlled"). But are these cognitive factors independent variables, or are they merely strongly correlated with some underlying emotional variable such as manifest versus suppressed anxiety? Or do both cognitive and emotional variables exert independent effects upon an individual teacher's or therapist's susceptibility to expectancy effects? Moreover, what role do these variables play in influencing the behavior of the handicapped child's able-bodied and handicapped schoolmates and in shaping the handicapped child's own susceptibility to the stigmatizing labels and stereotypes that he encounters in the classroom and elsewhere?

6. David L. Kirp, "Schools as Sorters: The Constitutional and Policy Implications of Student Classification," *University of Pennsylvania Law Review* 121, no. 4 (April 1973): 710.

7. For a useful overview, see T. Ernest Newman, "Psychological Assessment of Exceptional Children and Youth," in *Psychology of Exceptional Children and Youth*, ed. William M. Cruickshank (Englewood Cliffs, N.J.: Prentice-Hall, 1971), pp. 140–44. A sense of the poor predictive quality of IQ scores for children with cerebral palsy is provided by one of the rare longitudinal studies of such children, Zelda S. Klapper and Herbert G. Birch, "A Fourteen-Year Follow-up Study of Cerebral Palsy: Intellectual Change and Stability," *American Journal of Orthopsychi-*

atry 37 (1967): 540–47. The following table summarizes the authors' findings (Klapper and Birch, p. 543):

IQ Score in Childhood	IQ Score When Tested Fourteen Years Later in Adulthood			
	0–50	50–74	75–89	90+
0–50	100%			
50–74	6%	47%	18%	29%
75–89	—	7%	40%	53%
90+	—	7%	7%	86%

The individuals studied were virtually all white and came from generally lower-middle-class homes. The upward changes in scores fell within or somewhat above the mildly retarded range. See also Zelda S. Klapper and Herbert G. Birch, "The Relation of Childhood Characteristics to Outcome in Young Adults with Cerebral Palsy," *Developmental Medicine and Child Neurology* 8 (1966): 645–56.

8. See the useful discussion by W. K. Estes in "Learning Theory and Intelligence," *American Psychologist* 29, no. 10 (1974): 740–49.

9. Newman, "Psychological Assessment of Exceptional Children and Youth," p. 150. Newman's remarks on the serious difficulties that beset attempts to design tests that meet the traditional goals of intelligence tests developed for able-bodied children are apposite: "Our success in discovering those kinds of behavior that in combination are reasonably predictive of the learning behavior of children who are predominantly nonhandicapped . . . must be regarded as potentially restrictive of our perception of the . . . factors operating [in] . . . handicapped children. Because of perceptual or conceptual impairment or distortion and because of the unique communication problems of the various handicapped groups, certain behavior samples that are important with respect to the nonhandicapped may be of much less or no significance with respect to the handicapped, and vice versa" (Newman, "Psychological Assessment of Exceptional Children and Youth," p. 149).

10. For descriptions of the tests, see ibid., pp. 146–49; for discussions of studies that imply very poor correlations between IQ and academic achievement, see M. Vernon, "Potential, Achievement, and Rehabilitation in the Deaf Population," *Rehabilitation Literature* 31 (1970): 258–67.

11. Ivan B. Pless and Philip Pinkerton, *Chronic Childhood Disorder: Promoting Patterns of Adjustment* (London: Henry Klimpton: 1975), p. 106. Also see note 9 above.

12. Public Law 94-142, Section (612)(5)(B).

13. Jane R. Mercer, *Labeling the Mentally Retarded* (Berkeley: University of California Press, 1973), pp. 270–71.

14. The authors are equivocal about children who failed two of the five

tests. See Mortimer Garrison, Jr., and Donald D. Hammill, "Who Are the Retarded?" *Exceptional Children*, September 1971, pp. 13–20.

15. See Mercer, *Labeling the Mentally Retarded.*

16. Mercer's pluralistic criterion defines an IQ score in the retarded range as a score that falls more than two standard deviations below a given socioeconomic group's mean score (i.e., falling into the bottom 3 percent of that group's scores). Yet if one grants that conventional IQ tests discriminate against minority-group children, it seems odd to believe that this discrimination is confined to the way that the scores are conventionally interpreted (i.e., that the discrimination can be eliminated merely by changing the scale with which one "measures" the raw score). A much sounder working hypothesis would be that the test questions are inappropriate and that therefore entirely new tests should be constructed.

But even if we accept the rather odd assertion that the bias in the conventional intelligence tests can be minimized by a new scaling procedure, Mercer's choice of a 3 percent cutoff point seems arbitrary. Given the results of her attempt to check her strategy, a 2, a 4, or even a 5 percent cutoff would work about as well. At first glance, Mercer's social adaptation test seems to escape these objections because she constructed it in order to take into account different sociocultural norms of appropriate behavior. But a glance at the questions on her protocol raises the troubling possibility that very different questions are needed to assess social adaptation in different socioeconomic groups. For example, the work of Labov suggests that in some inner-city cultures, good behavior in school and adequate grades may, from about the fourth grade on, be a sign that one is socially maladjusted by the standards of the peer culture; the "adjusted" child scorns school and actively participates in the street culture. See William Labov, "The Relation of Reading Failure to Peer-Group Status," in *Language in the Inner City* (Philadelphia: University of Pennsylvania Press, 1972), pp. 241–54, especially Figures 6.1, p. 248, and 6.2, p. 249. By omitting questions about gangs, drugs, and other aspects of street culture, Mercer's protocols may inadvertently discriminate against children from certain subcultures. Just as perplexing is the use of the 3 percent cutoff point in assessing social adaptation. Why not 10 percent or 1 percent? The reason given is hardly convincing: 3 percent is the traditional cutoff point used for defining mental retardation by means of scores on conventional IQ tests.

17. Mercer, *Labeling the Mentally Retarded*, p. 260.

18. Mercer, ibid., distinguishes between two kinds of retardation as measured by her pluralistic approach—the "physically disabled retardate" and the "nondisabled retardate." While Mercer's failure to apply her pluralistic approach to physically handicapped children is disappointing, her pluralistic framework is certainly capable of admitting in principle the need for ways to perform the same kind of discriminations for physically handicapped children as for able-bodied minority-group children—i.e., to distinguish instances of genuinely low intellectual potential from instances when a child has the mental potential but fails

Mercer's pluralistic tests because of the special socialization experiences of handicap in his or her sociocultural group.

19. Ibid., p. 217.

20. Ibid. For a theoretical overview, see our discussion of Piagetian theory in chapter 7.

21. In England, most individuals who are labeled "mildly retarded" receive this label when they leave school (generally between the ages of fifteen and nineteen), at which time the Education Authority notifies the Mental Health Department that they are in need of supervision. The highly regarded Salford Study found that by age thirty, the prevalence rate had fallen to about one-quarter of its peak value. For an overview, see Albert Kushlick, "Assessing the Size of the Problem of Subnormality," in *Genetic and Environmental Factors in Human Ability*, ed. J. E. Meade and A. S. Parkes (Edinburgh: Oliver and Boyd, 1966), pp. 121–47. Also see A. D. B. Clarke, "The Prevention of Subcultural Subnormality: Problems and Prospects," *British Journal of Subnormality* 19 (1973): 7–20.

    Research in Sweden has approached the problem from a different perspective. Granat and Granat's work in the early 1970s suggests that perhaps two out of three schoolchildren with IQ's in the mildly retarded range (50–70) escape being labeled "retarded" because the children perform well enough in school to avoid calling special attention to themselves. See Kristina Granat and Sven Granat, "Below-Average Intelligence and Mental Retardation," *American Journal of Mental Deficiency* 78, no. 1 (1973): 27–32.

    As for the United States, Lemkau, Tietze, and Cooper found in their classic study of the Eastern Health District of Baltimore in 1936 that the peak incidence of mild retardation occurred between the ages of ten and fourteen. Prevalence rates for blacks and whites fell sharply for older age groups. See Paul Lemkau, Christopher Tietze, and Marcia Cooper, "Mental-Hygiene Problems in an Urban District," third paper, *Mental Hygiene* 26 (1942). Similar findings have been reported again and again in subsequent studies. Rates by the late twenties are usually less than one-third of the peak school-age rate. For an excellent compendium of U.S. data, see Ronald W. Conley, *The Economics of Mental Retardation* (Baltimore: Johns Hopkins University Press, 1974). The best overview of the decline of prevalence rates with age is still E. M. Gruenberg's chapter, "Epidemiology," in *Mental Retardation*, ed. H. A. Stevens and R. Heber (Chicago: University of Chicago Press, 1964).

22. See Edward F. Zigler and Susan Harter, "The Socialization of the Mentally Retarded," in *Handbook of Socialization Theory and Research*, ed. David A. Goslin (Chicago: Rand McNally, 1969), pp. 1080–88.

23. For a fascinating study—and a fascinating overview of the problem—see Robert A. Webb, "Concrete and Formal Operations in Very Bright 6- to 11-year-olds," *Human Development* 17 (1974): 292–300. Webb studied twenty-five children ranging in age from six years two months to eleven years four months, all with IQ's above 160. If high IQ were closely related to mental stage, many of these children should have been

able to solve problems at the level of formal operations (a stage that average middle-class children attain around age twelve). Instead, the children's cognitive level was what would be expected for an average IQ group of children of their ages. However, IQ did seem related to the *speed* with which a child learned to apply his most sophisticated cognitive strategies to new but logically similar tasks: i.e., *horizontal décalage* seems to proceed more rapidly in high-IQ children than in average children. One wonders if a similar relationship exists for IQ's that are determined by pluralistic measures.

24. Perhaps the clearest indication of Piaget's belief that the conventional intelligence test measures intelligence is still untranslated. See the references to intelligence tests in Piaget's 1955 Sorbonne Lectures, "Les Relations entre l'intelligence et l'affectivité dans le developpement de l'enfant." Notes of these lectures—reviewed by Piaget—appear in the following issues of the *Bulletin de Psychologie*: February 5, 1954, pp. 143–50; March 26, 1954, pp. 346–61; May 15, 1954, pp. 522–35; and June 17, 1954, pp. 346–709. The biographical essay that appears in Richard I. Evans, *Jean Piaget: The Man and His Ideas*, trans. Donald MacQueen (New York: E. P. Dutton, 1973), is also useful—see especially pp. 118–19. Also see Bärbel Inhelder, *The Diagnosis of Reasoning in the Mentally Retarded*, translation of the 2d French ed. by Will Beth Stephens et al. (New York: Chandler, 1968), especially the two prefaces by Piaget and chapter 1.

25. See Efthalia Walsh, "The Handicapped and Science: Moving in the Mainstream," *Science* 196, no. 4297 (June 24, 1977): 1424–26.

26. Ibid., p. 1424. One survey was conducted in 1975 by the American Association for the Advancement of Science's Project on the Handicapped in Science. The other survey was carried out in 1976 by Science for the Handicapped, a group that is associated with the National Science Teachers Association.

27. Ibid.

28. Ibid.

29. William M. Cruickshank, "The Exceptional Child in the Elementary and Secondary Schools," in *Education of Exceptional Children and Youth*, 2d ed., ed. William M. Cruickshank and G. Orville Johnson (Englewood Cliffs, N.J.: Prentice-Hall, 1967), p. 130.

30. Ibid. This passage immediately follows the preceding passage.

31. Gunnar Myrdal, with the assistance of Richard Sterner and Arnold Rose, *An American Dilemma* (New York: Harper & Brothers, 1944), p. 897.

32. T. Dembo, G. L. Leviton, and B. A. Wright, "Adjustment to Misfortune: A Problem of Social Psychological Rehabilitation," *Artificial Limbs* 3, no. 2 (1956): 39–40, quoted in Beatrice A. Wright, *Physical Disabilities— A Psychological Approach* (New York: Harper & Row, 1960), p. 137 (italics in original). Wright cites this passage from her paper to conclude the chapter entitled "Value Changes in Acceptance of Disability."

33. Abram Kardiner and Lionel Ovesey, *The Mark of Oppression* (Cleveland: World Publishing Company, 1962), p. 387. The book first appeared in 1951.

34. Lee Meyerson, "Somatopsychology of Physical Disability," in *Psychology of Exceptional Children and Youth,* ed. Cruickshank, p. 16.

35. Samuel J. Meisels, *Special Education and Development: Perspectives on Young Children with Special Needs* (Baltimore: University Park Press, 1979).

36. For more on these problems, see chapter 4 and the discussion of Piagetian theory in chapter 7.

37. See note 4 of this chapter.

38. Research Division, *Ability Grouping,* Research Summary 1968-Se (Washington, D.C.: National Education Association, 1968). A table summarizing the results of the fifty studies examined by the NEA group appears in Christopher Jencks et al., *Inequality: A Reassessment of the Effect of Family and Schooling in America* (New York: Basic Books, 1972), Table 3-1, p. 108. Jencks and his associates also concluded that elementary school tracking had very little effect upon student IQ scores (ibid., p. 108).

    The lack of any academic justification for tracking raises especially serious questions about the possible effects of tracking mainstreamed students in junior and senior high school, where the impact of the school upon a student's future goals and sense of his or her abilities is especially strong. We find Bowles and Gintis's discussion of the socialization functions performed by the school especially appropriate to handicap. See Samuel Bowles and Herbert Gintis, *Schooling in Capitalist America* (New York: Basic Books, 1976), especially pp. 131–41. Also see Ray C. Rist, *The Urban School: A Factory for Failure* (Cambridge, Mass.: MIT Press, 1973).

39. See Walter R. Born, "Ability Grouping in the Public Schools," *Journal of Experimental Education* 34 (Winter 1965): 2–97.

40. Joe Laskar, *He's My Brother* (Chicago: Albert Whitman and Company, 1974). For good recent reviews of stereotypes about disabled children and adults in books and other media, see Douglas Bikien and Robert Bogdan, "Media Portrayals of Disabled People: A Study in Stereotypes," *Interracial Books for Children Bulletin* 8 nos. 6 and 7 (1977): 4–9, and Albert V. Schwartz, "Disability in Children's Books: Is Visibility Enough?" in ibid., pp. 10–15.

41. Joan Fassley, *Howie Helps Himself* (Chicago: Albert Whitman and Company, 1975).

42. Stephen A. Richardson, "People with Cerebral Palsy Talk for Themselves," *Developmental Medicine and Child Neurology* 14, no. 4 (August 1972): 525.

43. Ibid.

44. The researches of Stephen A. Richardson and Richard Kleck are refreshing exceptions. See Stephen A. Richardson, "Attitudes and Behavior Toward the Physically Handicapped," *Birth Defects: Original Article Series* 12, no. 4 (1976): 15–34. Also see chapter 1, note 13.

45. The failure to connect what has been learned about race relations to disability is especially marked in the special education literature. See, for example, S. Kenneth Thurman and Michael Lewis, "Children's Re-

sponses to Differences: Some Possible Implications for Mainstreaming,"
Exceptional Children, March 1979, pp. 468–70.

46. Phyllis A. Katz, "Attitude Change in Children: Can the Twig Be Straightened?" in *Towards the Elimination of Racism* (New York: Pergamon Press, 1976), p. 213.

47. For an excellent compedium of this research, see Katz, ed., *Towards the Elimination of Racism*.

48. Significant differences in the content of the sick role in different cultures have been reported. See Talcott Parsons, *Social Structure and Personality* (New York: Free Press, 1964), Introduction, p. 11.

49. For a good overview, see Stephen A. Richardson, "The Effect of Physical Disability on the Socialization of a Child," in *Handbook of Socialization Theory and Research*, ed. Goslin, pp. 1047–63.

11 • The Psychological Effects of Medical Care

1. For a valuable, although sometimes polemical, update and historical overview, see Ivan Illich, *Medical Nemesis* (New York: Pantheon, 1976).

2. Franz Alexander, *Psychosomatic Medicine* (New York: W. W. Norton and Company, 1950), p. 23.

3. For a major attempt to redefine the physician's responsibilities in chronic care, see Ivan B. Pless and Philip Pinkerton, *Chronic Childhood Disorder: Promoting Patterns of Adjustment* (London: Henry Klimpton, 1975), especially chapter 5, "Therapeutic Intervention to Promote Adjustment," pp. 168–210.

4. For an overview, see Pless and Pinkerton, *Chronic Childhood Disorder*, pp. 78–81 and 91–95. Also see Group for the Advancement of Psychiatry, *Psychiatric Consultation in Mental Retardation*, Report no. 104, formulated by the Committee on Mental Retardation (New York, October 1979).

5. Gilman D. Grave and I. Barry Pless, eds., *Chronic Childhood Illness: Assessment of Outcome* (Washington, D.C.: U.S. Government Printing Office, 1976), DHEW Publication No. [NIH] 76-877, Part III, "The Impact of Chronic Childhood Illness on Sibling Development," pp. 221–32. Also see the report of much higher high school dropout rates among the siblings of children with cleft palates than among the handicapped children themselves: N. Demb and A. L. Ruess, "High School Dropout Rate for Cleft Palate Patients," *Cleft Palate Journal* 4 (1967): 327–33.

6. For a comprehensive discussion and literature review, see Pless and Pinkerton, *Chronic Childhood Disorder*.

7. D. Maddison and B. Raphael, "Social and Psychological Consequences of Chronic Disease in Childhood," *Medical Journal of Australia* 2 (1971): 1265–70.

8. Jerome D. Frank, *Persuasion and Healing*, rev. ed. (Baltimore: Johns Hopkins University Press, 1973). In some respects Frank's model overlaps the "guidance-cooperation" and "mutual participation" mode in Szasz and Hollender's three-part typology of possible doctor-patient re-

lationships; see T. S. Szasz and M. H. Hollender, "A Contribution to the Philosophy of Medicine: The Basic Models of the Doctor-Patient Relationships," *A.M.A. Archives of Internal Medicine* 97 (May 1956): 585–92. For a useful overview of the literature on doctor-patient relationships, see Samuel W. Bloom and Robert N. Wilson, "Patient-Practitioner Relationships," in *Handbook of Medical Sociology*, 2d ed., eds. Howard E. Freeman, Sol Levine, and Leo G. Reeder (Englewood Cliffs, N.J.: Prentice-Hall, 1972), pp. 315–39.

9. Stephen A. Richardson, "People with Cerebral Palsy Talk for Themselves," *Developmental Medicine and Child Neurology* 14 (August 1972): 534.

10. Interview conducted by the authors, Boston, June 1976.

11. See our discussion of the social pathology model in chapter 3 and our discussion of the parent-professional relationship in chapter 8.

12. See, for example, Erving Goffman, *Asylums: Essays on the Social Situation of Mental Patients and Other Inmates* (Garden City, N.Y.: Doubleday Anchor, 1961); Thomas S. Szasz, *The Myth of Mental Illness* (New York: Harper & Row, 1961); and D. L. Rosenhan, "On Being Sane in Insane Places," *Science* 179, no. 4070 (1973): 250–58.

13. This research suggests that psychotherapists, and indeed all professionals, are just as vulnerable to the biasing effects of information and stereotypes as laymen. (Recall our discussion of the factors that determine the layman's perceptions of a handicapped individual in chapter 1.) For example, Temerlin studied the effects of information about a potential client upon psychological assessments of the individual. One group of psychiatrists, clinical psychologists, and graduate students in clinical psychology were told by a prestigious confederate that they were about to hear a taped interview with a man who was very interesting "because he looks neurotic but actually is quite psychotic." A second group was told nothing. After listening to the tape, the misinformed group diagnosed the man in the interview as mentally ill significantly more often than did the controls, 60 percent of the experimental group diagnosing psychosis. See M. K. Temerlin, "Suggestion Effects in Psychiatric Diagnosis," *Journal of Nervous and Mental Disease* 147 (1968): 349–53. In another study Abramowitz, Abramowitz, Jackson, and Gomes found that political activism affected "nonliberal" counselors' estimates of the degree of maladjustment when asked to assess clinical case histories in which the "patient's" sex and political inclination were systematically varied: all other things being equal, the female radical activist was considered significantly more maladjusted than her male counterpart. See Stephen I. Abramowitz, Christine V. Abramowitz, Carolyn Jackson, and Beverly Gomes, "The Politics of Clinical Judgment: What Nonliberal Examiners Infer about Women Who Do Not Stifle Themselves," *Journal of Consulting and Clinical Psychology* 41, no. 3 (1973): 385–91.

Still more intriguing is Langer and Abelson's study of the biasing effect of information on the clinical judgment of behaviorist and psychoanalytically oriented therapists. Half of each group of psychotherapists were told they would watch a taped interview with a mental patient. The rest were told that they would witness an interview in which a man applies for a job. Afterward, all forty therapists were asked to evaluate the interviewee. Regardless of what they had been told, the behaviorist-oriented therapists described the man as fairly well adjusted. In contrast, psychoanalytically oriented therapists were swayed by the biasing information. When labeled "mental patient," the man was described as significantly more disturbed by these therapists than when he had been said to be a "job applicant." See Ellen J. Langer and Robert P. Abelson, "A Patient by Any Other Name . . . : Clinician Group Difference in Labeling Bias," *Journal of Consulting and Clinical Psychology* 42, no. 1 (1974): 4–9.

Studies such as these are suggestive and would be even more useful if such factors as experience and overall therapeutic success could be taken into account. For example, are experienced psychotherapists with a good track record less susceptible to the biasing effects of initial information about a patient or a potential patient? More generally, one would ideally like to see studies exploring real psychotherapeutic encounters and examining the evolution of the therapist's interpretations of the client's behavior over time. (Do some therapists function as scientists who regularly test their hypotheses, and is this mode of interaction at all relevant to successful outcome?) However, there is indirect evidence that the biasing effects reported in these and other studies play an important role in the ultimate success or failure of a psychotherapeutic encounter. Thus, Lerner and Fiske have found, in contrast to many earlier studies, that client attributes do not seem to be related to outcome in psychotherapy; rather, what appears crucial is the therapist's own response to these attributes, as this response is gauged after an initial interview: "Favorable outcome appears to be related not to any measured individual differences among clients but rather to differences among therapists in their democratic values, in their overall preference for working with lower-class and severely [emotionally] impaired clients, and in their self ratings of skill in working with such clients." Finally, we should add that these findings complement the fragmentary reports of social class effects in physicians' diagnosis of the severity of a disability noted in note 20 below, and the discussion of the potential importance of mobilizing placebo and other "suggestion effects" discussed in note 28. See Barbara Lerner and Donald A. Fiske, "Client Attributes and the Eye of the Beholder," *Journal of Consulting and Clinical Psychology* 40, no. 2 (1973): 272–77; see especially their discussion of possible confounding effects, pp. 275–76. Also see Barbara Lerner, *Therapy in the Ghetto: Political Impotence and Personal Disintegration* (Baltimore: Johns Hopkins University Press, 1972).

14. For comprehensive discussions of the many facets of this problem, see Grave and Pless, eds., *Chronic Childhood Illness*.
15. Robert J. Haggerty, "Foreword," in Pless and Pinkerton, *Chronic Childhood Disorder*, p. 11.
16. Barbara Korsch, "Outcome Data for Chronic Renal Patients," in *Chronic Childhood Illness*, ed. Grave and Pless, pp. 15–21. Also see B. M. Korsch, V. F. Negrete, J. E. Gardiner, C. L. Weinstock, A. S. Mer-

cer, C. M. Guskin, and R. N. Fine, "Kidney Transplantation in Children: Psychosocial Follow-up Study on Child and Family," *Journal of Pediatrics* 83 (1973): 399–408.

17. Korsch notes that there is a fairly high correlation between high self-esteem and a patient's degree of recovery and rehabilitation ("Outcome Data for Chronic Renal Patients," p. 16).

18. Ibid., p. 20.

19. I. Barry Pless, "Theoretical and Practical Considerations in the Measurement of Outcome," in *Chronic Childhood Illness*, ed. Grave and Pless, p. 5.

20. Fred Davis, *Passage through Crisis: Polio Victims and Their Families* (Indianapolis: Bobbs-Merrill, 1963); and John F. McDermott, Jr., Saul I. Harrison, Jules Schrager, Paul Wilson, Elizabeth Killins, Janet Lindy, and Raymond W. Waggoner, "Social Class and Mental Illness in Children: The Diagnosis of Organicity and Mental Retardation," *Journal of the American Academy of Child Psychiatry* 6, no. 2 (April 1967): 309–20.

21. See the discussion following Korsch's "Outcome Data for Chronic Renal Patients" in *Chronic Childhood Illness*, ed. Grave and Pless, pp. 20–21. For an excellent overview of personality factors in psychotherapy, see Frank, *Persuasion and Healing*. For more references see our note 4, chapter 10, and this chapter, note 13.

22. Robert Berg, "An Integrated Health Status Index and the Management of Outcome in the Care of Chronically Ill Children," in *Chronic Childhood Illness*, ed. Grave and Pless, pp. 9–13, and "Approaches to the Evaluation of Disability," ibid., pp. 109–12.

23. I. Barry Pless, "Theoretical and Practical Considerations in the Measurement of Outcome," in *Chronic Childhood Illness*, ed. Grave and Pless, p. 7. Also see, I. Barry Pless, "Measurement of Outcome: A Review of the Problem," in ibid., pp. 125–29.

24. See, for example, Marcia Millman, *The Unkindest Cut: Life in the Backrooms of Medicine* (New York: William Morrow, 1977); Eliot Freidson, *Profession of Medicine: A Study of the Sociology of Applied Knowledge* (New York: Dodd, Mead, 1970), and *Doctoring Together: A Study of Professional Self-Control* (New York: Elsevier, 1976). These books should be required reading for every prospective physician in chronic medicine.

25. Millman's study is especially useful in suggesting reasons why physicians in all areas of medicine have great difficulty in taking seriously complaints about medical care made by patients. See especially Millman, *The Unkindest Cut*, chapter 10, which, with a fine sense of irony, is entitled "The Enactment of Trust."

26. For more on the average physician's tendency to avoid speaking out in public against even his most incompetent colleagues, see Freidson, *Doctoring Together*, and Millman, *The Unkindest Cut*.

27. See Gregory Zilboorg, in collaboration with George W. Henry, *A History of Medical Psychology* (New York: W. W. Norton, 1941). Though characteristically polemical, Ivan Illich gives a useful compendium of information and references concerning the psychotherapeutic skills of

traditional physicians as well as the special emphasis traditionally placed upon helping the dying patient cope with death in *Medical Nemesis*. Shapiro's review of the history of the placebo effect also contains many useful sources: Arthur K. Shapiro, "A Contribution to a History of the Placebo Effect," *Behavioral Science* 5 (1960): 109–35. For an extraordinary recent statement of medical humanism, see Oliver W. Sacks's already classic study of Parkinson's disease, sleeping sickness, and the effects of the drug L-Dopa, *Awakenings* (Garden City, N.Y.: Doubleday, 1974).

28. The placebo effect and other "suggestion effects" deserve far more attention than they have received by those who specialize in chronic care. For useful overviews of the placebo literature, see Shapiro, "A Contribution to a History of the Placebo Effect," and Arthur K. Shapiro, "Placebo Effects in Medicine, Psychotherapy, and Psychoanalysis," in *Handbook of Psychotherapy and Behavior Change*, ed. Allen E. Bergin and Sol L. Garfield (New York: John Wiley and Sons, 1971), pp. 439–73. Also see Frank, *Persuasion and Healing*, and Henry Byerly, "Explaining and Exploiting Placebo Effects," *Perspectives in Biology and Medicine* 19, no. 3 (Spring 1976): 423–36. For an excellent traditional discussion of how the physician can employ suggestion effects on behalf of his therapeutic mission, see M. Levine, *Psychotherapy in Medical Practice* (New York: Macmillan, 1942).

Ultimately, we hope that physicians working with handicapped children and their families can use suggestion and placebo effects to enhance the efficacy of their medical interventions and to reduce the often unpleasant side effects of pharmacologically active drugs. However, here we wish to emphasize a point that is especially relevant to chronic medicine because of the field's general reluctance to confront the complex psychosocial dimension of long-term care.

Many studies have reported that an inert substance such as a sugar pill or a saline solution can sometimes possess potent physiological effects when administered by a doctor who presents it to the patient as a powerful medicine. With some individuals placebos have relieved intractable surgical pain as effectively as morphine; in others they have brought about reductions in swelling and other arthritis symptoms comparable to those achieved by heavy dosages of aspirin. There are also negative suggestion effects, often called nocebos. For example, a number of studies have found that harsh physical side effects can be induced in individuals who have received normally benign but physiologically active agents (note that this research shows that the psyche can sometimes modulate the way that the body reacts to a chemical that is not physiologically inert). Finally, there are many reports that placebo effects can play a striking role in determining the mood change induced by psychoactive substances. For a brief overview of work in all these areas, see Byerly, "Explaining and Exploiting Placebo Effects."

These findings suggest that the problem of ensuring that the parent actively and willingly implements the physician's management regime (see text, pp. 239–45) shades off into a gray area in which the actual efficacy of the physician's regime may in part depend upon the positive (placebo) or negative (nocebo) effects that are generated by his manner of relating to the child and the parent. Unfortunately, the resistance of the medical profession to taking psychological factors seriously would probably make it impossible to fund any study that systematically examined the effects of parents' compliance *and* suggestion (placebos and nocebos) on the child's physical (as opposed to psychological) responses to treatment—e.g., improvements in the child's underlying physiological functions, improvements in the child's functional abilities, and changes in the pattern of negative symptoms that reflect a real improvement in the child's medical condition and not a breakdown in what Pless and Pinkerton refer to as "symptomatic concordance" (*Chronic Childhood Disorder*, pp. 191–93). Furthermore, it is unlikely that many physicians could be found who possess the time, the interest, and the necessary expertise in social science to design and implement such a complex and difficult undertaking. But the fact remains that everything that has been learned about placebo effects with adults strongly encourages the view that suggestion effects of one sort or another may be just as important in determining the success of the management plan as parents' compliance with the plan—even when success is defined narrowly to mean the child's physical (as opposed to psychological) responses. (We also suspect that in many instances the only way to approach the problem of parents' compliance will be by taking into account the role that suggestion plays in persuading some parents to trust their physician and to believe in the efficacy of the management plan.) When one considers that everything psychiatry knows (or believes) about children is consistent with the view that children as a group are far more suggestible than adults, the importance of studying placebo and nocebo effects in chronic care would seem to be even greater—not, let us repeat, simply because of the obligation to do everything possible to relieve the stress and anxieties that may be aroused in parent and child by any medical intervention, but because the social or symbolic dimension of medical care is as real a tool and may sometimes be as valuable a tool for combating chronic disease as is the physician's armamentorium of physiologically active substances. For a useful discussion of some of the less frequently studied aspects of the social dimension of medicine, see Arthur Kleinman, "Medicine's Symbolic Reality," *Inquiry* 16 (1973), especially p. 209.

29. See James S. Kakalik, Garry D. Brewer, Laurence A. Dougharty, Patricia D. Fleischauer, Samuel M. Genensky, and Linda M. Wallen, *Improving Services to Handicapped Children* (Santa Monica, Calif.: Rand Corporation, 1974).

30. Korsch's remarks on the inability of some specialists to cope with "the frustrations of somebody who never gets well, who gets increasingly disturbed, who has many complications, and who may die" are apposite. Where the specialist has "a limited spectrum . . . for responding to that kind of challenge," asks Korsch, "are there things which he is no longer able to do for those patients that might make for a better out-

come? Would perhaps a general practitioner have something to offer a deteriorating, chronically ill child that a specialist would not?" ("Outcome Data for Chronic Renal Patients," p. 20).

12 • The Theft of the Future

1. A small proportion—perhaps 1 percent—of all children with Down's syndrome have IQ's that fall in the normal range.
2. Wolf Wolfensberger, *The Principle of Normalization in Human Services* (Toronto: National Institute on Mental Retardation, 1972).
3. Melvin Kohn, *Class and Conformity: A Study in Values* (Homewood, Ill.: Dorsey Press, 1969). Though not dealing with handicapped children, Kohn's work raises a host of important questions about the parents of handicapped children that deserve further investigation.

   Kohn sought an explanation for the observation, long commonplace to social scientists, that middle-class parents tend to emphasize values such as curiosity, self-direction, happiness, and self-control in raising their children, whereas working-class parents are more likely to emphasize such traits and goals as neatness, honesty, conformity, and obedience in their child rearing.

   To discover why, Kohn classified his adult subjects (a very large sample by the standards of social science) according to the kinds of work styles required by their work—such as whether they were closely supervised or expected to make decisions for themselves, whether they dealt with things, data, or people, and whether the work they did was complex and allowed scope for flexibility or whether it was repetitive and monotonous. Kohn found a strong positive correlation between parenting behavior and the values parents attempted to transmit to their children, on the one hand, and the values embodied in the structure of the parents' work experience, on the other. Parents whose jobs emphasized conformity emphasized conformity in raising their children and emphasized corporal punishment as well. Parents whose jobs required a great deal of initiative and self-direction encouraged these traits in their children and used less physical punishment. Kohn found that class differences between parenting styles mainly reflected the fact that working-class jobs tend to emphasize conformity whereas middle-class and professional jobs tend to emphasize initiative and self-direction (p. 163).

   Kohn concluded: "Whether consciously or not, parents tend to impart to their children lessons derived from the conditions of life of their own social class—and thus help prepare their children for a similar position. . . . Class differences in parental values and child rearing practices influence the development of the capacities that children will someday need. . . . The family, then, functions as a mechanism for perpetuating inequality" (p. 200).
4. For documentation of these assertions, see chapter 13, discussion and notes.
5. See chapter 13, note 22.

6. See chapter 13, especially note 33.
7. See chapter 13, note 24.
8. See the references cited in chapter 1, note 16.
9. See Gunnar Myrdal, with the assistance of Richard Sterner and Arnold Rose, *An American Dilemma* (New York: Harper & Row, 1944), chapter 19, "The War Boom—and Thereafter," pp. 409–26.
10. See, for example, Hans J. Eysenck, *The IQ Argument: Race, Intelligence and Education* (New York: Library Press, 1971); R. J. Herrnstein, *I.Q. in the Meritocracy* (Boston: Little, Brown, 1973); and Arthur R. Jensen, *Genetics and Education* (New York: Harper & Row, 1972).
11. Monroe Berkowitz, Jeffrey Rubin, and John D. Worrall, "Economic Concerns of Handicapped Persons," in *The White House Conference on Handicapped Individuals*, vol. 1: *Awareness Papers* (Washington, D.C.: U.S. Government Printing Office, 1977), p. 222.
12. A good overview of the history of federal legislation concerning architectural barriers appears in Frank Bowe, *Handicapping America: Barriers to Disabled People* (New York: Harper & Row, 1978), pp. 73–106.
13. For a nontechnical discussion, see Kenneth Keniston and the Carnegie Council on Children, *All Our Children: The American Family under Pressure* (New York: Harcourt Brace Jovanovich, 1977), pp. 93–99.

  For more technical assessments of the impact of fair employment laws (as traditionally enforced), see Richard Butler and James J. Heckman, "The Impact of the Government on the Labor Market Status of Black Americans: A Critical Review," in *Equal Rights and Industrial Relations*, ed. Industrial Relations Research Association (Madison, Wis.: The Association, 1977). Also see Andrea H. Beller, "The Impact of Equal Opportunity Laws on the Male/Female Earnings Differential," Discussion Paper Number 43677 (Madison, Wis.: Institute for Research on Poverty, University of Wisconsin, 1977).
14. Keniston, *All Our Children*, p. 94.
15. For different perspectives on the economic implications of the energy crisis, see Amory B. Lovins, "Energy Strategy: The Road Not Taken?" *Foreign Affairs* 55, no. 1 (October 1976): 65–96, and Barry Commoner, *The Politics of Energy* (New York: Alfred A. Knopf, 1979).
16. For an eloquent appeal for egalitarian strategies, see Richard H. de Lone, *Small Futures: Children, Inequality, and the Limits of Liberal Reform* (New York: Harcourt Brace Jovanovich, 1979).
17. For a brief discussion of the differential value of additional years of education for blacks in the 1960s, see Herman P. Miller, *Rich Man, Poor Man* (New York: Thomas Y. Crowell, 1971), pp. 179–87, and John U. Ogbu, *Minority Education and Caste: The American System in Cross-Cultural Perspective* (New York: Academic Press, 1978), pp. 160–62 and 165–76. Also see Christopher Jencks, Marshall Smith, Henry Acland, Mary Jo Bane, David Cohen, Herbert Gintis, Barbara Heyns, and Stephen Michelson, *Inequality: A Reassessment of the Effect of Family and Schooling in America* (New York: Basic Books, 1972), especially chapter 7, "Income Inequality," pp. 209–46, and chapter 9, "What Is to Be Done?" pp. 253–65. For an overview of recent economic studies of job discrimination, see Stanley H. Masters, *Black-White Income*

Differentials: Empirical Studies and Policy Implications (New York: Academic Press, 1975). For discussions of different models of job discrimination, see Kenneth J. Arrow, "Models of Job Discrimination," in *Racial Discrimination in Economic Life*, ed. Anthony H. Pascal (Lexington, Mass.: Heath, 1972). Also see Gary S. Becker, *The Economics of Discrimination*, 2d ed. (Chicago: University of Chicago Press, 1971).

18. Ogbu, *Minority Education and Caste*, chapter 5, "The Job Ceiling and Other Barriers to Rewards of Education," pp. 149–76.

19. Ibid. Also see Jencks et al., *Inequality*, pp. 216–18, and Samuel Bowles and Herbert Gintis, *Schooling in Capitalist America* (New York: Basic Books, 1976), p. 35.

20. This conclusion requires qualification in two principal respects. First, there is every reason to believe that the 1 to 5 percent of all handicapped children who are academically gifted may gain a great deal from education-centered job strategies. To begin with, it is almost certain that the psychometric procedures currently used to evelute the academic potential of disabled children underestimate the true proportion of handicapped children who are mentally gifted (see chapter 10). As assessment procedures improve, the percentage of handicapped children given special academic attention because they are gifted can be expected to approach gradually the percentage of able-bodied children labeled "gifted." At the same time that this improvement occurs, one can hope that the quality of the education provided these children will improve—especially in areas such as science that have been scandalously neglected in traditional programs. With improvement in the quality of their education, more handicapped children will be able to take advantage of the opportunities for a satisfying career provided by outstanding academic credentials in our society. Although the experiences of blacks, Spanish-surnamed Americans, and women provide every reason for believing that qualified handicapped individuals will encounter structural discrimination in the professions and sciences, this discrimination will scarcely compare in severity to the exclusion from professional and scientific careers of any sort that has been the traditional lot of many gifted individuals with severe handicaps. However, the economic relevance of education to the 1 to 5 percent of all handicapped children who are intellectually gifted should not obscure the relative economic unimportance of better education for the remaining 95 to 99 percent.

Second, where the education provided the individual actively promotes economically self-destructive behavior patterns and fails to impart even the most elementary skills (such as functional literacy), it seems self-evident that improved education will help the minority individual make the most of whatever economic opportunities exist in the system for individuals sharing his background. For example, improving the "negative education" presently provided many inner-city children will undoubtedly improve their ability to compete for jobs against *relatively* more privileged members of their ethnic community. Something similar may be the case for those lower-class and middle-class handicapped children who are now being actively socialized into economically self-destructive behavior by the schools, or who are not receiving an elementary grounding in basic skills such as reading. Here, too, ending the negative education provided these children may significantly improve their ability to compete for jobs with children who have received a better education, share their general social characteristics, and possess similar handicaps.

What is by no means clear—and it is a matter that requires much thoughtful research—is the relative importance of ending "negative education" in promoting a more equitable distribution of jobs and income among majority- and minority-group competitors for the same class of jobs. Does, for example, improving inner-city education make much difference one way or another to the inner-city youth's ability to take advantage of successful attacks on the patterns of discrimination that presently exclude him from all but the most marginal jobs in the "secondary labor force"? Or do the subsidized job experiments now being conducted by the Manpower Demonstration Research Corporation provide a more promising way to provide underprivileged individuals with the necessary skills and socialization to take advantage of such improvements? For a review of the M.D.R.C. research, see "Summary of the First Annual Report on the National Supported Work Demonstration," Manpower Demonstration Research Corporation, December 1976; and Rebecca Maynard with Irwin Garfinkle and Valerie Leach, "Analysis of Nine-Month Interviews for Supported Work: Results of an Early AFDC Sample," Mathematica Policy Research [MPR] and the Institute for Research on Poverty (Madison, Wis.: University of Wisconsin, November 1977).

Some mention should also be made of the evidence that the black middle class grew at a much more rapid rate than the white middle class in the decade spanning the late 1960s and the early 1970s. This apparent improvement is compatible with the view that when political and legal measures significantly reduce the impact of prejudice and structural discrimination, improvements in education (or, perhaps, simply the possession of some minimal level of educational experience) may play an important role in fostering a more equitable distribution of middle-class jobs and income. For a discussion of this new and still controversial evidence, see William Julius Wilson, *The Declining Significance of Race* (Chicago: University of Chicago Press, 1978).

13 • The Presumption of Economic Inferiority

1. Because James S. Kakalik and his associates devote a lengthy and quite favorable chapter to vocational rehabilitation (VR) programs for handicapped youths in their influential Rand Corporation study, it is essential to warn those with an interest in VR services for handicapped youths that the data presented in the chapter are extremely ambiguous and are perfectly compatible with a picture of the VR program that disagrees with the authors' evaluation on every point. See James S.

Kakalik, Garry D. Brewer, Laurence A. Dougharty, Patricia D. Fleischauer, and Samuel M. Genensky, *Services for Handicapped Youth: A
Program Overview* (Santa Monica, Calif.: Rand Corporation, 1973),
chapter 5, "Vocational Services to Handicapped Youth," pp. 49–88.
This warning is especially important, because as Kakalik and his colleagues note, "the quality of the data [concerning federal support of
VR programs for youths aged fourteen to twenty-two] is better than
that available for any other Federal program serving handicapped
youth" (p. 82).

The following table (based upon Kakalik et al.'s Table 5.2, p. 51)
provides a breakdown by disability of the 101,015 youths aged fourteen
to twenty-two who were accepted for rehabilitation in fiscal year (FY)
1970, as well as an estimate of fiscal year 1972 expenditures for these
groups.

Summary of Vocational Rehabilitation

Handicap Group	Number Accepted for Service, FY 1970 Closures	Number Successfully Rehabilitated, FY 1970
Blind	332	249
Partially sighted	1,235	964
Other visual impairments	5,197	4,443
Deaf, unable to talk	1,145	900
Deaf, able to talk	1,267	1,081
Hard-of-hearing	1,931	1,672
Orthopedic impairments or absence of extremities	16,465	13,520
Mental illness	24,032	15,974
Mental retardation	29,654	22,862
Other health impairments	15,987	13,249
Speech impairments	1,608	1,378
Other impairments	2,172	1,524
TOTAL	101,025	77,816

All told, 77 percent of individuals given training were pronounced successfully rehabilitated. Nearly two-thirds were male, four-fifths were white, and the median grade completed was eleven. The number of youths referred to rehabilitation agencies was 184,068. While 45 percent of this group were rejected, only 11 percent of the total referrals were adjudged not qualified: "The most frequent reasons given for not accepting youths was that they refused service; or were unable to be located or contacted or had moved; or failed to cooperate" (p. 52). Total public expenditures on VR for handicapped youths in fiscal year 1970 were on the order of $200 million, the state share being 13 percent and the federal share, 87 percent.

Three-quarters of the rehabilitated youths received job training, one-third received physical or mental restorative services, another third received income assistance, and a third received some other service.

of Youth, by Disability Group

Number Rehabilitated as Percent of Number Accepted, FY 1970 Closures	Percent of Basic Program Expenditures on Handicap Group, FY 1970	Approximate Total State and Federal Expenditures on Handicap Group, FY 1972 *
77	1.2	$ 2,427,000
78	3.3	6,674,000
85	5.7	11,528,000
79	1.5	3,034,000
85	1.7	3,438,000
87	2.2	4,450,000
82	23.7	47,934,000
67	16.5	33,372,000
77	23.7	47,934,000
83	16.7	33,776,000
86	1.9	3,843,000
70	2.0	4,045,000
77	100.0 †	$202,254,000 †

* Assumes total FY 1972 expenditures are distributed across handicaps in the same proportions as the FY 1970 Basic VR program expenditures were.
† Columns do not total exactly because of rounding.

Only 11 percent of all successfully rehabilitated youths worked in the week before their referral; they reported average weekly earnings of $51. By the end of their programs, 100 percent were employed and were earning an average of $76 a week. This latter figure is the same as the average weekly earnings of rehabilitated individuals of all ages. May 1970 weekly earnings of salaried workers ages sixteen to twenty-four were $112 and $88 for men and women respectively. Eighty-seven percent of the rehabilitated were employed in the competitive labor market and 4 percent in sheltered workshops. For a more detailed breakdown of employment data, see Kakalik et al.'s Table 5.18, p. 71.

The available information concerning the socioeconomic status of the youths referred to VR is summarized in the following table. In 1970, the monthly median income of families of referred youths was $300, or just about the official poverty line. About one-third of all families had incomes under $150 a month, and only 18 percent had monthly incomes above $600.

Percent of Young VR Applicants by Monthly Family Income, FY 1970*

Income Range	Not Accepted into VR	Accepted but Not Rehabilitated	Accepted and Rehabilitated
$ 0–149	30	34	21
150–199	6	6	7
200–249	8	8	9
250–299	6	6	7
300–349	7	8	9
350–399	5	5	6
400–449	8	7	9
450–499	4	4	5
500–599	8	7	9
600 and over	18	15	18
TOTAL	100	100	100

* From Kakalik et al., Services for Handicapped Youth, Table 5.15, p. 69.

In sum—and the point is of the greatest importance in what follows —the VR system for youths seems primarily to serve the poor and the near-poor.

Here, then, is something of the rich collection of data that exist concerning VR programs for handicapped youths. On the face of it, the system appears to accomplish a great deal, and in the words of Kakalik et al., "the program for older youth offers a very comprehensive package of services and appears generally successful in meeting the objective of gainful employment" (p. 53). But does it? It is our contention that existing data are unable to answer this question. The data concerning mentally retarded youths are especially troubling. Because only 4 percent of all VR clients in the age range fourteen to twenty-two were placed in sheltered workshops, we can assume that at the very least, 96 percent of the retarded clients were classified as mildly retarded. (Recall that in 1970, mild retardation was defined as possessing an IQ in the range 50 to 85 and that the median IQ of black schoolchildren is often found to be between 85 and 95.) Since the prevalence of mild retardation is about ten times higher among the poor than among the affluent, and since the VR population served was heavily weighted in favor of the poor and the near-poor, it seems plausible to believe (in the absence of additional information) that perhaps 90 percent of the retarded clients served were classified as mildly retarded and came from poor or near-poor families. However, as we saw in chapter 10, there is ample reason to believe that lower-class youths are frequently mislabeled "mildly retarded" by the schools because they present disciplinary problems or because they come from minority-group subcultures. Should most of the clients labeled "retarded" come from this group, *VR may be providing useful jobs to a needy group (lower-class youths), but not to the group (disabled youths) for whom the VR program is intended.* Moreover, although we are all in favor of job placement for disadvantaged able-bodied youths, we see no point in this service being provided by an agency that reinforces and perhaps brings home for the first time the reality of the highly stigmatizing label "mentally retarded."

"Emotionally disturbed" occupies a somewhat analogous position in the school system. Here, too, students who are disciplinary problems are frequently reclassified as handicapped—an effective way of segregating (and possibly punishing) disruptive youths by placing them in special education classes with youths having major—and generally highly stigmatized—handicaps. Because of the great overrepresentation of the poor and near-poor in the VR caseloads, it seems reasonable to assume that perhaps two-thirds of all the mentally ill youths enrolled in VR programs were basically normal youths given a handicap label either to protect the school or to protect the youths from some of the rigors of the juvenile justice system. Again, though we have no objection to finding these youths gainful employment, we do not believe that VR is the agency to bear this responsibility. Like retardation, mental illness is an especially stigmatizing label. Confirmation and reinforcement of a stigmatizing label should not be the price we make these young people pay for a job.

So far we have "accounted" for about 43,000 of the youths accepted by VR programs, or about 43 percent of the total. If one now adds to this population of needy but basically nondisabled youths two groups of mildly handicapped youths served by VR (hard-of-hearing and "other visual impairments"), the total rises to about 50,000, or half the youths served by VR in 1971.

We can now begin to appreciate the potentially misleading character of the figures concerning the family income of youths referred to VR. Overall, the figures suggest that VR is helping the most needy. In fact, the overrepresentation of the needy may reflect the 43 percent of "pseudo-handicapped" needy youths who were admitted into the program. Conceivably, the socioeconomic backgrounds of the 50 percent of youths who may be genuinely and rather severely handicapped is quite different.

We can also begin to gauge the ambiguity of the global figures on the race of VR referrals and trainees. Because of the vast overlabeling of poor and near-poor black youths as "mildly retarded" or "emotionally disturbed," it is possible that most of the black youths reached by VR were in these categories. As a consequence, it is perfectly possible that global statistics conceal preferential treatment given white children with severe handicaps.

Finally, note that our estimate of "creaming"—i.e., the selection of youths who are relatively easy to place in jobs and therefore to declare successfully rehabilitated—is conservative. The only handicapped categories presented by Kakalik et al. that can be assumed to exclusively contain seriously disabled youths—blind and deaf—compose barely 3 percent of all referrals to VR and 4 percent of all cases accepted for rehabilitation. It is perfectly conceivable—given the existing data—that most of the youths in the remaining handicap classifications (e.g., orthopedic impairments or absence of extremities) had relatively minor impairment of function.

The questions raised by this analysis are especially urgent because of two recent developments. On the one hand, the proportion of mentally ill and mentally retarded individuals of all ages receiving rehabilitation services has increased steeply since the late 1960s. (All figures concerning this increase are taken from chapter 2 of Sar A. Levitan and Robert Taggart, *Jobs for the Disabled* [Baltimore: Johns Hopkins University Press, 1977].) In fiscal year 1968 the mentally ill of all ages composed 19.6 percent of participants. By fiscal year 1974 this proportion had risen to 31.4 percent. The proportion of the mentally retarded also increased during this period—rising from 10.7 percent of all participants in 1968 to 12.6 percent in 1974. In contrast, amputees and persons with orthopedic disabilities declined from 24.2 percent to 19.5 percent. Concurrent with this shift was the provision of the Vocational Rehabilitation Act of 1973, which mandated increasing services to the more severely disabled of all ages. The proportion of severely disabled recipients (as defined by the VR administration) rose from 32 percent in fiscal year 1974, to 38 percent in the first quarter of fiscal year 1976; and the severely disabled compose 41 percent of cases newly accepted for services in this quarter. Unfortunately, we have not been able to obtain the corresponding figures for handicapped youths served by VR. But given the shift toward mental illness and retardation in the overall statistics, and given the new legislative pressure to serve the severely disabled, it would seem especially important to determine whether VR personnel are reclassifying mildly retarded and mentally ill clients as more severely disabled in order to meet the goals mandated by the new act. This possibility requires serious consideration because diagnosis and classification of youths in these two handicap categories is notorious for its subjectivity and inconsistencies in even the least pressured and least charged of circumstances.

Other important questions are raised by our partition of the referral population into a "pseudo-handicap" group (mentally ill and mildly retarded) and a genuinely but perhaps mildly handicapped group (all other disability groups listed by VR except the deaf and the blind). One of the most important of these questions concerns the kinds of jobs in which successful rehabilitants are placed.

We know that only one youth in five seen by VR is from a middle-class home. This strong bias in favor of the poor and near-poor may, in the absence of strong administrative measures, lead to a tendency for VR personnel to judge a youth's job abilities by what is "realistic" for working-class youths. What is involved here need not be deliberate: beliefs about the economic potential of people with disabilities may reflect the class background of the system's most numerous clients.

When one joins to this possibility the compelling evidence that a given degree of incapacity stemming from a handicap is relatively more economically disadvantageous for menial and manual work than for many kinds of middle-class and upper-middle-class work, a rather un-favorable interpretation of the job statistics follows. That interpretation is that the VR system is not very good at meeting the needs of middle-class youths with major disabilities. Instead of providing them with training for middle-class jobs, the VR system may underestimate the job potential of this group of youths and present them with a training and counseling program that represents a marked step downward on the social ladder.

An alternate reading of the data is more favorable to VR. It is that VR serves two very different groups of handicapped youth. The first, represented by the mildly retarded and mentally ill, come overwhelm-ingly from poor and near-poor homes. The second, represented by the remaining handicap groups, come from a range of homes reasonably similar to the distribution of families in the general population. In this case, the low average earnings of successful rehabilitants could conceal the fact that, in general, youths are being placed in jobs that in salary, occupational characteristics, and opportunities for advance-ment are similar to the jobs obtained by able-bodied peers with similar socioeconomic backgrounds.

A third possibility—and one that requires a further disaggregation of data by state programs—is that some states do very well by the potential of their rehabilitants while other states do very poorly.

In this note we have set forth a body of data which at first glance appears to paint an encouraging picture concerning VR for handicapped youths. Upon closer examination we have seen that the data beg virtu-ally all the important questions about the quality of existing programs. It is possible, however, that the data to answer all these exist. What is needed as a start is a reanalysis of the material collected by Kakalik et al. and presented in a highly aggregated form in their published tabulations.

2. For a brief overview of VR programs in the 1970s, see Richard T. Sale, "Employment," in *The White House Conference on Handicapped Individuals*, vol. 1: *Awareness Papers* (Washington, D.C.: U.S. Government Printing Office, 1977), pp. 205–16. For more technical discussions —all of which ignore the problem of job discrimination—see Levitan and Taggart, *Jobs for the Disabled*, and Robert Haveman, "Public Employment of Handicapped and Disadvantaged Workers—Lessons for the U.S. from the Dutch Experience," discussion paper (Madison, Wis.: Institute for Research on Poverty, University of Wisconsin, 1977)—a discussion of sheltered workshops. For a critique of the methodological flaws in existing attempts to evaluate the economic benefits of VR programs for adults and youths, see Monroe Berkowitz, Valerie Englander, Jeffrey Rubin, and John D. Worrall, *An Evaluation of Policy-Related Rehabilitation Research* (New York: Praeger, 1975).

3. See Sale, "Employment," and the Urban Institute, *Report of the Comprehensive Service Needs Study* (Washington, D.C.: Urban Institute, 1975), chapter 13, "Employment and Labor Force Participation of the Severely Disabled."

4. In the absence of a sufficiently powerful national commitment to end discrimination, even the much more ambitious federally sponsored retraining and placement programs for minority-group workers of the 1960s and 1970s have not succeeded in making significant inroads into employment problems of inner-city youths and other hard-to-employ groups of able-bodied individuals. See Richard H. de Lone, *Small Futures: Children, Inequality, and the Limits of Liberal Reform* (New York: Harcourt Brace Jovanovich, 1979), and our chapter 12, note 19.

   In any event, the *long-term* impact of the VR pilot projects is unclear. To our knowledge, no follow-up study has been carried out to determine if, once placed, the subsequent work experience of the VR graduates (e.g., pay raises, promotions, layoffs, etc.) is roughly commensurate to the experience of similarly qualified able-bodied workers in the same kinds of jobs.

5. For example, Frank Bowe, *Handicapping America: Barriers to Disabled People* (New York: Harper & Row, 1978), pp. 175–78.

6. A good overview of recent attempts appears in the Urban Institute, *Report of the Comprehensive Service Needs Study*, chapter 13, "Employment and Labor Force Participation of the Severely Disabled." Essentially similar conclusions were reached by Barker and his associates in their literature review a generation earlier: Roger G. Barker in collaboration with Beatrice A. Wright, Lee Meyerson, and Mollie R. Gonick, *Adjustment to Physical Handicap and Illness: A Survey of the Social Psychology of Physique and Disability*, 2d ed. (New York: Social Science Research Council, 1953), chapter 8, "Employment of the Disabled."

7. For discussions of the way that data about employment are collected, see Lawrence D. Haber, "Identifying the Disabled: Concepts and

Methods in the Measurement of Disability, *From the Social Security Survey of the Disabled: 1966*, Report Number 1, December 1967. This report also appeared in the *Social Security Bulletin* for December 1967. Also see Lawrence E. Riley and Saad Z. Nagi, *Disability in the United States: A Compendium of Data on Prevalence and Programs* (Columbus, Ohio: Division of Disability Research, Department of Physical Medicine, College of Medicine, Ohio State University, 1970).

8. It must be emphasized that virtually all economists and epidemiologists who have studied the disabled worker have traditionally employed this model. Luft's important monograph is typical: Harold S. Luft, *Poverty and Health: Economic Causes and Consequences of Health Problems* (Cambridge, Mass.: Ballinger Publishing Co., 1978). For more on the universality of the medical model in the economics of handicap, see Monroe Berkowitz, William G. Johnson, and Edward H. Murphy, *Public Policy towards Disability* (New York: Praeger, 1976).

9. For a stunning example of this oversight, see Luft, *Poverty and Health*, which does not even mention job discrimination against people with disabilities.

A small number of econometric studies have attempted to use existing data bases to demonstrate the existence or to estimate the extent of discrimination. But all of these studies are vitiated by a similar flaw, an inability to distinguish between effects due to job discrimination and effects due to the lower job productivity or work flexibility of disabled workers. A useful—but largely nonevaluative—review of the small econometric literature on this topic appears in the Urban Institute's *Report of the Comprehensive Service Needs Study*; see chapter 13, "Employment and Labor Force Participation of the Severely Disabled." Also see Saad Z. Nagi, William H. McBroom, and John Collette, "Work, Employment and the Disabled," *American Journal of Economics and Sociology* 31 (1972): 21–34; and A. L. Jaffe, Lincoln H. Day, and Walter Adams, *Disabled Workers in the Labor Market* (Totowa, N.J.: Bedminister Press, 1964). Though not specifically seeking to estimate the nature and extent of job discrimination, Berkowitz, Johnson, and Murphy's attempt to estimate the relative importance of different demographic variables on the employment experience of the disabled worker is useful; see their *Public Policy towards Disability*. Although its research review is more than a generation out of date, the best overall discussion of the obstacles facing the economic mainstreaming of the disabled worker is the chapter on employment in Barker et al.'s classic review of disability, *Adjustment to Physical Handicap and Illness*. One of the few discussions of childhood disability that seeks to follow the child into the adult world is Ivan B. Pless and Philip Pinkerton, *Chronic Childhood Disorder: Promoting Patterns of Adjustment* (London: Henry Klimpton, 1975). The scattered, small-scale follow-up studies reported by Pless and Pinkerton are tantalizing but inconclusive. In this regard see the two studies of children with cerebral palsy by Klapper and Birch mentioned in chapter 10, note 7.

10. Robert A. Scott, *The Making of Blind Men* (New York: Russell Sage Foundation, 1969).

11. For a good overview of the scope of the social service issues involved in disability, see Monroe Berkowitz, Jeffrey Rubin, and John D. Worrall, "Economic Concerns of Handicapped Persons," in *The White House Conference on Handicapped Individuals*, vol. 1: *Awareness Papers* (Washington, D.C.: U.S. Government Printing Office, 1977), pp. 217–45. For a recent estimate of the cost of public and private programs for disability, see Monroe Berkowitz and Jeffrey Rubin, "The Costs of Disability: Estimates of Program Expenditures for Disability, 1967–1975," mimeo (New Brunswick, N.J.: Disability and Health Economics Research, Bureau of Economic Research, Rutgers University, August 1977).

    For a representative idea of the special emphasis placed upon employment as a social welfare problem rather than a problem that also involves job discrimination, see the technical studies cited in note 2 of this chapter. Also see Berkowitz, Johnson, and Murphy, *Public Policy towards Disability*; William G. Johnson, "Multiple Benefits and the Efficiency of Public Programs," Health Studies Program Working Paper No. 27, paper presented at the Seminar on Issues in the Structure and Function of Disability Programs (Washington, D.C.: Brookings Institute, November 29, 1977)—a discussion of the need to increase the administrative efficiency of the more than eighty different public programs serving people with disabling illness and injury; and Paul N. Van de Water, "Improving Work Incentives in the Social Security Disability Insurance Program," paper presented to a seminar sponsored by the Disability and Health Economics Research Section, Rutgers University, November 29, 1977—a proposal for trying to reduce the number of disabled individuals claiming disability insurance by experimenting with various ways of lowering the benefits provided eligible adults.

12. Berkowitz and Rubin, "The Costs of Disability."
13. Berkowitz, Johnson, and Murphy, *Public Policy towards Disability*, p. 2.
14. The best discussion of this problem appears in Berkowitz, Johnson, and Murphy's *Public Policy towards Disability*.
15. See, in particular, Haber, "Identifying the Disabled," and Lawrence D. Haber, "The Epidemiology of Disability. II. The Measurement of Functional Capacity Limitations," *From the Social Security Survey of the Disabled: 1966*, Report Number 10, July 1970.
16. A particularly clear example of this approach is provided in the Urban Institute's *Report of the Comprehensive Service Needs Study*.
17. Berkowitz, Johnson, and Murphy, *Public Policy towards Disability*.
18. Berkowitz, Johnson, and Murphy have succeeded in introducing the distinction between *limitation* and *impairment* into the 1976 revision of the survey questionnaire used in the National Longitudinal Surveys of the Labor Force. This marks the first time that any survey of the employment of disabled persons has ever attempted to honor this distinction. See *Public Policy towards Disability*, p. 140. However, even in the survey revision, the category "Work Disability" is retained and continues to possess its traditional medical meaning. As a consequence, the economist interested in studying individuals with physical "limitations" but no work "impairments" can do so only at risk of considerable

semantic confusion—i.e., by speaking of the employment experiences of disabled individuals who are not "work-disabled."

Other serious problems with the survey questionnaire remain. These problems stem from the major methodological problems created by a reliance upon self-reports for estimates of physical limitation and work disability. See note 21 below for a discussion of the unreliability of self-reports of functional limitation, and note 22 for a discussion of the unreliability of self-reports of work impairment.

19. For overviews of the problem, see Nagi, McBroom, and Collette, "Work, Employment, and the Disabled," pp. 28–29; Henry Viscardi, Jr., "The Adaptability of Disabled Workers," *Rehabilitation Record*, May–June 1961; and Greenleigh Associates, Inc., *A Study to Develop a Model for Employment Service for the Handicapped* (New York: The Associates, 1969). For an excellent overview of older studies in this stagnant field, see Barker et al., *Adjustment to Physical Handicap and Illness*, chapter 8, "Employment of the Disabled," pp. 346–72.

20. See note 19 and the studies cited in notes 16 and 17 of chapter 12.

21. The importance of exploring the role of sociological factors on self-reports of function is illustrated by the following greatly oversimplified hypothetical example. Suppose, for the sake of argument, that regardless of social class, Jewish males tend to exaggerate the physical limitations imposed upon them by their chronic health problems, whereas WASP males of all social classes tend to understate their health-related limitations. Then, *ceteris paribus*, comparisons of Jewish and WASP workers matched for handicaps (e.g., diabetes, deafness, limb amputations), such economically relevant demographic characteristics as age and sex, and physical limitations *as measured by self-reports* would overestimate the productivity of Jewish workers and underestimate the productivity of WASP workers. This bias would translate into biased estimates of the degree of discrimination encountered by the two groups of workers. To take the simplest case, suppose that the matched groups of workers have similar average wages, days worked per year, unemployment rates, work force participation, etc. Then, while we could as yet say nothing about the job discrimination encountered by WASP workers, we would have to infer from these data that disabled Jewish workers were being systematically discriminated against because their higher average productivity (as estimated by the self-report method) was not being rewarded by the market.

There are many suggestions that self-reports of functional limitations are sensitive to social and psychological factors in the data obtained in the 1966 and 1972 Social Security Surveys of the Disabled (SSSD). Because data from the 1972 survey are only now beginning to be published, we will focus most closely upon the 1966 survey.

Before proceeding, however, we must signal a methodological shortcoming of both the 1966 and 1972 SSSD which renders much of these data almost uninterpretable. This is the failure of these and all other surveys before the 1976 Longitudinal Surveys of the Labor Force to include data on those handicapped people who did not believe that their disability in any way affected their ability to work (see note 18).

This omission means that the suggestions in the SSSD that demographic and economic variables significantly influence self-reports of degree of functional limitation may stem from the huge sampling error introduced into the SSSD by omitting all the handicapped who did not describe themselves as "work-disabled." To minimize the effects of this sampling bias, we shall focus upon the extremes of the distribution of functional ability reported by the work-disabled sample—those reporting no functional limitation and those reporting severe functional limitation or total physical dependency. We adopt this strategy because it seems reasonable to believe that the SSSD sample error is much greater for handicapped persons with minor physical limitations than for those with major physical limitations—i.e., a larger proportion of individuals with missing limbs are likely to be excluded by the "work-disabled" criterion than are deaf individuals or individuals with quadriplegia. Thus, if we find that self-reports of major and minor functional limitations seem to be affected in a mutually consistent way by social variables, we can assume as a crude first approximation that the patterns we have identified are probably not simply artifacts of the huge sampling bias built into the SSSD. Since we are interested only in making a persuasive *prima facie* case that the impact of psychological and sociological variables on self-reports cannot be assumed to be minor or to cancel each other out (i.e., to represent random "noise"), this precaution seems sufficient. However, it must be understood that our remarks represent only a point of departure for undertaking much more methodologically sophisticated analyses.

The evidence for an interaction between sex differences and social class is particularly suggestive. The evidence for sex differences in self-reports of work disability was noted by Haber a decade ago; see Lawrence D. Haber, "Disability, Work, and Income Maintenance: Prevalence of Disability, 1966," *The Social Security Bulletin*, May 1968.

On the one hand, women as a group seem to suffer more severe functional limitations from their disability than do men. This difference is most visible if one compares the proportions of the sexes at the two extremes of the spectrum of functional limitation. For example, in the age range eighteen to forty-four, 40 percent of all men report no functional limitation at all; the corresponding figure for women is 33 percent. At the other extreme, 19.9 percent of men report severe functional loss or total dependency, whereas 22.8 percent of all women fall into this category. The sex difference is most marked for the forty-five to fifty-four age group: about 27 percent of all men report no functional loss, while only 20 percent of all women report no loss. Severe loss or dependency is reported by 16 percent of all men and 29 percent of all women. In the fifty-five to sixty-four age category, the sex differences are smaller but still favor males. All figures are drawn from Haber, "The Epidemiology of Disability. II. The Measurement of Functional Capacity Limitations," Table 5, pp. 23–24. (We will subsequently refer to the study as 1966 SSSD Report Number 10.) Since women generally are more resistant to disease than men and live considerably longer than men, this finding is in itself curious. One would have expected men to be more severely limited in function and less frequently free of functional limitations than women.

However, if one accepts the finding that women are physically more frail than men, it seems reasonable to expect that the largest differences in functional limitations would occur in those social classes whose health is poorest and whose work is most physically demanding—i.e., individuals in blue-collar occupations at the time that they became disabled.

Surprisingly, the exact opposite is suggested by the 1966 SSSD Report Number 10. Roughly equal proportions of men and women in blue-collar occupations at the onset of their disability report that they have severe functional limitations or are entirely dependent. In startling contrast, the proportions of white-collar men and women are very different. Here the percentage of women in the most disabled category is 1.5 times greater than the corresponding proportion of men.

Confirmation of a sex and social-class interaction is suggested by looking at the other extreme of the physical limitation scale. The proportion of white-collar men with no functional loss is 1.5 times the proportion of women—the mirror image of the proportions for severe functional limitations. For blue-collar men the proportion is about 1.2 times the blue-collar women's rate. Thus, whatever is going on seems to make white-collar women (or men) give more extreme responses in self-descriptions of physical limitation than blue-collar men and women. (All data are from 1966 SSSD Report Number 10, Table 8, pp. 27–28.)

There is also indirectly a more ambiguous suggestion that self-estimates of functional limitation are sensitive to an individual's perceptions of the employment options open to him or her. Between 1966 and 1972 the economy went from boom to recession, and transfer payments to disabled adults greatly increased. Even when one takes into account the increase in disabled Vietnam veterans during those years, the shifts in the self-reports of functional limitations provided by men and women may require a sociological explanation, although the findings we report may simply represent the sampling bias of the surveys. Between 1966 and 1972 the percentage of men reporting no functional limitation remained constant at about 30 percent, but the proportion of men reporting severe limitation or total functional dependency increased by a third (from 21.7 percent to 29.0 percent). Self-reports of disabled women display a diametrically opposite shift. Severely limited and dependent individuals remained unchanged (28 percent in 1966 and 29.6 percent in 1972), while the proportion of individuals reporting no functional loss increased by 20 percent (from 23.8 percent to 28.6 percent). (All comparisons are from the 1966 SSSD Report Number 10, Table 5, pp. 23–24, and Kathryn H. Allan, "First Findings of the 1972 Survey of the Disabled: General Characteristics," *Social Security Bulletin*, October 1976, Table 4, pp. 27–28.)

Of course, sex, occupation, and economic climate are only three of the variables that one would want to examine more closely. Another is age. Still another is age of onset of the disability—especially onset in childhood versus onset in adulthood. Education, ethnic group, and religion are still other variables; so is modal personality type. Indeed, given the probable importance of the interaction of sex and class (as defined by occupation), it seems clear that a major task in obtaining comparable self-estimates of functional limitation must be to draw upon the rich medical (and psychiatric) literature documenting the impact of different social variables on expressions of feelings, degree of introspection, response to placebos, pain thresholds, etc., in order to single out the other most likely social factors involved in affecting self-reports of physical limitation. (See chapter 11 for a discussion of the literature on placebos and psychosomatic medicine.)

22. The shifts of self-reports of work disability between the 1966 and 1972 Social Security Surveys of the Disabled have been noted so often by economists and epidemiologists that we will not discuss them in any detail here. For the basic 1966 data, see Kathryn H. Allan and Mildred E. Cinsky, "General Characteristics of the Disabled Population," *Social Security Bulletin*, August 1972; for an overview of the 1972 survey, see Allan's "First Findings of the 1972 Survey of the Disabled." For a useful discussion of the significance of these shifts, see Levitan and Taggart's *Jobs for the Disabled*, chapter 1, "Disability and Employability." For an extremely interesting discussion of the biasing effects on self-reports of work disability that stem from the way questions about health and disability are framed and, indeed, upon the context in which nearly identical questions are asked in different surveys, see Riley and Nagi, *Disability in the United States*, pp. 3–8.

These studies show rather conclusively that inferences about employment that are based on self-reports of work disability are vulnerable to the same methodological objections as inferences based upon self-reports of functional limitations (see the preceding note for a brief critique). Luft's *Poverty and Health* brings out this point well. In his study Luft performs a sophisticated analysis of the data collected in the 1966 Social Security Survey of Disabled Adults and the 1967 Survey of Economic Opportunity. On the basis of his analysis he comes to many conclusions about the association of disability with socioeconomic factors such as race, sex, and education. Yet nearly all these conclusions are problematic because Luft simply ignores the possible existence of systematic biases in his self-report data.

For example, when age, income, and education differentials are held constant, Luft finds that black males tend to have a lower probability of becoming work-disabled than white males (p. 89). The difference is most striking for men with thirteen or more years of education. Here whites are 2.5 times more likely to become disabled than blacks. While some of this difference may reflect the larger sampling error for blacks in this category, Luft believes that some of the difference stems from the fact that "until very recently, only very exceptional black men went to college, and those who did were probably likely to have been exceptionally healthy to have 'made it out of the ghetto'" (p. 89). However, there is virtually no difference between the disability probabilities for black women and white women with thirteen or more years of education; are we then to conclude that the black woman has needed to be less healthy to fight her way out of poverty? We find it at least as plausible that social psychological factors have produced systematic biases in the self-reports of work disabilities (see the table below, which summarizes data presented in Luft's Table 4.4, p. 88). For example, many studies have found that white racism is often more destructive to the black man's sense of identity than to the black woman's sense of identity, thanks in no small part to an economy in which it has traditionally been easier for black women to find (menial) employment than black males. It is not difficult to imagine ways in which the possession of an elite credential (such as a college degree) might interact with these systematic differences in sense of self to produce very different patterns of bias in self-reports about the impact of health upon work experience.

Estimated Probability of Becoming Work-Disabled During 1967 in the United States

(by education, race, and sex)

	MEN		WOMEN	
Years of schooling	*White*	*Black*	*White*	*Black*
Less than 9	.0212	.0190	.0228	.0228
9–12	.0100	.0087	.0095	.0104
13 or more	.0090	.0038	.0083	.0081

The lack of any differential between black women and white women could also be ascribed to an equally complex mixture of sociological factors: differences in male and female sex roles in white middle-class society, the special economic responsibilities that black women have often been forced to assume in a racist society, and differences in male and female role ideals among blacks.

Of course, we have not even begun to mention all the sociological and social-psychological factors that *may* be responsible for the pattern of race differences displayed in the table; and any thorough investigation would have to take into account the fact that a crucial group of disabled people is excluded from the data base from which this table is constructed—those who rightly or wrongly do not believe that their health limits the kind or amount of work they can do or prevents them from working (p. 25). But that, after all, is our point. Until we can rule out the possible existence of systematic biases in self-reports of work disability, data collected by this method will be of uncertain value for the policy maker, the civil rights activist, and the economist.

23. If these factors canceled each other out, they would introduce random noise rather than systematic distortions. The random noise could be reduced by appropriate statistical techniques, and there is every reason to believe that rough estimates of the overall patterns of job discrimination against the disabled could be obtained. But if blacks, for example, systematically underestimated the severity of their physical disability

while Italian Americans and Jews systematically overestimated the severity of their physical limitation, self-reports could easily perpetuate a highly distorted picture of job discrimination. (Our example is purely hypothetical and is only meant to illustrate our concern about self-reports. The research that we call for would examine a huge number of social and social-psychological variables separately and in concert.)

24. Our concern about this point stems from the data about disability onset reported by Ralph Treitel, "Onset of Disability," *From the Social Security Survey of the Disabled: 1966*, Report Number 18, June 1972. These data are summarized in Treitel's Table 3 (p. 17), which we present opposite.

According to Treitel, about 2 million individuals aged eighteen to forty-four in 1966 reported that they were under eighteen years of age when they became disabled (ibid., Table 2, p. 16). Eighteen years earlier, in 1948, this group was under twenty-six years old. If one assumes for the sake of simplicity that these individuals were evenly distributed across age categories, one arrives at an estimate of about 1.5 million disabled individuals up to age nineteen. In order to compare this estimate directly with more recent estimates of the prevalence of childhood disability, certain disability categories must be excluded. These categories are those of mental illness and mental retardation (the prevalence of which the 1966 SSSD Report Number 6 seriously underestimates —see note 33), the category of "Other and unspecified conditions," and the category of visual impairment (this category includes 5 percent of all individuals disabled before age eighteen and must be excluded because no breakdown into legally blind and partly sighted is provided by Treitel). Discarding these categories leaves crippling and health conditions, a category that includes 74 percent of all individuals, or about 1.12 million people. This group represents about 2.2 percent of all individuals to age nineteen in 1948, or almost exactly the same prevalence estimate for crippling and health conditions offered by Kakalik and his colleagues for 1970 (*Services for Handicapped Youth*, Table A1, p. 274, and Table A2, p. 276; Kakalik et al.'s estimate of children in these disability categories in 1970 is about 2.3 percent of the total population).

However, our 1948 retroestimate must seriously underestimate the true number of handicapped people who, if asked, would report that their disability began before age eighteen, for the 1966 SSSD study excluded all handicapped people who did not describe themselves as work-disabled (see notes 18 and 22). Had these individuals been included (and one must assume that very large numbers of mildly disabled individuals were excluded), the total percentage of physically disabled or health-impaired children in 1948 suggested by the retroestimate would have been far higher. Finally, any estimate of the prevalence of these disabilities in 1948 based exclusively upon self-reports would have to be further increased in order to take into account the sizable (though indeterminate) number of individuals alive in 1948 who died before 1966.

There is also a consensus among medical men and women that fewer

Age at Onset of Disability by Diagnostic Condition and Functional Limitation: Percentage Distribution of Disabled and Severely Disabled Noninstitutionalized Adults Aged 18–64, Spring 1966

Diagnostic condition and functional limitation by severity of disability	Total	Age at onset of disability			
		Under 18	18–34	35–54	55–64
DISABLED					
Number (in thousands)	17,753	2,718	4,955	7,582	2,030
Diagnostic group and conditions					
Total percent	100.0	100.0	100.0	100.0	100.0
Musculoskeletal disorders	30.9	22.0	37.4	32.0	25.9
Arthritis or rheumatism	12.4	2.4	12.0	15.3	16.2
Back or spine	11.0	7.6	15.8	11.3	4.4
Impairment of limbs	4.9	9.1	6.5	3.3	2.0
Cardiovascular disorders	24.8	11.8	16.7	30.4	40.1
Heart trouble	11.4	4.3	5.1	15.9	20.3
High blood pressure	5.4	1.3	2.8	7.1	10.2
Respiratory and related disorders	11.2	20.3	12.3	8.1	6.4
Asthma	3.8	9.5	3.4	2.8	1.1
Mental disorders	6.3	11.0	7.8	4.5	2.8
Mental illness and nervous trouble	4.8	3.4	7.4	4.3	1.9
Mental retardation	1.2	7.5	.1	—	.1
Nervous system disorders	5.2	11.9	3.3	4.7	3.7
Epilepsy	1.0	5.1	.2	.3	—
Multiple sclerosis	.6	.4	1.2	.4	.1
Paralysis	1.0	2.8	1.2	.6	—
Digestive disorders	7.2	2.4	8.5	7.8	6.7
Neoplasms	1.7	.5	1.6	2.1	2.3
Urogenital conditions	2.5	2.8	3.6	2.1	1.6
Diabetes	2.7	3.0	1.3	3.5	4.8
Visual impairments	2.4	5.1	1.9	1.7	2.8
Other and unspecified conditions	4.9	10.2	5.6	3.3	2.9

handicaps were diagnosed (and treated) during childhood a generation ago than is the case today. This lower rate of diagnosis and treatment should be reflected in an underreporting of childhood disability in the 1966 SSSD. That is, one might reasonably expect fewer adults to remember being disabled in childhood than if present-day diagnostic and treatment techniques had been in effect during their childhood.

But should we expect the prevalence of crippling and health-related disabilities to have been considerably higher a generation ago than it is today? There is some reason to think that the answer is no. Many pediatricians believe that despite the conquest of crippling diseases such as polio, the overall impact of improvements in health care has been an increase in the proportion of children who are handicapped due to the increased survival rate of many children who would have died at birth or during childhood a generation ago. On the other hand, health surveys in the United States and the United Kingdom in the 1950s and 1960s have usually found that 10 to 15 percent of all children and youth had nonmental handicaps (including vision, speech, and hearing problems). In many of these surveys about two-thirds of all handicaps were physical, sensory, or a chronic illness. (See, for example, Ivan Barry Pless and James W. B. Douglas, "Chronic Illness in Childhood. Part I. Epidemiological and Clinical Characteristics," *Pediatrics* 47, no. 2 [February 1971]: 405–14, for a detailed discussion of one recent survey and—in Table IV—a summary of the results of many health surveys carried out in the 1950s and 1960s.) Unfortunately, the existing data are too crude to confirm or disprove the clinician's impressions.

25. The 1966 and 1972 Social Security Surveys of the Disabled contain data about adults who became disabled before age eighteen and who became eligible for the Social Security Administration's Old-Age, Survivors, Disability and Health Insurance program (henceforth referred to as OASDHI) when an insured parent died, retired, or became disabled. If these adults were representative of adults who grew up disabled, the SSSD surveys would indeed be a rich storehouse of information for those interested in the problems of handicapped children. However, published data for the 1966 SSSD suggest that the OASDHI group is highly unrepresentative of most adults who grow up handicapped. Three-quarters of this population suffered from mental retardation or nervous system disorders. Three-quarters of those not living in institutions were functionally dependent upon others for care, and more than one-quarter (56,000 out of a total 198,000) were institutionalized. See Lawrence D. Haber, "The Disabled Beneficiary—A Comparison of Factors Related to Benefit Entitlement," *From the Social Security Survey of the Disabled: 1966*, Report Number 7, June 1969, especially pp. 4 and 26.

26. Again this is a matter that cries out for careful research and cannot be decided beforehand. Moreover, even given a finding that, say, shifts in optimism about the future prospects of disabled adults strongly influence self-reports of physical limitation, it is still possible that the economist can devise ways of taking these shifts into account when viewing data based upon self-reports.

Note further that the question of optimism versus pessimism about the job prospects for disabled workers points to a potential way of greatly simplifying the kinds of social and social-psychological factors that must be taken into account in order to eliminate other systematic biases in self-reports. For example (again purely hypothetical), a tendency for black males to underestimate and Italian and Jewish males to overestimate their physical limitations may stem primarily from systematic differences in optimism or pessimism about employment among white and black males; biases stemming from ethnicity (being an Italian American, a Jew, or, for that matter, belonging to the black Jamaican subculture rather than to the southern black subculture) may be sufficiently small to be ignored.

27. See Fred Davis, *Passage through Crises: Polio Victims and Their Families* (Indianapolis: Bobbs-Merrill, 1963), and John F. McDermotts, Jr., Saul I. Harrison, Jules Schrager, Paul Wilson, Elizabeth Killins, Janet Lindy, and Raymond W. Waggoner, J., "Social Class and Mental Illness in Children: The Diagnosis of Organicity and Mental Retardation," *Journal of the American Academy of Child Psychiatry* 6, no. 2 (April 1967): 309–20.

A recent study of special education classification procedures by SRI International *may* speak to the same issues. This study reported an extraordinary lack of consensus among physicians, teachers, and parents about which children (aged six to eleven) had sensory or orthopedic handicaps. See Patricia A. Craig, David H. Kaskowitz, and Mary A. Malgoire, *Studies of Handicapped Students*, vol. 2: *Teacher Identification of Handicapped Pupils (Ages 6–11) Compared with Identification Using Other Indicators* (Menlo Park, Calif.: SRI International, February 1978). Common sense would ascribe the nearly perfect lack of any overlap between physician judgments and judgments made by the other two groups to teacher biases and parental anxieties. But the physician estimates are suspicious in one crucial respect: they report nearly uniform prevalence rates for these disabilities among all income groups and for all ethnic groups. Though the agreement in handicap identification between parents and teachers is not extremely high, both groups do report that sensory and orthopedic handicaps are very roughly twice as common among poor children and among black children as among other groups of children. This accords with our own beliefs about prevalence rates (but see our Introduction, note 12, for a review of the still very shaky statistical support for our view).

Interpretation of the SRI results is greatly complicated by the failure of the medical data to indicate the severity of the orthopedic disability and by the use of medical tests of vision and hearing (Snellen letters, pure tones) which may be nearly useless in detecting subtle problems in visual word and pattern perception and in auditory speech perception. These oversights mean that it is perfectly possible that the medical tests did a poorer job of identifying children with significant sensory or orthopedic disabilities than did either teacher or parents. Still, it is at least arguable—and well worth exploring as a hypothesis—that physician bias also played an important role.

28. This literature is a gold mine for possible ideas and techniques for opening up the marketplace to the disabled worker. Unfortunately, the literature does not contain any systematic attempts to study and to define the costs and benefits of attempting to increase the employment of disabled workers—a point to which we shall return later in the text. Attempts to evaluate the costs and benefits of vocational rehabilitation programs exist but—as noted by Berkowitz, Englander, Rubin, and Worrall's *An Evaluation of Policy-Related Rehabilitation Research* and Levitan and Taggart's *Jobs for the Disabled*, among others—the value of these efforts is vitiated by serious methodological shortcomings. Probably the best brief overview of the literature on demonstration projects and physical modifications of the work place appears in chapter 13, "Employment and Labor Force Participation of the Severely Disabled," of the Urban Institute's *Report of the Comprehensive Service Needs Study*. Also see the references cited above in note 19.

29. Gerald W. Scully, "Pay and Performance in Major League Baseball," *American Economic Review* 64 (December 1974): 915–30.

30. Lee Meyerson, "Somatopsychology of Physical Disability," in *Psychology of Exceptional Children and Youth*, 3d ed., ed. William M. Cruickshank (Englewood Cliffs, N.J.: Prentice-Hall, 1971), p. 9.

31. See the studies cited in note 11.

32. For an overview of European attempts to use wage subsidies to integrate disabled workers into mainstream jobs, see Beatrice G. Reubens, *The Hard-to-Employ* (New York: Columbia University Press, 1970).

At present, interest in wage subsidy programs in America focuses upon using such programs to provide individuals who have dropped out of the work force (or never entered it) with the socialization experiences and work record that will enable them to leave the subsidized programs and find employment in the competitive labor market. At least two projects being conducted under the aegis of the National Supported Work Demonstration concern reentry programs for two groups who are often classified among the disabled: former mental patients and alcoholics (see "Summary of the First Annual Report on the National Supported Work Demonstration," Manpower Demonstration Research Corporation, December 1976). Similar projects seem worth trying out for potentially employable individuals who have dropped out of the labor force or find themselves chronically unemployed because of physical or sensory disabilities or chronic disease.

However, by wage subsidies we also have in mind subsidy programs designed to accompany a disabled adult through his working life in the competitive economy. At least until substantial modifications in the physical structure of the work place and the organization of work occur, it is likely that the main potential beneficiaries of these permanent subsidies would be moderately disabled individuals who are somewhat less productive than able-bodied individuals of similar backgrounds but more productive than many severely incapacitated individuals. We suspect, for example, that a good number of the current nonworking or marginally employed disabled Vietnam war veterans fall into this category. For these and similar disabled groups, even a large "chronic" wage subsidy might substantially reduce the total burden they currently place on the public treasury, as well as provide them with the sense of independence and social adulthood that come from being gainfully employed in the able-bodied world.

33. Here are the disabilities surveyed by the 1966 Social Security Survey of the Disabled (see Lawrence D. Haber, "Epidemiological Factors in Disability: Major Disabling Conditions," *From the Social Security Survey of the Disabled: 1966*, Report Number 6, February 1969, p. 13):

1. Asthma	22. Thyroid trouble or goiter
2. Tuberculosis	23. Epilepsy
3. Chronic bronchitis	24. Multiple sclerosis
4. Emphysema	25. Chronic nervous trouble
5. Any other chronic lung trouble	26. Cancer
6. Rheumatic fever	27. Hernia or rupture
7. Hardening of the arteries (arteriosclerosis)	28. Prostate trouble
8. High blood pressure (hypertension)	29. Deafness or serious trouble with hearing
9. Heart trouble	30. Blindness or serious trouble with seeing, even when wearing glasses
10. Stroke	
11. Trouble with varicose veins	31. Missing legs or feet
12. Hemorrhoids or piles	32. Missing arms or hands
13. Tumor, cyst, or growth	33. Missing fingers
14. Chronic gall bladder or liver trouble	34. Palsy
15. Stomach ulcer	35. Paralysis of any kind
16. Any other chronic stomach trouble	36. Repeated trouble with back or spine
17. Kidney stones or chronic kidney trouble	37. Permanent stiffness or any deformity of the foot, leg, or back
18. Arthritis or rheumatism	38. Any allergy
19. Mental illness	39. Any condition present since birth
20. Mental retardation	
21. Diabetes	

While mental illness and mental retardation were included on the survey questionnaire, the self-reports of these disabilities vastly underestimated their prevalence. Only 1.2 percent of all work-disabled individuals stated that they were mentally retarded (or about 200,000 people in the age range eighteen to sixty-four). About 4.8 percent stated that they were mentally ill (about 850,000). As explained in note 24, we do not believe that self-reports concerning childhood disability can be trusted. However, for what they are worth, 7.5 percent of those who claimed to have been disabled before age eighteen classified themselves as mentally retarded (or about 200,000). About 3.4 percent in the disabled-before-eighteen group classified themselves as mentally ill (or about 90,000). In contrast, roughly 2.8 million children and youths up to age twenty-one are believed to be mentally retarded, of whom more than 2 million fall into the mildly retarded range. An additional 1.5 million children and youths are believed to be emotionally disturbed. See James S. Kakalik, Garry D. Brewer, Laurence A. Dougharty, Patricia D. Fleischauer, and Samuel M. Genensky, *Services for Handicapped Youth: A Program Overview* (Santa Monica, Calif.: Rand Corporation, May 1973), Table A1, p. 274.

When one recalls that the 1966 SSSD sampled an age range (eighteen to sixty-four) 2.2 times greater than the range covered by the Kakalik estimate, the conclusion seems inevitable that the survey failed to identify as such nearly all adults who were classified as emotionally disturbed or mildly retarded as children. For example, if one quite implausibly assumes that every adult classified as mentally ill had been classified as emotionally disturbed during childhood, the survey still would have missed three out of every four adults who were classified as emotionally disturbed as children. Again, even assuming that every adult counted as mentally retarded was classified as *mildly* retarded in childhood, the survey still identifies fewer than 5 percent of all adults who possessed this label during childhood.

14 • Increasing Employment Even When Discrimination Persists

1. Many economists view employment prejudice as the decision of a perfectly rational, profit-maximizing employer to sacrifice a portion of his potential profits in order to "pay" for his "taste"—his dislike of hiring, promoting, or retaining qualified black workers. See Garry S. Becker, *The Economics of Discrimination*, 2d ed. (Chicago: University of Chicago Press, 1971).

   For a taste theory of prejudice, then, the prejudiced employer is just as interested in the issues that we explore in this section as the unprejudiced employer. That is, any reduction in the uncertainty surrounding the economic value of a given handicapped individual will be taken into account in the prejudiced employer's rational assessments of the costs of indulging his prejudice against disabled people in his employment decisions. However, to avoid unnecessarily complicating our discussion for the nonspecialist (who is likely to find the compatibility of rationality with prejudice paradoxical), we shall refer only to unprejudiced employers in the text.

2. In the text we restrict ourselves to the simplest situations in which the signals broadcast by the handicapped person may adversely influence his employability. Other, more subtle, problems arise when one considers the effect that the handicap may play in impeding the individual's advancement within an organization. The role that one's social persona plays in corporate advancement has been admirably explored in a book about the employment problems of women, Rosabeth Moss Kanter's *Men and Women of the Corporation* (New York: Basic Books, 1977). Her argument's relevance to handicap is evident on every page. For a useful overview of the book, see Adeline Levine, "People and

Their Work," *Science* 198, no. 4320 (December 2, 1977): 920–22. Also see Michael Maccoby, *The Gamesman: The New Corporate Leaders* (New York: Simon & Schuster, 1977), and William H. Whyte, Jr., *The Organization Man* (New York: Simon & Schuster, 1956).

3. These tests suffer from the same kinds of conceptual flaws as the intelligence tests discussed in chapter 10. For an overview of test methodology, see Anne Anastasi, *Psychological Testing*, 4th ed. (New York: Macmillan, 1976). For a sense of the ways that standard personnel tests discriminate against any group of "nonstandard" workers, see James J. Kirkpatrick, Robert B. Ewen, Richard S. Barrett, and Raymond A. Katzell, *Testing and Fair Employment: Fairness and Validity of Personnel Tests for Different Ethnic Groups* (New York: New York University Press, 1968), especially pp. 29–39. Also see Kenneth M. Miller, "Nature, Advantages, and Limitations of Psychological Tests," in *Psychological Testing in Personnel Assessment*, ed. Kenneth M. Miller (New York: John Wiley and Sons, 1975), pp. 13–15.

4. See chapter 13, note 19.

5. Urban Institute, *Report of the Comprehensive Service Needs Study* (Washington, D.C.: Urban Institute, 1975), p. 325.

6. Roger G. Barker, in collaboration with Beatrice A. Wright, Lee Meyerson, and Mollie R. Gonick, *Adjustment to Physical Handicap and Illness: A Survey of the Social Psychology of Physique and Disability*, 2d ed. (New York: Social Sciences Research Council, 1953), p. 359.

7. Beatrice G. Reubens, *The Hard-to-Employ* (New York: Columbia University Press, 1970).

8. See chapter 13, note 32.

9. These tests are somewhat better at predicting success in job training programs: here there is an average correlation of about .50 between test scores and training program performance. If one looks at all personnel tests, rather than just the best ones, the average correlation between test scores and job performance falls to about .20; between test scores and training success the average correlation is about .30. See Edwin E. Ghiselli, *The Validity of Occupational Aptitude Tests* (New York: John Wiley and Sons, 1966), pp. 125–27.

10. See chapter 13, notes 1 and 2.

Appendix 2 • The Sexuality of the Severely Disabled

1. The discussion in Kinsey is confined to a paragraph in the work's chapter on prostitutes: "Some men go to prostitutes because they are more or less ineffective in securing sexual relations with other girls. This may be true of males who are unusually timid. Persons who are deformed physically, deaf, blind, severely crippled, spastic, or otherwise handicapped, often have considerable difficulty in finding heterosexual coitus. The matter may weigh heavily upon their minds and cause considerable psychic disturbance. There are instances where prostitutes have contributed to establishing these individuals in their own self-esteem by

providing their first sexual contacts" (Alfred C. Kinsey, Wardell B. Pom-
eroy, and Clyde E. Martin, *Sexual Behavior in the Human Male* [Phila-
delphia, W. B. Saunders, 1948], p. 608).

2. For example, Shere Hite, *The Hite Report* (New York: Macmillan,
    1976); Anthony Pietropinto and Jacqueline Simenauer, *Beyond the
    Male Myth* (New York: Times Books, 1977); and Alan Ebert, *The
    Homosexuals: Who and What We Are* (New York: Macmillan, 1977).
    Among popular magazines, *Penthouse Forum* is a refreshing exception
    to the general rule. Since 1977 its letter column has regularly carried
    letters from disabled individuals. Among professional journals, useful
    discussions of sexuality and handicap can be found in *Medical Aspects
    of Human Sexuality.*

3. See Mary Carson, "The New Baby Is Different," *U.S. Catholic* 42, no.
    9 (September 1977): 10–12. The generalization from severe retardation
    to all of handicap is even more marked when nonsexual topics are dis-
    cussed. Because the piece is condensed from a forthcoming book on
    retarded children, it is impossible to be sure if Mrs. Carson is respon-
    sible for the overgeneralization or if it stems from the editor's hand.
    But the fact that the article is introduced (both on the cover and
    within the magazine) by the caption "What you should know about
    retarded children" testifies that, whoever was responsible, the editors
    had second thoughts about using severe retardation as a touchstone
    for all handicaps.

4. Talcott Parsons has noted how the sick role represents a conditional
    legitimization of a social regression back to a state of dependency. See
    Talcott Parsons, *Social Structure and Personality* (New York: Free
    Press, 1964).

5. For a discussion of the marriages of mildly retarded individuals, see
    R. J. Kennedy, *A Connecticut Community Revisited: A Study of the
    Social Adjustment of a Group of Mentally Deficient Adults in 1948 and
    1960* (Hartford: Connecticut State Department of Health, Office of
    Mental Retardation, 1966). For the erotic character of some handicaps
    in women, see the letters column of *Penthouse Forum*, e.g., *Penthouse
    Forum* 7, no. 3: 122–23.

6. S. R. Lesser and B. R. Easser, "Personality Differences in the Perceptu-
    ally Handicapped," *Journal of the American Academy of Child Psy-
    chiatry* 11 (1972): 458–66.

7. For a full statement of our position on mainstreaming, see chapter 10.

8. Stephen A. Richardson, "People with Cerebral Palsy Talk for Them-
    selves," *Developmental Medicine and Child Neurology* 14, no. 4 (August
    1972): 525.

9. Robert C. Geiger, "Sexuality of People with Cerebral Palsy," *Medical
    Aspects of Human Sexuality*, March 1975, p. 78.

10. Ibid., pp. 76–78.

11. For estimates of the total number of psychotherapeutic schools in Amer-
    ica, see Boyce Rensberger, "Psychotherapy: Finding a Shrink to Fit,"
    The New York Times, December 28, 1977, p. C1. According to the
    American Psychiatric Association, there are thirty different schools of
    psychiatry alone.

12. Peter Blos, Jr., and Stuart M. Finch, "Sexuality and the Handicapped Adolescent," in *The Child with Disabling Illness*, ed. John A. Downey and Niels L. Low (Philadelphia: W. B. Saunders, 1974), pp. 538–39.

Appendix 3 • Typology of Motives

1. See chapter 1, note 15. Also see Gordon W. Allport, *The Nature of Prejudice*, abr. ed. (Garden City, N.Y.: Doubleday Anchor, 1958).
2. Georg Simmel, *The Sociology of Georg Simmel,* trans. and ed. Kurt H. Wolff (Glencoe, Ill.: Free Press, 1950).
3. Frank Kermode, *The Sense of an Ending: Studies in the Theory of Fiction* (New York: Oxford University Press, 1968), p. 138.
4. Robert A. Scott, *The Making of Blind Men* (New York: Russell Sage Foundation, 1969), pp. 25–32.
5. For key papers, see Stanley Milgram, *The Individual in a Social World: Essays and Experiments* (Reading, Mass.: Addison-Wesley Publishing Company, 1977).
6. See Philip G. Zimbardo, "Transforming Experimental Research into Advocacy for Social Change," in Morton Deutsch and Harvey A. Hornstein, eds., *Applying Social Psychology: Implications for Research, Practice, and Training* (Hillsdale, N.J.: Lawrence Erlbaum Associates, 1975); and Craig Haney, Curtis Banks, and Philip Zimbardo, "A Study of Prisoners and Guards in a Simulated Prison," *Naval Research Reviews* (September 1973), reprinted in Elliot Aronson, ed., *Readings about the Social Animal*, 2d ed. (San Francisco: W. H. Freeman, 1977).
7. See, for example, Georg Lukács, *Studies in European Realism* (New York: Grosset & Dunlap, 1964), and *Essays on Thomas Mann,* trans. Stanley Mitchell (New York: Grosset & Dunlap, 1965).
8. For an interesting example of this approach, see Jerome Siller et al., *Attitudes of the Non-Disabled Toward the Physically Disabled* (New York: New York University School of Education, 1967).
9. As noted in chapter 10, the work of Stephen A. Richardson and Richard Kleck is much more interesting. For a good overview, see Stephen A. Richardson, "Attitudes and Behavior Towards the Physically Handicapped," *Birth Defects: Original Article Series* 12, no. 4 (1976): 15–34.
10. For a brief discussion of some of these strategies, see chapter 10, pp. 229–32.
11. See Karl Popper, *Objective Knowledge* (London: Oxford University Press, 1972), and Imre Lakatos, "Falsification and the Methodology of Scientific Research Programs," in Imre Lakatos and Alan Musgrave, eds., *Criticism and the Growth of Knowledge* (London: Cambridge University Press, 1970).

Appendix 4 • Medicine and Handicap: A Promise in Search of a National Commitment

1. For excellent critical analyses of health services for children, see Children's Defense Fund, *Doctors and Dollars Are Not Enough: How to Improve Health Services for Children and Their Families* (Washington,

D.C.: Children's Defense Fund, 1976); Karen Davis and Cathy Schoen, *Health and the War on Poverty: A Ten-Year Appraisal* (Washington, D.C.: Brookings Institution, 1978); and Harvard Child Health Project, vol. 3, *Developing a Better Health Care System for Children* (Cambridge, Mass.: Ballinger Publishing Co., 1977).

2. National Academy of Sciences, Institute of Medicine, *Perspectives on Health Promotion and Disease Prevention in the United States: A Staff Paper* (Washington, D.C.: National Academy of Sciences, January 1978), pp. 21–22 (hereafter cited as IOM, *Prevention*).

3. Garry D. Brewer and James S. Kakalik, *Handicapped Children: Strategies for Improving Services* (New York: McGraw-Hill, 1979), pp. 115–21.

4. Stephen C. Schoenbaum, James N. Hyde, Jr., Louis Bartoshesky, and Kathleen Crampton, "Benefit-Cost Analysis of Rubella Vaccination Policy," *New England Journal of Medicine* 294 (1976): 306–10.

5. U.S. Department of Health, Education and Welfare, *Health United States, 1978* (Washington, D.C.: U.S. Government Printing Office, 1978), DHEW Publication No. (PHS) 78-1232, p. 51.

6. A. Minkowski and C. Amiel-Tison, "Obstetrical Risk in the Genesis of Vulnerability," in *The Child in His Family: Children of Psychiatric Risk*, vol. 3, ed. E. J. Anthony and C. Koupernick (New York: John Wiley and Sons, 1974), p. 144.

7. Margaret Wynn and Arthur Wynn, *Prevention of Handicap of Prenatal Origin: An Introduction to French Policy and Legislation* (London: Foundation for Education and Research in Child-bearing, 1976), p. 8.

8. Gerald A. Neligan, I. Kolvin, D. McI. Scott, and R. F. Garside, *Born Too Soon or Born Too Small: A Follow-up Study to Seven Years of Age* (Philadelphia: J. B. Lippincott, 1976), pp. 81–86 and *passim*.

9. *Eleven Million Teenagers: What Can Be Done about the Epidemic of Adolescent Pregnancies in the United States* (New York: Alan Guttmacher Institute, 1976), p. 10.

10. Ibid., p. 22.

11. Ibid., p. 62.

12. N. M. Morris, J. R. Udry, and C. L. Chase, "Shifting Age-Parity Distribution of Births and Decrease in Infant Mortality," *American Journal of Public Health* 65 (1975): 353–58.

13. *Eleven Million Teenagers*, pp. 34–40, and IOM, *Prevention*, pp. 55–56.

14. Gabriel Stickle, "The Health of Mothers and Babies: How Do We Stack Up?" *The Family Coordinator*, July 1977, p. 207.

15. University of North Carolina, School of Public Health, Department of Nutrition, *Medical Evaluation of the Special Supplemental Food Program for Women, Infants, and Children*, vol. 2 (Chapel Hill: University of North Carolina, 1976).

16. Wynn and Wynn, *Prevention of Handicap*, pp. 20–25.

17. Ibid., p. 8.

18. IOM, *Prevention*, pp. 58–59 and 209; Wynn and Wynn, *Prevention of Handicap*; and Steven L. Gortmaker, "Prenatal Care and the Health of the Newborn," *American Journal of Public Health* 69 (July 1979): 653–60.

19. National Academy of Sciences, Institute of Medicine, *Infant Death: An Analysis by Maternal Risk and Health Care*, ed. D. M. Kessner, Contrasts in Health Status, vol. 1 (Washington, D.C.: National Academy of Sciences, 1973).

20. Gortmaker, "Prenatal Care."

21. For a fuller discussion of these issues, see Kenneth Keniston and the Carnegie Council on Children, *All Our Children: The American Family under Pressure* (New York: Harcourt Brace Jovanovich, 1977), chapter 8, "Children's Health," especially pp. 162–67.

22. For the basis of this estimate, see the Introduction, note 12.

23. For two recent studies of the breakdown of medical accountability in even the most prestigious hospitals and group practices, see Marcia Millman, *The Unkindest Cut: Life in the Backrooms of Medicine* (New York: William Morrow, 1977), and Eliot Freidson, *Doctoring Together* (New York: Elsevier, 1975).

24. Jack Elinson and Ronald W. Wilson, "Prevention," in U.S. Department of Health, Education and Welfare, *Health United States, 1978*, pp. 36–37; and National Research Council, Committee for the Study of Inborn Errors of Metabolism, *Genetic Screening: Programs, Principles, and Research* (Washington, D.C.: National Academy of Sciences, 1975).

25. Wynn and Wynn, *Prevention of Handicap*, p. 8.

26. Ibid., p. 104, and IOM, *Prevention*, pp. 151–52.

27. National Academy of Sciences, Institute of Medicine, *Legalized Abortion and the Public Health: Report of a Study* (Washington, D.C.: National Academy of Sciences, 1975), p. 107.

28. Ibid., p. 103, and Elinson and Wilson, "Prevention," p. 37.

29. U.S. Department of Health, Education and Welfare, Public Health Service, *Forward Plan for Health: FY 1978–1982* (Washington, D.C.: U.S. Government Printing Office, 1976), pp. 73–74.

30. I. M. Rosenstock, B. Childs, and A. P. Simopoulos, *Genetic Screening: A Study of the Knowledge and Attitudes of Physicians* (Washington, D.C.: National Academy of Sciences, 1975); also, Elinson and Wilson, "Prevention," pp. 37–38.

31. IOM, *Prevention*, p. 150.

32. Wynn and Wynn, *Prevention of Handicap*, p. 8.

33. Minkowski and Amiel-Tison, "Obstetrical Risk," p. 141.

34. Edward R. Schlesinger, "Neonatal Care: Planning for Services and Outcomes Following Care," *Journal of Pediatrics* 82 (1973): 916–20.

35. For a summary of these studies, see ibid. Also see Wynn and Wynn, *Prevention of Handicap*, pp. 12–13; and Committee on Prenatal Health, *Towards Improving the Outcome of Pregnancy* (White Plains, N.Y.: National Foundation/March of Dimes, 1976).

36. *Regionalization of Perinatal Care*, Report of the 66th Ross Conference on Pediatric Research (Columbus, Ohio: Ross Laboratories, 1974).

37. Marshall H. Klaus and John H. Kennell, *Maternal-Infant Bonding: The Impact of Early Separation or Loss on Family Development* (St. Louis: C. V. Mosby Company, 1976), especially pp. 99–166.

38. Ibid.

39. Pamela A. Davis and Hazel Russell, "Later Progress of 100 Infants Weighing 1,000 to 2,000 gm. at Birth Fed Immediately with Breast Milk," *Developmental Medicine and Child Neurology* 10 (1968): 725–35.
40. IOM, *Prevention*, p. 142.
41. Leon Gordis, "Effectiveness of Comprehensive-Care Programs in Preventing Rheumatic Fever," *New England Journal of Medicine* 289 (1973): 331–55; A. C. Siegal, E. E. Johnson, and G. H. Strollerman, "Controlled Studies of Streptococcal Pharyngitis in a Pediatric Population. I. Factors Related to the Attack Rate of Rheumatic Fever," *New England Journal of Medicine* 265 (1961): 559–66.
42. Boston Children's Medical Center and Richard I. Feinbloom, *Child Health Encyclopedia: The Complete Guide for Parents* (New York: Delacorte Press, 1975), pp. 479–80.
43. Ibid., pp. 290–91 and 340; also Nancy E. Solomon and Jeff L. Harris, "Otitis Media in Children: Assessing the Quality of Medical Care Using Short-Term Outcome Measures," chapter 7 in Allyson D. Avery, Tovah Lelah, Nancy E. Solomon, Jeff L. Harris, Robert H. Brook, Sheldon Greenfield, John E. Ware, Jr., and Charles H. Avery, *Quality of Medical Care Assessment Using Outcome Measures: Eight Disease-Specific Applications* (Santa Monica, Calif.: Rand Corporation, 1976), pp. 588–90.
44. Brewer and Kakalik, *Handicapped Children*, p. 101.
45. R. G. Mitchell, "The Prevention of Cerebral Palsy," *Developmental Medicine and Child Neurology* 13 (1971): 137–46, cited in Wynn and Wynn, *Prevention of Handicap*, p. 2.
46. Robert J. Haggerty, "Foreword," in I. Barry Pless and Philip Pinkerton, *Chronic Childhood Disorder: Promoting Patterns of Adjustment* (Chicago: Year Book Medical Publishers, 1975), p. 11.
47. Pless and Pinkerton, *Chronic Childhood Disorder*, p. 15.
48. Brewer and Kakalik, *Handicapped Children*, p. 101.
49. P. J. Vignos, "Management of Duchenne Progressive Muscular Dystrophy," in *Ambulatory Pediatrics*, 1st ed., ed. Morris Green and Robert J. Haggerty (Philadelphia: W. B. Saunders, 1968), p. 741.
50. Carl F. Doershuk and LeRoy W. Matthews, "Cystic Fibrosis and Obstructive Pulmonary Disease," in *Ambulatory Pediatrics*, ed. Green and Haggerty, pp. 707–25.
51. L. W. Matthews, C. F. Doershuk, Melvin Wise, George Eddy, Harry Nudelman, and Samuel Spector, "A Therapeutic Regime for Patients with Cystic Fibrosis," *Journal of Pediatrics* 65 (1964): 558–75; C. F. Doershuk, L. W. Matthews, Arthur S. Tucker, H. Nudelman, G. Eddy, M. Wise, and S. Spector, "A 5-Year Clinical Evaluation of a Therapeutic Program for Patients with Cystic Fibrosis," *Journal of Pediatrics* 65 (1964): 677–93; and David M. Orenstein, Thomas F. Boat, Robert C. Stern, A. S. Tucker, Edward L. Charnock, L. W. Matthews, and C. F. Doershuk, "The Effect of Early Diagnosis and Treatment in Cystic Fibrosis," *American Journal of Diseases of Children* 131 (1977): 973–75.
52. In 1977 over 6 million persons were employed in the health care industry in this country, and almost 9 percent of our gross national

product was spent on health care services. Any comprehensive discussion of the health needs of the child with handicaps should take into consideration the vast literature that discusses the relative strengths and weaknesses of existing modes of health care delivery and of payment for health services. However, it is beyond the scope of this appendix to attempt such a review. The reader unfamiliar with the health care system and its financial and sociological structures may wish to refer to some of the following sources for further information: Karen Davis, *National Health Insurance: Benefits, Costs, and Consequences* (Washington, D.C.: Brookings Institution, 1975); Eliot Freidson, "The Organization of Medical Practice," in *Handbook of Medical Sociology*, 2d ed., ed. Howard E. Freeman, Sol Levine, and Leo G. Reeder (Englewood Cliffs, N.J.: Prentice-Hall, 1972), pp. 343–58; Charles E. Lewis, Rashi Fein, and David Mechanic, *A Right to Health: The Problem of Access to Primary Medical Care* (New York: John Wiley and Sons, 1976); and David Mechanic, *The Growth of Bureaucratic Medicine: An Inquiry into the Dynamics of Patient Behavior and the Organization of Medical Care* (New York: John Wiley and Sons, 1976).

53. Charlotte G. Schwartz, "Strategies and Tactics of Mothers of Mentally Retarded Children for Dealing with the Medical Care System," in *Diminished People: Problems and Care of the Mentally Retarded,* ed. Norman R. Bernstein (Boston: Little, Brown, 1970), pp. 73–105.

54. See, for example, Judith B. Igoe, "Bridging the Communication Gap between Health Professionals and Educators," *Journal of School Health* 47 (1977): 405–9; Francine H. Jacobs, "The Identification of Preschool Children with Handicaps: A Community Approach," unpublished doctoral dissertation, Harvard Graduate School of Education, 1979; I. Barry Pless and B. Satterwaite, "Chronic Illness in Childhood: A Regional Survey of Care," *Pediatrics* 58 (1976): 37–46; and Corinne J. Weithorn and Roslyn Roos, "Who Monitors Medication?" *Journal of Learning Disabilities* 8 (1975): 59–62.

55. See, for example, Constance Battle, "The Role of the Pediatrician as Ombudsman in the Health Care of the Young Handicapped Child," *Pediatrics* 50 (1972): 916–22; Francine H. Jacobs and Deborah K. Walker, "Pediatricians and the Education for All Handicapped Children Act of 1975 (P.L. 94-142)," *Pediatrics* 61 (1978): 135–37; Harold Kanthor, I. Barry Pless, Betty Satterwaite, and Gary Myers, "Areas of Responsibility in the Health Care of Multiply Handicapped Children," *Pediatrics* 54 (1974): 779–85; and I. Barry Pless, ed., *The Care of Children with Chronic Disease*, Report of the 67th Ross Conference on Pediatric Research (Columbus, Ohio: Ross Laboratories, 1975), especially pp. 57–90.

56. James S. Kakalik, Garry D. Brewer, Lawrence A. Dougharty, Patricia D. Fleischauer, and Samuel M. Genensky, *Services for Handicapped Youth: A Program Overview* (Santa Monica, Calif.: Rand Corporation, 1973), pp. 169–70.

57. For an excellent discussion of the range of functions that the pediatrician might perform, see Pless and Pinkerton, *Chronic Childhood Disorder*, pp. 202–10.

58. For a summary of the major federal-state financing programs for handicapped children and their limitations, see Brewer and Kakalik, *Handicapped Children,* pp. 255–80.

59. U.S. Department of Health, Education and Welfare, *Characteristics of State Plans for Aid to Families with Dependent Children under the Social Security Act Title IV-A* (Washington, D.C.: U.S. Government Printing Office, 1974).

60. In their discussion of employment in Part Four, Gliedman and Roth attack the definition of disability used by the Social Security surveys; I concur with their critique. However, none of us has any serious reservations about how the surveys were actually implemented. For one analysis from the Survey of Disabled Adults that focused on economic burdens, see Rachel F. Boaz, "Paying for Medical Care: The Burden on the Disabled," *Medical Care* 16 (1978): 705–22.

61. Brewer and Kakalik, *Handicapped Children,* pp. 205–54.

62. Our best estimate—and it is no more than an educated guess—is based upon the prevalence rates calculated by Brewer and Kakalik (*Handicapped Children,* pp. 78–97, especially Table 5.1). We have adjusted their calculations to remove some children whose handicaps probably require no special medical or psychiatric services. We thus estimate that the following numbers of individuals in the following disability groups have some handicap-related medical needs:

Visual impairment	193,000
Hearing impairment	490,000
Speech impairment (one-third of their estimate)	700,000
Moderately, severely, and profoundly retarded	700,000
Emotionally disturbed (two-thirds of their estimate)	1,000,000
Crippling or other health impairments	1,676,000
Multihandicapped	50,000
TOTAL	4,809,000

This is a total of approximately 4.8 million compared with Brewer and Kakalik's adjusted total of 9.5 million handicapped children and youths to age twenty-one in 1970.

63. See the Introduction for a fuller discussion of estimating prevalence rates. See also David H. Kaskowitz, *Validation of State Counts of Handicapped Children,* vol. 2: *Estimation of the Numbers of Handicapped Children in Each State* (Menlo Park, Calif.: Stanford Research Institute, 1977), pp. 1–48; William P. Richardson, A. C. Higgins, and Richard G. Ames, *The Handicapped Children of Alamance County, North Carolina: A Medical and Sociological Study* (Wilmington, Del.:

Nemours Foundation, 1965), pp. 13–37; and U.S. Department of Health, Education and Welfare, Office of Education, *Progress toward a Free Appropriate Public Education; a Report to Congress on the Implementation of P.L. 94-142* (Washington, D.C.: U.S. Government Printing Office, January 1979), DHEW Publication No. (OE) 79-05003, pp. 9–29.

64. Brewer and Kakalik, *Handicapped Children*, pp. 258–59 and 268–73.
65. Davis and Schoen, *Health and the War on Poverty*, p. 134.
66. Brewer and Kakalik, *Handicapped Children*, p. 272.
67. Ibid., p. 273.
68. Children's Defense Fund, *EPSDT: Does It Spell Health Care for Children?* (Washington, D.C.: Children's Defense Fund, June 1977).
69. "Summary of H.R. 6706: Child Health Assessment Act," *Washington Report on Health Legislation*, May 4, 1977, pp. 6–8; U.S. Congress, *Child Health Assessment Act*, Hearings before the Subcommittee on Health and the Environment of the Committee on Interstate and Foreign Commerce, U.S. House of Representatives, on H.R. 6706, H.R. 8794, H.R. 7474, and H.R. 8401, August 8–9, 1977 (Washington, D.C.: U.S. Government Printing Office, 1977).
70. Children's Defense Fund, *EPSDT*.
71. R. M. Gibson, M. S. Mueller, and C. R. Fisher, "Age Differences in Health Care Spending, Fiscal Year 1976," *Social Security Bulletin* 40, no. 8 (August 1977): 3–14.

Index